D0463976

"HAPPINESS
IS NOT
MY COMPANION"

"HAPPINESS IS NOT MY COMPANION"

The Life of General G. K. Warren

David M. Jordan

Indiana University Press / Bloomington and Indianapolis

This book is a publication of
Indiana University Press
601 North Morton Street
Bloomington, Indiana 47404-3797 USA
http://iupress.indiana.edu
Telephone orders   800-842-6796
Fax orders   812-855-7931
Orders by email   iuporder@indiana.edu

The paper used in this publication meets the minimum
requirements of American National Standard for Information
Sciences—Permanence of Paper for Printed Library
Materials, ANSI Z39.48-1 984.
Manufactured in the United States of America

Library of Congress Cataloging-in-Publication Data

Jordan, David M., date
"Happiness is not my companion" : the life of
General G. K. Warren / David M. Jordan.
p.   cm.
Includes bibliographical references (p.   ) and index.
ISBN 0-253-33904-9 (cl : alk. paper)
1. Warren, Gouverneur Kemble, 1830–1882. 2. Generals—
United States—Biography. 3. United States. Army—Biography.
4. United States—History—Civil War, 1861–1865—Campaigns.
I. Title

E467.1.W4 J67 2001
973.7'092—dc21
[B]

00–050641

1   2   3   4   5   06   05   04   03   02   01

To my grandson,
Augustus Francis Clearwater Born

"Happiness is not my companion."

—G. K. Warren to Emily Chase, July 27, 1862

"It is pitiful that one of his last requests was to be laid
in the grave . . . without soldierly emblems on his coffin
or uniform upon his body. The iron had entered his soul."

—Henry L. Abbot

CONTENTS

PREFACE

W ARREN? WARREN? WHO WAS GOUVERNEUR K. WARREN? His is not a name that resounds in the history of the American Civil War, but it seems to turn up all the time. One of the workhorses of the Army of the Potomac, he never commanded it, but his name pops up in the battles from Big Bethel to Five Forks, from the beginning of the war to almost its very end. Second Manassas, Chancellorsville, Bristoe Station, the Wilderness, Hatcher's Run—it is difficult to discuss a battle fought by the Federal army in the east without running into Warren's name in connection with it.

Sometimes Warren's name becomes very prominent indeed. Focus on July 2, 1863, the second day of the mammoth battle of Gettysburg. Longstreet has moved his Confederate corps around to the left of the Union lines, to throw two divisions upon Little Round Top, the capture of which will require Meade's army to retreat, because that height, in rebel hands, will dominate the Union line along Cemetery Ridge. Gouverneur K. Warren, the chief engineer of the Army of the Potomac, rides to the top of Little Round Top and finds that it is unoccupied by any force but a couple of signal corpsmen. On his own responsibility, he pushes troops up the hill. Arriving just in time, they save Little Round Top for the Union and Gettysburg for the Army of the Potomac. Without the quick eye and quicker action of G. K. Warren, the battle of Gettysburg would probably have ended on the late afternoon of July 2, 1863, resulting in an ignominious retreat by Meade's army. What reaction that would have caused in the body politic over which Abraham Lincoln presided is obviously a matter of speculation, but it would certainly have been serious, coming on the heels of the disasters at Chancellorsville and Fredericksburg, so close and threatening to the capital, where weariness with the war and defeatism were widespread.

Move on, then, to April 1, 1865. Although no one knows it at the time, Robert E. Lee's Army of Northern Virginia has but nine more days of existence. At an obscure country crossroads called Five Forks, southwest of Petersburg, Virginia, Major General Warren's Fifth Corps has combined with Philip Sheridan's cavalry to win an overwhelming victory over a Confederate force led by George Pickett. As the early darkness settles over the battlefield and the magnitude of the Union triumph is being recognized, Warren is stunned to receive an order from Sheridan, his temporary superior, relieving him from the command of his corps. Warren goes off in search of Sheridan, finds him, and asks him to reconsider the order, surely one made in the heat of battle under mistaken impressions. "Reconsider, hell," roars Sheridan. "I never reconsider my orders." And so Major General G. K. Warren rides off, out of the war.

Who, then, is Gouverneur Kemble Warren? What manner of man is this, who, from the absolute heights of heroism at Gettysburg, is plunged to the depths of humiliation as the great war is about to end? What kind of a soldier was he, what kind of a person? Warren has left numerous clues to his being, and many other men, members of the great army of which Warren was a leader, have left their remembrances of him. One man, signing himself "an old private," wrote of Warren years after the war, "He was very quiet and retiring in his manner, but somehow his men all loved him and had great faith in his ability." "He is smart," wrote a private in the Fifth New York; "there is no mistake in him." On the other hand, the provost marshal of the Army of the Potomac called Warren "a very loathesome, profane ungentlemanly & disgusting puppy in power." Charles Francis Adams, Jr., of the Massachusetts Adamses, not a man to bestow thoughtless compliments, called Warren one of "the very best of our army," while Abner Small of the Sixteenth Maine spoke of "the loved Warren." Yet Charles Wainwright, the commander of the Fifth Corps' artillery, marveled at Warren's excesses of temper and the "desperate blackguardism they displayed." A man who can produce such reactions can do with further examination. One of Warren's former aides wrote to him after the war, "[Y]ou know you can not escape the attention of the future historian."[1]

Warren was a man with a fine intellect, widely read, and of keen sensibilities. He was also an excellent engineer, mapmaker, and scientist. He was a soldier who cared much for the safety and welfare of the men under him, and he was sickened by the appalling carnage of the war in which he took such a prominent part. He was also arrogant and proud, and he hesitated hardly at all in putting down those of his colleagues he regarded as inferiors. His mind's eye took in much beyond what was his immediate concern, but this gift worked against him in the hierarchical realm of military life. Warren was prone to long sieges of depression, and he himself agreed that others found him to be morose and unsmiling. A complex and enigmatic man, Gouverneur Kemble Warren is not one to be easily categorized.

Warren's wife and daughter took the trouble to save everything they could find of papers relating to the general. They turned up family letters from his pre–West Point years, the records and journals of his prewar explorations in the Nebraska and Dakota territories, letters which Warren had written before he met his future wife, Emily, in Baltimore in 1862, and all the letters which he and Emily exchanged over the years, none of which apparently were ever discarded. Warren himself cooperated in this venture, because he was a saver, one who preserved all sorts of things over his career, from canceled checks and mathematical calculations for engineering projects to sketches of maps and orders received in the heat of famous Civil War battles. All of these items, and more, were carefully gathered by his daughter and turned over to the New York State Library in Albany.

With these aids we can make an effort at answering the question "Who is Gouverneur Kemble Warren?" I recognize that a different selection of quotations from the vast trove of Warren's letters might produce a different picture from the one I have developed in this book. It is the historian's task to choose what he brings forth in his work so that it presents a portrait as free of distortion as possible, and I have attempted to show the Warren with whom I became so well acquainted in the course of reading through his papers.

The primary resource, of course, has been the great collection of papers in the New York State Library, which I examined with the help of Jim Corsaro, Fred Bassett, Ed McGuire, and the rest of the fine staff there. As in any venture of this sort, however, there has been a great amount of additional assistance. Among those who have rendered it are Dr. James A. Hanson; Deborah McKeon-Pogue of the Special Collections Division and Judith A. Sibley of the Archives Division at the United States Military Academy Library; David Riggs; Leonard Levin, who found Warren's death certificate for me at the Rhode Island State Archives; William T. Lemmon, Jr., M.D.; Frank N. Schubert; Heather Briston at the Bentley Historical Library, University of Michigan; T. Sharon Defibaugh at the Alderman Library, University of Virginia; Tammy Peters and LaNina M. Clayton at the Smithsonian Institution Archives; Ruth Simmons and Al King at the Archibald S. Alexander Library, Rutgers University; Richard Baker at the U.S. Army Military History Institute; Scott DeHaven of the American Philosophical Society; Edith Prout and Bonnie Miller at the Jenkintown Library; Connie Wolf and Michael Long at the Missouri Botanical Garden Library; David Rowland and Joyce Root at the Old York Road Historical Society; Melissa Haley, manuscripts assistant at the New-York Historical Society; Steve Wright and his staff at the Civil War Library and Museum in Philadelphia; my secretary Liz Putnam; and the staffs at the Free Library of Philadelphia, the Historical Society of Pennsylvania, and Firestone

Library at Princeton University. Bill Nelson prepared the maps for me. I want to acknowledge the help and encouragement given me by Jim Bell, a National Park Service ranger at the (underdeveloped) Five Forks Unit, Petersburg National Battlefield, as well as the advice and counsel of Ned Hagerman, of York University, and Brian Pohanka, the authority on the Fifth New York. And, as so often before, I had critical editorial help from my daughter Diana, who came to share my belief that Warren, while not as good a soldier as Hancock, on whom we worked before, was a more interesting personality. Finally, my wife Barbara, while passing up numerous opportunities to visit scenic Albany, gave me valuable support and encouragement over the years this work was in germination.

DAVID M. JORDAN
Jenkintown, Pennsylvania

"HAPPINESS
IS NOT
MY COMPANION"

CHAPTER ONE

COLD SPRING AND
WEST POINT

A MALE CHILD WAS BORN ON JANUARY 8, 1830, to Phoebe and Sylvanus Warren, in the village of Cold Spring, New York, on the eastern shore of the Hudson River. The Warrens named their newborn son, the fourth of what would be twelve children, Gouverneur Kemble Warren, after a close friend who was one of the most distinguished citizens of Putnam County.

Gouverneur Kemble was a substantial citizen indeed. Born in New York City in 1786 and an 1803 graduate of Columbia College, Kemble had gone to Spain in 1816 to study methods of casting cannon. A fledgling casting industry had been set up by a group of local men in 1814, but the flowering of the business awaited Kemble's return from Europe. When he came back in 1818, he established the West Point Foundry, the lone industry in Cold Spring, where for the first time in the United States cannons were cast with any degree of perfection. A local historian called the foundry "the life of Cold Spring Village . . . and . . . it may be said, it feeds all, clothes all, and supports all."[1]

The foundry, in which Sylvanus Warren also made a fruitful investment, made Kemble's fortune, and he became the most influential Democrat in Putnam County, one who would serve two terms in the United States House of Representatives. Kemble, a lifelong bachelor, was also famed for his stag dinner parties, at which General Winfield Scott, hero of the 1812 and Mexican wars, was a frequent guest. Much would be hoped for from a newborn babe with a namesake of such exalted status.[2]

The baby Gouverneur arrived with some advantages, including a sturdy old New England heritage. His great-great-grandfather Samuel Warren was born in Boston in 1720 or earlier, became a physician, and came in about 1740 to Philipstown, New York, where he married and had two sons. No one seemed to know quite what it was, but there was apparently some kind of trouble or disgrace which caused Samuel to leave Boston.[3]

1

Gouverneur Kemble Warren. National Archives.

After his wife died, Samuel married again and moved on. His elder son, also named Samuel, sired a child named John Warren in 1765. Samuel, little more than twenty years old, was accidentally killed shortly afterward when he was thrown out of an overturning wagon. John, young Gouverneur's grandfather, was said to aspire "to no higher distinction than that of a plain, practical farmer, which he was," a man who "never gave just cause of offense to his neighbor." Though originally trained as a blacksmith, he farmed and also maintained a famous tavern on the Albany Post Road.[4]

Sylvanus, the youngest of John Warren's seven children, grew up in Cold Spring to become a solid and respected member of the community, a learned man, a prominent citizen, and a close friend of author Washington Irving. Sylvanus was associated with his friend Kemble in Democratic party affairs, working in support of the latter's successful campaign for a seat in Congress in 1836 as well as for his reelection in 1838. In 1839 Kemble suggested to Warren that he apply for the position of assistant U.S. marshal for taking the 1840 census, and both Kemble and Irving were instrumental in Sylvanus's securing the position. When *Washington Globe* publisher Amos Kendall needed subscribers to ensure the success of his paper, the organ of Jacksonian Democracy, Congressman Kemble was among those guaranteeing a certain number, and he immediately called upon his friend Warren "to assist in procuring subscriptions among our friends in the county." [5]

Sylvanus Warren was a big fish in the rather small pond that was Cold Spring. The town was named for a cooling spring at which George Washington had allegedly slaked his thirst, but it had not grown much since that time. In precolonial days, its site had been a fishing ground for the Wappinger Indians, but in 1697 a twelve-square-mile tract was granted by King William III to a wealthy New York merchant named Adolph Philipse. When the legislature in 1788 passed an act dividing the counties of New York State into towns, the area became Philipstown. Not until 1846 was Cold Spring carved officially out of Philipstown as a separate village. [6]

In 1817, fresh from his Spanish training in the casting of cannon, Gouverneur Kemble and a partner bought from the Philips family 178 acres of solid land, 27 acres of marsh, and the right to use the waters of Margaret Brook. A year later the West Point Foundry Association was incorporated and the foundry itself established on the site. Because of the quality of its product, the foundry in 1820 secured its first of many government contracts, and the town's prosperity was assured. In 1835 Captain Robert Parrott, the renowned ordinance engineer and inventor, resigned from the army to become the foundry's superintendent. Just upstream and across the river from West Point, Cold Spring faced the formidable Storm King Mountain on the western bank of the Hudson. Indeed, Kemble's cannons were tested by firing them at the face of the mountain across the water. [7]

Sylvanus Warren was married to the former Phoebe Lickley, and by all accounts the marriage was a satisfactory one. The Warren family lived in a comfortable though not luxurious house on Fair Street, seventy-five feet north of Main Street, just up the hill from the river, and here young Gouv and his brothers and sisters grew up. The Warren children had the advantages of a small-town, outdoor kind of life. Their basic necessities were well taken care of, and their parents inculcated in them a taste for literature and learning. Gouv was the eldest of the six Warren children who survived childhood, and he was looked up to by all of them.

Sylvanus Warren did the best he could for his children, and he arranged to send Gouv across the river to the care of a tutor named Kinsley, who specialized in the classics and mathematics. Here the youngster was well schooled in the fundamentals, and he later wrote, "I think I always applied myself as well as a boy could." [8]

It soon became apparent that young Gouverneur had an aptitude for science and mathematics. As the time approached to consider the further education of this bright young man, and how his talents could be properly developed, a solution appeared very close by, at the military academy at West Point. The academy's curriculum, strongly influenced by the Corps of Engineers, was attuned more to the development of engineers than of soldiers, and it offered a fine opportunity for Gouverneur Warren.

Sylvanus Warren's political activities over the years, the connections and friendships he had made, primarily through ex-congressman Kemble, were now to pay off. After the appropriate inquiries were made, the proper strings pulled, the right political IOUs cashed, a letter was sent on January 28, 1846, from local congressman William W. Woodworth to Secretary of War William L. Marcy (himself a good New York Democrat serving in the Polk administration) nominating young Warren for appointment to the military academy from the eighth district of New York.[9]

On March 5, 1846, Secretary Marcy dispatched a letter to the young man, advising him of his conditional appointment as a cadet, and on April 2, Gouv wrote formally back to Marcy "to inform you of my acceptance of the same." On the same document was the assent of Sylvanus Warren for his minor son and his permission to young Gouverneur "to sign articles by which he will bind himself to serve the United States, eight years unless sooner discharged." [10] Eight years would stretch eventually into thirty-six, years which would bring distinction, renown, achievement, ignominy, and heartbreak.

Gouverneur made the short trip across the river and up onto the great plain above the Hudson, entering the academy on July 1, 1846, not yet quite sixteen and a half. He was of medium height with a slight but wiry build. He successfully underwent the rigors of the encampment on the plain and the admission examination, and was soon accorded the status of a full-fledged cadet. Warren applied himself to his studies, and at the end of his year as a plebe he stood sixth in his class of eighty-nine, performing well in mathematics and English grammar, somewhat more poorly in French. He incurred only four demerits for violations of the Code of Discipline and stood eighteenth among the whole corps of cadets on the Conduct Roll. Warren's third-class, or sophomore, year saw him move up to second on his class roll, behind Frederic E. Prime, also of New York, who had led the class in its plebe year as well. He held his own in mathematics and French and was fourth in the class in drawing. Gouverneur's low total of eleven demerits stood him thirty-third on the Conduct Roll. He particularly enjoyed his introduction to Plato and the Greeks.[11]

There was a major flap in March 1848, when the third-year class put itself on the line to prevent the expulsion of one of its members, Henry C. Bankhead, for alcohol abuse. In exchange for leniency for Bankhead, the class members pledged themselves neither to bring onto nor drink on the post any intoxicating liquor, nor to partake of any when away from West Point "unless absent by authority for a longer period than three days." Warren signed the pledge on the morning of March 19; "my principal reason for signing it," he wrote, somewhat self-righteously, "was, that independent of its saving Bankhead, it will have the effect of making the members of our class sober men, when they get to be first-class-men, which is far from being the case with the present first class." Bankhead, saved by his peers, would years later perform valuable service on Warren's Fifth Corps staff.[12]

Gouverneur had admitted in early January that he had nine demerits, "which is considerable more than I had last. But we are more exposed this year to reports, and there is but one man above me who has less than myself." He told a story of being reported by one of the cadet captains, "evidently . . . out of some ill feeling, though what it was I could not tell, for I had never condescended to speak to the contemptible puppy." Warren went to the commandant and accused the captain of prejudice (not unlikely, if Warren's obvious feelings were made manifest), succeeding in having the reports removed from his record.[13]

In his junior year, with the class of 1850 now reduced by attrition to fifty-seven members, Warren moved into the first position, doing well in philosophy, chemistry, and drawing, while Prime dropped to third, stymied by drawing class. Gouv's four demerits for the year moved him up to twenty-first on the Conduct Roll.

In the following spring, Warren was alarmed to learn that his mother was ill, although it was to prove a passing malady. "Sickness in our family," he wrote to her, "always causes me apprehension, especially when it attacks Poppy or yourself . . . [L]et me beseech you do not over exert yourself . . . preserve your health at all hazard." As for himself, he assured her, "I am doing very well in my studies and never enjoyed better health in my life." [14]

Finally, as a first classman, Gouverneur had the academy at his feet. He graduated second in his class, behind young Prime, out of forty-five new officers, with excellent marks in engineering, ethics, artillery, and infantry tactics, and class leadership in mineralogy and geology. Gouv's twenty-five demerits for the year dropped him to sixty-sixth on the Conduct Roll, as his final year witnessed a perhaps-to-be-expected slackening of deportment.

In his first-class year, Warren came under the tutelage of the formidable Dennis Hart Mahan, the professor who instructed the budding soldiers in engineering, fortifications, and military tactics. The demanding Mahan stressed celerity of movement and common sense as the cardinal military virtues, and he felt that the progress of military technology increased substantially the importance of defensive field fortifications. Mahan's idea of offensive tactics was not the traditional frontal assault but the turning maneuver. Most of the textbooks and treatises on military doctrine in use for many years were written by Mahan, and his influence on decades of West Point graduates was immense. Warren, one of his brightest students, absorbed Mahan's teachings as the core of his own military thought, both in his senior year in college and through later reinforcement as a fellow faculty member.

As graduation neared, Gouverneur wrote to his father about finances. He had come to the conclusion, he said, "that it was wrong for me to be any longer a source of expense to you and that I ought to return to you whatever assistance you had afforded me since I became a Cadet." He calculated that in his first three years and the furlough following he had cost his father $256.50, with another $26 for his first-class year, or a total of $282.50. "This I intend to repay you as soon as I am *able*, and having once fairly made the resolution I shall keep it. The time however may be somewhat distant as I shall have to incur new debts which it will be necessary to pay up first." This, the future officer allowed, would start him "with some weight on my shoulders but it may lead me to contract economical habits." Another problem was that his postgraduation furlough would soon be upon him, and he did not "have the heart to deny myself all the pleasures I have promised myself on this occasion, even though they should be at the expense of some future privations." Lest Sylvanus be led to believe his hitherto strait-laced son was about to launch himself into a life of debauchery, Gouv said he would spend his furlough at home, but he wanted to have a horse at his disposal so he could go where he pleased. He hoped Sylvanus would put up half the cost of the horse; he would put up the other half, and his father could then sell the animal after the furlough was ended.[15]

The elder Warren furnished Gouverneur money to pay off his debt, buy a horse, and purchase the outfit he would need to get started in the regular army. Gouv was touched by "the evident interest and affection for me by which" the offer was dictated. Still, he was determined to repay his father for all financial assistance. "I cannot have a free conscience on the subject," he wrote, "nor feel like a man till I do." Besides, there were his younger brothers and sisters to think of. "I should be guilty of injustice to them if I did not all in my power to procure them equal advantages" to his own.[16]

And so Gouverneur K. Warren prepared to make his way into the world beyond the confines of the plain of West Point—a young man of achievement, with a strong sense of rectitude shading into self-righteousness, conscious of his mental attainments, with a condescending air of satisfied superiority.

Warren's high class standing was rewarded with a coveted assignment to the elite Corps of Topographical Engineers as a brevet second lieutenant. Following his furlough, he was ordered to report to the corps headquarters at Washington, where he arrived in October 1850, taking a room at Mrs. Peyton's boarding house, ready for whatever life had to offer.

TOPOGRAPHICAL ENGINEER

AFTER ARRIVING IN THE UNIMPRESSIVE LITTLE TOWN which served as the nation's capital and seeing to his lodging, twenty-year-old Gouverneur Warren reported to the headquarters of the Corps of Topographical Engineers, where he was directed to Captain A. A. Humphreys. Captain Humphreys informed the young officer "that he was preparing to make a survey and examination of the banks and bed of the Mississippi from the mouth as far up as the Red river, and that I was to assist him." [1]

Warren reported that Andrew Atkinson Humphreys, then forty years old and the product of a wealthy and respected Philadelphia family, was "an exceedingly pleasing man in manners and conversation." His meeting with Humphreys was the start of a close professional and personal relationship which would last the rest of his life, in the Topographical Engineers before the Civil War, in the Army of the Potomac, and in the Corps of Engineers after the war. Warren would be closely involved with Humphreys' controversial work on the Mississippi, and they would collaborate on Warren's mapping of the West. At Gettysburg, Humphreys was out on the Emmitsburg Road while Warren was holding Little Round Top. Humphreys was Meade's chief of staff in the 1864 campaign, and he saved Warren's neck at Spotsylvania on May 12. At Five Forks, Humphreys' corps was on the right of Warren's, and he was able to offer valuable insights in the later inquiry into that battle. Humphreys was Warren's superior in the postwar Engineers, and he worked closely with Warren and his attorney to force a resolution to the court of inquiry just before Warren's death. Through all the years and all their varied activities, the two men would remain close friends.

The project which Humphreys was about to undertake was one of immense importance, no less than a search for the means of taming the mighty Mississippi, bringing under control the devastating floods which periodically ravaged its lower watershed. For many years the civic and political leaders of the

Mississippi valley had bemoaned the destruction visited upon their land by the great river and demanded that the Federal government afford them some relief. Finally, in 1850, Congress passed a measure calling for a survey of the lower Mississippi and appropriated fifty thousand dollars to pay for it. The Secretary of War put Humphreys in charge of the project and was then chagrined to find President Millard Fillmore yielding to civilian demands that Charles Ellet, Jr., perhaps the most renowned engineer in the country, perform the survey. Under War Department pressure, Fillmore eventually directed that the appropriation for the survey be divided between Ellet and Humphreys, each to conduct the study independently of the other and to report separately.[2]

It was as an assistant on this project that Humphreys had recruited the newest member of the Topographical Engineers. Warren, having been briefed by Humphreys, described the planned survey to his father. The survey, he wrote, "is for the purpose of taking measures to prevent the inundation of the country, a great portion of Louisiana being at present covered by the waters of the Mississippi." From New Orleans to the mouth of the river they would be following up on work already done, "[b]ut from N.O. to the Red river it will have to be made with great accuracy, and will probably occupy more than one season." The expedition, which would consist of two army officers with the rest civilians, "will set out in the course of three or four weeks; until further orders I am to assist in forwarding the preliminary arrangements." The young second lieutenant was enthralled by the prospects: "This expedition will be capital practice in Civil Engineering on one of its most interesting subjects, and if I have my health nothing would please me more. Come what will I am bound to be pleased Anyhow."[3]

A week later Gouv wrote his father again, telling him of all the help he was getting from Humphreys in becoming acquainted with his new duties. He admitted that the book learning he was picking up was "of a very general character," but another officer told him he "would have no difficulty, in 'taking right hold' when I got in the field." The following week Warren was on his way, although the route taken to New Orleans from Washington was somewhat circuitous: to New York and Cold Spring first, for a visit home, then to Albany, to Buffalo (with a side trip to see Niagara Falls), then to Sandusky, Ohio, to Cincinnati and Louisville, and on to the Crescent City. On December 20, he wrote home again, saying that he enjoyed New Orleans but at present had "almost nothing to do."[4]

With the new year, Warren commenced the keeping of a personal journal in a small "daily reminder" book. He carefully inscribed inside the front cover, "Any body finding this will be suitably rewarded by returning to me. G.K.W." A New Year's Day hunting trip was spoiled by rain and hail, but Warren retrieved the day with dinner at the Florence House, drinking wine with many of his new acquaintances and spending the evening with several of the young ladies whose names turn up frequently thereafter in his journal.[5]

Through the early part of January the young officer recorded details of the New Orleans social whirl in which he gaily joined, noting champagne suppers, hunting expeditions, card games, evening soirees, and beautiful New Orleans belles. A young unmarried army officer was considered a great social asset, even if he spoke with the harsh accents of New York. On January 8, Warren shared his birthday with the celebration of Andrew Jackson's battle of New Orleans; "all the ladies [of] my acquaintance drank my health at dinner." The next day he ventured out into the bayous, where he "saw plenty of aligators [sic]."[6]

Warren would soon enough find work to keep him occupied. On January 17, 1851, Humphreys told him that he was to go to Bonne Carré Crevasse, forty miles upriver, "and stay there long enough to become acquainted with the routine there then do the same with the party coming down from the Red River, then go with him on an examination thro' the State, after which he would give me charge of a party." It was no doubt time to put the young man to work; he wrote to his sister Eliza that "I have now quite an extensive lady acquaintance with no less than *three* of which I am very much interested."[7]

On January 28, Warren set out up the river and reached Donaldsonville, about halfway to Baton Rouge, at 4 A.M. the next morning. He spent a couple of days there getting a gauge (which he persistently spelled "guage," then and for years to come) erected and then took a packet for Baton Rouge, where he arrived on the 31st. He worked hard during the days but had enough youthful energy left to go to a dance at ten in the evening, where he met a Miss Chambers and a "Miss I forget[,] with whom I flirted." After finishing the work in Baton Rouge, Warren proceeded up the river to Natchez, where he received a letter of further instructions from Humphreys. He set up another gauge at New Carthage, which he left with few regrets, calling it a "mighty rough looking place."[8]

Warren continued erecting gauges at various spots along the river, and on February 21 he noted his "first practical lesson in running circumferenter lines on a batture between Red River & Raccourci cut offs." On the 22nd he received his "first practical lessons in running regular lines of levels." On this day also he noted the arrival of Captain Humphreys ("very glad to see him"). Two days later, Humphreys having satisfied himself that the young man was up to it, Warren was given charge of his own party, running a line along a levee and in dense woods with thick underbrush and tangled vines. On a cold and rainy last day of February Warren was given his first test as a commander: "Men refused to work[;] finally induced to change their determination."[9]

Through March and April the work continued, and the young engineer's journal entries evidence a growing mastery of the procedures involved. On March 2, Gouv wrote his father that "I have under my immediate orders 3 men to chain and drive stakes 1 to carry the instrument 1 to carry the flags and 2 to cut the line. I have nothing very hard to do but I never was so busy in my life all day running up and down the line." "The men all like me," he continued, "and I am beginning to succeed very well. The duty suits my disposition exactly, and will I think be healthy." He admitted to himself on one occasion that the sight of "a pretty Creole at J. Lacone's . . . set me thinking about other things than my work," but most of the time he stayed at it with drive and determination. Warren was becoming closely acquainted with the mighty Mississippi River, with its great volume of water, its twists and loops, the incessant pressure upon its banks and levees, and its treacherous and changeable nature.[10]

The work continued through May, interrupted early in the month by what Warren called "rheumatic pains" in his chest and shoulder, which laid him up for a week, and in mid-month by a trip to Mobile and Pass Christian, where he was mildly involved with a "very pretty" young lady named Purnell. He told his father about the trip to Mobile and said, "I am getting to like Captain Humphreys more and more every day, and one cause is, I expect, he appears so well pleased with me."[11]

Lieutenant Warren continued to work hard on the river survey during the day, while he cultivated an extensive social life which often carried far into the evening. On June 24, he sent his brother Will a check to present to their father, to cancel his indebtedness for "certain money and assistance rendered me at West Point." He included an accounting showing a balance owed of $339.56. The check was for $340, but Gouv did not ask for the change.[12]

Late in June, Humphreys fell quite ill but still accompanied Warren on a trip to Pascagoula, Mississippi. While there, Humphreys' condition worsened, so the two officers spent a month in Pascagoula, with Warren having little to do but tend to his superior's needs and pay court to the local damsels. He had nothing to do, he wrote to Sylvanus, "but act my own pleasure consistently of course with the rules of society." He said he had won "quite a reputation for dancing, and can have for partner any lady I wish. My success here at the south quite astonishes me." Humphreys, he said, "thinks I am distinguishing myself in a new line for an engineer, but the truth is I have nothing else to do."[13]

On July 30, Warren left Pascagoula for New Orleans, where he packed up for a trip back east on leave. On the first of August, he sailed in the *Union* for New York, where he arrived on the 7th, returning on the 9th to Cold Spring. He stayed there until September 22, drawing maps and flirting with young ladies, with day trips to New York City and West Point.

One of the matters Warren considered during this time was a reported offer by Professor Alfred Church to join the mathematics department at the military academy. While this was reputed to be a great honor, Warren made it clear he was not interested. There were several reasons: "[S]ome of the young officers there I never could associate with . . . I disliked them when there, and

A.A.Humphreys, maj. Genl. Vols.
Chief of Staff Army of the Potomac
9th Jn. C. 1863 to Nov. 1864.

Andrew A. Humphreys, Warren's oldest and best friend in the army.
National Archives.

do still." More importantly, "I think it would be much better for me to keep away from there for four or five years, *as far as concerns my reputation in my Corps* . . . Our Corps has more duty than it can perform. My going there so soon would put me back in the profession to which I look only for success." Besides, he said, "I like Capt. Humphreys to [*sic*] much to think of leaving him if he wishes me to stay. At present I don't think he can get along without me." [14]

With the temptation of West Point behind him, Warren reported back to Humphreys in Philadelphia, on September 23, 1851. For the next couple of months he was engaged in writing up the surveys, studies, and data from his tour of duty on the Mississippi, all of which eventually contributed to the massive but controversial report Humphreys produced some years later, containing his conclusions and recommendations for dealing with the great river, conclusions and recommendations which did not always match those of other eminent engineers.[15]

Warren did not neglect either his cultural or his social life, however. He saw Edwin Forrest in *Othello*, he visited the Academy of Fine Arts, and he went to hear Bellini's *I Puritani* and *Norma*. Twice he went to see Madame Thillon, "the prettiest woman ever I saw," in a masterpiece called *Pride of the Harem*. He read Dickens. And for further diversion he paid court to numerous young ladies. "Saw O! such pretty girls," he wrote of one such occasion, "till was perfectly bewildered."[16]

Warren seems to have spent a good bit of time during his stay in Philadelphia with a young lady named Emily Lynam. In all of his courtly gallivanting as an eligible young officer he seems not to have formed any lasting attachments, but the scant evidence of his journals hints that Miss Lynam may have had a more serious feeling toward him. She continued writing him during the next year, until her name finally fades from the pages of Warren's record.

Gouverneur told his father that "my general health is excellent," and he had gained twelve pounds, to reach 137, since leaving New Orleans. For lack of funds the Corps of Topographical Engineers scratched that winter's planned sojourn in New Orleans, and Warren was told he would be leaving in the beginning of December for Louisville to spend the winter there. "I have had a most agreeable time in Philadelphia," he said, "with many delightful acquaintances." He reported spending the evening of December 8 with a lass named Emily Seymour "& was devilish sorry to leave her." At 8 A.M. the next morning Lieutenant Warren left Philadelphia for Louisville.[17]

As his second year in the Topographical Engineers closed, Warren could reflect upon his experiences with a good bit of satisfaction: he had made himself noticed as one of the coming young men in the corps and had gained a powerful sponsor and mentor in Humphreys. On December 31, 1851, he "spent the evening in jolly style and glided into the New Year."[18]

The year 1852, however, was for Warren one of marking time professionally. Congress starved the army financially, so that planned engineering projects were not carried out. He spent the year in Louisville, under the command of Colonel Stephen Long, doing paperwork, writing up more of the data compiled on the Mississippi, working on improvements to the Ohio River Canal around the falls of the Ohio, and carrying on an active social life.[19]

On one occasion Warren and Long argued over the calculation of pressures exerted against a lock gate under differing heights of water. Long had the principle reversed, and Warren refused to agree to it. Finally, the colonel exclaimed angrily, "I am not in the habit, sir, of having my opinions treated with contempt!" Warren coolly replied, "I don't know what you mean by a mathe-matical *opinion*." [20]

Gouv confided to his father that the young ladies competed with each other in the number of beaux "which they can have in their train." He was told that if he played his cards right he might "get some fine bids for my devotion. I shall take the hint and act like the toper on election day and not vote till pretty near dark. I'm not sure I shall vote at all." His journal records the names of many young ladies with whom he went to ice cream socials, to concerts, to balls and parties, even to church—Belle Sheridan ("the prettiest girl," he wrote), Lucy Long (daughter of his commanding officer), Lou Gross, Julia Bull, and others. What is clear, though, is that none of this was serious to him. [21]

In March 1853, Warren was detailed to New Orleans, to see to the sale of the property and equipment of the Delta Survey. By April 13, he was back in Louis-ville, marking time again until early June, when he was sent off to do a survey of rapids on the upper Mississippi River. Warren threw himself into this activ-ity, covering a stretch of river from Dubuque to Davenport, Iowa. He finished the work by November 18 and returned to Louisville on December 6. Back in the office the next day, Warren was ordered "to repair without delay to Wash-ington." When he reached the capital, he was told the Secretary of War wanted to see him. [22]

INTO THE WEST
WITH HARNEY

*J*EFFERSON DAVIS HAD A PROBLEM. Appointed secretary of war in 1853, when Democrat Franklin Pierce became president and ousted the Whigs from power, Davis was committed to advancing the cause of his native South within the Federal Union. One means of doing so involved the projected railroad to the Pacific Coast, a road which would enhance the economic interests of that part of the "civilized East" from which it departed. In the spirited sectional competition for the transcontinental railroad, Davis, a Mississippi planter and former U.S. senator from that state, was keenly interested in pushing the "southern route" as strongly as possible. Not only would the South benefit economically, but there would arise a golden opportunity to forge political ties between the South and the West. But before any route could be chosen, of course, the fullest information about the lands beyond the Missouri River had to be available.

The army had long been gathering information about the lands of the west on a piecemeal basis. For several years its officers and engineers had been compiling reports, data, statistics, and surveys of the western territories. But in order to make use of this mass of information, Davis needed it all pulled together. For this purpose he tapped Gouverneur Warren, who enjoyed a growing reputation both for accurate fieldwork and for meticulous handling of the data acquired.

Warren was assigned to the Pacific Railroad office within the War Department, with the overall assignment of preparing a great map of the West, utilizing the materials gathered in the field over the last several years. Warren, Davis later wrote, "has been especially intrusted with the preparation of the material and the construction of the General Map," along with the compilation of profiles of all the routes surveyed.[1] He started to work in the beginning of 1854 and was soon totally immersed in the task.

In August, Humphreys was placed in charge of the Pacific Railroad office. Upon taking command, he wrote,

> I found that the preparation of the material for the general map, a work of great labor, and the superintendence of its construction and drawing, had been intrusted to Lieutenant G. K. Warren, topographical engineers, whose zeal and ability in the performance of this and the general office duty, Major Emory [Humphreys' predecessor] acknowledged in warm terms. Lieutenant Warren has continued in charge of the office duties . . . In addition to this he has likewise largely aided me in making this report.[2]

"This laborious service," Humphreys concluded, "has been executed by him with great intelligence, zeal, and energy." Humphreys, of course, was not surprised by Warren's exemplary work but was glad to make it known to a wider audience than just the Topographical Engineers. The great map of the trans-Mississippi West was one of the signal contributions of the prewar army, and Gouverneur Warren was entitled to a major share of the credit for it. Warren, at this time and throughout his life, was a careful, painstaking, and energetic engineer and scientist, with a breadth of vision and understanding which impressed his peers. This same breadth of vision later proved to be a trait which, in a subordinate officer, was quite irritating to men like Meade and Grant.

While living and working in Washington, Warren made the acquaintance of Spencer F. Baird, a young man from Reading, Pennsylvania, already famous as a zoologist. Baird was serving as assistant to the secretary of the Smithsonian Institution, the eminent Joseph Henry, and he would succeed Henry as secretary at the latter's death in 1878. Baird made it a practice to befriend those who might be in a position to aid the Smithsonian, and a rising young officer in the Topographical Engineers was an obvious prospect. Baird and Warren became lifelong friends and correspondents. Warren brought Baird and the Smithsonian many items of value to that institution from his western explorations, while Baird helped to gratify Warren's interest in areas of science in which the military officer claimed no expertise.[3]

Warren wrote his brother Will, urging him to quit his dead-end job and come live with him in Washington, which Will was happy to do, eventually obtaining a job as a clerk in the War Department. Gouv also raised the possibility of leaving the army to make real money in the world of civil (and civilian) engineering, a possibility he considered many times over the years but never acted upon:

> There is no use not the slightest of either of us being in a hurry to get married [—] ten years yet will do, and before that time we can be well established in something. If I should ever go to civil engineering, and all the old officers advise it when I get a good opportunity, you would be just the person to go with me, one to attend to the financial and the other to the engineering.[4]

Warren worked in the Pacific Railroad office through 1854 and into the following year. On September 1, 1854, he was finally promoted to the full rank of
second lieutenant, shedding the "brevet" tag he had carried since graduation
from West Point. Davis was pleased with Warren's work; he referred to "the most
commendable diligence and intelligence" shown by the young topographical
engineer. On April 21, 1855, however, Warren received an order which would
bring about a substantial change in his life. Special Orders No. 72, from the War
Department, dated April 20, directed him to repair to St. Louis and report to
General William S. Harney for "duty with the Sioux Expedition . . . as soon as
his services in connection with the Pacific Railroad Survey can be dispensed
with." Warren was to replace Lt. Thomas Lee, who, believing the Sioux were
in the right in resisting white encroachment, resigned his commission rather
than participate in what he felt was an unjust mission.[5]

The purpose of Harney's mission was to punish the Sioux for the so-called
Grattan Massacre, an episode the previous August set off by an arrogant young
brevet second lieutenant named John L. Grattan. Grattan marched a thirty-
man unit into a Brulé Sioux camp to try to apprehend a brave who had killed
a Mormon emigrant's cow; when he failed to find the culprit, he opened fire
with his artillery upon the village and managed to shoot to death the Brulé
chief. The enraged Sioux then overwhelmed Grattan and his force, and all but
one of the soldiers were killed.[6]

William Harney was a crusty old Tennesseean, with long and distinguished
service in fighting Indians and Mexicans. He was no diplomat; his idea of
treating with Indians was to fight and whip them first and then to talk. He
moved up to Fort Kearney on the Platte River and began to organize his force,
which was to be composed of four companies of dragoons, six companies of
the Second Infantry, an artillery battery, and the Sixth Infantry, about six hundred men in all.

Meanwhile, Harney's assigned topographical engineer was back in Washington. On May 11, Warren noted that he "finished work in the P.R.R. office," and
the next day he called on Secretary Davis. He gained the secretary's approval
to employ assistants for his expedition and then had an hour's chat with the
future president of the Confederacy. On May 14, Warren hired J. H. Snowden,
from the Washington office of the corps, as a civilian assistant at sixty dollars
a month and on the 15th departed from Washington—to travel to Cold
Spring. Finally, on the 20th he left New York on the 5:30 Erie train, which
reached St. Louis at 2 A.M. on the 23rd.

The next day Snowden arrived in St. Louis. Warren called at Harney's office
and found neither the general nor "definite orders or instructions . . . for me."
Not until June 4 did Warren receive orders "to accompany the 2d Inf to Ft.
Pierre," up the Missouri. After hiring another assistant, the young officer left
by boat with the infantry regiment on June 7, for a trip which took five and a

half weeks to reach Fort Pierre, located on the west bank of the river, across from the present capital of South Dakota. Warren expected to reach Pierre by the end of June, he wrote his friend Professor Baird; "this season will probably provide little or no opportunities for me to make collections in your line," he said, "but I am prepared to do all that the opportunities offer for doing."[7]

The trip got off to a bad start when Warren discovered that they had left their theodolite in a repair shop and their clothes with a washerwoman; Snowden was set ashore to go back to St. Louis to retrieve these items. Nevertheless, Warren was, as he wrote Baird, "very glad to be on my way for the plains and leave St. Louis behind me." The steamboat encountered all sorts of problems, hitting sandbars and snags, running aground, and being buffeted by high winds. It reached Fort Pierre on July 16, bringing with it a very frustrated Gouverneur Warren: he was supposed to be with Harney, and Pierre was nowhere close to Fort Kearney.[8]

When Warren arrived, he immediately set to work surveying and laying out a position for a new fort, the work assigned him by Harney. He also mapped the Missouri upriver to the mouth of the Cheyenne as well as three miles up the latter stream. When these tasks were completed, the young second lieutenant debated with himself how best to reach Harney and his troops at Fort Kearney. He also had some unpleasantness with the post commander, a Colonel Montgomery:

> I was excessively annoyed by Col. Montgomery, for no cause, but some foolish idea of want of respect when I had been so occupied that had scarce a moment to myself. I took no offense at his conduct, but I must say he has in many respects treated me badly and made no provision for the necessities of my party. I owe him nothing in the way of politeness.[9]

Warren decided that he would join Harney by making an overland trek from Pierre south to Kearney, over three hundred miles of plains, sand hills, creeks, and—possibly—hostile Indians in country which he had never seen. It seemed an utterly harebrained, dangerous, and foolish venture for a young greenhorn, and the other officers at Fort Pierre warned Warren against it. Montgomery tried to detain him, but since Warren was not under his command Montgomery could not prevent him from starting out. Warren, in addition, felt that he had calculated his risks and chances well: "my intention . . . had not been formed without due consideration" of the possible dangers, which he thought should free him "from any charge of having acted with rashness or imprudence."[10]

With a party of seven Warren left Fort Pierre on August 8 at noon, moving rapidly but cautiously, stopping only to make observations of his position as well as sketches of the country's topography. He managed to avoid all possible hazards and on August 22 reached the Platte, eleven miles above Fort Kearney.

Later that day he reported to Harney, and he "slept that night in security without any guard." [11]

Warren got there just in time. On August 24, Harney's whole command marched out at 8 A.M. It headed northwest along the wide and shallow Platte, but it found no Indians at first. On September 2, Harney's force discovered some forty lodges of Brulés under Little Thunder, camped on a creek called the Blue Water. Harney decided to send his dragoons around the Indians to a position up the creek valley the next morning, so that the advance of his infantry would drive the Sioux into the mounted force. The infantry advanced at daylight, but Harney worried that the fight might begin before the dragoons were in position. In order to gain time for his mounted troops Harney initiated a parley with Little Thunder, which broke off when the Indians discovered the dragoons in their rear. Harney then moved the infantry forward, with the expected results. [12]

With the infantry moving north up the valley toward them and the mounted troops behind them, the Sioux attempted to flee to the east. "They were pursued at full speed by the Dragoons," Warren wrote, "for several miles between 8 & 12 and many killed. [A]ll the troops joined in the chase, but those not mounted were soon distanced." Warren rode with the advance guard of the infantry for his first taste of combat, one-sided as it was. At 9 A.M. the recall was sounded, and Warren with others went in search of the wounded. This meant primarily Indian women and children, many of whom had been shot during the infantry advance and few of whom had been able to flee with their warriors. Warren was appalled at what he found: "the sight . . . was heart rending—wounded women & children crying and moaning, horribly mangled by the bullets."

Warren offered succor to numerous wounded noncombatants, carrying several down to the creek to bathe their wounds and erecting a shelter to keep off the sun. He did not return to camp until 10 P.M., and even there he continued to dress wounds. He "was disgusted with the tales of valor afterwards told on the field, for their [sic] were but few who killed anything but a flying foe." Most of the eighty-five fatalities suffered by the Brulés occurred during the flight. [13]

For most of the next two or three days Warren was with Harney's force, camped near the scene of the fight. Although he does not mention it in his journal, Warren partially occupied his time by gathering up into his engineering wagon a large number of Sioux artifacts and clothing which had been abandoned by the flight of their owners. What he saved from Harney's order to burn everything has been called "one of the most significant Plains Indian collections ever made" and "the earliest intact, comprehensive gathering of Lakota material in existence." Delivered by Warren to Spencer Baird at the Smithsonian, it is one of the ethnographic gems in that great repository's vast collections. [14]

At Harney's direction Warren laid out a square wooden fort on the Platte near the Blue Water, named Fort Grattan, and then on September 9 the army moved northwest to Fort Laramie, which it reached on the 16th. On the 22nd "a large delegation of Brules and Ogallallah" came in to meet with Harney, who expressed in no uncertain terms what the future conduct of these tribes must be, failing which, as Warren wrote, "their buffalo would all be driven away, and . . . the Dacotahs would be no more." [15]

On September 29, Harney and his force left Laramie for an overland trek to Fort Pierre, on the Missouri. Warren recorded crossing the L'eau Qui Court River (now the Niobrara), marching along the White River, traversing "the Mauvaises terres" (the Bad Lands), fording Wounded Knee Creek, and reaching their destination on October 19. [16]

On the 22nd, Warren "told General Harney this morning that I desired to return to the states to close up my affairs and prepare for next year. He said yes and added . . . that any favor he could grant us he felt we were entitled to." The next day Harney issued the necessary order, and Warren and his party departed on October 27. He reached St. Louis on November 23 and spent several weeks there before heading on to Washington, where he promptly went to work on his maps and reports from the summer's and fall's travels. On the 21st, Gouverneur and brother Will journeyed home to Cold Spring for Christmas, but he "returned to Washington Friday Dec. 28, 1855 and resumed my labors." [17] It had been an eventful year for the young second lieutenant. He had accomplished much, he had developed a keen appreciation of the West, and he had increased his own sense of self-importance.

CHAPTER FOUR

THE BLACK HILLS

*T*HE REPORT WHICH WARREN WROTE ON HIS 1855 explorations was published the following year, accompanied by a laudatory letter from Secretary of War Davis. In its conclusion, Warren wrote, "Very little is known as to the accurate geography and topography of the Crow country and Black Hills, and, in fact, of any portion of Nebraska west of the Missouri, and the roads from Fort Pierre to Fort Laramie." He ended by recommending an appropriation by Congress of fifty thousand dollars "for military and geographical explorations in the territory of Nebraska." [1]

The high quality of the work Warren had performed in 1855, along with the recommendation in his report, was recognized by the War Department when he was ordered in 1856 to return to the West and continue his exploring work. He would once again be loosely attached to General Harney, but the focus of his efforts was to be on mapping the Missouri upriver from Fort Pierre.

In his travels in 1855, limited in funds, Warren had hired assistants for short periods—days or weeks—to help in performing various functions as he saw his needs come and go. The only exception had been J. Hudson Snowden, whom he had hired for his whole tour. For 1856, Warren benefited from more generous funding, although nowhere near the fifty thousand dollars he had suggested, and he was able to employ a three-man crew for the whole season: Snowden as a meteorologist and W. H. Hutton as a topographer, both from the Washington office, and Dr. Ferdinand V. Hayden, a geologist and naturalist, whom Warren wanted for his knowledge of the Sioux country. Hutton was hired at $100 per month, Snowden at $60 a month, and Dr. Hayden at $1000 for the year. [2]

Hayden, the geologist, was in the early stages of what would be a notable scientific career. He was born in Massachusetts in 1829 (three months earlier than Warren), graduated from Oberlin College in 1850, and made his first western journey in 1853, a trek into the Dakota Badlands with Fielding B. Meek. Hayden was outspoken, quick-tempered, and judgmental. He served with the Union army as a physician and taught at the University of Pennsylvania from 1865 to 1872. He spent many years thereafter surveying in the West and was considered one of the founders of the U.S. Geological Survey. He would have a peculiar relationship with G. K. Warren.

Hayden's biographer called Warren and Hayden "a dynamic pair" who shared many characteristics. "Both had eager, intelligent minds and slim bodies capable of enduring hardship," he wrote. "Both were bold in the face of adventure. Neither could tolerate fools, each could be tactless, and both yearned to make a name." They seemed fated to clash; "their similarities seem to have exacerbated their natural differences into a warm hostility." [3] Hayden, it might be noted, clashed with most of those with whom he came in contact, and the hostility seems to have existed primarily on his side. Warren's letters and diaries exhibit no corresponding feeling.

Warren's plan for his 1856 expedition was to pick up where his sketch of the Missouri had terminated the year before, "a short distance below the mouth of the Platte," and continue charting and sketching the river "as far up the Missouri as was in our power." Hayden expected to be "well fixed to do something in Natural History." [4] There was, of course, a built-in conflict. Warren's principal mission was exploration, while Hayden's main goal was to collect specimens of minerals, animals, and plants. Warren gave Hayden every opportunity to indulge his interests, but, when a choice had to be made, exploring new territory, which was what the army was paying for, took precedence. With a man of Hayden's temperament, this was bound to cause resentment and hard feelings.

Warren arrived in St. Louis April 14 and left two days later for the trip upriver on the *Genoa*. With the river falling, the trip was painstakingly slow, and Warren with his four assistants covered the last 150 miles on foot. Warren arrived at Fort Pierre on May 21, just in time for the end of Harney's treaty talks with representatives of most of the Sioux nation. The crusty old general, in concluding the peace treaty, once again warned the Sioux to leave white travelers unmolested. [5]

On May 24, Harney explained to the Sioux chiefs that he was sending Warren up the Missouri "to make a map, that they must respect us, that no harm was intended. Our Great Father wanted to know where all his people lived." Harney, Warren wrote, told the Indians of the goals of the exploring party "so that none of them will fear us as 'Medicine Men.'" Early in June, Warren received formal orders from Harney "to examine the Missouri above Ft. Pierre, and all required directions for men, ammunition, stores, transportation etc." [6]

Through the latter part of May and the first three weeks of June, Warren was back at Fort Lookout, downriver near the mouth of Crow Creek, surveying for a possible fort for Harney. He returned to Fort Pierre on June 25. Meanwhile

Hayden had been sitting around Pierre, stewing at his inactivity and the "sad deficiency in management of affairs." [7] The geologist would never become reconciled to the ways of the army.

On June 26 Warren hired two men who had been with him the year before, and on June 28 he and his party were on board the steamboat *St. Mary's* as it headed upriver. Harney provided an escort of two noncommissioned officers and fifteen privates. Warren did not know it at the time, but on July 1 he was promoted to first lieutenant. As they proceeded up the river, they encountered various Indian tribes, Sioux as well as the Sioux's frequent prey, the Rees (or Arikaras) and the Mandans. At one point Warren kept a band of Sioux off the boat because they had "evinced so much sauciness." [8]

The *St. Mary's* reached Fort Union, maintained by the American Fur Company at the junction of the Missouri and Yellowstone rivers, on July 10. On the 14th the steamer started back downriver, and Warren took this opportunity to send with it his accounts for the quarter ending June 30, a copy of the sketch of the river from the Cheyenne to the Yellowstone, and various documents and letters for Harney and officials in Washington. On the 18th he hired the famed mountain man Jim Bridger for a hundred dollars a month, and from Sir George Gore, an Anglo-Irish nobleman sojourning among the Crows, Warren purchased six mules, twelve horses, and two wagons.

On July 22, Warren's party crossed the Missouri and camped at the mouth of the Yellowstone, preparatory to ascending that stream as far as the mouth of the Powder River. They were now in country with plentiful buffalo, as well as "musquitoes so thick that the animals would hardly eat." [9] Warren reached the mouth of the Powder on August 1, and Bridger told him the Tongue River joined the Yellowstone about forty miles farther on. Warren, however, had reached his destination for the season; the country beyond this point would remain for the time being known only to its inhabitants, Lewis and Clark, and the wandering fur trappers. After resting his men and animals for a couple of days, Warren started on the return journey on August 4.

On October 4, on his way downriver, Warren sent a long letter from Fort Pierre to Spencer Baird at the Smithsonian, describing their efforts and the many specimens of deer, bighorn sheep, buffalo, and antelope skins collected. "Doctor [Hayden] has 3 wolf skeletons some six or eight skins and probably 150 skulls," he wrote, adding, "There are two bear skins one grizzly and one cinnamon, and some few skulls." [10]

After much strenuous effort and many meetings with Indians, Warren and his party arrived back in St. Louis on November 11. There was a dust-up in St. Louis, when Dr. Hayden gave several interviews in which it was made to appear, whether intentionally or not, that he and not Warren had been the leader of the expedition. After six months of their chafing each other, a flare-up like this was probably inevitable. An incensed Warren threatened to discharge the geologist, ordering him to desist from statements about the journey until given specific clearance.[11]

This contretemps taken care of, Gouverneur Warren headed on to Washington, secure in the knowledge that the accomplishments of the 1856 expedition had been substantial. He, Snowden, and Hutton reached the capital on November 16, having traveled in their western journey over nine degrees of latitude and sixteen of longitude.

The year 1857 was to be the culmination of Warren's career as an explorer. He was already making a name for himself as a result of his work of the previous two summers, and his superiors hoped to use him and his exploring talents to penetrate into places hitherto unknown. Warren received instructions from the secretary of war on May 7, which he summed up as

> to determine the best route for continuing the military road . . . westward to Fort Laramie and the South Pass; thence to proceed northward and make such examinations on the Black Hills as my time and means would permit, and to return by the valley of the Niobrara, and make a careful examination thereof.[12]

Warren departed the next day for New York City "to procure instruments and arms," visited Cold Spring, and returned to Washington on May 13. He left the capital on May 25 and arrived in St. Louis on the 28th, accompanied by his thirteen-year-old brother Edgar, who was in for a summer of adventure with his big brother. The Warrens left for Fort Leavenworth, Kansas, on June 5 and there Gouv purchased thirty-six mules and twenty-two horses. He and his brother headed upriver and arrived at Omaha on June 19, where he met the other members of his party, including Snowden, Hutton, and Hayden from the 1856 expedition. Also engaged were a physician named Dr. Samuel Moffett and general assistants named P. M. Engel and C. J. Carrington, both of whom had worked for Warren in 1855. Hayden had made efforts to hook up with some other exploring party, but, being unsuccessful in this, he had signed on for another summer with Warren.[13]

After a stop in Omaha, where he fended off a local politician who wanted to sell him overpriced horses, Warren and his party moved up the Missouri to Sioux City, meeting the escort of thirty men under Lt. James McMillan which had been assigned to him. McMillan's soldiers were an unruly lot. The organization of the pack train, Warren wrote, took almost a week, "during which time most of the escort were drunk and insubordinate and 12 of them deserted carrying off with them two of my horses." Warren's party finally started off, its escort much reduced, on July 7.[14]

Through July and into August Warren and his party marched wearily westward across Nebraska, through the sand hills, along the Loup River, to determine whether this could be a practical route from the Missouri to Fort

Laramie. On August 7, he noted, "We have now travelled the river from end to end and found its impracticability for almost any purpose so marked that it seems like a great waste of time to have made the exertions we have." Nevertheless, they sketched and mapped the land they traversed, they made careful note of its geological formations, and they meticulously recorded its flora, fauna, and insect life.[15]

On August 19, after being held up for several days because of the illness of Dr. Moffett, Warren reached the Platte and Fort Laramie, where he took dinner with the post commander that evening. He spent the next few days restoring the strength of his party, preparing for his ultimate assignment for the summer, exploration of the Black Hills.

On September 3 Gouv wrote his father that he had been detained longer than anticipated but was now ready to go, along with brother Edgar. "This trip," he said, "is one in which we anticipate much pleasure and some hardships." He mentioned that two regiments of infantry and a battery of artillery were at Laramie on their way to deal with Brigham Young and his Mormons in Utah; the Indians, he thought, were "completely overawed by the great display of troops made this season . . . and they begin to view us with great terror spreading over ever [sic] part of their hunting grounds." A band of Brulés under Little Thunder was on the Niobrara on the way to Fort Laramie, Warren said, "but all fled on my approach and have not been heard from since."[16]

Warren left the fort on September 4, at about 1 P.M., leaving behind Snowden and the military escort, who were to perform the explorations on the Niobrara ordered by the War Department and rendezvous with Warren later. Warren recognized the risk in dividing his party into two smaller, more vulnerable groups, but the season was late and it was the only way to complete his mission. "I deemed the case to justify the risk," he later wrote. He kept Dr. Hayden with his own group, though perhaps with some misgivings, because he expected to encounter more significant geological manifestations.[17]

By the following day Warren had reached the Indian agency maintained by Major Thomas Twiss on Rawhide Creek. Twiss told him the Indians "had been angry when they heard I was coming and spoke to him about it but he had told them it was all right and this quieted their excitement. They thought we were coming to make a road." Twiss concluded that "the indians would not trouble me."[18]

But these Indians were likely to be rather excitable as a result of the heavy traffic of that summer. Besides, the Sioux were particularly unhappy at the thought of white men penetrating the fastness of the Black Hills. These hills, formed by an upthrust of ancient rocks through the overlying strata, were considered sacred by the Sioux. The Black Hills covered an area in the southwestern part of Dakota Territory about sixty miles wide and one hundred miles from north to south. The dark and wooded canyons of the region alternated with limestone and granite cliffs, and travel through the hills was difficult. The Sioux did not reside in the Black Hills, for they were the domain of the Great Spirit.

The Sioux knew there was gold in the hills, and they feared, with good reason, the disclosure of this fact to whites. Earlier in the summer, at a great encampment at Lake Traverse and the Big Stone Lake, the tribes had enacted a law "that any Indian who should show the gold fields in the Black Hills to white men, should die, and the whites thus made aware of the presence of gold there should also die, for fear that the country would be taken from them." The Sioux cared little for the gold but they cared passionately about the country.[19]

Warren, knowing full well that an encounter with the Sioux was a distinct possibility, proceeded north from Fort Laramie, near the current eastern border of the state of Wyoming. He was on the western verge of the Black Hills, but on September 9, near the Cheyenne River, he was accosted by a band of Brulés. These Indians told Warren they objected to his proceeding as he was going, that he would drive away the buffalo, that Warren's horses would die for lack of grass, that the whites would get no meat. "I told them," Warren replied, "the President had told me to go and I was going and if they had any objections to make I would tell them to him if they wished but they gave me no message."[20]

Warren and his men continued heading north along Beaver Creek, along the west side of the Black Hills, although they were slowed somewhat by heavy rains. On September 16, as thick, misty clouds lowered over the hills, Warren and his men moved down the creek some six and a half miles toward an Indian encampment they had spotted.[21]

The whites pitched their tents in what was now pouring rain, and then Warren, Carrington, their interpreter, and two other men proceeded to the Indian camp, "causing no little consternation among them," Warren said, "as our advance had not yet been anticipated." He found about forty-five lodges of Oglala Sioux under a chief called Bird's Down, or White Feather. The Indians gave them some meat to eat, and Warren told them that he had been sent by the Great Father to look at their country "and tell him what was there." The Sioux took this in without much comment, asking only that the whites not drive away the buffalo farther down the creek they were on.

Warren then invited the chief and ten of his warriors to visit the white men's camp; "I was glad to find they were friends," he said. Warren's party had rigged up as good a shelter as they could with the materials at hand, and they had what he said was their usual meal, "coffee, hard bread, and beans." A couple of hours before dark they were visited by not ten but forty Oglalas as well as twenty Miniconjous and a Sihasapa from a village of eighty lodges which was not far off. The Indian telegraph system was working well. Warren got as many of them seated as he could fit "under our miserable shelter," after which the head man of the Miniconjous, Elk That Bellows Walking, and Black Shield, the Sihasapa, handed him papers that Harney had given them at Fort Pierre. Then they all settled in for a talk, for the Sioux were determined that Warren's party should turn back.

Warren later wrote that "the grounds of their objections to our traversing this region were very sensible, and of sufficient weight, I think, to have justified them in their own minds in resisting." They were camped near large herds of buffalo, whose hair was not yet long enough to make robes. The Indians were keeping these herds in the area so that when their skin was ready they could systematically kill off the animals one band at a time, and they did not want to risk the white men's stampeding them. "For us to have continued on then," Warren wrote in his report, "would have been an act for which certain death would have been inflicted on a like number of their own tribe had they done it." [22]

When the meeting began Warren had the interpreter tell his guests "that I had come to see the country as directed by their Great Father and that I wished to pass down the North Fork of the Shyenne [sic] to Bear Butte and then cross over to the L'eau qui Court." His intentions were friendly, he said, and he had no plan of making a road. [23]

Black Shield spoke for the Sioux in a voice "loud and earnest," and the Indians loudly supported his words:

> General Harney had told them no whites should travel in this part of their country any more. That if they found any doing so they should tell them four times to turn back the road they came and if they did not they should take all they had away from them whip them and turn them back by force.

Warren responded that Harney's words were about traders who had no paper from him, "but that I was one of Gen'l H.'s chiefs and had a paper from the Great Father which was better than any other paper. That he had told me to go and that it would be a disgrace to me to turn back that I must go on."

Black Shield said Harney had told him there was no chief over him, and what was the use of his paper from Harney if whites kept coming? "This place," he said, "was all that was left to them. They could not give it up. If they did they would starve." They had given the whites a road along the Platte, a road along the White River, and another along the Missouri. "This last spot," he repeated, "they could not give up."

Warren said again that he only came to see the country; "they might take all I had they might kill us all. That I came with a few men because I thought they were friends." If he were stopped, he said, "their Great Father would send a great force and then they would have to yield and many of them would be killed." Black Shield answered that if the whites kept coming all the Sioux would die "and they might as well die at once." He hoped that Warren would not go on but would return the way he came, for he did not want to see the whites hurt.

While this dialogue was going on one of the other Indians was heard saying they had better go and raise all their warriors and stop Warren at once. One chief told the young officer that eventually they would have to fight the whites and if he passed through the Black Hills the army would know how to fight them. Another complained of the roads the whites kept making through their country. Warren should go back and tell the Great Father in Washington that they would not allow passage through their country.

Warren concluded in his journal: "How true was all they said. The only security these indians can have in the possession of their country would be in its utter worthlessness to the whites." In his report he simply said that "I was necessarily compelled to admit to myself the truth and force of these objections." [24] Warren's conclusion, that of a humane and perceptive young man, reflected sentiments toward the Native Americans which he first felt after the Blue Water fight in 1855 and which he would hold all his life. Nevertheless, by the orders given to him by the army and his determination to carry them out, Warren was fated to serve the cause of Manifest Destiny in all too effective a manner.

On September 17, Warren again announced to the Indians his intention to proceed, and they went through their arguments all over again. The head men indicated to Warren that their young warriors might attack, "that I was deaf to all that was said and they feared for us." Warren asked to be taken to speak with Bear's Rib, who had been made head chief by Harney. Warren "promised that after talking with him I would turn back if he said so." Elk That Bellows Walking told Warren to stay where he was for two or three days and he would send Bear's Rib to him to talk. [25]

The next day Warren moved his camp five miles up the creek to a more defensible position, where there was good grass and wood. The Sioux departed, and Warren's men relaxed. The sun came out, and they dried out their clothes and bedding. "[W]ith fair weather secure position and the absence of our Red friends the usual good feeling and life of the men returned," Warren recorded. [26]

Warren waited two more days for an appearance by Bear's Rib, but the head chief did not come. Warren then determined to go around the Black Hills by the Cheyenne River "as far as circumstances would permit." He feared that the nonappearance of Bear's Rib "indicates a very hostile disposition at least of his tribe," the Hunkpapas. He felt that he "had much to lose by their interference in our proposed journey and quite as much to gain by the southern route. I would then have a chance to finish up the south side this year and leave the other for a further expedition." [27]

On the 21st and 22nd, Warren's party marched some thirty miles back to Beaver

Creek, giving the appearance to any watching Sioux that the whites were indeed going back the way they had come, and then "turned off in the Black
Hills to the east." They traversed 28 miles of the hills on the 22nd and another
23½ miles, heading slightly north of east, on September 23. A short time after
camping they were visited by two Indians, one of them the long-awaited Bear's
Rib, head chief of the Hunkpapas. Warren told the chief what he was about
and that he wanted to go as far as Bear Butte. Bear's Rib said they would discuss that in the morning, and the evening then passed in casual conversation
and reminiscence. Bear's Rib remembered Harney saying that Warren was to
"come into his country to look at it." [28]

After breakfast the next day, Bear's Rib told Warren "that what the others
had told me was right." Harney had told them no whites should come into
their country, and all the Sioux had agreed to let no whites into the hills. "That
if I went on," Warren recorded, "they would have to take what I had from me
and make me go back, that may be some bad ones of the nation would kill us."
Warren said that "if that was the way he was going to talk he had better go back
and let me go the way I pleased." He did not come to do the Sioux any harm
and asked nothing but to be left alone.

The chief retorted that "if he wished he could not help me that the others
would maybe kill him." Warren said that "if he could not do what he wished
then he was no chief and there was none among the Dacotas." Bear's Rib answered that he did not care to be chief since "the white men would not listen
to what he said." After more of the same the dialogue ended and Warren went
up on a nearby hill to look around. Bear's Rib came back in the evening and
said "that if it was any white man but me that was here with a party that he
would have gone and brought his soldiers here and take all we had, but he had
seen me at the treaty and would not." Why, he asked, do you want to go to Bear
Butte? Because it was a high hill, Warren said, "and enabled me to see far."

> After supper [Warren wrote] he said he had come to the conclusion to let
> me go where I pleased this time but that I must not come again. that at first
> he thought to stop me, but he feared I would go tell the President it was he
> made me do it, and would bring trouble on his people. What a hard position
> his is to fill. The whites to fear on one hand his own people on the other he
> can not well please both. He has my warmest sympathies.

Warren said that now he was talking like he should, "that I was sure his
people would never be worse for letting me pass." Bear's Rib asked plaintively
if anyone else would come again, and Warren said that he did not know but
he would tell the President his wishes "and I thought they would not." Bear's
Rib then launched into an extended rendering of his people's troubles, saying
he thought Warren would tell them to the president "just as he said." [29]

On the 25th Bear's Rib and his companion accompanied Warren as his party moved east about seven miles. The next morning at dawn the two Sioux went on their way, and the white explorers traveled on straight through the heart of the Black Hills. They met with no more opposition other than natural obstacles, and on September 30 they all climbed Bear Butte, a volcanic outcropping rising some fourteen hundred feet above the surrounding plain, about ten or twelve miles northeast of present-day Sturgis, South Dakota. "[T]he ascent," Warren wrote, "was steep and tiresome."[30]

The next day Hayden and Carrington went climbing in the Black Hills while Warren and a companion went on to the Belle Fourche, about thirteen miles from Bear Butte. On October 2 they set out on their return home. The path led across the Cheyenne, through the Badlands, across the White River and Wounded Knee Creek, and reached the Niobrara on October 13. On October 15 they were reunited with Snowden's party, which they had not seen since splitting up at Fort Laramie. On the 16th, Warren paid off the interpreter and five other members of the party. On October 30, he headed northeast toward Fort Randall on the Missouri, which he reached on October 31. "Were all very glad to find ourselves once more on the Missouri," Warren noted.[31]

Lieutenant Warren settled his accounts with the quartermaster at the fort, sold some horses and guns, and on November 6 moved on down the river, in increasingly cold weather. On the evening of the 15th, he and what remained of his party rode into Sioux City. The next day Warren wrote to Sylvanus, saying,

> We have gone safely and successfully through an expedition and are once
> more amongst white people and surrounded by friends. Edgar and myself
> never were in better health. Thanks be to Providence for all we have escaped.[32]

From Sioux City they had to make their way overland to Fort Leavenworth, since no boats were available because of ice in the river. Reaching Leavenworth on December 4, Warren was able to board a boat to St. Louis and then a train east to Washington. They had been fifty-six days from Laramie to Randall, during which time Warren "secured a vast amount of very important information." He discovered and named Harney Peak, the highest in the Black Hills, he traversed and mapped the western slope of the hills even before the first encounter with the Sioux, and after the confrontation of September 17 he still passed through, mapped, and studied the very heart of the region. Hayden's description of the plants and geology of the Black Hills area was substantial. And it was all accomplished because of Warren's cool head and considerable courage. One writer said that Warren "was not only a brilliant scholar but also a canny strategist and a quick thinker. Two of those qualities enabled him to complete his explorations and get home alive."[33]

Warren worked all through the winter of 1857 and 1858 on the report of his three years' exploring in the Nebraska and Dakota territories. Much of it was a narrative of his journeys, encounters, and accomplishments, and some of it was a recitation of the scientific results achieved. He included, too, descriptions of the agricultural and mineral possibilities of the area; in one place he wrote that "gold has been found in valuable quantities, and without doubt the more common and useful minerals will be discovered when more minute examinations are made." [34]

Gouverneur Warren also set forth his conclusions regarding the Indians living in the area explored, particularly the Sioux, or Dakota, whom he described as "still numerous, independent, warlike, and powerful," who "contain within themselves means of prolonged and able resistance to further encroachments of the western settlers." [35] He sympathized with these people, but he was a military officer writing a report for his military superiors:

> There are so many inevitable causes at work to produce a war with the Dakotas before many years, that I regard the greatest fruit of the explorations I have conducted to be the knowledge of the proper routes by which to invade their country and conquer them. The Black Hills is the great point in their territory at which to strike all of the Teton Dakotas . . . It will be perceived that in this plan I have considered a war with all the Dakotas to be on our hands, which at no distant day is probable . . . I believe a vigorous course of action would be quite as humane as any other, and much more economical and effectual in the end.[36]

He suggested that "many of the causes of war with them might be removed by timely action in relation to the treaties, which are from time to time made with them, and a prompt and faithful fulfillment of our own part of the stipulation," but clearly he did not really expect that course to be the one pursued. Finally, Warren said he had always found the Dakotas "extremely reasonable beings, with a very proper appreciation of what are their own rights." He said he had never heard a Sioux chief "express an opinion in regard to what was due them in which I do not concur." And, tragically, "many of them view the extinction of their race as an inevitable result of the operation of present causes, and do so with all the feelings of despair with which we should contemplate the extinction of our nationality." [37]

CHAPTER FIVE

THE EXPLORER
BECOMES A SOLDIER

W ARREN SPENT 1858 IN WASHINGTON, WORKING on his report
and his map. He pored over his daily journal, the notes he took, his drawings,
and his mathematical calculations, he reviewed the journal that Snowden had
kept of his separate journey along the Niobrara, and he urged Hayden to make
his contributions to the general report. His perfectionist nature drove Warren
to make his report a massive and comprehensive document, even though it
was titled a "preliminary report."

Warren felt that what he had accomplished in his three years in the West
was worthy of acclaim, and he was always pleased to see appropriate notice
taken of it. In February he commented that Dr. Joseph Leidy, one of the country's leading naturalists and a frequent correspondent of Hayden's, "thinks very
highly of our collection of vertebrate remains. New elephant & rhinoceros,
wolves, horses, deers, etc." [1]

Dr. Hayden was querulous in his comments on Warren. On November 19,
he complained to his friend Engelmann, "I have to make out a brief list of
plants for Lieut. Warren." A few days later, he wrote that "Lieut. Warren gave
me but a short notice to prepare a list of our collections to be published with
the Message and documents." He spoke of plants which he felt had been collected at other times, "so that they are not at Warren's disposal at all." The good
doctor worried about other things, too: "I saw him [Warren] and as I very well
knew before there is no money to pay for the examination of the plants. Indeed," he went on, "I do not think there will be any money to keep me at work
on the Geology. Lt. Warren will not promise to pay anything more." But Hayden did not despair: "I will however do all I can hereafter as he expects to start
out again next spring with a large appropriation." [2]

Warren did indeed expect to head west again in the spring of 1859. In the meantime, however, he wrote a long and heartfelt letter to his father, a letter which was emblematic of the feelings he had for that influential figure and of the strong interest he always took in his family:

> Will and myself who both have now a fair start in the world know that it has all been due to your efforts for us, in giving us the means of education and gaining us a position, and I believe we have not been unworthy of the advantages we have received. I know you have been the best of fathers to all your children and the more I see of the world the more I think you have one of the noblest natures God ever gave to man, and every body who knows you must think so. We all love you and mother very much—our dear mother whose whole life has been devoted to us.

Gouverneur went on to discuss the education of his younger siblings, stating that he and Will would each contribute a thousand dollars a year toward the education of Eliza and Emily. He thought that Edgar's education already was superior to his own when he went to Kinsley's school, but he added that "I have been a great deal of a student since I left West Point." [3]

Later, he wrote another letter to Sylvanus, summing up where he stood professionally, describing "the report of the Secretary of War in which you will see we are spoken of in very high terms." He went on to say,

> Our map of the Territory west of the Mississippi is now coming out and is very satisfactory. My map of Nebraska is most ready for publication (all my part is done) and you may have seen a late notice of it in the papers. I have during the past month written a report of 150 foolscap pages which will appear in the annual document. I have about 10 days work to finish another report that will be published with the maps of the P.R.R. Reports, and then I shall be free to finish my detailed report of explorations in Nebraska or to continue them next year as it may turn out . . . I have in fact every reason to believe I have gained for myself a good reputation as Topographical Engineer. [4]

The return to the West which Warren so eagerly anticipated, the assignment to the final mission to fill in those parts of the map still blank, a mission which Warren expected to consume two years, was not to be his. In February 1859 Sylvanus Warren died. "[I]n his last hours," Gouv wrote, "he forgot his dying agonies to say how hard upon me it was to leave the care of his family on me. I never could do too much to show what a pleasure that trust was to me." His son's career would be altered by that death, as he recorded:

> The death of my father has entirely changed my plans. I shall not now go to Nebraska again. I must stay awhile with my mother. His loss is a great one to us, besides my mother requiring me to be with her. I feel so sad about it, that all my ambition seems to have forsaken me. There was no person in the world whose death could make me so unhappy as my father's has. [5]

Sylvanus had died without a will, so the surrogate of Putnam County granted letters of administration to Phoebe Warren, the deceased's widow, on March 8, 1859. The estate eventually consisted of the house and lot on Fair Street in Cold Spring and two properties adjoining it, valued at $8,000, and personal property valued at $9,673, most of which was in railroad bonds and personal notes. Because of the intestacy, Phoebe inherited little more than a quarter of the estate, and she had to execute notes to her six children to gain title to all of her late husband's assets.[6]

The assignment for further western exploration which Gouverneur Warren had looked forward to receiving until his father's demise went instead to a pedantic, by-the-book soldier named William F. Raynolds, and Warren was ordered to report to West Point on August 25, 1859. The position of assistant professor of mathematics at the military academy which he now accepted was not only prestigious but entirely welcome to Warren, because of the post's proximity to Cold Spring and his bereaved mother.[7]

Warren was content with his teaching position at West Point, where he renewed relations with his former professor Dennis Hart Mahan, the country's leading military theorist. Warren shared mathematics duties with an officer of his own age from Maine, a pious graduate of both Bowdoin and West Point named Oliver Otis Howard. They were among thirty-six officers of junior rank at the Point in 1860 and 1861.[8]

There is little evidence that Warren paid much attention to the increasingly volatile political situation in the United States in the period leading up to the election of 1860. As an ambitious young officer interested primarily in advancing his career, particularly one who spent lengthy periods of time physically separated from the settled portions of his country, Warren left few traces in his prewar writings of positions on political or sectional subjects. Still, as a young man of keen intelligence and wide interests, Warren must surely have viewed the developing situation with some alarm. Having been raised in a Democratic household by a father whom he greatly respected, the young officer held views on the issues convulsing the country that matched those of the Democratic party at large, including the ambiguities which plagued the party, with its northern and southern wings. When, however, secession followed Lincoln's election, and South Carolina bombarded and then captured Fort Sumter, there was no hesitation on Warren's part.

The new president, Abraham Lincoln, called upon the states on April 15 to furnish seventy-five thousand volunteer troops, and politicians, businessmen, and civic leaders across the North were soon active in raising regiments to meet this call. On April 24, Warren, after hearing class recitations in the morning, was notified by telegram that he had been elected lieutenant colonel of a New York regiment called Duryée's Zouaves. Friends of the young officer had recommended him to the organizers of the regiment. Warren proceeded immediately to New York City, located the headquarters of his new regiment, and marched 340 of the regiment's recruits to Fort Schuyler, located on a peninsula where the East River flowed into Long Island Sound. He returned the next day to West Point and on the 27th secured a week's leave of absence. He headed to Washington to straighten out his military status, reaching the capital on April 30. There was at the time "a prevalent opposition to regular officers accepting commissions in the volunteers," and this opposition soon proved a barrier, temporarily at least, to Warren's accepting the proffered post. He found he "could not get permission to join the N.Y. regiment," so he turned around and headed back to West Point.[9]

As it became clearer, however, that the regular army could not begin to carry the burden of a war to coerce the southern states back into the Union, strong pressures were soon brought to bear upon the army to allow professional officers to lead volunteer organizations. On May 2, Warren arrived back at Fort Schuyler and reported the failure of his mission. The father of an officer in his regiment then went to Washington to put in a word for him. Whether by virtue of this solicitation, the endorsement of New York's governor Edwin D. Morgan and Senator Ira Harris, or a general change of policy, by May 8 Warren had received a leave of absence "for the remainder of the Academic Term" to go to war with his new regiment.[10]

Howard, his math co-instructor, said that Warren's promotion "seemed to the other lieutenants a wonderful advance. We had never met field officers who were not old and gray." They did not have long to admire their erstwhile colleague, for Warren was off to New York on the 8th to be mustered in as a lieutenant colonel of volunteers, which took place on the 14th. He returned to Fort Schuyler on May 15 and took over the effective leadership of the regiment; "the discipline," the regimental historian wrote, "was more severe and exacting after Lieut. Col. Warren entered upon his duties." By May 23 he and his regiment were on a boat on the Atlantic, headed for Fort Monroe, Virginia, after a march across Manhattan to the cheers of the New York throngs.[11]

After a full day on the ocean, Warren and his fledgling regiment landed at Fort Monroe, at Old Point Comfort on the southeastern tip of the Virginia peninsula, on the morning of May 25. They bivouacked that night and got their tents pitched the next day. Warren then resumed the task he had set himself even before leaving New York, that of converting his green but enthusiastic recruits into soldiers.

The regiment, which was officially designated the Fifth New York, had been raised by a patriotic New York businessman named Abram Duryée, a mahogany importer, who was commissioned its colonel. Duryée had long been active in militia affairs in the city, and it was thus natural for him to round up both officers and men from the ranks of existing militia units. High-spirited as they were, the members of the Fifth New York were almost totally ignorant of

real soldiering, which they soon found to be vastly different from militia service. It fell to Lieutenant Colonel Warren to open their eyes, for Abram
Duryée was in effect a figurehead at the head of the regiment. Warren was tireless in training first his subaltern officers and then the enlisted men in all the
elements of drill, discipline, weapon-handling, and tactics which were essential in turning civilians into soldiers.[12]

That Warren succeeded admirably in the work was testified to more than a
year later, when C. F. Cambrilling, a former captain in the regiment, wrote in
November 1862 to the *Times:* "To Col. Gouverneur K. Warren, who has been
in command almost from the battle of Great Bethel to Antietam, is due the
sole credit of having brought the Fifth Regiment to its present state of discipline." The letter spoke of Warren's "severe and exacting discipline, his unceasing efforts in the education of his officers and men, his stubbornness of
purpose, his incessant toil, his utter disregard of his own personal comfort,
(and that of his officers,) his wonderful example of endurance coupled with a
thorough contempt of danger and the most aspiring courage."[13]

There had barely been time for much of Warren's training to take effect
when the Fifth New York was thrown into battle, if battle is the proper name
to be given the engagement which took place at Big Bethel on June 10. Warren
noted in his journal for that day, "Joined the expedition under Genl Pierce just
this side of county bridge. Inglorious day great suffering and loss. No good result." A corporal in the Fifth New York wrote of it years later, "This battle had
it not involved loss of valuable lives, would have been one of the most ludicrous farces that I have ever had the pleasure of witnessing."[14]

Benjamin F. Butler, a prominent Democratic politician from Massachusetts
who had been given an early commission in the army as a reward for supporting Lincoln's war effort, was in command of the Union forces at Fort Monroe.
Ben Butler was to spend almost the entire war creating one folly and blunder
after another, but it was always thought too politically risky to get rid of him,
and his rank was so high (he was commissioned a major general in May 1861)
that he usually outranked any other general sent to work with him.

Big Bethel was one of the earliest of Butler's fiascos, a raid carried out for no
very good purpose by troops who were still woefully unprepared. Seven green
regiments in two columns, under the command of an inept militia general
named Ebenezer W. Pierce, marched out to attack a Confederate installation
at Big Bethel, twelve miles away. The two columns could not be coordinated,
and they wound up firing upon one another. When rebel artillery joined the
fray, Pierce ordered a retreat.[15]

The Federals retreated, in some disorder because Pierce neglected to establish a rear guard. Warren later wrote that he begged Pierce "to remain and see
that the rear was properly attended to," which Pierce thought unnecessary, for
he said he had ordered the First New York to do so. Warren said he had no

confidence in the commander of the First New York's doing what was required, and in fact, that regiment retreated with some haste. Warren "remained on the ground about an hour after all the force had left," rounding up a few men to gather the killed and wounded whom Pierce had abandoned. Warren personally carried the body of Lieutenant John T. Greble of the Second U.S. Artillery, the first Regular Army officer killed in the war, to an artillery limber and saw to the evacuation of Greble's remains. Warren was disgusted at the conduct of a number of his fellow officers, noting that "there was no pursuing force or the least cause for precipitancy." [16]

That was Big Bethel, soon trumpeted in Richmond as a great triumph of southern arms. What little credit accrued to any Federals from the skirmish came to Warren and those few men who assisted him in removing the wounded from the battlefield. Poor Will Warren suffered a great shock when he overheard, in Willard's Hotel in Washington, a messenger from Butler's army describing the battle and stating that the lieutenant colonel of Duryée's Zouaves had been killed at the head of his regiment. Will raced over to the War Department, to find there was no substance to the tale. [17]

Warren was later called before the Committee on the Conduct of the War and asked about Big Bethel. The plan for the movement, Warren testified, "from the very beginning involved a failure." He said, "it was planned for a night attack with very new troops, some of them had never been taught even to load and fire . . . to proceed from two different points, distant from each other six or seven miles." The map Butler furnished the expedition was from 1819, and the roads were "all laid down wrong." It *had* to fail. [18]

For the rest of June and most of July, Warren's diary records the minutiae and trivia of camp life, such as guard duty, reviews, distributions of weapons, scouting missions, work on the breastworks, and service on a court-martial. Simon Cameron, the secretary of war, showed up to review the troops on July 5, and on the 23rd the camp at Fort Monroe received the news of the battle at Bull Run. "Everybody gloomy," Warren noted. [19]

On July 26, the Fifth New York received orders to embark for Washington, and by ten o'clock that evening Warren and his men were on board the steamer *Adelaide*. On the 27th they reached Baltimore, not Washington, and camped on Federal Hill, relieving a Pennsylvania regiment. Here, it turned out, they were to stay for many months, because General Winfield Scott, the commanding general of the army, had decided that fortifications should be erected on Federal Hill, just south of today's Inner Harbor. This decision was not as fanciful as it might now appear, since Baltimore was not at that period of the war as far behind the lines as it would subsequently become. In addition, a part of the town's citizenry was considered of doubtful loyalty, and a stronghold of Union army power clearly seemed a good idea.

In Gouverneur Warren the army had selected an engineering officer of competence and skill for the job at hand. He set to work laying out the entrenchments and fortifications and followed with the assignment of work to carry through the project. His Zouaves worked through the winter, making many friends in Baltimore during their extended stay.

On August 19, Warren was startled to receive word that he would have to return to West Point, "as my leave would not be extended." On the 30th, however, he went to Washington and met with both Secretary Cameron and General Scott and got the nonsensical order rescinded, being formally "detached to serve with the Volunteers." Three days later Duryée was appointed a brigadier general, and Warren officially took command of the regiment which he had been unofficially commanding all along. Another piece of good news arrived on October 15, when Warren was notified of his promotion to the rank of captain in the Topographical Engineers, as of September 9, 1861. Brevet ranks and volunteer commissions were all well and good, but for the regular army officer his permanent rank—the status to which he would revert when the war came to an end—was always a matter of concern.[20]

In early November, Warren's regiment was shipped across the bay to join an expedition led by General Henry H. Lockwood to show the flag to the disloyal population of Accomack and Northampton counties, the part of the Delmarva Peninsula which was in Virginia. Warren and his men marched down the peninsula from Newtown to Eastville, accomplishing very little, before being transported back to Baltimore.[21]

One other noteworthy event took place during the extended stay of the Fifth New York in Baltimore: Warren fell in love. It might be recalled that he had written his brother Will in 1854 that there should be no thought of marriage for ten years at least, but even someone as organized and precise as Gouverneur Warren found that this was a matter over which he had far less control than he thought.

The officers of the regiment sponsored a party on St. Valentine's Day, February 14, 1862, "with Col. Warren's compliments," and one of the guests, arriving as an invitee of Captain Cambrilling, was a young lady named Emily Forbes Chase. Miss Chase was twenty at the time, the oldest of four children of a prosperous dry-goods merchant named Algernon Sidney Chase, a quiet and unostentatious gentleman, then fifty-three, who had started in business in New York, moved on to Boston, and settled in 1850 in Baltimore. Emily's mother, Mary Augusta Chase, was a Bostonian who had once been engaged to Hamilton Fish of New York. She was notable for having defiantly flown the Stars and Stripes from the family home when Union troops passing through Baltimore were attacked by Confederate sympathizers in the spring of 1861.[22]

Several years earlier Emily had been a bridesmaid in a wedding in which one of the groomsmen was an army officer from Virginia named Ambrose Powell Hill. Legend in the Chase family had it that Powell Hill, the future

Emily Chase, soon to be Mrs. G. K. Warren.
Warren Collection, New York State Library.

Confederate general, became an ardent swain of Emily's, but corroboration of such a story is scant. A. P. Hill *was* an unsuccessful suitor of Nelly Marcy, who eventually married George B. McClellan, but his losing another young lady to another future Union general is just too contrived.[23]

To the St. Valentine's ball came the belles of Baltimore, "but the Colonel of the regiment could see only Emily Chase," wrote the Warrens' daughter, no doubt basing her story on the family's oral history. The solid, sensible, scientific Colonel Warren was pierced by Cupid's arrow, as might have been expected on such an occasion on such a day, and he thereafter devoted his nonmilitary hours, both waking and dreaming, to young Miss Chase.[24]

For the rest of the tour of duty of the Fifth New York in Baltimore, Warren found whatever excuses he could to call upon Emily at her family's well-appointed home on St. Paul Street. The ardent feelings which had been called into being on St. Valentine's night developed into a deep and long-lasting love, which was soon to be frustrated by the demands of the war. The next week Warren even tried to march his troops by Emily's house for her inspection, but he abandoned the idea when some of his men complained that they would have a three-mile hike to get home.[25]

Warren's letters to Miss Chase, as he punctiliously addressed her at this early period, were those of an ardent young lover:

> But I don't know what to do—when I am with you it is 'sweet confusion' and when away it is bitter confusion, with all my intellect. Even while I write, I feel as if I have none, because I want to say so much to you, that perhaps I ought not to. I want to come and see you this evening if I can about 9 o'clock . . . It was very sweet of you to write me such a dear note late at night. If you are like me only those thoughts which are real, influence that hour, and whether I closed my eyes first or not my last thoughts were my darling of you and ever will be.[26]

Again, the next day, as the regiment's departure from Baltimore grew closer: "Won't you name some time very soon when I can go somewhere with you and be with you a while. Let it be for a visit, a walk a ride, a concert, a visit, the theatre, to church or anything only say when and let me know." [27]

On March 30, the regiment marched through Baltimore, to the fitting strains of "The Girl I Left behind Me," and boarded a steamer headed back to Fort Monroe. A reporter watched the departure of "Col. Warren's Zouaves, long stationed here, and so deservedly popular with our loyal citizens." He described the mass of spectators who had come to see the regiment off and concluded, "Success and glory to the Zouaves wherever they go. They will not be forgotten in Baltimore, and we believe, will not forget the many friends they have left behind them here." [28] Particularly was this true of their commanding officer.

CHAPTER SIX

ON THE VIRGINIA PENINSULA

*T*HE FIRST FLUSH OF MARTIAL GLORY—the "On to Richmond!" stage— was past, gone with the tragicomic battle of Bull Run. Winfield Scott, the relic of America's wars of old, was gone, too, pushed into retirement by his own infirmities and the ambitious nudging of George Brinton McClellan, who succeeded him as general in chief. McClellan set about building and training an army, a job for which he showed an exceptional aptitude. Eventually, however, when it appeared to Abraham Lincoln that McClellan had little stomach for risking his new creation in battle, the president forced his general's hand and pressed him to present a plan for a spring 1862 campaign. McClellan eschewed the difficult task of fighting his way from Washington to Richmond overland, electing instead to transport his army by water to the tip of the Virginia peninsula, where Federal control of Fort Monroe gave him a secure jumping-off point.

It was to participate in McClellan's march up the peninsula that Warren's regiment was shipped back to Fort Monroe at the end of March, arriving on the 31st and going into camp five miles from the fort, near the division of regulars under General George Sykes to which the Fifth New York was attached. The scene around the "huge and frowning" Fort Monroe was chaotic. "Negroes were everywhere," wrote one arriving soldier, unused to seeing such a concentration of black men, "and went about their work with an air of importance born of their new-found freedom." The beaches were jammed with guns, wagons, and pontoon trains, and the land behind the beaches was crowded with tents. The observer saw "the red cap, white leggins, and baggy trousers of the Zouaves mingled with the blue uniforms and dark trimmings of the regular infantry-men," along with cavalrymen, gunners, engineers, laborers, and teamsters, "all busy at something." [1]

Gouverneur Warren was kept busy with the myriad organizational chores required by an untried unit about to advance against the enemy, but he found time to write a hasty note to Emily back in Baltimore, saying, "With many things to look after I have little time to write or I should have written you before, but I think of you enough to make it up to you. I wish you could be near me." [2]

On April 2, Warren noted the arrival of McClellan and the receipt of orders to advance the next morning. "Our Regt," he wrote, was "unable to do so for lack of wagons." His wagons finally arrived on the 5th, along with four days' rations, which had to be cooked. It rained hard all that night, so that when the advance actually started the next morning the roads were heavy with mud and filled with stuck wagons.[3] An infantryman described how "the foot sank insidiously into the mud, and came out again reluctantly; it had to be coaxed, and while you were persuading your left, the willing right was sinking as deep." Walking in this slop, he said, sounded like "a suction-pump when the water is exhausted." Mud, he said, "took the military valor all out of a man." [4]

Warren's regiment, after struggling eighteen miles in the mud, camped and awaited better weather for several days until the rain stopped. Warren reconnoitered on April 10 and found "seas of mud everywhere." On the 11th the Fifth New York was ordered up two and a half miles closer to Yorktown, where McClellan's army had come to a halt, confronted by a skimpy set of Confederate defenses along Warwick Creek. "Right here," wrote one observer, "begins that month's delay at Yorktown." Never considering an assault to chase away the defenders, McClellan settled down for a siege, preparing trenches and angles of approach, and ordering siege guns to be shipped from Washington. Confederate general Joseph E. Johnston, considering his defensive line at Yorktown to be defective, said, "No one but McClellan could have hesitated to attack." [5]

Another officer later wrote, "From the very first, the majority of the generals had advised forcing the Warwick lines without delay." McClellan, though, "engineer officer in all his instincts, preferred digging ditches, opening parallels, and placing batteries around Yorktown . . . the scientific method, so dear to special schools." [6]

Since the Confederate line lay essentially across the Peninsula, McClellan's could not be a siege in the ordinary meaning of the word: not being surrounded, the enemy could get up and leave any time he chose. Still, the commanding general felt his quasi-siege to be the proper way to take the position without substantial casualties. The men under him were not so sure. "On this narrow peninsula," Warren wrote to Emily, "200,000 men are now arrayed against each other striving by every exertion to render the day of battle terrible . . . I suppose my chances are about the same as others." Though he longed to be with her, he said, "I am very proud to be here . . . part of a great army in the field and there must be glory to be won, and shared with you hereafter." The regimental historian noted that "we see very little of Colonel Warren," because he was frequently with McClellan or the general's staff, "by whom he is

highly esteemed." Warren returned the esteem, and henceforth he would always be "a McClellan man."[7]

On April 27, Warren received a message from the assistant to Brigadier General William F. Barry, Chief of Artillery: "If you can report at once for duty as
Heavy Artillery we have some important work for you to be done at once." He
duly marched his regiment off to General Barry, who soon had them hard at
work on the construction and placement of the siege batteries. "My regiment
has been put in charge of a portion of the siege batteries," Warren wrote to
brother Will, "and you can fancy what a sight I have to do." Warren, his con-
cept of military fieldwork shaped by Mahan, welcomed such duty. He and his
men did excellent work for Barry, hauling the heavy cannons through deep
mud into place at Battery No. 1, and they watched with pride when the mon-
strous guns opened on the enemy on April 30. On the night of May 3, observing that the rest of McClellan's heavy guns were about ready to open on his
lines at Yorktown, Johnston ordered the lines abandoned. The rebel army retreated back up the Peninsula.[8]

The men of the Fifth New York felt frustrated seeing the fruits of their strenuous labor abandoned as useless while the army took off in pursuit of
Johnston's army, but they would quickly learn that this was the military way
and nothing could be done to change it. As a slight consolation they received
plaudits from a Baltimore reporter who remembered them well from Federal
Hill, writing that they were "admitted by general consent to be the crack regiment of the service . . . Colonel Warren's Zouaves have been assigned the post
of honor of the army, being connected with the division of regulars, and . . .
they have . . . received expression of admiration from the Commander-in-
Chief [McClellan, not Lincoln]."[9]

"The evacuation of Yorktown took the Union army by surprise," one staff
officer wrote, and as a result the pursuit of Johnston's army was slow to develop
and leisurely at best. McClellan made his way cautiously up the Peninsula, after two of his corps were bloodied by the Confederate rear guard at Williamsburg. It took his army sixteen days to move the fifty-two miles from Yorktown
to the banks of the Chickahominy River, within view of the spires and steeples
of Richmond. On May 7, Warren wrote expansively to Emily that "we will be
in Richmond in a few days. Virginia is already ours but we will not anticipate
too much victory for then we shall have too little to rejoice over when it
comes." (It did not take long for Warren to recognize his overconfidence.) He
enclosed a rose, which "like my love for you blooms amid the strife that sur-
rounds it."[10]

On May 15 and 16, McClellan established a supply depot at White House,
on the Pamunkey River, and shortly thereafter he reorganized the Army of the
Potomac, the name which he had given to his eastern army. He divided it into
five corps, with Generals Edwin V. Sumner, Samuel P. Heintzelman, Erasmus
D. Keyes, William B. Franklin, and Fitz John Porter as corps commanders.

Porter's Fifth Corps was composed of two divisions, under George W. Morell and George Sykes, and the Reserve Artillery. Warren's Fifth New York was a part of Sykes's division, along with all the regular army regiments.[11]

On May 26, McClellan said he had learned of a rebel force in the vicinity of Hanover Court House, to the right and rear of the Union army, "threatening our communications, and in position to . . . oppose McDowell, whose advance was then eight miles south of Fredericksburg." Lincoln had insisted upon keeping Irvin McDowell's corps in front of Washington, to protect the capital, as a condition for permitting McClellan to sail away with his army. McClellan, who imagined against all the proof to the contrary that he was outnumbered by a much larger Confederate army, felt that McDowell's joining the Army of the Potomac before Richmond was crucial to the capture of that city, and he wanted no possible obstacles to that joinder. He ordered Porter to move on the 27th to dislodge whatever Confederate force was at Hanover Court House.[12]

Porter took Morell's division and a cavalry brigade north to Hanover Court House by way of Mechanicsville, and he created a provisional brigade, commanded by Warren, made up of the Fifth and Thirteenth New York, the First Connecticut Artillery (serving as infantry), the Sixth Pennsylvania Cavalry, and a Rhode Island battery, to move there along the Pamunkey River from Old Church, where Warren's regiment had been camped.

Warren's brigade was delayed by bad weather and the necessity of repairing bridges along the way, and Porter reached Hanover Court House ahead of him on the rainy afternoon of the 27th. After fierce fighting and sloppy leadership on both sides, the Federals prevailed, driving the enemy away and taking numerous prisoners, just as Warren arrived on the scene. The next day Warren's men, he noted, "worked hard burying dead, etc." On the 29th they headed a few miles west to Ashland Station, to break the telegraph, tear up some railroad tracks, and capture more prisoners. Warren then turned his brigade around and marched it back to Old Church; two days later he rejoined Porter's corps near Cold Harbor.[13]

In his journal for May 31, Warren recorded, "Heavy battle commenced on opposite side of Chickahominy." This was the battle of Fair Oaks, or Seven Pines, a two-day affair in which Johnston attempted to take advantage of McClellan's division of his army between the two sides of the Chickahominy to isolate and destroy Keyes's corps. Poor coordination and confused generalship frustrated the Confederate leader, who was put out of action by a wound suffered on June 1. The battle was essentially a draw, but Johnston's disability brought to the command of the Confederacy's eastern army the redoubtable Robert E. Lee, who would lead the Army of Northern Virginia, as he now named it, to the end.

None of Porter's Fifth Corps troops participated in the fighting at Seven Pines, and June brought a lull in the campaign. While Lee reorganized his army and built up the defenses of Richmond, McClellan complained to the president, to the press, and to anyone who would listen that he was being forced to fight a vastly larger southern army with one hand tied behind his back, as it were, referring to the absence of McDowell's corps. In fact, one of McDowell's divisions, under George McCall, arrived at White House, McClellan's supply base on the Pamunkey River, and marched to join Porter's corps.

Warren wrote to Will on June 2 that "the sound of firing has become quite monotonous, there has been so much of it, and the slaughter has been considerable." Nevertheless, he added, "we are all reduced to excellent fighting trim." A few days later, however, he noted that "there seems to be a standstill at present, waiting for something." In addition, he said, "the army is suffering from sickness very much, principally fever." The fetid swamps of the Chickahominy in June were prolific breeders of feverish diseases. He also told Will that he now had command of a brigade, the Third Brigade of Sykes's division, consisting of the Fifth and Tenth New York regiments. Though small, it was "a very good Brigade." [14]

On June 13, it was the ill fortune of Warren's brigade to be in just the wrong place when Confederate cavalry commander Jeb Stuart made his famous ride around the Union army. Lee ordered Stuart and his cavalry to conduct an armed reconnaissance to determine what was behind McClellan's right flank. He was planning to bring Thomas "Stonewall" Jackson's force from the Shenandoah Valley to participate in the battle for Richmond, and he needed to know the country over which Jackson would march. He also wanted Stuart to examine how well the Federal supply line to the Pamunkey was guarded. Stuart, who had been waiting for just such a chance, hoped that, instead of riding around the Union right and then fighting his way back the way he had come, he could keep going, across the Chickahominy, all the way to the James, and return to Richmond that way. He made the actual decision to keep going when he reached Old Church the afternoon of June 13, but clearly he had had it in mind all the time.

At 5 P.M. on the 13th, Warren's brigade was ordered to arms "to repel an advance of the enemy on our flanks." He was told to report to Brigadier General Philip St. George Cooke (who happened to be, of all things, Jeb Stuart's father-in-law), and Cooke ordered the brigade to march off after the rebels. Warren soon discovered that the invaders were cavalry and that there was no chance of his infantry brigade catching them, but Cooke had heard (erroneously) that they included five or six regiments of infantry, so he ordered Warren to keep on. Early the next morning, Warren again told Cooke the chase was futile; exhausted infantrymen stood no chance of catching cavalry, and it was clear there was no rebel infantry.

Cooke told him "to keep on until further orders, and we did so, he remaining with our column." The morning was brutally hot; the men were dog-tired after only an hour and a half of sleep, and many of them fell out, some with sunstroke. Finally, about noon, Warren's brigade reached Tunstall's Station, close to White House, and learned that Stuart had left there twelve hours or so earlier. Cooke at last allowed them to march back to camp. Warren let his men sleep until midnight, and they reached camp at 7 A.M. "We were very tired and a good drink of whiskey soon set us all asleep," he wrote to Will. Warren called it "a weary tramp (and an unsuccessful one foolishly managed)." Cooke, he said, "had more cavalry than the enemy, and yet he was afraid to leave the infantry and follow up." Stuart's Ride became legendary in Confederate mythology, and Warren was not happy with the part he and his men played in the story, although they knew that their role had been prescribed by Philip St. George Cooke's bumbling leadership.[15]

Warren and his men remained in their camp at New Bridge until the 26th, waiting for McClellan's drive on Richmond to resume. When something did occur, though, it was Robert E. Lee who stirred the pot, and the Union army could only react. McClellan's only contribution was a timid push forward at Oak Grove on June 25, what one historian called "a fight over advanced picket lines," although this made the 25th technically the first of what would later be called the "Seven Days."[16]

On June 26, at Mechanicsville, north of Richmond, Lee fell upon the extreme right of the Union army. The assault was not all that Lee expected, since his plans were based on a surprise attack by Jackson on the Fifth Corps flank, and Jackson never made it to the scene of battle that day. But A. P. Hill initiated the fighting, crashing into an impregnable Union defense at Beaver Dam Creek manned by McCall and his division of Pennsylvania Reserves. Warren noted in his journal, "Enemy attacked McCall at Mechanicsville[; he] held his own. We were ordered out to his support—were under arms all night sleeping." McCall and his supports stopped every Confederate advance cold.[17]

Beaver Dam Creek was a solid Union victory—yet that night McClellan determined to end his campaign for Richmond and retreat to the safety of the James River, where his army would come under the protection of Union gunboats. The sudden attack by Lee, the looming presence of Jackson, Stuart's ride around his army, the possible threat to his supply base, his conviction that he was greatly outnumbered—all of these factors played on McClellan's mind. The peculiarities of the commanding general's psyche are beyond the purview of this work, but his decision to "change his base," really to retreat, is one of the strangest in the annals of the Civil War. He had four army corps south of the Chickahominy, seventy-four thousand fighting men, opposed by only twenty-one thousand Confederates under General John B. Magruder, while the bulk of Lee's army was north of the river. Yet McClellan barely considered an attack upon Richmond, so fixed was his mind on the dangers he imagined.[18]

At 2:30 A.M. Warren's brigade, together with the rest of those who had defended Beaver Dam Creek, was marched back some six miles to a position on a plateau named Turkey Hill, overlooking Boatswain's Swamp, near Gaines's Mill. Warren's Third Brigade was on the left of the division's line, but in the virtual center of the Fifth Corps, connecting with the right of Morell's division. It was another strong defensive position, and it had to be, for here Porter with one corps was to hold off most of Lee's army. Warren's brigade, with the aid of artillery, repulsed an initial, tentative advance around 1 P.M. After a lull, at around three o'clock, "suddenly a regiment burst from the woods with loud yells, advancing at double quick upon us." The attackers were from Maxcy Gregg's brigade of A. P. Hill's division. The Tenth New York fired effectively upon the oncoming enemy, and then the Fifth New York "charged back turning his charge into a flight, killing and wounding nearly all of those who fled." The Confederates gazed in awe at the assault of the "red legs," as they called the colorfully garbed Zouaves.[19]

Warren later described the clash in a letter to Emily:

> Oh I wish you could have seen that fight on the 27th of June when our regiment rushed against a South Carolina one [Gregg's] that charged us. It was the opening of bitter fighting. Nothing you ever saw in the pictures of battles excelled it. The artillery which had been firing stopped on both sides, and the whole armies were spectators. In less than five minutes 140 of my men were killed or wounded and the other regiment was completely destroyed.[20]

Warren reformed his brigade as well as he could in the confusion following, and his men turned back another advance, though "the enemy continued to throw forward fresh troops." General John F. Reynolds came up with his brigade to relieve Warren's tired men. Nevertheless, they took up a position in support of a threatened battery and kept up the fire upon the Confederates. As darkness fell John Bell Hood's Texans finally broke through Morell's division and the southerners captured the position which Porter's Fifth Corps had defended all day through nearly nine hours of attacks, though Warren's brigade and Sykes's division stood firm to the end. The Federals moved slowly back toward and across the Chickahominy. Still, Gaines's Mill, as the conflict was called, was a spectacular day for Fitz John Porter and his men, for they were alone on the north side of the river, assailed by most of Lee's army, under Longstreet, Jackson, and Powell Hill.[21]

Warren, who suffered a slight contusion from a spent bullet, and his men received particular plaudits for their gallant conduct on this day. Warren, it was said, "was everywhere conspicuous on the field, and not only directed the movements of his own brigade, which he handled with consummate skill, and placed in the most advantageous positions, where they could produce the most effect on the enemy, but directed the movements of other regiments."[22]

On the morning of the 28th Warren withdrew across the Chickahominy and stayed till late in the afternoon, supporting the artillery which was defending the passage of the river. McClellan's army was now in full retreat toward the James, and Warren's men crossed White Oak Swamp on the morning of June 29. They stayed there all through the day and night to defend the bridge against any rebel thrust out the Charles City Road. On the next morning they moved with the rest of the division to the James.

Porter posted Warren's men, "greatly in need of rest" after having "suffered greatly at Gaines's Mill," along the river road. Here, at about four o'clock, Warren's brigade participated in the artillery and gunboat barrage which blunted and then turned back an abortive attack by a Confederate division under Theophilus Holmes. McClellan later wrote, "A concentrated fire of about thirty guns was brought to bear on the enemy, which, with the infantry fire of Colonel Warren's command, compelled him to retreat, leaving two guns in the hands of Col. Warren." Warren maintained his position at the far left of the army the next day during the fierce fighting on Malvern Hill but did not really participate in it. Even though Malvern Hill was a signal Union triumph, McClellan ordered a final retreat to the sanctuary of Harrison's Landing, where the Army of the Potomac hunkered down under the protective guns of the Union Navy.[23]

The great campaign against Richmond was at an end, and all the bright expectations of early spring had disappeared. Colonel Francis C. Barlow, a regimental commander in the Second Corps, wrote home, "McClellan has been completely outwitted and . . . our present safety is owing more to the severe fighting of some of the Divisions than to any skill of our Generals . . . I think all confidence in McClellan is gone with the majority of the Army." Regis de Trobriand, a Frenchman who led a brigade in the Third Corps, said disgustedly, "We ought to have been victorious. Any general of ordinary capacity, in command of the army, would have led us into Richmond." Alexander Webb, in his later history of the campaign, summed it up as "a lamentable failure— nothing less." [24]

In New York City, diarist George Templeton Strong recorded on June 30, along with other bad news from the Peninsula, "Duryea's Zouaves have lost their colonel (Warren) and many more." In truth, as Andrew Humphreys wrote to his wife a few days later, "Warren was very slightly hurt not enough to keep him out of his saddle." [25]

Gouverneur Warren had some time, at Harrison's Landing, to attend to correspondence of his own. He told Will he had not time "to give you any detailed account of our operations and efforts for the last 10 or 12 days," but he summed things up for him: "I am very well; escaped with only a bruise from a spent ball, and the loss of my horse, shot twice in the neck." One captain killed and six officers wounded, he said, and the brigade lost 60 or 70 killed and 150 wounded. "I think I have now secured a recommendation for promotion," he went on, "for I never have been so praised as I have by all the officers from Genl McClellan down." [26]

He wrote a lengthy letter to Emily after receiving a despairing one from her, telling her that

> I am very, very sorry that you should have been so unhappy about recent events. I think darling that much good to us all will come from them and I have gone through, without harm and with credit though having to mourn the loss of many of our brave comrades . . . you were unhappy while I was full of life and hope and exertion and in the place of all others on the face of the earth where I would choose to be. In the last few days of peril and sleepless nights long marches and ceaseless vigils I have never felt better never been in better health never desponding.

He told her that he had won "golden opinions from all who know my acts." McClellan, he wrote, said no men ever fought better than Warren's brigade and no one fought his men better than Warren did. That evening McClellan had introduced him to President Lincoln on review and publicly praised him. "Genl Sykes," he wrote, "says he don't see how I escaped being killed. I was struck once on my knee with a spent ball."

After describing Gaines's Mill and the rest of the fighting, he concluded

> Do you fear I will trifle with your love? If so banish it . . . Are we not both now as we would have ourselves. You safe at home and well. Do you not sleep better to know that one you love is directing his efforts to his country now in its hour of need. Would any less devoted to it be worthy of your love. Could I slink away from here at such a time No darling, I could not. I sleep sweeter wrapped in my blanket here on the turf in the front rank with those who meet their country's foes, than I could at home on a couch of roses locked in your own dear arms." [27]

A couple of weeks later, with the army still sitting idly in the camp on the James, Warren took pen in hand again and wrote Will, telling him he was glad to learn from Will's letters "that our regiment is so well spoken of. It has certainly worked hard enough and suffered enough. If every regiment was as good as ours and performed as much, the war would long since have closed." He went on to comment on the developing political situation: "The feeling that is springing up now between the conservative men and the radical Republicans is I think getting very intense and I fear old Abe trembles at the prospect much as old Buck [former president James Buchanan] did in his day."

He felt Lincoln should "discard the New England and Greely [sic] Abolitionists entirely; this would remove the cause for resistance from the minds of the masses South, and we could crush out the Secession Leaders." The army, he said, was not suffering as it was for an abolitionist program. "It is fighting for the Union, which is unattainable without allowing the Southern people their constitutional rights." He concluded by saying, "I am not speaking of my own sentiments and ideas, but our men are beginning to feel that with disease and battles their chances of seeing the end is small." [28]

What Warren did not reveal to his brother was that he was earning a reputation as a commander who refused to let sick men be removed from field hospitals to their homes. They "must either get cured here or die here," Warren's position was characterized by one in the ranks. "What did they come here for? Did they not come to die?" Presumably, this seemingly heartless attitude was adopted to encourage malingerers to return to duty.[29]

Warren wrote Emily a long and revealing letter a few days later, saying,

> It makes me almost tremble when I read some parts of your last letter to see how much you trust your happiness to me. I am too frail a barque in life's ocean of storms and hidden shoals to dare to trust myself with such a precious jewel as a cargo . . . It is as you say dear 'it may be' a pleasure to love you. It is an irresistible impulse. To try and win yours, is, to aspire to the performance of worthy deeds. To be worthy of you is to be perfection.
>
> I aspire Emily to be a soldier. I am (I am sorry to say) 'full of strange oaths' I strive to fight for our country, but what is it! Is it the country of the Abolitionists or the Secessionists? It seems to belong to one or the other but that is not my country. I care for neither. If as a soldier I strive for glory it must be for the Union, a union that leaves both north and south as they were and dishonors neither . . . I have been in the war from the beginning in a place of some responsibility. I have always acquitted myself with respectable ability at least. I have been in four hard fought battles and one siege, and those of the General Government who recognize devotion to its service have done *nothing* for me. Where is the hope of advancement as a soldier[?] I tell you just this little to give you a clue to some of my inner thoughts, 'who' as Byron says 'would—dare unmask man's heart, and view the hell that's there.'

There was more: "Don't dear Emily trust your earthly happiness with one like me." Circumstances, he said, "have fixed my career, and though I expect it is for good I feel as if I must keep on though unhappily like Milton's fiends I be found warring against heaven itself. Don't it almost make you shudder to think of it. It does me—" Bleakly he went on, "Dear one happiness is not my companion. It might be found with you but I cannot be there." He wrapped it up with "I wish I could be more loveable to day but I cannot. Yet I feel well and brave enough." [30]

A week later Gouv, clearly worrying about the effect this remarkable missive might have had on its recipient, wrote Emily again, saying, "[I]t was a very mean letter I wrote you last time & was concentrated selfishness on my part." Then he received a letter from her enclosing her photograph, and he responded: "You have no idea how happy I feel to have your photograph to look at as I do almost all the time and when I put it in my bosom I feel as if an angel was at my heart . . . I cannot look at it and realize that you have said your fate was bound up in mine for better or for worse." [31]

A few days later, still stalled at Harrison's Landing, Warren wrote again to Emily, saying, "We have not left here yet and don't know what fate has in store for us." After saying, "I know you love me dearest and I know I love you," he continued, "[I]f I am killed don't you mind it in any public manner. Don't wear mourning for me as some have done for their dead lovers." He had heard that people in Baltimore thought they were engaged. But, he told her, "I wish you to remain perfectly free in the public estimation. Darling you do a fearful thing when you trust anything so sacred as yourself to any man or let the public think you do. You make me tremble with the weight of my own responsibility as regards your happiness." Warren, though apparently unskilled in the arts of love, knew exactly how to thrust prospective guilt upon his beloved should she presume to take his self-denigrating words at face value. [32]

That evening at dusk, August 14, Sykes's division finally left Harrison's Landing, marching eastward back down the Peninsula. Warren ticked off the familiar names in his journal as his brigade marched by—the Chickahominy, Williamsburg, Yorktown. On the 18th they reached Newport News, and on the 20th they were on a steamer heading north up the Chesapeake. On August 22, after sailing up the Potomac, they were set ashore at Aquia Creek and put on trains for Fredericksburg.

Warren, Sykes, and all of Porter's Fifth Corps were about to become part of the Army of Virginia, a new structure Lincoln had created, pulling together the bits and pieces of the Union army which had chased Jackson fruitlessly up and down the Shenandoah Valley, McDowell's First Corps, and such parts of McClellan's Army of the Potomac as arrived pursuant to an order from Washington of August 4 to leave the Peninsula and join the new army.

The commander of the new creation was John Pope, an 1842 graduate of West Point who had served previously with the western army in Missouri and Mississippi. Pope had earned the immediate enmity of his new command with a pompous, bombastic, and patronizing address to his new troops, saying, "I have come to you from the West, where we have always seen the backs of our enemies; from an army whose business it has been to seek the adversary, and to beat him when he was found; whose policy has been attack and not defense." There was a good bit more of the same kind of bluster, all aimed pointedly at McClellan. The new commander also issued orders decreeing harsher treatment of southern civilians, thereby arousing fiercer enmity and even angering the gentlemanly Robert E. Lee. Pope added to the picture by responding to a reporter's question that his headquarters would be "in the saddle." His soldiers said that his headquarters were where his hindquarters should be. [33]

CHAPTER SEVEN

FROM SECOND MANASSAS TO FREDERICKSBURG

T HE SEEDS OF THE DISASTER TO COME at Second Manassas were planted in the new organization of the eastern army. Pope was despised by friend and foe alike, and McClellan was not disposed to offer the western general any kind of cordial cooperation. In addition, the corps commanders of the Potomac army units directed to join the Army of Virginia were McClellan confidants, who took their cues from Little Mac. McClellan's inclination "to let Pope get out of his own scrape" was well known to them all. Pope himself, after an initial good start in dealing with Lee's tactics, ultimately became confused at the key points of the ensuing battle and his army came to grief as a result.

Once Lee became aware that the Army of the Potomac was leaving Harrison's Landing, he attempted to destroy John Pope before the troops coming up from the James could unite with the Army of Virginia. With the aid of McClellan's foot-dragging, he very nearly did it. In a situation where the need for celerity of movement was glaringly obvious, McClellan moved even more slothfully than usual. One historian of the battle of Second Manassas wrote that "McClellan would determine how long Lee's window of opportunity remained open. McClellan's plodding evacuation of the Peninsula gave Lee additional days to operate against Pope." [1]

The first scrap of the campaign took place at Cedar Mountain on August 9, when Jackson defeated N. P. Banks on the strength of a crushing counterattack by Powell Hill. Lee then moved to join Jackson with Longstreet's corps, but Pope was able to avoid the trap the Confederate leaders prepared for him, moving back north of the Rappahannock. On August 22, Stuart's cavalry struck Pope's headquarters at Catlett's Station, on the Orange and Alexandria Railroad, seizing John Pope's best dress coat and all his papers, including recent communications with General Henry Halleck and the War Department.

These messages confirmed Lee's understanding that Pope was obliged to extend his left flank toward Fredericksburg, whence units of the Army of the Potomac were supposed to be coming.

Lee then boldly split his force, sending Jackson's corps with Stuart's cavalry on a sweeping movement around the right of Pope's army. Jackson left the Rappahannock on the morning of August 25, marched fifty miles in two days, poured through Thoroughfare Gap in the Bull Run Mountains, and captured the great Union supply depot at Manassas Junction on the night of the 26th. Stonewall Jackson's lean and hungry troopers were astounded the next morning by the immensity of what they had seized. August 27 was a day of unparalleled revelry for the men of Jackson's corps. They ate what they could, gathered up as much as they could carry, and burned and destroyed everything else they could get their hands on—warehouses and boxcars loaded with foodstuffs, weapons, ammunition, supplies of every kind conceivable and inconceivable.

John Pope learned, a little belatedly, that Jackson had marched around him and was sitting comfortably on his supply line. He ordered the units under his command to head east from Warrenton toward Gainesville and Manassas, to catch Jackson before he could unite with the rest of the rebel army. McDowell's and Franz Sigel's corps marched east along the Warrenton Turnpike, Jesse Reno's division with a portion of Samuel Heintzelman's Third Corps made up the center column of Pope's three-fold advance, and Joseph Hooker's division, followed by Fitz John Porter's Fifth Corps, marched northeast along the Orange and Alexandria Railroad.

Porter's corps, of course, included Gouverneur K. Warren and his brigade, which had been marching about the map of northern Virginia for several days without knowing what was afoot. On the 24th, Gouv wrote to Emily from near Fredericksburg, "We march westward this evening. Where to is uncertain but I suppose our prospects of another battle are good." On the 26th, Warren recorded that they "marched on towards Bealton." The next day he noted that he "marched to Warrenton Junction found that the rebels had cut the R.Rd at Bristoe & Manassas Junction." His letter of that day to Emily said, "We are here all well," but warned of "battles in prospect of which you will hear probably before this reaches you." [2]

Pope told Irvin McDowell, "[I]f you will march promptly and rapidly, we shall bag the whole crowd." He would soon learn that Stonewall Jackson did not "bag" quite that easily. He expected Jackson, the very exemplar of rapid movement in the war so far, to sit and wait at Manassas Junction while Pope's forces converged on him. He also expected to "bag" Jackson before Longstreet, following with the rest of the Army of Northern Virginia along the same track that Jackson had previously taken, could arrive for the fray. [3] And Pope expected more from his patched-together army than it could possibly give him, especially with George McClellan now sitting in Alexandria hindering further reinforcements from joining him.

On the morning of August 28, some of Pope's forces arrived at Manassas Junction and found Jackson gone. Jackson had moved to the north and west, to the vicinity of Groveton, where a fierce but indecisive fight took place on the 28th as the Confederates struck Rufus King's division of McDowell's corps, moving eastward toward Manassas. Pope mistakenly believed that Jackson was retreating toward the Shenandoah Valley and that King had collided with the head of his column. He determined to pursue his fleeing foe. Instead, Jackson had taken up a strong defensive position behind a railroad embankment north of the Warrenton Turnpike. The stage was set for the climactic battle of the campaign.

As August 29 opened, John Pope had arranged for a three-pronged attack on the retreating corps of Stonewall Jackson. Porter was directed to lead the Fifth Corps, augmented by King's battered division, to Gainesville, west-northwest of Manassas, where the road from Thoroughfare Gap met the Warrenton Turnpike. Here Porter presumably would be in position to cut off Jackson's "retreat."

The evening before, elements of Porter's corps awakened men of the Sixth Wisconsin, sleeping after a hard day's fight. Porter's men expressed something close to contempt "for us as of 'Pope's army.' They said: 'We are going to show you "straw feet" how to fight.' . . . There was one regiment of Zouaves with baggy trousers (Duryea's, I think). I remember one of our men said: 'Wait till you get where we have been. You'll get the slack taken out of your pantaloons and the swell out of your heads.'" [4] The feeling of superiority inculcated by McClellan and his subordinates would soon be put to the test.

The morning's fighting consisted primarily of Sigel's uncoordinated attacks against Jackson, while the Fifth Corps was marching toward Jackson's right flank, out the Manassas-Gainesville road. In the meantime, the remaining half of the Confederate army, under Longstreet, made its way through Thoroughfare Gap and linked up with the right of Jackson's corps. The Confederate army was now reunited, although John Pope did not know it. Porter, recognizing that he had a major force in front of him, brought his troops to a halt along a creek called Dawkins' Branch, about three miles short of Gainesville.

The Confederate line was some three and a half miles long, with Jackson on the left, solidly entrenched behind his railroad cut, and Longstreet to the right, available for offensive movements. "Shaped as it was like a huge pair of gaping jaws," wrote a recent historian of the battle, the position "offered Lee great opportunity against a reckless, unwary foe." Longstreet, however, was concerned, probably unduly, about the unknown Union force (Porter's corps) out on the Manassas-Gainesville road, a force which could threaten his right as he moved against the unsuspecting remainder of Pope's army. Much to Lee's dismay, Longstreet decided that an attack on the 29th was too risky. [5]

Porter, after consulting with McDowell and trying to fathom a confusing message titled a "joint order" which Pope had addressed to the two of them, decided to stay put and await developments. Fitz John Porter was a staunch friend of McClellan, and he regarded Pope with something akin to contempt. He expected Pope to be defeated, and he was indiscreet in letting his views be known. Porter was also a conservative soldier, not given to risk-taking, and it seemed to him, in light of both what was contained in the "joint order" and the situation he found himself in, a couple of miles away from the rest of the army, that sitting still was the best course to follow. He set out his artillery and he put out skirmishers, and everyone else settled down for the afternoon.[6]

Porter's position on the Manassas-Gainesville road had a substantial effect on the course of the battle when it convinced Longstreet that he could not safely attack on the 29th. It had another effect, however, in that Pope expected Porter to reach Gainesville, turn east, and fall upon Jackson's right flank. Pope ignored the fact that the "joint order" directed no such thing; indeed, it did not contain the word "attack." Pope was unaware when he wrote the order and for some time after of the presence of Longstreet. The rest of the afternoon of the 29th Pope had his army make a series of disjointed but bloody efforts against Jackson to keep him in place for the Fifth Corps attack which was expected at any minute.

At 4:30 in the afternoon, still having heard nothing of Porter's expected attack, Pope sent him another order, this time directing an attack on the enemy's flank and, if possible, his rear. Porter received this order at around six o'clock. The hour was late, and the order was impossible to obey, reflecting only John Pope's hopelessly inaccurate picture of the battlefield. Porter once again stayed where he was, unaware that his failure to carry out the flawed order would bring an end to his military career.

Warren was disappointed that Porter chose to remain inactive after halting the morning's march. He wrote in his journal, "Marched to Manassas then back along the road to Gainesville[;] found the enemy but not allowed to attack him." Many years later, someone who signed himself "Duryea Zouave" wrote a letter to a newspaper about that August 29th idleness, decrying Warren's support for Porter's rehabilitation.

> General G. K. Warren also has changed his opinion much since the day of the battle. While in command of my regiment [actually, the brigade of which the regiment was a part], and in full hearing of the battle then going on, with his drawn sword in his hand, he was cutting down the high grass in madness and said: 'it is our business to go in on the flank of the enemy, why we don't do it I can't say; but mark my words tomorrow you will have to suffer for it.' and we did.[7]

Late in the day, when Pope finally realized that there was to be no Fifth Corps attack upon Jackson's flank, he peremptorily ordered Porter at 8:50 P.M. to bring his corps to the main battlefield. At 8:17 the next morning, August 30, Porter arrived at the head of his corps, to find a commanding general who was convinced the Confederates were retreating. Porter tried to reason with Pope, whom he now met for the first time, to explain to him what the rebel line really looked like, to warn him of the great danger of Longstreet enveloping his left, but Pope refused to listen. He had made up his own mind, and, besides, he felt Porter, a friend of McClellan who had refused to attack when ordered the day before, was little better than a traitor.

Porter, left to his own devices, took position in the center of the Union army, on Dogan Ridge. He did not have his whole corps with him, for Morell had gotten lost and taken a portion of his division to a location where it would see no action. Nevertheless, Porter took up a strong position on the ground north and south of the hamlet of Groveton. At 11:30 in the morning, Pope sent orders to attack, to pursue the retreating enemy. Porter prepared to carry out this illogical order, leaving Warren's brigade to guard the corps artillery at the foot of Dogan Ridge. Porter, with ten thousand men, would attack Jackson's entrenched position behind the unfinished railroad cut.

Meanwhile John Reynolds's division, holding the area around Groveton, was ordered to withdraw from this sector. Warren did not know why this withdrawal was ordered, but he saw that it meant that Porter's left was unprotected. On his own hook Warren decided to occupy with his small two-regiment brigade the ground abandoned by Reynolds's division. With Warren went the battery of Lt. Charles E. Hazlett of the Fifth U.S. Artillery. "I knew the enemy was in the woods and on the high ridge . . . all around toward our right." reported Warren later, "but high authority [read: Pope and McDowell] reported him retreating and that this was only his rear guard . . . I immediately assumed the responsibility of occupying the place Reynolds' division had vacated, and made all the show of force I could." Porter, when Warren informed him of this movement, told Warren to "hold on." [8]

Warren's little brigade had unknowingly placed itself squarely in the path of Longstreet's long-delayed assault upon the left of Pope's army, an assault which was no less powerful for its having been held back. While Porter's attack, launched at about three o'clock in the afternoon, was bloodily repulsed by Jackson from behind his railroad embankment, Longstreet bided his time. Finally, at 4 P.M., Longstreet, Lee's "old warhorse," struck, with a massive attack led by Hood's Texas Brigade. The only Union troops south of the Warrenton Turnpike when the assault commenced, aside from a brigade eight hundred yards farther east on Chinn Ridge, were Warren's two regiments, the Fifth and Tenth New York, about eleven hundred men.

The Tenth New York—the "National Zouaves"—was hit first, overwhelmed by the strength of Hood's surge. The men of the Tenth fired a few futile volleys and then took to their heels. Unfortunately, as Warren wrote, they fell back "at the position held by the Fifth New York before the enemy, and in such a manner as to almost completely prevent the Fifth from firing upon them." Warren tried unsuccessfully to get them to clear out from in front of the Fifth New York but was unable to do so before "the enemy in force opened fire from the woods on the rear and left flank of the Fifth with most fearful effect." Warren warned Hazlett of his battery's jeopardy, and the artillerist was able to limber up and leave the field. "Although opposed to an overwhelming force," Hazlett reported, "Colonel Warren's men stood their ground until the battery was removed, though at a cost of half their number."[9]

Warren ordered a retreat but was only partially heard in the uproar of battle, and his two regiments suffered fearful losses before being extricated from their dreadful position, called "the very vortex of hell" by one participant. The Fifth New York suffered the loss of more than 300 men, while the Tenth lost 133 men killed or wounded. "Braver men than those who fought and fell that day," Warren reported, "could not be found. It was impossible for us to do more." One observer in the Fifth Corps wrote, years later, "At the second battle of Bull Run Warren's regiment and brigade, commanded by him, sustained heavier losses than any command on that disastrous field." Alas, the gallant and bloody sacrifice of Warren's brigade was almost wholly in vain; Longstreet's powerful advance was barely slowed at all.[10]

Indeed, Longstreet's assault brought about the rout of Pope's army, which was saved from total destruction only because Reynolds and Sykes were able to get their divisions to Henry Hill, the position which dominated the Warrenton Turnpike and Pope's line of retreat, and hold it against the surging Confederates. The Battle of Second Manassas was a substantial southern victory, with the Army of Virginia fleeing to the outskirts of Washington, but the temporary retention of Henry Hill assured that the Union army would survive to fight another day, though assuredly not under John Pope.

Warren noted in his journal for August 30, "Disastrous battle to our regiment . . . Fell back to Centerville." And, indeed, there was nothing to be done but to gather together the remnants of his brigade and move it back across Bull Run, to Centreville, on the road toward Washington. Warren stayed there on the 31st, and over the next two days marched back to the capital, after Lee's move around the right flank of the Union army brought on the sharp fighting at Chantilly on September 1. Sykes's division went into camp just across the Potomac from Washington for a few days. Lincoln and Stanton arranged to transfer Pope to a command in Minnesota, where he would encounter few Confederates, and reluctantly gave the eastern army once again to McClellan, at least to reorganize it for the defense of Washington.

Warren took pen in hand to bring his brother Will up to date on the recent activities of the army. "We are getting well worn out," a discouraged Warren wrote, "and I expect the next battle will finish us all." He set down the wanderings, marches, and countermarches of the Fifth Corps after reaching Aquia Creek on August 22, the confused generalship of Pope and McDowell, and the results of the fighting. He went on,

> Oh that our strength and power could be brought properly to bear on the enemy instead of being wasted in useless and senseless marches. Several times we could have whipped the enemy had all our army available been brought into action at once: but we never engaged with more than one fourth of it at a time, and we were repulsed in detail . . . A more utterly unfit man than Pope was never seen. Every dispatch he sent to the Department was, as published, a gross lie. McClellan's were never overdrawn. I begin to think that nothing but the withdrawal of the protecting hand of God could ever have brought us to our present state. McClellan is again in control but I fear the opposition to him will nullify all his good as it has done since Stanton became Secretary of War.[11]

What this letter clearly demonstrates, of course, is that Gouverneur Warren was firmly in the camp of George B. McClellan. To what he could see and experience himself he added the party line circulating from McClellan to his favorites like Fitz John Porter, i.e., the unflinching opposition of Stanton, the clarity of McClellan's dispatches, etc. Pope's dispatches, of course, were not lies at all but reflections of his totally mistaken conception of the field of conflict, the whereabouts and intentions of the enemy, and the progress of the fighting. And no one was more responsible for the divided state of the army than McClellan, who did his best to withhold Franklin's and Sumner's corps from Pope.

Although Warren shared in the general gloom pervading the army, as the cause of the Union faced its darkest hour after Second Manassas, he tried to keep this feeling out of the letter he wrote the same day to Emily. "I have only time to say I am well," he wrote. "Will write you more soon." After describing his exhausted state of the day before, he went on, "Don't feel disheartened if you can help it. We have done all we could to save the army and the country, and have nearly all perished ourselves."[12]

Even as Gouverneur Warren was writing these letters, Robert E. Lee's Confederates crossed the Potomac into Maryland to initiate their first invasion of the North. McClellan would have precious little time to reorganize the battered and discouraged units of the eastern army, and President Lincoln, who had apparently thought of the restored general as a temporary stopgap to pull things together after Pope, had no choice but to permit McClellan to lead the army into battle again.

On the 6th of September, Warren's brigade took up the march into Maryland on the trail of the Confederate army. It reached Tenallytown, a few miles beyond Washington, and stayed there for a few days. The rest of the division moved on to Rockville, while Warren went into Washington to arrange for arms and clothing. On September 9, the Third Brigade moved on to Rockville, and Warren wrote a note to Emily, saying, "I should be so happy to see you." Responding to her plea, he said, "Dear one you are free to tell your friends our relationship if you choose." He was frustrated by being so close to her and yet unable to get away for a brief visit. In a letter to Emily on the 12th from Hyattsville, Maryland, he complained that he was in the only division in the army from which he could not have a short leave to see her.

In the same letter, Warren told of a long confidential talk he had had with McClellan on the evening of September 11, in which the general assured him that "he has recommended me first of all volunteer colonels for promotion and that it was promised him it should be made at once." He also mentioned that two new regiments recruiting in New York were to be added to his brigade. "Secesh," he said, "will have a hard time fighting us in our own country as they will soon find, and I am sure they will soon be driven back and perhaps we can overwhelm before they can recover." Finally, he promised Emily that he would "take the very first opportunity" to see her; there would be a battle first.[13]

On they marched through western Maryland, to Frederick, to Middletown, over the Blue Ridge, and to a position on Antietam Creek on September 15. McClellan had received the famous "Lost Order," Lee's Special Orders No. 191, two days earlier, providing him a clear picture of the disposition of Lee's widely separated corps. Although McClellan's actions based on this find were rather sluggish, they were still rapid for Little Mac, and they disconcerted Lee, who did not know the Union commander was privy to his order to his corps commanders.[14]

After catching up with the main portion of the Confederate army on September 15, McClellan wasted the 16th in arranging his forces for battle. Jackson completed his conquest of Harper's Ferry and started his troops toward Sharpsburg, where Lee awaited them with his army arrayed between Antietam Creek and the Potomac. On the morning of the 17th McClellan launched his men forward, with sequential attacks on the right, then in the center, and finally with Ambrose E. Burnside's corps on the left. The timing of the Union advances made it possible for Lee to move defenders from one threatened area to the next, and finally to stop Burnside with Powell Hill's troops as they arrived from Harper's Ferry.

The men of both armies fought savagely and gallantly, and they left many thousands of dead and wounded comrades on the field at Antietam. There was no lack of heroism and devotion to duty in the Federal regiments, and it was not the fault of the men in the ranks that McClellan once again let them down. His plan for the battle seemed unwittingly to be designed to give the enemy the maximum opportunity for countering it, and Robert E. Lee was no man to be given an opportunity like that. In addition, McClellan kept two of his corps, Franklin's and Porter's, in reserve, in effect keeping them out of the fight. At one point in the afternoon, Warren's brigade, in McClellan's words, "was detached to hold a position on Burnside's right and rear." The net effect of this posting was that Warren had just one man wounded on what turned out to be the bloodiest single day of the war.[15]

On September 18, Lee's battered army stood at Sharpsburg with its back to the Potomac. McClellan, with two fresh corps untouched by the fighting of the day before available, chose to do nothing. The two armies glared at each other, buried their dead, gathered up their wounded, but there was no further combat. The next day McClellan discovered that Lee had recrossed the Potomac. The invasion of Maryland was over, terminated by a most ambiguous and unsatisfactory Union victory.

A reporter watching the Army of the Potomac pass through Sharpsburg after the battle noted that, as the Fifth Corps moved through the town, "McClellan and his staff came galloping up the hill. Porter's men swung their hats and gave a cheer; but few hurrahs came from the other corps—none from Hooker's," which had suffered devastating losses. "A change had come over the army. The complacent look which I had seen upon McClellan's countenance on the 17th, as if all were going well, had disappeared," replaced by a troubled look, "a manifest awakening to the fact that his great opportunity had gone by. Lee had slipped through his fingers."[16]

For Gouverneur Warren, there were a couple of days of duty at one of the fords of the Potomac and then, on September 22, an order to go to New York to recruit. Earlier in the day he wrote to Emily, "I think there must be a lull in the storm of war . . . and I expect to get a leave of absence for a day or two. If so I shall be in Baltimore tomorrow evening." That schedule was a bit optimistic, but, setting out on horseback, Warren reached Washington on the afternoon of the 24th. The next day he learned that his name had been sent in for promotion to brigadier general, "for distinguished conduct at Gaines Mill June 27th '62," and the promotion was approved on September 26. Warren was now a general, at the age of thirty-two. Sick in bed with a cold on the 26th and 27th, he was in no mood for celebrating his elevation. His spirits improved when he left for Baltimore the evening of the 27th. He sent Emily a note from Barnum's Hotel at seven-thirty that evening, apologizing for being "too fatigued with my journey to come and see you tonight."[17]

The next morning Warren was able to get to the Chase home for a long-awaited reunion with his young sweetheart. It was just one short day, but the long-separated couple made the most of their time together. The next day Gouv went on to New York, and on the 30th of September he reached Cold Spring and his family. From then until October 18, he moved back and forth between New York and Albany, with side trips when possible to Cold Spring, as he tended to the business of getting new regiments organized for his brigade.

On the 18th, Warren returned to Baltimore, where he was able to combine business and time with Emily until the 23rd. Then it was off to Harper's Ferry for a couple of days and back to Baltimore on the 26th. He stayed there until October 31, when he left at 4:45 P.M. to return to Harper's Ferry to rejoin his command. There would be another separation from Emily, but their time together in late October strengthened the relationship between the two lovers.

Early in November the 140th New York joined Warren's brigade, on Bolivar Heights outside Harper's Ferry. An officer in the new regiment, Porter Farley, described joining the veterans of the brigade, particularly the Fifth New York, which he said "at this time and until the expiration of their term of service . . . remained the best drilled regiment in the army." [18]

After Warren rejoined his brigade, it marched around northern Virginia as McClellan dithered and hesitated and did everything but fight. Warren wrote to Will on November 5 that "there seems to be a grand game going on between the two great armies, and I hope we shall have some good results to us." The game seemed less than grand to Abraham Lincoln, and late at night on November 7 he sacked McClellan for good, turning the command of the army over to Burnside. There was some quasi-mutinous muttering among McClellan's friends in the officer corps of the Army of the Potomac, but nothing overt transpired. The man had had every opportunity, on the Peninsula and at Antietam, and some peculiar quirk of his personality caused him to squander them. [19]

Burnside, of course, was another matter. He protested to the authorities in Washington that he was not competent to command the army, and they should have listened to him. The day after Burnside took command Stanton and Halleck relieved Fitz John Porter of command of the Fifth Corps, with Hooker as his successor. Porter was ordered to face a court-martial on charges that he had deliberately disobeyed orders from Pope and caused the debacle at Second Manassas. Porter, close friend of the now-deposed McClellan, was set up as the scapegoat for Pope's defeat. Despite the fact that Pope's orders in question were virtually impossible to obey, Porter was convicted and cashiered from the army, and it took many years for him to clear his name.

Burnside planned a late-season campaign and quickly marched his army to Falmouth on the Rappahannock, opposite the town of Fredericksburg. He needed pontoons for bridges to get his army across the river, and the pontoons, ordered from Washington but snarled in military red tape, did not arrive. Warren, with his brigade, made it to Falmouth on November 23, and then he, with the rest of the army, sat in camp opposite Fredericksburg, waiting. Although the pontoons failed to arrive, Lee's army eventually did. While the Union soldiers waited for a way to get across the Rappahannock, the Confederates busily built up the defenses on their side of the river.

Warren had time to write a long letter to Emily, having just received one from her which, he thought, "seemed to indicate that you were going to act as if you were forgetting me and to *do* something to leave others in no doubt of it." He said, "I should almost despair of the favor and protection of kind Providence if your gentle pure spirit should cease to plead for me." He went on,

> My evil nature keeps down my better I know and is so strong I should fear for yours if linked with it in destiny. My better nature clings to you, my evil one leads me from you, and I am only too contemptible in yielding to its influence. You should despise me and yet you do not, not as you should. Oh that my life had left me pure enough in thought, action and ambition to be worthy of your everlasting companionship.

What the young lady in Baltimore made of all this is hard to imagine. Warren then switched gears, to discuss the problems of the army:

> We are waiting here for the completion of some arrangements for future movements, but I don't know what they are to be. I am somewhat discouraged at our prospects . . . The authorities seem bent on sending us to Richmond by land when we should go by way of James River [this, of course, was the gospel according to McClellan] and they are scattering and dividing up our forces when every man should be concentrated around Richmond . . . It may be that our present movements are designed to deceive the enemy as to the real ones but if not God help us poor fellows here and save the country for we are going to certain misery and perhaps destruction. McClellan I fear will not be vindicated till a ruined country calls him again in the field to find the bones of his old soldiers strewing the ground.

He concluded, "Victory to our cause would be so easy with good management. Why is it the will of Providence that we should go on as we do?" [20]

Warren was sick all through the first week of December, but on the 9th he complied with a request from Emily and sent her "a little lock of my hair." With another battle looming, he wrote her "a kind of farewell till the fate which it brings me is over." [21]

Burnside's pontoons finally arrived, and December 11 was occupied with getting them in place across the Rappahannock. This effort involved fierce resistance by the rebels, as their sharpshooters picked off the men putting the pontoons together, a massive Union artillery barrage which nearly destroyed the town, and an amphibious assault to drive off the Confederate resisters. December 13 was the day Burnside planned for his attack. When it came, it made Gouverneur Warren appear very prescient in his expectations of the outcome.

On taking command, on November 14, Burnside had divided the Army of the Potomac into three wings, called "grand divisions." The Left Grand Division was placed under General William Franklin, the Right Grand Division under sixty-five-year-old General Edwin V. Sumner. The Center Grand Division, consisting of the Third and Fifth corps, was entrusted to General Joseph Hooker. In the assault at Fredericksburg, Franklin's wing was to attack the Confederate right, below the town, while Sumner's and Hooker's were to seize the commanding hills behind the town, known as Marye's Heights, by frontal assault. Burnside's senior commanders were leery of the plan, but the commanding general insisted upon it. Unfortunately, the orders he wrote out to his wing commanders were fuzzy and imprecise, and Franklin, on the left, showed little enthusiasm for any but the most minimal compliance with the order that came to him. In the town itself, Sumner's divisions attacked with vigor, but succeeded only in piling up casualties at the foot of Marye's Heights.

Unknown to Burnside, at the base of Marye's Heights was a stone wall behind which ran the main road to Richmond. Confederate defenders twenty-five hundred strong lined up behind this wall and fired with virtual impunity across the wide field which the Union attackers had to cross. In addition, massed Confederate artillery on the top of the hill pelted the attacking Federals with shot and shell. No Union soldier reached the stone wall, while the divisions of William French, Winfield Scott Hancock, and O. O. Howard, Warren's former West Point colleague, came to grief in the attempt.

Hooker's Center Grand Division, to which belonged Sykes's division of the Fifth Corps, was held in reserve on the eastern bank of the river. "All day long," wrote the historian of the 146th New York, which had recently been incorporated into Warren's brigade, "we watched the progress of the slaughter. Fighting against a foe located in a position that was naturally one of great strength and which had been fortified by a triple tier of batteries, the Union troops never had the least semblance of a chance." [22]

Between three and four o'clock, the Fifth Corps, led by its temporary commander, General Daniel Butterfield, crossed the river, clambered up the banks on the western side, and double-quicked through the town, encountering as they did mangled and bleeding survivors of the earlier assaults who had managed to get away from the deadly field. Hooker, under orders from Burnside to continue the direct assault upon Marye's Heights, tried to remonstrate with the commanding general about the futility of such further attempts, but to no avail. Hooker sent forward the division of Andrew Humphreys, which attacked gallantly but with no greater success than its predecessors. Finally, Hooker, deciding that he had "lost as many men as my orders required me to lose," directed Humphreys to fall back, calling up the First and Second Brigades of Sykes's division to cover the retreat.[23] Warren's brigade thus had no real part in the fighting at Fredericksburg. His total casualties from December 13 through 16 were six wounded and twenty-seven missing.

Burnside was dissuaded from leading a renewed assault by his old Ninth

Corps the next day, and the battered Army of the Potomac gradually pulled back into the town. On the night of the 15th of December, Warren was directed to arrange "a line of earthwork defenses on the south side of the city" to cover the withdrawal of the Union army back across the Rappahannock. Using troops borrowed from both Humphreys' and Sykes's divisions, as well as a detail from his own 146th New York, "battery epaulements and rifle-pits, connecting with brick houses and walls, intended to be loop-holed, and barricading all the streets, were built," presenting "to the view of the enemy the next morning a complete line." There was a paucity of tools available for the work, and it all had to be done in the dark, but it was accomplished in the time required. Warren, always at his best in engineering work, received from Butterfield "honorable mention and reward for his energetic and efficient services in the duties intrusted to him." [24]

There was a glitch at the end, as the engineers responsible for one of the pontoon bridges cut it loose from the Fredericksburg side of the river before Warren's brigade, the rear guard, reached it. "Nothing remained for us but to march with all haste to the upper bridge," reported Porter Farley, "in the hope that it had not yet been taken up." The last units of the army were crossing and the bridge was still intact, so Warren's brigade was able to get across, with the Fifth New York bringing up the rear.[25]

Warren wrote despairingly to Will a couple of days later that "our troops are rushed about managed and manoeuvred little better than a mob." He knew the remedy: "We *must* have McClellan back with unlimited and unfettered powers. His name is a tower of strength to every one here; and the repose of winter is absolutely necessary to discipline, and reorganize and rest." Decrying generals who assault when they should besiege, he said, "My heart sickens when I think of the way our affairs seem to be going." [26]

The Army of the Potomac licked its wounds and contemplated a dubious future. Gouverneur Warren was occupied with many tasks which took up his time, performing inspections, drawing maps, fixing up tents, and visiting other headquarters. He dined with Butterfield on Christmas, after writing another long and gloomy letter to Emily.

He first recalled that he had spent the prior Christmas stationed in Baltimore, although he had not yet met her, and contemplated with wonder the fact that it was less than a year since they *had* met.

I today feel very desponding about our government and the management of
affairs. We cannot succeed as affairs now go, and all our manhood will be
impeached in the eyes of the world. It will not suffice that our men endured
unutterable trials from cold, storms and privations sickness and death in the
field, and vainly assaulted with naked breasts time after time impregnable
defenses. The world will judge only by success and that through ignorance
and mismanagement are wanting. Our esteemed leaders [McClellan and

Porter] are ostracised and their words of commendation are an injury to their patriotic followers. Jealousy supplants ability—patriotism languishes and baffled valor droops.

"I like Burnside as a man," he wrote. "He is noble in generosity and heart, but his letter assuming the whole responsibility of this movement, seems to me to show a disregard of the consequences of his acts that astonishes me." His fate, Warren went on, "should be such as to make fools fear to rush in where angels bashful stand. To be accountable to God for a failure which every one over him and beneath him predicted is a most fearful thing. Were I the author of such a thing, such a hecatomb of victims, I would seek some cave away from the haunts of men."

> I left my home without ambition to save a noble cause. I have seen that cause almost betrayed—I know of bleeding hearts, desolate homes, and un-numbered nameless graves of noble men that have vainly perished. What have we done as a nation to suffer as we do. There must be a just God[.] Why does he permit these things. Is he the jealous God to us now that visits the sins of the fathers upon the children.

"Dear Emily write to me soon," he concluded. "I do not despair of our cause. I know that all would go right if we had ability and unity in our counsels and perhaps we may yet have them both."[27]

So stood the unreconstructed McClellan man at the end of the second year of the Civil War.

WITH HOOKER

*E*IGHTEEN SIXTY-THREE BEGAN WITH THE ARMY of the Potomac hunkered down at Falmouth, Virginia, staring across the Rappahannock at its adversary in Fredericksburg. Gouverneur Warren spent a good bit of time at Burnside's headquarters, in his temporary capacity as division commander in the absence of George Sykes. Sykes returned to camp on January 9, and Warren resumed his duties with his brigade.

On January 20 the army began the celebrated movement known to history as the "Mud March." Warren noted in his journal that his brigade "marched only about a mile, road so occupied by troops." The heavens had opened up on the Army of the Potomac and Ambrose E. Burnside, and the pouring rain persisted until about noon on the 23rd. "Everything stuck in the mud," Warren recorded on January 22, the same day that Burnside called off the advance, which was designed to go around the right flank of Lee's army, crossing the Rappahannock at Banks's Ford.[1]

It was not a bad plan, but it was bedeviled by bad luck. Warren's friend Humphreys wrote to his wife, "If we had only marched a day earlier, and could have attacked the enemy's intrenchments in that storm, we should have carried them. It would have been a glorious fight." But it was not to be.[2]

Burnside never stood a chance. The latter part of December and early January witnessed the growth of a near-mutinous sentiment among many of the senior officers of the Army of the Potomac, symbolized by the secret visit of two generals to the White House, bearing tales against Burnside. As the advance began on January 20, some of these officers publicly ridiculed the commanding general in front of their men, and the morale of the army declined precipitously. When the rains started and the whole army bogged down in the Virginia mud, morale hit rock bottom. On January 26, Lincoln reluctantly relieved Burnside of the command and, with great misgivings, bestowed it upon Joseph Hooker, although he was well aware of Hooker's disloyalty to his chief.

The army and his fellow officers had serious reservations about "Fighting Joe" Hooker, as he was known. After a couple of weeks, one newspaper correspondent wrote that Hooker's appointment "is variously received by the army," but that everyone felt that Hooker would either "destroy the rebel army, or our own." General John Gibbon called Hooker "a strange composition . . . essentially an intriguer. In his intrigues, he sacrificed his soldierly principles whenever such sacrifice could gain him political influence to further his own ends." The historian Palfrey called Hooker "brave, handsome, vain, insubordinate, plausible, untrustworthy," and said, "As an inferior, he planned badly and fought well; as chief, he planned well and fought badly." [3]

Hooker, as he took command, was cognizant of the fact that the army required reorganization and restoration if it was to function again in a proper manner. He named Butterfield his chief of staff, abolished Burnside's "grand divisions," and regularized furlough policy in an effort to cut down on the problem of desertions. He instituted long-overdue sanitary reforms and directed the distribution of soft bread and fresh vegetables on a regular basis. He consolidated the cavalry into a single corps and reduced the head of the artillery, General Henry J. Hunt, to an administrative role. "Whatever his merits or his shortcomings as a commander," one staffer later wrote, "Hooker was surely an ideal inspector-general." [4]

Such a shakeup was overdue in the Army of the Potomac. Even Warren and the officers of his brigade were said to be "getting to be regular Gin heads, in such dreary times as we have just gone through, they keep their skins full of Commissary Whiskey." [5] How the private reporting this fact came to know it is not revealed, but the role of the grapevine and scuttlebutt in any army should not be underestimated.

On January 30, Warren wrote to brother Will that Hooker "offers me the place of Chief Topl. Engineer on his Staff, and I have the matter under consideration." He said that he wanted to consult Sykes and Humphreys about the offer, and both were away. "I asked to be Chief Engineer of the whole and Genl Hooker will give it to me if it can be arranged." [6]

After a little more thought Warren agreed to accept the position offered, which was not as chief engineer but as topographer. He told Will that "I can do more good there perhaps than I can here," and Hooker assured him "that I shall not lose in advancement by the change." On February 4, 1863, he formally assumed his place on Hooker's staff. [7]

Hooker's headquarters may seem like a strange place for Gouverneur Warren to be, for it quickly developed a bad reputation. Joe Hooker was notorious for his heavy drinking and for consorting with women of easy virtue, and he attracted as associates men of the same kind. Warren's correspondence and journals, however, make no reference to any such activities. His eyes were focused strictly on his engineering duties, and his heart was off in Baltimore, with the young lady he loved.

Warren did get to know Daniel Butterfield, and closer acquaintance with the former New York businessman, most famous as the composer of "Taps," did not prove rewarding. Warren called Butterfield "the most obviously mean and contemptible moral specimen, for he lacked physical courage." Humphreys said Butterfield was "the most detested and despised man in the Army, false, treacherous and cowardly." [8]

Regardless of his relations with the rest of the staff, Warren immediately immersed himself in his new duties, examining and preparing maps, requisitioning supplies, and getting acquainted with the men under him: draftsmen, civil engineers, "civil assistants," and laborers. "We live together in a very mixed up way as yet," he told Emily, "eating, sleeping, working, writing, talking & all in one tent—so that I have no time or chance to enjoy private thoughts nor write to friends *or* sweethearts." He asked the Topographical Engineers Corps for $1,430 monthly to run his office and was pleased to be furnished with $1,500, "charged to the appropriations for surveys for military defences." [9]

On February 26 Warren was granted a leave, and by the 28th he was in Baltimore with Emily. A month earlier he had written to her, telling her that he agreed with her father, who said he had "convinced" her, rather unwillingly, "that it is best painful as it may be to postpone any union or engagement while prospects are so gloomy." Gouv added, "That is what I told you was best, Emily, but you were *not* 'convinced.'" Then he said, "You used to think you would be more happy if our relations were acknowledged, if so acknowledge them. If the event is deferred let not the hope be." In this uncertain state of affairs, she was surely happy to share his ten-day leave. After a day in Baltimore, they left together on March 1 for New York and Cold Spring, to meet Gouv's family, returning to Baltimore on the 8th. Warren then reported to Washington and telegraphed her the next day that he had to return to camp. [10]

On March 10, Warren noted that a recently enacted law abolished the Corps of Topographical Engineers and transferred all of its officers to the Engineer Corps. Unfortunately, no orders or directives promulgating or implementing the act had been issued, so Warren found himself in a sort of limbo. [11]

He wrote Emily about the problem: "I as the ranking officer when I came here would have been chief . . . But the order promulgating the law . . . has not yet been given and things remain." Thus valuable time which could have been spent in consolidating the functions of the hitherto-separate engineering departments was wasted. "I could go on and prepare myself as if the change were already made," he said, "were it not that while I was home Genl. Hooker got Genl. [Henry W.] Benham who is Lt. Col of Engns. ordered here prior to the consolidation, and I do not know what position he is to have: if as an engineer he will rank me and I shall feel compelled to leave."

There was really not that much topographical work to be done, he told her, and, in light of the consolidation, he would not allow himself to be assigned to it. He could not serve under Benham, he said, "who is personally a disagreeable man and one in whose judgment I have not much confidence." If he went back to a line command, he felt he was entitled to more than the little brigade he had commanded previously, and if there were to be some other command "I should be with it at once so that I can be becoming familiar with it and it with me." With active operations approaching quickly, something should be done; "I sit here a prey to procrastination like one in a nightmare who sees some frightful thing approaching without power to move." [12]

A couple of days later Warren was ordered up to Washington, and he took advantage of this trip to squeeze in a day and a half with Emily in Baltimore. In mid-April, in a letter to her, Warren analyzed his feelings in their separation: "The feeling of lost companionship is strongest amid toils and sorrows, and perhaps those love each other most who share the most of the hardships of life together. To be the one to caress you, when you are no longer pleased with excitement and gaities, is happiness far enough for me." [13]

Warren wrote another letter the same day, addressed to "my dear wife," expressing his disgust with the politics of army rank:

> Genl Humphreys, a soldier by education by nature and by experience, who has proved his title to being a gentleman and soldier in every way, whose *mind* has made him an enduring ornament to *society & science*, whose years place him in the prime of life (my senior by 12 years) He commands only a small division of 4000 men. While Danl Sickles (a defeated democratic politician, tried for murder, morally debased, and of no military experience) is in command of an army corps. Simply because he is smart as a political maneuverer.

He went on to discuss the new army commander: "Genl Hooker is in every respect a soldier and I know him well. Under him this army will succeed if under anyone. I know he appreciates his position with regard to the enemy, and I am devoted to aiding him all in my power. He will succeed if anyone can." [14]

As the Army of the Potomac prepared for its spring campaign, the anomaly of Warren's position began to wear on him. "I am in very good health," he wrote Emily, "but feel somewhat out of spirits. I am getting very tired of the constant camp life I have led for two years." He felt that "my occupations have not kept pace in importance with my impatience." He longed for "another sphere of action or a more satisfactory one here." He begged her to write often, even if she had nothing to say "but that you love me." [15]

As Emily's now-acknowledged fiancé, Warren felt freer in opening up his innermost feelings to her, as when he denied to her that he could any longer be regarded as "a rising young man with a bright future."

> [I]gnoble as it may seem to think so, I am beginning to lose some of the confident hopes in the future which I indulged in, in my earlier years, when

no position was envied because I felt I could aspire to it and win by worthy efforts. Now I see that I am too stupid and weak to gain by my energy and ability—and too honest and stupid to gain by the usual means of success. And I never feel the apprehension of failure so much as when I think of your being linked to it. That makes me write so to you. It is very wrong to make you unhappy about our relation but I would fully have you appreciate the worst before our relations become irrevocable. So too I feel that if you gave up wealth for me you lost a substance for a shadow.

He went on to discuss the inscrutability of reasons for advancement:

Look at Burnside. A good fellow certainly, manly honest and comely. But of only moderate mind and attainments. Who has made our cause suffer more in battle than any other Genl—who has been friendly to McClellan, himself hunted down—who wanted to dismiss Genl Hooker and several other Genls, whom the President has advanced—who told the President that neither the army nor the people had any confidence in Stanton or Halleck, and yet *he* retains his position. Neither blunders & inefficiency—personal animosity in higher sources—nor friendship with the proscribed has lowered him, while one like Genl Porter was dismissed in the vilest disgrace.

He then wrote lines which may have come back to him at times over the years:

I believe in eternal justice and in the ultimate triumph of truth and virtue, but this often comes after the victims to malice and ambition have long mouldered in their graves, or the time of life is past when pleasure was had in the world or its opinions. I always try to think that one has but to do his duty, hide his repinings in consciousness of duty performed and trust to the future.[16]

Later, Warren wrote to Emily again, responding to her question whether his family depended on him pecuniarily. "I answer you plainly no," he said, "not at all essentially." He then went on to discuss why he had not told his family when she accompanied him to Cold Spring that they were engaged, a rather lame explanation that their visit home was to close up his father's estate and if he had said at the same time that he was engaged to Emily "I would have been mingling you with an apparent monied transaction." This way, he said, it takes away "any possible cause of unpleasant feeling towards you, which I believe brothers and sisters always feel towards their son's and brother's wives." Besides, he said, his sisters Emily and Eliza "have the most kindly feelings towards you."[17]

On April 27, Warren wrote his fiancée that "we are now on the move and great events are on the gale . . . I feel full of hope in our success and if we do succeed it will be a great advance towards closing the war." The next night his letter said, "It is a momentous night this darling . . . I hope heaven will be propitious for it is to be a telling day in the annals of the war . . . We must win or be destroyed ourselves." He added that "no prominent place is yet assigned to me and in the preliminary struggle I shall be at most a spectator."[18]

The next day, April 29, Warren reported to Emily that "a large part of our army crossed the Rappahannock last night and this morning with but slight loss in which the rebels suffered as much as ourselves. Tomorrow if we succeed is to be a grand day." For Joseph Hooker had commenced his great secret flanking movement around Lee's army. Warren described the start of the plan in his post-action report: "Three corps, the Fifth, Eleventh, and Twelfth, were put in motion on April 27 to pass around the enemy's left flank, crossing the Rappahannock at Kelly's Mills, a distance of 30 miles from Fredericksburg, thence to cross the Rapidan by Germanna and Ely's Ford."[19]

Hooker recognized that the Confederate defenses before Fredericksburg were vastly more formidable than they had been when Burnside hurled his army against them in December. Hooker's plan was a bold division of his army, with the bulk of it moving secretly north and west, to cross the Rappahannock and its tributary, the Rapidan, and come in *behind* the rebel army at Fredericksburg, where the foe would be fixed in place by the Union Sixth Corps crossing the river and threatening an attack on the old ground.

Various feints and ruses were designed to draw off Confederate defenders at the crossing places, and Hooker kept his plans to himself until virtually the last minute. Warren later told the Committee on the Conduct of the War that "I did not know any of his plans until I saw them being carried into operation."[20] Success depended on secrecy and speed, as well as some good old-fashioned luck. Incredibly, it all came together for Joe Hooker—for a while.

The Rappahannock was crossed by the morning of April 28, the Rapidan by the morning of the 30th. In the meantime, the Sixth Corps, under General John Sedgwick, crossed the river to Fredericksburg the night of the 28th. Warren left the Falmouth headquarters at 5 P.M. on the 29th, to get a pontoon bridge laid at U.S. Mine Ford. Though the approaches to the crossing-place were difficult, by 3 P.M. the next day "the bridge was laid and the Second Corps was crossing the river." Warren wrote Emily, "We have had good success so far and all are in good spirits. I have had a hard day's work, but accomplished what I undertook."[21]

By the evening of the 30th of April, four corps of the Union army, under Hooker's personal command, were assembled at a place called Chancellorsville, a clearing in the dark and tangled second-growth forest called the Wilderness. Hooker that evening issued a general order to the army, stating his "heartfelt satisfaction" that "the operations of the last three days have determined that our enemy must either ingloriously fly, or come out from behind his defenses and give us battle on our own ground, where certain destruction awaits him." The soldiers cheered when the order was read to them, but they looked warily at the Wilderness surrounding them.[22]

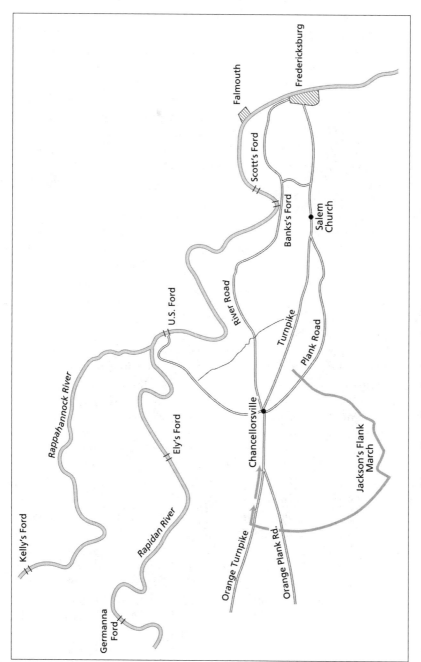

Chancellorsville and Salem Church, April 29–May 5, 1863

The Wilderness. There had once been an iron industry there in those woods, and the original timber had been cut to provide charcoal for the furnaces. The second-growth forest was a dark and gloomy tangle of stunted trees and impenetrable undergrowth. "Dense woods and thickets of black-jack oak and pine," Warren described it, and, he said, "no one can conceive a more unfavorable field for the movements of a grand army than it presents." There were, however, two usable roads through the Wilderness, both running roughly east and west: the macadamized Orange Turnpike and the Orange Plank Road. "Between Chancellorsville and Fredericksburg the country becomes more open and clear as you approach the latter place," Warren wrote, "and for several miles along the Plank road the country is clear and even-surfaced, and affording a fine field for the use of all arms." It was thus imperative for Hooker to move his army out of the Wilderness toward Fredericksburg.[23]

The following morning Warren rode out to reconnoiter some three miles toward Fredericksburg on the turnpike, which road he found "good and broad." The country was still wooded on both sides for the first mile and after that was more open to the right of the road. He returned to headquarters at about ten o'clock and learned that an advance along the pike had finally been ordered. Darius Couch, commander of the Second Corps, complained that "somehow things dragged," and he received no order to move "until hours after light." At last, two divisions of the Fifth Corps under George G. Meade were to move along the river road to Banks's Ford, the uncovering of which would substantially reduce the problem of communications between the two parts of Hooker's army, while Sykes's Fifth Corps division, backed up by part of the Second Corps, was to march out the pike toward Fredericksburg. The Twelfth Corps under Henry Slocum was to move in the same direction on the plank road. A line of battle was to be formed two and a half miles in front, ready to advance at 2 P.M.[24]

Warren rode along with Sykes and his old division, which encountered the Eleventh Virginia about a mile and a quarter east of Chancellorsville. Sykes attacked vigorously, drove back the enemy, and reached the position assigned to him by Hooker's orders, a ridge with a good field of fire in front. He was soon joined by Hancock's excellent division of the Second Corps, which, according to Couch, "took up a strong position." Sykes, however, discovered that a substantial body of rebels in his front overlapped both ends of his line, and he was unable to connect with Slocum, off to the right on the plank road. Warren rode back to headquarters to fill Hooker in on the situation. Lee had reacted to the movement of the Army of the Potomac by sending a substantial force west from Fredericksburg, but this was just what the Federal generals had long been seeking, a fight in open ground. At this point Hooker, to the astonishment of all, instead of supporting Sykes, decided to abandon the position already won and directed Sykes and Hancock to fall back to Chancellorsville, to the line held the night before. "Unfortunately," as Warren wrote, "this line had been taken up the day before by tired troops toward the close of the day and without much prospect of fighting a pitched battle upon it. It was a bad line, and had several commanding positions in its front for the enemy to occupy." [25]

When the order to withdraw reached Couch, Hancock, and Sykes, they exploded in outrage. Warren felt the position held by Hancock's division was a strong one, and he suggested to Couch that he not order the retreat until he (Warren) went to see Hooker again. He did so, but Hooker reiterated the order, and the two divisions were withdrawn, back into the Wilderness, back to Chancellorsville. "All the other columns"—Meade's as well as Slocum's Twelfth Corps—"withdrew to the vicinity of Chancellorsville without having engaged the enemy," Warren wrote. The overconfident Joe Hooker seemed to have lost his nerve with the first appearance of opposition, and the initiative passed quickly from Hooker to Robert E. Lee, who knew far better what to do with it. [26]

William Swinton, in his history of the Army of the Potomac, wrote that

> Till he met the enemy, Hooker showed a master-grasp of the elements of war, but the moment he confronted his antagonist, he seemed to suffer collapse of all his powers, and after this his conduct, with the exception of one or two momentary flashes of talent, was marked by an incomprehensible feebleness and faultiness; for in each crisis, his action was not only bad—it was, with a fatal infelicity, the worst that could have been adopted. [27]

Darius Couch wrote to Warren after the war that when the commanding general "found Lee disputing the advance Hooker lost confidence in his ability to maneuvre so large an army in presence of the enemy, and concluded it was best to fight where he was partially enveloped and hidden by woods." [28]

Whatever the reason, Hooker's army marched back into the Wilderness, although he does not appear to have had any definite idea what to do with it there. After the new line was established around the Chancellorsville intersection, Couch, Meade, Sykes, and Hancock sat on their horses, behind Hancock's division, and Meade, comparing where they were with where they had been, exclaimed, "My God, if we can't hold the top of a hill, we certainly cannot hold the bottom of it!" [29]

Since the position retired to "formed a very bad line of defence," Warren and others expected that an order would be forthcoming to make arrangements for battle by forming a better and stronger line. Warren had urged on Hooker an advance "with our whole force of five corps" in the morning, a plan he "urged with more zeal than convincing argument." The commanding general was adamant, however, that he would assume the defensive and force Lee to make a move. [30]

Warren was astonished, however, when Hooker went to bed with his door locked at 10 P.M. without making any specific provision for the next day. Sometime after midnight two corps commanders, Meade and Sickles, came to Warren, pointed out the lack of adequate disposition of the troops for battle the next morning, and in frustration suggested to Warren that he, "as a staff officer of the Commanding General . . . should take the responsibility of giving the necessary instructions to meet the great emergency of the case."

Warren recoiled at the suggestion, as he later recalled to Sickles:

> I stated that I might thus in case of disaster be found guilty of a treasonable offense, and that my insignificant position before the country would not protect me, but that if you Corps Commanders would agree among yourselves what was best to do and act upon it, I thought the emergency would justify you and your positions secure you from any imputation of unpatriotic motives. That at any rate it would be fool-hardy for me to assume to do what exceeded your power and responsibility.[31]

Nothing came of the Meade/Sickles initiative, and in the morning the Army of the Potomac lay relatively inactive, awaiting developments. During the day there were occasional glimpses of Confederates moving to the south and west, out in the woods below Chancellorsville, but Hooker decided that these were retreating troops—he had convinced himself that Lee was going to have to retreat—and he did little more than send Sickles's Third Corps out to hurry the withdrawing rebels along. In fact, this was Jackson with half the southern army, marching through the forest on obscure woodland trails out of sight of the Federals, moving around and beyond the unsuspecting and unprepared right wing of the Union Army, General O. O. Howard's Eleventh Corps.

Jackson's late afternoon attack upon Howard, coming from a completely unexpected place, was devastating, and the resultant rout left Hooker's army in a shambles. Warren reported that he "tried in vain to assist some of the officers" of the Eleventh Corps "in rallying their men, but soon saw it was a waste of precious time." He then rode back to Fairview, just south of Chancellorsville, where he helped to organize a line of artillery to bombard the enemy. "General Warren," wrote the historian of a Michigan regiment, "with Hooker's old division and fifty pieces of artillery, stemmed Jackson's advance after dark." This artillery barrage as well as Jackson's accidental wounding by his own men brought affairs to a standstill. The Union line was stabilized, and a new defensive perimeter established. In addition, Hooker directed Warren and Captain Cyrus Comstock of the engineers to lay out a new defensive line to the rear, back toward the fords of the river, should the Chancellorsville position be given up.[32]

At the close of the day on May 2, the Army of the Potomac had contained Jackson's attack, and it had received the addition to its strength of the First Corps, now across the river. The position of the Third Corps, at the high ground of Hazel Grove south of the turnpike, effectively cut off communication between the two halves of Lee's army.[33]

Hooker's situation was in fact much better than it deserved to be. Hooker now decided the time had come for Sedgwick, with the Union force at Fredericksburg, to fall upon Lee's rear. Warren, "knowing much of the road that General Sedgwick would thus have to march over in the night," was directed to "go and guide the column, and give such information and assistance as I could." In effect, he was to be Joe Hooker's proxy in hurrying along the often slow-moving Sedgwick.[34]

Warren set out with an aide at about 10:30 P.M. and reached Sedgwick, crossing the Rappahannock, at 3 A.M. He found it difficult to prod Sedgwick and later told Hooker that had he not been there Sedgwick might not have moved at all. The Sixth Corps troops moved slowly and by daylight had not yet passed out of the town to position themselves for the attack on the hills beyond. The Confederates defending Fredericksburg were under the command of the irascible Jubal A. Early, who concentrated his force south of the town, where he assumed the Federal attack would come.[35]

With daylight Warren could see that Marye's Heights was defended much more lightly than it had been in December, held in fact by just two Mississippi regiments from the brigade of William Barksdale. Warren knew that Hooker did not want Sedgwick to drive Early's force back toward Lee, so at 8:30 A.M. he suggested to Sedgwick that "the only thing left for us to do was to carry Marye's Hill by main force as speedily as possible." This, if accomplished, would leave Early's troops south of the town while Sedgwick headed west. A couple of hours later the assault was finally set in motion; the rebels were driven from the notorious stone wall at the base of the hill, and the hill itself was quickly captured. Warren sent a 1 P.M. dispatch to Butterfield, reporting that "the heights were carried splendidly at 11 A.M. by Newton . . . Our loss, though honorable proof of a severe contest, is not very severe."[36]

From Fredericksburg Sedgwick moved his troops slowly westward out the plank road, to strike Lee's rear if possible, after taking time to shuffle the divisions of John Newton and William Brooks, with Brooks now taking the lead. On a slight ridge five miles west of the town and six miles east of Chancellorsville stood a red-brick Baptist church called Salem Church. Lee, who had no idea of sitting still while Hooker maneuvered around him, detached the division of Lafayette McLaws from his force at Chancellorsville and moved it back to meet the oncoming Sedgwick at Salem Church. Cadmus Wilcox marched his Alabama brigade rapidly down from Banks's Ford to take up positions along the plank road, where he delayed Sedgwick's advance a couple of times, giving McLaws time to arrive and move into place at Salem Church.

At five o'clock the Union attack commenced. Wilcox's Alabamians and Paul Semmes's brigade of Georgians received the charge, yielded ground, lost the church and a nearby schoolhouse, and then, led by the Ninth Alabama, hit the Federals with a fierce countercharge which broke them and won the day for the rebels. Although Sedgwick outnumbered the enemy before him by about 20,000 men to 10,000, he made the attack at Salem Church with only the 4,100 men of Brooks's division. Newton was too far behind to give effective support, and the defeat followed. There is little evidence that Sedgwick had any real notion of the size of the enemy force he was attacking. This repulse marked the end of John Sedgwick's advance to Chancellorsville. "The day closed," Warren wrote, "with the enemy holding his position." [37]

For Gouverneur Warren, the long day had not yet ended. He was to return to headquarters, and he promised Sedgwick to send back instructions for the latter's guidance. Sedgwick's advance had, as noted, caused Wilcox to withdraw from his position at Banks's Ford, and the Federals had thrown a bridge across the Rappahannock, actually at Scott's Ford, a mile downstream. By this bridge and then by United States Mine Ford, Warren rode back to Hooker's headquarters, which he reached at 11 P.M. He discovered that matters had not gone well for the Army of the Potomac while he was gone.

In the early morning of May 3, Hooker had pulled the Third Corps back from Hazel Grove, a disastrous mistake which enabled the Confederates immediately to seize that commanding position for their artillery. From there the rebel gunners were able to shell both Fairview and Chancellorsville, and the barrage at the latter place even managed to disable Hooker temporarily when he was hit on the head by a falling pillar. The concussion did not do anything to improve the commanding general's tactical sense, and he soon ordered a withdrawal north from the turnpike, back toward the fords over the Rapidan. Hancock's division covered the retreat as the rear guard, and the army pulled back to the defensive line about a mile north which Warren and Comstock had laid out the night before. The casualties incurred by both armies in the three battles fought that day, at Marye's Heights, at Chancellorsville, and at Salem Church, made it the second bloodiest day of the war, surpassed only by Antietam.[38]

At headquarters behind the new line Warren found Hooker, whom he had some difficulty awakening, particularly after the latter's concussion earlier in the day. "After reporting to the general, and getting his ideas," Warren said, he felt he should let Sedgwick know how things stood, since no one else seemed to be doing anything to keep the Sixth Corps commander informed. Hooker made it clear that he had no instructions for Sedgwick. Although Warren was totally exhausted, having been in the saddle almost continuously for twenty-four hours, he composed the following message and sent it on its way to Sedgwick:

> I find everything snug here. We contracted the line a little, and repulsed the last assault with ease. General Hooker wishes them to attack him to-morrow, if they will. He does not desire you to attack again in force unless he attacks him at the same time. He says you are too far away from him to direct. Look

well to the safety of your corps, and keep up communication with General Benham, at Banks' Ford and Fredericksburg. You can go to either place, if you think best. To cross at Banks' Ford would bring you in supporting distance of the main body, and would be better than falling back to Fredericksburg.[39]

Having forwarded the dispatch to Sedgwick, Warren stretched out without an overcoat or other cover over him and fell into a sound sleep.

This message was not phrased as felicitously as it might have been—Warren's exhaustion had certainly dulled his mind somewhat by the time it was written—and it was less helpful to Sedgwick than it could have been. For one thing, due to the scrambled state of Union army communications, Sedgwick did not receive the dispatch until 6:30 the following morning. The sentence about contracting the line a little sounds like a Hooker euphemism and certainly does not present a true picture of the army's situation. That Hooker might attack the enemy was by this time extremely unlikely. The message did tell Sedgwick he was to maintain his communications with both Banks's Ford and Fredericksburg, and it appeared to leave to his discretion where he should go next. But it was somewhat fuzzier than the Sixth Corps commander would have liked.

On May 4, Hooker, with the major part of the army, remained inactive, waiting and hoping for Lee to attack him in his strong defensive position. Sedgwick, with his three divisions forming a salient running from the plank road back to Banks's Ford, learned early in the day that the Confederates had recaptured an undefended Marye's Heights, so that he was now effectively cut off from Fredericksburg. Late in the afternoon three southern divisions under McLaws, Early, and Richard Anderson attacked Sedgwick's position, but despite fierce fighting they were unable to break his lines. Sedgwick sent word to Hooker, in a message that reached Fighting Joe at about 11 P.M., that he was preparing to cross the river.

Hooker had not let Sedgwick in on his plan for May 5, which was to recross the Rappahannock at U.S. Mine Ford, march to Banks's Ford, and then join Sedgwick for a grand turning movement against Lee's flank. Sedgwick was unaware of the importance of his salient to Hooker's plan, and Warren's message of the night before seemed to permit him to cross to the safety of the north side of the river when he felt it best to do so. Now, as he prepared to cross the river, Hooker's plan for the following day (and the climax of the battle) was falling apart.

The night of May 4, Joe Hooker called his corps commanders together, to "consult" with them on what the army should do next. Those in attendance were Meade, Reynolds, Howard, Sickles, and Couch, as well as Butterfield, the chief of staff, who had just recently arrived from Falmouth, and Warren. Slocum of the Twelfth Corps could not be found and arrived only as the conclave was breaking up. Hooker laid out the situation of the two armies, and he presented two courses of action, a forward movement against Lee's force in his front or a withdrawal across U.S. Mine Ford, bringing an end to the campaign. Significantly, he said nothing about recrossing at Banks's Ford to join Sedgwick for a flank attack. He drew the bleakest picture he could of any possible offensive movement, and then he and Butterfield withdrew, to permit a free discussion.

Warren, who had already "strongly urged an attack in force next morning" in a private consultation with Hooker, remained, "thinking that some information might be desirable from me about the field of operations generally." Meade, Reynolds, and Howard spoke in favor of an attack; Reynolds and Meade knew that their corps had seen hardly any action since the campaign began and were still fresh, while Howard was hoping for an opportunity to redeem his corps' lost honor. Couch said that he did not have enough information to make a judgment, and Sickles advised a withdrawal; "the uncertainties," he said, "were against us." Sickles went on to denounce Hooker "in the most abusive language" for "getting the army where it was, through his unfitness for command," and then throwing the responsibility to the corps commanders. At this point, with criticism of Hooker increasing, Warren felt it best to leave the meeting, "on account of my confidential relations to the commanding general."[40]

When Hooker rejoined the conference, he set forth his arguments for a withdrawal and was chagrined to find his corps commanders voting 3-2 in favor of an attack. He then said that it was his responsibility and the army would march back across the river at U.S. Mine Ford. John Reynolds was put out by the whole business: "What was the use of calling us together at this time of night when he intended to retreat anyhow?" In any event, the Sixth Corps crossed to the north side of the Rappahannock at Banks's Ford that night.[41]

In the meantime, at Hooker's direction, Warren prepared on May 5 "a new and shorter line in our rear, to secure us against any attempt of the enemy to interrupt the move." He and Comstock carried out this directive, constructing "a continuous cover and abatis . . . from the Rappahannock at Scott's dam around to the mouth of Hunting Run, on the Rapidan, a distance of 3 miles." They also put the roads in good order and laid a third bridge. A heavy rain began to fall at 4:30 P.M., three hours before the withdrawal was to begin, and a sudden rise in the river jeopardized the bridges. Warren and Comstock took up the third bridge, using it "to piece out the ends of the other two," and the crisis passed.[42]

A detail from the 155th Pennsylvania was sent to Warren to help dig the final line of fortifications. The work was arduous and the difficulty was increased by rain. Warren, seeing the work progressing slowly, got down into the trenches with the men and, "as if he were a brother of the soldiers, took shovels and picks from their hands and showed them the knack and skillful way to use the same in throwing up earth." He moved along the line, helping out those who needed instruction. Reported the Pennsylvanians, "At first so modest was he and kindly in his action that no one suspected him of holding the rank of Brigadier-General, as he had no sword or epaulettes or style indicating his rank."[43]

Warren's accomplishments in the Chancellorsville campaign were considerable. In less than forty-eight hours, he threw up "five miles of the most formidable entrenchments yet constructed under battlefield conditions," fortifications which astounded and amazed the Confederates who came upon them after the Federals had departed. He helped to stem the rebel tide after the Eleventh Corps had been overrun, and he practically pushed Sedgwick up Marye's Heights the next day. Abner Doubleday, a division commander in the First Corps, wrote that Warren "made almost superhuman exertions to do without sleep and perform the important duties assigned him."[44]

Regardless, however, of Warren's work, or Couch's, or Hancock's, the Army of the Potomac was beaten again, once again outgeneraled rather than outfought. The great army of Fighting Joe Hooker passed over the bridges to the other side of the river, the last unit crossing at 8 A.M. on May 6, and the Chancellorsville campaign came to an inglorious end. [45]

CHAPTER NINE

TO LITTLE ROUND TOP

GOUVERNEUR WARREN WAS HEARTSICK AFTER the Army of the Potomac recrossed the Rappahannock and returned to its camps around Falmouth. He wrote to his brother Will that "it was unnecessary for us to retreat . . . There was a want of *nerve* somewhere in carrying out the movement." He said that he had "urged and counselled activity and rode from one end of our long lines over and over again to push things." Unfortunately, he said, his advice was not taken "and here we are again . . . 30,000 men weaker than before we moved."[1]

Warren's letters to Emily after Chancellorsville, at first somewhat matter-of-fact as to his activities and duties, became more despairing as days passed. On May 11, he told her, "My mind is suffering from a great reaction and disappointment." Filled with high hope and courage, he said, "we grappled with the foe" in what he thought was to be "the great victory that was to close the war." He "knew not fatigue nor want of sleep and little regarded danger," but steady purpose in the high command was wanting. "We halted, we hesitated, wavered, retired." He thought about his own position in the army's affairs:

> I feel how little one man like me can do after all. I have been in this war with all my energies, enthusiasm, hopes, happiness, all through it. I brought a good military education & a youth spent in active life in national pursuits. No word of censure has ever been recorded against me, and I have been praised and complimented till I am sick of it. Position not praise is what I want. Power to do good not to pleasure myself with.[2]

Although this was surely not what Warren was talking about in his letter to Emily, his position on Hooker's staff was clarified somewhat the next day, May 12, when Special Orders No. 128 named him as chief engineer "on the staff of the major-general commanding," which of course made him chief engineer of the Army of the Potomac.[3]

Several days later, Warren wrote to her, "War is a horrible thing but such a war as this army has waged for nearly two years most horrible of all. Battle after battle has been given and no decisive victory." Between the two armies, he said, no less than 150,000 men had died. The man of science in G. K. Warren was appalled at what the soldiers had wrought, although at bottom he blamed the politicians.[4]

A couple of days after that, Warren wrote to her about the enemy: "[t]hose men of the Southern Army who have behaved honorably still have my esteem for their conduct though I feel sorry that we should ever have been arrayed against each other." Although, he said, he rejoiced at Jackson's death "as a gain to our cause . . . yet in my soldier's heart I cannot but deem him the best soldier of all this war and grieve at his untimely end." He said that those southerners who now led their armies "were once many of them my associates and together we deplored the political debasement and malignity that was bringing on this war." Now the South had put down its radicals, but not until the North did the same would God give it the victory. "Now as it stands, unrelenting cruelty would be practiced by a triumphant north," he wrote, having in mind the wanton looting of Fredericksburg by Burnside's troops. The disappointed McClellan adherent was fast becoming a demoralized general.[5]

At the same time Warren was trying to set up a wedding date. Hopes for early May were dashed by his duties after Chancellorsville, and he soon felt that "we would have to delay it till the month of July." On May 17, after discussing the uncertainty of the army's staying near Washington, he wrote that "the war will not cease, perhaps for years, so we can hardly wait its termination for our union." The question becomes "shall we be married soon?"[6]

On May 20, Warren wrote to Emily about the news that General Ulysses S. Grant had captured Jackson, Mississippi. "Oh that we could have such a commander for perseverance who should also combine ability with the firm faith in success that removes mountains and turns rivers aside," he wrote, in words that would have horrified him a year or so later. "Hooker I am afraid has been too wicked a man to succeed in a great and holy cause. In the hour of trial he lost that support which a good man would have felt even if he were not great." Hooker, Warren noted, "has told me since he wished he had followed my advice. Nor was I alone in giving it, so many of us were agreed that I do not see how he acted against our opinion." He spoke of the defects of character of Hooker and his cronies, Butterfield and Sickles, and asked, despairingly, "[C]an a cause be holy which is entrusted to such hands? Can God smile upon them and bring defeat upon such Christians as Lee and Jackson fighting for their own Virginia?"[7]

Still hoping to set a wedding date, Gouv wrote to Emily on May 21 that "I am one of the workers in this hive and cannot easily leave." The next day he said, "Darling I must when I do come to marry you have time enough not to

leave you at once, and I have full confidence that by the time your preparations can be completed our affairs here will take such definite form as to enable me to demand for once in my soldier's life some consideration for myself
and you." On the 26th, Emily wrote to him, setting June 18 as the day. Four
days later he got some time off and went to Baltimore to see his betrothed.[8]

In the meantime, Fighting Joe Hooker was trying to figure out what Robert
E. Lee was planning to do. Hooker had about exhausted his supply of offensive
ideas and was simply waiting to react to the enemy's moves. Warren noted "important indications of movements in the lines of the enemy calling for corresponding preparations by us." Hooker, he said, told him it was "impossible for
him to tell whether I can be spared on the 15th or not." (The wedding had
been moved up to the 15th; now it was set back to June 18 once again.) Warren
was complimented, he said, when Hooker said "that when we did move he
could not spare me for a *minute*."[9]

On the 11th Warren reported on "quite a persevering talk" with Hooker, who
"finally agreed we could announce the day of our marriage and nothing but
actual battle should keep me away." So, he said, the wedding should be firmly
fixed on the 17th or 18th; "that will give time enough to inform our friends."
He asked Emily to make sure that the members of his family were invited.[10]

In the meantime, while Gouverneur Warren was privately venting his
frustrations to Emily and at the same time trying to arrange a suitable time
for their nuptials, the army, the enemy, and the war were not standing still.
Disillusionment with Joe Hooker was general throughout the Army of the
Potomac after its return to Falmouth. President Lincoln and General in
Chief Henry W. Halleck appeared at army headquarters on May 6, and the
commander in chief was soon made aware of the widespread dissatisfaction
with Hooker. Couch asked Lincoln to relieve him from his corps command,
stating that he would no longer serve under Fighting Joe. A few days later,
Couch joined Slocum and Sedgwick in sending word to George Meade that
they would be pleased to serve under him instead. Meade refused to join any
such movement, but his frank conversation with Governor Andrew Curtin
of Pennsylvania about Hooker's shortcomings cost him the goodwill of the
commanding general when the latter learned of the talk.

A senior artillery commander, Colonel Charles Wainwright, reported hearing from numerous officers, all of whom "agreed on Meade as the fittest man
in this army, with Warren as chief of staff." The artillerist agreed with the assessment of Meade but added, "of Warren I know but very little." He would
come to know Warren very well. Such a consensus, of course, reflected a high
regard for Warren's competence among those familiar with him. Several generals in addition to Meade, including Couch, Sedgwick, Hancock, and Reynolds, were reported to be under consideration to head the army. John F.
Reynolds in fact was offered the command of the Army of the Potomac, an of-

fer he turned down on June 2 because he could not be promised a free hand, independent of any political considerations.[11]

On June 3, Lee began moving his army away from Fredericksburg, leaving A. P. Hill in command of the fifteen thousand men left there, gathering the bulk of his command around Culpeper Court House, some thirty miles to the northwest. Lee and Jefferson Davis had agreed upon a strike north, into Maryland and Pennsylvania, as the movement likeliest to relieve the pressure upon John Pemberton's besieged army at Vicksburg. Unfortunately for the Confederacy, it was far too late to save Vicksburg and its doomed garrison.

President Lincoln had to restrain Hooker from attempting to cross the Rappahannock and attack the well-entrenched Hill, pointing out that the larger force under Lee should be his main concern. Over the next week Hooker stretched his army to the northwest, to counter Lee, so that it covered a span of about forty miles from south of Fredericksburg to Beverly Ford, on the upper Rappahannock.

While Lee's infantry moved toward the Shenandoah Valley for its advance north, Hooker pulled the Army of the Potomac back from the Rappahannock, to concentrate at Dumfries, twenty miles north of Fredericksburg, there to await the future movements of the enemy. One wing of the army, made up of the Second, Sixth, and Twelfth corps, covered the removal of government property from the huge supply depots at Aquia and Potomac Creeks.[12]

Warren was put in charge of the withdrawal of the supplies. Spurred on by an officious and unnecessary dispatch from Butterfield, stating that "a shameful waste and abandonment of property, entirely unnecessary and uncalled for, may possibly occur if vigorous measures are not taken," Warren took control of the situation.[13]

He wrote to Emily on the 14th from Aquia Creek, telling her "the whole army is in motion," but that "I confidently expect to be with you on . . . the morning of the eventful day." Under Warren's efficient supervision, the job of loading up the surplus property and moving it back up the Potomac was carried out. He wrote to Hancock late on the 15th that "everything has been removed" down to "the window sash out of the depot windows." By 9:45 on the morning of the 16th he was in Alexandria, sending word back to Hooker's headquarters: "I have just arrived here. I left Aquia last night, 11 P.M. Everything is removed but a little rolling-stock, which will be away today."[14]

The next day two New York regiments were ordered to the mouth of the Monocacy, up the Potomac in Maryland, above Washington, to protect the bridges and fords at that point. "They will receive special instructions," their orders read, "from Brigadier-General Warren after reaching their destination." Warren, of course, would not be there, so provision was made for an interim commander until his arrival.[15]

From Alexandria on the 16th, Warren was ordered to report to headquarters.

He reached Fairfax Court House, where Hooker was now located, at noon, "worked all day on notes and orders," including a careful and detailed survey of fords across the Potomac, and "at dark received permission to go to Baltimore and be married next day." First, though, he had to deliver some dispatches at Alexandria. He reached there at midnight, made his delivery by 2:30 A.M., and got to Washington by daybreak. He caught the 6:30 train to Baltimore, arriving at 9 A.M. on the 17th.[16]

At noon, Gouv Warren's wedding to Emily Chase, so long jeopardized by military contingencies, took place in the drawing room of the Chase home on St. Paul Street. The ceremony was performed by Emily's uncle, the Reverend Henry Burroughs, rector of Old North Church, Boston. A brief reception concluded by three o'clock, and the families sat down to a wedding supper at five.

While at table, the bridegroom was handed a dispatch from headquarters, summoning him to the Monocacy to post those two regiments. Warren set out with Emily for Washington, where they spent their first night of wedded life at Willard's Hotel. On the next day, Warren ascertained that the troops he was to post were no farther than Rockville, so he won a reprieve of another day. Late on the 19th, however, he received a peremptory order to "join Head Quarters at once." On June 20, he sent Emily back to Baltimore, in the care of his sisters, and rejoined the war at Fairfax Court House.[17]

Next morning Warren wrote to his bride, telling her that General Hooker "was much amused at hearing of the difficulties I overcame in reaching you in time to be married." He said that "the events of the past few days will long be the central point of all my thoughts, and my heart now is warmed with the emotions with which I beheld you first dressed for the bridal." He thought the rise in the Potomac from a recent rain would trouble the Confederates, "and you must not be alarmed for we are not."[18]

After writing his letter, Warren set out on a reconnaissance ride of more than fifty miles, to Chantilly, Centreville, Groveton, Gainesville, Manassas, and back to camp. He was sorely affected by the scene at Manassas, where "the hastily formed graves of my men almost covered the ground where they fought, formed as each was by covering him with earth where he fell." In some places swine had "rooted them from their scanty tombs." Brave heroes, he called them, "sacrificed to the imbecility of favorites . . . in their deaths they have been thrown as pearls before swine." He said his scrutiny of the field confirmed his thoughts about that battle, the history of which he hoped to write. "God smites a nation for the sins of its rulers," he continued. "We suffer now for the sin of slavery and we must suffer still till favor, ambition avarice and envy hatred and malice shall all disappear under God's chastening influence and patriotism and purity alone survive."[19]

On the 23rd of June Warren's letter to Emily conjectured that Lee might move into Pennsylvania and threaten both Philadelphia and Baltimore "and make a great panic I have no doubt, but I think it will ultimately ruin him." Such a crisis, he said,

> will demand new men and measures and in the changes I must be advanced. I have served the country faithfully and disinterestedly while those who have brought so many misfortunes upon us have been working for themselves. They'll get their reward and I'll get mine.
>
> The longer the war lasts now the better it is for me until I have a more potent voice in its control, for I have become a thorough soldier and need a field to display my knowledge and experience, which would all be lost in peace.[20]

The next day Warren sent a letter to Emily using his new chief aide, Lieutenant Washington Roebling, as a courier. He described Roebling, the son of John A. Roebling, the famous engineer and wiremaker from Trenton, New Jersey, as "a splendid young man rich and talented and accomplished." On June 25, he told her, "we move at daybreak tomorrow and I expect hard stirring times soon again."[21]

Joe Hooker had finally concluded that Lee's army was carrying out a major movement through Maryland and into Pennsylvania. It had taken him some time, because he had effectively lost contact with Lee. Concerning the maneuvers of the two armies in May and June, one historian wrote of the irony that, "neither commander knowing the other's movements, Hooker maintained a position designed only to prevent a march on Washington which Lee never intended, and Lee, to protect his march to the upper Potomac and to tempt Hooker to battle, executed maneuvers which Hooker never discovered."[22]

Warren, at Hooker's request, presented the commanding general on June 24 with a paper setting forth the desirability of moving the army toward Harper's Ferry. Whether influenced by Warren's paper or not, Hooker finally moved. On June 25, he named Reynolds to command the advance elements of the army, the First, Third, and Eleventh corps with Julius Stahel's cavalry division, and directed him to guard Crampton and Turner's Gaps in South Mountain, so that Lee could not come through these gaps and fall on his left flank as he marched the Army of the Potomac into Maryland.[23]

The rest of the army, following Reynolds, got under way on the 26th, crossing the Potomac at Edwards' Ferry. Cumbersome baggage trains, drizzling rain, and clogged roads made the day's march a difficult one, but at least the Federals were on the move. By this time Ewell's and Hill's corps of the Army of Northern Virginia were in Pennsylvania, and most of Longstreet's corps was across the Potomac into Maryland. Hooker's delay in making up his mind to follow Lee meant that his troops would have to make forced marches to catch up.

Warren reached the new headquarters of the army, at Poolesville, Maryland, by 10 A.M. on the 26th. The next day, June 27, he and Hooker rode to Harper's Ferry, the cause of a gathering conflict between Fighting Joe and his superiors in Washington. Hooker wanted to abandon Harper's Ferry and add its garrison to his own force. Harper's Ferry and Maryland Heights, overlooking the town from across the Potomac, had long been regarded as important possessions, and Halleck told Hooker that they were not to be given up unless absolute necessity required it. The journey to the town on the 27th was apparently an effort to find such a necessity.

Finding none, and learning that General William French, commanding the garrison at Harper's Ferry, had received instructions from Halleck that he was not required to obey any orders from the commander of the Army of the Potomac, Hooker rode back to his new headquarters at Frederick, Maryland, and, at 1 P.M., fired off a telegram to Halleck. Complaining that he could not protect Harper's Ferry and Washington *and* face Lee's army "with the means at my disposal," Hooker asked to be relieved. He surely did not expect his request to be accepted, since a collision with the enemy was clearly only days away. Hooker's wire was designed to coerce Halleck into affording him freedom to handle the army as he pleased. Nevertheless, in Washington the resignation was greeted with relief. That evening Halleck sent a dispatch to General George Gordon Meade, received well after midnight, advising him that he was now in command of the army. "Considering the circumstances," Halleck said, "no one ever received a more important command." [24]

That Hooker's resignation was accepted is not all that surprising, although Hooker himself was apparently astonished by the sudden turn of events. The administration, from Lincoln on down, was unhappy at the thought of its eastern army giving battle to Lee again with Fighting Joe still in command. Disappointment with the way the army was handled at Chancellorsville was widespread, and the president was well aware that many of the highest-ranking generals in the army were disgusted with Hooker. Halleck and Hooker were bitter enemies, and Hooker's own conduct toward his superiors, before attaining the army command, ensured that there would be no hidden sympathy for him. He still had the support of the Radical Republicans, and Lincoln would not remove him from command as he marched to battle. When he presented the president with a resignation, though—over a minor issue which never should have called forth such a dramatic gesture—he solved a myriad of problems for Lincoln.

Meade, a Philadelphian, was not as well known as some other generals, either to the public (he tended to ignore reporters and so had little press) or to the soldiers of the army, but he was the proper choice for such a dramatic change. An untheatrical, even drab-looking, figure, he was an energetic, clear-headed, and competent soldier of the old school, a gentleman and a good friend to his intimates. Without charisma or magnetism, he could be counted on to carry out his mission in a careful but thorough manner. Meade's most conspicuous failing was a quick and violent temper, which flared up and then subsided rapidly, a temper which earned him the nickname of "Old Snapping Turtle." Reynolds having declined the command earlier, Meade was the obvious choice to succeed Hooker with the enemy just thirty or so miles away. He was not requested to accept the post, he was ordered to do so, and George Gordon Meade always obeyed orders.

The first thing Meade did upon receiving his new command, even though it was after three in the morning, was to go to Warren's tent and awaken him. Meade and Warren had come to know, like, and trust one another, one engineer to another, particularly since Warren's transfer to the staff. The two men talked briefly, and Meade asked Warren to become his chief of staff. After discussing the situation for a few moments, Warren turned him down, urging Meade to keep Butterfield on because of his better knowledge of current army affairs. While this seemed like good advice at the time, Meade long regretted his decision to retain the treacherous Daniel Butterfield. Warren later said he preferred to continue as chief engineer because the position of chief of staff "always kept a man away from the front in battle and the other took him there. My experience that was valuable, was in the fighting I had seen or taken part in." [25]

Warren called the change of commanders an "extraordinary change at such a time." He went on, "I do not know what effect this change will have on me. I was spoken to about being Chief of Staff but I prefer not to take it. I may continue as Chief Engr., or I may get command of a Division." [26]

It is interesting to speculate whether the course of Warren's career would have been changed materially had he accepted Meade's offer. His talents clearly suited him for staff work, as his colleagues recognized, but his preference was for field command, and he likely would have prevailed upon Meade for such a command eventually.

Meade's first order of business, after determining that his important staff positions would remain unchanged for the moment, was to concentrate his forces and continue the pursuit of the Army of Northern Virginia, which was now spread across central Pennsylvania. Rebel units were nearing Harrisburg, had passed through York, and had reached Columbia on the Susquehanna River. The Confederates were gathering supplies as they went, by purchase (with Confederate currency) or by requisition; they seized specie where they could; and when they came across free black men they took them into custody and shipped them south into slavery. A sense of panic was growing in the North as the Confederates rampaged through Pennsylvania.

Meade's army was scattered across western Maryland, between Middletown, five miles west of Frederick, and Poolesville, twenty miles to the south. Meade's first orders pulled the pieces together, and by the end of June 28 most of the army was in or around Frederick. Meade worked out his plan for moving the army north toward the Pennsylvania border, and on the morning of the 29th he had the various corps on the move. Despite numerous hardships, not the least of which was the fact that many soldiers had gotten drunk in the fleshpots of Frederick, Meade made great progress in moving his army forward, with its flanks covered and its rear protected.

On June 30, Meade moved the Second Corps under Hancock to Taneytown and Reynolds's First Corps to Emmitsburg, just south of the Mason-Dixon Line, where Reynolds was to take charge of the two corps already near there. He sent Warren to Reynolds, to aid him in selecting a position.

Later that day, Warren and Henry J. Hunt, the army's artillery commander, checked out the area from near Uniontown, Maryland, to Manchester, where they spotted a potentially fine defensive position, along a winding stream called Pipe Creek and a high ground called Parr Ridge, eight hundred to a thousand feet high with widths of four to ten miles. This line, if it should become necessary for defense, was between the enemy's known position and Baltimore. Working from the information given him by Warren and Hunt, Meade issued what became famous (or notorious) as the Pipe Creek Circular, in which he laid out for his corps commanders certain contingencies which would cause the Union army to take up a strong defensive position along this line. A fair reading of the Pipe Creek Circular makes clear that this was just one of several alternatives Meade was considering, since he could not know the intentions of the Confederates or the outcome of his moves toward the Pennsylvania border, but his enemies after Gettysburg used the Circular in unfair attacks upon Meade's reputation.[27]

Warren wrote to his wife that "our rapid movements have relieved the attack on Harrisburg we hope and believe," and "we are we think all right now. Our Pennsylvania people have suffered some, but they must expect something as well as ourselves that we don't like."[28]

At the same time Meade moved his army north, Lee was drawing his forces together, and fate, as well as the never-ending Confederate quest for replenishment of supplies—in this case, shoes—would soon bring on a clash of the two great armies. On July 1, General Henry Heth, commanding a division in A. P. Hill's corps, sent a column from Cashtown southeast into Gettysburg, the county seat of Adams County, Pennsylvania, and a town where numerous roads converged, to check a report that there was a sizable supply of shoes stored there. Before reaching the town Heth's men clashed with Union cavalry under General John Buford and fell back. When the rebels came on again they were held off by Buford until units of the First Corps, under Reynolds, arrived on the scene. Reynolds was killed early in the fighting northwest of Gettysburg, but his steadfast veterans, now under General Abner Doubleday, made a good showing against what soon became superior numbers.

In the meantime, the Eleventh Corps of O. O. Howard marched through

Gettysburg and took up a position due north of the town. The First Corps was retreating slowly back toward the center of town, resisting stubbornly, when the Eleventh was attacked on its right flank by Jubal Early's division, returning from the Susquehanna. The men of Howard's corps broke and ran once again, in their flight through the town overwhelming the orderly retreat of the First Corps. The Union withdrawal turned into a rout. Many Federal soldiers were taken captive in the labyrinth of streets, and those who escaped streamed in disarray up a high ground called Cemetery Hill south of the town, where Howard tried without success to reorganize them.

Fortunately, when Meade learned that Reynolds was wounded or perhaps killed, he sent Winfield Hancock from Taneytown north to Gettysburg, with orders to take command of the Union forces there. Hancock arrived on Cemetery Hill at about 3:30 P.M. and assumed command from a resistant Howard; Hancock's very presence helped to stiffen the resolve of the disorganized Union soldiery. With his inborn air of authority and a keen tactical sense, Hancock restored order to the Federal position, organizing the Union soldiers he found into a defensive line strong enough to deter Confederate general Richard Ewell from attacking again. Hancock then sent word back to Meade that the position was a strong one, and Meade ordered the rest of the army to move toward Gettysburg.

Shortly before Meade sent Hancock to Gettysburg, he dispatched Warren to the same place. Traveling by way of Emmitsburg, Warren arrived at Cemetery Hill a few minutes after Hancock and was able to assist in reorganizing the army's lines there. He and Hancock, the two men there without specific units to look after, galloped about the hill pulling the scattered Union forces into a cohesive whole.

Warren sat down the following morning and wrote to his wife that "we are now all in line of battle before the enemy in a position where we cannot be *beaten* but fear being turned." He said all were "worn down by hard marching, want of sleep, and anxiety," and he "never felt our cause so much endangered." He wrote darkly of the day possibly being his last and lamented "my dear wife so soon being made a widow before she hardly ceased to be a maid." In any event, "God's will be done & I will try to do my duty. Do not grieve too much for me."[29]

With this gloomy missive behind him, Gouverneur Warren went to work. July 2, 1863, would be a busy day for him, as it was for so much of Meade's army. The Army of the Potomac was aligned in what was essentially a defensive position, its right anchored on Cemetery Hill and a nearby height called Culp's Hill. The Twelfth, Eleventh, and First corps, the latter two of which had been badly mauled the day before, were posted on these two hills. To the left of the First Corps, Hancock's Second maintained position on a ridge which ran south from Cemetery Hill, called, with a certain lack of imagination, Cemetery

Ridge. To the left of Hancock the Third Corps, under its amateur commander Daniel Sickles, was supposed to extend the line along the decreasing ridge to a wooded hill called Little Round Top. (There was, just to the south of it, another hill some 135 feet higher, called Big Round Top.) Little Round Top had a panoramic view of most of the field, and it overlooked and dominated the whole Union line.

Most of Meade's army was on the scene by noon of July 2, with the major exception of Sedgwick's Sixth Corps, which had been farthest from Gettysburg and was laboring along the Baltimore Pike toward the town. The Fifth Corps, under George Sykes, had reached Gettysburg with some difficulty, but it was now in position in reserve, awaiting developments.

A suggestion the evening before by Henry Slocum, commanding the Twelfth Corps, that Ewell's right flank might be attacked from the position on Culp's Hill, resulted in Meade's ordering Slocum and Warren in mid-morning to scout out the terrain around Culp's Hill for possibilities. After checking the rugged nature of the ground both Warren and Slocum advised against any such assault.[30]

The crisis of July 2 was to develop at the other end of the long Union line from Culp's Hill. Dan Sickles did not like the position to which Meade had assigned his Third Corps, between the Second Corps and Little Round Top. Sickles preferred another line, about three-fourths of a mile to the west. He spent much of the morning trying to get his orders changed, working on young George Meade (the commanding general's son and aide), Hunt (the artillery commander), Warren, and even Meade himself to effect a change, but without success. Finally, in mid-afternoon, without sanction from Meade and without notice to Meade or to Hancock, with whose corps he was supposed to connect, Sickles, in a glaring act of insubordination, moved most of his corps out almost a mile to the position he desired, along the Emmitsburg Road.

Lee, in the meantime, had been having some difficulty in getting his army started. He determined to make his major effort of the day on his far right (the Union left) with Longstreet's corps. It took hours, however, for Longstreet to get his units into position, for he had to keep them out of sight of Federal signalmen on Little Round Top, and this necessitated several lengthy and time-consuming detours and backtrackings. Finally, though, at 4 P.M., Longstreet had two divisions, under McLaws and Hood, ready to attack the Union left, and he sent them forward against Sickles's corps.

Meade and Warren rode out at about three o'clock to see what had become of the Third Corps. Warren, probably more familiar with the whole field than anyone else in Meade's army, and deeming the Third Corps "very badly disposed on that part of the field," suggested to Meade that he be sent to the left "to examine the condition of affairs," particularly Little Round Top, the importance of which he keenly recognized. Meade agreed, and Warren was

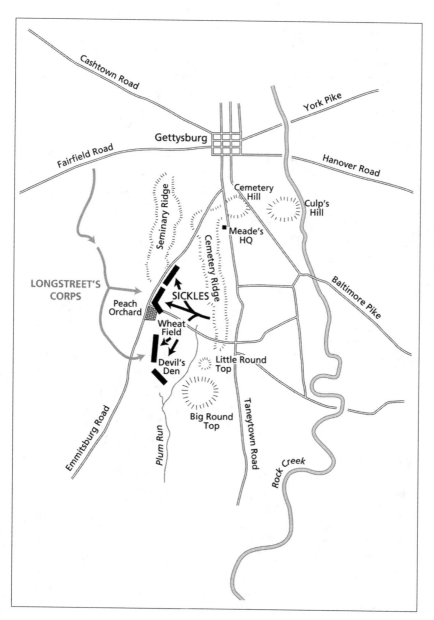

Gettysburg, 4 P.M., July 2, 1863

quickly on his way, with his aides (Roebling, Captain Chauncey B. Reese, and Lieutenant Ranald S. Mackenzie) and a couple of orderlies.[31]

On climbing Little Round Top, Warren discovered that it was bare of troops except for a few signalmen with their semaphore flags. "I saw that this was the key of the whole position," wrote Warren, "and that our troops in the woods in front of it could not see the ground in front of them, so that the enemy would come upon them before they would be aware of it." He observed the woods on the near side of the Emmitsburg Road as "an excellent place for the enemy to form out of sight." To test this suspicion, Warren said he sent an orderly to Capt. James E. Smith's rifle battery, the Fourth New York, in Devil's Den, a jumble of huge boulders just west of Little Round Top, directing that a shot be fired into those woods. When this was done, the sound of the shot caused the Confederates in the woods to turn their heads, which motion caused the sun to glint off of gun barrels and bayonets and confirmed Warren's worst fears—that the rebels were there and that their line of advance to Little Round Top was unopposed.[32]

"I have been particular in telling this," Warren said, "as the discovery was intensely thrilling to my feelings and almost appalling." He immediately sent off an aide, probably Reese, to ask Meade "to send a division at least to me," and he sent Mackenzie to Sickles for help. (Sickles refused, saying he had not a man to spare, which was probably true, considering the fix he had gotten himself into.) Meade, receiving the message from Warren, at first ordered Humphreys to move his Third Corps division to Little Round Top, but this order was canceled when Meade learned that a part of the Fifth Corps was going there. Mackenzie, rebuffed by Sickles, found Sykes and asked for help. Sykes, whose troops were already engaged in the deadly fighting in the Wheatfield, where the Third Corps was suffering severely, detached the brigade of Brigadier General Strong Vincent to Little Round Top.[33]

Vincent, a graduate of Harvard College and a lawyer in Erie, Pennsylvania, had commanded the Eighty-Third Pennsylvania since its original commander was killed at Gaines's Mill, and he was given the brigade after the fight at Chancellorsville. In his first test of high leadership, Vincent quickly moved his regiments around behind Little Round Top, up the slope between it and Big Round Top, and into position beneath the crest of the hill along the southwestern slope. The order, from right to left, was the Sixteenth Michigan, the Forty-Fourth New York, the Eighty-Third Pennsylvania, and the Twentieth Maine, led by a former college professor named Joshua Lawrence Chamberlain.[34]

Though Vincent's brigade had arrived as a result of Warren's solicitation, he did not see it arrive and take position, because he was at the northerly end of the hill; the configuration of the surface of Little Round Top prevented him from seeing activity below the crest at the southern end. When bullets started flying around their station, the signalmen started to pack their flags, preparatory to vacating the area; Warren bade them stay, to mislead the enemy into thinking there was a Union presence on the hilltop. While the right of Hood's force crashed into Vincent's brigade, his center and left prepared to ascend Little Round Top virtually uncontested. The moment of supreme crisis had arrived.[35]

Warren quickly rode down the back side of the hill, seeking troops who could be pressed into immediate action. By the sheerest coincidence he came upon the Fifth Corps brigade which he himself had previously commanded, now led by Brigadier General Stephen H. Weed. The troops, greeting their former commander, started cheering, but Warren had no time for accolades. Not seeing Weed, he rode up to Col. Patrick H. O'Rorke, leading the last regiment in line, the 140th New York, and told him in an excited manner what he needed. "Paddy," he shouted, "give me a regiment!"[36]

O'Rorke said, "General Weed is ahead and expects me to follow him," but Warren answered, "Never mind that! Bring your regiment up here and I will take the responsibility." Without hesitation, O'Rorke turned aside and led his regiment up Little Round Top, following Roebling. As O'Rorke and his men climbed the rocky hill, six guns of Lt. Charles Hazlett's battery of the Fifth Artillery moved up among them. The guns had to be hauled and manhandled up the slope with great difficulty, Warren himself pitching in to help with the heavy work.[37]

The 140th New York reached the top of the hill and surged down the other side. O'Rorke was killed instantly and his regiment suffered fearful losses, with 183 men killed or wounded, but they managed to throw back the Texans. The adjutant of the 140th estimated that they came within sixty seconds of losing the top of the hill. Soon the rest of Weed's brigade was arrayed to the right of the 140th New York, and that end of the line was secure.[38]

The right portion of Hood's Confederates had commenced their attack and were met by Vincent's brigade. The fighting was fierce and bitter as Hood's veterans fought their way partly up the hill, only to be rebuffed by the stern resistance of Vincent's men, and then with renewed effort pushed up the slope again. Meanwhile, on the top of the hill, Hazlett's battery was firing away at the Confederates in Devil's Den, although its guns could not be depressed enough to have any real effect on the assault on Little Round Top. Warren was grazed in the throat by a rifle bullet, but the damage was minimal. Warren bound up the wound with his handkerchief and carried on.[39]

For a little more than an hour the bloody fighting went on. Vincent, Weed, Hazlett, and O'Rorke were all killed, and Chamberlain and his men won glory with a final bayonet charge when their ammunition was exhausted.[40] When the fighting was done, though, Little Round Top remained in Union hands. The heroism and gallantry of the leaders and the men in the ranks were responsible for the Union victory. But, clearly, without the quick thinking and

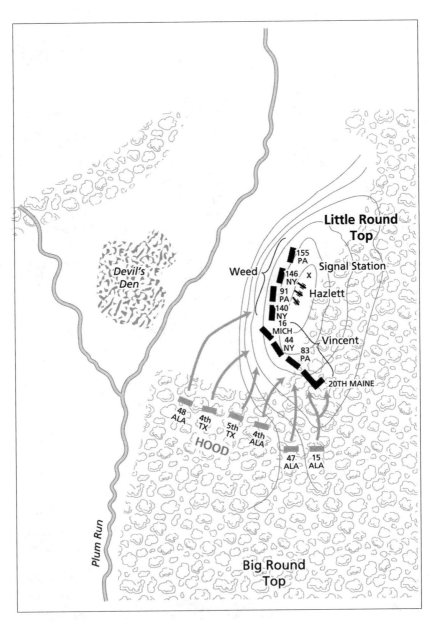

Little Round
Top

155
PA

146
NY

Signal Station

91
PA

x

Hazlett

Weed

140
NY

16
MICH

44
NY

Vincent

83
PA

20TH MAINE

Devil's
Den

48
ALA

4th
TX

5th
TX

4th
ALA

HOOD

47
ALA

15
ALA

Plum Run

Big Round
Top

Defense of Little Round Top, July 2, 1863

instantaneous activity of Gouverneur K. Warren, there would have been no opportunity for the others to shine. Without Warren's actions, Little Round Top would have been lost and, with Confederate artillery on its heights, so too must have been the Union line on Cemetery Ridge.

Warren was conscious and justifiably proud of what he had done at Little Round Top, but he did not vaunt or boast about it. He did not mention saving the hill in his letters to Emily or in his personal journal, and even years later he wrote simply, "There was no merit in my actions except to secure for our army a position if I could, which would prevent our lines from being flanked and this when attacked was but giving an opportunity for a fair fight front to front, and there our opponents did not win." [41]

The armies, though, soon realized what Warren had done. Union general Abner Doubleday, writing about the battle, said, "This eminence . . . was the key of the field, but . . . nothing but Warren's activity and foresight saved it from falling into the hands of the enemy." Armistead Long, Lee's military secretary, wrote that "the prompt energy of a single officer, General Warren, chief engineer, rescued Meade's army from imminent peril." And General Samuel Crawford, a Fifth Corps division commander, wrote to Warren in 1872, "Your name ought to be forever connected with the saving of our left, for Round Top was *saved* by your foresight." [42]

There were many heroes in the Federal army at Gettysburg—Meade, the army commander, whose prompt actions in moving units to threatened positions far exceeded what any previous commander of the Army of the Potomac had done; Hancock, who seemed to be everywhere in the thickest of the action, who bailed out Sickles on July 2 and repulsed Pickett's attack the next day; Buford, whose cavalry held off Heth's division on July 1; Gibbon; Humphreys; Colville of the First Minnesota; Stannard and his Vermont brigade; and many others. Among the very brightest of stars in that battle, considering how serious the loss of Little Round Top would have been and how much its retention was due to his efforts, was the army's chief engineer, G. K. Warren.

Poor Warren! How could he know that Little Round Top was to be the apogee of his career?

THE AFTERMATH OF GETTYSBURG

THE BATTLE OF GETTYSBURG, OF COURSE, did not end with the defense of Little Round Top, although it might have if Longstreet's Confederates had captured the hilltop. Meade and Hancock, now in command of the entire left wing of the Union army, had anxious moments before all the results of Dan Sickles's foolish move were countered. As the sultry July afternoon waned and the sun set in a fiery red glow through the dark smoke of battle, there was fierce fighting along Plum Run and in the woods and fields between the Emmitsburg Road and Cemetery Ridge. At the end of the day the Union line was intact and perhaps stronger than it had been at noon.[1]

That night, after Confederate probes at the positions on Cemetery Hill and Culp's Hill had been repulsed, General Meade called together his corps commanders to assess the army's condition and plan for the morrow. The meeting began around nine o'clock in the stuffy little bedroom of the house where Meade had his headquarters. Butterfield and Warren were present with Meade, as were Slocum and Hancock, who had led the right and left wings respectively of the army, and seven corps commanders. The consensus reached was for the army to stay in its present position and, at least for the next day, wait for Lee to resume offensive action. Warren took no part in the conversation; worn out by his exertions, by the heat, and by the pain of his neck wound, the chief engineer curled up in a corner and slept through the meeting.[2]

The next morning, rested and refreshed, Warren rode with Meade and Hunt from Culp's Hill to Little Round Top, inspecting the dispositions of the various corps. Satisfied with what they saw, the generals could only wait to see what Lee had determined to do. At about one o'clock in the afternoon, a single cannon shot from the rebel artillery concentrated on Seminary Ridge gave the signal for the start of the greatest artillery barrage ever seen on the American continent.

Colonel Porter Alexander, in charge of the Confederate artillery, had gathered about 170 guns with which to pound the Union lines before Lee's planned infantry attack. Alexander's guns, Lee hoped, would knock out the Union artillery on Cemetery Ridge and demoralize the Federal infantrymen waiting to receive the rebel attack. When the mighty barrage began, it was soon answered by the Union guns, and the deafening noise was, it was said, like no sound ever heard before.[3]

After about an hour of the barrage, Warren, from his observation post on Little Round Top, sent a message to Meade, suggesting that the Union batteries cease firing. He felt that they were doing the Confederates "very little harm" and filling the valley between the two armies with smoke which would provide cover for the impending infantry attack. Henry Hunt, the Union artillery commander, had reached the same conclusion, and he brought the firing to a close.[4]

As the Union guns fell silent, Alexander felt that his cannonade had accomplished as much as it was expected to do, so he brought it to an end also. Longstreet gave the word for the infantry assault to begin, and a force variously estimated at from ten to fifteen thousand men, under the tactical command of George E. Pickett, emerged from the woods behind Seminary Ridge and started across the valley intervening between it and the Union line.

Warren watched from his post on Little Round Top as the Confederate force slowly crossed the fields between the two armies and converged toward a point where a portion of Hancock's Second Corps huddled behind a low stone wall near a copse of trees. As the southerners advanced toward Cemetery Ridge, Union artillery and then musketry tore great holes in their ranks. Still, the men in gray came on, their numbers much reduced, with a relatively small portion of Pickett's force swarming up and over the stone wall as its defenders fell back. In a few moments, though, hundreds of Union soldiers were rushed to the spot and the Confederates who had pierced the line were shot, captured, or put to flight. Pickett's men retreated back across the field, to the sanctuary of Seminary Ridge, and the great assault was defeated.

With the repulse of Pickett's attacking force, the battle of Gettysburg was essentially over, except for an ill-conceived Federal cavalry charge which did nothing but increase casualties. Meade, after learning of the victory on Cemetery Ridge, joined Warren on Little Round Top. The two generals were soon under fire from rebel sharpshooters, with one bullet passing just under Warren's arm. They quickly retreated down the hill.[5]

The next day was the nation's birthday, and the Army of the Potomac celebrated its triumph, as well as the news coming from the west that Vicksburg had surrendered to Grant. Some, of course, reflected ruefully that even when the eastern army won a great victory it had to share the glory of it with Grant in the west. Warren wrote to Emily that "I believe we have completely beaten Lee and that he has nothing to do but fly to Virginia. We shall be after him."[6]

There was the rub. Lee was beaten and must be pursued, and many, including the president of the United States, expected that the follow-up to the great triumph at Gettysburg must be the destruction of Lee's army. There were already those who wondered why Meade had not counterattacked after the repulse of Pickett's attack, although they ignored as Meade could not the condition of his army. Victorious it may have been, but it had suffered severely in three days of fighting. Three of his corps commanders were gone, Reynolds killed on the first day, Sickles badly wounded on the second, and Hancock seriously wounded on the third. After long, hard marching and bitter fighting, often without adequate sustenance, Meade's army was worn out. The units of the various corps were jumbled and scattered as a result of battlefield improvisations, and it took time to get brigades and divisions back to their proper corps again. Lines of command were badly scrambled. For all these reasons, Meade elected not to throw his army upon Lee's beaten but still dangerous legions, to Lee's disappointment. Warren noted in his journal for July 4, "Both armies quietly occupied their positions, firing only on the picket lines and with a little artillery."[7]

The Army of Northern Virginia waited for attack on July 4, its lines shortened and strengthened, its position on Seminary Ridge entrenched and concealed on the western side of the slope. There was plenty of fight left in Lee's army, and Meade chose not to attack its breastworks. Warren wrote to his wife, saying, "We are enthusiastic but cautious in our eagerness to improve our advantage—we must not spoil our greatest triumph."[8] And so they waited.

Late in the afternoon of July 4, having decided regretfully that Meade was not going to assail his position on Seminary Ridge, Lee started his wagons and ambulances over the mountains into the Cumberland Valley, to get a head start south before the infantry moved out. During the night, in a pouring rain, the rebel army followed, southwest toward Fairfield, Pennsylvania. Meade, before committing his army to a definite route to follow the retreating Confederates, decided to have Warren take a division from Sedgwick on a reconnaissance to ascertain Lee's intentions.[9]

Warren and Sedgwick elected to utilize the whole Sixth Corps for the reconnaissance on July 5, in effect converting it into a pursuit. After a march of about six miles Sedgwick's advance encountered the rear of Ewell's corps near Fairfield late in the afternoon. There was some exchange of gunfire with Gordon's brigade, but that was all the fighting for the day, as a cautious Sedgwick did not push matters. Warren returned to Gettysburg to report what he knew to Meade, telling the commanding general that he and Sedgwick thought Lee had most of his army around Fairfield and was prepared for a fight. Meade, whose army had started south toward Middletown, Maryland, had to redirect his troops. He sent word to Sedgwick at 2 A.M. on the 6th, after conversation with Warren, to "push your reconnaissance, so as to ascertain, if practicable, how far the enemy has retreated." [10]

With Butterfield having been wounded and sent home, Warren and cavalry commander Alfred Pleasonton acted jointly as chief of staff until Meade appointed Humphreys to the position on July 8. Warren resumed his engineer's duties, although in actuality he seemed at times to be Meade's chief advisor. At the same time, he was cheered by a letter from Emily, responding to one of his periodic self-pitying epistles, saying, "Oh dearest you do not think for an instant that I could ever forget you or love any one else. You do not know me if you think so." [11]

In the meantime, Meade had determined to push after Lee's army, and with the Potomac still too high from recent rains to ford, and Lee's only pontoon bridge damaged, there was a good chance he could catch it. For the next five days Meade moved his troops about, trying to get them into a good position for an attack, while Lee established a sturdy defensive line from Hagerstown to Falling Waters, on the river. On the night of July 12, Meade was prepared to issue orders for a reconnaissance in force, convertible into an assault, but was dissuaded by his corps commanders in a council of war, even though Warren argued strongly in favor of the movement.

Finally, on July 13, Meade ordered for the next morning the push he had called off the day before. That night, however, Robert E. Lee, with his pontoon bridge repaired and the river reduced to fordable depths, moved his army across the Potomac and back to Virginia. Warren set forth what happened in his journal: "Whole line advanced early in obedience to orders sent out the night before. Found the enemy had nearly all crossed the Potomac. Captured his rear guard." [12]

Meade's failure to prevent Lee's army from returning to Virginia without a fight, especially after yielding to the vote of the council of war on the night of July 12, gave his enemies much cause for finger-pointing, and it bitterly disappointed Lincoln, who held a rather unrealistic view of the two armies and their capabilities after Gettysburg. Nevertheless, Gouverneur Warren, who recognized that what was done was done, moved on to take up his duties. While other officers went to look at the fieldworks which Lee's army had thrown up to receive an attack, Warren rode "as fast as I could to Harper's Ferry, where all our Engineer troops were already to restore the bridge communications across the Potomac and Shenandoah rivers and the canal communication with Washington." Warren soon had the bridges back in operation. That afternoon, he sent a message to the War Department, saying, "The Maryland campaign is ended. Have sent to me at Harper's Ferry, as soon as practicable, all the maps you can spare of the Shenandoah Valley and the routes east of the mountains to Gordonsville." [13]

At this time Warren found himself messing with a young officer on Meade's staff named Morris Schaff. Schaff, who spoke of seeing Warren "day after day at close range," said that however proud Warren may have been of his work at Little Round Top, "it altered not his bearing—which was that of the thoughtful, modest scholar rather than the soldier—nor did it kindle any vanity in look or speech." Schaff did note Warren's delight in limericks and his puzzlement that his messmates did not find them as entertaining as he did. Schaff recorded Warren's small and jet-black eyes, "one of them apparently a bit smaller than the other, giving a suggestion of cast in his look." Warren's most striking characteristic, Schaff said, "was an habitual and noticeably grave expression which harbored in his dusky, sallow face," a look of gravity which deepened "as he rose in fame and command."[14]

While Warren was supervising the projects which restored mobility to the Army of the Potomac, an effort which would affect him profoundly got under way in another area. Winfield Hancock had been badly wounded in the groin at the time of Pickett's attack at Gettysburg, and it was clear that he would require a lengthy period of recuperation at his home at Norristown, Pennsylvania. The Second Corps was temporarily under the command of William Hays, but he was a lackluster figure who was certainly not the man to lead this famous organization. On July 19, Meade wrote to Halleck, stating his anxiety "to have a competent commander for the Second Corps," and, in view of "the very valuable services and most efficient assistance rendered me," he nominated Warren for promotion to major general, in order to command the Second.[15]

Earlier, when Meade told Warren of the recommendation, Gouv wrote to Emily about the upcoming promotion, saying, "I consider it almost certain so that I can tell you it is done tomorrow." He said he was proud that "my efforts and self denial during the month that love and marriage would have directed to my own happiness should have met with so rich a reward." On the 21st he told her that they had had no word from Washington, "so I cannot say whether I have been appointed Maj. Genl. or not." His tune had changed somewhat, as he added, "But don't be disappointed if I am not. I have won all the honor the place can give me except as I might make it the chance of future glory."[16]

On July 22, Warren poured out his gloomy thoughts and bitter feelings in a letter to his wife, noting how strange it was that Meade's request for "a suitable commander" for the Second Corps "should not have been noticed":

> If it is denied me I shall cease to expect any further promotion. I have worked
> very hard under every commander and invariably with the most honorable
> mention . . . If those who stay all the time in Washington deny this to me I
> shall consider it very unjust and further if that spirit is to rule I shall cease to
> hope for great commanders to our corps or speedy success to our cause.

When I think how weary I am of this constant campaigning now in its third year, deprived of all enjoyments and oppressed with labor and care and dangers and contrast the peaceful happy life I would have with you, I feel the necessity for some military reward to sustain me, some mark of appreciation at least.[17]

Halleck responded to Meade on July 26 that "it is impossible to promote General Warren at present. There is no vacancy. I have recommended the discharge of certain useless major-generals, but it has not been acted on." Humphreys showed Warren this dispatch, and Warren wrote to Emily about it. He told her he had heard indirectly that Stanton had spoken in his favor, "so that . . . if the road to promotion is not blocked up I may get the position." But with Halleck saying "it was impossible to promote me as there was no vacancy. . . my anticipation and philosophy were timely." [18]

By July 30, while Warren was writing to his brother Will that "I have quite given up promotion now," his letter to Emily barely mentioned the subject. He thanked her for telling him she had heard people praising him, he wrote about the heroes of the poet Ossian, whose ghosts wandered the earth restlessly till they heard their praises "worthily sung," and he mentioned the two horses he had sent to Baltimore in retirement. "Take off their shoes, turn them out on grass." He wrote particularly of the big white one he had ridden all through the war except at Gaines's Mill, where his other horse was killed. The white horse had never received so much as a scratch, although he was often an obvious target. Warren said he hated to part with him "from long companionship. I had begun to feel safe when on his back." But there was a problem: "He is not however a kind animal in disposition and he and I have had many a fight which should be the master." [19]

On August 3, Warren was ordered to Washington. He wasted no time in obeying this directive, arriving in the capital by 5 P.M. and immediately taking the train to Baltimore and Emily. He spent the next few days shuttling between Baltimore and Washington, and on August 8, he met with President Lincoln and Secretary Stanton, to be advised that his promotion had come through after all, to date back to May 3, in recognition of his estimable service at Marye's Heights and Salem Church. On August 10, Warren returned to Meade's headquarters at Warrenton, Virginia, and two days later received the order assigning him temporarily to command of the Second Corps.[20]

On August 16, having taken the necessary time to close up his engineering and staff affairs, Warren relieved Hays and assumed command of the fabled Second Corps. Organized on March 13, 1862, by General Orders No. 101 of the Army of the Potomac, the Second Corps was the only one of Lincoln's five original corps which maintained an unbroken existence until the end of the war. Sumner, Couch, Hancock, and Hays (briefly) had commanded the corps before Warren, and Dick Richardson, John Sedgwick, O. O. Howard, John Gibbon, and Alexander Hays had been among its illustrious division commanders. The corps whose leadership Warren had assumed had attained a high degree of excellence under Hancock.[21]

Gouv wrote to Emily on August 16 that "this day finds me in my new position." Overcome with elation, he went on, "I am delighted with my present position. So much power to do good. So independent . . . So far from feeling I have reached as the Times says the highest round, I feel as if while before I but climbed now I have wings." Patriotism, honor, and justice, he said, would be his guides. The month before, when the newspapers had erroneously identified Warren as Meade's chief of staff, he had written to Emily, "I did not want it. So do not feel disappointed. I shall do better I hope in the end." And so he had—or at least so it appeared. So much power, so independent, he thought. For a professional soldier, a command of troops was the ultimate desideratum. Gouverneur K. Warren had performed admirably as a member of the staffs of Joseph Hooker and George Meade, at Chancellorsville and at Gettysburg. Would he do as well as an infantry corps commander?[22]

A week later Warren wrote to Emily that "I am sure we shall for a long time when ever we meet be just such 'foolish lovers' as you say we were last time. Indeed I don't know what you are good for but to love." He spoke of having won commendations from McClellan, Burnside, Hooker, and Meade and "the confidence of the War Dept," representing "golden opinions from all sorts of people." He indulged in a bit of false modesty, saying, "I wish I was really half as good as my friends flatter me I am." [23]

The Army of the Potomac was doing little but attempting to cope with its manpower problems during the latter part of July and August. With troops sent off to New York City to deal with the draft riots, and with the expiration of the enlistments of many regiments, Meade recognized that his army was shrinking rapidly. Still, vigilance was required with Lee's army just south of the Rappahannock. On the 27th of August, Warren wrote Emily, "I cannot be spared now, and when the army is ready to move I would not go away if I could. There will be no chance of my seeing you probably till we suspend operations in the winter." A few days later he said, "After all our troubles to get married is it not too bad that we should be so separated. I don't know yet when I can get away. I feel ashamed to ask for a leave." So he awaited the chance to lead his new command in action.[24]

CHAPTER ELEVEN

SECOND CORPS INTERLUDE

T HE TIME OF IDLENESS WAS COMING TO AN END. Early in September
Meade heard rumors that Longstreet's corps had been pulled out of the Army
of Northern Virginia and sent west to Tennessee. To try to confirm this story,
Meade settled upon a reconnaissance in force, to be carried out by Pleasonton's cavalry with the Second Corps right behind. Instructions went out to
Warren the evening of September 11 to "move your entire corps, in the course
of tomorrow, to Rappahannock Station, prepared to cross the river Sunday
morning, in support of a cavalry reconnaissance." [1]

The Second Corps was ready to start on its first mission under its new commander. The First Division was traditionally one of the crack outfits of the
whole army, commanded in the past by Richardson and Hancock, its four brigades now under Brigadier General John C. Caldwell. The Second Division,
three brigades, was under Brigadier General William Harrow while Gibbon
recuperated from his Gettysburg wound. The Third Division, under Brigadier
General Alexander Hays, one of the heroes of the July 3 fighting, also had
three brigades but was a little smaller than the other divisions. The corps was
blessed, in its chief of staff, with one of the best staff officers in the army, Colonel Charles H. Morgan; Warren would come to appreciate Colonel Morgan.

The corps moved out on the morning of the 13th, following Pleasonton's
cavalry as it crossed the Rappahannock. Pleasonton's troop encountered only
rebel cavalry and artillery and drove the enemy beyond Culpeper Court
House, nine miles south of the river. Warren's men followed and occupied the
town. Pleasonton had been warned by Meade that the mission was strictly a
reconnaissance; "I do not desire to bring on a general engagement." Pleasonton followed the Confederates to the banks of the Rapidan River but found
the crossings well guarded. Lee's army took up quarters below the Rapidan.
Warren felt that the mission "has been very successful the most valuable information having been gained." [2]

On the trek to Culpeper Court House, one of the members of the staff, Thomas Livermore, received a short but memorable lesson in military etiquette as practiced by his new chief. Warren, he said, was riding along ahead of his staff. In jumping a ditch or stream, Livermore's horse shot ahead of the general's, and he was rewarded with "a ferocious look," one which caused him to be "careful not to repeat the offense." [3]

Meade's whole army soon advanced to Culpeper. A plan to cross the Rapidan was set in motion but suspended on orders from Washington. Pleasonton's mission had confirmed the rumor that Longstreet's corps had been sent to the west, where it would soon be instrumental in the Confederate victory at Chickamauga. The Eleventh and Twelfth corps were detached from the Army of the Potomac and sent to Tennessee, to help Rosecrans's beleaguered forces. The eastern army would sit still for the time being. [4]

One day in the autumn of 1863 a deputation of citizens from Cold Spring showed up with a handsome and expensive sword to present to their most famous soldier. Appropriate speeches were made and responded to, and, it was reported, "there was much merriment." The Second Corps staffers felt it was their duty to make the members of other staffs who showed up "as merry as possible," so they mixed up a washtub full of whiskey punch. "When the visitors arrived," Livermore wrote, "its consumption began and many ludicrous scenes ensued." He does not tell what happened to the delegation from Cold Spring. [5]

Another rowdy, if somewhat more private, scene took place a few nights later. Warren was occupying a small house, with the tents of his staff members in the yard. He, Livermore, and two other members of his staff, Frank Haskell and Henry Bingham, were sharing whiskey punch in one of the tents, telling tall tales and laughing uproariously. Livermore went off to the mess tent to find more lemons, and when he returned he found Warren outside the tent with his legs entangled in the tent ropes while Haskell and Bingham looked on. Haskell offered to help, but the general said, "No assistance is required." When he staggered up and started for the house, he tripped over a small sapling, literally falling-down drunk. Haskell ran to help. Warren grabbed him and, calling for the guard, started shouting that Haskell had knocked him down. Bingham sent off the sentry who rushed up, while Livermore got both Warren and Haskell to their feet and to the door of the house, where Wash Roebling took over. The next night, Warren invited Livermore to dinner and asked him what had happened the night before. Livermore told him "in as mild terms as I could invent," and the general "vowed he would touch no more whiskey." [6]

Inactivity soon sapped Warren's spirits. After mentioning to Emily that he was in an abandoned house at Mitchell's Station, south of Culpeper, enjoying a blazing fire, he commented, "It seems a strange kind of life, to be living in other people's homes." A few days later, he wrote,

Warren the young major general. National Archives.

I repine a good deal. I begin to feel myself giving out in spirit. I so need rest where I could be contented. So long now my life has been one continued worry or excitement that, I am losing my elasticity and I am getting almost afraid of myself for I am apprehensive I cannot uphold my position. I need such rest as I would have at home with my mother, soothing companionship without excitement, and perhaps I could not live that way either.

Having given Emily that thought to consider, he went on:

Every day shows me more and more how this war is severing my old affiliations and making me lonely . . . here I sit all alone in this great camp (for so

I feel) and the memory of my dear absent friends comes over me and I am morbidly depressed. Indeed I feel I am a very small man that I cannot endure more, for I am well and not a prisoner . . . and have been honored more than I deserve. I have not the heart of a good soldier.[7]

The war was wearing down Gouverneur Warren, and it was doing so just as he was attaining higher position and greater responsibility. Nevertheless, he was still a soldier—a good soldier, whether he had the heart of one or not— and he would carry on as he had to.

Early in October, Warren wrote to Emily that he was "in solemn truth dying to be with you," and the next day, "I *must* come to see my consoler my darling yourself soon. I cannot live here much longer unless I do." Fortunately, on October 5 the Sixth Corps relieved the Second of its front-line duty, and the next day Warren and his men marched back to Culpeper. On the 8th Gouv left Culpeper on leave and reached Baltimore by 8:30 that evening. He had just a couple of days off before being summoned back to duty, but it sufficed for the moment.[8]

Warren returned to his corps at Culpeper just in time for the next phase of the eastern war. With both armies reduced in size by reason of the detachments sent to Tennessee, Lee began a movement north on October 10, heading around the right flank of Meade's army. At 6 P.M. that day, Warren got back, and at 4 A.M. the next morning he and the Second Corps left Culpeper and marched northeast to Bealeton, along the north side of the Orange & Alexandria Railroad.

On the 12th the army turned around and went back as far as Brandy Station on the basis of a faulty cavalry report to Meade. At 11 P.M. word came to reverse again; the corps headed north once more, marching all night and being retarded by the inefficient march of the Third Corps. While on the move, the irrepressible men of the Irish Brigade saluted and delighted Warren by going through the manual of arms as they passed by him.[9]

Lee's overall plan was to pass Meade's right and interpose his army between the Army of the Potomac and Washington, forcing Meade to fight him at a disadvantage. Thus, speed was crucial to both armies, and the early backtracking and bungling of the Union march handicapped Meade in this race. Once he ascertained the general thrust of the southern army, however, Meade had his men undertake forced marches, in an effort to secure the heights of Centreville and frustrate his opponent.[10]

On the evening of October 13, Lee was in Warrenton, and Warren's Second Corps reached Auburn, just five miles to the east, where it camped on the south side of a stream called Cedar Run. To protect against attack from the west, Warren posted Caldwell's First Division on the heights above Cedar Run. Unknown to everyone, Jeb Stuart's rebel cavalry was bivouacked in the valley some four hundred yards from where Caldwell's division lay. In the morning, when Caldwell's men on the hilltop lit their fires to make breakfast, Stuart's guns opened on them from the fog-shrouded valley, doing considerable damage at first. Caldwell's men kept their cool, however, and moved to the other side of the hill.

On the opposite side of the hill, though, the First Division shortly came under fire from the west, where the head of Ewell's corps was coming up from Warrenton. While matters looked chancy for a few minutes, and Warren later reported with some exaggeration that "to halt was to await annihilation," things soon cleared up. Two regiments from Hays's division chased off Stuart's cavalry, and Caldwell was able to fend off what turned out to be much less than the full strength of Ewell's force, while Warren got the corps across Cedar Run and back to its prescribed line of march.[11]

From Warrenton Lee had determined to move in two columns. The left, under A. P. Hill, would move to New Baltimore by the Warrenton Turnpike, then turn to the east to strike the railroad at Bristoe Station, cutting off Meade if it could seize the road ahead of the Union army. Meanwhile, the right-hand column, under Ewell, (as we have seen) marched eastward of Hill, by way of Auburn and Greenwich, hoping to join Hill at Bristoe Station.

At 10 A.M., Humphreys sent word to Warren, warning of the "probability of a jam, arising from the crossing of Broad Run at Bristoe," but he added that "Bristoe would be a good position, if the road is clear beyond you." At noon, Humphreys sent a dispatch from Bristoe Station to Warren, advising him to "move forward as rapidly as you can as they may send out a column from Gainesville to Bristoe." Sykes and the Fifth Corps, he said, would remain at Bristoe "until you are up." [12]

The Second Corps tramped up the road toward Centreville, the rear guard of the Army of the Potomac, and as the afternoon of October 14 wore on, most of the rest of the army had reached the safety of the heights there. The Third Corps under French was at Manassas Heights with Sykes's Fifth Corps trailing behind it. "I am at Bristow waiting to see the head of your column," Sykes wrote to Warren at 2 P.M. "I shall move on the moment I see it. There is a long interval between French and I which I ought to close up as soon as possible." Later, Sykes sent Warren a message urging speed: "The longer you delay the more force they can bring against you & if Lee army is on your left two corps are little better than one." [13]

In the afternoon of the 14th, A. P. Hill's corps hurried east toward Bristoe Station, hoping but not expecting to cut off the Federal army there. As he rode up to the crest of a plateau overlooking Bristoe Station and Broad Run beyond it, Hill was overjoyed to see Yankee soldiers spread out in front of him: George Sykes's Fifth Corps, slowly fording the swift stream. He gave orders to the commander of his lead division, Henry Heth, to attack without delay.

Heth's three brigades, Hill wrote, "advanced in beautiful order and quite steadily. [John R.] Cooke's brigade, upon reaching the crest of the hill in their front, came within full view of the enemy's line of battle behind the railroad embankment . . . and of whose presence I was unaware." For Warren and the Second Corps had arrived just ahead of Hill's rebels; Sykes, hearing of Warren's arrival, had quickly moved on, so eager to be on his way that he did not even hear the Confederate attack upon the rear of his corps. Warren, his own troops shielded from view by the woods they were moving through, saw Heth's division off to his left and saw as well a railroad cut and embankment which could serve as a ready-made protection for his battle line. It was a moment for quick and decisive action.[14]

From his saddle, Warren quickly ordered Alexander Webb, temporarily commanding the Second Division, to put his men behind the embankment and then barked, "Tell General Hays to move by the left flank, at the double-quick, to the railroad cut." When these movements were carried out, Warren had a near-impregnable battle line in place. Hill, recognizing that Cooke's brigade would be subjected to devastating fire on its right flank if it continued on to Broad Run, ordered a halt for ten minutes, then, in ignorance of just what force of Federals was behind the embankment, directed the advance be resumed. Two well-sheltered Union divisions awaited Heth's two brigades in what one of Hill's biographers called "one of the neatest traps arranged in the Civil War."[15]

Heth had his brigades veer toward the embankment, but it did no good. Raked by the fire of Webb's and Hays's well-protected infantry and pummeled by the Union artillery posted on the hill behind the railroad line, Heth's troops suffered severe losses. "We . . . were driven back with considerable loss," Heth said. "We inflicted but little loss upon the enemy." The rebels soon fell back, but not before leaving in Union hands 450 prisoners, two flags, and five guns. In forty minutes of fighting, Heth lost 1360 men killed or wounded, while Warren's loss was 350.[16]

As dusk gathered over Bristoe Station, an officer from Sykes's staff galloped up with a message for Warren. "I have halted on Manassas heights, but think it best to go along slowly," Sykes wrote, "unless you need the assistance of the 5 Corps." Warren, who had been advised by Humphreys to expect the Fifth Corps at Bristoe Station, steamed as he read Sykes's note. "I don't think you ought to stay there too long," he read. "Let me hear from you as soon as possible. I understand there are but few infantry opposed to you." Warren, reading this, looked out and saw Hill's corps in front of him and Ewell's corps moving up the railroad behind him. "If so of course you can manage them with yr corps." Warren exploded at the unfortunate staff officer who had delivered the note and sent him on his way.[17]

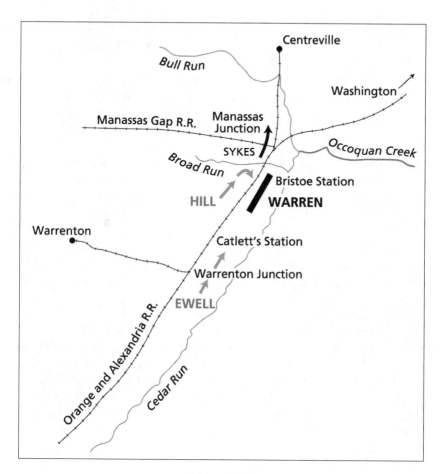

Bristoe Station

Gouverneur Warren had no more time to think about the Fifth Corps at that moment, for, despite his overwhelming victory and the arrival of Caldwell's division at the end of the battle, he was still in a tight spot. He was faced with Lee's entire army, and the rebel artillery commanded the road which Warren must take to escape. At dusk, the head of the Fifth Corps, ordered by Meade to render assistance, arrived. Fortunately, darkness fell, and Lee could make no dispositions for another attack. Warren sent off the now-unneeded Fifth Corps, and at 9 P.M., ordered his corps to withdraw.

The Second Corps crossed Broad Run as silently as possible—"the only sound we heard as we left the field was the groans of the Rebel wounded," wrote one staff member—and made its escape. "No one will forget the anxiety of the evening of the 14th of October," wrote one participant, as Warren imposed utter silence on his troops so they could make their getaway. "In ghostly silence the army was to steal away, marching by the flank across the enemy's front within three hundred yards of their skirmishers." By 4 A.M., after an exhausting march, the last of Warren's command crossed Bull Run at Blackburn's Ford, and the whole of the Army of the Potomac was safely out of harm's way.[18]

Meade the next day issued to the army an announcement of the Bristoe Station victory, concluding that "the skill and promptitude of Major General Warren and the gallantry and bearing of the officers and soldiers of the 2d Corps are entitled to high commendation."[19]

There was an unfortunate aftermath to Bristoe Station, initiated by George Sykes, who wrote on October 27 to Warren complaining about William Swinton's *New York Times* article on the role of the Fifth Corps in the fight. Swinton wrote that just as the Second Corps was engaged in battle, Warren received from Sykes word that he was "moving off leisurely." Warren replied to Sykes on the 29th, explaining that Swinton had shown up at the Second Corps on October 20. Warren had "talked freely with him and so did many of the officers of this corps," most of whom were aware of what had occurred on October 14. Warren denied to Sykes that the offending phrase had come from him, because he would have "given your exact words." He went on to explain why he had been upset with Sykes's actions and he "regretted exceedingly" having vented his anger upon Sykes's staff officer. Warren said he had "no personal feeling . . . in the matter" but believed there was "an interval as wide as that between Bristoe and Manassas between, what you did under Genl Meade's instructions and what I expected you to do from his dispatches to me." What, he asked, if as a result the Second Corps, alone and unsupported, had been annihilated by General Lee's army?[20]

Sykes could not let it go at that, of course. He wrote back the next day, saying he had written to Warren, not because he suspected him of being a party to Swinton's report, but because "being the officer most conversant with what occurred, I looked for a refutation [from you] of the inferences which that individual in his letter saw fit to draw." Sykes offered a long apologia showing that he really had not intended to leave the Second Corps in the lurch. "This is the whole story so far as I am concerned," he went on.[21]

Warren evidently regretted the passage with Sykes, a good if somewhat cautious old soldier whom he knew well as his former division commander, and he wrote back soothingly the next day to bring the exchange to a close.[22]

Lee, frustrated in his effort to get between Meade and the capital, realized as soon as the Army of the Potomac achieved the heights of Centreville ahead of him that the game was up, so he turned back and recrossed the Rappahannock. Meade followed behind him at a cautious distance. Warren told Emily, "The enemy has all run away across the Rappahannock. The victory was all mine. I think now there will be a lull in operations here, and I may get to see you soon again, my dear love."[23]

The Second Corps went into camp at Turkey Run, near Warrenton, and its commander sat down on the 26th of October to write up his report of the recent campaign. He praised his division commanders, Caldwell, Webb, and Hays, as well as several exemplary brigade commanders, and went out of his way to single out the "invaluable" Morgan. "His untiring energy, knowledge, and intelligence, under all circumstances," Warren wrote, "show him fitting for a high command," and Warren recommended that he be promoted to brigadier general.[24]

At the same time Warren received a letter from Captain Cornelius Hook, in Wilmington, Delaware, asking the general "to give me your sister Eliza to be your wife." Warren was concerned about Hook's health, which had been bad, but the ardent suitor assured him that he was improving and hoped soon to return to his duty station at Key West, Florida. Hook and Eliza were married at Cold Spring on November 24, 1863. Brother Gouv was hopeful of getting away to attend the nuptial festivities, but neither he nor his brothers in the service could do so.[25]

The only activity for the Army of the Potomac was a movement forward on November 7 to retake the area between the Rappahannock and the Rapidan. There was some desultory fighting by the Sixth and Third corps, but Lee declined to oblige and pulled his army back behind the Rapidan. Everyone sat down again to await what would happen next.

Frank Haskell, of the Second Corps staff, wrote home that "Warren is a man of the right sort, and I am getting to like him much." Citing Warren's "able and judicious" handling of the corps, Haskell said, "Such men as he are required to end this War—men who will not hesitate to strike when a chance occurs, and who will *hanker* after a chance, and run forward to meet it."[26] Haskell was no doubt correct about the kind of leaders needed; whether Gouverneur Warren fit the description only time would tell.

With hostilities in suspension in the east, Warren's depression returned. He wrote to Emily that "I fear I too am losing my mind, for I really feel quite desperate at being so long kept away from you, at the weary lengths to which the war is prolonged, and at my utter powerlessness to make things go as I should." He said he had thought of quitting the service and going public with his views on how the war should be handled. "I thought yesterday I could get away tomorrow," he continued, "but a long talk with Genl Meade quite dashed my hopes not only of that but everything else. For I find a most radical difference in my plans and his and his estimate of results." He said that Webb, brigade commander Sprigg Carroll, and others had asked for leave for various personal reasons, with the army inactive. Warren would have granted them all, but Meade turned them all down.[27]

"You see dear one," Warren wrote, "I am not in very good spirits. I cannot be. I feel as if all my usefulness is wasted by the way in which things are managed . . . I really wonder at myself for feeling so depressed at times and can only account for it that the constant effort and anxiety of a temperament constantly hoping, striving and laboring is destroying my mental elasticity." If he were alone in the world, he concluded, he would rather be a wandering gypsy. Next day he wrote that "I feel sometimes as if I were not of the proper nature for the times in which we live." Saying that he had been hard at work since age fifteen, he felt "the peevishness of age is already upon me while the fires of youth still burn." This last must have been deeply reassuring to his young bride, just out of her teenage years.[28]

On November 18, Warren told Emily about a cavalry skirmish between the Confederate Wade Hampton and George Armstrong Custer, quoting Custer's overblown report of the encounter. "What a *lie:* And yet that is the style of many of our cavalry reports and shows the horrible mismanagement. So is a great deal of the cavalry." Warren had shown little feeling toward the mounted branch until this time.[29]

Late in November the army moved forward again. "This morning we move against the enemy once more for another life and death struggle, if he will meet us," Warren wrote his wife before daylight on November 26. Meade's plan called for his army to cross the Rapidan in three places, move quickly south by a stream called Mine Run, along which the Confederates had built their fortifications, and surprise Lee by outflanking him. The plan was knocked askew by bad weather—rain which turned the roads muddy and caused the river to rise so that the army's pontoon bridges did not quite span it—and the unpardonable blundering and delays caused by William French, commander of the Third Corps.[30]

The effect of these combined factors, coupled with the time given to Lee to make adjustments in his defenses, was to place the Union army opposite the Mine Run fortifications on the night of November 29, looking for some place to attack the enemy with some chance of success. Warren's Second Corps was on the far left of the line, Sedgwick's Sixth on the right. The Third, First, and Fifth corps were posted in the center. Sedgwick came to Meade's headquarters that night and said there was a point opposite him which he thought might be vulnerable, and Meade began preparing plans for three concerted attacks. At this point, Warren joined the meeting and reported that he had pushed his corps, strengthened with a division from the Sixth Corps, beyond Lee's defenses. He had run out of daylight before he could make an attack, but he strongly urged that the main attack be made there in the morning, against Lee's right.[31]

Meade, his trust in Warren's judgment high, concurred. Since French, in the center of the line, said an attack by him would be fruitless, Meade transferred two of his divisions to Warren. The attack by the Second Corps would commence at 8 A.M., at which time artillery on the right of the line would open, preparing for Sedgwick's advance at 9 A.M. It was assumed that by then the force in front of Sedgwick would have been thinned to meet the assault on the right of the rebel line.[32]

Warren returned to his corps and he and Morgan worked through the night, laboring on all the details of placement and disposition. The night was bitterly cold, and one regimental commander avowed that "more deaths resulted from that one night's exposure than were lost in many a battle of magnitude." Well before dawn, the whole staff was up, sitting around a fire with the general and eating a meager breakfast. Warren told them of the planned assault and said, "If I succeed today I shall be the greatest man in the army; if I don't, all my sins will be remembered." [33]

At about dawn, with the moon still up, Warren and Roebling crept on their hands and knees close to the rebel lines, where Warren was shocked to see that all had changed. "I found that the line had been re-enforced with all the troops and artillery that could be put in position; the breastworks, epaulements, and abatis perfected, and that a run for eight minutes was the least time our line could have to close the space between us, during which we would be exposed to every species of fire." His troops, too, could see what changes the night had wrought, and Warren saw them writing their names on pieces of paper and pinning the papers to their blouses, for easier identification of their corpses.[34]

Just as Warren was struggling with this grim new reality, an orderly rode up with Meade's instruction to attack at once. Warren gave the order to do so to his division commanders but in a few moments rode himself to the front to order a delay. Back at Meade's headquarters, time passed and nothing was heard from the far left. French, jealous of Warren's increased prestige and angry at the run-ins he had had with the younger general in the past few days, jeered as he asked Meade, "Where are your young Napoleon's guns? Why doesn't he open?" Shortly before nine, Roebling rode up to tell the commanding general that Warren had canceled the attack. Meade exclaimed, "My God! General Warren has half my army at his disposal!" [35]

Meade had to send word instantly to Sedgwick to call off his attack, and he then rode angrily off to see Warren. There was a stormy scene between the two men. Marsena Patrick, the provost marshal of the army, was not surprised, "for Meade has a fearful temper & Warren has been so puffed & elated & swelled up, that his arrogance and insolence are intolerable." A reporter, looking on from a little distance, wrote that "Gen. Meade seemed to be administering a rebuke to Warren, judging from the demeanor of both." Meade calmed down enough for Warren to take him to the front to demonstrate the strength of the enemy defenses, and Meade sadly recognized that Warren was right: an attack against those defenses would have been suicidal. [36]

The commanding general called off the operations for the day, and on the following day he turned the army around and marched it back over the Rapidan, to winter quarters. The Mine Run campaign was over, but its repercussions were just beginning. [37]

CHAPTER TWELVE

FALLOUT, 1863–1864

THE ARMY OF THE POTOMAC MARCHED BACK from Mine Run and the Rapidan and moved into winter quarters. Warren wrote to Emily, saying, "Our army accomplished but little on the late movement. We drove Genl Lee into his intrenchments when finding him too strongly posted for us to assault we came back." He told Will, "You must not be disturbed by any attacks you may see on me in the newspapers. I have warning, that there is to be a regular charge on me because I declined to attack the enemy's breastworks on the morning of the 30th November. But I am master of my position and good will come of it." He warned Emily of "a grand newspaper assault on me" but hoped that out of it all "things will come before the public and I hope evils corrected that have long affected us."[1]

Warren was anticipating the storm that would descend because of the abortive Mine Run campaign, but he was confident that his actions were immune to criticism. "Don't let the late movements worry you," he told his wife. "Thank heaven they were all right as far as I was concerned and the failure was to the plans not having been carried out by those with us, and then it fell upon me to decide we should not waste our men's lives in hopeless assaults to make up for previous blunder. Rest assured I did right and all in the army will say so."[2]

The fallout was not long in coming. The march to Mine Run and back brought upon the head of the commander of the Army of the Potomac a torrent of criticism for his failure to bring Lee's army to battle. How could Meade have marched the entire army all the way down past the Rapidan and then retired with nothing more than a few skirmishes with the rebel force? The Radical Republicans, who had no love for Meade because he was not one of them and had displaced Hooker, who was, thundered against him for having wasted resources, time, and opportunity. Meade, they said, was just a pale imitation of McClellan in his reluctance to carry the fight to the enemy.

Once the facts of the campaign were revealed, not least by his enemies such as French, Warren came in for his share of the heat. His rapid rise in the ranks of the Army of the Potomac had inspired much jealousy and bitterness among his fellow officers, and he had not always handled himself in the most appropriate manner. Conscious of his own talents, all too intolerant of shortcomings in others, and aware of the prerogatives of his rank, Warren at times was arrogant and overbearing.

On December 3, for example, Warren wrote a twelve-page letter to Humphreys, now Meade's chief of staff, which he had "no objection to Gen. Meade seeing," setting forth some of his ideas for conducting a campaign and running an army, and adding that the army was badly hampered by "the retention . . . of certain corps & Div. commanders and of our present artillery force." He specifically named French and two elderly division commanders as liabilities to be gotten rid of. All three had helped to botch the recent movement. It is, however, questionable how much Meade appreciated receiving this advice from this particular source just at this time.[3]

One evening in winter camp, Warren was playing cards with his staff and losing heavily, to the point where he borrowed twenty dollars from one of his staffers. He got into a dispute with Morgan at the table and told his chief of staff that he would not stand for being contradicted, that he ranked him in both the regular army and the volunteers, and that he should be paid due respect. Morgan quietly replied that when the general condescended to play cards with his staff he laid aside his rank and would be treated as an equal.[4]

Within the army, however, Warren heard little but applause for his decision at Mine Run. Although Meade, in a letter to his wife on December 2, obliquely blamed his corps commander for the failure to attack, and henceforth held him in lesser esteem than he had, the men in the ranks found it a praiseworthy and courageous exercise of judgment. One of his regimental commanders called Warren's action "one of the noblest acts of humanity on your part ever enacted . . . a mark of Generalship worthy of great credit." Another colonel, writing home, said simply, "The slaughter would have been great and we feel thankful to have been spared."[5]

The colonel of the First Pennsylvania Reserves said, "The army, perhaps the Union cause, was saved, due to the clear judgment and military skill of those grand officers, Meade and Warren . . . Had the two armies fought at Mine Run the result would have been the greatest slaughter in the history of the United States." Livermore, of the Second Corps staff, felt that Warren's "boldness was greater than it would have been if he had charged that formidable position." Warren had nearly half the army under him, with orders to attack that would have protected him in the event of a fiasco, with a command that would have charged with courage and resolution, and with the anticipation of great personal reward if he should succeed; for an ambitious young general officer it was a nearly ideal situation—except for those Confederate defenses. Ambitious as Warren was, his realism and sympathy for his soldiers forced him to call off the attack and accept whatever consequences might arise.[6]

The army marched away from Mine Run in good spirits, realizing what it had been spared, and moved into winter quarters at last. For Gouverneur Warren, the winter of 1863–64 would be dominated by the comings and goings of Winfield Hancock, for the latter's convalescence and ability to resume active command would dictate the length of Warren's tenure with the Second Corps.

As early as the end of September, Hancock had written to Warren, saying, "I hope to be well in three weeks," although "my wound has not healed yet, and I am still lame." Hancock's hopes were clearly unrealistic, but he did return to the Second Corps on December 29, still in considerable pain. Hancock was ordered north again on January 8, 1864, to continue his convalescence and aid in recruiting, and Warren resumed command of the Second Corps.[7]

Earlier, Warren had sent Emily his report of the Mine Run campaign with instructions to put it away with his other papers. After discussing the culpability of French for the campaign's failure, he said, "they have all tried to throw the blame of their own slowness on my shoulders. But the effort will not succeed." He went on to say that "much of the gloomy feeling I have heretofore expressed in my letters to you" was caused by his recognition of the incompetency of French and others and the knowledge that this would cause failure. "When my efforts to have these men changed have failed," he said, "I have felt despondent and unhappy." In addition, "I do not feel very kindly towards Genl Meade," because he could have made the changes and did not. "Now," Warren said, "he must suffer for it and I for a time with him in the public prints." He went on to say that "all my Corps think a great deal more of me than they did before, and men from other corps come and tell me I was right. They all feel that for once there was a senseless slaughter saved by the action of their commander."[8]

A couple of days later, Warren wrote her that a benefit of the Mine Run controversy was "to make my individuality stand out in *better* light than I ever did before." He also denied a quarrel between himself and Meade, saying that Meade's reported rebuke was "only his earnest way of speaking to me. It was not a reproof."[9]

Warren was able to secure a leave and departed the army, accompanied by Wash Roebling, on December 14, arriving in Washington that night and Baltimore the next day. He and Emily were thus able to spend their first married Christmas together, despite the uncertainties of their future. At the end of the month Warren made a trip to Philadelphia, Cold Spring, and New York City, returning to Baltimore on January 5. Secretary Stanton told Warren he could remain in Washington (with Emily) to finish his reports if Meade consented, so he headed to Culpeper to see the commanding general. When he arrived back at headquarters on the 7th, he learned to his chagrin that he would celebrate his thirty-fourth birthday the next day by resuming command of the Second Corps, "till Genl Hancock returns from Washington to which place he is going for some temporary duty," he told Emily. If Warren thought that meant a few days, he would soon learn better.[10]

A few days later he mentioned to Emily that Webb, Morgan, Sprigg Carroll, and Alex Hays all had their wives in camp with them. "And yet I do not wish for you to be here now," he said. "It is too cold and cheerless and damp and you might get sick . . . and then you cannot be spared from home now." Emily's mother was ailing, so she was needed in Baltimore. On the 13th, Warren said he now understood that Hancock would be away for another six weeks, and the fact that his own confirmation for major general was pending in the Senate made him feel that his place was on duty with the army. Warren knew there was to be a consolidation of the Army of the Potomac, but he was dubious of his chance of getting command of a corps in the reorganization.[11]

On January 27, Warren received a telegram advising him that Mrs. Chase had died that morning. He left immediately for Baltimore where he lent what assistance he could to the bereaved family. He was not given much time to comfort his wife and her family, for there were military affairs afoot. Butler's Army of the James was to make a lunge for Richmond, and as a diversion the Army of the Potomac was to essay a small effort across the Rapidan.[12]

Warren was, as he said in his report, "very unwell" on the morning of February 6, and since the operation was to be but a demonstration, he put Caldwell in charge of the corps. The overall plan, designed on short notice by Sedgwick, temporarily commanding in Meade's absence, was for the cavalry to cross the Rapidan at Barnett's Ford and Culpeper Ford, the First Corps to demonstrate at Raccoon Ford, and the Second Corps to cross at Morton's Ford.[13]

Caldwell's demonstration at Morton's Ford did not go well, and Warren, arriving on the scene at about 3 P.M., decided to wait until dark and then to withdraw his forces to the north side of the river. The corps lost 255 men, mostly in Hays's division. Warren wrote angrily to Emily that the demonstration was in aid of Butler's effort to capture Richmond. Butler, Warren wrote, got as far as the Chickahominy river, then turned around and came back. "So I sacrificed 200 men to aid that fool. I have such a contempt for his military abilities, that I could not express it in decent words."[14]

Aside from occasional diversions like Morton's Ford, the winter dragged along. The Second Corps held a ball at Culpeper on Washington's Birthday, called "brilliant, successful, and very well attended" by one reporter and "quite a success" by Meade, who complained that he did not get back to his quarters until 4 A.M. Warren's sister Emily came down from Cold Spring for the ball, at which she met Wash Roebling. Almost at once, the general's aide and his sister fell in love. On February 28, his wife Emily's brother Sidney died, after a long and painful illness, but the next day Warren was cheered by a letter from Senator Edwin D. Morgan of New York, advising him that his promotion had been confirmed by the Senate.[15]

Warren was much gratified by the confirmation, writing Emily that "now that the hard trial my character has borne and my position secured I shall be more than ever able to bear the buffets of fortune." He sent Senator Morgan's letter to her with instructions to keep it, "as I prize it very much." [16]

March was an eventful month for the young general. He left for Baltimore on the third, had a couple of days with Emmie, and reported as directed in Washington on the 7th. On March 9 and 10, Warren found himself testifying before the Committee on the Conduct of the War, answering questions and offering opinions on the army's operations.[17]

Warren's performance before the committee won him few friends in the army. He dutifully defended Meade's performance at Gettysburg and after, although admitting that he himself might have done things differently from Meade on occasion. He was critical of Sedgwick, Hooker, Sykes, Halleck, Howard, French, and Sickles, as he answered questions from Senator Ben Wade, the committee chairman, about actions at Chancellorsville, Gettysburg, Williamsport, Bristoe Station, and Mine Run. Candid and forthright in discussing the shortcomings of his fellow soldiers, as he usually was, he opined at one point that "the corps have not been commanded by soldiers—that is, that the corps commanders have not been the men they ought to be . . . have not all of them been equal to their positions." He said corps commanders "do not go enough to the front to see for themselves." On two occasions, when Warren mentioned that the army had suffered grievous losses at Gettysburg with the death of Reynolds and the wounding of Hancock, Wade interjected the name of Sickles, the committee's favorite, as another serious loss; Warren ignored the first mention of Sickles but, the second time, rather gently put down Sickles as brave and well-intentioned, but an amateur in a military setting.[18]

When he finished with the committee, Warren stopped by Matthew Brady's establishment to sit for his photograph. The next day, March 11, he returned to the army, this time taking Emily with him, along with his sister Emily, to the immense gratification of Roebling. There is no record of the reaction of the general's wife to army life, but she did accompany Gouv on the 16th to a divisional ball. A week later, on the 23rd, the two Emilys were sent back to Baltimore, for Winfield Hancock was returning, big things were brewing in the Army of the Potomac, and the decks had to be cleared.[19]

Hancock did get back on the 23rd, although he did not show up at the Second Corps that day, since, as Warren was told, "he does not wish you to put yourself to any inconvenience on his account." Hancock's return, however, was the trigger for a major reorganization of the Army of the Potomac. It represented the fallout from the operations of the prior year, and the repercussions were substantial.[20]

The principal development was the reduction of the Army of the Potomac to three corps, the Second, Fifth, and Sixth, because Meade felt that he had only three generals capable of handling a corps. Two of the corps which had fought at Gettysburg, Howard's Eleventh and Slocum's Twelfth, had previously been sent west. Now, the First and Third corps were wiped off the organizational charts, with their divisions allotted among the survivors. Hancock resumed command of the Second Corps, while Warren was given the Fifth, replacing Sykes. Warren, Roebling wrote, won command of the Fifth Corps "in the face of bitter jealousies and opposition which pursued him and maligned him through the whole Wilderness campaign." [21]

Sykes, French, Newton of the First Corps, Pleasonton of the cavalry, and several division and brigade commanders were detached from the Army of the Potomac, turned out to pasture or sent off to areas of lesser responsibility. Only Meade's strong intervention saved Sedgwick from the same fate. Humphreys, the chief of staff, wrote his wife that "the changes are taken in very good part by the Army," but that was a judgment from headquarters. Another officer wrote that "the thing will no doubt cause a great deal of ill feeling in the First and Third Corps." Six Third Corps officers, bitter at the disappearance of their unit, defiantly sewed their new corps badges on the seats of their trousers. [22]

On the 24th, rejoicing "over the opportunity given to me," Warren, who was said to be "fairly worshiped" by the men of the Second Corps, turned over that command to Hancock. He then rode to Culpeper for the uncomfortable meeting with Sykes, who had advised his corps that he was reluctantly "obeying an order so wholly unexpected." One of the causes of the change was certainly the mixup at Bristoe Station and Warren's reaction to it, and it made his removal more painful for Sykes. That his young replacement had once been a regimental commander under him surely added to Sykes's discomfiture. The formalities and civilities duly undergone, the old regular rode sadly away and left Warren with his new command. John Newton issued his farewell order to the First Corps and similarly departed. [23]

Warren told Emily that "I do [not] fear I can do as well as others. I am now fairly before the world as a General either to make or break." The next day he and Meade paid a visit to the recently arrived commander of all of the armies of the United States, Lieutenant General Ulysses S. Grant, who had decided that he would accompany the Army of the Potomac in the upcoming campaign. Warren thought "he seems to be much more vivacious than I supposed and did not look *at* me with any apparent eye to discerning my qualities in my face." Grant would have plenty of opportunity to make his judgment of Warren's qualities. [24]

Warren may not have taken note of it at the time, but the removal of Pleasonton gave Grant the opportunity to name as cavalry commander for the eastern army one of his protégés from the west, a blunt, aggressive young man named Philip H. Sheridan. Theodore Lyman, of Meade's staff, described the new cavalry commander as "a small, broad-shouldered, squat man, with black hair and a square head. He is of Irish parents, but looks very like a Piedmontese." Meade and Sheridan would clash early in the campaign, and Meade would quickly learn that Sheridan could do no wrong in Grant's eyes. For the time being, Warren and Sheridan had no more than limited and perfunctory contact.[25]

On the 26th, Warren established his corps headquarters in the "very dirty and disorderly" Virginia Hotel in Culpeper and went to work. "I have today got my new corps machinery running," he wrote to Emily, "and shall begin to make my mark as soon as my new officers and myself get well acquainted and all my staff get here."[26]

Concurrent with the War Department order reducing the eastern army to three corps was an order from Meade's headquarters directing that the three divisions formerly composing the old First Corps be transferred to the Fifth Corps, where they would be consolidated into two divisions. To Gouverneur Warren fell the responsibility of making this reduction, which necessarily entailed pain to displaced officers, to accompany the general feeling of unhappiness which afflicted all those in the disappearing corps. As he went about this unpleasant business, Warren was cheered by a letter from Samuel W. Crawford, one of his division commanders, who wrote, "I have heard that you are to be assigned to the command of the Fifth Corps. I assure you that nothing has given me greater pleasure than the hope that this may be true. I for all of the officers of rank in the corps hail the change with the greatest satisfaction."[27]

With the assistance of Colonel Fred Locke, the chief of staff who had been with the Fifth Corps virtually from the time of its creation, Warren worked out the new organization. He recognized that it "was unpalatable to some," and he also was conscious of the fact that "the appointment of myself junior in years to many of the Generals under me produced unpleasant reflections in their minds." He was not happy that officers like Romeyn B. Ayres and Lysander Cutler, "who had long commanded divisions," were forced to return to brigade command. But the imperatives of numbers and rank required the results he reached.[28]

Brigadier General Charles Griffin, a gruff, hardbitten old artilleryman, retained command of the First Division, composed of three brigades from the Fifth Corps. Griffin was a superior soldier and would continue to give satisfaction. The Second Division would be made up of three First Corps brigades and be commanded by Brigadier General John C. Robinson, a professional soldier.

The Third Division, led by Crawford, was made up of two brigades from the old Fifth Corps. Crawford, a graduate of the University of Pennsylvania and its medical school, had been a doctor in the prewar army but switched to the infantry when hostilities began. One man serving under him wrote that "we didn't think too much of Crawford . . . a tall, chesty, glowering man, with heavy eyes, a big nose, and bushy whiskers; and he wore habitually a turn-out-the-guard expression, which was . . . fairly indicative of his military character." [29] Crawford's performance was often unsatisfactory, and Warren would eventually pay the price for his failures.

Brigadier General James S. Wadsworth commanded the Fourth Division, composed of three brigades from the old First Corps. Wadsworth, a wealthy, fifty-six-year-old New York patrician, was an amateur soldier of great valor who refused payment for his services. He had taken leave to run as the Republican candidate for governor of New York in 1862 but returned to the army after his defeat. [30]

Warren also ordered out of camp all of the stray and unattached officers who had quartered themselves there. On the 27th he took a long ride around "my lines." Warren was feeling "light hearted and confident," he told Emily. "We are going to have a magnificent campaign and I have a situation commensurate with it. Let me have a fair chance where I now am and I do not fear the result." [31]

A few days later Warren complained to his wife that "I have a very laborious command to look after." Sedgwick and Hancock had their corps concentrated in one place, whereas his was "scattered for 50 miles" and "all new to me and needs especial looking after." "I seem fated always to get the hardest of these things if there is any difference," he went on. But never mind, he continued; "I find my command well disposed towards me, [and] the newspapers generally support me." Roebling wrote to his Emily that "your brother is working quite hard . . . he gets along now by going to sleep at 6 o'clock on three chairs drawn up to the fire, whether he falls off during the night I don't know." [32]

There was a great deal of work to be taken care of, as Warren settled in with his new command. He became better acquainted with the commanders of the divisions, brigades, and regiments of the Fifth Corps, and he tested and tried his new staff. He learned that he had a very touchy artillery commander, a suspicious New Yorker named Charles Wainwright, who had been with the First Corps and added to distrust of infantry commanders generally an unhappiness at the displacement of his old corps. When Grant reviewed the corps at the end of March, Wainwright sniffed, grudgingly, "Warren knew enough to put the artillery on the right of the line where it belonged . . . When we arrived Warren was already on the ground to assign each command its position: he promises to be a very different man from Newton in this respect." Wainwright went on to describe Warren to his diary as "a small man, about thirty-five years old, dark complexioned, with black eyes, and long, straight black hair; he has a little look of an Indian, and evidently is of a nervous temperament." [33]

Warren went over, approved, and sent back to Washington the transcript of his testimony before the Committee on the Conduct of the War, and he even

Samuel W. Crawford, whose handling of his division
caused trouble at Five Forks. National Archives.

took off a couple of days in early April to go snipe hunting. He received a letter
on the 8th from his sister Emily, asking, "Now that you have found another
Emily all your own, are you willing to transfer this Emily to Roebling's keeping?" She said, "You have always been more to me than a brother and I should
dread to undertake so serious a step without your consent and approval." She

need not have worried, as Warren found Wash Roebling an eminently suitable candidate for brother-in-law. A couple of weeks later Warren presented Roebling with a fine sword.[34]

Late in April, Warren wrote to his wife that "I suppose we shall not see each other again till after the next battle." A few days later, he wrote that she should not worry about him, "for I never entered upon so splendid an opportunity as I do now and may never again have a more exalted station."[35] The Army of the Potomac was getting ready to march. Grant directed that all of the Union armies should move against their Confederate enemies in unison, or nearly so, and the beginning of May would be the time.

As the Union armies prepared for the campaign, there was a difference in their composition from three years earlier. One regimental commander noted it: "It was the men who went in '61. The school-boys filled the ranks in '64. The large majority of the new soldiers who filled the ranks of the . . . [regiments of the Army of the Potomac] were innocent of a beard, but they were the bravest and the best."[36]

CHAPTER THIRTEEN

INTO THE DEEP, DARK WOODS

*T*HE ARMY OF THE POTOMAC, NEARLY A HUNDRED thousand strong, renewed by an invigorating winter, the return of many men wounded in the 1863 battles, and the addition of new recruits, "in health, in spirits, and in discipline," as one of its members wrote, "never in better form for strong and stubborn work," moved out early on May 4, 1864. At 2 A.M., James Wilson's cavalry division reached Germanna Ford at the Rapidan, dispersed a few Confederate pickets guarding the crossing, and made the ford available to the pontoon bridge which quickly took shape.[1]

Gouverneur K. Warren's Fifth Corps followed the cavalry, having marched away from its camps around Culpeper. Griffin's division reached Germanna Ford at about 6 A.M. and quickly moved across the river, to be followed by Crawford's division, the forty-eight pieces of artillery commanded by Wainwright, and then Wadsworth's and Robinson's divisions. Warren, with Meade, Grant, and their staffs, stood on a bluff overlooking the ford, watching the corps as it crossed. The Fifth Corps entered the Wilderness.[2]

As it did so, expectations were high for the corps' new commander. One observer said, "Of a subtle, analytic intellect, endowed with an eminent talent for details, the clearest military *coup d'oeil*, and a fiery concentrated energy, he promised to take the first rank as a commander." Grant later wrote that "at that time my judgment was that Warren was the man I would suggest to succeed Meade should anything happen to that gallant soldier to take him from the field." Clearly, G. K. Warren was the rising star of the army as the 1864 campaign got under way.[3]

The command structure of the eastern army was curious and somewhat awkward. Meade was the commander of the Army of the Potomac, but Grant, the army's overall commander, was with it and would give strategic direction. Whether he could restrain himself from getting into tactical decisions remained a question. Another complication was the Ninth Corps, with nineteen thousand men under Burnside, which was following behind the Army of the Potomac, was expected to fight with it, but was not a part of it. Since Burnside outranked Meade, Grant kept the Ninth Corps as a separate force, subject only to his orders.

Grant had determined to move against Lee by taking a route to the east of the rebel army, so that the Chesapeake Bay could serve as his supply line. In selecting this line of advance, Grant recognized that Lee would be free to utilize his twice-used invasion route to the north, but he felt, correctly, that the Confederate commander would not be in any position to consider incursions into Maryland or Pennsylvania. Grant hoped to pass through the Wilderness and get around Lee's right flank before the Confederate commander could react.

Warren had been up all night two nights earlier suffering from indigestion, but now he was ready. Just prior to departing from Culpeper, he wrote a last letter to Emily, consoling her on the death of her younger brother, coming soon after the deaths of her mother and her brother Sidney. He said his noble army, "strong in numbers in armament and equipment, in the intelligence of its officers and men and their consciousness of the nobility of their cause," was ready for its great hour. "Do not fear my sweetheart for me. I am only too happy in the high place I fill and if I am to die I can never do so more gloriously than in the now opened campaign."[4]

Warren had called together his division commanders and Wainwright, the artillery chief, on the afternoon of May 3, going over his orders, explaining the army's projected movement and its attempt to get around Lee. Wainwright made a curious notation in his diary, saying that Warren "paid especial deference to Griffin, whom he evidently fears." At this he did not wonder, as Griffin "is such an inveterate hater, and so ugly in his persecutions." Griffin was a tough, harsh soldier, and Wainwright was invariably resistant to infantry commanders (even old artillerymen like Griffin) who presumed to regulate his precious guns. Still, it was an odd comment, reflecting the antipathy toward Warren which became a feature of Wainwright's diary. Nevertheless, the marching orders as given were followed to the letter the next day.[5]

Sedgwick's Sixth Corps followed Warren across the Rapidan at Germanna Ford, while the Second Corps under Hancock utilized Ely's Ford, a few miles to the east. The Army of the Potomac thus bypassed the fearsome defensive works the rebels had constructed at Mine Run, off to the west.

The Fifth Corps moved from the Rapidan down the Germanna Plank Road to its intersection with the Orange Turnpike near the site of an abandoned inn called Wilderness Tavern. This was its destination for the first day's march, so the corps went into camp upon arrival at two o'clock. A soldier in Robinson's division wrote that he started out the morning on "a glorious spring day," but when he crossed the Rapidan he felt that, though "the day had not been oppressively warm, . . . in the narrow defile no air was stirring." In the increasing heat and the enclosing forest, overcoats and blankets soon became burdens to be cast aside, and the army's route could be marked easily by its discarded equipment.[6]

The Wilderness of Spotsylvania, to give the area its full name, was not un-familiar to those men in Meade's army who had struggled at Chancellorsville almost exactly one year earlier. To those soldiers, however, as well as to those who were encountering it for the first time, the Wilderness presented a dark, gloomy, and forbidding appearance. Of the dense, second-growth forest, a member of the Fifth Corps staff wrote that "generally, the trees are noticeably stunted, and so close together, and their lower limbs so intermingled with a thick underbrush, that it is very difficult indeed to make one's way through them." Another soldier called it "a wild, desolate region . . . covered with a dense growth of scraggy oak and pines, sassafras and hazel, interlaced with an entanglement of vines that rendered its recesses almost impenetrable."[7]

There were few roads penetrating the forest fastness, and those that existed were often nothing more than paths through the woods. Two east-west roads, the Orange and Fredericksburg Turnpike and the Orange Plank Road, ran roughly parallel, a mile or so apart, but even these had seen better days. With the lack of roads and open areas, cavalry and artillery were of little use in the Wilderness, and even infantrymen experienced excruciating difficulty in moving through the dense woods.

Why, one wonders, did Grant stop the first day's march, unimpeded as it was by enemy resistance, at such an early hour in the afternoon? Passage through and out of the Wilderness was certainly a prime objective of the Union army. Unfortunately, the marching army was followed by a creeping one, more than four thousand supply wagons in great, slow-moving trains, and Grant was fear-ful that his infantry might get so far ahead of these trains as to render them defenseless in face of a sudden enemy raid. Hence the decision to halt early in the afternoon. Besides, Grant believed that he had truly stolen a march on the rebels and that he could indeed exit the Wilderness before they could menace him.[8]

Roebling wrote bitterly many years later that the orders for the march pre-sumed that there would be some sort of opposition to the passage of the river, that the Fifth Corps should have been kept going to the plank road, which it could easily have reached on May 4, and that this failure on Grant's part— "Grant's first great fizzle," he called it—doomed the army to the kind of bloody but inconclusive struggle which took place over the next two days.[9]

Warren made his temporary headquarters at the Lacy house, near the inter-section of the turnpike and the road from Germanna Ford. Griffin's division was bivouacked a little to the west, along the turnpike, with Crawford's slightly southwest from the Lacy house. Robinson's men were north, toward the ford, while Wadsworth threw out a picket line to the east, toward Chancellorsville, where the Second Corps was encamped. The Sixth Corps was spread out along the Germanna Plank Road, three miles south of the ford. A staff officer said that Warren, at supper that night, was "cheerier at heart, I believe, than ever afterwards, unless it was on the field of Five Forks just before he met Sheridan." [10]

Orders for the next day called for the Fifth Corps to move through the forest, over an obscure woods trail, in a southwesterly direction, to a place on the Orange Plank Road called Parker's Store. Crawford's division was to take the lead, followed by Wadsworth and Robinson, with Griffin bringing up the rear. Warren was instructed to "keep out detachments on the roads on [his] right flank," that is, in the known direction of the enemy. [11]

There would be no need, however, for the Fifth Corps to seek out the enemy. Robert E. Lee had put his army into motion when his observation posts picked up signs of Union army movement on the north side of the Rapidan. He knew the Wilderness well, and he considered it a good place to go after Grant's army; the impenetrable forest would nullify the great difference in numbers between the two forces. As a result, on the evening of May 4, Powell Hill's corps was on the Orange Plank Road, east of Mine Run; Longstreet's corps was moving swiftly from Gordonsville; and Ewell's corps was encamped on the turnpike, just a few miles from Griffin's outposts.

A curiosity of warfare kept the Union army ignorant of Ewell's position on the turnpike. Wilson's cavalry division had scouted west on that road almost to Robertson's Tavern, near Mine Run, on the afternoon of May 4, had encountered nothing, and had been withdrawn to the plank road just in time to miss Ewell's advance in the evening. Warren later wrote that "I was informed however that our mounted troops held Robertson's Tavern so that I apprehended nothing." [12]

The Fifth Corps got underway on May 5 as ordered, at about 5 A.M., with Crawford's division moving slowly down the woods trail, somewhat widened the previous afternoon by the engineers, toward Parker's Store, to be followed by Wadsworth and Robinson. Warren sent a message to George Getty, commanding the leading division of the Sixth Corps, that Griffin would hold the pike until Getty arrived, then follow the rest of the corps. Mounted on a big dapple-gray horse and bedecked in the yellow sash of a major general, Warren was anxious and somewhat snappish as his corps began its march, assigned to claw its way five miles along a narrow, sinuous path through the jungle, with the Army of Northern Virginia somewhere off to its right, hidden by the deep woods. Just as Warren was about to head off behind Wadsworth's division, a staff officer from Griffin rode up to him with a startling message. [13]

Three regiments of Griffin's division, the 140th and 146th New York and the First Michigan, were posted about a mile out on the turnpike west of Wilderness Tavern, waiting to be recalled to join the day's march. About an hour after daybreak, observers spotted dust rising above the road off to the west. Squinting into the distance, they were soon able to pick out horsemen and, behind them, gray-clad infantrymen, who seemed to be filing off into the woods north of the road. Colonel David Jenkins of the 146th New York sent in word that "the rebel infantry have appeared on the Orange C.H. Turnpike & are forming a line of battle ¾ of a mile in front of" Griffin. What they saw was Edward Johnson's division of Ewell's corps.[14]

Warren promptly notified his division commanders that Griffin had reported rebel infantry on the turnpike but, "until it is more definitely ascertained, no change will take place in the movements ordered." He ordered Griffin "to push a force out" to see what strength the enemy had out there. Warren also reported the sighting on the turnpike to Meade, adding the type of unsolicited advice which came to exasperate the commanding general: "Such demonstrations are to be expected, and show the necessity for keeping well closed and prepared to face toward Mine Run and meet an attack at a moment's notice."[15]

Meade passed the word on to Grant:

> The enemy have appeared in force on the Orange pike, and are now reported forming line of battle in front of Griffin's division, Fifth Corps. I have directed General Warren to attack them at once with his whole force. Until this movement of the enemy is developed, the march of the corps must be suspended. I have, therefore, sent word to Hancock not to advance beyond Todd's Tavern for the present. I think the enemy is trying to delay our movement, and will not give battle, but of this we shall soon see.[16]

Grant, acknowledging receipt of Meade's note, told his army commander, "If any opportunity presents itself for pitching into a part of Lee's army, do so without giving time for disposition." Grant neglected to comment on Meade's tacit admission that, if Lee's intention was "to delay our movement," Meade's order to stop played into the southerner's hand.[17]

Meade sent Grant's message to Warren, adding that "[Horatio] Wright [commanding a Sixth Corps division] is advancing on the Spotswood road," a road which angled down southwestwardly from the Germanna Plank Road to the Orange Turnpike. A march down the Spotswood Road would bring Wright's division in on Warren's right flank. "Attack as soon as you can," Meade said, "and communicate, if possible, with Wright."[18]

Warren thought this directive foolish. No one in the Union army knew the strength of the Confederate force spotted out to the west, although Meade apparently assumed it was a small party. Warren had been hearing from his officers that it looked like a force of some substance and that it was erecting unseen defensive works in the woods, and he knew his corps was well spread

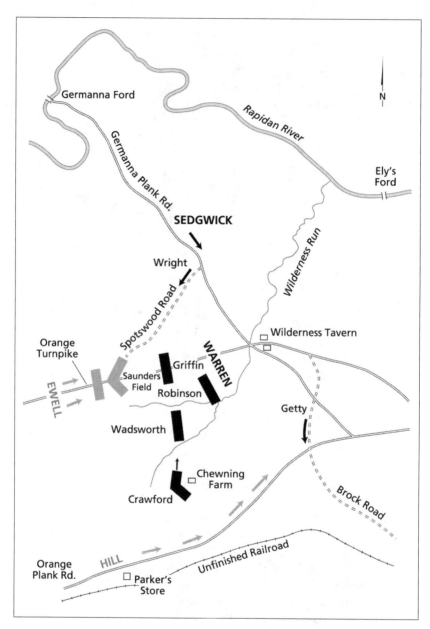

The Wilderness, mid-day, May 5, 1864

out by this time. Crawford's division had reached a clearing called Chewning's Farm, which overlooked Parker's Store and the plank road, and Crawford had reported seeing a skirmish on the plank road between Union and what he thought was Confederate cavalry. Roebling, who had ridden down to Crawford, felt that the plateau at Chewning's was a key spot which should be held.[19]

Wadsworth's division was laboring through the woods behind Crawford, and part of Robinson's division was in the same woods, with the rest back at Wilderness Tavern. Until he made a connection with Wright's division, supposed to be coming down the Spotswood Road, Warren knew, Griffin's right flank was in the air. Arranging for an attack against the enemy west on the turnpike was more than simply a matter of saying "Go!"

Warren later said that the order to attack at once with Griffin's division was "the most fatal blunder of the campaign." He suggested to Meade that he needed time to get his corps turned around in the right direction for an attack through the thick forest and that such an attack should await the arrival of the Sixth Corps on his right. Meade, no doubt desiring to demonstrate to Grant the aggressive spirit of the Army of the Potomac, expressed his impatience at the delay; when he found Warren at his headquarters, Meade said, "If there is to be any fighting this side of Mine Run, let us do it right off."[20]

At 7:30 A.M., Warren had sent word to Crawford that "the movement towards Parker's Store is suspended. You will halt, face towards Mine Run, and connect with Genl Wadsworth on your right." Around 8 A.M., Crawford was ordered to leave Chewning's, march back up the path his corps had traversed, and join Wadsworth's left, preparatory to attacking toward the west. Crawford was reluctant to abandon his strong position at Chewning's Farm, so he sent word back about the advantages of the position and did not move, waiting to see if someone back at headquarters might change his mind and order him to hold it. Warren, under mounting pressure from Meade and Grant, fired off another order to Crawford, directing, "You will move to the right as quickly as possible," and again, as noon approached and the attack on the turnpike had not yet materialized, "You must connect with Gen. Wadsworth and cover & protect his left as he advances."[21]

Crawford, in response to these peremptory orders, detached four regiments under Colonel William McCandless to try to find and link up with Wadsworth, whose division had in the meantime clawed its way through the jungle to form a shaky connection with Griffin's men below the turnpike. Warren with some of his staff rode about a mile through the woods to where Wadsworth was forming his division. Warren pointed into the woods and said to his elderly division commander, "Find out what is in there." Wadsworth's skirmishers tracked through the woods until they came upon rebel pickets, and a sharp little fight ensued.[22]

Warren, with his corps still entangled in the woods and certainly not in anything approaching a line of battle, with his right flank unprotected, was loath
to initiate an attack. Meade, as the hours passed with still no attack against the
Confederates on the turnpike, continued to press Warren for action. "Again
and again," Schaff wrote, "inquiries were made of Warren, when Griffin
would move, and each time with more edge." Grant and Meade and their
people continued to think it was some sort of rebel rear guard out there on the
pike, and they could not see why Warren was taking so long to go out and deal
with it. In addition, from where they were, they had no idea of the difficulty,
the near impossibility, of putting regiments and brigades in line for battle in
the Wilderness, where "once a division left the roads or fields it disappeared
utterly," out of sight of its commander.[23]

Warren was hearing from Griffin and from Brigadier General Romeyn B.
Ayres, a sound and intelligent officer of long experience, that it would be suicidal to advance without having the right flank of the corps (which meant the
right flank of Ayres's brigade) protected, as they could see that the Confederate
forces awaiting them stretched far beyond Ayres. Warren understood this, but
he was under intense pressure from Meade to get an attack going. When
Griffin said he "was averse to making an attack," he was told to go ahead with
it. He sent a staff officer again to Warren, who responded with remarks questioning Griffin's courage. "It was afterwards a common report in the army,"
wrote the staff officer, "that Warren had just had unpleasant things said to him
by General Meade, and that General Meade had just heard the bravery of his
army questioned." [24]

By 11:30 A.M., having completely lost patience with the long hours it was taking to get the Fifth Corps in line of battle, Meade ordered Warren to send his
corps into the attack, Griffin on the turnpike, Wadsworth and Crawford into
the impenetrable thickets south of the pike. "We are waiting for you," Warren
was told, sternly. If he did not attack, he was advised by an emissary from
Grant, he would be cashiered on the spot, relieved of his command and disgraced forever. Forget about the Sixth Corps. Bag that rebel force before it gets
away! Reluctantly, for he feared the result, Warren gave Griffin his direct orders: advance, with Ayres's brigade on the north side of the turnpike and Bartlett's on the south. Wadsworth would attack on his left, Crawford beyond that,
but there was nothing, Warren told him, on his right.[25]

Out in front of Griffin's division was a cleared area called Saunders' Field,
about eight hundred yards from east to west and about four hundred yards
from the turnpike to the woods on the right. There was a swale about halfway
across it, and the ground then rose to the western edge of the field. The division scrambled forward through the woods. By the time it reached Saunders'
Field, at about one o'clock, "all semblance of line of battle was gone," a witness wrote, "and there were gaps everywhere between regiments and bri-

gades." Commanders tried to reform their jumbled lines, and Warren rode up to urge his men onward.[26]

As Ayres's veteran, well-disciplined brigade, led by the 140th New York and a regiment of U.S. Regulars, reached the center of the cleared field, from the enemy ranks, hidden in the woods, came a line of fire slowly moving from left to right. The first volley did little damage, but a second and a third cut great gaps in Ayres's line, blasting it from in front and on its unguarded right flank. By the time Ayres's men reached the woods, they recognized the futility of the attack and fell back. In ten minutes, Ayres's big brigade of thirty-seven hundred men was reduced to barely two thousand.[27]

On the other side of the turnpike, Bartlett's brigade moved forward at the same time as Ayres's, but other than that there was no coordination between the two attacks. Bartlett's men were in the woods, where they encountered the Virginia brigade of John M. Jones. Bartlett's first line, the Eighty-Third Pennsylvania, Eighteenth Massachusetts, and Forty-Fourth New York, enjoyed a momentary success: Jones, the Confederate brigadier, was killed, and his men fell back upon their support, Cullen A. Battle's Alabama brigade. One of the Virginia officers lost his head and shouted, "Fall back to Mine Run!" and Battle's regiments began retreating. Bartlett, however, had to stop his troops, who were hopelessly snarled in the dense woods, to reorganize them. While they were regrouping, they were hit hard by fire from their right and rear, where the Confederates who had repulsed Ayres were now on Bartlett's flank. The hard-pressed brigade about-faced and fled back toward its own lines, General Bartlett himself being wounded and nearly captured.[28]

During the course of the attack, two guns from Winslow's battery were ordered forward into Saunders' Field and beyond the swale. Their fire, which raked friend and foe alike, only served to confuse things further in the hellish fighting. Eventually the gun crews were driven off and the guns were captured by the Confederates, who were unable, however, to get them off the field under the incessant musketry. The guns were retaken by the Union army, lost again, and eventually dragged away by the rebels after dark.[29]

Meanwhile, to the left of Griffin, Wadsworth's division was faring no better. The famous Iron Brigade, under General Lysander Cutler, advanced with Bartlett's brigade but soon became separated from it in the woods, with its own right flank being exposed as a consequence. The Georgia brigade of George Doles shattered the right flank of the Iron Brigade, and a strong counterattack by John B. Gordon's brigade of Early's division forced the westerners to break and run for the first time in their illustrious history. Colonel Roy Stone's Pennsylvania brigade, to the left of Cutler, was led into a swamp, and its confused regiments wound up firing at one another. Many of its members were captured. Wadsworth's third brigade, under Brigadier General James C. Rice, on the division's far left, became disoriented in the forest, drifted northward, and ran into Junius Daniel's North Carolina brigade at an angle, so that the Confederates poured their fire into Rice's exposed left flank. Rice's men, with Daniel's rebels on their left and Stone's brigade gone on their right, soon broke for the rear.

McCandless's brigade, dispatched by Crawford to find Wadsworth's left and connect with it, found instead the right of Ewell's corps and more Confederates than it could handle. Apparently surrounded, McCandless's men had a choice of fighting their way back to the rear or surrendering. Some did one, some the other, and Colonel McCandless himself barely made it safely to the rear. Other parts of Crawford's division, ordered to attack into the dense woods, moved forward and disappeared from sight. Some of his regiments wound up firing upon each other in the murky forest, some units were captured, and others simply wandered about, not knowing where they were.[30]

Griffin rode back to Meade's headquarters, in a vile humor after seeing his division so roughly handled, complaining bitterly that he had driven Ewell but with no flank support from Wright and Wadsworth had been forced to fall back. When he "blurted out something . . . mutinous about Warren," Grant, listening nearby in amazement, turned to Meade and asked, "Who is this General Gregg? You ought to arrest him." Meade, so often prey to bursts of anger himself, maintained his composure and said soothingly to Grant, "It's Griffin, not Gregg, and it's only his way of talking."[31]

Warren's attack was completely repulsed. The Fifth Corps gathered to lick its wounds back near the Lacy house, a "worn and somewhat dilapidated house" in the midst of "wild, sparsely cultivated land . . . fully as dismal as the forest itself," as one participant wrote. Warren had Wainwright put some of his guns in position there, and the artillery drove the pursuing Confederates back into the woods on the western side of the Lacy clearing.[32]

Ewell's and Warren's forces settled down to the maintenance of a noisy and bloody equilibrium along the turnpike, with sporadic firing and periodic small-unit charges and countercharges. Warren ordered the remainder of Crawford's division, stranded near Chewning's, back toward the Lacy farm. The battle flared up in intensity to the south, where Hancock's Second Corps, with Getty's Sixth Corps division, defended the intersection of the Brock and Orange Plank roads from A. P. Hill's corps. At about 3:30, Sedgwick, this time unsupported by Warren, fought Ewell's corps north of the turnpike, with the same lack of success as the Fifth Corps had suffered. Along the turnpike, the major fighting was over, but not the dying, as wounded soldiers lying on the field died because it was too dangerous for anyone to attempt to rescue them. Many men on both sides were burned to death when the woods caught fire and the flames engulfed those unable to move away from them.

Warren's substantive part of the battle of the Wilderness was over. There would be minor actions taken or not taken by him over the next day and a half, but his major effort had failed, and more than three thousand men had been lost. Wadsworth's division of his corps still had a leading role to play, one which would cost the division commander his life, but that would come when it was detached to serve under Hancock on the plank road. Warren, in the eyes of Grant and Meade, had been found wanting, and his star ascended no higher. He took too long, they felt, and while two of his divisions suffered severe losses, he got few of Crawford's or Robinson's units into the fighting. Still, it is hard to find Warren wrong when he wrote,

> If we had waited till the 6th Corps or two divisions of it had got up with the enemy on the road the 6th Corps was taking we should have begun the attack on Ewell's flank. I should have had Robinson's division also in supporting line, and we should have utterly crushed Ewell's corps. Hill would then have stood alone and nothing except retreat could save him. Longstreet was not up, and if General Lee had made any attempt to hold on in the Wilderness we should have finished him there.[33]

Late in the afternoon, Warren's signal officers spotted "a heavy column of the enemy's infantry moving in a field this side of the plank road and going towards Genl. Hancock." What they saw was Cadmus Wilcox's division of Hill's corps, ordered by Lee to abandon the Chewning plateau in order to rescue the beleaguered men of Harry Heth's division, just about fought out against Hancock and Getty. Grant, hearing this, reached two conclusions: that the time had come to throw a new force into the plank road struggle, striking at Hill's rear; and, since he erroneously assumed that the rebel reinforcements must have come from Ewell's corps, weakening it, that there should be a renewal of the fighting on the turnpike.[34]

The troops ordered to Hancock's assistance were Wadsworth's division plus a brigade from Robinson's division. Wadsworth, the old warrior from the Genesee Valley, chagrined at the earlier performance of his men, was anxious to have another go at the rebels, and he asked Warren for the assignment. Robinson, pleading that he had missed out on the earlier fighting, asked to accompany Wadsworth, so he was directed to bring along Henry Baxter's brigade. Wadsworth's orders were to advance toward the heavy firing going on around the Brock and plank road intersection and, if all went well, strike the enemy on his left and rear. Wadsworth's force marched off and disappeared into the woods at about 6 P.M.[35]

At the same hour Warren was directed to "renew the attack on the pike immediately. Sedgwick is ordered to renew Wright's attack at once." Sedgwick had put in motion an attack on what he supposed was Ewell's unprotected left flank, but once his men got through the woods to their objective they found well-entrenched rebels waiting for them. Sedgwick's advance was called off. Back at the Lacy house, Warren never ordered the Fifth Corps to move at all.

He conferred with Meade shortly after the six o'clock order to attack had been issued and presumably convinced him that a new advance on the turnpike would be futile, simply another needless effusion of blood.[36]

Meanwhile, Wadsworth's force struggled through the woods, ran into and dispersed rebel pickets, "and steadily pushed until it was too dark to see, when the troops halted in line of battle for the night," as Wash Roebling reported. "The resistance of the enemy had not been very severe," he said, and indeed A. P. Hill was nearly done. With Wadsworth coming in on his left and Barlow's tough Second Corps division moving on his right, Powell Hill had about reached the last extremity when he was saved by the darkness, which brought an end to organized fighting for the day. Soldiers on both sides simply lay down where they were, for moving around in the deep woods was fraught with peril.[37]

After supper that night, Lt. Morris Schaff dropped into the Lacy house, where he found Warren, Locke, and the corps' chief surgeon, trying to figure up the losses for the day. Warren's "coal-black hair," reported Schaff, "was streaming away from his finely expressive forehead, the only feature rising un-clouded above the habitual gloom of his duskily sallow face." As Schaff passed, he heard the surgeon give a figure from the data he had gathered at the corps field hospitals. "It will never do, Locke," he heard Warren say, "to make a showing of such heavy losses." The young officer noted with wonder "the earnest, mournfully solemn lines" of his corps commander.[38]

The first day's fighting in the Wilderness was a standoff, with Lee having brought Grant's movement to a halt and Grant having fought the rebels on the two roads to stalemate. One participant wrote later, "Is it not clear that a battle in the Wilderness was not expected, was not prepared for?—that Grant and his army were surprised in the very heart of the Wilderness, where Nature's ob-stacles were more to be dreaded than mortal foes?"[39] And, surely, Grant *was* surprised by Lee in the Wilderness. But Grant, in his imperturbability, simply adjusted to developments and fought the battle there. He would continue the fight there the next day, for he regarded May 5 as just the prelude to the battle.

Grant directed Meade to attack with the Army of the Potomac at 4:30 the next morning, Hancock and Wadsworth on the plank road, Warren and Sedg-wick on the turnpike, and Burnside, with his Ninth Corps, filling the gap be-tween Warren and Hancock and seizing the Chewning plateau. When Meade met with his generals, they were convinced that Burnside, notorious for his tardiness, would not be up on time, so they asked Meade to move the attacks back to six o'clock. When Meade asked Grant for a delay, suggesting that the early daylight was needed to make some troop adjustments, Grant grudgingly moved the starting time to five A.M.[40]

The Fifth Corps, less Wadsworth's division, was again deployed above and below the Orange Turnpike, with Griffin along the eastern edge of Saunders' Field. Bartlett's brigade was north of the pike this time, with Ayres below it, and Colonel Jacob B. Sweitzer's brigade in support behind the two front brigades. Crawford's division was on Griffin's left, while Robinson's, less Baxter's brigade, which was with Wadsworth, was back near the Lacy house, held in reserve. At 5:30 A.M., Warren sent off a report to Meade's headquarters, that "all Genl. Warren's troops are disposed for the assault" except the two brigades of Robinson held in reserve. "Judging by the firing the attack began as ordered at 5 P.M.[sic]. I have no reports." He mentioned also that the head of Burnside's column was just then coming into view.[41]

Meade reported to Grant at 6 A.M. that Sedgwick and Warren had been engaged since 5 A.M. This was only partially true. Sedgwick and Ewell had pitched into one another at five o'clock and reached another standoff. Warren, declining to throw his men into the same suicidal situation they had faced the morning before, fired off his guns and pushed up to the rebel entrenchments but made no attempt to assault them. "Genl. Griffin," Warren reported, "has moved up close to the enemy's position and drives him to his lines . . . I think it best to not make the final assault until the preparations are made." The final assault was not made at all. "The enemy was found to be entrenched," he said, "and but little impression could be made." Headquarters tried to make the best of the situation: at 6 A.M. Humphreys sent word to Warren that Meade "desires that you will throw your pickets and skirmishers well out to the front."[42]

Meade and Grant were concerned at this time that Ewell be kept engaged, or at least worried about being engaged. At 7:15 Meade told Warren it was "of the utmost importance that your attack should be pressed with the utmost vigor. Spare ammunition and use the bayonet." Down on the Orange Plank Road, Hancock, with assistance from Wadsworth, was driving Hill's corps back in what was fast turning into a rout, and the Union commanders did not want reinforcements coming to Hill from the turnpike. Warren, however, noted no change in circumstances on the turnpike to cause him to modify his course, so he continued firing his artillery and occasionally feigning an advance by skirmishers.[43]

As it developed, as Hill's troops streamed to the rear in defeat while Union regimental and brigade leaders tried to sort out and regroup their victorious units, James Longstreet's long-awaited corps arrived on the plank road. Smashing into the unsuspecting Federals, Longstreet's men quickly redressed the balance of power on the plank road. A while later, using an unfinished railroad cut which gave them unseen access to Hancock's left flank, the rebels sent the Second Corps and its auxiliaries reeling back to their defensive position along the Brock Road. In the course of this struggle the gallant James Wadsworth was mortally wounded, and Cutler's brigade sent pelting back up the road toward the Lacy house in disarray. As the Confederates prepared another assault, which they hoped would seal the defeat of their northern adversaries, Longstreet was severely wounded by fire from his own men and the planned attack was postponed.[44]

While this drama was playing out along the plank road, the antagonists near the turnpike settled down to watchful waiting. In mid-morning, Meade directed that Warren's and Sedgwick's "attacks" be suspended. "You will throw up defensive works to enable you to hold your position with the fewest possible number of men—and report at once what number of men you will have disposable for an attack upon Hancock's right." [45]

Eventually it was Burnside's Ninth Corps which was supposed to make the attack on the enemy opposite Hancock's right. The Ninth Corps, however, after a leisurely scramble through the forest, made a desultory and unsuccessful attack and then entrenched. Hancock was essentially left to fend for himself, which he was well able to do. Late in the afternoon, Lee ordered a direct assault upon Hancock's Brock Road defenses. After a brief success when the felled trees in the works caught fire—a breach in the line which caused a panicky Meade to order and then recall reinforcements from Warren—Lee's attack failed.

There was one last flare-up of fighting that day, just as darkness was beginning to settle upon the Wilderness. A sudden and unexpected attack upon the right flank of the Sixth Corps gave the rebels a solid little victory at the far northern edge of the field. John Sedgwick, however, was soon able, with the assistance of the impending night, to restore order on his right.

On the Fifth Corps front, as darkness fell on the army's third night in the Wilderness, Warren's engineers had thrown up strong defenses of log and earth breastworks. The works were virtually impregnable, but so were those of the Confederates down the road. The two armies had achieved stalemate in the dark forest, and Grant knew that he would not maneuver Lee into a decisive battle there. Early the next day, May 7, Grant made up his mind to extricate the Army of the Potomac from its Wilderness lines and move away after darkness fell that night. Surreptitious preparations for the movement were carried on throughout the day, and Gouverneur Warren wrote to his brother Will, assuring him that "I am very well" and bemoaning the "great loss" of Wadsworth and Alexander Hays of the Second Corps.[46]

BLOODY SPOTSYLVANIA

*I*N THE EARLY AFTERNOON OF MAY 7, 1864, Meade's headquarters, after getting the word from the lieutenant general, issued orders for a movement southeast from the stalemated battlefield along the turnpike and the Brock Road. The march was to begin when darkness fell, with the Fifth Corps in the advance.[1]

Pulling away undetected from a front with the enemy just a short distance away was a tricky business, to be handled with great discretion. It was essential to the plan worked out in Grant's mind that he reach Spotsylvania Court House before the Confederates did, in order to place his army between Lee and Richmond, forcing Lee to a fight on what would presumably be unfavorable terms for the rebels. While Grant's army lay in place in the Wilderness the Confederates were uncertain whether it would offer further battle where it was, retreat across the Rapidan, backtrack toward Fredericksburg, or move east and south, toward Spotsylvania. The very uncertainty of his next movement in Lee's mind was an element of strength to Grant.

The order of march called for the Fifth Corps to lead the way south, passing behind the Second Corps, which would then follow it on the Brock Road, while the Sixth and Ninth corps took a more indirect route, moving east through Chancellorsville and then south along a road called the Piney Branch Church Road. The Sixth Corps should arrive at Spotsylvania Court House shortly after Warren.

Warren started his corps on the march at about 8:30 P.M., as directed, with Robinson's division in the van, followed successively by Griffin, the Fourth Division (now under Cutler after Wadsworth's demise), and Crawford. The men silently left their lines, marched eastward along the turnpike past Wilderness Tavern to the Brock Road, and then turned right onto that southbound roadway. "The night was very dark, no moonlight," recorded Roebling. The first of many obstacles was encountered when the marchers discovered the men of the Second Corps lying in the road behind their entrenchments, forcing the Fifth Corps soldiers moving behind them into the mud off the road, "causing the men to straggle very much."[2]

A slight detour around the sleeping Second Corps soldiers would prove to be the least of the delays afflicting Warren and his men the night of May 7–8. At one point a driverless artillery team followed by fifty or sixty pack mules careened down the road in a bizarre cavalcade, the panicky animals stampeding back to the rear of the column. Fortunately, their route was on the other side of the road from where the Second Corps was sleeping. "The road, which was not wide . . . , was literally jammed with troops moving one step at a time," recorded Wainwright. "Never before did I see such slow progress made," he said, "certainly not over half a mile an hour, if that." Another participant wrote, "This was one of the most fatiguing marches of the campaign, the night being intensely dark and the roads in an almost impassable condition."[3] Porter Farley, of the 140th New York, said, "Our progress during the night was slow; halt after halt was made, and yet none long enough to admit of any sleep. All night we kept it up—marching a little way then halting, then marching on again."[4]

At about 10:30 P.M., the head of Robinson's division encountered General Meade's mounted provost guard clogging the intersection of the Brock and Orange Plank roads, bringing the march to a halt. Many of the men took the opportunity to catch a brief bit of sleep. Robinson, after waiting some fifteen or twenty minutes for Warren, got Grant and Meade and their staffs to move forward toward Todd's Tavern, thus permitting the Fifth Corps to resume its march at about midnight.[5]

Further trouble lay ahead. Sheridan, the new cavalry leader, had been ordered to clear the road of rebel cavalry, but he had failed to do so. As the Fifth Corps made its way slowly down the Brock Road, Fitzhugh Lee's horsemen were still in a blocking position south of Todd's Tavern, felling trees across the road to slow the Union advance. Meade, arriving at Todd's Tavern, found David Gregg's cavalry division camped there, with Wesley Merritt's cavalrymen in camp about a mile further on, both waiting to hear from Sheridan what they were to do. Meade angrily dictated orders directly to the two division commanders, bypassing the absent Sheridan, ordering Merritt to clear the Brock Road for the Fifth Corps advance and Gregg to move out westward. "It is of the utmost importance that not the slightest delay occur in your opening the Brock road beyond Spotsylvania Court-House," Meade told Merritt, "as an infantry corps is now on its way to occupy that place."[6]

The head of Warren's column reached Todd's Tavern at 1 A.M., and some additional time was lost in getting Gregg's cavalry out of the way. When the Fifth Corps reached Merritt's encampment a couple of hours later, they found that the cavalry leader had just received the order from Meade directing him to clear the way. At 3:30, Merritt's men moved out, and the Fifth Corps divisions camped along the side of the road, waiting to learn that the road was clear. Some men took the opportunity to sleep, while others lit fires for cooking breakfast. At about this time Wainwright, the corps artillery commander, arrived on the scene. "When I reached General Warren, who had halted Robinson's division about a mile and a half beyond the Tavern," he sniffed, "I found them all quietly eating their breakfast, waiting for Merritt to open the way with his cavalry." Since this was what they had been ordered by Meade to do, it is hard to see why Wainwright was so disapproving, but he went on to say that he "felt chagrined; . . . I certainly thought then that both Warren and Meade were not pushing matters as much as they ought." [7]

Whether the officious artilleryman expressed himself on the subject to Warren he does not say, but he did remark that "the General appeared decidedly crusty this morning," and then added, disingenuously, "Why I do not know." Warren, with Meade and Grant urging him to hurry, with the road narrow, dark, and obscure, and with the way blocked by obstacles of all sorts, including the cavalry of two armies, could hardly have been in the mood for carping about the obvious by a self-important subordinate. [8]

At 5 A.M., Warren reported that Merritt had been skirmishing about a mile in front of him "for some time," but Warren did not know the result of it. He was "aware of the importance of getting on to Spotsylvania Court-House as soon as may be," and he suggested that if Merritt was unable to clear the road he should make way for the infantry. Finally, well after six, Merritt conceded that Warren could do a better job of pushing the rebels, so he yielded to the Fifth Corps. [9]

Warren sent Robinson's division ahead, with two batteries, while ordering Wainwright to stay behind and send up other batteries as needed. (Wainwright got his nose out of joint with this order: "This I did not consider my business; it was for me to make arrangements to have the batteries brought up as needed, but my own place at the opening of a fight is undoubtedly alongside of the corps commander." Perhaps, though, Warren did not want him alongside.) Robinson quickly drove the rebel horse out of the way, and Warren reported that "the opposition to us amounts to nothing as yet; we are advancing steadily." He added, "If there is nothing but cavalry, we shall scarcely halt, if our troops can be made to move, but they are exceedingly hesitating, I think." [10]

Robinson's leading brigade emerged from the woods at 8:30 A.M., stepping out into the open fields of Alsop's farm, where the Brock Road forked into two tracks which ran parallel for about a mile before coming back together alongside a place called the Spindle farm. Warren sent Robinson's division out the eastern Brock Road fork and Griffin, when he arrived on the scene, out the western fork. The men of the Fifth Corps, after a full day's activity on May 7 followed by an enervating night march, were not in good shape.

"The men were very much blown," wrote one regimental commander, and Roebling reported them "very much hurried and excited . . . ; the tendency to stampede was so great that Gen. Warren himself had to go to the front of the leading brigade." [11]

Warren, resplendent in his dress uniform with the yellow sash, had a close call at this point. Morris Schaff, of his staff, standing right behind the general, heard "the ping of a passing shot." When two more shots came from the same direction, each coming closer and after an interval equivalent to the time needed to reload, Schaff said, "General, that man is getting the range on you." Warren said nothing but started to move to the right, when the next shot killed his horse. [12]

The Fifth Corps infantrymen pushed wearily forward, and Fitz Lee's cavalry fell back to a low ridge south of the Spindle farm, where they started constructing fieldworks. This ridge enjoyed the euphonious name of Laurel Hill, but it would, over the next several days, take on a dark and ugly meaning to the men of the Fifth Corps.

While the Army of the Potomac was on the move, the enemy was not idle. After the severe wound suffered by Longstreet, Lee had settled on Richard H. Anderson of South Carolina to assume command of the First Corps. He told Anderson to pull back out of line and, on the morning of the 8th, march his new corps to Spotsylvania Court House. When Anderson pulled his corps back, however, between the burning woods and the stench of dead bodies from the Wilderness fighting, he was unable to find any suitable place for his troops to bivouac. As a result, rather than stopping, he continued his troops on the march, toward Spotsylvania. Without this happenstance, Warren's men would have found only cavalry between themselves and the courthouse; as it was, when Fitzhugh Lee's horsemen retired, they were replaced by Longstreet's veteran foot soldiers. At Laurel Hill.

Robinson's leading brigade, commanded by Colonel Peter Lyle, prepared to advance, although Robinson preferred to wait until more of his division was up. Warren rode up to him and, after about fifteen minutes waiting, watching the rude breastworks going up on the rebel line, impatiently ordered him forward with the men available, the five regiments of Lyle's brigade and the Fourth Maryland, saying, "We must drive them from there, or they will get some artillery in position." The Federal officers assumed that they were just facing cavalry, and Warren wanted to drive the Confederate horsemen away before they could get entrenched. Robinson gave the order to Lyle to attack. [13]

Lyle's men moved ahead, with some difficulty because of small gullies which broke up their formation. Two sharp volleys from Joseph B. Kershaw's South Carolinians staggered the tired Federals, and it became clear that they were now facing not dismounted cavalry but infantry. Lyle's men recoiled from the foot of the hill and then fled back to the trees in their rear.

Warren had ridden back to the Alsop house, to see where Robinson's other brigades were. When Richard Coulter's brigade and Andrew Denison's Maryland Brigade came on the scene, Warren hurried them forward to the front. To the Seventh Maryland, he shouted, "Never mind cannon! Never mind bullets! Press on and clear this road. It's the only way to get your rations." Without pausing, the two brigades, led by Robinson and Denison, moved to the attack. Blasted by both artillery and musket fire, they were soon halted. General Robinson was shot from his horse, severely wounded in the knee, and Denison was downed as well. The attackers turned and fled the four hundred yards across the clearing, back to the trees.[14]

On Robinson's right, Bartlett's brigade of Griffin's division wearily moved forward to follow up the attack, but it was subjected to the same withering fire which had repulsed Robinson's men and soon fell back, although a number of men of the Eighty-Third Pennsylvania managed to climb the Confederate field-works before being killed or captured. As Bartlett's men retired, Griffin's remaining brigades under Ayres and Sweitzer attempted the assault, but they were equally unsuccessful.[15]

Warren, appalled at the devastation visited upon his corps, rode onto the field and seized the ragged flag of one of the fleeing regiments in an effort to inspirit the troops. He was able to rally enough men around a section of the Fourth United States Artillery to repel a Confederate counterattack, but there was no hiding the fact that the Fifth Corps had suffered a major defeat. Roebling wrote that "the enemy's fire was not heavy enough to justify the breaking of the men, it was chiefly owing to their being excited, somewhat scared, and hurried entirely too much." Warren reported that "General Robinson's troops fought with reluctance," as did part of Griffin's command. With Robinson out of action, his division was subsequently broken up, Lyle's brigade going to Cutler's division, Coulter's to Crawford, and the Maryland Brigade coming under the direct supervision of the corps commander.[16]

In the meantime, Crawford and Cutler arrived on the field, and their divisions were moved to the left and right, respectively, of Griffin's division, located at the juncture of the two forks of the Brock Road. They took their turns as attackers, with no more success than the other two Fifth Corps divisions. Cutler's men made a gallant effort but were driven back, while Crawford's made hardly any headway after the division commander was stunned by a tree limb knocked down by an artillery shell. Three brigades of Horatio Wright's Sixth Corps division arrived, in response to Warren's request for help, and Warren met them at the fork near Alsop's farm "in a very excitable state."[17]

At noon Meade, having just received Warren's 10:15 dispatch (on which he noted, "I hardly think Longstreet is yet at Spotsylvania"), sent back a dispatch urging the Fifth Corps to "attack vigorously." But Gouverneur Warren was through for the time being. At 12:30 P.M., he sat down and wrote out another message to Meade, stating, "I have again suffered heavily, especially in stragglers . . . I have lost no prisoners; the men simply straggle back into the woods fatigued and wounded. I have done my best, but with the force I now have I cannot attack again." He asked for troops from Sedgwick and Hancock to be brought up. He said he had fought at least two of Longstreet's divisions. "My position is good enough if I am not attacked in some unprepared point on my flanks. I incline to think, though, that if I let the enemy alone he will me. I cannot gain Spotsylvania Court-House with what force I have." He concluded by saying, "I am out of ammunition," then added in a postscript, "I dare not fall back, for then I shall disclose my feeling of weakness."[18]

Warren's performance on the morning of May 8, for which he was justly criticized, was very much out of character for him. The general who believed in careful preparation, who had called off an attack at Mine Run rather than charge into a suicidal situation, who had resisted for as long as he could making an assault along the Orange Turnpike when his divisions were not in place, threw his brigades in piecemeal, unsupported attacks against the rebel fieldworks on Laurel Hill.

His reasons for doing so are not known but can be guessed at. He was certainly very tired, after the stress of the all-night march from the turnpike, with all the obstacles overcome along the way, and perhaps this fatigue affected his thought processes. (His rambling, unfocused dispatches of that morning would seem to confirm this.) During the three days in the Wilderness, with his headquarters so close to those of Grant and Meade, Warren undoubtedly heard the muttering of their staff members, criticizing his efforts and those of his corps, implying that they had not the stomach for Ulysses Grant's style of warfare, whispering that he was not up to the job. Through the night of May 7–8 he had Meade after him to get through to Spotsylvania Court House before the Confederates. So he moved his corps ahead with all the speed it could muster when he took over the lead from Merritt's horsemen, and he pitched into the rebels with Robinson's brigades as soon as he could get them going. At least with Lyle's brigade and probably with Coulter's and the Maryland Brigade, Warren thought he was attacking dismounted cavalry. He continued sporadic assaults after he knew that Confederate infantry was opposite him, when his other divisions became available, perhaps because he knew it had been said that he did not get all his men into the fight on the turnpike on May 5. Numerous observers, from Wainwright to the men of the Fifteenth New Jersey, commented on Warren's agitated or irritable manner that morning, so it can safely be said that he was not himself on the morning of May 8 at Laurel Hill.[19]

Warren perked up a little later. At 1:30, Meade sent him word that John Sedgwick's whole corps would join him for an attack and that "it is of the utmost importance the attack of yourself and Sedgwick should be made with vigor and without delay." At two o'clock, Humphreys told Warren that ammunition was on the way, and at the same time Warren notified Meade that "I will do my best to smash Longstreet up when General Sedgwick comes." He said he no longer feared an attack because "the rebels are as tired out as we are." [20]

Meade, however, goaded by Grant, wanted another attack to be made by the Fifth Corps early that afternoon, in conjunction with the Sixth Corps. He went to see Warren and told him to "cooperate with Sedgwick and see what can be done." "General Meade," responded Warren, wearied and perhaps unnerved by the events of the morning, "I'll be damned if I'll cooperate with Sedgwick or anybody else. You are the commander of this army and can give your orders and I will obey them; or you can put Sedgwick in command and he can give the orders and I will obey them; or you can put me in command and I will give the orders and Sedgwick will obey them; but I'll be God damned if I'll cooperate with General Sedgwick or anybody else." Meade, who had just come from an angry shouting match with Sheridan, chose to let this tirade pass.[21]

The afternoon passed by as Sedgwick cautiously moved his troops into position, while the Confederates on Laurel Hill strengthened and reinforced their defenses. Officers and men alike were moving and thinking at half-speed, all of them sorely in need of rest after the strain, the fighting, and the lack of sleep of the last days, but Grant was insistent upon another attack and seemed angered by the delay. After six o'clock, a line of battle was ready, and Meade ordered the advance. Warren and Sedgwick had six divisions to Anderson's two, but the well-constructed fieldworks on Laurel Hill served as a great equalizer. The Sixth Corps units charged ahead but were quickly brought to a halt by the deadly fire of the enemy. Crawford's Pennsylvania Reserves made some progress in getting around Anderson's right flank, only to run head-on into the advance of Ewell's corps, arriving on the field at exactly the right time to have the maximum effect upon the fighting. After suffering substantial losses, Crawford's men fell back.

The fighting for May 8 was finished. At nine o'clock, Warren wrote out one last almost incoherent message to Meade, concluding, "I am so sleepy I can hardly write intelligently." Then he was finally able to lay his weary head down.[22]

At 6:30 A.M., Meade resolved his problem of getting Sedgwick and Warren to "cooperate." He notified Sedgwick (and Warren) that "in any combined operation on the left by both the Fifth and Sixth Corps," Sedgwick, the senior, was to be in command. An hour later Sedgwick, meeting Roebling in the breastworks, said to him, "Just tell General Warren to go on and command his own corps as usual. I have perfect confidence that he will do what is right, and knows what to do with his corps as well as I do."[23]

The Fifth Corps maintained its position on May 9, while its members tried to keep out of the sights of Confederate sharpshooters. Sedgwick, however, was not so fortunate. At about 9:30 in the morning, just after chiding some of his men for trying to dodge enemy bullets and saying, "Why, man, they couldn't hit an elephant here at this distance," Sedgwick was hit and killed by a sharp-shooter's bullet just below his left eye. The men of the Sixth Corps, and the rest of the army, mourned their beloved "Uncle John," and Meade named Horatio Wright to the corps command.[24]

At just about the time Sedgwick was killed, Gouverneur Warren was writing a long letter to his friend Andrew Humphreys, marked "confidential," with his opinions on the conduct of the army, the operations of the day before, and his fellow corps commanders. Warren said,

> I would venture to suggest an opinion as regards future operations of the fol-lowing import . . . It is . . . to make a move with the whole army in two or three columns towards some *desirable point* and disregard every other consideration as far as possible. That is, not to hazard this main movement and not make a change next day to meet any minor consideration. For instance if we yesterday had moved according to the programme of the Genl Orders for the day Genl Sedgwick would have been so close to me that we should have undoubtedly whipped Longstreet and all of Ewell that came to his support.
>
> As it was the delays in halting Genl Sedgwick made his arrival here too late . . .
>
> I fought yesterday with all the rapidity possible, and know I could have kept going if supports had been close by, and when Genl Sedgwick came I urged my plan, which he took time to have explained and adopt. And here I would venture another opinion that Genl Meade should accompany the column moving to *the desirable* point as I was yesterday. Whether he thinks I am ca-pable or not, my want of rank makes me incompetent when two corps come together, and I don't think our other two corps commanders are capable. Genl S[edgwick] does nothing of himself. I have lost confidence in Genl H[ancock]'s capabilities to do it from his failing with all the force he had in our first and second days battles, especially on the latter day when he gave to Genl Wadsworth the command of the column of attack. I think if he had moved out with his whole command directing near the head in person he could have won.[25]

Before this epistle got into circulation, Warren obviously received the news of Sedgwick's death, so he carefully folded it up and put it away.

Later that morning, Warren told Wainwright to stay with the artillery re-serve: "I want you to remain here so that when I want any batteries I can send for them." The artillery commander treated this simple directive as a slur on his manhood or his parentage. "I have been feeling ugly all day" as a result, Wainwright told his diary. "I cannot understand this . . . I do not know how to act in the matter . . . I do not know whether it would be best to demand an ex-planation now or to wait patiently. I certainly cannot and will not occupy any such position longer than is necessary, but if things are to go on in this way will ask to be assigned somewhere else, so soon as this campaign is over." Another problem Warren did not need was awaiting him in the outraged person of the touchy New Yorker.[26]

During the afternoon Grant moved Hancock's corps from Todd's Tavern to a crossing of the Po River, west of the Confederate line, in an effort to hit the enemy's left flank. A second crossing of the little river was required to reach the rebel flank, and Hancock was unable to accomplish this before dark. In the meantime, Meade had ordered Warren to make a demonstration toward Laurel Hill to prevent Lee from sending troops from there to the Po crossing. Crawford moved forward and was promptly pushed back, evidencing that Laurel Hill was still strongly held by Anderson's corps.[27]

Lee took advantage of the nighttime to send Mahone's division from the Third Corps, temporarily under Jubal Early (due to A. P. Hill's illness), to contest Hancock's crossing, and he sent Heth's division to cross the Po below Hancock and surprise him on his right flank. Grant had allowed Sheridan to take the Union cavalry off on a raid toward Richmond, so he had no information about Lee's movements other than what his infantry units could see. The movement of the Second Corps across the Po was an ill-planned, ill-advised operation, and it was endangered by Grant's lack of knowledge of his opponent's movements.

The plan for the morning of May 10 was for the Second Corps to move across the Po and smash the left flank of the Confederate army while the Fifth and Sixth corps attacked the weakened enemy in their fronts. Hancock, however, was unable to get across the Po because of the dug-in resistance of Mahone's division, while Heth's movement on the Second Corps' right presented an unexpected jeopardy. While this scenario played out across the river, Warren directed various probing efforts against the enemy in his front. These probes merely confirmed the continuing strength of the Laurel Hill defenses, while costing a few hundred Fifth Corps casualties.

In mid-morning, Grant shifted gears. Recognizing that Hancock was getting nowhere on the enemy's left flank, Grant figured that Lee must surely be weakening his line somewhere to strengthen it on the left. He decided to liquidate Hancock's movement, pulling two of the three divisions back to the main Union line (leaving Barlow's division to disguise the pullback), and then throw Hancock's two divisions and the Fifth Corps against a presumably weakened Laurel Hill. At 10 A.M., Meade sent Warren word of this new plan, with the attack "on the enemy in your front" scheduled for 5 P.M. Hancock, he added, "will by virtue of seniority have the command of the combined operations." [28]

John Gibbon's division was the first of the Second Corps units to fall into line on the right of the Fifth Corps. Warren, for some reason, had it in his mind that an attack should be made earlier than the one Grant had ordered. Gibbon and Warren moved through the woods to a place where they could, they hoped, examine "the proposed place of attack." Gibbon did not like the looks of it—a forest of dead cedar trees, "their stiff ragged arms standing out like so many bayonets, in such a way that a movement by a line of battle . . .was entirely out of the question." He and Warren then rode to Meade's headquarters, where Gibbon stated his objections. Meade, though, "seemed to rely wholly upon Warren's judgment in the matter" and Warren "seemed bent upon the attack."[29]

Meade sent word to Grant at 3:30 that Warren, because of some progress and the taking of some prisoners, "indicates the enemy were shaky." Accordingly, "I have ordered him to attack at once." Word went out to Hancock, who had recrossed the Po to help Barlow extricate his threatened division, that "the opportunity for attack immediately is reported to be so favorable by General Warren" that an attack had been ordered, with Gibbon participating. Whatever Warren saw must have been a chimera; the attack was made and "repulsed with heavy loss; the enemy were well-entrenched with plenty of Artillery in position, enfilading both Cutler's and Crawford's line." Gibbon's men "made a feasible effort to get through the woods and stem the storm of bullets hurled against them, then gave it up." General James C. Rice, the commander of Cutler's Second Brigade, was killed in the failed assault.[30]

During the assault the men of the Sixth Wisconsin were lying flat on the ground under the brow of a hill less than two hundred feet from the rebel works. Suddenly they saw Warren and Sprigg Carroll, commander of a brigade in Gibbon's division, running up the hill to get a closer look at their objective. Colonel Rufus Dawes, the regimental commander, said, "If Genl Warren's head had appeared over the hill he would certainly have been shot at once." Dawes jumped up, grabbed at Warren's yellow sash, and "fairly jerked him backward." It was a "ludicrous affair," Dawes said, "and we all laughed at it afterward," but he was still convinced that he had saved his corps commander's life.[31]

This first assault, of course, was not Grant's planned attack, which would proceed as scheduled, no matter what the repulse of Warren's attack may have demonstrated. Roebling noted that "this preliminary attack showed that the enemy was all set for us, and that the subsequent attack would have but little chance." Nevertheless, though the second attempt was moved back to 6:30, then 6:45, it was duly made. Gibbon's division and one brigade of David Birney's joined the Fifth Corps in another forlorn-hope assault on Laurel Hill. By this time, none of the attackers, picking their way through the bodies of those who had fallen earlier, had much enthusiasm for the effort.

Neither Gibbon's nor Griffin's division made much of an attempt to advance. J. H. Hobart Ward's brigade, of Birney's division, actually managed to break the Confederate line, but those who did it were either shot or captured, for there was no support. Warren attempted to rally Crawford's men personally, waving

Spotsylvania

the corps flag, when they came running back. "The little general looked gallant enough at any rate," Wainwright wrote, "mounted on a great tall white horse, in full uniform, sash and all, and with the flag in his hand." [32] It was no use; the attack was a dismal failure, serving only to augment the roll of dead and wounded in the Army of the Potomac.

Warren's part in the affair drew a snide comment from Charles Dana, reporting to Stanton, saying, "I witnessed it in Warren's front, where it was executed with the caution and absence of comprehensive *ensemble* which seem to characterize that officer." Even Grant's aide, Adam Badeau, when he came to write the military history of his patron, which was none too complimentary of Warren, commented that "this criticism appears to me too severe." [33]

Warren did unknowingly make amends to his chief of artillery, when, late in the day, he directed Wainwright to "bring" a battery to the front. Wainwright immediately complied and, reaching the front, visited all his batteries wherever they were. Even though "the compliment of calling upon me when he was in trouble" did not atone for "the insult" of leaving him in the rear for two days, Wainwright said, "From Warren's manner and all, I do not believe he meant it as an insult in any way." Still, the artilleryman thought he should "remonstrate with him . . . but feared it would tend to make him obstinate, and my position worse than ever." [34]

There was little activity on May 11; "one day fighting and then a day of rest seems to be the new order," commented Wainwright. It was on this day that Grant sent his famous dispatch to Washington, proposing "to fight it out on this line if it takes all summer." In the afternoon, Grant directed Meade to move the Second Corps under cover of darkness far to the left, to attack the next morning in conjunction with Burnside's Ninth Corps a Confederate salient known from its shape as "the Mule Shoe." "Warren and Wright," Grant said, "should hold their corps as close to the enemy as possible to take advantage of any diversion caused by this attack, and to push in if the opportunity presents itself." [35]

The fighting of the next day, May 12, is the most renowned of the Spotsylvania campaign—the assault by the massed Second Corps early in the morning, appearing out of the fog to overrun the Confederate works at the salient, capturing three thousand prisoners including two generals and twenty guns, the counterattack by Gordon which pushed the disorganized Federals back over the breastworks, the savage fighting which lasted all day and into the evening at what came to be called the "Bloody Angle," the trees cut down by the unrelenting gunfire, and the bodies of the killed and wounded piling up on either side of the breastworks. The initial overwhelming Union victory turned by the end of the day into stalemate.

While Hancock's troops battled at the head of the salient, and the Ninth Corps made ineffectual lunges at the eastern side, efforts were made by Grant and Meade to bring the Fifth and Sixth corps into the struggle. At 5 A.M., Warren notified his division commanders of Hancock's success and instructed them to "have your command in readiness to advance, if possible." An hour later Meade told Warren to "keep up as threatening an attitude as possible to keep the enemy in your front. Wright must attack and you may have to." At 6:15, Warren reported that his artillery was firing and his skirmishers had been ordered to push their lines forward wherever possible.[36]

At 7:30, Meade told Warren that Wright and the Sixth Corps needed support. "Your attack will in a measure relieve him," he said. A half hour later, Meade, under intense pressure from Grant to have attacks made all along the front, was a bit more direct: "Attack immediately with all the force you can, and be prepared to follow up any success with the rest of your force." Warren read this, then told the commanding general, "Your order to attack immediately with my whole force leaves me no time to attack the key points first," but, he said, "Your orders have been issued and reiterated." He then added, pointedly, "It does not take many men from the enemy to hold the intrenchments in my front."[37]

Warren, of course, knew from the bitter experience of previous assaults on the defensive works erected on Laurel Hill that there was no way of capturing the strong point, and the men in his corps knew it too. His units made sporadic efforts to move forward, but there was no all-out push. Roebling noted that the attack was "quickly repulsed as was anticipated." By the fourth or fifth attempt at Laurel Hill, he said, "it is not a matter of surprise that they had lost all spirit for that kind of work." Shortly after nine, Warren sent word that "I cannot advance my men farther at present." Moments later, he reported, "My left cannot advance without a most destructive enfilade fire . . . My right is close up to the enemy's works and ordered to assault. The enemy's line here appears to be strongly held. It is his *point-d'appui* if he throws back his right."[38]

At 9:15, Warren received another message from headquarters (it may have been the French that got to Meade this time): "The order of the major-general commanding is peremptory that you attack at once at all hazards with your whole force, if necessary." A few minutes later, he got a "Dear Warren" note signed by "Your friend, A.A. Humphreys," who could see and hear the reactions around Meade's headquarters, and who knew how thin the ice beneath Warren was becoming: "Don't hesitate to attack with the bayonet. Meade has assumed the responsibility, and will take the consequences." Warren knew that the consequences would in actuality be taken by the men being sent to charge an impregnable position, but he now had no choice. To his division commanders he sent word that the order to attack was peremptory and must be obeyed. "Do it," he told them.[39]

So they did it. All three division commanders got their men up once again, pointed them toward Laurel Hill once again, and again ordered them forward. The attacks were made with a surprising amount of vigor, considering the circumstances—the Confederates called them "two violent assaults" in the official corps diary—but they were driven back with the predictable slaughter. By the time the results of the attacks had gotten back to corps headquarters, Humphreys was there, dispatched by Meade to watch Warren. Humphreys recognized the futility of further assaults and called them off. Meade, however, had his blood up by now, and he sent a message to Grant, saying, "Warren seems reluctant to attack." Grant promptly replied, "If Warren fails to attack promptly, send Humphreys to command his corps, and relieve him." [40]

When Andrew Humphreys called off the Fifth Corps attack, headquarters finally got the idea that there was no profit in continually attacking the Confederate entrenchments on Laurel Hill. Instead, Warren was directed to hold his line with one division and send the other two to support the other corps. Cutler's was sent to the Sixth Corps, where it was supposed to be used to bolster a column of attack. Wright, however, simply used it to relieve his own troops and made no attack. Warren was not the only corps commander to give his own reading to attack orders on May 12. Griffin's division was sent to Hancock, and Warren had nothing more to do that day but watch his line.

Humphreys' presence and concurrence in Warren's opinion provided cover for the Fifth Corps commander, but it had been a close call. Worse, Grant had been fully prepared to sack him, as had Meade. Whether Humphreys knew just how close they had come to relieving Warren and communicated that to his friend is not known; there appears no evidence in Warren's correspondence that he knew just how near he had come to disaster.[41]

Whether Warren knew it or not, however, the idea had certainly been planted in Grant's brain, and it would stay there. "I feel sorry to be obliged to send such an order in regard to Warren," Grant supposedly said, to a member of his staff. He spoke of the high regard he had formerly had for Warren, even as a successor to Meade, but, he went on, "I began to feel, after his want of vigor in assaulting on the eighth, that he was not as efficient as I had believed, and his delay in attacking and the feeble character of his assaults today confirm me in my apprehensions." [42]

This assessment was ironic. On the eighth, Warren *had* acted vigorously, perhaps too much so, in his initial assaults; he pushed ahead with attacks before his whole corps was up, and he was stymied by troops who were too tired to accomplish what he wanted them to do. On May 12, Grant was the one who was wrong, insisting upon repeated suicidal charges against a position which clearly could not be taken. Warren tried to explain the situation but, when given no further leeway, made the assault he was ordered to make. That it was once more bloodily repulsed simply confirmed what Warren had tried to tell his superiors. Unfortunately, it mattered not that Warren may have been right and Grant wrong. Grant was the commanding general, and he had marked out Gouverneur Warren as a reluctant warrior. Warren would one day pay the price for that conclusion.

CHAPTER FIFTEEN

AROUND LEE'S RIGHT

THE FIGHTING AROUND SPOTSYLVANIA COURT HOUSE continued for another week after the day and night of the "Bloody Angle." While it did not match the sustained carnage of May 12, the combat reflected Grant's continuing belief that he could flank Lee out of his position and force a battle outside the rebel defensive works.

On May 13, the armies rested. The Confederates had pulled back in the early morning hours from the salient to a new line constructed about two miles in the rear, and the Union army spent the morning looking for them. Warren wrote to Emily that "I am yet very well," and "yesterday was a fearful day of battle." He sent Meade an unsolicited (and probably unappreciated) suggestion for crossing the Po again and perhaps flushing Lee out for a fight. Wainwright groused in his diary that "I have found no previous commander who did not shew me more consideration." And Meade ordered a night movement by the Fifth Corps all the way around the army, to take up position on the left of the Ninth Corps and stage an assault at 4 A.M., "if practicable."[1]

According to Roebling, "we were expected to march all night, get into position on the left of Burnside's in an unknown country, in the midst of an Egyptian darkness, up to our knees in the mud, and assault the enemy's position which we had never seen, at 4 o'clock in the morning, in conjunction with the 9th Corps who had been whipped the day before, and felt in fine spirits for such work." After a night march Warren described as "one to be remembered by all my Corps as one of horror among the horrible ones," confounded by heavy rain, intense darkness, mud, floods, and swamps, he arrived at the designated spot with only about a thousand weary men. Other thousands had fallen by the wayside through sheer exhaustion. "I have not more with me than would make a good skirmish line for the corps," he reported to Meade at 4 A.M., and at 6:30 he said his men were not "in condition to fight to advantage." The planned attack was called off, and the day was occupied in capturing, losing, and retaking a single hill on the Myers farm.[2]

On May 18 the Second Corps was moved around to the right for an attack with Wright's corps against Lee's left, the last major engagement of the Spotsylvania campaign. The Fifth Corps was expected to participate only with an artillery barrage. Before long Colonel Wainwright was complaining about a waste of ammunition, "but Warren repeatedly ordered me to fire." Wainwright sent word to the army's artillery commander, General Henry J. Hunt, who "managed to make Warren less exacting on this point." The Second and Sixth corps' attack, like so many others before it, went nowhere.[3]

On May 19, Lee sent Ewell's corps on a reconnaissance in force to determine where the Union right was located, since there were clear indications that Grant was preparing to move to his left again. Around four o'clock in the afternoon, Ramseur's brigade of Rodes's division collided with Federal heavy artillerymen under Colonel J. Howard Kitching, who was soon supported by additional heavy artillery from the division of General Robert O. Tyler. The "heavies" were untrained in infantry tactics, and most were undergoing their first combat. Nevertheless, stiffened by the more experienced Maryland Brigade of the Fifth Corps, sent over by Warren when he learned of the fighting, they held their own and eventually sent Ewell's veterans back across the Ny River. The fighting was somewhat confused, but the good conduct of the "heavies" was gratifying to the Union high command. "It was the enemy's best troops," Warren said, "and what we supposed were our worst ones."[4]

Warren wrote that day to Emily, complaining about the irregularity of mail delivery, and said, "The intense mental anxiety I have to occasionally endure is very trying indeed but having made up my line of duty I try to await the result of our efforts resignedly for better or for worse." A corps commander "resignedly" waiting to see what happened was probably not what Grant had in mind for his movements; this was an early sign of the mental strain taking its toll on Warren.[5]

On May 21, Hancock's Second Corps was able to break away from its position undetected and move around far to the left, beyond Guinea Station and the Mattaponi River. Warren followed, and the horrors of Spotsylvania Court House were left behind. The Fifth Corps suffered casualties from May 8 to 21 totaling 4,480 second in number of the four Union corps to those of the Second, which had losses of 6,642 men. What lay ahead, Warren's men knew, could not be pleasant, but they felt that nothing could be worse than Laurel Hill and Spotsylvania. Warren told his wife that "we are going to make a movement today which will bring about some result or other," hoping "to get . . . a battle in an open field without breastworks if possible."[6]

The Fifth Corps, Crawford in the lead, started moving south on the Telegraph Road at 10 A.M., and part of the corps reached Milford by the end of the day, across the Mattaponi. "We have had a long march today," Warren wrote to Emily, "and have succeeded in my part of the programme perfectly having got possession of the place I was sent to in advance of the enemy." Lee, he said, would have to abandon his entrenchments, "either to attack us or go back towards Richmond."[7]

On May 22, Warren proceeded south to Harris' Store, at the intersection of the road from Milford to Chilesburg. Next morning the corps, despite woefully erroneous maps, marched through "open country abounding in fine fertile farms." Nearing the North Anna River, Warren was fortunate enough to come across a knowledgeable black man who warned him of the well-entrenched Confederate force waiting at the place designated for the Fifth Corps' crossing and who guided the corps to another rarely used ford which was not defended. Jericho Ford was not much of a crossing place, with precipitous banks, a rocky bed, and a swift current—"a ford in name rather than in reality," Swinton called it—but the lack of enemy opposition made it quite appealing.[8]

Bartlett's brigade waded over first, chasing away a few enemy pickets, and a pontoon bridge was promptly begun. By 4:30 P.M., the whole corps was across, with Crawford's division sloshing across the stream (its men carrying their shoes and stockings on the ends of their bayonets far above the water) while Cutler's marched over the bridge. The men of the Twenty-Fourth Michigan, in the Iron Brigade, doffed their clothes to wade across, soon found themselves slipping on the smooth rocks, and "soldiers, weapons, and uniforms—all went down in a sodden mass." This caused much frivolity and intentional ducking, until the regimental officers shouted sternly to the skylarking troops that "to make a river crossing in the face of the enemy was hardly an occasion for horseplay."[9]

The enemy was caught by surprise by Warren's reaching the North Anna so far to the west, while Hancock's crossing farther down was hotly contested. Warren's men were not to be spared the rebels' attention, however. One observer wrote, "Time was when the first thing to be done after a halt was to make coffee . . . Now the first thing the men do is to entrench."[10] It was fortunate that they did so, for the center of Warren's line was soon struck by a furious rebel assault.

A member of Lee's staff, speaking a few years after the war, said that the Confederate commander was still seeking ways to attack the Army of the Potomac at this time, and he hoped for much from the assault he launched against Warren late on the afternoon of May 23, with the Fifth Corps "in a hazardous position, separated from the rest of the army." A. P. Hill sent the divisions of Wilcox and Heth to the attack, hoping to drive Warren back into the river. The rebel assault was heaviest on the Union right, where Cutler's men, just getting into position, had not dug any entrenchments. Part of Cutler's division broke to the rear, but the pursuing Confederates were driven back by the corps artillery, "served under the eye of General Warren," one witness wrote. Wainwright felt "very exultant, for I do believe that the artillery saved the day," but he sulked that "General Warren has not given me one word of commendation for myself or my batteries." Griffin's division, in the center, sternly repulsed the attack, and Hill's men fell back to their entrenchments on the Virginia Central Railroad. While the killed and wounded were about equal, the Confederates lost about six hundred prisoners.[11]

Warren reported the engagement to Emily, saying, "our advance was so rapid, that the enemy did not expect us and we got foot hold before he knew it. He made desperate efforts to drive us back but we routed his attacking force." Mentioning that Meade had sent a congratulatory note, he said that the enemy kept Hancock from crossing the river at all, "so that we have all the honor of the day, I think." [12]

This day Warren was presented with a supercilious and "high-toned" Virginia gentleman, a captive looking for his wounded brother. When the Virginian refused polite offers of help, Warren sent him off with two other prisoners, remarking that his company was not agreeable. To this the Virginian responded that he had heard that "Genl Warren was a good soldier but not a gentleman." Considering the source, Warren told Emily that he was proud to be found guilty on that charge; "in time of war a gentleman should be a good soldier and be satisfied with that." [13]

The next day Hancock's corps crossed the river on the bridge at Chesterfield Ford, and part of the Sixth Corps crossed over at Jericho Ford, where the Fifth had made its passage. At Ox Ford, however, midway between the two crossings, Burnside's Ninth Corps found its passage heavily disputed and was unable to get across at all. Investigation soon showed that Lee's line was in the form of an inverted "V," with its apex solidly anchored on the river at Ox Ford. Warren and Wright on the Union left could not connect with Hancock on the right, because the Confederates were squarely interposed between them, with the advantage of interior lines.

After a couple of days probing here and there, Grant decided that there was no way he could make progress or even fight to advantage at the North Anna. Once again, beginning after dark on May 26, he surreptitiously extricated the Army of the Potomac from its lines facing Lee's force, recrossed the river, and moved it far around the Confederate right. "I write you a few words just as we are starting on another night march," Warren jotted to his wife. "The roads are muddy and the night dark and it makes a disagreeable prospect." [14] The Sixth Corps led the way on a wide swing east and then south, over the Pamunkey River, formed by the North and South Anna. By the morning of May 28 the Fifth and Ninth corps joined the Sixth south of the Pamunkey, with Hancock crossing later that afternoon. This movement had the advantage, for Grant, of bringing his supply depot much closer, to White House, at the head of the York River (at the confluence of the Pamunkey and Mattaponi rivers).

Lee's army followed and with the benefit of a direct line was able to interpose itself between the Army of the Potomac and Richmond, retiring behind
a creek called the Totopotomoy. The Fifth Corps, led by Griffin's division,
crossed the Totopotomoy and advanced about a mile and a half toward Shady
Grove, skirmishing with the enemy all the way. Warren, on the 28th, directed
that entrenchments be dug, and he laid out the lines himself. Wainwright
commented that "for once they were made with some knowledge." Warren,
he said, "liked the work and was consequently in good humor, so that I had a
very pleasant time aiding him." Throwing himself into engineering projects
gave Warren's mind a welcome hour or so away from his problems with Grant
and Meade and the carnage of the campaign.[15]

Warren's corps was on the Union left, opposite Ewell's rebels, and on the 29th
Crawford was threatened by a movement around his left flank by Rodes's divi-
sion. "It was an anxious time for fifteen or twenty minutes," Wainwright noted.
With the aid of a well-served battery, however, and some brigades placed in line
on his left by the corps commander, Crawford was able to beat back the attack.
Warren was unhappy: Sheridan's cavalry had been ordered to protect the Fifth
Corps flank but had been nowhere in sight. When Warren complained to
Meade, Sheridan replied, "I have had troops on the left of General Warren's
corps all day and connected with him." Warren knew that this was not so and
the next day told his division commanders that "the cavalry do not co-operate
with us in any reliable way, as far as I can learn." This repeat of the flare-up on
the road to Spotsylvania boded ill for future relations between the two men.[16]

On the 29th there was imposed upon the Fifth Corps Brigadier General
Henry H. Lockwood, a fifty-year-old West Pointer with a spotty record but considerable rank. Warren had served under Lockwood early in the war in a
poorly conducted campaign on the Delmarva Peninsula, and he was not
much impressed with the man. Since Lockwood outranked the other officers
of the corps, Warren was forced to reconstitute the Second Division (formerly
Robinson's) and put Lockwood in command of it.[17]

May 30 was marked by a late-afternoon attack on Warren's left flank, near
Bethesda Church, which was repulsed handsomely, and May 31, a beautiful
warm summer day, was a day of rest and reorganization for the Fifth Corps.
The term of enlistment for the Pennsylvania Reserves ended that day, with the
result that nearly four thousand men, most of Crawford's division, left for
home. Elsewhere, Grant and Lee moved their units around, as Grant prepared
to force and Lee to defend the Chickahominy River, once again a focus of battle as it had been two years earlier. Warren wrote to Emily of the battle of the
day before, saying, "we had a good fight and whipped them." He added that
Meade, who had chided him for not maintaining a connection with Burnside's corps, "is very nervous & disagreeable lately and one would think from
his tone we were doing nothing."[18]

The first day of June was not a good day for Gouverneur Warren. Still upset with Meade, he took his anger out on those around him. Wainwright said Warren "has been in one of his pets all yesterday and today, as ugly and cross-grained as he could be." "He has pitched," Wainwright wrote, "into his staff officers most fearfully, cursing them up and down as no man has a right to do, and as I wonder that they allow." In the morning Warren was supposedly directed to attack a column of Confederate infantry passing down the road toward Cold Harbor, near the old battlefield of Gaines's Mill, but all he did was push out skirmishers and open with artillery. Charles Dana reported this back to Stanton in scathing terms and, after mentioning a similar dereliction of the Sixth Corps, added that both Grant and Meade were "intensely disgusted with these failures of Wright and Warren." Meade, he went on, said "a radical change must be made, no matter how unpleasant it may be to make it," but Dana doubted that he would try.[19]

Later in the day, with Wright and William F. "Baldy" Smith's Eighteenth Corps, detached from Ben Butler's Army of the James and brought to the area of battle developing around the Chickahominy, striking Lee's right wing, Warren was ordered to attack in his sector. Instead, the enemy assaulted Griffin in three waves, each one being turned back with terrible loss. Of the corps commander's handling of his forces in these encounters, Grant later wrote, "There was no officer more capable, nor one more prompt in acting, than Warren when the enemy forced him to it," although Meade, in a late-night report to the lieutenant general, said sourly, "Warren does not seem to have effected anything in his front, except repulsing attacks made on him."[20]

In the meantime, Warren ordered Lockwood to extend to his left and to prepare for an attack in conjunction with Wright and Smith. Somehow—and no one seemed to be able to figure out how he managed this—Lockwood marched his whole division to the rear, around a swamp, and turned up at dark two miles to the rear of the fighting, the sound of which could be plainly heard. It was the perfect end to a lovely day for Warren, who wrote disgustedly to Meade of Lockwood, "He is too incompetent, and too high rank leaves no subordinate place for him. I earnestly beg that he may be at once relieved from duty with this army."[21]

The next day, Grant's headquarters issued an order relieving Lockwood from duty and directing him to report to Baltimore to await further orders. Warren immediately named Crawford to command the Second Division and transferred to that division what was left of the former Third Division after the departure of the Pennsylvania Reserves.[22]

There was no major combat on June 2. An attack on the main rebel line by the three corps of Hancock, Wright, and Baldy Smith, originally planned for the morning, was ordered to take place at 5 P.M., with the Fifth Corps cooperating by attacking in its front, but because of the late arrival of the Second Corps the assault was postponed to the next morning, giving the Army of Northern Virginia additional time to perfect its defenses. Wainwright commented that Warren seemed in better humor, and he supposed that the general "may not have been well yesterday, which would be some, though not sufficient, excuse for his behavior." [23]

When the attack at Cold Harbor did take place, on the morning of June 3, it was a disaster for the Union army. An uncoordinated frontal assault by three army corps against a well-entrenched defensive position, it gained nothing and cost a fearful toll in dead and wounded. A Confederate officer called it "one of the most . . . murderous engagements of the war. Along the whole Federal line a simultaneous assault was made on the Confederate works, and at every point with the same disastrous result." Even Grant said of it, "I have always regretted that the last assault at Cold Harbor was ever made . . . [N]o advantage whatever was gained to compensate for the heavy loss we sustained." Union losses in the few moments of the assault were nearly seven thousand killed and wounded, while the Confederates lost no more than fifteen hundred. When further attacks were ordered by the Federal high command, the men in the ranks, already pinned down by enemy fire, simply declined to move. Finally, after noon, Grant ordered "a suspension of further advance for the present." [24]

The Fifth Corps, with Burnside at the northern end of the Union line, away from Cold Harbor, moved forward with the attack, but it was not opposed to the heavily entrenched Confederate position and consequently suffered comparatively few losses. Warren peppered Meade's headquarters all day with reports of his minor and essentially irrelevant activities, as well as those of the Ninth Corps.

Gouverneur Warren's ill humor got the best of him again on the evening of the third, causing Wainwright to feel that he was "standing on the edge of a volcano which may burst at any moment." He said, "This evening I saw it in its fury." Warren, he said, had gone to Burnside's headquarters before dark, leaving no orders for the night. The Fifth Corps staff were afraid to put up tents or even order their supper "without his consent." When the general returned late in the evening and found no preparations made for the night, he exploded, ripping "out at his staff generally and poor little [Capt. A. S.] Marvin [the assistant adjutant general] in particular." After describing the profanity of other celebrated swearers, Wainwright said, "I never heard anything which could begin to equal the awful oaths poured out tonight; they fairly made my hair stand on end with their profaneness, while I was filled with wonder at the ingenuity of invention and desperate blackguardism they displayed." [25]

Assuming the veracity of Wainwright's diary writings, and there appears no reason to doubt them, even granting the fact that the artilleryman seemed

160 HT'THET HT
HT'
AROUND LEE'S RIGHT

Warren and his Fifth Corps staff, Virginia 1864. National Archives.

cool to Warren from the start of their relationship, there must be some attempt
to come to grips with Warren's displays of choler. He had begun the campaign
with high hopes for glory and distinction, the protégé of Meade and the favored of Grant. Conscious of his own intellectual attainments and his knowledge of military science, a follower of Dennis Hart Mahan, he did not hide
the pride and arrogance which others noted. Disillusionment quickly set in,
as Warren learned from the start of the campaign that it would be conducted
in a manner far different from his model and repugnant to his deepest feelings. For a commander who had always cared about the welfare of his men,
the necessity of ordering them to their deaths in what his military mind told
him were fruitless endeavors wore deeply into his soul. Worse, it soon became
apparent to Warren that Grant and, to a lesser degree, Meade were actively unhappy with his conduct and that, far from his being the army's rising star, his
continued command of his corps and his good name were at risk. Constant activity and lack of sleep drained his physical strength, and continued absence
from his young bride sapped his spirit.[26]

Under all these circumstances, exacerbated by the necessity of dealing with
incompetents like Lockwood and the departure of some of his best troops, it
did not take much of a trigger to set Warren off in what appeared to be an al-

most ungovernable rage. Perhaps, too, the hypersensitive and condescending attitude of the artillery commander he had inherited with his corps command contributed.

In any event, there could be little doubt that the campaign of the Army of the Potomac from the Rapidan to the Chickahominy in May and early June 1864 had seen the eclipse of G. K. Warren's star, just as it had seen the devastation of the Union army and Lee's force as well. Grant's campaign for Richmond had come to a halt at nearly the same place as McClellan's in 1862, with little more to show for it than many more deaths and maimings than McClellan's drive had generated. The attrition of the Army of Northern Virginia was now well advanced, of course, and the destruction of Lee's army was Grant's major goal, but Cold Harbor had contributed almost nothing to the advancement of Grant's plan. Meade's order to move "against the enemy's works by regular approaches" was rightfully considered absurd by the army, a mere effort by Grant to save face.[27] What would happen after the debacle of Cold Harbor would determine the fate of the Army of the Potomac and, as well, of the commander of the Fifth Corps.

CHAPTER SIXTEEN

STANDOFF AT PETERSBURG

A FTER THE BATTLE OF COLD HARBOR THE FIFTH CORPS had several days of welcome rest near Bethesda Church, while Warren revamped his corps organization, a move made necessary by the hasty departure of the unfortunate Henry Lockwood.[1]

Griffin remained in command of the First Division, consisting of the brigades of Bartlett and Sweitzer and a former Fourth Division brigade, now headed by Colonel Joshua L. Chamberlain of Maine. Romeyn Ayres was placed in command of the Second Division, consisting of his own former brigade, the Maryland Brigade, and Kitchings's heavy artillery brigade. The Third Division under Crawford had in it the veteran brigade of the Pennsylvania Reserves (those who remained after most of the Reserves went home), and the brigades of Lyle and Bates. Cutler led the Fourth Division, made up of the brigades of Robinson and Hofmann. The new regime was to take effect immediately on June 5, with a movement to a spot about two miles behind Cold Harbor scheduled for that night.[2]

There was another run-in with the cavalry on June 5. Early that morning, Warren notified headquarters that the nearest cavalry picket was two miles from his right flank; "I am not capable," he said, "of maintaining any position whatever, if that is all the co-operation I am to have." Humphreys duly shipped Warren's complaint off to Sheridan, who never admitted mistakes. Sheridan responded characteristically, with a note saying the reason for the break of Wilson's connection with Warren the night before was "the withdrawal of some army corps without notification to the cavalry." He then added, gratuitously, "infantry commanders are very quick to give the alarm when their flanks are uncovered, but manifest inexcusable stupidity about the safety of cavalry flanks." Humphreys promptly responded that there was no reason for the cavalry to have lost contact with Warren's flank, and that, while infantry commanders are "instructed to keep in communication with the commanders of cavalry on their flanks," they were frequently unable, "with

Romeyn B. Ayres, a solid and reliable soldier. National Archives.

the means at their disposal, to do so, and . . . they could find neither the cavalry pickets nor the commanders of them." This was just another round in the hostility between the cavalry under Sheridan and Meade's headquarters, but once again Gouverneur Warren was the immediate target for the angry young cavalry commander.[3]

The night march of June 5 was marked by all the problems of earlier night marches, and at four-thirty in the morning Warren expressed his opinion of these efforts to headquarters:

> It is almost useless I think to attempt marching these dark nights, unless it is for the mere object of safely retiring from a position. It was 3 A.M. before the rear of my column got on the way, and it was so on all our previous efforts . . . The men being unacquainted with the roads, on all descents step out just as one does in a strange house when they go down stairs. It is unavoidable, the inclination to feel before planting the foot, and the frequent tumbles they get off of banks and other places makes them do it in spite of every effort of their officers; then, too, in the night an officer cannot be distinguished, nor those who disobey him, so that practically an army on one of these dark nights marches a little better than the crowd that walks the streets, as far as organization is concerned.[4]

While the corps remained relatively inactive for several days, the men digging rifle-pits and throwing up defensive works, Wainwright felt that Warren had "sunk into a sort of lethargic sulk, sleeps a great part of the time, and says nothing to anyone." The artillery commander thought "these fits of his must be the result of a sort of insanity; indeed, that is perhaps the most charitable way of accounting for them." Warren, he thought, had "not got along well at Meade's headquarters lately, though I know nothing as to wherein the trouble has lain." Warren, in the meantime, wrote to Emily on June 10 that "we have been having a few days of rest but movements are soon to begin again. I want them to do so and continue, and speed the time, whether in defeat or triumph, a finished war restores us all again to our friends and loves."[5]

The following morning the Fifth Corps began its march away from Cold Harbor, preceded by Wilson's cavalry division, moving in an eastward direction along the north bank of the Chickahominy. Warren was ordered to get to a spot called Moody's on the 11th, to rest there for a day, and in the darkness on June 12 march to Long Bridge and there cross the Chickahominy. By late afternoon of the 11th, Warren was able to report from Moody's that "my command is all in camp as ordered."[6]

The movement the next day began at around six in the evening, and the corps moved out nicely. Wainwright reported to his diary that he "rode most of the way with General Warren, who was in a good humor today, and quite conversable." The artilleryman found "something exhilarating" in the air so that "everyone moved along most cheerfully." The site of Long Bridge was reached in good time, though the bridge for which the crossing was named was long gone by this time.[7]

There was a delay in getting a pontoon bridge laid at the Long Bridge crossing. Warren understood that Wilson, whose cavalry reached the river first and was to cross first, would lay the bridge, while Wilson thought Warren's engineers were to get the bridge down for the horsemen to use. Wilson said that he sent two messengers to Warren, advising that the bridge was not ready and the advance could not begin. The first two messages achieving no result, Wilson sent another aide, a youngster named Yard, with the same message, only to have the boy return shortly in tears. "General," he allegedly reported to Wilson, "I gave your compliments and message to General Warren, exactly as you gave them to me, but, instead of receiving me politely, he cursed me out and then with a loud and insulting oath said: 'Tell General Wilson if he can't lay that bridge to get out of the way with his damned cavalry and I'll lay it.'"[8]

Roebling tells a different story. "Gen. Wilson had charge of the crossing," he wrote, and there was "a brisk fight" against a small detachment of Confederate defenders before Wilson won control of the crossing by 10 P.M. "The bridge was commenced at once by Maj. Ford," Roebling wrote in his report, "and completed by 1 P.M. [sic]." Roebling's account is not as colorful, certainly, as Wilson's, but it *was* written contemporaneously, while Wilson's came out in 1912, long after Warren was dead.[9]

In any event, Wilson soon sent his men to get the bridge down, and at 10 P.M. Warren reported to Humphreys that "General Wilson has crossed over some men, and they are commencing to lay the bridge." He added that Ayres's division was "waiting for the cavalry to get out of the way," while Crawford was massing his. At 5 A.M., Warren said, "The bridge was not so that [Wilson] could cross in force until 1 A.M."[10]

Eventually, the Fifth Corps crossed to the south side of the Chickahominy during the early morning hours of the 13th, rested and boiled coffee for a short while, then pushed out the road westward past White Oak Swamp, toward Richmond, until confronted by a sizable force of rebels near a place called Riddell's Store. Both sides then entrenched, glared at each other, and awaited attack.

In the meantime, Grant had the rest of his army on the move. Baldy Smith's Eighteenth Corps marched to White House to board steamers for the long trip around the peninsula to the south side of the James. The Second Corps crossed the Chickahominy at Long Bridge behind the Fifth Corps, and the Sixth and Ninth corps crossed at Jones's Bridge, lower down the sluggish stream, all unseen by the enemy. The three corps marched rapidly toward the James, while the Confederate commander was misled by Warren's movement into thinking that Grant might be advancing upon Richmond north of the river. Warren was "stretched across the only road by which General Lee could assail our flanks," one participant wrote, which gave the rest of the Army of the Potomac nearly complete protection during its move.[11]

When dark came on the 13th, Warren pulled in his pickets and set his corps in motion again, now following the Second Corps toward the James, its mission of deceiving Robert E. Lee completed. Charles City Court House on the James was reached the afternoon of June 14. The Second Corps was being ferried across the river, while the other units would cross on a lengthy pontoon bridge being put in place by the army's engineers. The river was twenty-one hundred feet wide at this point, fifteen fathoms deep in the middle of the channel, with high, steep banks and a strong tidal current with a rise and fall of four feet. The construction of the bridge was an engineering marvel, but it took time. The Fifth Corps accordingly had a day to put up tents, rest, and lounge in idleness.[12]

On the evening of June 15 Warren was notified to move at daylight the next morning, and by 6 A.M. the ferrying of his troops across the James had begun. By 1 P.M. the corps was across, with the artillery and wagons going over the pontoon bridge. An hour later Warren's men began the hot and dusty trek toward Petersburg, "the Cockade City," a small town twenty-five miles south of Richmond. Petersburg's misfortune was that it held the key to the capital, for through it came all of the railroad lines supplying Richmond from the south and west.[13]

Grant's plan for disengaging from the lines at Cold Harbor, feinting toward Richmond with the Fifth Corps, and moving the other corps rapidly to the south side of the James and on to Petersburg worked splendidly. Lee was fooled, and the Army of the Potomac marched toward a Petersburg defended by a ragtag army of invalids, clerks, and whoever else could be thrown into the virtually unmanned defenses by Beauregard, in command of the town. Still, the malign spirit which seemed to hover over the Union's eastern army made itself felt once again. Smith, first to reach Petersburg with his corps, delayed fatally in attacking the defenseless city, and when Hancock reached Smith on the evening of the 16th, after being handicapped by a faulty map and imprecise orders, he deferred to Smith's supposed superior knowledge of the situation, with the result that no attack was made that night. The great opportunity to seize Petersburg while Lee's veterans were still many miles away was lost.

At noon on June 16 Warren was directed to "push forward . . . as rapidly as possible toward Petersburg," moving out each division as soon as it was ready without waiting for the whole corps. At 2 P.M., Warren reported to Meade that the Fifth Corps was "on the road" and would "make as good time as possible." He could not, of course, be expected to be there before dark, "but I certainly will be before morning." After some confusion, Warren was directed to take position on the left of the army, to the left of Burnside, along the railroad line from Norfolk.[14]

On the 17th there were desultory attacks by Hancock in the morning and Burnside in the afternoon, with Crawford's division being thrown in at dusk on Burnside's left in support. Crawford's men blundered through some unexpected ravines in the gathering darkness, but they captured prisoners and a flag from an Alabama regiment. Failure to capture Petersburg on the 17th was decisive for Grant, for the Army of Northern Virginia was rapidly working its way south to fill the defenses around the Cockade City. Warren had been within sight of the Jerusalem Plank Road, off to his left, but had not been ordered to occupy it. Beauregard had no troops at all in this area, and a Union corps marching up the Jerusalem Plank Road might have captured Petersburg without opposition, forcing its evacuation by the Confederates. The Fifth Corps, however, was under the direction of Grant and Meade, and its commander had been warned of the perils of independent thinking. That evening Warren wrote to Emily, reminding her that it was the first anniversary of their wedding. "I am now awaiting every minute for an attack to begin upon Petersburg," he said, "and it may be a very heavy battle. My preparations are all made." [15]

For the next day, Grant and Meade wanted a general assault, in the vain hope that Lee's army had not yet fully arrived at Petersburg. It was to be a day of frustration for the high command. At 5:15 in the morning, Meade asked Warren, "[W]hat is the delay in your attack?" Thirty-five minutes later Warren reported that Cutler's skirmishers had just struck the enemy but that the rebels had retreated to a new defensive line. At 6:30 A.M. Meade told Warren, "I have ordered the whole line forward." At 7:10 he told the Fifth Corps commander that he had heard of no force in the Confederate lines but Beauregard's. At ten o'clock, he asked Warren to "please advise me at what time your columns of assault will be prepared to attack the enemy in your front." Half an hour later Warren responded, "At present I am not well enough informed to say when I can be prepared to assault, nor to advise one at any place we have yet approached, but I hope to receive information from my left soon." A frustrated Meade then sent a peremptory order to all his corps commanders to attack punctually at noon. [16]

When, at 11:36, Warren notified Meade that "I cannot be ready to attack in line or column before 1 P.M.," the angry commander fired back, "I cannot change the hour in the order of attack just issued. Everyone else is ready. You will attack as soon as possible after the hour designated, and endeavor to be ready at that hour." Five minutes later Warren said, "I will have my right advanced probably by the time, and keep up the connection." Meade resignedly wired back that "the advance of your right will answer all purposes." [17]

On the right of the Union line, David Birney, temporarily leading the Second Corps, and John H. Martindale, commanding the only Eighteenth Corps division left at Petersburg, attacked as ordered, with mixed results, but Meade continued to have trouble with his left. At two o'clock, Warren reported, "I thought the attack at 12 m. was to be a rush. My left had not then got up close enough . . . I think it would be safe for all of us to make a rush at, say, 3 P.M. That will give time to notify all to make another effort. I am willing to try alone." Burnside endorsed this message, "I fully concur in the statement of General Warren." This drew a fiery response from Meade at 2:20 P.M. to both corps commanders: "I am greatly astonished at your dispatch of 2 P.M. What additional orders to attack you require I cannot imagine. My orders have been explicit and are now repeated, that you each immediately assault the enemy with all your force, and if there is any further delay the responsibility and consequences will rest with you." [18]

The attack was duly made by the Fifth Corps, beginning at 3:15 P.M., with moderate success—an advance of about two miles but no penetration of the enemy's main line—but considerable loss. Chamberlain led the assault on Rives' Salient, commanding the Norfolk Railroad and the Jerusalem Plank Road, but, as he wrote, "it was too late; all Lee's army were up and entrenched." Chamberlain said his "veterans were hurled back over the stricken field, or left upon it." A regimental commander called the attack "a horrid massacre of our corps" and said it was "awfully disheartening to be ordered upon such hopeless assaults." [19]

At 6:30 Meade notified Warren that Birney had been repulsed and that he should straighten his lines and make his connections secure. "I am quite satisfied we have done all that it is possible for men to do, and must be resigned to the result." The effort to capture Petersburg by frontal attack had failed, and a resumed stalemate was the net result. Wainwright wrote that "never has the Army of the Potomac been so demoralized as at this time." [20]

Sunday, June 20, was a day of discord between Warren and his superior officer. At 9:30 in the morning Warren sent an unsolicited advisory on how the enemy could be attacked. Exactly what happened after that is not precisely known, but Dana picked up something, reporting that evening to Stanton that "General Meade notified Warren this morning that he must either ask to be relieved, or else he (Meade) would prefer charges against him." Dana's rumor was not quite right, but a letter Warren wrote to Emily about the day's events gives further clues:

> Darling late events have been very trying to me personally as well as the other trials incident to this severe campaign.
>
> A rupture is probable between me and Genl Meade who has become very irritable and unreasonable of late, and with whom I had a square understanding today, to the effect that I was no creature of his. I am so well satisfied with my efforts and integrity—that I would not fear to run against Genl Grant if necessary. At any rate I will not allow myself to be made anyone's scapegoat and you must be as prepared to see me disgraced . . . as well

as to see me honored. I feel no security to honest efforts patriotism or daring
if certain influences succeed . . .

My darling I may have a fierce ordeal to go through between some one else
becoming a hero and I a nobody. And I am as prepared to die that way as
ever I was by the enemy's bullets.[21]

Warren did not understand that Meade could have been dissatisfied with the
performance of the Fifth Corps, and particularly its commander, on June 18. Ar-
mored as he was in his own layer of cocksure self-confidence, Gouverneur Warren seemed oblivious to the forces which could bring about, and indeed almost
had brought about, his downfall. It was the third time since the army had
headed into the Wilderness that Warren's tenure was threatened, and he
seemed in his letter to Emily to recognize this at last, but there was no consciousness in his words that he could be in any way responsible for his situation.

A week and a half later Dana wrote to Stanton that "Grant thinks the
difficulty between Meade and Warren has been settled without the extreme
remedy which Meade proposed last week." Dana's problem in getting the
story straight, it would appear, was that he was picking up rumors from Grant's
staff at City Point, about things someone thought he had overheard. There was
trouble between Meade and Warren, but the particulars got a bit strained by
the time they reached the ears of Charles Dana.[22]

The contretemps between Meade and Warren made it into the public press
several weeks later, when the *Pittsburg Commercial* of July 14 reported "that
General Meade and General Warren have had a disagreement" and, echoing
Dana, that Meade had preferred charges for "disobedience and tardy execu-
tion of orders." The writer went on to decry "a great deal of jealousy, fault-
finding, and mutual derogation . . . in the army." Warren sent the slip from
the paper to Meade, asking that "some public denial of the statement" be
made. He said that Baldy Smith, two weeks earlier, had told him "it was common talk at General Grant's headquarters that you had told General Grant
that you had threatened me with a court-martial if I did not resign." As Meade
had never done so, Warren said, he could not believe "that you had ever said
so to General Grant."

Meade wrote back to Warren the same day, giving him a short note, to
"make any use of you think proper," stating that the newspaper accusation of
bringing charges was "entirely without foundation in fact." This note was enclosed in a longer letter, in which Meade said he "could not deny the existence of a disagreement, because there was a serious one between us on the
19th ultimo." He was not surprised that there was publicity, because the argument between the two men had been in the presence of Crawford and within
hearing of several other officers.[23]

"I was very much irritated," Meade said, "and felt deeply wounded by the tone and tenor of your conversation on that occasion, and fully determined, on leaving you, to apply to have you relieved." He did speak to Grant about relieving Warren ("I have frequently spoken about you" to Grant, Meade said), and even went so far as to write an official letter giving his reasons for doing so, but "upon further reflection, in view of the injury to you, and in the hope the causes of disagreement would not occur in the future," he kept the letter and took no other action.[24]

Meade continued:

> I have never entertained any but the most friendly feelings toward you, and have always endeavored to advance your interests, but I cannot shut my eyes to what I think is wrong in you, and on several occasions I have differed from you in what you seemed to consider was your prerogative. In your conversation of the 19th ultimo I thought you exhibited a great deal of temper and positive ill-feeling against me, not justified, as I think, by anything I have either said or done. It is my earnest desire to have harmony and co-operation with my subordinate officers, but I cannot always yield my judgment to theirs, and if it is impossible to have these relations, necessary for harmonious co-operation, a separation is inevitable. I do not make these remarks for any other purpose than to explain the reason I felt called on to speak to General Grant about you.[25]

But this exchange was several weeks in the future. In the meantime, Warren was called upon to referee a dispute between Griffin and Crawford as to movements between their two divisions on the 18th. "It was a very trying day to me," the corps commander concluded, "and I am willing to assume the whole or any fault rather than any feeling should exist between two divisions." He added, "With so great difficulties as we have to contend with, annoying occurrences of this kind must be met with mutual forebearance." [26]

On the 23rd Warren sent Meade another suggestion for a movement, if the army's goal now was to cut all the railroads coming into Petersburg. He proposed that Meade abandon the position presently held and march the whole army west to the Weldon Railroad, forcing Lee out of his defenses. "If this succeeds," he said, "we will then know how to reach the next road." Meade sent this on to Grant, while replying to Warren that an objection to his plan would seem to be the probability of Lee's seizing a strong position athwart the Union army's communications, "where we shall have all the work to get back, which our experience gave us in the Wilderness, Spotsylvania, North Anna, and the Chickahominy." Warren responded that "I see the plan has the risks and objections you point out." Nevertheless, he said, "with our unparalleled losses and exhausting efforts we can scarcely say we are much nearer destroying Lee's army than when we were on the Rapidan . . . [W]e must make some decisive movement, in which, throwing all our weight in the battle, we are willing to run the risk of losing all by a failure." Needless to say, Grant, who felt that he now had the Confederate army in a position to squeeze the life out of it, was not about to risk all on one throw of the dice, no matter how weary Warren thought the army was becoming.[27]

This exchange came the day after a disastrous movement in which a rebel thrust got in between the Second and Sixth corps, with great Union losses, including a large number of captives. On the 24th, Warren reported to Humphreys that Gibbon's Second Corps division was "in a very bad state of demoralization," four regiments of it having surrendered to one Confederate regiment on the 22nd.[28]

The next day a disconsolate Gouverneur Warren sat down and penned a despairing letter to his wife:

> Our losses on this campaign are not less than 70,000 and at least that many northern homes are bereaved or suffering in anxiety, and war to utter submission seems the only plan our rulers can devise. I cannot but think that with ability virtue and magnanimity an easier solution of the difficulty might be brought. But in the rivalry of political faction neither party can adopt moderate views without being at once stigmatized as sympathizers and traitors, forgetting that sympathy for our patriot soldiers and their friends might claim to mitigate their rage, and lessen the effusion of blood. Our men are getting very weary and nervous that are left . . .

> I am afraid to despond and scarce dare to hope. I fear we have not yet the Generalship we should have. I know it is not what I would want. I dread to think of the disaster that is necessary to make the American people think so, the popular idea of Genl Grant is I believe very wrong but still it governs all men more or less here. There is scarce a man to be found to show now the moral courage I did in stopping the battle of Mine Run. Times have often been here when some one should have done the same, but I had not the power. To sit unconcerned on a log away from the battle field, whittling, to be a man on horseback or smoking a cigar seems to exhaust the admiration of the country, and if this is really just, then Nero fiddling over burning Rome was sublime . . .

> And then disregarding the useless slaughter of thousands of noblest soldiers, the country grows jubilant, and watches the smoke wreathes from Grant's cigar as if they saw therefrom a way to propitiate a God.

> Emmie I believe we could win by good management but I fear we shall never see the Union restored, and I mention this seriously for Mr Chase to consider in his business so that such a termination may not carry ruin to his business and leave you in poverty for most likely the same end would ruin me.

On and on he went:

If there were no limit to the number of men we could continually waste in battle I might be more hopeful. But we have been so senselessly ordered to assault intrenchments that the enemy suffer little in comparison with us and may outlast us. Genl Meade is very nervous and unreasonable and I quite regret he commands. He has keen perception and ability but lacks nerve and has offended almost everyone. You know I told you that he and I have had an understanding to the effect that his tone towards me must change and it has. He admitted great anger produced by his vexations and did not mean to censure me when I thought he had. My nature broke out against it.[29]

Later in the day he sent Emily another letter, stating that his "self reliance had increased since" his encounter with Meade but despairing of the country's future stability. "I am glad," he said, "that no fears of opposition or desire of place can make me sacrifice my self respect or submit to unjust censure from a responsible source." [30]

This brace of letters clearly represented the cry of a deeply depressed and troubled soldier, who as stalemate became only too clear could see no prospect of the war coming to any satisfactory end within the foreseeable future. In addition, Warren now knew he was in trouble with his superiors—unjustly so, he felt—and this knowledge could only have deepened his gloom. One can easily sympathize with Meade in his patient tolerance of such a troubling subordinate.

The army's activities now concentrated on strengthening its lines south of Petersburg, turning the entrenchments into fortifications, straightening works so that there were no weak points to serve as possible targets for enemy attacks, all so that the lines could be held securely with the fewest number of men, freeing Grant to move other units around the flanks of Lee's army. Much of the work being done, of course, was engineering work, Warren's specialty, and he threw himself into designing and overseeing the erection of redoubts, parapets, bombproofs, and other fortifications, "where I find my rank and experience combined . . .very much needed." "General Warren is now in his element," Wainwright noted; "so far as I can learn he is his own officer of the trenches, and commander of the working parties." He commented upon Warren's great good humor and, contrasting that with the black moods he had earlier recorded, said he was "more than ever convinced that he has a screw loose, and is not quite accountable for all his freaks." [31]

Warren's headquarters at this time were located in a fine old colonial mansion known as the Avery House, not far from the firing line and, as a result, somewhat damaged by Confederate artillery fire. The corps headquarters comprised much more than space for Warren and his personal staff. Also located there were the corps quartermaster, commissary, provost guard, and medical director, as well as a company of sharpshooters, a cavalry company, mounted and unmounted orderlies, clerks, telegraphers, signal corpsmen, postal clerks, wagoners, teamsters, cooks, and servants: three or four hundred people, along with horses, mules, wagons, and supplies. It was a sizable contingent that followed the corps commander about.[32]

At the beginning of July, Warren received two pieces of news, one good, the other sad. On July 1 he was notified of his promotion to major in the Corps of Engineers, his permanent rank.[33] A couple of days later, he learned that Captain Hook, his sister Eliza's husband, had died of yellow fever; Eliza had returned home to Cold Spring, where she remained disconsolate.

On the morning of July 3, Grant asked Meade, "Do you think it possible, by a bold and decisive attack, to break through the enemy's center, say in General Warren's front somewhere?" Meade responded that "before replying it will be necessary I should see both Warren and Burnside to obtain information." At noon he sent Grant's query on to Warren for his views, and Warren quickly answered, "I shall have to make a careful personal examination today before I can give a proper opinion on so important a question as that proposed." Then, having in mind the views he now knew were held about him at headquarters, he added, "I would rather the opinion of some one independent of me should decide the question, as circumstances in the past leave me without much strength in declining any proposed attack whatever."[34]

The next day Warren reported to Meade that General John G. Barnard, Grant's chief engineer, had visited him and talked "as if he thought we could carry the enemy's line along the plank road [the Jerusalem Plank Road, running south from Petersburg]." Once again, Warren said he wanted the subject considered by competent staff officers, "so that the opinion can rest on mere military grounds and not hereafter be a question of individual willingness, ability, or boldness."[35]

Later that morning, Warren saw the instructions with which Meade had armed his artillery chief and engineer in sending them out to inspect the lines, and he took exception to the part which read, "Major-General Warren does not deem any [offensive operations] practicable in his front." Conscious now that his reputation was no longer what it had been, he wrote to Meade that "I am sorry to be troublesome, but fear to let this statement of my opinion stand as it appears above . . . [I]n the hands of those unfriendly to me hereafter it may be made a source of injury and unhappiness." He said that his opinion, which he believed confidential because it was in reply to a "confidential" request, was an answer specifically to Grant's question about "a bold and decisive attack" possibly being successful. "The possibility, of course, could only be settled by trial. My opinion was that it was not advisable to do it by assault; not that I could not carry on 'any offensive operations' in my front."[36]

Meade's position itself was none too secure. The trouble-making Dana wrote to Stanton on July 7 that "a change in the commander of the Army of the

Potomac now seems probable. Grant has great confidence in Meade . . . but the almost universal dislike of Meade which prevails among officers of every rank who come in contact with him, and the difficulty of doing business with him . . . so greatly impair his capacities for usefulness and render success under his command so doubtful that Grant seems to be coming to the conviction that he must be relieved." Hancock, Dana said, would be put in command. Once again, Dana was picking up scuttlebutt from Grant's headquarters, where the officers of the Army of the Potomac were regarded largely with disdain, and relaying it as information to the secretary of war. Meade stayed on.[37]

On July 12, Warren had his headquarters circulate an order that "the officer in charge of the Coehorn mortars on General Ayres' right will serve the mortars and receive orders while in his present position according as General Ayres directs." He hardly thought that this simple directive would stir up a hornet's nest of controversy, but he reckoned without the egocentricity of his artillery commander.[38]

On the 15th Wainwright complained to Hunt, the army's artillery commander, about the transfer of authority over the Coehorn mortars, adding that "nor was I in any way notified that the control of the Cohorn [sic] batty' was taken out of my hands." On July 18 Hunt wrote to Humphreys—he "slashed out a letter," according to his biographer—requesting "that the use of all the corps artillery employed on the lines be placed under the general direction of the chief of artillery of the Corps, through whom all orders . . . be given." This, he said, would "secure some system in the operations." Hunt said the Coehorn mortars were not part of the division field artillery but were placed under a division commander who delegated his authority to a brigade commander. Finally, he said, the mode employed in carrying out this transfer was "not merely wanting in courtesy to the chief of artillery of the corps" but was "calculated to destroy on the part of his subordinates the respect due to his position, and to impair his just authority."[39]

Hunt's complaint was passed on to Warren, whose response was relatively mild, addressing some of Hunt's specifics and then concluding, "I do not agree with Genl Hunt in many things concerning the management of artillery but presume a discussion on these points is not wanted. I do not think Genl Hunt right in the tone of the communication which virtually charges me with bad management, with producing mischief, with discourtesy, and so forth, which would make me feel very bad if I thought they could be substantiated."[40]

Back in early June, when Wainwright and Hunt made an issue of the right of the corps commanders to regulate the use of their artillery, Meade had sustained Warren's authority. Now, with Warren himself in disfavor at headquarters, things were different. The Fifth Corps commander was ordered to "give as far as practicable the direction of the artillery of your Corps to the Chief of Artillery"; when it was imperative to give direction of a battery to a division commander, "the order should be sent to the battery thru the Chief of Artillery." Meade felt "that with conciliation and harmony and a disposition to co-operate there need be no difficulty in having all proper orders given and executed." [41]

Wainwright, as might be expected, crowed over his apparent triumph, suggesting that Warren's answer to Hunt's charges "was very queer," making him "think of the wail of a whipped school boy more than anything else." The letter from headquarters, he wrote, "gives me assurance that I may act as if his [Warren's] order had distinctly placed all the artillery in position under my control." With that the "crisis" ended. [42]

On July 20, Warren wrote to Emily, disapprovingly, that "Genl Griffin goes home tomorrow playing sick at least making that the reason." He then added, "I think it very likely I should die before I would leave the field from sickness." [43]

His next letter home came after the exchange with Meade of July 24, Warren saying that Meade's letter "contained many other things so disagreeable to my feelings that I have framed several different replies to him and am not yet decided what is the most patriotic and manly to do." He found Meade "an unjust and unfeeling man." He went on, "I dislike his personal character so much now that it is improbable we shall ever have again any friendly social relations. I have also lost all confidence in his ability as a general. He has quick perceptions but does not know how to act with patience and judgement. He would expect to hatch a chicken from an egg in the same time you could boil it."

After mentioning that "Genl Meade has I think lost the good will of nearly every body including most of his own staff," Warren said, "I have now with myself a conflict of opinion as to how I should act in the present state of affairs." He felt either he or Meade should go, although that might not suit Grant.

> I have no friend I feel like consult [sic] in this unfortunate matter and it being one where my personal interest and my patriotism are both so much concerned I hardly can trust to myself to make a determination which my own judgement and that of the country may not approve hereafter.
>
> So I have been studying the tone of the things around me and keeping quiet. But it occupies so much of my thought that I almost forget you. [44]

Thus passed the days during the siege of Petersburg.

CHAPTER SEVENTEEN

THE MINE AND THE RAILROAD

T HROUGH JUNE AND JULY A PROJECT HAD BEEN underway which promised a possible break in the Petersburg stalemate. The commander of a regiment in the Ninth Corps made up primarily of miners from Pennsylvania's anthracite region had suggested digging a mine from the Union lines to a spot under the rebel position and there exploding a large amount of powder, with the hope of blowing a hole in the Confederate defenses. Burnside agreed to the plan—to keep his men occupied if for no other reason—and won grudging approval from Meade and Grant for the project. No one really expected much to come of the digging, but as the end of July approached so too did the end of the mine, and suddenly there was all sorts of interest in it. When there appears no other way to break a deadlock, any plan may seem attractive.

A few days before the expected detonation of the mine, Hancock's Second Corps and two divisions of Sheridan's cavalry were sent off to the right, to Deep Bottom, a bridgehead on the north bank of the James, to threaten Richmond from there and, it was hoped, draw off some of Lee's army from Petersburg to meet the threat. The Confederates did in fact move substantial forces north of the James to counter the movement of the Second Corps. As the time for the bomb drew near, Hancock's men were brought back to Petersburg.[1]

On July 29, comprehensive orders in preparation for setting off the mine went out from Meade's headquarters. For the Fifth Corps, Warren was directed to reduce to a minimum the number of troops holding his entrenchments, in order to concentrate "all his available force on his right and hold them prepared to support the assault of Major-General Burnside." Burnside was ordered to spring his mine at 3:30 A.M., with his assaulting columns immediately moving "upon the breach" to "seize the crest in the rear, and effect a lodgment there." The Ninth Corps "will be followed by Major-General Ord [commanding the Eighteenth Corps, detached from Butler], who will support him on the right, directing his movement to the crest indicated, and by Major-General Warren, who will support him on the left."[2]

This followed an earlier communication from Meade to Warren, telling him that his part in the assault "will be co-operating, by the use of all the artillery possible along your line, the holding of your corps in readiness to take part in the action, and particularly all available reserve free for the immediate support of Burnside, if necessary." Warren responded that he could hold his front line with Griffin's division and one brigade of Cutler's, leaving Cutler's other brigade and Ayres's division to support Burnside. In addition, he said, Crawford's division would be well placed to follow up a success on Burnside's front.[3]

Warren's orders to his corps directed Ayres and Cutler's reserve brigade to get into position by 3:30 A.M. the next morning, "to support the column of attack, whenever it may be required and await orders," with Baxter's brigade from Crawford's division in readiness to move up, "but to await orders." Clearly, the Fifth Corps units were to await subsequent orders, after the attack of the Ninth Corps had developed. These subsequent orders would come from Warren, after he received further direction from Meade, the army commander, or Burnside, whose attack he was to support.[4]

Warren wrote to Emily, "Tomorrow morning another assault is ordered and if it is boldly made we shall have a success or another slaughter. We are all prepared Genl Burnside has the lead and in fact it is mainly his plan."[5]

Burnside had prepared for the attack by giving the lead division of Edward Ferrero special training for two weeks, so that the men would know what to do when the mine was exploded. There was one problem: Ferrero's division was made up of recently recruited black soldiers, and, the day before the mine was to blow, Meade, with Grant's concurrence, told Burnside that he could not spearhead the attack with black soldiers. In the event of a disaster, the political fallout would be too great; it would appear that the freedmen had been purposely sacrificed. Burnside then drew names from a hat to determine whose division would lead the assault, and the name drawn was that of the worst of his division commanders, James H. Ledlie, a man who had little competence, little respect from those under him, and a drinking problem. Ledlie, for some reason, failed to acquaint his brigade commanders with what their men should do the next morning other than charging ahead; Burnside's most recent biographer speculates that Ledlie may have been drunk when he received his orders at corps headquarters.[6]

At 4:44 A.M., on July 30, the earth rumbled and trembled, then, with a muffled roar, the mine exploded under a Confederate fort, throwing the fort, its guns, and those manning them, an infantry regiment and a battery of artillery, a hundred feet or so into the air. For nearly five minutes debris from the great explosion rained down upon the area around the site.

When the fallout ceased, Union artillery opened on the Confederate lines, and Ledlie's division started forward, in no particular order, hindered by the fact that Burnside had neglected to have obstructions in front of the lines removed. The division commander himself retired with a bottle to a bombproof, and his men moved forward into the crater left by the explosion. Since the brigade commanders did not know they were supposed to take the crest beyond the crater, the men stayed where they were, despite the lack, for the time being, of any meaningful opposition from the stunned rebels. Potter's and Willcox's divisions followed Ledlie's, and they too wound up in the crater, although several regiments had attempted to go around it but had been pushed back by the now-reviving Confederates. Next came Ferrero's black soldiers, all crowding into the pit.

At 5:50 Humphreys notified Warren that "Burnside is occupying the crater with some of his troops," and asked how things were in front of him. "If there is apparently an opportunity to carry their works take advantage of it and push forward your troops." Warren, receiving this, said, "It is difficult to say how strong the enemy may be in my front," but "I will watch for the first opportunity." A few minutes later, he told Humphreys, "None of the enemy have left my front that I can see."[7]

At 6:05, Meade asked Burnside "what is going on on your left, and whether it would be an advantage for Warren's supporting force to go in at once." Burnside's equivocal response fifteen minutes later was, "If General Warren's supporting force can be concentrated just now, ready to go in at the proper time, it would be well. I will designate to you when it ought to move. There is scarcely room for it now, in our immediate front." An exasperated Meade answered that "Warren's force has been concentrated and ready to move since 3:30 A.M. . . . What is the delay in your column moving? Every minute is most precious, as the enemy undoubtedly are concentrating to meet you on the crest, and if you give them time enough you cannot expect to succeed."[8]

At 6:30 A.M., Warren was instructed to make a movement to his left, where "none of the enemy's troops are visible in their works," and attack if he thought it "practicable." Warren then sent Crawford a copy of this dispatch, with the direction that he take a brigade and a half "and make the demonstration indicated in the dispatch, if practicable," a slight but perhaps significant modification of Meade's order. Crawford thought even such a demonstration was impractical, and nothing was done on the left.[9]

Warren then went to see Burnside, and the two of them moved up as close to the front as they could to see what was happening. Warren pointed out that the main impediment to Burnside's troops advancing was a two-gun battery south of the mine crater (on its left), whose fire enfiladed the Federal troops. Burnside asked if he could take it. Warren noted that the approaches leading to the mine were jammed with Burnside's troops, which meant the Fifth Corps would have to cross an open field. At 7:50 he wired Humphreys that he thought the battery should be taken, and shortly thereafter he received word back from Humphreys to "go in with Burnside, taking the two-gun battery." A short while later came back word from Meade that "the attack on the two-gun battery is suspended."[10]

By this time, Grant and Meade had recognized the failure of the attack and the futility of throwing more men into the combat, and Burnside had been ordered to pull his men back. For many of them, this order came too late. The Confederates had arrived in force to seal the breach in their lines, and their firing down into the jammed crater found targets impossible to miss. Many Union soldiers surrendered, while Ferrero's blacks were slaughtered by the rebels, who refused to accept their surrender. It was a complete Union fiasco, made all the worse by the golden opportunity it had offered to break the stalemate.

Warren wrote to his wife about the disaster:

> Yesterday there was another attempt made against Petersburg by Genl Burnside and the design was for the rest of us to support him but he failed to accomplish anything and so the others were not brought in. It was a disgusting failure and resulted in quite a quarrel between Meade and Burnside and perhaps something will come yet as it was badly managed like I think all Burnside's undertakings are. He lost over 2000 men for worse than nothing.[11]

When Warren testified at the court of inquiry Meade ordered after the mine failure, he made two principal points: first, that "some one should have been present to have directed my command as well as General Burnside's and General Ord's, some one person," to which Meade took exception, and second, that as he was supposed to be supporting the Ninth Corps, he waited in vain for Burnside to give him any directions. "If General Burnside had given me any orders," he said, "as I was there for the purpose of supporting him, I would have obeyed them; but he seemed to act as if what we did was to be done after consultation." [12]

Burnside's biographer sneered at this: "This sudden subordinate attitude of Warren's seems wonderful, considering his customary condescension, but Burnside had no orders giving him specific authority over other corps, and . . . [h]e therefore declined to act without consulting army headquarters." Nevertheless, the investigation resulted in the relief of Burnside and the effective termination of his Civil War service.[13]

Meade, in his testimony to the court of inquiry, summarized Warren's role as follows:

> He was authorized to attack if he could see a good chance to attack. When he reported no chance to attack and was asked what force he had available, he reported that he had no force available except he moved Ayres. He was directed not to move Ayres until information was received from Crawford, only if he could attack the two-gun battery in his front he was ordered to attack it, and then the operations were subsequently suspended.[14]

Years later, Grant told a reporter that Warren's penchant for questioning orders rather than obeying them "led to our disaster at the mine explosion before

Petersburg. If Warren had obeyed orders we would have broken Lee's army in two, and taken Petersburg. But when he should have been in the works, he was worrying over what other corps would do. So the chance was lost." This was rewriting history at its worst. There were no orders which Warren disobeyed at the mine crater. While Warren certainly displayed no very aggressive spirit at the mine, the court of inquiry, headed by Hancock, concluded that "the Fifth Corps did not participate at all in the assault, and General Ord's command only partially, because the condition of affairs at no time admitted of their co-operation as was contemplated by the order of assault." [15]

One staff officer recounted meeting Warren, early in the day, and passing a few words with him. "He seemed very anxious to be allowed to assault (this was early in the fight), but was not allowed to." Major J. C. Duane, Meade's chief engineer, testified at the inquiry that he did not understand that the Fifth Corps was to advance on its front but that it was "to have advanced on the Ninth Corps front." And that front, of course, was so clogged with Ninth Corps troops that no advance by other troops was possible there. Warren him-self later told the Committee on the Conduct of the War that "my place in the programme was rather insignificant." [16]

At the time, Grant's letter to Halleck simply called the follow-up to the mine explosion "the saddest affair I have witnessed in the war." One observer noted that the brigade commanders "were not informed of any design further than the occupation of the exploded salient." He went on to say that there was no evidence "whether the commanding general proposed to push on and oc-cupy the city or simply to occupy the fortified crest." If such a plan existed, he added, "it could only have been accomplished by the advance of Warren's line on the left of Burnside, a movement certainly never ordered and probably never suggested to General Warren." Charles Wainwright simply called the whole thing "a most miserable fizzle." [17]

With the failure of Burnside's mine, the Army of the Potomac settled back into its siege, the monotony relieved primarily by the postmortems of the July 30 failure. On August 14, his corps having been moved back in reserve, Warren wrote to Emily, "We are still as miserable as ever here and not much prospect of doing better." He complained that Burnside, the author of the most recent failure, had been given a twenty-day leave; "I think I shall have to do some-thing bad and get away too." He finished by saying, "I sometimes feel I can hardly stand it here, always in the presence of the enemy, cut off from all chance to be enterprising and having no enjoyments but on the contrary con-tinual longings." [18]

The Fifth Corps, accompanied by the cavalry brigade of Gen. August V. Kautz, was ordered to march at 4 A.M. on August 18. With four days' rations, Warren was directed westward, to "endeavor to make a lodgment upon the Weldon railroad," as near the enemy's line as possible, "and destroy the

road . . . as far south as possible." Warren should consider the movement a reconnaissance in force but should not "fight under serious disadvantages or assault fortifications." There would be no reinforcements available, and "you
must depend entirely upon your own resources." [19]

Warren wrote to Emily that "I have a very nice set of instructions" for the
next day's activities "and I ought to do well if ever." He added that he felt
"much softened towards Genl. Meade for making them without my solicitation so much in accordance with my idea of the way things should be." He
even sent a dispatch to Humphreys, telling him how "exceedingly pleased" he
was with his instructions. [20]

The Weldon Railroad, or the Petersburg and Weldon, to give it its full name,
was one of the two railroads still supplying Petersburg and Richmond from the
south. Its maintenance as a conduit to the embattled capital was essential to
the Confederacy, and every previous suggestion of a Union movement against
the line had triggered a ferocious rebel response. Lee was reputed to have said
that the Weldon Railroad was worth half his army to the South. Gouverneur
Warren had been handed a major assignment.

The corps moved out the next morning, Griffin in the lead, followed by
Ayres, Crawford, and Cutler, initially heading south on the Jerusalem Plank
Road to deceive the enemy. It was a lean and spare column, with ordnance
trains and supply wagons cut to the bare essentials. After going south for two
miles, the corps turned off to the west on an intersecting road. The country
through which the Fifth Corps marched was heavily wooded, with here and
there open fields and small farms. [21]

By 9 A.M., Warren reported that he had encountered nothing but cavalry
and that the head of the corps had reached the railroad. The heat of the day
was intense, making marching slow and causing many cases of sunstroke, but
by 11 A.M. the last division had reached the railroad, at a place called Globe
Tavern, on the Halifax Road, which ran parallel and close to the railroad. The
corps then changed direction, moving north toward Petersburg, tearing up
track as it moved. Rainfall began at 1:15 in the afternoon, and at about two the
Confederates of Henry Heth's division of Hill's corps attacked, some six thousand men in two lines. Ayres broke the first rebel line, but the Maryland Brigade gave way before the second wave, and this caused Ayres to be outflanked.
After falling back, and with Cutler's division in support, Ayres stabilized his
line. Crawford was also attacked but not as strongly, and he held his own. The
rebels fell back to the line from which they had begun their advance. [22]

Warren summed up the day's activity for Meade by saying, "[T]he enemy's
proximity to his fortified line enabled him to act with boldness, and I do not
think he considered us strong and made his effort to drive us from the railroad.
He has taken some prisoners from us to-day and now knows our strength. If he
tries again, it will have to be with a very large force to succeed." To Emily, he

said, "we have had a very hard day's work and some hard fighting. We however maintained ourselves well, and have accomplished our main object in getting possession of the Weldon Railroad." [23]

Possession of the Weldon Railroad was indeed a signal achievement, as Warren knew. The importance of the road was marked by the rapid response of General Lee in pushing a division out from his lines to try to recapture the endangered railroad, and it would be emphasized in the next several days by his further efforts to drive the Fifth Corps off the line. As Grant wrote to Halleck, "Taking possession of the Weldon road has made the enemy apparently very nervous." [24]

With Warren on the Weldon Railroad, Meade wanted to make sure he stayed there. Warren was notified that Gershom Mott's Second Corps division had been ordered (from Deep Bottom, north of the James) to relieve some five or six thousand troops of the Ninth Corps, now under John G. Parke, who would then come to Warren's support. This support was not immediately available, however, as Mott's men could not show up for some time. Parke had an additional fifteen hundred men who were being sent immediately to the aid of the Fifth Corps. The Ninth Corps was closest to Warren, and efforts were made to connect the picket lines of the two corps, although ultimately an interval of more than a mile existed between them, which had to be picketed by cavalry. [25]

Late at night on the 18th, Grant instructed Meade to "tell Warren if the enemy comes out and attacks him in the morning not to hesitate about taking out every man he has to repel it; and not to stop when the enemy is repulsed, but to follow him up to the last." Meade promptly sent this message on to his Fifth Corps commander. [26]

The morning of August 19 found Warren still trying to establish a connection with the Ninth Corps on his right while his men erected earthworks. He advised Meade that with the expected reinforcements from the Ninth Corps, now counted at six thousand men, "it will be safe to trust me to hold on to the railroad." He had sent General Edward Bragg's brigade of Cutler's division, the famed but now sadly depleted Iron Brigade, to fill the gap between the right of the Fifth Corps and the left of the Ninth. "This order General Bragg did not execute as directed," Warren wrote, "but took up another line a mile or more to the rear." Learning this, Warren sent staff officers to correct the line, but before that was done, at 4:15 P.M., William Mahone's Confederate division struck Bragg. Into the thinly held space, only lightly timbered, swept Mahone's rebels, "until," as one participant wrote, "completely carrying away our right flank, he had swept quite into our rear, taking in his track nearly all of four regiments." It was a scary moment, as the Iron Brigade "had crumpled like paper in a matter of minutes." "[C]onfusion worse confounded" threatened "not only the loss of our hold on the railroad, but of most of the corps." [27]

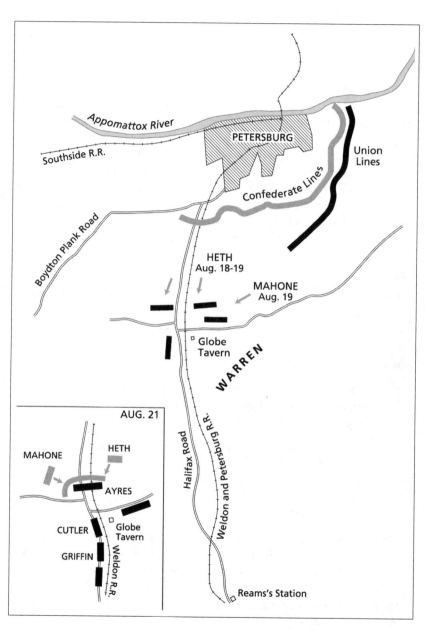

Weldon Railroad and Globe Tavern, August 18, 19, 21, 1864

But Colonel Charles Wheelock ordered his brigade of Crawford's division, unseen by the onrushing rebels, to change front and charge the enemy, and his unit's point-blank volley so deranged the unsuspecting Confederates that they broke and ran. Ayres's division, struck by the same flank attack of Mahone, saw a part of one brigade cut off and captured, including Brigadier General Joseph Hayes, the brigade commander. Ayres then initiated a fierce counterattack which drove the Confederates back. Twice more the enemy came on and twice more Ayres, with help from Griffin and part of the Ninth Corps, drove them back. After the last repulse, the Confederates returned to their own works, their major effort to retake the Weldon Railroad having been frustrated. The Fifth Corps lost heavily on August 19, including some twenty-five hundred men captured, but it held its position. "We have lost in numbers," Warren told Meade, "but not in morale." Wash Roebling said "the night closed finding us still in secure possession of the Weldon R.R. and one Div. almost unengaged yet. We were still good for another fight."[28]

Warren was not happy about the day's activities. He wrote in frustration to his wife:

> A line that I expected to establish by 9 AM was not reported done till 4 PM and before I had time to do anything further in relation to it, the enemy broke through in very heavy force and . . . captured quite 2000 men. The command being taken in the rear gave up easily and in the woods as they were commands could not be given in turn.
>
> We fought them heavily for about two hours and drove them all back, but I have been unhappy ever since at the loss and have had to make redoubled exertions to make up for it . . .
>
> . . . I feel so dissatisfied with the result and yet I find no special fault with my command. All did as well as they could. But it is very trying to stand battles as commander where there is so much giving way, and you cannot conceive my position at such times . . . But I believe I have the best set of men and officers in this army.[29]

August 20 saw little fighting in Warren's area, but he knew that Robert E. Lee had not given up his efforts to regain the Weldon Railroad. The day was occupied by the Fifth Corps (and Willcox's division of the Ninth) in making their defensive works ever more secure, with earthworks, trenches, abatis, and wires. Warren's front line was formed across the railroad, but the left was refused, almost parallel with the tracks and about two hundred yards from the woods to the west of the railroad. His rear line under Griffin was about three hundred yards beyond the first, and formed in echelon to it, with the artillery posted on a high spot on the right bank of the railroad cut. Wainwright's guns perfectly covered the open plain to the left of the first line. Warren, one observer wrote, "seems to have calculated to a certainty where and how the at-tacks of the enemy would be made, and every part of his programme thus far had been admirably played, and now the last, most decisive and concluding act was about to be enacted." [30]

The morning of the 21st, beautiful and sunny after the heavy rains of the preceding days, opened with a half-hour rebel artillery cannonade, and then Mahone's veteran Confederate infantry moved out of the woods off the left flank of Warren's line, its "heavy and compact columns in grand array," as one witness wrote. "Time was given them to swing clear of the woods and open out on the plain towards the left of our main, front line. It was a grand sight; with their steady, firm tread now just begun, and their colors floating in the breeze." Now the time had come: "Warren's batteries open and this living mass of humanity become a mass of mangled flesh and bones; and the living drop with the dead and dying." [31]

Roebling noted that it was Hoffman's and Bragg's brigades which did the damage, along with the artillery, and he called it "a clear victory for us, achieved with trivial loss." Bragg's Iron Brigade, in fact, exacted sweet retribu-tion for its humiliation of two days before, creating "a field of carnage" in front of its lines. Wainwright, of course, felt that the damage was done mainly by his artillery; "even Warren," he wrote, "is said to praise it." [32]

Regardless, the day's Union loss of three hundred was far outmatched by the Confederate total of three thousand. Even Patrick, the crusty provost marshal general of the Army of the Potomac, no fan of Warren's, admitted that "their repulse by Warren [on August 21] is regarded by them as the bloodiest they have had recently." [33] Such losses as the enemy had sustained in trying to drive off the Fifth Corps were unacceptable to an army with no means of replacing those lost. Lee had to acknowledge, reluctantly, that the Union army was irre-trievably ensconced on the Weldon Railroad, and he immediately cut his army's rations in half. After this the Confederates could run supplies safely only so far north on the rail line before they had to be transferred to wagons for a long and laborious detour around the Union army.

Warren still managed to find a dark cloud beneath the silver lining. He told Emily that "the enemy attacked me again yesterday with very heavy force but I had everything well arranged and whipped them easily." He complained, though, that after all he and his corps had accomplished in the movement to secure the railroad and repel the enemy's efforts to drive him away the only word of acknowledgment he had received "was a note from Genl Grant to Genl Meade saying it seemed to him I ought to have done more." He con-cluded that he had "no confidence in Genl Grant's abilities to use an army," but he hated to have himself proven right in his judgment. "We cannot afford to prove the incapacity of our commanders at such cost of men and means. So I do hope that I am mistaken in my estimate of his ability." [34]

In the meantime, in response to the repeated innuendoes from Grant that the Fifth Corps should get out of its entrenchments after repulsing Confederate attacks and chase the rebels all the way back to and beyond Petersburg, Warren pointed out to Meade that "on my north front he [the enemy] falls back at once into his intrenchments, and if I move west with my whole force I must make another detour to avoid a flank attack while doing it. I lose all the advantage of my artillery as soon as I move and get the effect of his." He concluded by saying, pointedly, "I believe I have fought against the army opposed to me to know pretty well what to do here on the field." [35]

The siege of Petersburg continued, and the rebels began to feel the real privations of a siege. As Lee had long foreseen, it had become a matter of time.

CHAPTER EIGHTEEN

WEST TO PEEBLES' FARM

GEORGE GORDON MEADE WROTE TO HIS WIFE on August 24, "We have had some pretty hard fighting to secure our lodgment on the Weldon Railroad. Grant and Warren are the heroes of the affair," Grant for his conception of the movement, Warren for carrying it out successfully. Still, he said, "we lost a good many men in killed and wounded, but principally in prisoners. Our army is becoming much weakened by these repeated losses, and our only hope is that the enemy suffers proportionately." [1]

Meade now brought Hancock's Second Corps back from Deep Bottom, north of the James, and directed two divisions of it to Reams' Station, on the Weldon Railroad below Warren's position at Globe Tavern, to tear up tracks and make the railroad useless to the enemy as far south as could be done. Warren's corps, meanwhile, was busily engaged in building redoubts, battery positions, and whatever else was needed to make its position on the railroad impregnable. [2]

Throughout the 23rd and 24th of August, reports came in of Confederate troop movements to the left of the railroad. There was conjecture at both the Fifth Corps' and Meade's headquarters as to whether these movements threatened Warren or Hancock, and both commanders were alerted. Warren felt that the troops observed were probably working parties for the construction of a new line for General Lee, but Humphreys thought that a force of eight to ten thousand men was somewhat excessive for a working party. [3]

After a day of destroying about eight miles of railroad, the Second Corps was attacked on the 25th by A. P. Hill's corps at Reams' Station, the attack confirming that these were not working parties. Hancock was able to drive off several efforts by the rebels, but late in the day a portion of Gibbon's division gave way, eight guns were lost, and a fierce fight took place before Hancock could stabilize his position. It was a dark day for the Second Corps, for many of Gibbon's men, mostly untried conscripts or substitutes without much incentive to sacrifice their lives for the cause, surrendered meekly or refused to fight. "About as thorough a thrashing I guess as the Second Corps has ever had," Wainwright observed, and Hancock was shattered by the day's reverses.[4]

Meade ordered Warren to send Crawford's division down the Halifax Road to support the Second Corps, along with a division from the Ninth Corps, but before they were very far along Hancock sent word that he was withdrawing and the reinforcements were not necessary. His only purpose in being at Reams' Station was to tear up tracks, and his men could not do this with the interference from the enemy.

The next day there were reports and rumors about possible assaults against Warren's position, but nothing came of them. Over the course of a week, the Second, Fifth, and Ninth corps had all been bloodied to some extent, but Gouverneur Warren's Fifth Corps still sat solidly upon the Weldon Railroad, the great prize of the week's activities. In fact, the Confederates were never to regain possession of the road.

Warren's comment to Emily was that "the newspapers have not done the 5th Corps justice in our late movements." So much attention, he said, had been paid to the Second Corps' efforts north of the James, of which nothing came, that the reporters failed to appreciate what he had done. "Yesterday's work proved that we are so far the only ones that have maintained their selves 'on this line.'" A couple of days later Wainwright was astounded to read accounts in the New York papers that made Reams' Station almost a Union victory. "Twice as much is made in the paper of this fight," he said, "as of ours of the 21st, for which there are two good reasons. First, Hancock keeps a reporter and seeks newspaper reputation, while Warren does neither; and second, Hancock's fight needs bolstering, ours does not." He added, "Somehow that fight of ours seems to be very little talked of, though it was really one of the most brilliant and perfect affairs of the whole campaign."[5]

The next day Warren reported to Emily that Grant and Meade had visited his lines. "I think late operations have improved their estimate of my opinions very much and lately they are carrying out the very plans I urged here in June." He still felt, though, "that I could have made better plans for this army than any that have been adopted."[6]

With the Weldon Railroad now denied to the Confederates in Petersburg and Richmond, combat along the siege line settled down once again. Sharpshooters and snipers were always a problem, but an informal truce prevailed along the respective picket lines, and warnings were given before hostilities directed from higher echelons were resumed. On the 27th Warren sent word to his division commanders to clean out the drainage ditches in their areas; "we must make every effort," he said, "to secure good drainage in order to prevent sickness."[7]

The Fifth Corps had by this time been reduced to the three divisions it would retain to the end of the war. Lysander Cutler, citing ill health and the effects of several wounds, had asked to be relieved from active duty, and his division was merged into the other three, now commanded by Griffin, Ayres, and Crawford. Much work was done in constructing four redoubts on the newly won line, and, as Wainwright noted, "General Warren has taken them in hand himself and pushed them on with great rapidity." [8]

On September 10 Warren pleaded with headquarters for a break from the incessant labor of building roads and constructing fortifications, since "as much of our attention as possible" should be given "to drilling the recruits and restoring the discipline and morale of the troops." The Fifth Corps, like the others, had received its share of green and untried newcomers, and military training and discipline were necessary to make real soldiers of them. All of the hard labor imposed on the men, Warren said, "makes us neglect purely military matters of greatest importance." One thing was certain, and that was that much hard fighting lay ahead before the South would give up. For that work soldiers, not pick-and-shovel laborers, would be required. [9]

Grant's next plan for nipping at Lee's flanks centered on a proposed drive against Richmond by Butler's army, to be carried out at the end of September. He told Meade that "on the morning of the 29th instant a movement will take place intended to surprise and capture the works of the enemy north of the James River and between Malvern Hill and Richmond." He admitted that he did not think Butler could "force his way to Richmond," but, at the other end of the long Union line, he wanted Meade to have his army "under arms at 4 A.M. on the 29th," with three or four days' rations and sixty rounds of ammunition per man, "ready to move in any direction." As to what the Army of the Potomac might do, Grant said, "I leave the details to you, stating merely that I want every effort used to convince the enemy that the South Side road and Petersburg are the objects of our efforts." [10]

An appropriate order went out next day from Meade's headquarters, directing, *inter alia*, that Warren should be prepared to move "with not less than two divisions of his corps," while Parke was to concentrate two of his Ninth Corps divisions at a spot south of Globe Tavern, "ready for movement." At 11 A.M. of the 28th, Warren sent to headquarters information obtained from two deserters, that the rebels had extended their entrenchments southwest from Petersburg to Poplar Spring Church. "They are building works on Mr. Peeble's farm," Warren said, "and how far south they do not know and think there is a considerable infantry force in that direction." The deserters said the enemy troops were "pretty thick." William Peebles's farm was a little under two miles west of Globe Tavern and slightly to the northwest of Poplar Spring Church. [11]

The orders to move on the 29th were pushed back a day, and shortly after midnight on the 30th Warren was directed to have his corps ready to move at eight o'clock that morning. After some further delay he was ordered at 8:50 A.M.

to "move out past Poplar Spring Church and endeavor to secure the intersection of the Squirrel Level road, so as to enable us to gain a position on the right
of the enemy." The Ninth Corps would follow in support "and also try to open
a route across the swamp below Poplar Spring Church." [12]

A few words on the geography of the area are necessary for orientation here.
As has been noted, the Weldon Railroad ran straight south from Petersburg,
with the Halifax Road parallel to and just west of the railroad. About a mile
south of Petersburg, and roughly halfway between the city and Globe Tavern,
where Warren now had his headquarters, the Vaughan Road branched off
from the Halifax Road in a southwesterly direction, toward Dinwiddie Court
House. A half mile to the west the Squirrel Level Road paralleled the Vaughan
Road, also running southwestwardly. From a spot on the Halifax Road a half
mile south of Globe Tavern there ran a road called the Poplar Spring Road,
angling west by northwest, and intersecting, first, the Vaughan Road and, second, the Squirrel Level Road, two miles west from the Halifax Road. Below
the Poplar Spring Road was a sluggish, meandering stream called Arthur's
Swamp. Just west of where the Poplar Spring Road met the Squirrel Level
Road sat the Peebles farm, a large open field in a generally wooded area. The
Confederates had extended their defensive line just behind the Squirrel Level
Road, west of the Peebles farm.

Finally, about a mile farther west, was the Boydton Plank Road, now uti-
lized by the rebels for wagons carrying supplies into the city from Stony Creek
Depot, eighteen miles below Petersburg and the northernmost point on the
Weldon Railroad still controlled by the Confederacy. Beyond that road was the
South Side Railroad, the last rail line still supplying Petersburg. These were
Grant's ultimate goals in this area, but he recognized that they would have to
be reached in increments.

On the 29th Warren had sent Baxter's brigade, from Crawford's division,
west to verify for Meade that the rebels were in force at the Peebles farm. Baxter determined that Heth's division was indeed there, with four guns, and he
returned to his original position. The Confederate line at the Peebles farm,
and the infantry holding it, were the objects of the next day's activities. [13]

One of Warren's brigades saw some action on the 29th. David Gregg's Union
cavalry got into a heated fight with Wade Hampton's rebels during the day, farther to the south and west, and the Federals were getting the worst of it. At
about 5 P.M. Meade told Warren to send some help to Gregg, and Colonel
Edgar Gregory's brigade of Griffin's division was quickly rushed down to lend
a hand. Gregory arrived in time to help the Union cavalry fend off the final
rebel charge in the gloaming; his brigade then turned around and marched
back to Globe Tavern to prepare for the attack of the next morning.

At around 9 A.M. on the morning of September 30, Warren set his force in
motion, south on the Halifax Road and then west on the Poplar Spring Road,

toward Poplar Spring Church and the Peebles farm. The force of twenty thousand infantrymen consisted of Griffin's and Ayres's divisions of the Fifth Corps in the van, followed by a large part of the Ninth Corps. Ten batteries (or forty-two guns) rolled along as well, and some forty-three hundred of Gregg's cavalry completed the Union attacking force. Warren was in command of his men, Parke in command of his, and the two were supposed to cooperate in overall tactical leadership—not the best arrangement, as Warren had tried to make clear to Meade as far back as Spotsylvania Court House.

The movement went slowly, as all of these men were required to use just one road, which, just west of the Vaughan, went through a dense forest. Warren, as the principal historian of this battle has written, "met the technical demands of the new situation well." He put his pioneers, picked troops skilled at such tasks as clearing roads, building bridges, and erecting fortifications, to work building another rough road alongside the narrow Poplar Spring Road. He threw his leading regiment, the Eighteenth Massachusetts, out in front of his column as skirmishers, and when rebel fire was drawn he pushed out three more regiments in support of the Bay Staters.[14]

Marching cautiously through the forest, Griffin's division did not reach Poplar Spring Church until 11 A.M., at which time Warren notified Meade of this arrival and said that "I am widening out the road and getting my command up and in order."[15] It took another two hours before he had his command "in order," and this delay has drawn upon Warren some serious animadversions by historian Richard Sommers:

> His hesitancy to force a battle on September 30 . . .was almost characteristic of his conduct on semi-independent missions during the last twelve months of the war. Such conduct, despite its many fine features, drew unfavorable comment from others, including Grant himself. The General-in-Chief later attributed the subordinate's shortcomings to a tendency to 'see every danger at a glance before he had encountered it' . . . [T]he General-in-Chief's estimate, while accurate in itself, does not get to the root of the problem. Nor does the New Yorker's desire for perfection more than complement, if not stem from, the basic cause. Warren was hesitant not just because he feared danger, not just because he feared imperfection, but also because he feared responsibility. Not the responsibility for minor tactics—his technical know-how made him justifiably confident there; nor was it the responsibility for meeting an emergency, which summoned forth his latent talent without leaving time for self-doubt. What bothered Warren was the responsibility for grand tactics, that realm of military art dealing with movements just outside the actual field of combat. Making the awesome decision to precipitate battle and concerning himself with potential enemy responses beyond the site of fighting were what made him hesitate.[16]

Well, now, that is a stern assessment. There is no doubt that Warren seldom moved his corps with the speed of a Hancock or a Stonewall Jackson; he knew from his training the precautions that were to be taken on a march, and he took them. As a result, he did not blunder into things he was not prepared for. He tried to avoid going into battle without being sure that his flanks were covered, that everything he could put in order *was* in order, and he had the lessons of the Orange Turnpike and Laurel Hill to show him what happened when this was not done. How many "semi-independent missions" did Warren lead, in which this shrinking from responsibility supposedly disabled him? The North Anna, where his corps acquitted itself nobly? The night march to Spotsylvania, where he hesitated not at all in throwing his units forward, perhaps even too rashly? The December raid south to Hicksford, to destroy more of the Weldon Railroad, a movement which even Grant's man John Rawlins called "a great success"?[17]

Perhaps, after all, it is just at Peebles' Farm that this fatal characteristic showed up. Warren did, after all, write to Emily the evening of October 1 that in any fighting the next day, with Meade on hand, "I shall not have the anxiety of responsibility upon me as on yesterday." Recall, though, that at Peebles' Farm Warren commanded only his own corps; for support from the Ninth Corps he had to depend upon John Parke's cooperation, a fact which may have caused him some "anxiety." At Peebles' Farm he had responsibility, but he did not have the authority that should have gone with it.[18]

In addition, there were other impediments at Peebles' Farm. The terrain was terrible, "even more difficult west of the church than east of it," as Sommers says. In addition to the thick woods, there were ravines, swamps, creeks, and tangled undergrowth. These all blocked Warren's view of the farm and caused delays in his troops' getting into position for the assault. Warren, who understood that at least Heth's division was present behind the rebel fortifications, also felt it important to wait for the Ninth Corps to come up, and he made a key decision which speeded up this process. He shifted Ayres's division out of the way of Parke's corps by moving it a short way north on the Vaughan Road to face northward, where it could protect the right flank of Warren's advance. Once he did this, the Ninth Corps made much better time.[19]

When Griffin got his division ready for action, in a steep ravine along the southeastern part of the farm, he directed that each brigade, as it emerged from the ravine, should make a half-right wheel to shift its front northwest toward the main Confederate fortification, called Fort Archer, which would keep the rebels from enfilading the Union ranks with fire from the fort.[20]

The men of the First Division, when they received the word to advance, surged out of the ravine, made the required turn, crossed the Squirrel Level Road, passed the abandoned farmhouse, and ran the remaining distance across an open field to the Confederate line. The distance from the ravine to the enemy works was more than six hundred yards, and by running they cut down substantially the time they were exposed to the defenders' fire. Griffin's men climbed over the enemy earthworks and over Fort Archer and in a few minutes overwhelmed the Confederates present. Warren called Griffin's charge "one of the boldest I ever saw . . . 600 yards over a clear field defended by infantry against a parapet flanked by an enclosed redoubt." His loss, Warren reported, was "not very great," although Colonel Norval E. Welch of the Sixteenth Michigan Veterans was killed on the parapet.[21]

What made the charge a bit less impressive in retrospect was the fact that the overwhelmed defenders were not the tough infantrymen of Heth's division but a small cavalry brigade and a few artillerymen, adding up to about a thousand men. Of course, Warren and Griffin did not know this when the assault was ordered, and the men of the First Division indeed acquitted themselves handsomely. Griffin received a great cheer from his men when he climbed up into Fort Archer, and a few minutes later Warren was applauded noisily as he joined his troops in the captured fortification. Griffin pulled his men together around Fort Archer to rest and regroup.

Fort Archer was the key to the whole southern line along the Squirrel Level Road, and the Fifth Corps had rammed right through it. The way now lay open to the Boydton Plank Road, and the Ninth Corps should have made the move. Of the two Fifth Corps divisions, Griffin's was spent and Ayres's was situated off to the right of Griffin, along the Squirrel Level Road, on the opposite side from the way to the Boydton Plank Road. The Ninth Corps, behind and slightly to the left of Fort Archer, was in position to move ahead, but Parke had his men take up a defensive position around Peebles' Farm. He and Warren were both concerned about a possible Confederate counterattack— as had taken place so often in the preceding months after a successful charge—so appropriate defensive measures were taken. Also, at this point, Warren took steps to make sure his connections back to Globe Tavern and the railroad were secure.

For an hour or more there was no effort made to follow up the victory at Fort Archer. Richard Sommers suggests that "had either Parke or Warren commanded the strike force instead of acting as coequals, they might at least have achieved a greater measure of co-ordination," though he speculates that "their individual hesitancy would likely have still retarded the advance."[22] Meade did not show up until 3 P.M., far too late to move his army effectively to the Boydton Plank Road.

The Ninth Corps did now move out to the north and west, toward what was called the Pegram farm and beyond toward the Jones farm, just shy of the Boydton road, but then Parke stopped again, for another two hours. Warren rode up, perhaps after receiving a spur from Grant ("If the enemy can be broken & started follow him up closely"), and urged Parke to resume the advance, but of course he had no authority to order the Ninth Corps forward. "Warren was urging him all in his power," Wainwright, who was present, said, "[though] it was no avail." Parke evidently wondered why Griffin's division did not move up on his right, but it continued to pull itself together back at Fort Archer.[23]

In the meantime, however, the Confederates recognized the serious threat to their vital line of supply, and they hustled Hampton's cavalry down into some rudimentary works between the Jones farm and the plank road. Next, from A. P. Hill's corps, came Heth's two infantry brigades and two under Cadmus Wilcox. The rebel infantry far outnumbered the small portion of the Ninth Corps which had reached the Jones farm, and the southerners soon counterattacked, chasing the bits and pieces of the Ninth Corps back toward the Pegram farm. At this point, however, Griffin's division emerged from the captured works and, under Warren's direction, joined with the Ninth Corps to put together a solid defensive line. Warren ordered Wainwright to create a second line with his artillery on the knoll on which the Pegram house stood. If these defensive lines failed to hold, the Army of the Potomac would lose everything it had gained earlier in the day. But, with Griffin's division making the crucial difference, the line held after savage fighting; Wilcox's thrust was checked and pushed back. The combat for the day ended, with the Union holding its gains at Peebles' Farm and the Squirrel Level Road.

Warren lauded Griffin again, for the "gallant manner in which he advanced and met the enemy's attack this evening . . . effectually checking their most persistent efforts to advance." Earlier, he had written that "the Fifth Corps has done splendidly today; principally Griffin." Warren's corps lost 626 men that day, while the Ninth Corps, at the Jones and Pegram farms, lost almost two thousand.[24] The Union line, as a result of the day's activities, now reached to Peebles' Farm, and the troops soon set to work incorporating Fort Archer into the Union defensive works. The day's long-term objective, the Boydton Plank Road, was not attained, although it is questionable whether two small corps, stretched out in a line back to Globe Tavern, could have held that road even if they had reached it.

In the early evening of the 30th Meade directed Warren to "occupy the intrenchments taken from the enemy today, your left holding the redoubt in Peebles' field and your right connecting with your works on the Weldon railroad . . . You will intrench." Several hours later word came down to the Fifth Corps commander to send out a strong reconnaissance at daylight to find where the enemy was, and a little after that Warren and Parke were advised that if their reconnaissance showed a weakening of the Confederate forces in their fronts a new effort should be made for the plank road. At 8 A.M. the next morning, though, Warren sent word to Meade that the enemy was still in position near the Pegram house, "where they were last night," and they were demonstrating against Ayres.[25]

Warren had fashioned a strong defensive line, with Griffin to the right of the Ninth Corps, Ayres to the right of him, facing north on the Squirrel Level Road, and Crawford brought up to fill the gap between Ayres and the Halifax Road. Through the rainy night of September 30–October 1, the men of the Fifth Corps marched into their positions and dug what entrenchments they could in the mud. While these were not elaborate, they were, as matters developed, sufficient. Hill put together a force of some 4,750 men under Heth to smash what he expected to be the flank of Ayres's division, and Wilcox, with about 2,400 men, was to feint an attack at the Pegram farm. Intelligence reports of the gathering Confederate offensive came to the corps commanders, who felt that such a showing of rebel strength answered the question which the ordered reconnaissance was supposed to determine, so there was no need for it. Sommers comments that Warren and Parke "now had their pretext for not attacking. Let Hill try whatever he wanted." [26] The fact is that Warren and Parke were right: they had a strong defensive position, and they were fully prepared to face whatever Powell Hill could throw at them.

Wilcox made his feint at the Pegram farm, and Harry Heth, after some initial hesitation when he realized he was hitting Ayres not on the flank but frontally, sent his three brigades forward at around 9 A.M., one after the other, and saw them suffer one-sided losses with no corresponding gains. He then called off the assault, and his decision to do so, as Sommers says, "confirmed Federal possession of their newly won foothold on Peebles' farm." Warren sent word back to headquarters that "General Ayres has repulsed the assaults upon him." [27]

The Fifth Corps spent the rest of the day digging in, strengthening its defenses, and ensuring that the Peebles farm would henceforth be an integral part of the Union line. It rained hard all day, but Warren's men kept at it, digging down into the mud.

He wrote that evening to Emily, telling her, "This morning the enemy attacked me early but he was easily driven off." While he was at it, Warren wrote to Meade, giving him once again the benefit of his strategic thinking, suggesting "the establishment of a very strong position on the Weldon railroad, with a supply of stores and competent garrison . . . [T]hen, assembling all our force, place ourselves on the South Side Railroad and destroy it. This would undoubtedly bring on a general battle, which would decide whether General Lee could keep the field against us or not." Warren continued with this written lecture, reminding Meade of the time required "to get our new levies in order" with "the rudiments of their drill and discipline." Finally, he said, "operating at the same time on two such distant flanks" makes "the commander at each point apprehensive of being outnumbered by the enemy, which is always practicable for him to do at one or the other, and thus inevitably produce want of boldness and vigor on our part, unless we neglect more than any of us are willing to do." Meade perhaps read this as a justification for the failure to capture the Boydton Plank Road the day before.[28]

Grant was willing to call off offensive operations after the repulse of Heth on October 1, but Meade wanted to try again the next day. He ordered Warren and Parke to attack in the morning, "as soon after daylight as practicable," using "your whole force in attacking." Mott's Second Corps division had been brought up by military railroad, arriving at Globe Tavern early in the evening of October 1, so it was to participate as well. However, Warren was not to attack any entrenched lines.[29]

In the morning, Mott advanced on the left, while Parke and Warren advanced on their own fronts. What they found was that the Confederate army had gone back inside its defensive line, and the only way they could force a battle was to charge the Confederate works. Humphreys, at 11:15, wrote to both Warren and Parke, saying, "Appearances indicate that the enemy has withdrawn to his main line of intrenchments." This being so, Meade wanted them "to take up the best line for connecting with the Weldon railroad, and making the left secure, and then to intrench." The battle of Peebles' Farm was over.[30]

Richard Sommers, analyzing the results of the fighting around the Squirrel Level Line, gave high marks to Griffin and Ayres, as "master tacticians, able both to co-ordinate and to inspire their forces offensively and defensively." And he applauded Warren, too, except for his reluctance to accept the responsibility of giving battle and exploiting success. "Below the grand-tactical level," he said, "the New Yorker again performed well, especially when the Butternuts forced battle upon him." Overall, "his tactics were flawless. Few corps commanders then in Virginia could handle combat as well as Gouverneur Warren—if only a senior officer was around to free him from grand-tactical responsibility."[31]

CHAPTER NINETEEN

TO THE END OF 1864

W ith peebles' farm and the weldon railroad now solidly in Union hands, Gouverneur Warren wanted a rest. He wrote to Emily that "we accomplished everything expected of us splendidly, and are now straitening [*sic*] things out, repairing damages, etc." Of course, they did not seize the Boydton Plank Road, which had been one of the goals of the movement, but Warren was justifiably proud of what his men succeeded in doing, cutting the rebels' Squirrel Level Line.[1]

He applied promptly for a leave and, after first being turned down by Meade, was then given eight days, "to be extended by telegraph if possible." Crawford took over acting command of the corps, and Warren had what turned out to be almost two weeks with Emily. The young general and his even younger wife finally had the opportunity to celebrate for more than a hastily seized day or two what young married life had promised them. A fortnight of bliss with Emily left Warren even sadder at one more leave-taking. Stopping in Washington on the way back to the army, he wrote of how much he loved her and how miserable he felt at being separated once again. "Yet," he said, "I feel rejoiced when I think of what a blissful time I have spent with you and what a happy life we'll have when war no longer compels us to be separated." He reported back to the corps on October 21, only to be told by Meade that he might as well have stayed away four or five days longer. "That was a mighty mean thing to tell a man *after* his return," Roebling wrote.[2]

That Gouv and Emily had an exhilarating reunion is evidenced by a letter he wrote in answer to one of hers, saying, "I think strangers would think it right naughty to see the letter you wrote me addressed to your 'lover' if they did not know I was your husband which they would never imagine being called by that title. Yes I like it very much. It seems to have so little of being your wedded lord about it. I would rather to be bound to you by the affection that often causes sinful attachment than by any less tender tie."[3]

Not everyone was overjoyed by Warren's return. Wainwright, his artillery chief, wrote in his diary that "ten days with his wife does not appear to have sweetened his temper at all, from what I hear." He added, then, "I see very little of him myself, except when obliged to officially. Our notions are not at all similar, so I deem it best to keep on the most punctilious terms with him." This reaction may, of course, reflect what Warren told Emily after he got back, that there was much work demanding his attention; presumably, his staffers, who would complain to a sympathetic ear like Wainwright's, were kept busy in doing what was required to relieve these matters.[4]

In addition, the men of the Iron Brigade, to relieve monotony, had laid out a race track in the rear of their camp. The track proved quite popular with the men until several regimental commanders complained about it, claiming that it was a demoralizing influence. On the 22nd, the day after his return from leave, Warren dispatched a detail to the track which arrested all the enlisted men who were there enjoying themselves. This action was not a popular one on the part of the corps commander, but on the whole he was well regarded by his men. One day Warren was out checking on work details, and he came to a group from the Iron Brigade which was making very slow progress. Proclaiming that his staff could cut down more trees than the men of the famous midwestern unit, Warren said, in mock indignation, "I never saw a lazier set of men in my life, they are good for nothing but fighting!" The men howled in appreciation.[5]

That Warren was still highly regarded by the army, if not perhaps at its headquarters, is attested by a letter from cavalry captain Charles F. Adams, Jr., to his brother Henry in London, on October 15, describing reports of a possible push by land against the Confederate fortress at Wilmington, North Carolina. Adams thought its capture likely "if a dashing General is in command—say Warren."[6]

Wilmington was not to be, but soon after Warren returned to his post, Grant ordered another push westward, seeking still to get astride Lee's last lines of supply. This time Hancock's Second Corps would be the main strike force, with support from the Fifth and the Ninth. The objective, again, was the Boydton Plank Road and beyond that, if possible, the South Side Railroad.

Hancock was ordered to start at 2 A.M. on October 27, moving by the Vaughan Road, crossing Hatcher's Run well to the south of the rebel works, and marching to the Boydton Plank Road. From here, it was hoped, the Second Corps could reach to the South Side Railroad and capture that vital line. Parke's Ninth Corps, on the right of the Union thrust, was to attack the unfinished rebel line, and Warren was to support Parke if he broke through and support Hancock if Parke did not succeed. North of the James, Ben Butler was to attack at the same time with his army, although no one really expected much of Butler by this stage of the war.[7]

It was a complex plan, plotted over country poorly understood, and too ambitious by far. Parke was unable to make any progress on a rainy day against the
main Confederate line, and the Ninth Corps' "movement" did not convince
the rebel command that it was a credible threat. The Fifth Corps initiative,
along Hatcher's Run by Crawford's division, bogged down in the dense and
soggy thickets along the stream and never connected with Hancock. The honors of the day went to the Second Corps commander, in his last fight before
yielding to the continuing agony of his Gettysburg wound and relinquishing
the corps command. Hancock, cavalry commander David Gregg, and division
commanders Gershom Mott and Thomas W. Egan won laurels in repulsing
the surprise attacks of Heth and Mahone. During the night, low on ammunition and out of contact with the rest of the army, Hancock was given permission to withdraw.[8]

Another shot at the South Side Railroad had come to naught. Summing it
up, Meade said that Hancock "made a glorious fight and . . . punished the enemy severely."[9]

The next morning Grant sent a testy dispatch to Meade, with an underlying
criticism of Warren, asking, if the enemy crossed the run below Hancock,
"where was Crawford during this time? If he had followed your repeated instructions to Warren this could not have happened. Even after Hancock was
attacked Crawford must have been in a position where, by boldly pushing up,
he could have annihilated all of the enemy south of the run." Perhaps there
was an explanation for this, but he wanted to know what it was.[10]

Meade responded that there were several factors preventing the division
from getting up, all really beyond Crawford's control. First, he said, "the character of the country" was "worse than the Wilderness"; next, Crawford was in
fact engaged with the enemy; and, finally, the distance between Crawford and
Hancock was, "owing to a bend in the stream," greater than had been thought.
Meade said he agreed with Warren that there was no way Crawford could have
gotten up in time, and he hoped that the explanation would relieve Grant's
mind "of any impression unfavorable to General Crawford." Perhaps it did,
but once again Grant harbored an unfavorable impression of Warren's Fifth
Corps, whether there was reason for it or not.[11]

Gouv summed up the Hatcher's Run fight to Emily, calling it "a very hard
days work and some considerable fighting . . . The results were not very important either way, though our loss and the enemy's must have been considerable."
He added that no other day's battle had "so exhausted me." A day later he told
her "it was about a drawn game." He wrote to Will that criticism of Crawford
was unwarranted, since "the 5th Corps did its share in the work beyond question." He added that "too much is expected of us: we always have a duty assigned us, and then must perforce take all the blame if somebody else fails." He
would, he said, "enter the arena if anything is said against this Corps."[12]

Back in the lines, Warren told Emily about a long conversation with his friend Humphreys at Meade's headquarters, "about affairs in general." There were strong rumors, which would shortly turn out to be true, that Humphreys would succeed to command of the Second Corps when Hancock stepped aside. Warren told his wife that "since I left you I have become quite philosophical about the war and begin to think of it as my occupation for life. At any rate I have ceased to worry about its long continuance or look eagerly for its termination." This sense of fatalism, comforting as it may have been to Warren at the front, must have proven worrisome to his dutiful Emily at home.[13]

That such thoughts were rather ephemeral for Warren was proven a few days later when he reported to Emily that Hancock was to be sent north recruiting again, as he had been last year. Overlooking the fact that Hancock's recruiting assignment the year before was the result of his severe wound and that this year it followed his surrender of his corps command, Warren said, "How fortunate he is in these respects. I fear such chances never will come to me."[14]

After writing to Emily on November 7 that "I could hardly think of bringing you to the army this winter," on the next day he wrote of fixing up his headquarters for her. "Don't I wish I could take you in my arms . . . and wouldn't it make me so happy, and so I will be one of these days won't I my darling." Of the presidential election, he wrote with disappointment that only two of his regiments, both from Michigan, had voted for McClellan. Speaking obviously for himself, he wrote, "Our people must, if they aspire to self government have the nobleness to stand by the result of the ballot to which they certainly pledge themselves when they go into an election." Still, the reelection of Abraham Lincoln, with the Republican administration of which he so much disapproved, was just one more disappointment to Gouverneur Warren.[15]

A few days later, Warren was having a "very quiet time" at the front, which gave him the opportunity for "reading and working up maps and papers to great advantage." He spent nearly a full day with Andrew Humphreys, just talking; Humphreys reported that "it is very refreshing to have Warren with me many hours." When Emily wrote to him of going to dinner and the opera, Warren said, "They both make me feel heart sick and desolate to think now everybody can be with you and I so far off. I have been almost brooding over it all day. When will our separation be at an end[?] My position seems to chain me here irrevocably."[16]

Late in November he told Emily that he expected important campaigning yet before the cold of January settled upon them. "I think after all the trials of the campaign," he said, "I have brought my corps out No. 1 and really beaten Hancock who is going home so that hereafter I shall have a chance more than before and be more kindly treated." The next day Warren had a long talk with Meade, who felt that the end of the war was still a long way off; "the prospect . . . of ever enjoying home and love seems so hopeless that nothing but a sigh can tell you how I feel." Still, he concluded, "in this hour of trial to our nation, one should try to be pleased with the post of trial and danger, and be worthy of 'freedom's home or glory's grave.'" [17]

When Emily wrote him of having been in the company of August Belmont, the financier and leader of the Democratic party in New York, Warren wrote back, warning her to "be careful of yourself not to get too much interested in mere fashionable people and fine things, for it makes nine tenths of the people miserable and is the cause of much crime. There is that in the very atmosphere of New York that makes me dread it. The worship of the almighty dollar there is so great that aspiring emotions, noble impulses and intellectual efforts languish." He was glad, he said, that she was making friends for him, "but of course at the risk of no suspicion against yourself. You must be like Caesar's wife." He advised her to cultivate people like the Hamilton Fishes or Governor Morgan or the Seymours, people "of the highest respectability and wealthy," whose friendship might be of service to him.[18]

On December 4 Warren wrote to Emily in an apparent effort to discourage his twenty-three-year-old wife from thoughts of children. "Heaven only knows," he said, "what might be in store for us of happiness or misery in a child. If it made absence more supportable to you it would not at least to me, and I always think of the curse put upon poor Eve 'in sorrow shalt thou bring forth children.'" If they could only live together, he admitted, "it might seem different." [19]

Inaction seemed to induce in Warren a brooding, hectoring, morose sort of humor, as evidenced in his letters home, so an expedition fixed for early December was not unwelcome, even though he called it "a not very important piece of work." He said he was glad to go, for "it gives me busy occupation and enables me to keep my longing thoughts a little more for you." [20]

With his whole corps, Mott's Second Corps division, three brigades of cavalry, and a pontoon train, Warren was to march due south, cross the Nottoway River, and take up the task of further destroying the Weldon Railroad as far as the town of Hicksford, on the Meherrin River. Every mile farther south that the northern terminus of the railroad was pushed was that much more strain imposed on the Confederate supply system. With the army essentially doing nothing, Grant felt that a renewed effort against the Weldon line was in order.

The Sixth Corps, recalled from service in the Shenandoah Valley, arrived back at City Point on December 4. Meade ordered the Sixth to relieve Warren's men in the position held by them, so that the Fifth Corps could then concentrate between the Halifax and Jerusalem Plank roads.[21]

Warren's command, some twenty-five thousand strong, set off at 7 A.M. on the morning of December 7, taking the Jerusalem road south to the Nottoway River. It rained heavily until noon, but the men made steady progress, and a bright late-afternoon sun sent "a spirit of cheerfulness throughout all the ranks." Crawford's division started crossing the Nottoway at around 4 P.M. and, with the cavalry, bivouacked for the night near Sussex Court House. The rest of the force settled down north of the river, having encountered minimal rebel opposition other than cavalry.[22]

The march was resumed early the next morning, and the men were impressed with the countryside through which they were marching, country which "had been entirely free from the ravages of war" and which contrasted sharply "with the desolate, almost desert, land in which we had been accustomed to operate." Warren's infantry reached the railroad in mid-afternoon, to join the cavalry in the work of tearing up the track. After a meal and rest, with Mott's division guarding the trains and watching for possible enemy attacks, the three divisions of the Fifth Corps went to work at 6 P.M., their labors illuminated by the bonfires of burning ties, over which rails were placed until they were bent out of usable shape. By midnight, when Warren called off work for the day, the railroad had been effectively destroyed from the Nottoway to below Jarratt's Station.[23]

"The work of destruction," Warren wrote, "was renewed early on the morning of the 9th by forming a line of battle on the railroad, each division destroying all on its front, and then moving to the left alternately." Gregg's cavalry got rid of any Confederates to the south and picketed north and east, while Griffin's division took over the role of guarding the wagons and watching for any major rebel effort. The destruction was carried to the Meherrin River, at Hicksford, where the enemy was discovered with some force and three artillery batteries dug in on the south bank. Since forcing a crossing was deemed impracticable, the men's rations were close to exhausted, and the Meherrin was as far as he was directed to go in any event, Warren turned back at this point, giving orders to depart the next morning. A half day's ration of bread and a full one of beef were dispensed that evening, and the men had a less than comfortable night, as it began sleeting about eight o'clock.[24]

The return trip was unpleasant in many ways. The sleet in which it started caused slow going, the freezing weather created many hardships including lack of sleep, rations were low, and rebel cavalry harassed the sides of the column. A number of Union soldiers, stragglers who had fallen out of the column heading south, were discovered shot or with their throats cut, murdered apparently by rebel irregulars. "A spirit of vindictiveness [now] pervaded the entire column," one participant wrote. In retaliation, many houses which had been spared on the way south were burned by the angry Federals. When the bodies of several more Union soldiers were found lying in front of the court house at Sussex, the enraged cavalrymen who discovered the victims set fire to the court house and the town, burning much of it to the ground before Warren arrived and put a halt to the destruction.[25]

On the 10th, Robert Potter's division of the Ninth Corps was sent south to aid Warren, reports having come in that A. P. Hill's corps had gone off in search of the Union raiders. Warren, in his report, noted that, "General Hill's corps, the people thought would attack us, but we saw nothing of it." Hill had gone off to the southwest, toward Dinwiddie Court House, on the supposition that the raid was aimed at the South Side Railroad. By the time Hill's men reached Jarratt's Station, all they found were burnt crossties and bent rails. Warren was long gone. Potter reached the Nottoway with his division, learned that he was not needed, and returned whence he had come. On the afternoon of December 12, Warren marched his force back into camp, its mission successfully accomplished, "a great success," as John Rawlins called it. Almost twenty miles of track had been destroyed, at a cost of fewer than a hundred men killed, wounded, and missing.[26]

Back in camp, "weary and exhausted" from the Hicksford raid, he admitted to Emily that "the life I lead is telling on my nerves." He complained that the war might last another three years, and he despaired of the "miserable hirelings that scarce can be made to fight" who were now filling up the army. Warren noted that Mrs. Grant had a fine house on the banks of the James with a steamboat at her disposal, but found that "no reason to bring my little wife who is twice the lady in to the center of our lines in an ambulance over a corduroy road to share a tent or a log cabin."[27]

Warren had another run-in with Meade on December 14, telling Emily that he was "quite indignant . . . the way he talked to me and acted but kept down my passion enough to hear him through bid him good evening and come away . . . But I am getting to hate him for what I regard as unreasonable arrogance and selfishness." Ten days later, all was changed. He reported that Meade had made him a long visit and agreed that Warren should go home in January. "I was glad I had suppressed my feelings when he so offended me a few days ago," Gouv wrote his wife, "for unfriendly personal relations greatly interfere with our official duties and we have not time to quarrel with each other."[28]

A few days earlier Warren had sent to headquarters applications for leaves for himself, Griffin, Ayres, and Crawford, explaining the timing and necessity for each, and showing that the corps "will never be without as good and competent generals as there are in it present for duty." He was accordingly gratified when the staggered leaves were allowed, with his own granted on December 31.[29]

Warren spent most of a month happily with his wife. One feature of his leave was the wedding of his sister Emily to Washington Roebling at Cold Spring. Gouv celebrated his thirty-fifth birthday on January 8, 1865, and, refreshed but reluctant, returned to the army on January 27. He had no inkling of what awaited him in the next couple of months.

CHAPTER TWENTY

BEGINNING OF THE END

"*I* FEEL SO WELL AND STRONG SINCE I CAME BACK that I could be quite happy if I can keep so and never again afflict you with such miserable letters." So did Gouverneur Warren begin his first letter to his wife Emily after returning to the army at the end of January 1865. Backsliding immediately, he then told of visiting Romeyn Ayres, commander of his Second Division, just back from a twenty-day leave to his home in Portland, Maine, and complaining about it. Ayres, he said, "found his leave . . . so short he was sorry he went at all." He and Ayres then visited Griffin, who had brought his wife back with him on a special pass from Stanton, the secretary of war. When they arrived at Petersburg, Griffin received a note from Meade saying he "presumed she was here by authority superior to him." Mrs. Griffin took the hint and went home. Meade, Warren complained, had a rule "that ladies may visit the army but on no account will be allowed to stay all night in camp but must go back the same day to City Point."[1]

On January 31, Warren, in the log cabin that served as his headquarters, hosted a dinner for Humphreys, Crawford, Griffin, Ayres, Wainwright, Lt. Col. Henry C. Bankhead (his corps inspector general), and former Supreme Court Justice Archibald Campbell, now seeking admission to the Union lines as a peace commissioner for the Confederacy. Warren described to Emily the menu planned—oysters on the half shell, whiskey, soup, sherry, oyster patties and fish, roast beef and boiled mutton, macaroni *au gratin*, corn, beans, tomatoes, potatoes, venison or prairie chicken, "and whatever else can be got." Then dessert, fruit, coffee, and music by the band. Afterward, he said that his dinner "passed off very beautifully," and added, "My cook is splendid."[2]

The commission of which Campbell was a member, with Confederate Vice President Alexander Stephens and Senator Robert M. T. Hunter, gave Warren momentary hope that the war could be brought to an end without further fighting. "From what the talk is," he told Emily, "I should not wonder if terms could be agreed upon; the south agreeing to give up slavery at once or prospectively, and come back into the Union." As it stood, he said, "the mass of the southern people probably are as little satisfied now with the Confederacy as they ever were with the old Union." When the peace commissioners left empty-handed a couple of days later, though, Warren recognized that this view was hopelessly optimistic: "I hardly can see how the war can terminate till we disperse Lee's army." [3]

Early in February Grant decided to try again for the Boydton Plank Road, with a combined effort using Gregg's cavalry division, two divisions of Humphreys's Second Corps, and all of Warren's Fifth. Gregg was to ride around the end of the Confederate lines to reach the Boydton Plank Road at Dinwiddie Court House, while Humphreys moved north of Hatcher's Run, shielding Warren's operations south of that stream, supporting the cavalry. Warren advised Emily that "we are going to make a movement tomorrow morning early out to Dinwiddie Court House to see what is going on and try to capture the wagon train they are said to be using hauling provisions from Hicksville." He expected little fighting. [4]

On the morning of the 5th the Fifth Corps set out at 7 A.M., following Gregg's cavalry south on the Halifax Road, then west on the Stage Road. Rowanty Creek became a major obstacle, as the bridge over it was down and there were about a hundred Confederates on the other side of the sixty-foot wide, ice-covered stream. The ice, unfortunately, was not thick enough to bear a man's weight, so most of the infantry got across by swimming the frigid stream. A bridge was constructed for the cavalry, artillery, and wagons, the rebel defenders were quickly driven off, and the entire command was over the creek by 4 P.M. The men marched on in their icy-damp uniforms until they reached their designated positions, Griffin's division about two miles east of Dinwiddie Court House, Ayres's at the Vaughan and Quaker roads intersection, and Crawford at the junction of the Vaughan and Stage roads. With no rebels in sight, most of the men built big fires over which they dried their clothes. Warren told Emily, "We have had some little fighting with my column today and some adventures." [5]

Gregg's horsemen, preceding Warren, reached the Boydton road and gathered in the eighteen supply wagons they encountered there, a disappointing haul. That afternoon Heth's division of Hill's corps smashed into a gap between the two Second Corps divisions, but Brigadier General Robert McAllister's brigade, plugged hurriedly into the gap, was able to drive the rebels back after repeated attacks. [6]

Meade, who had never had much confidence in this movement ordered by Grant, noted with alarm the ferocity of the southern response to his movements. He became concerned about the safety of Gregg's cavalry and the Fifth Corps, strung out toward the Boydton Plank Road, so at nine o'clock that evening he ordered them to pull back to the spot where the Vaughan Road crossed Hatcher's Run. Warren passed this order on to Griffin, whose division had the farthest to return, starting at 11 P.M. on a bitterly cold night. Ayres and Crawford had correspondingly shorter distances to travel, but they still suffered from the freezing weather. "It was a cold winter's night and past midnight before we were fairly on the march," wrote one participant. "The roads were frozen hard and we keenly felt the cold."[7]

There was a mixup on the morning of February 6, caused in part by the misapprehension of Alexander Webb, now Meade's chief of staff, that Humphreys outranked Warren. Dispatches sent to Humphreys apparently never reached Warren, although by 8 A.M. the Fifth Corps commander did receive notice "to feel the enemy along my front, and fight him if outside his lines." Warren interpreted this to refer to the enemy in front of the Second Corps, where the fighting had taken place the day before and where an attack was expected. Since he was the senior officer present, Warren felt that "my front" encompassed Humphreys' front as well as his own. "This left me in some doubt," Warren said, "and before I could make any definite arrangements I received notice from General Humphreys that he was about to attack the enemy if outside his works; and then I thought it best to await the result of his operations and hold all the Fifth Corps and cavalry in hand to co-operate with him if needed."[8]

Around noon Meade showed up at Warren's headquarters and made clear to the Fifth Corps commander that the reconnaissance ordered had been for both Humphreys and him. Accordingly, at 1:15 P.M. Warren sent Crawford out on the Vaughan Road and then west toward Dabney's Mill, to be followed by Ayres. Gregg's cavalry moved south along the Vaughan Road. Gregg ran into Confederate cavalry and then two brigades of infantry, but, with the support of Winthrop's brigade of Ayres's division, he managed to bring things under control by late afternoon.

Out on the road to Dabney's Mill, however, Crawford struck a rebel infantry brigade, soon reinforced by the divisions of General Clement A. Evans and Billy Mahone, led on this occasion by General Joseph Finegan. Crawford's men were successful at first, capturing what they thought was a large fortification but which turned out to be a huge pile of sawdust. When Evans's men hit, however, Crawford reeled back until two of Ayres's brigades came to his assistance. Then, ammunition running low, the Fifth Corps units were overwhelmed by the fierce assault of Finegan's division. They broke and ran, running through the Sixth Corps division of General Frank Wheaton which was marching to their support. Wainwright quoted officers who had seen the rout as saying that "it was disgraceful beyond anything they have ever seen on the part of the Fifth Corps before."[9] With Wheaton's division and Griffin's a new line was established east of Dabney's Mill.

Warren wrote later to Emily that "we are now getting to have an army of such poor soldiers that we have to lead them everywhere and even then they run away from us. I was four hours under musket fire in the battle of the 6th even riding in front of our own line of battle to make the men steady and yet we could not keep them up." In his official report, he put the best face he could on the affair: "[O]ur line, despite all the exertions of the prominent officers and much good conduct among those in the ranks, gave way and fell back rapidly." He summed up: "[O]n the whole, it was not a bad fight and in no way discouraged me in my willingness to try the same thing again with the same men." [10]

The next day, in sleet and hail, Crawford moved his division forward again, pushed back the rebel pickets, reformed, and at about 6 P.M. drove the enemy back to Dabney's Mill. Crawford captured part of the prior day's battlefield, and his men buried the dead from that fight. Meade, who had not encouraged Warren to undertake any offensive operations on this day, reported to Grant that Warren "had recovered most of the ground he occupied yesterday," which "accomplishes all I expected him to do." In the meantime, the Union entrenched line was extended to Armstrong's Mill, on Hatcher's Run. The second battle of Hatcher's Run was over. [11]

Meade wrote to his wife that "the result on the whole has been favorable to our side," while Warren felt that he had "just lost the victory" when his troops broke on February 6, resulting in "a drawn battle." [12] Other observers have called the second battle of Hatcher's Run a Confederate triumph, because the rebels kept Grant from seizing the Boydton road and Union losses were heavier. Still, the Union line was extended a bit farther, and Lee lost another thousand men he could not afford to lose.

Warren and his corps moved back away from the front, into another stretch of inactivity. "At present we are just existing and that is all," he told Emily, " . . .very uncomfortable and hard at work." And again, "I am in a miserable camp in the mud eating off of the ground and sleeping as best I may." On the evening of February 14, though, he wrote, "It is at this hour almost exactly 3 years ago that I first saw your lovely self on Federal Hill and lost my heart. Long years they have been of care and hardship and danger in all of which you have been my angel in the most trying hours. In the hours we have spent together I have been only too happy for my peace of mind in our separation." [13]

On the 16th Gouv sat for an artist making medallions of all the prominent officers of the Army of the Potomac (Warren ordered one of the fifteen-dollar tin models, passing up the $150 bronze jobs), and the next day received Emily's wire saying she would be in Baltimore on the 18th. Warren obtained permission to meet her there and bring her back for a short visit to the lines. He returned via City Point on February 23, and Emily stayed with him until the 26th. Next day, he wrote to her that "you cannot think how utterly bleak everything here seems to be without you." [14]

Warren had another long (and friendlier) talk with Meade on March 5, during which Meade said he had told Grant "he thought I had the first claim in the Army of the Potomac to promotion as Brig. Genl. in the regular army and that I ought to have the vacancy made by his [Meade's] promotion" to major general, confirmed by the Senate on February 2. Warren, of course, was still a major in the regular ranks. "I believe it is a fact," he told Emily, "that my corps alone since last May has done more fighting than all of Sherman's army together, judging by my killed and wounded. Genl Meade said . . . that if I kept my place till the war was closed they could not leave me out." [15]

Warren was dismayed to learn that the regular brigadier appointments had gone to Alfred Terry, John Schofield, and O. O. Howard; he felt that Lincoln often made such appointments without consulting Grant and "merely to please political friends." It apparently never occurred to him that Grant might not pass on Meade's recommendation. Will wrote to him from Washington, "If they would not give you a Brig Genl's appointment in the regular army for what you have already done I suppose you must expect something besides merit to secure it for you." [16]

Through the month of March preparations went forward for the next campaign, with hopes for its outcome rising every day. Warren told his wife that "everything looks hopeful but we must expect a sanguinary campaign this spring." There was now a steady stream of deserters from the Confederate lines, many of them veterans who had fought throughout the war but who now saw their cause as hopeless. This hopelessness was demonstrated to them daily, as rations in the rebel army sank to starvation level. [17]

In the meantime, there had been an exchange of letters which boded ill for Gouverneur Warren, arising out of an embarrassing situation in the Department of West Virginia. Generals George Crook and Benjamin Kelley, the commander of the department and his second-in-command, were unceremoniously snatched from their beds in Cumberland, Maryland, by rebel irregulars early in the morning of February 21 and carted off to Libby Prison. Grant promptly wrote to Stanton suggesting either Warren or Humphreys, preferably Warren, to succeed Crook as department commander. At the same time he wired Sheridan, who was still operating in the Shenandoah Valley, that he had recommended Warren or Humphreys to take Crook's place and said, "If you want any change from this, telegraph me at once before assignments are made." Sheridan quickly telegraphed back that he preferred John Gibbon to either Humphreys or Warren. "If not," he said, "I prefer Humphreys to Warren." The hostility which had begun on the road to Spotsylvania and been aggravated by several later incidents was alive and well in Sheridan's mind. [18]

Before the final campaign of the Army of the Potomac began, Robert E. Lee unveiled one last surprise. In an effort to force Grant and Meade to relax their grip on Petersburg and its lines of supply, Lee planned an assault designed to blast a hole in the middle of the Union lines and to disrupt communications behind them. He quietly gathered nearly half of his army and placed it under the command of General John B. Gordon, a Georgian who now led the Second Corps of the Army of Northern Virginia. Gordon made his carefully planned attack in the predawn hours of March 25 against an earthen fort called Fort Stedman, held by John Parke's Ninth Corps. An overwhelming initial success was followed by hesitation, confusion, and regrouping by the surprised Federals. Warren soon had Crawford's division on the march toward the Fort Stedman area, with Ayres right behind, but at 8:20 A.M. headquarters told him to stop his troops, because the attack had been contained and then thrown back. Parke, who had wired Grant at 6:10 A.M. that "the enemy have attacked and broken through our lines near Fort Stedman," reported at 8:30 that "Fort Stedman and whole line [are] reoccupied." Between casualties and prisoners, Lee, in this last throw of the dice, lost what was estimated to be another four thousand men.[19]

Warren, in describing the Fort Stedman affair to Emily, noted the peculiar circumstance that President Lincoln was present at the time, having been invited down from Washington by Grant, and that Lincoln "reviewed one of my divisions which was out under arms . . . at the time." The president, he said, "received me very kindly." Warren went on to say that in the planned advance the Fifth Corps would be in front. "I have the advance again," he wrote, "in which I am always so fortunate for when the war is over it will be a proud thing for me to have led the grand army from the Rapidan to the end of this campaign. It will be proof enough of my ability that that post of honor has always been mine and that my conduct has merited its being so long reposed in me."[20]

CHAPTER TWENTY-ONE

TO THE WHITE OAK ROAD

WARREN ON MARCH 28 WROTE TO EMILY, "[T]omorrow morning long before day break we begin our march, and the sun will rise on the smoke of rattling musketry I have no doubt." [1]

As the Fifth Corps prepared to launch its final campaign, Charles Griffin still commanded its first division, with three brigades led by Joshua Lawrence Chamberlain, Edgar M. Gregory, and Joseph J. Bartlett. The solid Romeyn Ayres led the Second Division, its three brigades commanded by Frederick Winthrop, Andrew W. Denison, and James Gwyn. Crawford, described by one brigade commander as "somewhat lofty of manner, not of the iron fiber, nor spring of steel, but punctilious in a way, obeying orders in a certain literal fashion that saved him the censure of superiors," continued in command of the Third Division, his brigades headed by John A. Kellogg, Henry Baxter, and Richard Coulter, "fiery Dick Coulter bold as a viking." Wainwright still led the corps artillery. [2]

The campaign plan for the Fifth Corps involved its moving along with Sheridan's cavalry far to the left of the Union works, in another effort to stretch Lee's ever-thinning line to the breaking point and cut off the last railroads into Petersburg. The Second Corps, now led by Andrew Humphreys, would follow and stay on Warren's right. As early as March 19, Grant wrote to Sheridan, summoning him back from the Shenandoah Valley to City Point. "When you start out from here . . . ," Grant told his protégé, "your problem will be to destroy the South Side and Danville roads." [3]

On March 28, Meade's headquarters issued orders for the movement to begin at 3 A.M. on the 29th, with Warren and his corps to cross Hatcher's Run and, when the Second Corps was in position, to advance on the Boydton Plank Road, with the right of the corps to connect with Humphreys. Grant's orders went to Sheridan, advising him that "the Fifth Army Corps will move by the Vaughan road, at 3 A.M. tomorrow morning." The intention, Grant said, was to force the enemy out of his entrenched position, then to "move in with your entire force in your own way and with the full reliance that the army will engage or follow the enemy as circumstances will dictate." If Sheridan was unable to entice the Confederates out of their defenses, he was to tear up both the South Side and Danville railroads to the extent possible.[4]

Precisely at 3 A.M. on March 29, Warren's corps started to move, with Griffin in the lead. The morning was mild and clear, although clouds in the afternoon presaged the rain which began around sundown. The march was made difficult only by the soggy character of the roads, and Hatcher's Run was crossed with little difficulty. The head of the corps reached its destination, about two miles from Dinwiddie Court House, at about 8 A.M., where it halted. At 10:20 A.M., Warren received a message from Meade "to move up the Quaker road to Gravelly Run crossing." At 10:30 Warren answered by saying that "my skirmishers are out on the Quaker road as far as Gravelly Run. They had been ordered there, and I'll see that it is done."[5]

Upon receiving this, an angry Meade had Webb fire off another dispatch to Warren, saying he inferred from the latter's response "that you did not understand his last order." Warren was to move his *corps,* not skirmishers, up the Quaker Road across Gravelly Run, north toward the Boydton road, there to take position facing north and connecting on his right with Humphreys. Warren's confusion undoubtedly arose from Meade's changing the whole direction of the movement in such an offhanded way. As Wainwright noted, "we certainly were moving farther off from Sheridan, whose operations we were supposed to be supporting." In his next message, at noon, Warren said that Griffin's division was now on its way up the Quaker Road, with Crawford to follow.[6]

Meade joined Warren at the junction of the Vaughan and Quaker roads, and the two generals rode north toward Gravelly Run. Late in the afternoon, after crossing the run and about a mile from the plank road, at a place called Lewis's Farm, Chamberlain's brigade of Griffin's division encountered the main Confederate force, Gen. Bushrod Johnson's division of Richard Anderson's corps. Initially repulsed, Chamberlain's men gallantly held their ground until Gregory's brigade came to their support. After some back-and-forth movements, Griffin's forces pushed Johnson back to the Boydton road, and another assault at dusk drove the Confederates to their fortifications on the White Oak Road, the extreme end of the thirty-seven-mile-long line of Confederate works defending Richmond and Petersburg. "The engagement," Griffin reported, "lasted over two hours with great severity." Meade sent a 7 P.M. message, congratulating Warren and Griffin upon their success in taking possession of the much-sought-after Boydton Plank Road. Warren, in the meantime, had located Chamberlain, to tell him, "General, you have done splendid work. I am telegraphing the President."[7]

Sheridan's cavalry, meanwhile, had occupied Dinwiddie Court House without significant opposition, entering the town at about 5 P.M. The Second Corps, starting at a later hour than Warren, was spread out north of the Vaughan Road, from Hatcher's Run to Gravelly Run, connecting to the Fifth Corps by means of pickets.[8]

Warren had a difficult evening, with troubles he did not need after the rebuke from Meade earlier in the day. After telling Emily that "we had a hard fight for a while and won it," he said that "my wagons do not come up and I sleep out in the air with rain threatening and little to eat."[9] Colonel Wainwright added some details to that bare-bones description:

> Corps headquarters waggon was not up for some unknown reason, and when Warren came back from Meade's headquarters there was a scene. I was just near enough to catch a word now and then; they fell on Locke and everyone around, and were fearful . . . The devil within him [Warren] seemed to be stirring all day, and I presume something had been said at Army Headquarters which he did not like.
>
> Presently Locke came over to me, and asked me to invite the General to supper with me. This I had already resolved to do, but thought that it would sound most easy, and as if I had not heard any of the goings on, did I wait until just as it was being served.
>
> Accordingly when all was ready I walked up, and said, "General, I am lucky enough to have a pair of broiled chickens for supper tonight, and as I see your waggon has not yet arrived, should be glad if you will come over and help eat them." He, however, refused, and for him, politely; but could not help damning his staff. "If a corps commander could not get his own supper," he did "not see why they should sponge on their subordinates, and he'd be damned if he would." I did not attempt to reason, but tried to tempt him by praising my supper, and saying that Fitzhugh [his aide] was absent and I should have to eat it almost alone; but could get nothing more out of him.
>
> Later and just before I turned in, I again tried to tempt him with the offer of a bed, but it was the same answer: "If I can't sleep in my own tent, I'll be damned if I sleep in someone else's"; and the last thing I heard as I went to bed were his mumbled oaths as he sat under a tree in the same spot he had been in for two hours.[10]

During that night and all the next day, March 30, the rain came down steadily, with the roads turning into quagmires. There was little fighting but considerable maneuvering. Warren was instructed to extend the corps' left, which he did with Ayres's division. He was somewhat perplexed by the vague directions he was getting from Meade, since he was not told whether or not he should extend to the White Oak Road. Late in the day Warren rode out personally to inspect Ayres's dispositions and found the Second Division pickets almost up to that road.[11]

Robert E. Lee, quickly recognizing the danger the Union movements held for his army and its precious supply line, ordered Pickett's division, augmented by a part of Bushrod Johnson's, out of the Confederate trenches to oppose the Federal thrust. Pickett was supported by three divisions of cavalry under the overall command of Fitzhugh Lee. The Confederate force moved out on March 30 to a nondescript spot on the map called Five Forks (because five roads came together there) and deployed along the White Oak Road. During the afternoon, Sheridan's cavalry had moved up from Dinwiddie Court House toward Five Forks.[12]

"Today," Warren reported to his wife that evening, "it has rained quite hard nearly all the time and the roads are almost impassable. Yet we have been marching and fighting all day. The fighting has been light and everywhere we have driven the enemy back." Wet through at the end of the day, he was quite comfortable as he wrote, in dry clothes in a warm, dry tent, with a good dinner under his belt "and clear starlight overhead." Sheridan, he said, "came to see me today, his cavalry being in operation on my left. He looks very well and bright."[13] Warren and Sheridan had encountered each other only rarely to this time, but the few times they had met had not been pleasant occasions. As we have seen, Sheridan was not an admirer of the Fifth Corps general, but they were now supposed to be working together.

Phil Sheridan was a hard case. Grant's cavalry commander in Virginia was Warren's antithesis in just about every way imaginable. In background, in intellectual attainment, in attitude toward war and its requirements, in social status, Sheridan and Warren could hardly have differed more completely. Sheridan was aggressive, blunt, and crude, and he carried a huge chip on his shoulder against just the kind of educated, cautious, and genteel sort that Gouverneur Warren represented to him. There was another way in which the two men were far apart, and that is that by the start of the 1865 campaign, Sheridan, as a favorite of Grant, was a rising star in the Union army, while Warren was on the decline, his best days at Gettysburg and Bristoe Station now well behind him.

At the start of the Civil War, Sheridan, who had completed a spotty West Point career three years behind Warren, was stationed in a remote outpost in California. Recalled to the east as a quartermaster, he soon had command of a cavalry regiment. The young man made a name for himself as an aggressive, hard-riding fighter. A brigadier's star appeared on his shoulder, soon followed by appointment to command of a division. Sheridan led his division at Perryville, Stone's River, and Chickamauga, and his forceful and aggressive assault on Missionary Ridge at the battle of Chattanooga made a lasting impression on Grant, soon to become commander of all the Union armies.

When Grant came east to assume his new role, he brought Sheridan with him to take charge of the cavalry of the Army of the Potomac. Notwithstanding Sheridan's run-ins with Meade, his nominal superior, he always enjoyed Grant's full support, another disturbing factor in the peculiar command arrangements of the eastern army in 1864. In the fall of the year Grant gave Sheridan an independent command in the Shenandoah Valley, and the implacable cavalry commander enjoyed himself thoroughly watching his army ravage the heretofore fertile Valley, burning farms, barns, and grain mills, and slaughtering thousands of sheep and cattle. "We destroyed the enemy's means of subsistence, in quantities beyond computation," wrote Sheridan with satisfaction.[14]

Grant brought him back from the Valley to utilize the cavalry in the campaign of late March 1865, and it was in this campaign that Sheridan and Warren were to become entangled with one another. The crude and aggressive Sheridan and the perfectionist intellectual from Cold Spring would not make a good match.

On the night of March 29, Grant had sent a message to Sheridan, changing his mission from one of getting to the enemy's railroads to that of getting onto the right rear of the Confederate line. "We will act together as one army here," Grant said, "until it is seen what can be done with the enemy." "One army," of course, would bring Sheridan back into his long-abhorred position of subordination to Meade, who outranked him, so the cavalryman quickly rode back to Grant's headquarters for a meeting with his patron. As a result, Sheridan was directed to take Five Forks in the morning. His command would continue to be independent and subject to no one's orders but Grant's.[15]

At the start of activities on March 31, Sheridan was several miles to Warren's left, near Dinwiddie Court House. Pickett's reinforced rebel infantry division was at Five Forks, a couple of miles north, with his lines extending back along the White Oak Road toward Petersburg (and the Fifth Corps). Warren's corps was spread out from near the White Oak Road, where Ayres was located, back to where Crawford's division was, behind Ayres and to the right, with Griffin further to the right, behind Crawford, connecting with the left of Humphreys's Second Corps. Swinton, in his history of the Army of the Potomac, points out that Warren's disposition of his troops, in masses *en echelon*, "was perfectly conformable to correct principles" and superior to the usual long, thin, and unsupported lines. So disposed, "they could meet attack from any direction, and readily re-enforce any point assailed."[16]

At 8:15 A.M., Warren warned Ayres that he should be alert to possible Confederate infantry showing up on his left, where Pickett was reported to be, although at 8:40 he received a dispatch from Webb, at Meade's headquarters, advising that "there will be no movement of troops today." This was no surprise, as the drenching rain continued and "the whole country round was one vast swamp, holding fast . . . everything on wheels," as one participant wrote. The smallest

Philip H. Sheridan. National Archives.

streams had by now become raging torrents. An hour later Warren advised
Webb that, having learned from Ayres that the rebel pickets were still on his side
of the White Oak Road, he had instructed Ayres to drive them off, though Ayres
had told him there was the risk of an enemy attack. At 10:30 A.M., Warren was
instructed by Meade that if he could get possession of the White Oak Road he
was to do so, "notwithstanding the order to suspend operations to-day." [17]

Ayres's movement was meant to be a reconnaissance by one brigade to deter-

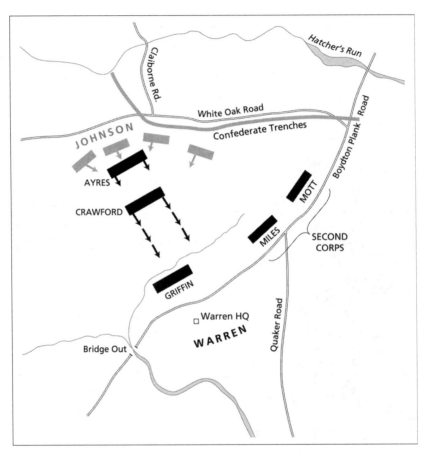

Battle of White Oak Road, morning, March 31, 1865

mine how strongly the road was held. At 10:30 Winthrop's brigade advanced toward the White Oak Road but was quickly forced back and overrun by four
Confederate brigades thrown at it by Anderson, under the personal supervision
of Robert E. Lee. The heavy and unexpected rebel assault flanked Ayres, whose
division quickly retreated, and then struck Crawford, whose men also fell back,
to form up again behind Griffin, who stopped the oncoming enemy cold.
Here, as Swinton pointed out, "the good effect of the *echelon* arrangement was
now seen." Warren, who had been at his headquarters exchanging telegraphic
messages with Meade until 10:30, crossed a swollen stream and attempted personally to stem the retreat, seizing a regimental flag and riding up and down
the lines. In this he was unsuccessful, but "Griffin's troops," as Warren reported
to Webb, "held the enemy at the run [a branch of Gravelly Run], west of the
plank road." Warren sent word of the reverse to Humphreys, who quickly sent
General Nelson Miles's division forward on the right flank of the Fifth Corps.[18]

While Crawford was reforming his scattered division, according to Sylvanus
Cadwallader, a reporter of somewhat suspect reliability who had attached
himself to Grant, Warren rode up to the Third Division commander, "white
with rage," and unleashed "the most abusive tirade on Crawford that mortal
ever listened to." As written by Cadwallader, "he called him every vile name
at his command, in the presence of officers and privates." Crawford sat stol-
idly on his horse, absorbing the verbal assault, and made no reply as Warren
finished and rode away.[19]

Warren, in his report, downplayed the setback of the morning: "The temporary result of this attack by the enemy was such as different portions of our
army had experienced on many former occasions in taking up new and extended lines, but our loss was not great, and was probably quite equaled by the
enemy." Grant, nowhere near the fight but always ready to see the worst in
anything Warren did, wrote sourly that "I do not understand why Warren permitted his corps to be fought in detail. When Ayres was pushed forward he
should have sent other troops to their support." A reconnaissance by three divisions, of course, would have been a rare animal indeed, but this seems to
have been missed by the ever-critical general-in-chief.[20]

Sometime after 2 P.M., the Fifth Corps began its advance back toward the
White Oak Road, with Chamberlain's brigade of Griffin's division once more
in the van. Crawford's division on the right and Ayres's on the left, both having
regrouped from their run of the morning, supported the advance. Confederate
opposition was not as hearty as expected, Lee having chosen to pull back
toward the defenses of the White Oak Road, and soon that road was in
sight. Warren halted Chamberlain temporarily, in order to get the whole corps
up, and then the advance resumed. When the 198th Pennsylvania, one of
Chamberlain's regiments, wavered under artillery fire from the rebel works,
Chamberlain requested that Gregory's brigade make an attack from the right.

This movement succeeded splendidly, and Griffin's line advanced three hundred yards across the White Oak Road, blocking the Confederate route to the west, taking position by about 3:15 P.M.

Warren personally scouted the enemy's works to see if an opportunity existed for carrying them, but he concluded that the defenses, which angled north from the road back to Hatcher's Run, were too formidable for a frontal attack. The Fifth Corps' fighting for March 31 was over, Warren remarking pointedly in his report that "Thus far my operations had been quite independent of those of General Sheridan." [21]

Sheridan's cavalry had put in a busy day, starting with a move forward from Dinwiddie Court House toward Five Forks, soon to be interrupted by Pickett's infantry and Fitz Lee's horsemen. The rebel force stopped Sheridan in his tracks and soon pushed him back to a position in front of Dinwiddie Court House, about where he had started the day. It was a tactical victory for Pickett, but the Virginian's infantry division was dangerously isolated from the rest of Lee's army. Warren's corps was closer to him than were Anderson's Confederates, who found the Fifth Corps across the White Oak Road, between them and Pickett.

Now, however, began a long and mystifying night of travail for Gouverneur K. Warren, what Grant's aide Horace Porter called "one of the busiest nights of the whole campaign," with "generals . . .writing dispatches and telegraphing from dark till daylight." [22]

For a little background, note should be made of a dispatch Sheridan sent to Grant the morning of the 31st, in which he suggested, "If the ground would permit I believe I could, with the Sixth Corps, turn the enemy's left or break through his lines, but I would not like the Fifth Corps to make such an attempt." The Sixth Corps had worked with Sheridan in the Shenandoah, which accounts for his preference, but not for his slur upon the Fifth Corps. This dispatch followed a brief meeting between Grant and Sheridan, at which both generals apparently expressed their unfavorable opinions of Gouverneur Warren. In any event, Grant replied that it would not be possible to give him the Sixth Corps. [23]

Around five o'clock in the afternoon of the 31st, Warren received a message from Webb, suggesting, "if you think it worth while," that he "push a small force" down the White Oak Road to communicate with Sheridan. At quarter to six, Warren was ordered "to push a brigade down the White Oak road to open it for General Sheridan," who by this time had been pushed far back from the White Oak Road by Pickett. Bartlett's brigade had already been sent by Warren to see if it could help Sheridan, with orders to march across country following the sound of the firing. [24]

A little while later, Webb told Warren that he had heard that Pickett had gotten between Sheridan and the Fifth Corps, so he said, "Let the force ordered

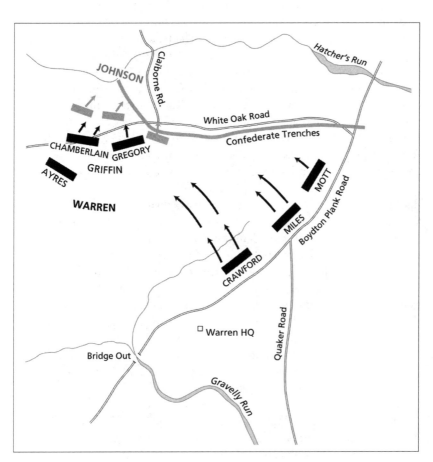

Battle of White Oak Road, afternoon, March 31, 1865

to move out the White Oak road move down the Boydton plank road as promptly as possible." Since Bartlett had already been gone almost an hour when Warren received this latest message at near 6:30, the Fifth Corps commander sensibly left Bartlett alone and sent three regiments under Brig. Gen. Alfred L. Pearson down the plank road. As darkness came on, Bartlett's brigade had followed the Crump Road through the woods to take up a position near Gravelly Run on the plantation of Dr. James P. Boisseau, actually in the rear of the Confederate force. Pearson's unit marched down the plank road to Gravelly Run, where it was discovered that the bridge over the rain-swollen stream was gone. At 8 P.M., Warren received a message from Meade, telling him that Sheridan had been forced back to Dinwiddie Court House, and the force sent down the plank road should stop at Gravelly Run (which it could not cross in any event, although Meade did not know this).[25]

At 8:20 P.M., Warren advised Meade of the strong positions held by Bartlett and Pearson and said, "It seems to me the enemy cannot remain between me and Dinwiddie if Sheridan keeps fighting them, and I believe they will have to fall back to the Five Forks." In fact, when Pickett and Fitz Lee learned of Bartlett's presence, mistakenly believing it was a division rather than a brigade, they immediately ordered their troops to start withdrawing back to Five Forks on the White Oak Road. Fifteen minutes later Warren was told by Webb that the Union force probably would have to "contract our lines to-night." This prospect was not pleasing to Warren. He promptly sent off another message saying he wanted to "move down and attack the enemy at Dinwiddie on one side and Sheridan on the other." "Unless Sheridan has been too badly handled," he said, "I think we have a chance for an open field fight that should be made use of."[26]

General Grant, in the meantime, seemed consumed by the idea that his pet Sheridan might be defeated, so that at 8:45 P.M. he told Meade that Warren should move back to the Boydton road and "send a division of infantry to Sheridan's relief," starting "at once." An hour later Meade suggested to Grant, "would it not be well for Warren to go down with his whole corps and smash up the force in front of Sheridan?" Grant responded, as generals far from the front and unfamiliar with conditions are wont to do, "Let Warren move in the way you propose and urge him not to stop for anything."[27]

At 9:17 Warren was told by Webb to "move back at once to your position within the Boydton Plank Road and to send a Division down to Dinwiddie C House to report to Genl Sheridan." He then specified that it should be Griffin's division, and it should go by the Boydton Plank Road. At 9:35 Warren issued orders to his corps: for Ayres and Crawford to pull back to the Boydton road, for Bartlett to rejoin Griffin, and for Griffin to move to Dinwiddie Court House and report to Sheridan. At 9:45, Warren received another dispatch from headquarters, directing that "the division to be sent to Sheridan will start at once."[28]

Warren responded promptly, as follows:

Your dispatch of 9:20 is just received. I had already sent out my orders, of which I send you a copy. You asked General Griffin to be sent to General Sheridan and at once. It will take so much time to get his command together that I withdraw the other divisions first, they being unengaged, but this will not retard General Griffin. The bridge is broken on the plank road, and will take I hardly know how long to make passable for infantry. I sent an officer to examine it as soon as your first order was received. He now reports it not fordable for infantry. It requires a span of forty feet to complete the bridge, and the stream is too deep to ford. Nevertheless, I will use everything I can get to make it passable by the time General Griffin's division reaches it.[29]

The engineer who looked at the washed-out bridge site, Captain W. H. H. Benyaurd, later wrote to Warren that "when I examined the bridge [site] that night the water was just about up to the top of the banks," about ten feet high, "below the bridge while above the water was over the bank." He moved downstream some 150 yards to find a suitable site for a new bridge and started to work. "We built the bridge as quickly as possible under the circumstances," Benyaurd recalled, and it actually was ready by the time Ayres's division reached it.[30]

Meanwhile, the flurry of dispatches continued. At 10:15 Warren received another message from Webb, saying that another brigade in place of Bartlett's should be sent with Griffin. At 10:48, Warren got a dispatch from Meade, directing him to send Griffin on the plank road and the other two divisions by the Crump Road Bartlett had taken earlier, to "strike the enemy in rear." Meade stressed that "you must be very prompt in this movement." A few minutes after receiving this last message, Warren responded to Meade that "I issued my orders on General Webb's first dispatch to fall back, which made the divisions retire in the order of Ayres, Crawford, and Griffin, which was the order they could most rapidly move in." Now, despite Meade's orders, "I cannot change them to-night without producing confusion that will render all my operations nugatory." So he would send Ayres to Sheridan and put the other two divisions on the Crump Road. "Otherwise," he said, "I cannot accomplish the apparent objects of the orders I have received."[31] A night attack, which Meade's order seemed to contemplate, was out of the question, given the conditions and the impossibility of coordinating such a movement between Warren's and Sheridan's widely separated forces.

Warren, in his report, pointed out that "the obstacles to overcome in carrying out so many orders and changes of orders in the darkness of a stormy, starless night, when the moon had set," were considerable. Under any circumstances, withdrawal of an army force in the immediate face of the enemy was fraught with danger. Because the corps was so near the Confederate entrenchments, he said, bugle calls, drum rolls, and shouted commands were out of the question; "each order had to be communicated from each commander to his subordinate—from the general till it reached the non-commissioned officers, which latter could only arouse each man by shaking him." [32] Once this "whisper down the lane" process was put in motion, of course, countermanding the order became difficult.

In the meantime, Grant sent Sheridan a message at 10:45 P.M., telling him "the Fifth Corps has been ordered to your support" and "should reach you by 12 to-night." Sheridan was to "assume command of the whole force sent to operate with you." There was no realistic possibility for the Fifth Corps to reach Dinwiddie Court House by midnight, even if the bridge over Gravelly Run had still been in place, and Grant should have known this. Unfortunately, all he did was give Phil Sheridan another reason to distrust the commander of the Fifth Corps, when midnight came and went with no sign of Warren or his men. [33]

Around one in the morning, Warren received another message from Meade, saying, "A dispatch, partially transmitted, is received, indicating the bridge over Gravelly Run is destroyed, and time will be required to rebuild it." Meade suggested sending the troops by the Quaker Road, which would have meant one more backtracking detour. "Time is of the utmost importance," Meade said. "Sheridan cannot maintain himself at Dinwiddie without reenforcements, and yours are the only ones that can be sent." [34]

Warren said he "felt much anxiety about what to do" upon receiving this dispatch, with its solicitude for Sheridan's apparent danger. In fact, that danger was actually past. Pickett's retreat back to Five Forks, caused by Bartlett's position on the Crump Road, was already well underway. During his withdrawal, Pickett received word from General Lee that he was to "hold Five Forks at all hazards." He was to prevent Union forces from getting at the South Side Railroad. "Regret exceedingly your forced withdrawal," Lee said, "and your inability to hold the advantage you had gained." [35]

Warren decided to ignore the suggestion, impractical as it was, to go around by the Quaker Road. He would keep Ayres on the Boydton road, moving south to reinforce Sheridan as soon as the bridge was completed, which in fact it was by 2 A.M., and leave Griffin and Crawford where they were, with their men getting some rest for the morrow's business.

One more message passed through the night, this from Philip Sheridan to Warren, sent off at 3 A.M., and received at ten minutes to five. "I am holding in front of Dinwiddie Court-House, on the road leading to Five Forks, for three-fourths of a mile, with General Custer's division," Sheridan said. "I understand . . . you are in rear of the enemy's line and almost on his flank. I will hold on here. Possibly they may attack Custer at daylight; if so, have this division attack instantly and in full force. Attack at daylight anyway, and I will make an effort to get the road this side of Adams' house, and if I do you can capture the whole of them. Any force moving down the road I am holding, or on the White Oak road, will be in the enemy's rear, and in all probability get any force that may escape you by a flank attack. Do not fear my leaving here. If the enemy remains I shall fight at daylight." [36]

This was all fantasy, totally ungrounded in reality; as Warren later wrote, "this suppositious state of affairs . . . promised most brilliant results if true, but it was not." "Attack at daylight anyway," Sheridan said, even though he did not know where the Fifth Corps was and Warren probably did not know where the enemy was or where Sheridan and his cavalry might be. Just attack. Warren was left to his own devices, to figure out from all the conflicting orders, all the dispatches based upon incorrect assumptions, what he should do. He felt that what he had already decided to do promised the best results, so no changes were ordered as a result of the Sheridan dispatch. [37]

CHAPTER TWENTY-TWO

ALL FOOLS' DAY

A T DAYLIGHT ON APRIL 1, 1865, ROMEYN AYRES and his division joined Sheridan near Dinwiddie Court House. For all the nocturnal messages about Sheridan's peril if he was not immediately reinforced, he and his cavalry were in no danger when the Fifth Corps division appeared on the scene. Indeed, Ayres as he arrived noted the departure of the last Confederate cavalry pickets, heading off to join the rest of George Pickett's force near Five Forks. Around 7 A.M., the other two divisions of the Fifth Corps, Griffin's and Crawford's, showed up midway between Dinwiddie Court House and Five Forks, having been ordered by Warren at 5 A.M. to join Sheridan by way of the Crump Road.[1]

When Chamberlain reported as the head brigade of Griffin's division, he got a little taste of Phil Sheridan as the cavalry commander was reacting to the world on the morning of All Fools' Day. Sheridan was sore from the ill treatment his cavalry had suffered the day before, he was naturally impatient, and he did not care for Gouverneur Warren. When Chamberlain reported with the usual courtesies, Sheridan responded, "Why did you not come before? Where is Warren?"

"He is at the rear of the column, sir," said Chamberlain.

"That is where I expected to find him," responded Sheridan. "What is he doing there?"

"General," said Chamberlain, "we are withdrawing from the White Oak road, where we fought all day. General Warren is bringing off his last division, expecting an attack." With his superior Charles Griffin arriving on the scene, Chamberlain was allowed to withdraw from an extremely uncomfortable situation. The leader of a brigade, hearing the physical courage of his corps commander challenged by the army commander, was placed in an impossible situation. While Grant, in all of his writings about Warren, never professed any doubt of his courage, Sheridan, before Warren's subordinates, in effect accused him of cowardice. It was not a good start to the day.[2]

At 11 A.M., Warren reported to Sheridan. There is no adequate explanation of the period between 7 and 11 and why Warren was unable during this time to present himself to his commanding officer. In his report, Warren says he was waiting with Griffin "for instructions from General Sheridan," and he did utilize the time to have his breakfast. He later testified that since Sheridan had ordered Griffin's division to halt where it was, he felt that order applied to him as well, a very shaky explanation. This delay was unwise on Warren's part, as subsequent events would show, as well as being disrespectful to the general commanding. "Were Warren a mind-reader," wrote Chamberlain, "he would have known it was a time to put on a warmer manner toward Sheridan." Warren, however, was being Warren, and, having no high regard for Sheridan, he let the cavalryman wait.[3]

In the meantime, Grant intervened again, once again basing his action upon misinformation. Early on the morning of April 1, an artillery captain named E. R. Warner was detailed by General Hunt, the artillery commander, on a mission to the Fifth Corps headquarters. Rawlins, Grant's chief of staff, told Warner to find out for him just where the Fifth Corps was. When Warner reached his destination, he found there Wainwright and Colonel Fred Locke, the Fifth Corps adjutant. Warren had told them and other members of his staff to get some sleep during the night and to rejoin the corps in the morning, Asked by Warner where the corps was, Locke, apparently not yet fully awake, said that when he had last heard it was waiting for a bridge to be built over Gravelly Run, for that was indeed the situation when Locke went to sleep. Unfortunately, Warner, misconstruing this bit of stale information, returned to Grant's headquarters at about ten o'clock and told Rawlins that the Fifth Corps was still delayed because of a bridge being out. When Grant heard this story, he exclaimed that he should have gotten rid of Warren when he had intended to earlier but that Meade had saved his corps commander then.[4]

Grant assigned Orville Babcock, another aide, to go to Sheridan with a verbal message, as follows: "General Grant directs me to say to you, that if in your judgment the Fifth Corps would do better under one of the division commanders, you are authorized to relieve General Warren and order him to report to General Grant, at headquarters." Just before noon, Babcock delivered this message to Sheridan, and Gouverneur Warren's fate was sealed. The "authorization" was in effect an invitation, a reminder of Grant's feelings about Warren delivered to a man Grant knew also harbored a low opinion of the Fifth Corps commander.[5]

Warren himself later wrote that he felt sure "that it was a predetermined thing to injure me, which I could not avert by any good service or success." Colonel Charles Morgan, chief of staff of the Second Corps, later agreed with Warren in this conclusion, saying "the cards were stacked against you . . . [Y]ou could do nothing to satisfy Grant or Sheridan in the frame of mind they were in."[6]

At eleven o'clock Warren reported in person to Sheridan. He later described the encounter:

> As I approached the place, I think he had been lying down on a blanket, and he rose up. I spoke to him, [he] half reclining or maybe sitting upon the blanket. I know there was a log between me and him, and I sat down upon it, and we had some conversation there together.

Sheridan, although doubtless still perturbed by what he perceived as delays in getting the Fifth Corps to him, about which he had earlier that morning spoken to Grant's aide Porter, told Warren to hold his units at the Boisseau place on the Crump Road, refresh his men, and be ready to move when necessary. In an effort to make conversation, and to stress that his corps had engaged in a hard fight the day before, Warren remarked that the Fifth Corps "had had rather a field day of it since yesterday morning." Sheridan, in no mood for polite talk, said harshly, "Do you call that a field day?"

Warren "saw by the tone of his remark that he was not very well pleased with what I had said, so I, in a measure, apologized for it by saying that it was perhaps a little ironical." On a day intended for little activity, he said, "the dispositions General Lee had made had given us about as lively a time as I had in my experience." Sheridan, unimpressed, turned away to talk to a scout and then rode off.[7]

Soon after this encounter, Gen. Ranald Mackenzie, commanding a cavalry division of about a thousand men from the Army of the James, arrived on the scene, and Sheridan sent him off to scout eastward on the White Oak Road, to make sure no relief was coming up in the Federals' rear, on its way to Pickett. Mackenzie completed this mission successfully, driving off some rebel cavalry on the White Oak Road, and, later in the afternoon, was able to return toward the fighting at Five Forks.

At about one o'clock, Sheridan said, he "ordered up the Fifth Corps . . . to turn the head of the column off on the Gravelly Church road, and put the corps in position on this road obliquely to and at a point about a half mile from the White Oak road and about one mile from the Five Forks." Two divisions, Ayres on the left and Crawford on the right, were to form the front line, with Griffin in reserve, to the rear and right of Crawford. Warren told Sheridan that his corps would be ready by 4 P.M. Sheridan's plan was for the Fifth Corps to hit the enemy's left flank, behind the White Oak Road, while the cavalry attacked in front and on the right of the rebels. Crawford's division, it was expected, would crash into the rebel breastworks from the right, while Ayres would engage the line on the left with his division.[8]

Sheridan, who had been restless all morning long, now became even more impatient as he anticipated the coming fighting. He said later that he rode over to where the Fifth Corps was forming up, by the Gravelly Run Methodist

Episcopal Church, "and found them coming up very slowly." "I was exceedingly anxious to attack at once," he said, "for the sun was getting low"—a dubious statement, around three o'clock on an April afternoon—"and we had to fight or go back." Warren, cautious and precise, nevertheless urged expedition upon his division commanders, and they moved their units as quickly as they could, given the heavy mud and cavalry horses on the roads and the thick woods through which they marched.[9]

Warren arranged his units in order, and he rode out toward the White Oak Road to look at the ground over which his men were to proceed. One of Grant's favorites, writing long after the war, took great exception to this standard precaution, saying this showed Warren "distrusting Sheridan's judgment, and rebelling against his authority." This criticism, aside from being absurd, overlooks the fact that Sheridan was actually in error regarding where the Confederate line ended, a miscalculation which had serious consequences when the attack commenced.[10]

Pickett had arranged his force behind breastworks stretching a mile and a quarter along the White Oak Road, with Matthew W. Ransom's brigade of North and South Carolinians, of Johnson's division, at the far left, George Steuart's Virginians to their right as far as the Five Forks intersection, then Colonel Willie Pegram's battery, Joseph Mayo's Virginia brigade, more of Pegram's guns, Montgomery Corse's brigade of Virginia infantry, and, on the far right, two brigades of Rooney Lee's cavalry.

Early in the afternoon, Pickett and Fitzhugh Lee, the Confederate infantry and cavalry commanders, respectively, rode back from their defensive line at Five Forks about a mile north on Ford's Road to a spot across Hatcher's Run, where cavalry general Thomas Rosser had invited them to a shad bake. Rosser and General James Dearing had caught "some fine shad . . . in the Nott[o]way two days before," and it seemed only appropriate that Pickett and Lee should join them in consuming the tasty fish. Unfortunately the Confederate officers left in command at the front had no good idea where Pickett and Lee had gone. With bottles of bourbon and brandy on the table before them and a confident feeling that there would be no real fighting that day, the rebel commanders sat under a tent, enjoyed the succulent shad, washed it down with a libation of choice, and passed several lazy hours of the early spring afternoon.[11]

At four o'clock, with the southern commanders still north of Hatcher's Run, digesting their elegant repast, Warren's Fifth Corps was in line and ready to move forward. As Warren attacked the enemy left, the Union cavalry would keep up offensive fire along the White Oak Road, pinning the rebel infantry in place. The order to advance was given at about 4:15, and Ayres and Crawford moved their men forward, with Griffin behind them. When they reached the White Oak Road, at its intersection with Gravelly Run Church Road, it

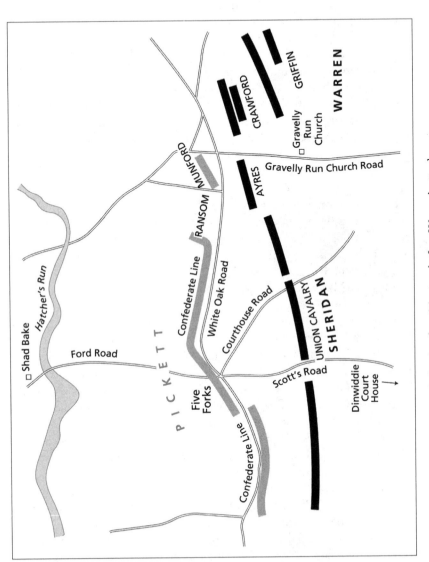

Five Forks, April 1, 1865, just before Warren's attack

quickly became apparent that the Confederate line did not reach that far, contrary to what Warren had been told by Sheridan.

Finding no rebel line where it was expected, Warren spotted a dense wood some three hundred yards north of the road, concluded that there was most probably the enemy position, and continued the advance. As the Federals proceeded, Ayres's division was staggered by heavy fire on its left flank, revealing that the Confederates were actually some three-quarters of a mile to the west. Ayres had his division make an abrupt left turn, facing to the Confederate fire. The three divisions here began to diverge from the alignment originally assigned to them, Ayres's men moving to the left and Crawford drawing away from Ayres as his division continued to move northward.[12]

At the end of the Confederate line on White Oak Road, Ransom's brigade had swung back northward, so that the line formed an angle or "return" with the road, running some 150 yards into the woods. It was toward this angle that Ayres's division now marched, with the brigades of Bowerman and Gwyn in the lead and Winthrop's brigade just behind. As the other two Union divisions marched through the woods, contact was lost and Crawford wandered off to the north, drawn in that direction in part by firing on his right from cavalry colonel Thomas Munford's skirmishers.

"Soon after crossing the White Oak road, finding the enemy's fire to come from the left," wrote Ayres, "I changed front to the left by facing the Second Brigade [Bowerman's] to the left and filing it to the left." Warren ordered Winthrop's brigade into the front line, on the left of Bowerman. Bowerman's brigade, which had originally received the unexpected fire upon its left flank, showed some unsteadiness as a result, with some additional confusion resulting from Winthrop's men coming on at the double-quick. Sheridan, who was at this time with the advance of Ayres's division, later made much of this momentary faltering on the part of Bowerman's men, but, urged on by both Sheridan and Ayres, they soon moved up and, as Ayres reported, "bore their part in the action in a handsome manner."[13]

As Crawford's division wandered farther away from the fighting, disoriented by Ayres's sharp swing to the left, Griffin, alerted by messengers coming from Warren, noted the widening gap between Ayres, now hotly engaged, and Crawford, and sent Chamberlain's and Gregory's brigades through this gap to strike the enemy line. As Chamberlain approached, he encountered Sheridan again, who exclaimed, "By God, that's what I want to see, general officers at the front!"[14] This comment reflected Sheridan's personal style, but his style may not have been universally suited to an army which had lost many of its best generals—Reynolds, Mansfield, Reno, Sedgwick, Kearny, and Hancock, among others—to enemy fire.

Ayres's attack, coupled with the assault of the cavalry along the White Oak Road, caved in the Confederate line. Ayres, wrote a correspondent, "fought like a lion in this pitch of battle, making all the faint-hearted around him ashamed to do ill with such an example contiguous." Winthrop, the gallant commander of Ayres's first brigade, was killed as he entered the rebel lines, but his brigade's charge met with great success. On its right Griffin's division drove the rebels before it; Gwyn's brigade of the Second Division, which had lost its direction, was taken in hand by Chamberlain and thrown into the fray, where it helped in the rout of the Confederates. Enemy soldiers surrendered in great numbers, and those who did not fled to the rear.[15]

In the meantime, Warren was doing his best to get Crawford into the fight. After his staff officers were unable to get the errant division turned around, Warren himself went to deal with the problem. He first found Kellogg's brigade, and he placed it as a "marker," a pivot on which the division should turn, with the intention of bringing Baxter's brigade in on its right. He then rode off to locate the balance of the division. The "marker" disappeared, however, when one of Sheridan's staff officers found it and ordered it forward. As a result, Crawford's brigades fought independently rather than in concert. Warren, meanwhile, found Crawford and got the rest of his division faced in the proper direction. As his brigades advanced they found themselves in the rear of the southern lines, in a position to effect the capture of many fleeing rebels. Crawford advanced across the Sydnor field to Ford's Road, coming close to capturing Pickett as he belatedly attempted to rejoin his command. Coulter's brigade did capture at least three of the four guns of Captain William M. McGregor's battery, and Crawford made prisoners of hundreds of men from Mayo's brigade. Warren then ordered Crawford to move his division by the right oblique, toward the White Oak Road, in hopes of cutting off that potential escape route.[16]

Warren sent Locke, his chief of staff, to find Sheridan, to explain his position, and to solicit further orders. Locke soon met Holman Melcher, of Warren's staff, and together they rode up to the cavalry general with the message to "give Gen. Warren's compliments to Gen. Sheridan, and tell him the enemy's lines are broken and I am in full pursuit." Locke was astounded to see the cavalry general rise up from his saddle and shout angrily, "Tell General Warren, by God, that I say he wasn't at the front; that's all I've got to say to him!" Locke was so startled by this outburst that he took care to write out Sheridan's answer in his notebook.[17]

After slogging through woods and swamps, Crawford reached the White Oak Road and faced his division to the west, perpendicular to the road. Montgomery Corse formed what was left of his brigade of five Virginia regiments on the edge of a cotton field along the western edge of the Gilliam farm, just below the road, quickly throwing up a line of rough breastworks to try to stop the blue infantry.

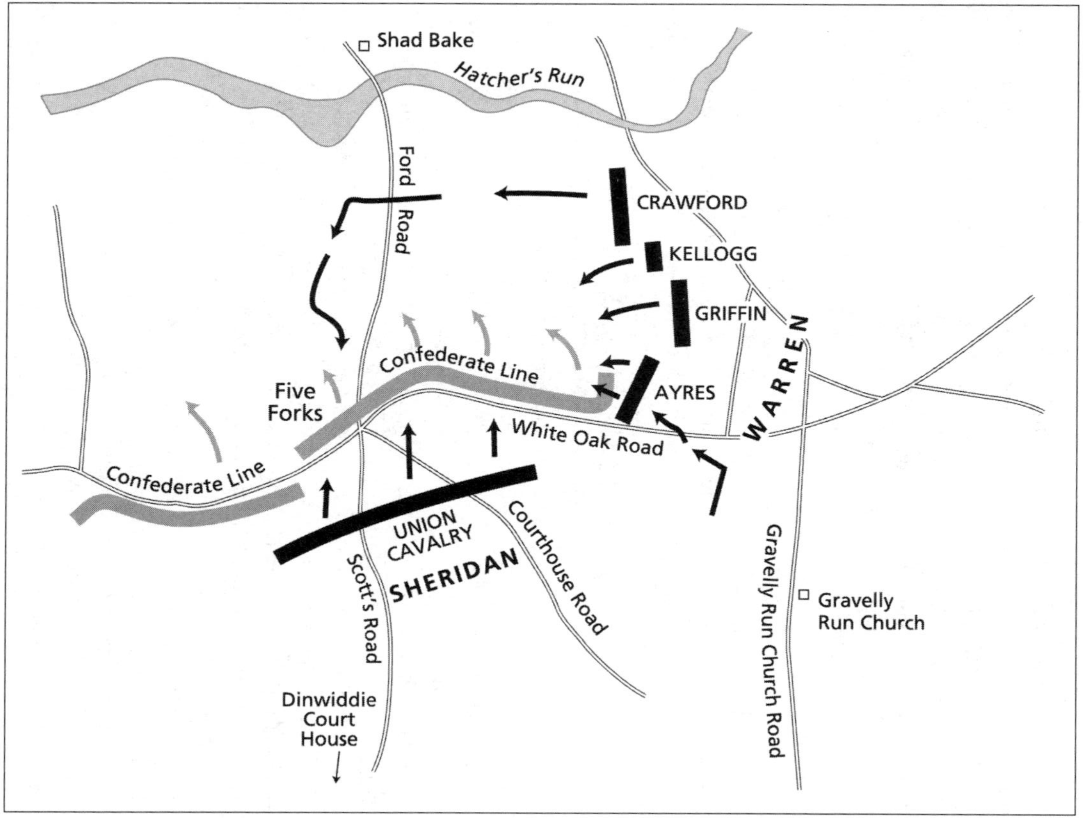

Five Forks, April 1, 1865, the battle

Shad Bake

Hatcher's Run

CRAWFORD

KELLOGG

GRIFFIN

WARREN

AYRES

Gravelly Run Church

Gravelly Run Church Road

White Oak Road

Courthouse Road

Confederate Line

Ford Road

Five Forks

Confederate Line

UNION CAVALRY

SHERIDAN

Scott's Road

Dinwiddie Court House

Confederate Line

Crawford's men were grimy, sweaty, and disheveled after their long march; "our connections are not firmly kept," wrote one of Crawford's aides. When they came to a stop before Corse's defensive line, Warren, who had just had Sheridan's outburst reported to him, took matters personally in hand. Under the setting sun, he snatched up the corps flag, shouted for the men to follow him—"Now, boys, follow me, this will be the last fight of the war!"—and rode straight toward the rebel line. His horse was shot and killed, and Colonel Hollon Richardson of the Seventh Wisconsin was wounded as he tried to shield his corps commander when he toppled to the ground, but Crawford's men followed Warren, driving Corse's brigade off and taking a good part of it prisoner. "Everywhere along the front," Warren reported, "the color-bearers and officers sprang out, and . . . our men advanced, capturing all the enemy remaining." [18]

The battle of Five Forks was over. Some of the defeated Confederates were able to make their escape by an obscure woods road west of Five Forks, while others fled up Ford's Road or ran through the woods. What was left of the Confederate force gathered at the Church Road crossing of the South Side Railroad, but it was just a shadow of what Pickett had started the day with. Approximately 545 rebels were killed or wounded, and well over two thousand were captured. It was a great victory for the Fifth Corps, which did the major part of the fighting. The divisions of Ayres and Griffin were the hammers which broke the Confederate line, and even Crawford, after Warren got his division pointing in the proper direction, found himself in position to make a major contribution. [19]

As darkness fell over the Virginia woods, at about 7 P.M., Brig. Gen. James A. Forsyth of Sheridan's staff rode up to Warren, handed him a message from Sheridan, and told him its contents. Warren took the paper and read with disbelief: "Maj. Gen'l Warren, com'd'g 5th A. C., is relieved from duty, and will report at once for orders to Lt. Gen'l Grant, Com'd'g armies of the United States." [20]

The stunned Warren, confused but sure that some kind of hideous mistake had been made, rode off to find Sheridan. When he located the cavalry general, Warren suggested that he reconsider his action. The hot-tempered Sheridan, his blood still up from the just-concluded fighting, shouted, "Reconsider, hell! I never reconsider my decisions! Obey the order!" [21]

With this, the crestfallen Gouverneur Warren, whose troops had actually won the battle that day, rode slowly away from the field, his career shattered by the action of the crude little Irishman. The thoughts coursing through his brain as he rode through the darkness must have been black ones indeed.

Late in the night Warren reached Grant's headquarters, to be told by Grant that it was *his* idea, passed on to Sheridan in the form of a verbal authorization, to remove him from his corps command. Grant told him that "he thought well of my judgment but that I was too much inclined to use it in

Charles Griffin, placed in command of the Fifth Corps
by Sheridan. National Archives.

questioning orders before executing them; that I did not co-operate well with
others, doubted too much the sense of my superiors, and interfered with my
subordinates." Warren replied that even if all these things were true, which he
denied, "I had not been guilty of any of them with Genl Sheridan, and that a

victory won could not fairly furnish a reason for punishing passed [*sic*] alleged offenses not known." He went on to argue the other points made by Grant, but it became clear that the lieutenant general was not listening. Grant, admitting that Warren had "striven hard," said he would not send him home as other relieved officers had been.[22]

Warren then went to see Meade and was chagrined to learn that Meade had been finding fault with him to Grant with the same kind of complaints. Meade told him that he had intended to have him relieved but had been waiting until he could find a suitable successor. ("He would not have Griffin under any consideration," Warren quoted him as saying of the officer to whom Sheridan turned over the corps.) Meade said his major complaint was that Warren "was too much inclined to cavil at orders that I should have gone ahead to obey and let the consequences be where the orders originated." Meade said he often "differed in judgement with the orders [from Grant] he had to transmit." Warren said that while it might "satisfy his [Meade's] conscience and sense of duty to see men slaughtered by order that there was a hope of modifying even at the risk of a sacrifice of position, my sense of duty compelled me to act as I ever had done in these matters."[23]

Gouverneur K. Warren's career with the Army of the Potomac was at an end, and his future service in the military was thrown into doubt. But the real fight of his life—the struggle to restore his good name—was about to get underway.

CHAPTER TWENTY-THREE

A SOLDIER'S GOOD NAME

W ARREN'S RELIEF WAS THE TALK OF THE ARMY for a brief time. The men in his corps were generally outraged at Sheridan's high-handed action. Capt. Charles H. Porter, of a Massachusetts regiment, said that "the most ardent friend that Sheridan has cannot explain away the insult conveyed to one of the bravest and most devoted of soldiers in the Army of the Potomac." Another regimental historian noted that the absence of Warren from the head of the column on the morning of April 2 was "the first intimation to the troops that the general had been relieved of the command." The men of the Fifth Corps, he said, "have never forgiven [Sheridan] for his hasty action toward their well-tried commander." Regarded at the time "as a freak of temper rather than the dictate of calm and sober judgment," a year later "the removal of General Warren remains . . .without the justification of reason or expediency." [1]

Lieutenant Colonel A. B. Farnham of the Sixteenth Maine told Warren his removal was regarded by the corps "as an act of the grossest injustice, a great wrong to you its beloved commander as well as an insult to every member of the corps." Brigadier General Henry Baxter, of the Third Division of the corps, said he was "astonished beyond measure" to learn of the removal. Another soldier wrote that the victory at Five Forks had been "considerably dampened" by Sheridan's action. "As our corps commander," he wrote about Warren, "all his men had learned to love and respect him, for although his bravery and gallantry were beyond all question, he was never impetuous to the point of rashness nor was he ever guilty of needlessly sacrificing his men to gain glory for himself." These qualities, it should be noted, led to the caution which debased Warren in the eyes of the army commander. [2]

Even Wainwright was astonished at the unforeseen change of command. His first thought was that "Warren might have got into one of his ugly fits and said what he ought not to," but he realized that could not have been the cause or the relief would have taken place on the spot, not after the battle. Indeed, he told Warren of "seeing you in apparently amicable conversation with Gen. S. within half an hour of the time the works were carried." "To me," the artilleryman wrote in his diary, "his removal at this time, and after the victory had been won, appears wrong and very cruel." Indeed, to those in the army with a sense of history, the removal from command of a triumphant general at the moment of victory seemed both unprecedented and illogical.[3]

The *New York World*, on April 4, noted that Warren was, at Five Forks, "dark, dashing and individual as ever," but was "for some reason or other," relieved of his command after the fight was over. "We shall probably have an explanation of this fall from grace very soon," its correspondent wrote.[4]

The rival *Herald*, the same day, carried two strikingly disparate notices of the change in command of the Fifth Corps. L. A. Hendricks's dispatch of April 1 stated,

> Unexpectedly to many, General Warren was relieved from command of the corps today. . . Various reasons were given for this change. The general understanding is that it was on account of alleged disobedience of orders. One thing is certain, that he has always had the respect and confidence of his troops. His courage is of the highest order.

Meanwhile, Sylvanus Cadwallader, Grant's sycophant, sent this dispatch on April 2:

> But the most unexpected event of the day or of the season was the removal from command, in the presence of his troops, and in the face of the enemy, by General Sheridan, of Major General Warren, so long commanding the Fifth army corps . . . But little has transpired as to the immediate provocation, or justification, but it is understood to have been because of General Warren's tardiness or refusal to obey orders, by charging the rebel lines. From a tolerably thorough acquaintance with General Warren's usual behavior in somewhat similar circumstances, I have not a particle of doubt that his removal was right and proper.[5]

Cadwallader's remarkable piece of poisoned journalism was typical of the reaction of Grant's people, who made sure that the stories coming from headquarters cast Warren in the most unfavorable light. Rawlins wrote his wife the night of April 1 that Sheridan's relief of Warren "should have been done yesterday," and Charles Dana reported to Stanton that "General Grant relieved Warren from Fifth Corps Sunday for disaster of Friday." Warren long felt that John Rawlins, whom he called "a personal coward in danger, but a bold liar and firm believer in the value of a lie," was "the active principle" on Grant's staff against him.[6]

Warren reported to his wife the day after his relief that "greatly to my astonishment just at dark *after the fighting was all over* Genl Sheridan ordered me to report to Genl Grant." He described his meetings of the night before with Grant and Meade; Grant, he said, "spoke very kindly of my past services and efforts, but thought I was too self reliant in executing my duties and did not stoutly obey orders and co-operate in his general plans closely enough," surely a bland rendering of his conversation with the lieutenant general. He said, "I am not altogether unprepared for this. Ever since Genl Grant came here every chance and favor has been given to the western generals and they have shown a spirit that is extremely sectional . . . It made me see sometime ago that I should never gain any advancement . . . and it has been a great source of un-happiness." Now that the act had been done, he said, "now that it is to be en-dured certainly I feel better already. Adversity proves men, and their friends." He said, "My operations yesterday were very successful and I believe it was one of the most glorious day's work of my life. I feel glad I should have had that day for the last of the command of my corps." [7]

The Confederates abandoned Petersburg and Richmond after the debacle at Five Forks and the Union army's seizure of the South Side Railroad. Grant assigned Warren to the command of Petersburg as well as City Point, Bermuda Hundred, and the line of the South Side Railroad, all of what was now the backwater of the war, as the pursuit of Lee's army moved west. On April 4 War-ren wrote to Emily, "Petersburg is a nice place, and all the houses in town are open to me, and if the war as it ends finds me here or in such a place you must come and stay a little with me, and sun your lovely face in this sunny land." [8]

As Emily in New York and brother Will in Washington, not yet having heard from Gouv, attempted to sift facts from rumors to learn what had truly oc-curred at Five Forks, Warren tried to make sense of his new situation. On the seventh he wrote to Meade's headquarters, pointing out that various other gen-erals had actual command of areas theoretically within his jurisdiction, and stating that "I have virtually no command, except a cavalry picket under Colo-nel Sanders." On the night of April 5, he said, Rawlins told him to await in-structions from Grant, "which I have since been doing." Meade sent this on to Grant, but nothing was forthcoming in reply. [9]

On April 5, Emily wrote that her heart and mind were "torn with anxiety on your account." "The account we get of your having been relieved of your com-mand in the face of the enemy and front of your troops," the result of Cadwal-lader's mendacious report, "has been a great shock to me and the suspense of not hearing any thing from you has been terrible to bear." She assured Warren that she loved him "through good or ill fortune, in joy or in sorrow you are all the same the pride, love and joy of my life." The next day Gouv wrote to her, "Don't let my being relieved grieve you it will all come out right. The Herald correspondent made it out much worse than it was." A couple of days later he told her, "It is very hard for me to bear my present position and have to await my vindication which must come . . . My countrymen cannot allow me to be treated so when they shall know the whole truth even if Genl Grant should fail to do me justice." On the 9th he assured her that "I will have justice done me yet." Writing about Lee's surrender of that morning, he said he had "lost no battle field of my corps as it has been in no fight since I left it. I feel glad of that." [10]

Warren fully expected redress for the injustice at the hands of Sheridan, and he anticipated that it would be forthcoming promptly. On the 11th he told Emily, "I shall learn something definite of my future soon, I expect. I have written Genl Grant requesting a full investigation." He heard from Will, who told him "the whole country was astounded by the news that you had been relieved from your command on the battle field . . . I have not seen the first person yet who does not believe that the most outrageous injustice has been done you." Gouv wrote back to Will, explaining that "I have purposely kept quiet, expecting justice would set me back to my old place without any effort of mine, in due time . . . I have now some assurance that I shall be returned to my Corps soon." [11]

Indeed, on April 18, George Meade wrote to Grant, calling his attention to the necessity of appointing a permanent commander for the Fifth Corps and saying, "Should you be disposed to reassign General Warren I shall make no objection thereto." Here was the perfect opportunity for Grant to set matters right, at no risk to the country, even if as he claimed he regarded Warren as unsafe in combat as a corps commander (despite the latter's almost two years of service in that role). The war was over for the Fifth Corps, and if Grant was speaking the truth to Warren the night of April 1, the reappointment could easily have been made, with no jeopardy to the public interest. But Warren's restoration would have implied that Sheridan's action was perhaps either hasty or unnecessary, and Grant would countenance no criticism, implicit or otherwise, of his pet. Meade was told to continue Griffin in temporary command of the corps; "orders will be sent to General Warren in a few days." [12]

Meade, who undoubtedly felt regret and perhaps a trace of guilt for the predicament of the subordinate with whom he had maintained a touchy relationship but for whom he still felt friendship, wrote again to Grant on May 1, saying, "Permit me, if you have not already acted, to call your attention to the case of General Warren." Grant wrote back that evening, saying, "I have this day ordered Maj. Gen. G. K. Warren to report to me in person for orders." And indeed orders were cut that very day, assigning Warren to command of the Department of the Mississippi. [13]

Before heading south, however, and while Emily visited him at Petersburg, Warren was given one gratifying display of esteem. On May 3, the Fifth Corps passed through Petersburg on its journey back to Washington for the great review of the Union armies. Griffin sent word to Warren that the corps wished to give him a salute of honor, so Warren with Emily and members of the staff took their places on the balcony of the Bolingbroke Hotel to review the corps as it passed before him. Chamberlain described what transpired:

> Drums ruffled, bands played, colors dipped, officers saluted with their swords; but for the men it was impossible to hold the "carry," or keep the touch of elbow and the guide right. Up turned the worn, bronzed faces; up went the poor old caps; out rang the cheers from manly hearts along the Fifth Corps column;—one half the numbers, old and new together, that on this very day a year ago mustered on the banks of the Rapidan . . . One half the corps had gone, passing the death-streams of all Virginia's rivers; two hundred miles of furrowed earth and the infinite of heaven held each their own. Warren, too, had gone in spirit, never to rise, with deeper wound than any who had gone before.[14]

Having Emily with him was a comfort to Warren in Petersburg, as he pushed for the inquest which would exonerate him. She worried about leaving him alone, for, as she wrote to her father, "he is almost crazy some times over this affair of his." She said, "he has pretty much determined to leave the army," but that determination, of course, assumed that he would shortly receive the official inquiry he was seeking. As he wrote, at about the same time, "When this affair is disposed of . . . I shall seriously take into consideration the prospect of quitting the army entirely." He would not do anything "that can separate me for a long time from Emily." [15]

Gouv got a letter from Will, expressing hope that Grant would find the time to give him a fair hearing, as requested, "and I have no fear of the result." Will thought that Sheridan was "so puffed up that his conceit ran away with his judgment," but he was particularly hard on Meade, for letting one of his commanders be treated the way he was. "I believe him to be a mean, selfish man," Will wrote, "and is a friend only to those who do not require his friendship." [16]

Warren's expectation that he would be granted the investigation to which he was entitled was soon quashed. He addressed a letter to Rawlins, as Grant's chief of staff, on April 9, requesting an investigation of his conduct at Five Forks:

> The order of Gen. Sheridan, taking from me the command of my corps on the evening of the 1st of April, after the victory was won, assigns no cause, and leaves me open to the inferences now finding expression in the public prints, and which are in every way to my prejudice. I am unconscious of having done anything improper or unbecoming to my position or the character of a soldier, or neglected any order or duty. I therefore request a full investigation of the matter as soon as the exigencies of the service will admit. I make this application now, while awaiting orders, which I deem the most appropriate time; but I do not intend nor desire to press the matter upon the consideration of the lieutenant-general until he can give it his attention

without interfering with more important duties. The regard already shown
me in immediately assigning me to another command on the 2d instant
gives me the assurance that he will not deem it an intrusion to solicit [an
opportunity] to vindicate the honor and reputation of a faithful soldier of
the Union, who waits in silence under an unmerited injury, till such time
as his superior shall be ready to give him a hearing.[17]

Hearing nothing in response, on April 22 Warren wrote to Bowers, Grant's
adjutant, with a copy of the April 9 letter and a request to be permitted to pub-
lish it. On May 2, he wired Bowers a query, to learn whether his two letters had
been received. Bowers answered that they had been, and that orders had been
sent to him. The next day Warren received the order sending him to Mississippi; he immediately went to Washington to see Grant. On May 6, he received from Grant a brief note, stating that "it is impossible at this time to give
the court and witnesses necessary for the investigation." Grant, however, had
no objection to Warren publishing the correspondence. Warren did not suspect but in time would learn that this was the only response he would ever get
from Grant.[18]

There was nothing for him to do but to head south to take up his new duties.
Reaching Cairo, Illinois, on May 10, Warren dropped Emily a hasty note simply
telling her where he was as he took a steamer down the Mississippi. He wrote
the next day from Memphis, describing "the darkies all the while singing an old
Mississippi song I had not heard for ten years before." He said he was enjoying
the journey, "everything being so different from my past four years life." By the
14th he had reached his new headquarters at Vicksburg and was acquainting
himself with his duties, which consisted mainly of furnishing military police
and watching for Jefferson Davis, if the fugitive Confederate president should
venture into his jurisdiction. Warren worried about the long trip and "prospective warm weather," which could mean yellow fever, if Emily were to join him.[19]

Once Davis was captured, Warren's duties boiled down to paroling prisoners, receiving and transporting them, and looking after surrendered public
property. His staff actually took charge of these affairs, and Warren did not
need to concern himself greatly with them. The state governor called for a
meeting of the legislature at Jackson, and, though Warren was urged to prevent it, he resolved to "let it take its own course ignored by me." He felt that
if the seceded states were allowed to return to the Union under their present
governors and laws the president could settle any terms he liked upon them,
but if these local governments were upset and replaced by imposed administrations there would be "a perfect pandemonium for some years." This of
course is what took place, but Warren was no part of it. "If the first [course] is
adopted," he said, "such position as mine will be unnecessary," and if the second, "I shall ask to be relieved."[20]

It was not long before Warren decided that Vicksburg was no place for him. On May 20 he wrote to Emily, "I have finally decided to resign and 'the die is cast.' You could not stand it here I know, and I could not without you. I have asked for a leave of absence as Major of Engineers for 30 days, in which I can arrange either for pleasant duty, a longer leave, or resign that too." He added that "I fully anticipate a state of affairs down here in the reconstruction which will be revolting to my feelings." He had received an order that day from General E. R. S. Canby, commanding the Division of West Mississippi, that he was to prevent by force if necessary any attempt on the part of the legislature to assemble and to arrest and imprison any persons who might attempt to exercise governmental functions. This was the last straw for Warren, and he sent off his resignation. In addition to the war's being over, he said, he had become "much exhausted" and felt unable "to properly continue on duty in this hot and debilitating climate." [21]

It then became a matter of waiting for his resignation to be accepted. In the meantime he sent off a letter to several newspapers, in an attempt to vindicate his reputation in the face of unfriendly journalistic reports like that of Cadwallader. Warren's letter was published in the *New York Times* and *New York Herald* on May 25, as well as in the *Vicksburg Daily Herald* on May 30:

> The only reason I have heard assigned for relieving me at that time were the surmises of newspaper correspondents, which there is no authority for. But an unfriendly spirit toward me apparently dictated their suppositions, and they have done me much injustice. I was relieved only after the battle was over, and while at the head of my troops, and when not even a fugitive of the enemy was in sight. I personally sought of Gen. Sheridan a reason for his order, but he would not or could not give one, and declined to do so.

He then recited his efforts to have an investigation initiated and his assignment to the Department of Mississippi, after which he described in eight paragraphs the course of his corps' actions from the night of the 31st to the conclusion of the battle the next day, and then followed with his letters to Rawlins and Bowers and Grant's reply, refusing his request. The Vicksburg paper commented that the letter was "a complete vindication of this gallant and distinguished soldier, against the unjust aspersions which correspondents of some of the newspapers have circulated in regard to him." [22]

Unfortunately for Gouverneur Warren, the public at large had lost interest in his sacking and his charges of injustice. There was simply too much happening for Warren's relief to stay in the forefront of public attention. The victory at Five Forks had been followed closely by the abandonment of Petersburg and Richmond and the pursuit of Lee's army, the surrender at Appomattox, and the assassination of the president. The fate of Booth, the capture of Jefferson Davis, the capitulation of the remaining rebel armies, and the gathering storm in Mexico occupied most people through the rest of April and into May, and few had much interest in the complaints of Warren against two of the leading heroes of the Union army.

On May 27, Major General Peter J. Osterhaus arrived in Vicksburg, to take over Warren's command as soon as his resignation was accepted. In the meantime Warren had some strange visitors. The famous rebel cavalry leader Nathan Bedford Forrest came to see him, and Warren sent Forrest's autograph to Emily. "You know," Warren told her of the future founder of the Ku Klux Klan, "his treatment of the colored soldiers when he captured Ft. Pillow makes him a marked character." On the 31st Warren reported that "Genl Sheridan's staff are here today and his brother and Genl Forsythe [sic] called to see me." Treating them "with distant formality," Warren "wondered that they could come," particularly Forsyth, whom he looked upon as "one who has been exceedingly unfriendly to me." [23]

On June 6, his resignation having been accepted at last, Warren left Vicksburg, wiring Emily that "I shall be home about June fourteenth." Having obtained a leave of absence and being reunited with his young bride, Warren said later, "I passed the whole summer on the sea shore resting during which time I gained weight from 137 pounds to about 165 pounds." Warren's resort of choice was Swampscott, north of Boston, where he began to gather together all of the papers and information he could find pertaining to the Five Forks campaign. He needed to prepare his official report and, even more, prepare for whatever procedure would be given him to justify his actions.

CHAPTER TWENTY-FOUR

AN ENGINEER, AGAIN

G OUVERNEUR WARREN'S POSTWAR CAREER breaks down into three fairly distinct periods. In the first one, he traveled all over the midwest and western United States on various engineering projects for the Corps of Engineers. After that, he was transferred to Newport, Rhode Island, and settled in there. Finally, he was involved in and consumed by the court of inquiry at last called at his request. In all three of these phases the be-all and end-all of Warren's existence was his passion for vindication, for the chance to tell the world what had happened at Five Forks.

Philip Sheridan published his report of the campaign from Dinwiddie Court House to Appomattox in the *Army and Navy Gazette* of June 13, 1865. If Warren had harbored any faint expectations that the cavalryman might admit to some sort of inadvertent mistake in relieving him, these were rudely dashed. Sheridan's report dripped with vitriol. He said that Grant told him the Fifth Corps would report to him by midnight on March 31. Ignoring the manifest fact that this was impossible, Sheridan wrote, "Had General Warren moved according to the expectations of the lieutenant-general, there would appear to have been but little chance for the escape of the enemy's infantry in front of Dinwiddie Court-House." [1]

Sheridan spoke of the assembling of the Fifth Corps on April 1:

> I then rode over to where the Fifth Corps was going into position, and found them coming up very slowly. I was exceedingly anxious to attack at once, for the sun was getting low, and we had to fight or go back. It was no place to intrench, and it would have been shameful to have gone back with no results to compensate for the loss of the brave men who had fallen during the day.

> In this connection I will say that General Warren did not exert himself to get up his corps as rapidly as he might have done, and his manner gave me

the impression that he wished the sun to go down before dispositions for the attack could be completed.

Describing the attack made by the Fifth Corps, Sheridan continued:

> During this attack I again became dissatisfied with General Warren. During the engagement portions of his line gave way when not exposed to a heavy fire, and simply from want of confidence on the part of the troops, which General Warren did not exert himself to inspire. I therefore relieved him from the command of the Fifth Corps, authority for this action having been sent to me before the battle, unsolicited.[2]

Little of this scraped-together hodge-podge made much sense to anyone who examined it closely, particularly the last charge, which apparently accused Warren of not acting like a company commander when a portion of Bowerman's brigade faltered early in the attack, and then was misleading as to when Warren was relieved. Curiously, Sheridan's report, while accusing the corps commander of all these derelictions, described the Fifth Corps "burst[ing] on the enemy's left flank and rear like a tornado," and he said he could not speak "too highly of the conduct of the troops in this battle and of the gallantry of their commanding officers," including Griffin, Ayres, Bartlett, and Crawford. No wonder he had to make it somehow appear as if Warren had had nothing much to do with the fight, having been disposed of early on.[3]

With this report now in the army's records, Gouverneur Warren felt that he had no alternative to obtaining an official inquiry to clear his name. Grant and Sheridan had each been given an opportunity to redress the injury to Warren at little cost to themselves, and both men, for whatever reason, had declined to take advantage of it.

Warren at first tried to counter his traducers in the court of public opinion. On February 21, 1866, he sent to army headquarters his official report of Five Forks, dated December 1, 1865, and asked that it "be given the same publicity" as Sheridan's report. Next, Warren wrote a long letter to the editor of the *Army and Navy Journal* citing various articles written about Five Forks which were factually wrong about his role in the battle, and he prepared a pamphlet refuting Sheridan's imputations.[4]

Warren had the pamphlet privately printed.[5] Later, a publisher named Van Nostrand printed up additional copies for sale to the public. In his introduction, Warren said he had trusted that Sheridan's report "would do me justice," acknowledging "that his treatment of me was hasty and based on erroneous impressions." Sheridan's report when it appeared showed that trust to be badly misplaced, and since no investigation had been ordered Warren had prepared a narrative to let "all fair-minded men" decide the case for themselves.

Warren's pamphlet, copies of which he sent to leading military figures and journalists, as well as to those who requested it, was well received, with particular comment being made on its dispassionate tone. Hancock told him that, even before reading it, all those he had spoken with felt that Warren had been treated harshly, "based on knowledge of your character as a soldier, and of your important services to your country." Now, after reading the pamphlet, he said, "I consider the matter is settled in your favor." Warren's good friend and fellow engineer officer Henry Abbot said "the array of facts are so irresistible as to place Genl Sheridan in a very unfavorable light." What answer Sheridan could give, he said, "I can hardly imagine, and to let the matter stand thus convicts him of great haste & bad planning, or of wilful injustice." Sheridan was already guilty of the latter charge, Abbot said, "for his official report must have been prepared deliberately with the essential facts before him." [6]

Theodore Lyman, who as a member of Meade's staff had experienced much of the hostility coming from Grant's headquarters, wrote Warren, "Why Sheridan so treated you I could never understand." Calling the cavalryman "a hot ambitious man," he said, "I suppose it was a compound of a good many prejudices and dislikes." [7]

The *New York World* commented that Warren's writing "certainly makes out a very strong case, which his acknowledged bravery and former success as commander of the Fifth Corps will go far to strengthen." E. L. Godkin, editor of *The Nation*, recalled the public's surprise on learning of Warren's removal and the general impression that there had been some sort of difference between the two generals "peremptorily settled by the superior authority of Genl. Sheridan." Now, Godkin said, Warren's pamphlet, "in a manner . . . dignified and temperate," refuted the imputations contained in Sheridan's report. "No candid person," he said, "in our opinion, can read General Warren's defence without feeling that his grievance is a real one. The question of facts is easily settled against General Sheridan," whose motives, however, remained unknown. The next week, *The Nation* published a letter signed "A Staff Officer," defending Sheridan and attacking Warren, but Godkin noted editorially that "we have compared it carefully with the latter's [Warren's] pamphlet, and see no reason to reverse our previous decision." [8]

Warren read with pleasure William Swinton's book on the history of the Army of the Potomac, particularly Swinton's treatment of the movements of March 31 and April 1. Warren wrote to the newspaperman, and Swinton responded on April 6 saying, "your wrongs are deep." Swinton said in his book, "After the close of the action, General Sheridan, for some reason as yet unexplained, relieved General Warren from duty. . . . In saying that this act is 'as yet unexplained,' it will hardly be interpreted in the sense that I am unaware of the reasons stated by General Sheridan in his official report, but that these reasons are wholly inadequate to justify that officer's conduct." [9]

These expressions of regard from men whom he respected gratified Warren, but they did not take the place of the army's official investigation, which he felt he must have. In the early part of 1866 Warren decided on his course to get Grant to reverse his decision. Edwin D. Morgan, governor of New York during the first half of the war and now a United States Senator, a respected Republican businessman who had long been on friendly terms with Warren, agreed to be his go-between with Grant. Late in March Warren wrote to Emily from the capital, "I am so sure of full justification hereafter that I am not much depressed by delays and difficulties." He added that Grant was to be in town the next couple of days, "but I doubt if Gov Morgan sees him before Saturday as the Senate does not sit Saturdays." [10]

On April 9 Warren again saw Morgan, who had done nothing and apparently had not understood what he was supposed to do. Warren gave him a letter setting forth his grievances and what he hoped the Senator would do for him, and Morgan said the course proposed was "eminently proper" and he would undertake it "with pleasure." He said he was on "very friendly terms with Genl Grant but [had] never spoken on the subject to him." He said that Thurlow Weed, the ancient prewar Whig leader of New York politics, had in fact spoken with Grant about the case and that Grant had said that in differences between Sheridan and another Sheridan could hardly be in the wrong, a discouraging reaction. Five days later Warren wrote that he had heard nothing yet from Morgan. [11]

In the meantime, Warren received a query from his old military science professor Dennis Hart Mahan, a survey he was taking on good generalship. Warren said in part, with some bitterness, "Genl Grant Genl Sherman and Genl Sheridan have won all their successes only by having overwhelming numbers, and they sneer at the more heroic efforts of those who long years maintained an equal contest. They sneer at the Army of the Potomac for not sooner taking Richmond." Warren, having written what he believed, then thought better of it and did not send this response on to Mahan, putting it away in his papers. [12]

A few days later Warren told Emily that he had not yet heard from Morgan but would not like to leave Washington, where he was finishing up engineering paperwork, "till I have a full understanding about the course Genl Grant intends to pursue in regard to Five Forks." On April 20 he told his wife he thought he could get home "if Gov. Morgan will let me know how his mission succeeds so that I can say what next." [13]

The next evening Warren called upon Morgan and was disheartened to learn that the senator "had done nothing about my request for him to see Genl Grant." Worse, Morgan "seemed to have almost *entirely forgotten* about it— apparently having trouble to recall what it was." Warren went over the whole matter again, and Morgan assured him that he would call on Grant, but in the meantime the lieutenant general had left town to go to Richmond. "I almost regret that I asked Gov. Morgan to do anything in the matter," a despairing

Warren wrote, "for I have lost important time, waiting for him, and if he shows the same indifference in speaking of the matter to Genl Grant, he will do me more harm than good." [14]

On April 27 Warren wrote Emily that he expected Morgan to see Grant for him the next day "and then I shall learn something definitely about what to expect or do next." If he got his court of inquiry, he expected, it would be a very trying time "for days and days," an interesting comment in light of the many months the actual court consumed when it was finally convened. After he was vindicated, Warren said, "I shall follow it up with counter charges of injustice and misrepresentation." [15]

Morgan finally did see Grant but, as Warren said, "got nothing from him at all satisfactory to me." Grant offered to write a public letter speaking well of Warren in general terms but "so carefully worded as not to relieve me from Sheridan's imputations at Five Forks." If Warren accepted such a letter, he feared, he might be estopped "from any further proceedings." [16]

Frustrated by Grant, Warren drew up a letter to the secretary of war request-ing his court, but Stanton was reluctant to run afoul of Grant and there was little chance that he would reverse the lieutenant general's decision. Indeed, Warren was kept waiting for a full day in the secretary's anteroom in a vain effort to present his letter to Stanton in person. There was to be no court of inquiry.[17]

While making his efforts to obtain an official investigation, Warren took up his engineering duties for the army. With the war behind it, the American economy was ready to expand into the west, and the key to this expansion was transportation—along the rivers which flowed there and by way of railroads which were to come. The Army Corps of Engineers was primed to play a cru-cial role in this expansion, and Gouverneur K. Warren was one of the best of the army's engineers.

Warren had been promoted to the rank of major in the Corps of Engineers on June 25, 1864, and with his volunteer rank and his brevet rank behind him it was as Major Warren, officially, that he took up his postwar duties. Infor-mally, it should be said, he was usually addressed as "General Warren," except in official communications.

Warren was sent west in late 1865, came back to New York City to work on his papers and reports, and then in July 1866 was assigned to make surveys of the Minnesota, Wisconsin, and upper Mississippi rivers. Early in August, as he prepared to leave for his station in St. Paul, Minnesota, Warren wrote to Emily about an offer he had rejected for a civilian engineering job, telling her that his army assignment "concerns all the Railroads from St Louis to St Paul and the navigation of all the streams and would make me acquainted with all these interests and the men concerned in them which I much desire in taking my position in civil life. I can get a good look at that country without expense." What he did not say, in explaining all the advantages of staying in the army for the time being, was that he would be entitled to a court of inquiry only as an officer still serving in the army.[18]

Warren arrived in St. Paul on August 17, 1866, telling Emily, who was pregnant at home, that there was not anything to eat on the boat that she would have liked and that the mosquitos were bad. Of St. Paul, he said, "I don't think you would like this place at all, to stop in, and so am not on your acct sorry you are not here. I wish though that you were for mine in my leisure hours."[19] One of the curiosities of Warren's postwar life, it will be noted, is how little time he and Emily actually lived together, after all the longing, loving letters of their wartime separation. There was little evidence in their correspondence of any lessening of their mutual devotion, only the odd circumstance that they so often seemed to be apart, even when this did not appear to be required by Warren's assignments.

From St. Paul Warren commented to his wife on what he saw and experienced in the Minnesota region, called President Andrew Johnson a "scurvy" politician, described his "gratification in having the great rivers and the interests connected with them under my control," and reported with pleasure that "all have treated me with much respect and kindness." He was outraged that someone back east had used his name as a supporter of a pro-Johnson meeting, and he reported with some pride that even an attack of diarrhea had not prevented him from sending out his required working parties.[20]

At times Warren's true feelings came through to his wife. "Indeed the past year," he wrote early in September 1866, "was one of great despondency to me . . . I somehow don't wonder that persons often remark how seldom I laugh, but it is really seldom I do." His future, in the army or out, oppressed him. "[T]he casting about for what to do continually occupies my mind. The offer of Mr. Richardson," who had pressed him to resign in order to take a job in the civilian world, "seemed to promise something but it only introduces me to another case of hard work . . . which gives me much anxiety as to the means necessary for final success." To the worry whether he could make a proper living in civilian life was added, always, the necessity of remaining in the army to be entitled to a court of inquiry.[21]

"Ambition," he said, "is the most harrowing thing one ever set their hopes upon," and his consolation for "the harsh treatment I received" was the resulting freedom "from any desire for high position," or, really, any hope of the same.[22]

Still, Warren was able to immerse himself in his work, work which he found "delightfully interesting to me," and he made great progress, completing his study of the upper Mississippi, surveying bridge sites at Burlington, Quincy, and Hannibal, and running into Winfield Hancock in St. Louis for a pleasant get-together. He finished at Hannibal on November 2, 1866, left the next day for Chicago, and departed Chicago for New York on the 8th, only to be summoned to Washington by Humphreys, once again his superior in the Engineers, for consultation.[23]

Late in the month, with Gouv back in New York to be with her, Emily gave birth to a baby boy, a healthy little fellow who was, almost seventeen months later, named Algernon Sidney for Emily's father, though he was always called Sidney.[24]

Early in December Humphreys, now commander of the Corps of Engineers, told Warren, "You have opened up or are opening up a new region of river improvements, which of itself must be a source of interest." After the words of commendation came the hook: "When do you propose making up your maps & reports." Unfortunately, the maps and reports always trailed several years behind the fieldwork—Warren had not yet finished his final report on the treks through Nebraska and Dakota from the late 1850s, the war having gotten in the way—so the public at large, even the public which read such documents, had little conception of what Gouverneur K. Warren was doing now that the Civil War was over. A month later Humphreys reported that Senator Alexander Ramsey of Minnesota had been to see him twice, inquiring about Warren's reports on his summer's work. "Can you see your way sufficiently to say about when you can get through a preliminary or full report?" Humphreys asked. Warren was as meticulous about the accuracy of his reports as he had been about the dispositions of his troops, so the reports progressed slowly.[25]

Pressure for the completion of his paperwork kept Warren in the capital, away from Emily and the baby. He wrote her that she should "wean the little fellow and save your strength," and then admitted that his own 9 A.M. to 11 P.M. workdays were exhausting him. A note from his brother Will chiding him for not visiting while he was in Washington showed the pressure Warren was under. In April 1867, he headed back to the upper Mississippi again, arriving in Chicago on the 16th, in Keokuk, Iowa, the next day, and in Davenport on the first of May.[26]

During the day Warren worked very hard at his engineering work, particularly on his supervision of the progress of the bridge over the Mississippi from Rock Island, Illinois, to Davenport, Iowa. This great bridge, the first double-deck drawbridge over navigable waters, was to remain one of Warren's most lasting monuments, but it took a toll upon his physical well-being.

The bitter past impinged upon his sleep. From Davenport, he wrote to Emily that "I wish I did not dream so much. They make me sometimes dread to go to sleep. Scenes from the war, are so constantly recalled, with bitter feelings I wish never to experience again. Lies, vanity, treachery, and carnage." Late in the month he called upon Sherman in St. Louis, a visit he must have viewed with some distaste in light of Sherman's close connections with Grant and Sheridan, but he described Sherman as "very cordial and polite."[27]

Family problems occupied Warren from time to time. He had the major responsibility for making sure that his mother's continued tenure in the family home at Cold Spring was untroubled, while a good deed that he had done, buying his Aunt Hannah's home (and taking out a mortgage to do so) so that she could continue to reside there, became a source of grief to him, with his aunt irrationally suspecting him of trying to turn her out. Emily and his sister Eliza both gave him concern about these dealings, to the point where he wrote, "It is a very troublesome thing to do business with women." [28]

In late June, Warren left St. Paul, returning to New York to bring Emily and the baby out to visit him. He had his family with him until early August, and then they came out again in the fall. These were happy times for Warren, and he missed those times when he could see the stages of his baby son's development. On the 12th of December, with his family back in New York, he wrote, "I am glad baby is so well. Does he talk any real talk yet?" [29]

The paperwork connected with his engineering duties Warren described as "an enormous incubus upon my spirits," and he told Emily that "it has been my misfortune to be all the time since you have known me overtasked," but he hoped that "in a year more," that is, by December 1868, he would have "our affairs all arranged so that I shall get rid of all that now worries me, and we can be together afterwards as much as we please." This was always the hope that he held out to her, that after the present burdens were overcome all would be well, the army would be left behind, and they would live together in joy and prosperity. Always in the background, however, was the need for vindication in the eyes of the army. Warren knew that Grant was in the ascendancy in Washington and that he could hope for nothing while that situation obtained, but he assumed that Grant's power must come to an end sometime. In the meantime he would wait. [30]

Warren spent the better part of 1868 in the west, except for a period in the late spring when he was in New York and Washington. While there he wrote to ex-governor Morgan, asking for confirmation in writing of what Grant had said to Morgan at their meeting in 1866, denying Warren a court of inquiry, and Morgan obliged. In the west, Warren wandered from Pittsburgh to Salt Lake City and Laramie, with many stops in between. He recorded his meetings with a number of prominent persons, including Brigham Young in Salt Lake City, Hancock in St. Louis, and the famous Swiss naturalist Louis Agassiz, touring the west with Judge (later Justice) Ward Hunt and Senator Roscoe Conkling of New York, in St. Paul. Warren described his congenial personal visit with Agassiz but had little to say about the flamboyant Conkling, who was a friend and supporter of both Grant and Sheridan. [31]

In early October Warren was appointed a commissioner to examine the Union Pacific Railroad. He was to be paid an extra three hundred dollars over and above his salary, so he was happy to have the appointment, until he discovered that the assignment of the commission was to review the whole line—

some eleven hundred miles—rather than the twenty-mile stretch he initially thought was to be covered. "This has been a much harder piece of work than I expected," he wrote.[32]

In mid-November he had to deal with the news that Grant had been elected president, although the nomination by the Democrats of the ineffectual Horatio Seymour had given Warren time to adjust to the probability of Grant's success. "I think it is quite likely that the same influences that drove me so unjustly from my position in the war will be used to push me out of anything desirable I may have here. I have always had this contingency in view and they cannot hurt me much if they do." He expected Grant to oppose "these public improvements which I am connected with," although he thought that it might be politically risky for Grant to do any more than "disconnect me from them." In any case, Warren wrote, "I am prepared for what comes."[33]

Sitting in a bleak hotel room in Omaha, Nebraska, Warren wrote despairingly to his wife that the railroad survey was "a long tedious task." "I am very tired of being here so long in such an out of the way place," he told Emily, "all alone as far as intimate acquaintances goes and it makes me feel uncomfortable to find that all the work of my life has not enabled me to avoid some of the disagreeable things I am compelled to go through with." If she were with him, he said, "I would not mind it," but then their combined expenses would be more than his pay. The next day he assured her that "next year if I am in the west you can be with me all the time."[34]

When he heard that his old commander McClellan had gotten an engineering job at a ten-thousand-dollar annual salary, Warren said, "I am glad he has it, but how I would like to get something like that." A couple of days later, while admitting that he felt "very churlish" where he was and would be very glad never to see that part of the country again, he felt that he was improving his engineering prospects so that he would "be able to get a salary of $10,000 before a great while." He said the great labor he had been performing "has been in making myself familiar with such an extent of country and so extensive operations. I feel pretty well established now, and I believe the work I have done the past three years will bear fruit soon."[35]

Gouv had promised to be home for Christmas but did not quite make it. He left St. Paul on December 24 and was in Chicago on the holiday heading east. After a brief visit home to New York and a stay of several days in Washington with Emily, observing his thirty-ninth birthday, Warren was soon on his way west again, on more railroad business: a special joint commission examining the Union Pacific and Central Pacific lines. He reached Chicago on January 22, Omaha on the 24th, and Salt Lake City on the 28th. "[I]t seems all like a little dream, the short visit I made home, and having you with me alone in Washington. Like a pleasant dream, all too short." On he went, with his fellow railroad commissioners, getting to Stockton, California, on February 1, 1869.[36]

Warren met with ex-governor Leland Stanford and Charles Crocker, two of the great California railroad-builders. He was gratified in San Francisco to "find a disposition to honor me for what I did in the war greater than I expected." Crossing the Sierra Nevadas, he noted that the snow was about ten feet deep, and he wrote, "I enjoy our work very much." In Utah, Warren's party received word of the appointment of Grant's cabinet, an undistinguished group, and Gouverneur commented bitterly, "I believe it is the success and flattery and adulation that attend Grant, who is nothing but a worthless drunkard, that is causing so much mischief." [37]

On March 18, Warren wrote from Salt Lake City that the railroads east of there were so blocked with snow that no mail was going out. He noted that a three-thousand-dollar payment on the mortgage he had placed on his mother's home was due on April 1, that he had sent checks for the amount in question, but he feared they might not reach the intended recipients. Would Emily have her father make the payment until he could take care of it? "There is no trouble about it," he said, "only I am so poor everybody requires security in dealing with me. I am determined it shall not be so much longer." [38]

Ordered back to New York, Warren arrived in mid-April. The rest of the spring, summer, and early fall of 1869 he spent in the east, working on his reports and actually spending a comparatively large amount of time with his family. In the midst of all his other work, Warren supervised the preparation of a meticulously exact map of the battlefield of Gettysburg, a map which was not finally completed until early 1871. [39]

In October, Warren reported back to his headquarters at St. Paul and resumed supervision of the construction of the Rock Island bridge. His work on the bridge contributed to a severe impairment of his health, and he was very sick for several months in the early part of 1870. Emily and Sidney came out to see him, but late in January they departed for the east, and Warren was left to suffer alone. Another worry presented itself when the assignments of all the leading engineer officers were changed around and Warren was ordered from St. Paul to Detroit, to take charge of the Survey of the Lakes. When Humphreys learned how unwell his friend was, he delayed the transfer to Detroit, ultimately canceling it. [40]

Warren's doctor in St. Paul told him he was suffering from "an engorged state of the liver and digestive organs." Perhaps; Warren knew that he had a great deal of pain in his chest, had "trouble in lying in but few positions," and needed morphine to get to sleep. Hancock came to see him several times and said there was concern that Warren might be getting typhoid fever, but by mid-February he seemed to be over the worst of his illness. As time went on, however, he was very slow in regaining his health; "the muscles of my whole body are as sore as if I had been pounded," he told Emily, "and I am very weak and the weight of my own flesh is a burden to me." Later he wrote her, "I never recuperated so slowly from sickness," and he suffered from persistent headaches.[41]

Cross words from Emily produced a rebuke from Gouverneur:

> If there is any want of sympathy between us, I think it is because you do not sympathize with my efforts to overcome the troubles that I have had to undergo. We must keep up the struggle. If we stop our efforts we shall sink. There is no use bemoaning for it can't be helped. The consolation is that we don't deserve so hard a lot even if it has fallen to us, and it cannot last always.[42]

After Humphreys wrote Warren that the latter's sickness must have come from overwork, Warren wrote bitterly to his wife, "If I am who put the work on me[?] Why was last summer's work at the R.I. bridge added[?]" He said, "I am really afraid that hard work has exhausted the nervous forces. My head is clear and comfortable but I have no animal strength." [43]

In late March, he made a trip east for several weeks, "to confer with the Chief Engineer about the Rock Island Bridge," but in April he was out west again. He got back to St. Paul on April 30, although he still felt sick and was troubled by headaches. By this time, though, he knew that his orders had been changed and that he would be going ultimately not to Detroit but to Newport, Rhode Island, an assignment that was much more congenial to him. The formal order was issued on May 3.[44]

Warren had another month of work on the Rock Island bridge to oversee. Before boarding his boat to go down the river, he stopped on May 2 to see the Hancocks in St. Paul. Hancock, who had run afoul of Grant in his service as a Reconstruction commander in New Orleans, was smarting from ill treatment by the new president in the command assignment he had received. When he complained, he received from Sherman what Warren called "a spiteful . . . indiscreet as well as malicious letter" explaining that he (Hancock) need not expect any attention to be paid to his personal preferences.

On May 17, Warren finished his engineering work on the Rock Island bridge. He was headed back east by the end of the month, although still complaining of his sickness, and arrived at Newport by June 11. He was back in the east to stay.

Gouverneur Warren was a thorough, conscientious, and capable engineer, and the work he did in the American west in the years after the war was well regarded by his superiors in Washington, by the civilians with whom he came in contact, and by his peers. He enjoyed fieldwork and the open-air activities involved in it, finding that only here could he push to the back of his mind the bitterness of what he regarded as the continuing injustice of Five Forks.

CHAPTER TWENTY-FIVE

NEWPORT

*J*UST BEFORE STARTING EAST, WARREN RECEIVED a note from his father-in-law, advising him that the city of New York had created a Department of Docks & Piers and was looking for a first-class engineer to head it. Warren asked Humphreys for a letter of recommendation, and the latter said he would "do all in my power to support you for the place you mention or any other in which I can serve you." Humphreys furnished him with a letter to the city Superintendent of Docks, saying that Warren was "gifted by nature with brilliant talents . . . in a service of twenty years a hard student, a close observer, an indefatigable worker, a man of . . . energy and zeal." Nothing, however, came of the overture. Warren noted that he "never had occasion to use" Humphreys' letter, apparently because he felt the position would be too political, and he remained in the army, though he was forever considering—so he said—various ways to make big money in civilian life.[1]

Warren settled into his new life at Newport and found engineering duties there considerably less stressful than those on the upper Mississippi. The Corps of Engineers rented a house on Mary Street for its director. The Brenton House was named for Jahleel Brenton, who had built it around 1720. In earlier days the house had been visited by George Washington and James Monroe and been occupied by Commodore Oliver Hazard Perry. Now it came with the job for G. K. Warren, as both residence and office.[2]

Officially, Warren was in charge of everything along both sides of Long Island Sound to Cape Cod, along with the offshore islands. Consulting on breakwaters on Cape Cod, harbor improvements at Martha's Vineyard, piers and docks on Narragansett Bay, wharves at Bridgeport—projects like these were not as exciting to Warren as building a bridge over the mighty Mississippi or examining the great railroad lines across the plains and mountains of the west, but they were less of a strain on his physical resources.

Even after arriving at his new station in Rhode Island, of course, Warren found himself detailed on assignments to boards and commissions, investigating a bridge in Buffalo in October and serving on the board on Ohio River bridges, working out of Cincinnati, in November. Family concerns continued to worry him. Brother Will importuned Gouv for financial assistance, and Warren noted to Emily that Will's problems "make me think how much you and I are relieved by having a home with your father." There were constant worries about Emily's younger brother Lewis, a black sheep if ever there was one. Lewis was court-martialed by the army for excessive drinking, was reinstated at Gouv's earnest request, and then was thrown out again after an embarrassing binge. Warren did what he could to aid Lewis, but one gets the feeling his heart was no longer in the effort, after numerous earlier intercessions on Lewis's behalf. He did give Lewis a job, much to his later chagrin. Finally, in December, Warren's mother died at Cold Spring, a widow of long standing who had lived out her life quietly and graciously. Once again, Gouv took charge of family business, administering her estate as executor.[3]

Gouv, as the senior with the prestigious record of his wartime service and great rank, remained the head of the family. Financially, however, few of the Warrens prospered after the war, and the general, with his meager salary as a major or lieutenant colonel of engineers, considered himself a poor man. He was considerably embarrassed when little Sid, whom Warren tried to talk out of a tricycle he desired, asked earnestly "if I hadn't money enough to buy it."[4] His brother-in-law and former aide, Washington Roebling, became wealthy after the war, through his bridge-building (the Cincinnati Bridge and the great Brooklyn Bridge) and the family wire-manufacturing business in Trenton. Warren's sister Emily, naturally, shared in her husband's new status. She had always looked upon her brother Gouverneur with great adoration and respect, and this attitude never changed, although of course it mellowed as she grew into middle age. When the Roeblings gave Warren financial assistance, as they did from time to time, it was always done with the greatest delicacy in order to preserve the general's self-respect and his sister's feelings.

Warren was frequently troubled by financial problems. A colleague who had just resigned from the army wrote to Warren, advising, "You ought not to remain in the service an hour longer than it will take you to find business suitable to your tastes & talents, and this I should not think very difficult." But it was a step he could not bring himself to take. He told Emily from Cincinnati that he was a fool for being away from her, "but then I know that it is because I want to do more for you than I could if I did not go." His greatest crime, he wrote, "is working too much without profit, judged in any human point of view." Still, he felt he had to discharge his share of "the uniform distribution of responsibility . . . demanded of our corps," and he had in his mind at all times his entitlement to a court of inquiry.[5]

Warren spent much of his time alone. Emily and Sidney lived at Mr. Chase's home in New York City, making periodic visits to Rhode Island. They visited with Warren from mid-January to mid-February in 1871, returned to New York, and then came back again in July, when Warren rented a house. In between, he made occasional weekend visits to the city. In mid-August 1871, though, he was sent off again to Cincinnati, and then was detailed to Chicago on a commission regarding the Illinois Central Railroad. Warren did not return to Newport until October 17. In the meantime, he worked away on maps and reports from earlier assignments. At one point, he said, "I wish I had never had any thing to do with the Wisconsin River but having begun it, I feel my reputation is at stake to go fairly through with it."[6]

Litigation arose concerning the Rock Island bridge, and Warren was called to Washington in January 1872 to testify in the case. The next month he went to St. Louis to serve on a board with General John Newton, who had lost his First Corps command in the 1864 reorganization but held no grudge against Warren for it. Back in Newport, Warren slaved away at the mountain of unfinished business on his desk. In April he felt he had "worked down to the bottom of the well and will soon finish it," but on Christmas Day he was still struggling with paperwork in Newport while his family celebrated the holiday in New York. He told Emily that "I know that I have given up a great deal of my life to thankless public service but I do not regret it. I could not have been myself and do otherwise as I was placed." He hoped finally by January 15, 1873, to "take up the Wisconsin River which I have never been able to finish since I laid it down when I was sick at St. Paul. What a long time to keep so huge a matter on the mind."[7]

Lewis Chase continued to be a problem. After he was ousted from the army, he was given a job by his brother-in-law, working as an engineer. On June 22, 1872, Lewis and three other men were working on a survey of the river and harbor at Westport, Connecticut, under the supervision of Henry N. Babcock, when they suddenly ran amuck. They hauled a sulky belonging to the local hotel out and left it on the bridge, hurled a rock through a barbershop window, removed a gate from a residence and dumped it across the road, and threw several barrels from a liquor store into the river. Lewis was jailed overnight, and Babcock had to pay a fifty-dollar bail for him. Mr. Chase later wrote to Warren, saying, "I believe Lew is very sorry too & he don't say much to justify it, but says it was not a drunken frolic at all, for that none of the party had been drinking any," which, if true, made the whole affair that much odder.[8]

Warren had an unexpected request from James H. Dwight, secretary of the American Palestine Exploration Society, in June 1872, asking if he would like to participate in an exploratory and archaeological expedition in the area east of the Jordan River and Dead Sea. Warren turned the offer down, saying that he was "not qualified for the work you propose . . . My pursuits as an engineer and as a soldier and my early education, have not only kept me from preparing for antiquarian researches, but have filled my mind with other materials for working upon." [9]

The years took on a familiar pattern for Gouverneur Warren. He sent his crews out on the projects under his immediate care, on the rivers and harbors of New England. He went off on various assignments around the country when the Corps of Engineers wanted boards of experts to inspect bridges, rivers, or dams. And when he had time, back in Newport, he worked on the reports and studies which he owed the corps for past inspections and projects.

In 1873, for example, he was sent to Detroit, Chicago, St. Louis, back to Detroit, then on to Louisville and New Orleans. In the latter city, he ran into a friend of Senator Matthew Ransom of North Carolina, the same Ransom who had commanded the left end of the Confederate line at Five Forks. Senator Ransom had told his friend he knew that Warren had acted properly in that battle "and that he meant to say so in a speech in the Senate as soon as the opportunity occurred." In November, Warren had to go to Antietam in connection with a six-hundred-dollar claim by a farmer there for materials belonging to him which Warren had used to build a bridge over Antietam Creek in July 1863. [10]

Once again Warren spent Christmas alone in Newport, working on his reports. 1874 was much the same for him, with a couple of delightful bonuses. In April, Emily gave birth to a little girl—to be named Emily, as if the family did not have a goodly supply of Emilys already—and the general wrote his wife that "I am going to dress up very elegant and go up to the club tonight and receive congratulations." [11]

A month later, he went to a Ninth Corps reunion held at Harrisburg, Pennsylvania, and received a tumultuous reception. Warren's entry, a reporter noted, "was the signal for uproarious applause, and when he attempted to take a seat in the body of the hall he was carried enthusiastically to the platform where the general officers were seated." What made this reception even more delicious was that Sheridan was present and forced to witness it. Warren told Emmie, "You have no idea of the talk my reception at Harrisburg has made in Army circles." [12]

In December 1874 an engineering board on which Warren was sitting in Washington made a ceremonial call on the president. Warren reported that he was shocked at Grant's "broken down appearance. His right eye is dreadfully blood shot and his face is red and bloated with a kind of trembling shake all over him." He made no further comment on his nemesis except that "we made the call very short." [13]

Warren did what he could to help out as an absentee parent. He asked Emily to "tell Siddy his father expects him to grow into a man. He need not imitate the . . . big boys. If he does as we want him . . . [they will] come to him and ask for work." A few weeks later, hearing that Sidney, slight of build like his parents, had been picked on, Warren wrote, angrily, "I am very sorry Siddy has been hurt again and if the boy knocked him down maliciously. . . I will bring prosecution against his parents or guardians. I am enraged at the tyranny of the big boys over the small ones." [14]

In 1875, Warren's sister-in-law Cornelia, his brother Edgar's wife, died, as did the ancient and revered Gouverneur Kemble. Warren wrote to Kemble's nephew to "pay tribute to the great public worth of his long life," adding that he could "never forget his kindness to me in my early life." [15]

In September 1875, Mr. Chase asked Warren for a letter of recommendation for Lewis. Lewis was seeking a position with General Joseph E. Johnston, who was expected to become commander in chief of the Egyptian army; Chase suggested that Warren might "be willing to aid him in getting a situation which would give you & him separate paths in life, which I believe is what you would like." Whether Lewis would have made a new life for himself in the shadow of the Pyramids will never be known, because Johnston did not obtain the position, and Lewis Chase was next heard of as a haberdasher in Chattanooga, Tennessee. [16]

Early the next year Warren was stunned to learn of the death of his brother Robert on January 23. An army officer stationed at Camp Douglas, Utah, Robert died suddenly "of apoplexy" at the age of twenty-nine. Robert had enlisted initially in the Fifth New York in 1861 and had risen gradually in rank until he was breveted major for the battle of Five Forks. He remained in the army after the war and was a first lieutenant in the Fourteenth Infantry at the time of his death. He died virtually penniless but survived by tales of his impulsive generosity. Emily Roebling wrote to Gouv that "Eliza and Rob seem to have inherited from Father a most reckless generosity." Emily was able to check Eliza, who lived with the Roeblings, "but Bob has been left free to carry out his impulses and I have no doubt that one great source of his money embarrassment was because he gave away money when he ought to have used it for himself." The general and the Roeblings took care of Robert's debts. [17]

On a more positive note, Warren was overjoyed to complete his report on the Wisconsin River and to set it on its way to publication. This completion eased the burden upon him, and he was further gratified by election to the National Academy of Sciences, which he called "the kind of endorsement I wanted." Nevertheless, he was ordered off on another commission inspecting bridges over the Mississippi between St. Louis and St. Paul, which involved a month-long sojourn in the upper midwest in September and October 1876. [18]

Warren took a keen interest in the presidential contest of 1876, which would pick the successor to Grant after eight years. (Grant was perfectly willing to continue in the White House, but party leaders heard from back home that such a continuance was not favored by the electorate.) Warren took the trouble to paste in his letter book a full front page from a Washington paper calling for the Democrats to nominate Hancock, but that was not to be. Samuel J. Tilden of New York had things all his way in the Democratic convention, while a surprise choice, Rutherford B. Hayes of Ohio, snatched the Republican nod from James G. Blaine of Maine and two Grant supporters, Oliver Morton of Indiana and Roscoe Conkling of New York.[19]

Warren felt both nominees were good and said, "I think between the two parties and their candidates there is not much choice." He went on to set out "some reasons why I prefer that the next president should be a republican." With Hayes, "there will be a change in the management of the party." Before the Republican party left office, he said, it should purify its ranks "that the good of the party not be swamped with the bad," which of course was Grantism and all its manifestations. He was pleased to see Hayes ultimately elected, after the resolution of the electoral stalemate. For Hayes meant the end of Grant and a government no longer dominated by Grant and his cronies.[20]

Life was somewhat relaxed for Gouverneur Warren in 1877. He was confident in his ability to handle the routine business of his office and the normal exigencies of the rivers and harbors of southern New England. He found a place for Andrew and Becky Humphreys to rent for the summer, and their presence in Newport was a tonic for him, as it was for Humphreys. "I have not had so much Army-operations talk in years as we had last evening," Humphreys said in a note to Warren on the 10th of July. "I hope no one was bored . . . by my reminiscences." In August, Warren dined with George McClellan, and in September he and Emily were guests of the city of Boston for the dedication of its Army and Navy Monument. Chamberlain gave the main address, and Warren was pleased to hear a great ovation for McClellan.[21]

He wrote to Nelson Miles, after Miles stopped the Nez Perce tribe in its flight to Canada at the Bear Paws Mountains in Montana. He congratulated Miles on the humanity shown by him to Chief Joseph and his desperate followers, and he recalled, "My first experience in war was with the red men, and it was in a successful campaign too; but the result was that my sympathies were largely with the red man in his wrongs and claims for justice." He hoped that Miles would treat the Indian "as deserving the rights of a man. I feel so most emphatically." [22]

In the spring of the next year Warren finished his report on bridging the Mississippi between St. Louis and St. Paul, submitted it to the department, and was gratified to have it printed. On June 13, Emily's father died at the age of sixty-nine after a lingering illness. He had been a bulwark of Warren's family for many years, furnishing a home to Emily and the children. He named Warren executor of his estate, although that estate turned out to be far less sizable than expected. With Emily no longer needed to make a home for her father, she and the children were at last able to move to Newport, to the house her husband occupied on Thames Street, and to take up a normal family life.[23]

Warren was not present at the death of his father-in-law, for he had been sent by the Corps of Engineers on June 4 to Manassas and Groveton to start on the preparation of a comprehensive map of that historic field. Later in the summer he was back on the Mississippi, reporting on the prospects for improving navigation in its upper reaches.

What Warren was primarily interested in now, though, with his major reports and Grant both out of the way, was a court of inquiry. The need for a formal investigation to clear his name had been uppermost in his mind ever since the fateful moment in which Sheridan relieved him, despite repeated evidence over the years that most knowledgeable observers agreed that an injustice had been done him. Their good opinion did not alleviate the mental distress which afflicted Warren. So long as the army persisted in the action of April 1, 1865, so long would he insist that the army must redress the injury.

Warren knew that it was futile to push for a court during the eight years of Grant's presidency, but now, he hoped, prospects should be brighter. On November 10, 1878, he prepared a letter to Humphreys setting forth the history of his efforts at vindication, saying, "On the election of a successor to Genl Grant I have always intended to apply again." [24] Humphreys took this letter to a meeting with the secretary of war, George W. McCrary, an Iowa lawyer-politician with no ties to Grant.

McCrary listened carefully to Humphreys as he read portions of Warren's letter. McCrary, Humphreys reported, "evidently entertains a high opinion of you and of your services." All those years working to improve navigation and transportation on the Upper Mississippi certainly helped his image in the eyes of a former Iowa congressman. McCrary suggested that an application for the court should be made to the president, emphasizing that the facts of the battle at Five Forks were not known ("not even to Genl Sheridan") and that "the facts are what you want established." [25]

Warren was handicapped slightly when he sprained his wrist early in 1879, but Humphreys consoled him in mid-February with the thought that his application should not go in to Hayes during the current session of Congress in any event. "You will not be able to get a hearing until Congress has dispersed," he wrote. "I mean a consideration of your request to have a hearing." In the meantime, Humphreys suggested, perhaps Warren should come to Washington and see influential persons who might put in a good word for him with McCrary and Hayes. [26]

Warren spent much of March and April in Washington, meeting people, gathering papers and what he hoped would be evidence, and working on his application. When Emily wrote him that she was feeling "forlorn" in Newport, he replied coldly: "Newport is next to death to me. Here I am in the midst of life and really enjoy it . . . There is no end of interesting people and subjects here for me. I am seeing lots of friends every day. It is the world for me." He said he was "gathering a great deal of valuable information," and he had help from his friend Henry Abbot. At length, though, even the capital began to pall. "I am tired of being here now," he wrote in late April to Emily, who was staying then with the Roeblings in Brooklyn. "I don't feel very well and my occupation is depressing." [27]

He and Humphreys worked closely on the all-important application. They decided that a detailed presentation of the facts and his reasons for an inquiry was to be preferred over a bare-bones statement of the case. This was so because Hayes and McCrary really knew nothing of the battle and "they must necessarily... have a disinclination to open the subject since Genl Grant persistently refused the investigation." They discussed whom they would hope to have on the court if the application was granted. "What do you think...," Humphreys asked, "of Hancock, Wright Ord or Hunt or Gibbon or Ruger?" [28]

Henry Hunt, who had become a close friend despite their wartime differences over the uses of Hunt's artillery, was in fact advising Warren in the preparation of his application. Though he would be happy with both men on the court, Warren was afraid that Hancock and Hunt could not "act harmoniously together," since they were engaged in a bitter public dispute over Hancock's employment of the artillery on the third day at Gettysburg. "Ord and Ruger," Warren said, "I do not know much about." He was afraid that Wright could not serve because of his own differences with Sheridan, but he thought there could be no objection to John Parke. "I would like to have two men from the Army of the Potomac at least," he said. Schofield, Terry, Abbot, and Upton were others he would feel comfortable with. Warren also had a list of those who should not be chosen: cavalrymen, members of Grant's inner circle, blighted officers like McDowell and Pope. He dismissed Howard and Auger as not having "much character as tried soldiers." What he really wanted, he said, was "men of character as soldiers, possessed of independent judgments, and capable of action without fear favor or affection." The latter quality was important, of course, because of Sheridan's position as the second-ranking officer in the U.S. Army. [29]

There was a question of timing. The retrial of Fitz John Porter had recently taken place, resulting in a vindication of that Fifth Corps commander, but there were other proceedings required to complete the case, including congressional action. Warren did not want to appear as coming too closely on the heels of the Porter case. On the other hand, Secretary McCrary had been named by Hayes to a circuit court judgeship, and, if quickly confirmed, he would be leaving the War Department, his successor an unknown quantity. Warren hoped to have his request considered while McCrary was still in office, "for I have formed so good an opinion of his sense of fairness," but felt it could wait until autumn. [30]

Early in October Warren had a long meeting with ex-governor Morgan in Newport. Morgan said Grant had told him the trouble with Warren was that he wanted to command too much. The former president also said that he could not give Warren a court of inquiry without offending Sheridan and that, of course, he would not do. Morgan told Warren that when the latter was ready to apply he would put in a good word with President Hayes.[31]

On the night of November 17, Gouv and Will worked late to get the letter of application into final form, and the next day Warren and Humphreys called on Secretary McCrary and formally placed the document in his hands. "Now that the matter is fairly launched," Warren wrote, "I feel better satisfied." [32]

On the 21st, Warren and Humphreys called upon President Hayes, who received them very cordially. Hayes had already received the promised letter from Morgan, asking that the application be granted, "for his own sake and the sake of his State." The president promised to give attention to the application "in a week or two," and Warren decided to wait in Washington for a while longer. He was now very hopeful that the long-awaited court would be granted him.[33]

Finally it came. The commanding general of the army, Sherman, approved the application, and the adjutant general's office announced on December 9, 1879, fourteen years, nine months, and eight days after the battle, that it had received the following order of the same day from the White House:

> On the application of Lieutenant Colonel Gouverneur K. Warren, Corps of Engineers, (late Major General of Volunteers), a Court of Inquiry is hereby appointed to assemble at Governor's Island, New York Harbor, on the 11th day of December, 1879, or as soon thereafter as practicable, for the purpose of inquiring into Lieutenant Colonel Warren's conduct as Major General, commanding the 5th Army Corps, at the battle of Five Forks, Virginia, on April 1, 1865, and into the operation of his command on that day and the day previous, as far as they relate to his, Lieutenant Colonel Warren's conduct, or to imputations or accusations against him.

> The Court will consist of the following three members:

> —Major General W.S. Hancock, U.S. Army
> —Brigadier General C.C. Augur, U.S. Army
> —Colonel Z.B. Tower, Corps of Engineers

> —Major James McMillan, 2d Artillery, Recorder.

> The Court will report the facts and its opinion in the case.

> R.B. Hayes[34]

CHAPTER TWENTY-SIX

THE COURT BEGINS

O N DECEMBER 11, 1879, WARREN ATE BREAKFAST with Emily and Wash Roebling in Brooklyn and then took the ferry to Governor's Island, where he called on Winfield Hancock. Hancock, Warren reported to his wife, received him very kindly, "and he seems to not take it as a hardship that he has this lengthened investigation before him." [1]

Hancock then convened the court of inquiry for the first time and immediately adjourned, in view of the absence of his two fellow court members. On December 12, Augur appeared but Tower, who was sick, failed to show. When the same situation prevailed the next day, Hancock adjourned the court to January 5, 1880.

Warren took advantage of the hiatus to journey with an aide to Petersburg and then on to Five Forks, to refamiliarize himself with the terrain and the landmarks in and around the field of battle. Even this trip was controversial. On December 15, Warren requested orders to go to Five Forks, so that his trip need not be at his own expense. On the 17th, Sherman declined, saying that Warren's examination of the battle area would "be *ex parte* and may be disputed." Assuring Warren that he would "give any order that will enable him to make the truth manifest," Sherman said the order Warren asked for would have to come from the court itself. [2]

So Warren expended his own limited funds to go south. He spent Christmas at the Gilliam mansion, near the site of his final charge late in the battle. He and the Gilliam family celebrated the holiday and Mrs. Gilliam's birthday with an egg nog toast before breakfast. Warren rented two saddle horses for four days as he moved back and forth over the old battlefield. He returned to New York several days later and then went on to Willets Point, where he sat down with Henry Abbot to go over some final items for the inquiry, returning to New York City on New Year's Eve. [3]

When the inquiry reconvened, in a large room in the barracks at Governor's Island, the court itself had changed from the one set up in the president's

Henry L. Abbot, fellow engineer and confidant. National Archives.

order. General John Newton was substituted for Tower on December 16. On January 5, 1880, Hancock called the proceedings to order and, after Warren said he had no objection to any member, the court was sworn. The next day, asked to state his case, Warren said

In now bringing my case before the court, I am under a great disadvantage in feeling that I am required to present both sides of the controversy; and it was for this reason that I requested that Lt. Gen. Sheridan should be asked to attend and state any and all the grounds of complaint, and the reasons that led him to remove me from my command. Thus far it can hardly be said that he has made any satisfactory statement.

He then presented an official copy of Sheridan's report of the Five Forks battle and the campaign against Lee's right.[4]

Winfield Scott Hancock, first president of the Warren Court.
National Archives.

The next day Sheridan's report was read into the record. Warren, surrounded by maps and papers, sat at a table a few feet away from Major McMillan, the recorder, with one aide at his side. Warren followed the reading of Sheridan's report closely, tracing the described movements on a map before him, and he considered the three men who composed the court which he had been seeking for such a long time.

Hancock, of course, he knew well and considered a friend, but he also knew the Pennsylvanian would consider the evidence with an open mind. Hancock had, in the past, expressed sympathy with Warren for the treatment he had received, and he was no friend of Sheridan or Grant, with both of whom he had experienced personal or political, though not military, differences. He had gained much weight after his Gettysburg wound, but he still looked impressive at fifty-five, wearing a yellow major general's sash across his chest.

Christopher Columbus Augur, a fifty-eight-year-old New Yorker, had been stationed at West Point when Warren taught there, but otherwise Warren knew little of him. Augur, more of an administrator than a fighting soldier, had led a division under the ill-starred Nathaniel Banks in 1862 and 1863 and commanded the Department of Washington thereafter. That he had worked closely with Sheridan after the war had to concern Warren.

Newton, the new member, was born in Virginia in 1822, graduated from the Military Academy in 1842, and joined the Corps of Engineers. He made a good record during the war, primarily in the Sixth Corps, and commanded the First Corps at and after Gettysburg until the 1864 reorganization. Newton had been one of the objects of Warren's strictures about the incompetence of corps commanders in the Army of the Potomac, although Warren had not mentioned him by name. He and Warren had worked together on occasion on postwar engineering projects and boards, and Warren hoped to receive from Newton a sympathetic hearing for a fellow engineer.

On January 9, the court announced that the summons for Sheridan requested by Warren would be granted, but in view of the former's current status on sick leave an indefinite adjournment was taken. The court would reconvene when Sheridan, who was at the time in Florida, could be present.[5]

When a lawyer friend offered his help, Warren said he had "not yet reached the point were [sic] I want legal advice and assistance." He changed his mind within a few days and, on the advice of Henry Abbot's lawyer-brother, engaged a New York lawyer named Albert Stickney to serve as his attorney. Warren had learned that Sheridan would have legal counsel in the form of Major Asa Bird Gardner, of the army's judge-advocate corps, at government expense. Stickney offered to serve at no cost to Warren, which offer the general refused as a matter of principle. Warren laid out for Stickney his entire financial picture: his annual pay and allowance of $4,576; Emily's income of $420, possibly to in-

crease by $800 if her father's estate could be settled properly; and his owner-
ship of the family home in Cold Spring, worth from five to ten thousand
dollars, which he had purchased from his siblings after his mother's death. He
added that he had wealthy friends who were willing to contribute to the expenses of his court. He wanted to get the compensation question settled, he
said, "so that I may have a right to some of your time and aid, without robbing
you or those depending upon you." [6]

The lawyer suggested that $2,000 or $2,500 would be about as high as his
fees would go. Warren borrowed $500 from his sister Emily to give Stickney as
a retainer, and he later placed a mortgage on the house in Cold Spring, to de-
fray further legal costs. He hoped thus to be neither an object of Stickney's
charity nor dependent on contributions from his friends. [7]

On his fiftieth birthday, January 8, Warren wrote to his wife from New York
that nearly fifteen years after Five Forks, he was still "fighting that same battle
. . . now for the honor of my name, as an inheritance for our children." As
long as there was an unwarranted imputation against him, he said, "I never
will cease to strive while I live, so that no reproach can be made when I am
gone, that I tamely acquiesced or submitted. If Syddie ever grows to appreciate
me in his manhood, he will follow it up if by death I leave my part
unfinished." He went on to something which bothered him. "While I am
worked to the point of physical endurance to sustain my character, and compelled to spend money beyond my means my real accuser is seeking restoration of health and absents himself while I who am sick myself have to stand to
fight against his unsupported accusations." Never fear, though; "I am the man
for all this, I hope. If I cannot enjoy life myself I will spend it as my manhood
youth was spent in fighting for what I thought was right." [8]

The long delay in the court enabled Warren to return to Newport, where he
put his small staff to work on the maps he would need for his trial. With his
engineer's mind, he worked systematically at getting together everything he
would need for the court—dispatches, maps, the placement of each regiment,
brigade, and division on the field, and, crucially, witnesses who could testify
to every movement he made on March 31 and April 1, 1865. "I believe," he told
his counsel, "that when I am thoroughly known and understood there [on the
actual battlefield], all the other insinuations and imputations fall off." Recognizing that it was essential for Stickney to have knowledge of the events in
question as complete as his own, Warren outlined his preparations, vowing "to
present the matter to you solid rather than as a disjointed skeleton." [9]

Warren mentioned to Stickney where Crawford was living in New York.
Crawford, he said, "seems disappointed that I don't tell him more what I am
doing, but in reality I have told him all that it is necessary for him to know."
Perhaps Crawford would be mollified if Stickney called him in for a brief conference. "He was not educated as a soldier," Warren went on, "and has not a

high military reputation, but I believe he is better than reputed . . . He has always been very friendly to me, but some of my friends think [him] a source of weakness. I do not think so, if he has just consideration shown to what he has done." Crawford was an important witness: Charles Griffin having died in 1867, Crawford and Ayres were his only surviving division commanders.[10]

By March, Warren was back in New York City, where he set up in the Stevens House as his headquarters for the duration of the inquiry. His work of preparation was arduous and strength-sapping, and a touch of malaria at the end of March did not help. As he continued to work under great, albeit self-imposed, stress, there seemed no end to the series of illnesses, of greater or lesser severity, which Warren had suffered since the war. More and more, his letters reflect his declining strength and vitality and his doubts about the length of life left to him.

Brother Will, working again at the War Department in Washington, was helpful in obtaining documents, and Humphreys, always a staunch friend, kept his eyes and ears open for whatever of assistance he could pick up.[11]

Finally, in mid-April, the court was ready to resume. Colonel Loomis L. Langdon sat now in the position of recorder, with McMillan relieved because of illness. Sheridan, back from sick leave, asked the court to permit him to catch up on army business before devoting his full attention to Warren's matter, so there was further delay. On April 13, however, the court reconvened at Warren's request to take the testimony of the former artillery officer E. R. Warner, who was about to sail for Europe. Warner described his ill-fated mission of the morning of April 1, when he found Locke and got an erroneous description of where the corps was. It was on the basis of this error, reported to Grant, that the lieutenant general sent Babcock to Sheridan with the authorization to relieve Warren. After hearing Warner, the court adjourned to May 3, and Gouverneur Warren headed back to Five Forks for another examination of the field.[12]

When he returned from Virginia, Warren spent a few days in Newport with the family and then returned to New York, telling Emily, "No rest I suppose till the investigation is over." On May 2 he noted that Sheridan was in New York, so the court of inquiry would be starting in earnest.[13]

As Gouverneur Warren approached the inquiry which was the culmination of his postwar years, he was confronted with another previously unconsidered possibility. Ulysses S. Grant was again a candidate for the Republican presidential nomination, and his support by many of the party bosses, led by Roscoe Conkling, put him in front of all other candidates. The party convention meeting in Chicago early in June would determine whether Grant would once more be put on the path to the White House, with whatever unhappy consequences that might hold for Warren and his court of inquiry.

July 11. 1880

G.K Warren

Lieut Col. Engrs &
Bvt Maj. Genl.

An artist's drawing of Warren during the Court of Inquiry. National Archives.

Hancock reconvened the court on May 3, and much of the day was taken up with correcting the record of the previous hearing. Sheridan was present, as were many other military figures. After the correction of the record, Sheridan presented a letter to the court, introducing Gardner as his counsel. Frederick C. Newhall, formerly of Sheridan's staff, then testified briefly in connection with a map of the battle. The court adjourned to the following day for Sheridan's evidence.[14]

Sheridan occupied a great part of the proceedings on May 4 with a long prepared statement giving his view of Dinwiddie Court House and Five Forks and his reasons for dismissing Warren. He made much of the fact that the Fifth Corps did not reach him by midnight of March 31, as Grant had said it would, and "the diversion of Crawford" the next day that "destroyed the plan I had in my mind on making the attack." He said he was worried after the battle that his force, isolated from the Army of the Potomac, was in danger from "the main rebel army," and that Warren "was not the man to rely on."[15]

Stickney, on cross-examination, elicited an admission that Sheridan had never read Warren's pamphlet on the battle. When he asked Sheridan whether "there was any human possibility" for the Fifth Corps to have marched the six miles to Dinwiddie Court House in less than two hours, under the prevailing conditions, Sheridan replied, "It can be done. I have done it myself . . . I have marched at the rate of nearly five miles an hour . . . for twelve hours and over . . . in Oregon; on the frontier . . . in 1858 or 1859." This statement drew guffaws from the audience.[16]

Warren reported to Emily that evening that "matters are going on as well could be expected." He said the inquiry "will end my efforts to make the record right, and whatever the result may be, I shall live the life that is left me with you and the children, without worrying more over this matter." He added that through "the action of Grant and Sheridan . . . I for the first time realized *the devil on earth*. There is something dreadful in the realization when you find him in the highest places."[17]

The court reconvened at 11 A.M. on May 5, with Sheridan on the stand for cross-examination, his pitchfork left behind, his forked tail tucked up under him. He testified all that day and for four more days after that, finishing on May 11. Stickney in his questioning established that Sheridan had little or incorrect information about Warren's actions before meeting him on April 1, was ignorant of Meade's orders to Warren the night of the 31st, had no idea what Warren had done after the battle started, and had made no effort to find out. He had judged the corps commander at Five Forks on the basis of what he had seen with just one part of the smallest of the three divisions of the corps. "The examination," said a reporter, "was at times exciting," "the fencing was adroit on both sides, and the contest at times dramatic."[18]

On May 10 Sheridan quoted Warren as telling him, after the cavalry general set forth his hopes for a smashing success on April 1, not to count too heavily on victory, as " 'Bobby Lee' was always getting people into difficulties." Sheridan said he thought "it was very strange that a man would talk that way when he knew he had to fight. I thought he ought to talk the other way and encourage those who were about him and not depress me." At that moment, Sheridan said, he decided to accompany the Fifth Corps in its attack. Of the men in Ayres's division, Sheridan said, "The poor fellows had been fighting behind breastworks for a long period, and when they got out to attack breastworks they seemed to have been a little timid," a statement which would come back to haunt him.[19]

Stickney had mastered the facts of the case, and Warren was content to let his attorney pursue it as he saw fit. "Warren," it was noted, "seldom prompts his counsel, or interposes in any way. Judged by his manner, he is the most indifferent of all the spectators in the court-martial room. He sits motionless and silent, without the slightest symptom of interest save an occasional flash of his deep-set, dark eyes."[20]

Despite the hostility and animus evident throughout his testimony, Sheridan denied having any prejudice against Warren. "I don't know what his reputation was," he said, disingenuously; "I had not served with him especially."[21] This statement surprised those who knew of the friction between Sheridan and Warren after the night march to Spotsylvania. Indeed, Warren, thoughtful, cautious, educated, was just the kind of man whom Sheridan would have disliked almost instinctively; though there is no evidence of it, Sheridan may have noted and resented Warren on the plain of West Point, a polished and superior cadet from the east who could rouse feelings of malicious envy in a crude and struggling underclassman from the hinterland.

Warren was particularly pleased with the performance of his attorney, making Sheridan squirm on the witness stand and, in effect, making his case through Sheridan's words. Stickney, he told Emily, "is winning golden opinions, and has suddenly gained a national reputation." Sheridan's testimony ended with an answer to Hancock that, without the message from Grant, he would not have had authority to relieve the Fifth Corps commander. Warren considered this "a tremendous point gained for me for it is already in chain of proof that Grant sent that order under an entire misapprehension."[22]

Outside the narrow confines of the courtroom on Governor's Island, Sheridan's story about the twelve-hour sixty-mile march generated much unbelieving mirth, incidentally casting a shadow over the rest of his testimony, and his slurs on the fighting qualities of the Fifth Corps infuriated Warren's veterans, who had little regard in any event for the man who had fired their commander. With Sheridan finished, Warren said, "I now feel perfectly assured of my fame at Five Forks . . . [F]or the first time since the battle . . . I cease to worry over it."[23]

On May 12, Newhall, from Sheridan's staff, did what he could to bolster his chief's case, testifying that Warren appeared to be "passive and indifferent" while his divisions were coming up to Gravelly Run Church and that Sheridan was very annoyed. Day after day the inquiry went on. W. H. H. Benyaurd the engineer testified to the necessity for rebuilding a bridge over Gravelly Run. Jimmy Wadsworth, then on Warren's staff, now the controller of New York State, described how he too checked the swollen stream that night, how he carried Warren's orders to bring up the divisions promptly the next day, and how Warren sent him off to bring Griffin's division back into line. James Forsyth, Sheridan's chief of staff, described giving Warren the order of relief, and George Forsyth, also of Sheridan's staff, claimed he rode across Gravelly Run without getting wet above his stirrups. John A. Kellogg, one of Crawford's brigade commanders, told of Warren's finding his brigade and putting it into place as a pivot and his orders' being overridden by Forsyth.[24]

Joshua Lawrence Chamberlain took the stand on May 15, not just a retired soldier but president of Bowdoin College and former governor of Maine. His testimony was strong as he described the Fifth Corps fighting on the 29th and 31st of March. Asked about Warren's demeanor as his corps was assembling near Gravelly Run Church on April 1, Chamberlain said

> General Warren's temperament is such that he, instead of showing excitement, generally shows an intense concentration in what I call important movements, and those who do not know him might take it to be apathy when it is deep concentrated thought and purpose . . . [A] stranger, looking at General Warren and not seeing indications of excitement and resolution on his face, might judge him to be apathetic, when, in fact, that conclusion might be far from the truth . . . I do not think he was apathetic that morning. He was energetic.[25]

Charles Dana's *New York Sun* provided an editorial summation of the first two weeks of the hearing, concluding that, although the bulk of the testimony thus far had been provided by Sheridan's side, "yet its general result is decidedly in Warren's favor." Dana, who as undersecretary of war had been scornfully critical of Warren in the letters he sent back to Stanton from Virginia, now averred that "Sheridan's treatment of Warren, both on the battle field and in his report, was plainly based on ignorance of Warren's actual conduct." The *Times*, too, had produced an editorial a few days earlier, stating that enough evidence was in the record—"the strongest possible testimony that could be adduced against Gen. Warren," that of Sheridan himself—"for the formation of a preliminary judgment," which was in favor of Warren on all points. The *Brooklyn Eagle* commented that "General Warren, after a patient waiting of fifteen years, has at last proven by several witnesses that he was at the place he should have been and that every order of his superiors was carried out literally." [26]

On Monday morning, May 17, Romeyn Ayres took the stand and testified to the actions of his division on March 31 and April 1. He contradicted Sheridan's slur upon his men by pointing out that one day at the Weldon Railroad was the *only* time his men had fought behind breastworks. He quoted the exact language of George Forsyth on meeting his division a mile south of Gravelly Run on the morning of April 1: "[I]t was not expected that you would get up as soon as this, or I would have been here sooner to meet you." Of the movement to Gravelly Run Church, Ayres declared, "The road was full of cavalry and all sorts of impedimenta and wagons on the road, so the movement was very slow." He denied that his division was thrown into confusion at the start of the attack, stating that one brigade came up at the double-quick and created a small bit of disorder, quickly corrected. Gardner's cross-examination did Ayres no harm, after which the court adjourned for the day.[27]

The next morning Ayres was recalled for a few questions by Hancock. He testified that Griffin "came riding through the woods very rapidly, and he says, 'Ayres, what is up?' I said, 'There is nothing new, Griffin; Crawford has taken his division away and left me to fight alone. The same old story.'"[28]

Chamberlain followed Ayres and concluded his testimony, describing the conference Warren held with his division and brigade commanders, detailing the plans for the assault, while the troops were assembling at Gravelly Run Church on April 1. He disputed Sheridan's contention that the battle would have been lost if Ayres had been repulsed; Griffin, he said, would have come in on his right, with Crawford on the right of the First Division. He also denied Sheridan's claim that the battle was really over when Ayres carried the Confederate return. Chamberlain was followed by Col. W. W. Swan, Ayres's adjutant, who confirmed what Forsyth had said when he met Ayres, and R. M. Brinton, from Griffin's staff, who described Sheridan's putting Griffin in command of the corps and also told of seeing Warren make his final charge at dusk.[29]

The court took a couple of days off, and Warren promised to take the boat to Newport to see his family, a promise on which he soon reneged, saying he needed to work over the brief adjournment. "Every day's testimony goes in my favor more and more," he said, "and the interest increases. The public begins to think there was a Little Butter Cup at Five Forks that 'mixed them babies up.'"[30]

Three days later, on May 21, the court reconvened. Colonel H. R. Richardson of the Seventh Wisconsin was called. As a part of Kellogg's brigade, he attested to the confusion caused by Forsyth's ordering the brigade forward from where Warren had placed it preparatory to lining up the rest of Crawford's division on it. "From that time on," Richardson said, "we were fighting as an independent brigade, right straight through until we reached the Ford road." He also described the last charge, when he rode close to Warren and was wounded at the same time Warren's horse was killed. E. B. Cope, of Warren's staff, was the next witness, testifying to the movements of the corps and to the efforts

Warren made to get Griffin and Crawford back into place after they lost contact with Ayres on his wheel to the left. At the end of the day, Recorder Langdon read off a list of Confederate generals whom Warren wished to call. After listening to sparring between Gardner and Stickney over the request, Hancock announced that they would call a limited number of the witnesses first and see what transpired. The court then recessed for the weekend.[31]

On Monday, May 25, the witnesses were all Warren's people: Bankhead and Locke from his staff; Richard Coulter, one of Crawford's brigade commanders; and Coulter's adjutant. They testified to Warren's diligent efforts at Five Forks, particularly in getting the troops organized before the assault. Locke also described his encounter with the irate Sheridan near the close of the battle, when the cavalryman accused Warren of not being in the fight. Both Bankhead and Locke witnessed (and Locke participated in) Warren's final charge at the Gilliam farm, with Locke saying on cross-examination that this took place after he reported Sheridan's angry words to his commander. The next day the court heard from a member of Ayres's staff, who said the disorder at the start of the attack was so trifling he with a few other officers straightened it out himself.[32]

Montgomery D. Corse, a former Confederate brigade commander, appeared on May 28 as the first former rebel soldier to testify. The following day, Colonel Thomas T. Munford described the activities of his Confederate cavalry. Asked by Newton how the Fifth Corps advanced at the start of the battle, Munford said, "I think it was very steady, very regular; that is, the men came along fast enough for me." Holman Melcher of Warren's staff, who was with Locke at the late-afternoon meeting with Sheridan, finished up the day's business.[33]

On June 1, Fitzhugh Lee appeared on the stand to describe the situation of March 31 and early April 1 from the rebel viewpoint. Lee admitted that he had not seen the fight of April 1, being back with General Rosser "where our wagons were," though he managed to avoid mentioning the shad bake. Colonel W. W. Wood, of the Fourteenth Virginia, followed, describing the hard attack of Ayres's division. Gardner tried to get Wood to admit that some of the attackers may have been dismounted cavalry, but the witness said they certainly did not look or fight like cavalry. The court adjourned until the following Monday, six days away, in order to let Newton attend to engineering duties.[34]

Two more Confederates testified on June 7, as did Meade's aide Theodore Lyman. Joseph Mayo, a brigade commander at Five Forks, said the only reason the Confederates retreated from Dinwiddie Court House on April 1 was the word received by Pickett that a strong Union infantry force was coming down the Boydton Plank Road. Mayo described the heavy infantry attack, and, when Hancock asked him, "Your impression, then, was not that the whole of the fighting was at the angle?" the witness replied, "No, sir." He said, "[I]t seemed to be all the way around. But the heaviest of it, where an attack in force was indicated, came from our left and rear." That is, from both Ayres *and* Crawford.[35]

On June 8, General William H. F. Lee—"Rooney" Lee, son of the Confederate commander—took the stand and testified about the fighting at both Dinwiddie Court House and Five Forks, emphasizing that the rebels' retreat was forced by the attacks of the Fifth Corps and that the fiercest fighting took place after five o'clock, in the Gilliam field. The most important event of June 8, however, took place in Chicago, where a deadlocked Republican convention thwarted Grant's ambition and awarded the party's presidential nomination to Congressman James A. Garfield of Ohio on the thirty-sixth ballot. Grant had led the voting all the way, and he still had 306 votes on the final ballot, but this total was not quite enough to give him a majority. Warren wrote joyfully to Emily that "the great bug-bear, Grant, who has so frightened my bravest friends, is killed." [36]

On June 15, Samuel W. Crawford took the stand. The *Times* reporter wrote, "His evidence has been anticipated in military circles as decisive upon certain points at issue between Sheridan and Warren; but it was less important than had been expected, and, indeed, was mainly corroborative of what has been already given." There had been some concern about Crawford's testimony, and the relief in Warren's camp was obvious when the Third Division commander concluded his appearance with no harm done. Warren said Crawford "gave a good clear military account of himself." Mentioning to Emily that Crawford was going soon to Newport, he said, "Tell him I said he gave his testimony like a soldier." [37]

Over the next couple of days General Wesley Merritt of the cavalry and two Confederate brigadiers, R. L. T. Beale and Eppa Hunton, both current members of Congress, testified, without adding much startling to the record. Warren wrote to Emily, "I feel now pretty well satisfied that my position cannot be shaken in the matters before the Court, and can meet the future without being nervous." Warren told Will that Hunton "gave today in court a very clear account of the battle on Mch 31st . . . The way he puts it makes it appear to invite admiration instead of censure upon all parties engaged." [38]

There was another break, until June 28. Warren wrote a despairing letter home, one which indicated that indeed the prospect of a Five Forks investigation had become the end-all of his existence. He said, "I am in a measure getting weaned from home, which I thought when this investigation began would be all that would be left to me. Nor do I see anything to take its place. I suspect I have been caught in the whirlwind which destroys all we build. But I will try to save the children anyhow" in "the little of life that is left to me." [39]

The next day, to the surprise of many, particularly the professionals of the Democratic party, Winfield Scott Hancock won the Democratic presidential nomination at the party's convention in Cincinnati. What this would mean

for Warren's court of inquiry was not immediately apparent; Humphreys indeed wrote to Warren that he was delighted with Hancock's nomination.
"Nothing could be more satisfactory," he said. Warren, worried as he had been
about a possible Grant nomination but never expecting Hancock to be chosen, was not so sure.[40]

CHAPTER TWENTY-SEVEN

THE COURT RESUMES

*T*HE COURT RECONVENED ON JUNE 28 AND HEARD from three witnesses. E. W. W. Whittaker talked about what Custer's cavalry did at Five
Forks, while Nelson Miles, commander of the Second Corps division on the
right of the Fifth Corps, and Confederate general Samuel McGowan testified
about the fighting on March 31 at the White Oak Road. The testimony of all
three witnesses bolstered Warren's case, although he was troubled by some
parts of what Miles said, feeling that he claimed for his division some of what
the Fifth Corps had done. At the end of the day Hancock announced that he
had sent a message to the War Department on June 26, asking to be excused
from the court "for personal reasons." [1]

The next day Hancock was still in his place, no word having come back
from Washington. Before the day's proceedings began, Hancock said, "There
is a doubt in my mind as to whether I can be relieved." He pointed out that
there could be no appointment in his place, because a successor could only
read transcripts and would not have seen the demeanor of the witnesses.
"There is a provision of law," he said, "that in case of the death of a member
the other members shall constitute a legal court," but whether this rule would
apply to a resignation was unclear. That said, he turned to the day's business.
Alexander Pennington, commander of one of Custer's brigades, testified, as
did Samuel T. Gilliam, who was a lad of sixteen when the battle of Five Forks
was fought around his family's plantation and he was pressed into service by
Rooney Lee as a scout. [2]

On June 29, 1880, the War Department announced that Hancock had been
relieved from duty on the Warren Court of Inquiry at his own request. Warren
wrote Emily that "it is probably all for the best though I do not like to lose his
opinion in the matter." Will and General Humphreys regretted Hancock's
step; "I cannot tell you how sorry I feel that Genl Hancock did not make up
his mind to see the thing through," Will wrote. Such a view was short-sighted;

the last thing Warren needed was to have his investigation mixed up with the presidential election.[3]

With General Augur assuming the chair, the sessions resumed, Warren himself now taking the witness stand to conclude his case in chief. His testimony took several days, ending on July 3. There was little surprise in what he said, as the outline of his position had become clear in Stickney's presentation up to that time. Speaking about the hectic night of March 31, Warren said,

> Another great source of uncertainty to me about how to act at this time was the disjointed manner in which my dispatches went to General Meade and General Meade's would come to me. An order would come from him on a certain supposition and be countermanded when mine gave him the true situation. We were separated by an interval of an hour . . . I was continually in possession of facts that my superior did not know.[4]

Regarding the morning of the first, he said he waited with Griffin until about 11 A.M., when "I thought it was best for me to go up the road and find General Sheridan and see what he would require of me." Of this meeting, Warren testified,

> I found him on the west side of the road that leads up to Five Forks . . . As I approached the place, I think that he was lying down on a blanket, and he rose up. I spoke to him, half reclining or maybe sitting upon the blanket. I know there was a log between me and him, and I sat down upon it, and we had some conversation there together.

STICKNEY: Did he show any impatience in his manner then?

WARREN: No; he showed no impatience. I met him as I usually meet men, without anything particular to remark . . . [H]e appeared to have been asleep or trying to get asleep.

STICKNEY: Did he say anything as to your having been delayed in your march?

WARREN: He made no remarks at all about that that I recollect . . . I felt a good deal elated that such a night as we had had had turned out so well; that everything had turned out so successfully. So I made the remark to General Sheridan that we had had rather a field day of it since yesterday morning. He said to me, 'Do you call that a field day?' I saw by the tone of his remark that he was not very well pleased with what I had said; so I, in a measure, apologized for it by saying that it was perhaps a little ironical, and I referred to the fact that we had been directed to cease operations and have a quiet time of it, but the dispositions General Lee had made had given us about as lively a time as I had had in my experience. That was the only allusion that I recollect making to that subject, and we ceased conversation . . .

STICKNEY: How long were you with him?

WARREN: I was with him but a few minutes, I think, when one of his scouts . . . came up, and they had a whispered conversation together, which I did not hear. Then General Sheridan got on his horse and rode away towards Five Forks.[5]

At one o'clock, he said, he rode up the road toward Five Forks to find Sheridan, and when he met him the cavalryman told him how he wanted the Fifth Corps to move. "We talked that over until I understood it, I think; and he was convinced that I understood him," Warren said. A bit later, "I told him that in my opinion it would take until four o'clock" to get his troops into position for attack. Sheridan was impatient, as he thought his cavalry were running out of ammunition. Warren said he gave his men "as much stirring up as I thought would do any good. I thought they moved up as well as men could . . . They had been doing very severe work; and they had suffered very great privations."[6]

Stickney offered a letter the now-deceased Charles Griffin had written to Warren on June 26, 1865, attesting to Warren's call for dispatch in forming up and Griffin's opinion that "the division was formed without any halting or unnecessary delay." Gardner objected to this as an unofficial letter, "from one gentleman to another . . .written with the idea of using that as evidence." The court, which had a few days earlier declined to accept into evidence an unofficial letter from Custer, ruled Griffin's inadmissible.[7]

When Griffin and Crawford lost connection with Ayres, Warren continued, "I sent staff officers after Crawford to tell him that he must make a wheel to the left at once and keep closed in to the left of the brigade [Kellogg's] that I had already established in the new direction." When Sheridan seemed anxious about Griffin and Crawford, Warren said they were "too good soldiers to go very far away from the fire if there was no enemy on their front." He then went after them himself, soon coming upon Griffin's division and ordering its attack, then "with a first-rate horse" he located Crawford and "told him to change his direction at once to the southward and move down upon those guns that were firing south of us."[8]

Finding the rebels retreating to the west, he told Crawford to pursue the enemy in a westerly direction.

I think I did that before I came in sight of the Gilliam field. I had no idea that there was such a field there until I came to the east edge of it. When I came there there was considerable many of our men ranged along that woods [on the east side], and the firing that came across from the other side—west side—against them was considerable . . . There were a great many men shouting to go forward, but there was no advance at all. I saw that the only way to get the troops to advance was to get the color-bearers out . . .

I took my own flag, went out into the field; then the color-bearers went out with me. The firing at that point was not very heavy, but it was enough to stop the men who did not have some one to lead them, in their disorganized condition. We then began to move across the field, everybody coming on with a great deal of eagerness again; and the firing was comparatively mild until we got more than half way across the field. [At that point he met a staff officer from Custer, south of him, who said Custer would advance with him.] By that time the firing was beginning to be very lively.

As we kept moving on, we moved steadily—no double-quick—when we approached the angle in the northwest part of the field, there was, behind the breastworks, a regular line of battle that held its fire until we were close to the angle; then it gave us a volley which killed a good many men. That was very severe at that point, but before they could load their arms again we were inside of their works; and we captured many men . . . I think that there were in line fully 500 or 600 men, with arms in their hands, and two or three battle flags.[9]

Warren then described receiving the order for his relief, his encounter with Sheridan, and his subsequent meetings with Grant and Meade. A summation of the losses of the corps on the 31st and April 1 concluded his direct testimony.

Gardner began his cross-examination late on the afternoon of July 2. The next morning he grilled Warren on the various orders of the night of March 31 and his actions in response to them, but Warren easily held his own. Gardner asked him, "Did you say to him [Sheridan] or in his hearing . . . in language substantially as follows: '"Bobby Lee," or General Lee, as you please, is always getting people in tight places?'" Warren answered, "I believe that is an invention, if anyone ever says I said it. I never spoke of General Lee in those terms."[10]

Gardner asked, who was responsible for Crawford and Griffin's getting so far to the right? The most important cause, Warren said, was Sheridan's mistaking "the real position of the enemy. Not finding the enemy where we supposed, and having a skirmish fire in our front [from Munford's cavalry], it was natural that our troops should push on towards that fire, thinking that the line of battle would be there," continuing "until a large portion of Crawford and Griffin's divisions were in the woods, and by that time we discovered that General Ayres was receiving a heavy fire on his left flank." Ayres, he said, "on his own responsibility, with great promptitude and skill, without waiting for orders from anybody, immediately faced his command . . . to meet that ascertained position." Warren then went at once "to Crawford's division, the left of which was still in that field, and established a pivot for it immediately, to make a turn to the left."

The second cause of confusion was the removal of that pivot. Had that not been done, "there would have been no farther going to the right on the part of any of my troops, unless the necessities of battle compelled them to go." After some verbal sparring with Gardner, Warren was able to finish his thought by saying that "the next responsibility for the others getting away rested with the authority that moved that pivot"; i.e., Forsyth, acting for Sheridan.[11]

A few minutes later Gardner asked about the message which Warren sent Sheridan late in the battle. "Where were you?" he asked. "I was on the Ford road in that Boisseau field, or near there," Warren replied. "I cannot be positive about the time; I should think it was in the neighborhood of six o'clock."

GARDNER: You received back from General Sheridan a message by Colonel Locke?

WARREN, indignantly: I received an insult . . .

GARDNER: Can you recall the substance?

WARREN: I prefer not to recall it.

GARDNER: It was to tell you that you had not been to the front, or something to that effect?

WARREN: Yes; with an insulting gesture and oath . . .

GARDNER: It was after that that you came down to the White Oak road, and finally, as you say, moved in across the Gilliam field?

WARREN: It was.

GARDNER: Up to that time you had not been in action with Ayres's division?

WARREN: I had not.

GARDNER: Nor with Griffin's division?

WARREN: I had not.

GARDNER: Nor with Crawford's division?

WARREN: I had with Crawford.

GARDNER: Where?

WARREN: As he moved down the Ford road.

GARDNER: That was after Colonel Locke had gone to General Sheridan with your message, that you moved down the Ford road?

WARREN: Well, I do not know exactly what you mean to say—being in action—I was under fire along with the rest of the troops when we crossed the Ford road, and when the attack of Ayres began I was under fire. I was the first one that was under fire in the Sydnor field.

GARDNER: This fire as you crossed the White Oak road, was that a skirmish fire?

WARREN: Exactly.

GARDNER: And then when you were up in the Sydnor field you met fire?

WARREN: I did . . . I should think that any implication that I was not under fire, and was not to the front, could not be made out from any position I was in that day.

GARDNER: No one questioned the fact that in the whole course of your military career, as far as I know, you were as brave an officer as the Army had, and General Sheridan does not intend to dispute it.

WARREN: He did dispute it at that time.

GARDNER: The fact appears that you were not with either of those divisions up to the time when you joined Crawford to move down the Ford road. That is so, is it not?

WARREN: I was with them alternately, each one in its turn, and saw them go into action. I did not lead the charge. It is the division commander's business to fight his division. I did not want to interfere with him. My object was to direct these divisions on the points of the enemy that were to be attacked.

GARDNER: You were really traveling around the field most of the afternoon trying to get them in position?

WARREN: I was, except General Ayres; he took position for himself. I directed the positions of all of them or of the other two and part of the cavalry.[12]

After a few more questions about the dispositions of Crawford's division, Gardner concluded his cross-examination. Stickney had several questions on redirect, and then the court adjourned, with Warren's testimony on the record.[13]

Gouv wrote the next day to his wife, "My testimony is now all in . . . On the whole I am very well satisfied with the case as it stands. It is so strong that Sheridan will no doubt try his best to break it down." There would be no more evidence taken at this time, he said, since much time would now be required to correct and print the record already made. In the fall the court would meet to hear Sheridan's witnesses. "So far," he said, "I fear nothing from them."[14]

A couple of days later Warren advised Emily that he would have to stay in New York while Langdon and the court went through all the papers before them. "Friendly interest in me seems to increase," he said, "and I am sure that Sheridan's prestige is broken." On July 8 he wrote, "I am happy in the condition of the case, but I have long, longing dreams at night for home, for you, and Siddy and Emily."[15]

On July 13, Warren suffered an attack of what he called "cholera morbus" and had to leave the court room. Augur, too, was unwell, Newton and Langdon and the court reporter were worn out, and it was time for a break from the mid-July heat on Governor's Island. Gardner asked for the adjournment to run, for Sheridan's convenience, to October 1. Stickney suggested September 1; "I have seen so much of these delays," he said, "that I dread them very much." Augur equivocated, saying the court would meet after Sheridan had a chance to examine the record. The major parties to the drama thereupon dispersed for the summer. Gouverneur Warren repaired to Rhode Island for a welcome reunion with his family.[16]

Warren reached Newport on July 21 after a soothing cruise down Long Island Sound, during most of which he slept soundly. He passed the summer in
relaxing as much as he could—fishing for bluefish with Sidney, walking on the
beach with his wife, reading with little Emily. He kept up correspondence on
the inquiry with Stickney and Humphreys, and in September Colonel Langdon came to visit, to go over Warren's testimony with him before submitting it
to the printer.[17]

During the summer Will reported to Gouv that his name was mentioned as
a possibility for head of the army's Signal Bureau, the chief of which had recently died. Warren wrote back, "After thinking the matter over I do not think
I would take the head of a Bureau if it were offered to me. I want rest more
than anything." He thought that "an appointment of me to anything not in
the regular line of promotions would be decried by some as an attempt to fore-
stall the opinion of the Court of Inquiry." [18]

Warren and Humphreys had a minor disagreement over some of Miles's testimony regarding his division's movements on March 31. Warren felt that
Miles claimed too much, to the denigration of the Fifth Corps. Humphreys
defended Miles but said he would look into it further. Then, reacting to Gardner's questions to Warren about being "at the front," Humphreys went on,

> A corps commander goes where he deems is best that he should be, even to
> the suppression of his inclinations & promptings to take part personally in
> the fight of any one of his divisions or brigades! To attribute to you a disin-
> clination to go where the fight was hottest seems to me simply monstrous,
> for your reputation for courage was among the highest in the Army of the
> Potomac.[19]

As the court prepared to resume its deliberations, one New York paper
called the case "a remarkable one in many respects. More distinguished
officers are either directly or indirectly interested in it than in any previous
military court in the history of this country." The court reconvened on October 1, moving from Governor's Island to the Army Building in the city. "Phil
Sheridan's friends are going to have their say now about the battle of Five
Forks," a newsman wrote.[20]

The three witnesses on October 1, all from the cavalry, were General Ranald
Mackenzie, Captain Henry C. Erich, and Captain Henry C. Alvord. Mackenzie, formerly on Warren's engineering staff before being transferred to the cavalry, and Erich were, Warren wrote, "as good witnesses for me as I could wish."
Mackenzie, he said, "was the real warm friend to me that I thought he was."
Alvord, though, he called "a conceited blower" whose testimony "with sensible persons . . . will do me no harm. He knew altogether too much." Alvord,
a cavalry captain, seemed to have been in all the right places on April 1 so that
he could testify on all of the contentious issues. He said he was sent back

numerous times from Sheridan to Ayres to have his men hurry into position, he saw the infantry finally move forward at about five o'clock, he saw the serious disorder and confusion into which Ayres's men fell, and he saw Sheridan himself bring order out of chaos. He observed Warren but once during the day, when the Fifth Corps leader met with Sheridan during the infantry's forming up, and he just happened to be near enough to hear what was said. Sheridan, he said, expressed great displeasure, using strong profanity, at the tardiness with which the Fifth Corps was advancing. Stickney, with disdain, asked a few perfunctory questions, and Alvord was dismissed.[21]

Gardner produced a large number of witnesses, although often just one or two a day, who were either cavalrymen or members of Sheridan's staff. They all seemed to have seen Warren, either meeting with Sheridan or otherwise, and nearly all of them testified that the Fifth Corps commander appeared listless, indifferent, gloomy, despondent. Their fund of adjectives seemed bottomless. (Two of them, however, strayed from Gardner's program. George L. Gillespie on October 13 said Warren appeared to him "cool and collected," while five days later A. J. McGonnigle called Warren's manner "cool, imperturbable, and quiet.") Almost all testified to the important fighting the cavalry had done at Five Forks, and many of them said they saw Custer's division getting around the Confederate right, thus casting doubt upon the rebel stand at Gilliam's field. Warren was not much troubled by these witnesses, but was more provoked by the delay engendered by Gardner's slowness in producing them, resulting in days being consumed by a very few inconsequential ones.[22]

A sensation was produced in the presidential campaign on October 5 when an interview with Grant was published in which the former president viciously attacked Hancock, the Democratic candidate. Grant called Hancock "ambitious, vain, and weak," and made numerous charges, factually incorrect, about Hancock's Reconstruction command in Louisiana and Texas. Warren felt that this attack lined Hancock up with himself in the public eye, and he said, "It is for reasons like this that it was probably best that Genl Hancock retired from my Court." Humphreys agreed and conceded that he was wrong in decrying Hancock's withdrawal; "sometimes that which appears to us at the time unfortunate turns out in the end to be the very reverse."[23]

The stream of cavalry witnesses was interrupted on October 12, when a large crowd turned out to see Orville Babcock and Horace Porter, two of Grant's former aides. Porter did not testify on this day but Babcock, tainted by his connection with the Whiskey Ring frauds during the Grant administration, did. His testimony, however, was brief and was concerned mainly with the oral message he carried from Grant to Sheridan, authorizing the latter to relieve Warren if he saw fit.[24]

The next day was Porter's turn, and the former aide gave evidence on the fordability of Gravelly Run, the meeting in the morning between Sheridan and Warren, and the alleged confusion on the part of Ayres's troops. He said that he crossed the run the evening of March 31 on horseback, with the water above his horse's belly, but he admitted that he went about two hundred yards along the bank before he found a place where he could cross. He did not hear the conversation between Sheridan and Warren, although he recalled that Sheridan was impatient, and he said it was Ayres's skirmish line that lay down at the start of the attack, not an unusual thing, and that Ayres's men were "rallied rather than re-formed." Warren's not-quite-unbiased comment on his testimony was that "Horace Porter made a painful impression today," though Porter's testimony hardly harmed him.[25]

He also suggested, in his letter to Emily, "Don't you think sometimes, how nice it would be to go off with some nice lovely fellow with plenty of money and a home in Europe . . . leave behind everything of the name of Warren. My life has been so hard, and so unsatisfactory; and I am older than you; and you can't live but once. Get away off beyond the sea: in another clime and forget your native tongue and nagging children, and unloveable husband." Presumably Emily shrugged this off as just another gloomy effusion.[26]

The next several days were taken up by more cavalry witnesses, producing not much of great importance to the inquiry, but Stickney was concerned that his client was disappearing in the mass of evidence about the mounted arm. On October 15 he surprised observers with his statement to the court that "I do not question before this court a single point of General Sheridan's conduct. It is not open to me to do so. I shall assume that General Sheridan acted with the best intentions; and, as far as this court is concerned, I shall assume that no act of his on that day is to be questioned, at all. There is no one to be criticised before this court except General Warren." Thus Stickney moved adroitly to refocus the inquiry on Warren, which was the whole point of it from the beginning.[27]

The inquiry was clearly dragging at this point. One reporter said, "The sparseness of the audience gave token that the interest in the case is flagging." It was announced, however, that Grant had been subpoenaed and would appear shortly, and this prospect was guaranteed to ratchet up public anticipation by more than a few degrees. In the meantime, an officer named Jonathan Tarbell, formerly the colonel of the Ninety-First New York in Crawford's division, currently holding a patronage job as deputy first comptroller of the Treasury, appeared as a witness on October 21, criticizing nearly everything the Fifth Corps did in its two days on the White Oak Road. Tarbell had had a checkered career, having been dismissed from the service in 1862 and reinstated the following year, but he was anxious to weigh in against Warren. Stickney destroyed him on cross-examination, where Tarbell "exhibited but little knowledge of localities or of the formation of the troops. He could not name division or brigade commanders he met; he could not tell the relative position of other brigades with his own, and appeared to have no idea of the plan of the battle." Warren called him "an astonishing witness" who "says I offended him by a remark at Five Forks." Warren dismissed Tarbell's testimony as "absurd." [28]

October 23 saw the much anticipated appearance of Ulysses S. Grant in the Warren inquiry. For the convenience of the ex-president the Court convened at 10 A.M., an hour earlier than was customary. Gouverneur Warren did not record his feelings at seeing before him the man he regarded as the source of all his troubles, but surely they were intense. Gardner began by asking Grant to state the circumstances that led to his sending Warren's corps to the aid of Sheridan. Grant said that he wanted Sheridan to capture Five Forks; Sheridan's force was insufficient for that purpose, and so he sent the Fifth Corps to his relief. [29]

Asked about the message he sent Sheridan authorizing the relief of Warren, Grant replied,

> I notified General Sheridan that he was authorized to relieve General Warren if, in his judgment, it was for the best interests of the service to do so; that I was afraid he would fail him at a critical moment. That was the substance of my message. I cannot recollect the words. Of course, I had to judge of that fact by my knowledge of General Warren previous to any of these movements . . .
>
> It was simply my reflection as to General Warren in this critical position, which I then expected to make the last battle of the war, that he would probably fail him, and I wanted to warn General Sheridan of the danger he was in. The authority was not sent to General Sheridan in consequence of any report that was brought to me—it was simply that I knew General Warren's defects.
>
> STICKNEY: What you considered his defects.
> GRANT: What I considered his defects. And his was the only corps I could send promptly; that corps would not have been sent if I could have gotten another one as conveniently—and I was just thinking of the consequences of a failure there, and wanted to put General Sheridan upon his guard, and I sent him that authority, so that he might feel no hesitation in removing an officer if it was necessary to his success. [30]

The next question was put and answered so quickly that Stickney had no time to object before it was recorded. Gardner said, "Will you state to the court your reason for sending that message?" Grant responded, "While appreciating Gen. Warren's courage and his qualities as a soldier, from what I knew of his previous conduct I was apprehensive that he might fail Gen. Sheridan at the critical moment, and I sent the message so that the General might feel at liberty to take any measures essential to success."

Stickney then objected to the answer unless Grant's judgment of Warren was based upon the events which were the subject of the inquiry, those of March 31 and April 1. After much contentious wrangling between counsel, Grant interjected that his judgment was formed before the fight on the White Oak Road.

> STICKNEY: General Grant's action was dictated by his opinion of General Warren. Of course that opinion was based on his understanding of what General Warren had done in the past history of the war, upon General Warren's past acts, as they had come to General Grant's knowledge. No one would admit more readily than General Grant that he might have been misinformed upon many of those points.
>
> GRANT: Well, no. I don't think I will admit that. I have probably made many mistakes in the course of my life; but I don't think I was mistaken in my judgment of General Warren.
>
> STICKNEY: But you may have been mistaken?
>
> GRANT: Possibly; but I don't think I was.

The argument resumed, ended finally by the court's ruling that Grant's opinion, not being based on Warren's actions on the two days in question, should be stricken from the record, though it had certainly been recorded by the newspapers for public consumption. This ended Gardner's direct examination.[31]

On cross-examination, Stickney tried to get specific answers from Grant on several points but Grant said he had no particular recollections.

> It would be impossible for me to answer now from recollection just what I did. I know, through the whole of the day, from the time General Sheridan was sent off to my left flank, until Five Forks was carried, I was watching their every movement and everything that was done, doing all I could to aid. I was sending orders here and there, to one army and another, wherever I judged there was an opportunity of putting it in, and I wanted my orders promptly obeyed . . . But where officers undertook to think for themselves, and considered that the officer giving them orders had not fully considered what everybody else was to do, it generally led to failure and delay.

"And that you did not like?" said Stickney.

"That I did not like," Grant replied, "and that kind of conduct led to the removal finally of one officer." At this answer, Stickney strode up to the court and demanded that the last remark be stricken. Grant said, "Leave it out," and it was removed from the record.[32]

There was some fencing over the timing of orders sent from Grant's and Meade's headquarters on the night of March 31, and Grant stubbornly refused to admit that he had been wrong in understanding that Warren had delayed to build a bridge over Gravelly Run, although he said his knowledge was based on reports brought to him.[33]

Asked whether Warren had requested a court of inquiry, Grant smiled grimly, according to the *Sun* reporter, and answered, "I cannot recollect. That was not much of a time to be holding these courts of inquiry." With this, Grant's examination was ended, and he immediately left the room.[34]

Warren reassured Emily, "Let not Grant's testimony concern you. We caught him in several important errors. He made no points of fact against me and fell back upon his opinion upon former events which the Court ruled out. As stands Stickney and I are not dismayed nor even disconcerted."[35]

There was nearly a month more of witnesses (with a break of about a week along the way), but nothing could match the drama and interest of Grant's appearance. On the 25th James Forsyth returned, with the usual cavalryman's testimony that Warren's countenance was "gloomy and despondent" when meeting with Sheridan on April 1. Forsyth also testified that, when Locke rode up with Warren's message to the commanding general near the close of the fighting, Sheridan first reviled Warren for not being in the action, then asked where he was, and Locke, Forsyth testified, said he was a mile and a half to the rear.[36]

The next day the only witness was another member of Sheridan's staff, who claimed that he heard Warren, after receiving the order relieving him, defiantly give Sheridan "so many minutes to reconsider your determination." After that Gardner presented another long written statement from Sheridan, explaining why he removed Warren from command. Stickney declined to object formally, stating that it was simply argument to help Sheridan's case. The *Brooklyn Eagle* said editorially that Sheridan's statement lacked one essential: "[I]t fails to demonstrate that any change was really necessary, and the treatment Warren received seems as unjustifiable now as it has done since the facts were made known to the public." Augur then recessed the court to November 4, with the presidential election to be held in the interim.[37]

The election was a great disappointment to Warren. In a very close finish, Hancock lost to Garfield, the Republican nominee, by 214-155 in electoral votes and by little more than 7000 votes in the popular tally. Hancock was done in by the machinations of Tammany Hall and the Democratic organization in Brooklyn, which cost him the electoral vote of New York State. With New York added to his total and subtracted from Garfield's, Hancock would have been the next president. Warren's consolation was that Garfield was not Grant and would not be beholden to Grant or his friends.

"Don't be despondent," he wrote to Emily. "Think how much less disappointment we have to bear today than the Hancocks although so much better off than ourselves. His feeling today is the chagrin at disappointed expectations, at receiving a fatal blow to all future aims of ambition. I *never* had such."[38]

The court resumed on November 4, with one inconsequential cavalryman on the stand. Another followed on the next day, after which Gardner introduced Custer's official report, in an attempt to counteract the earlier testimony of Warren's charge against the rebel line in Gilliam's field.

Stickney then produced in rebuttal Ayres and Chamberlain. Both men were strong witnesses, reiterating and emphasizing their earlier testimony that there was no delay on the part of the Fifth Corps on April 1. Chamberlain, questioned again about Warren's manner, said it was "peculiar to himself—a deeply earnest manner. Those of us who knew him understood it . . . He seemed to be intense." [39]

Captain J. W. Felthausen of the Ninety-First New York took the stand and contravened several of the statements of Colonel Tarbell, his commander. Felthausen graphically described advancing at dark into the Gilliam field, ordering his men to lie down before pretty hot rebel firing, then seeing a lone horseman with a flag in his hand advancing. Though it was dark, he said, the horseman rode close enough that he recognized it as Warren. "He got scarcely in the field more than twenty yards," the witness said, "when the entire line moved forward, and the fire from an opposite piece of woods ceased when we got pretty near it." [40]

The final witness on November 5 was Captain Holman S. Melcher, Fifth Corps postmaster on Warren's staff. Melcher was with Locke when Warren's message presenting his compliments to General Sheridan was transmitted. Gardner objected to Melcher's testimony, but Stickney pointed out that Forsyth had quoted Locke at this time saying Warren was a mile and a half to the rear, and Melcher could establish that no such statement was made. The court allowed the testimony, and Melcher, on cross, averred that there was no conversation between Sheridan and Locke that he did not hear. He was with Locke when Sheridan's insulting message was delivered to Warren, and he then observed the charge led by the general. [41]

After taking Saturday and Sunday off, Augur and Newton reconvened their court on Monday, November 8, at which time they heard two members of Warren's staff, Bankhead and Wadsworth, who fixed Warren's location when he received the notice of relief. Both men put the general on the White Oak Road west of Five Forks and west of the Gilliam field.

Over the next couple of days Stickney presented Locke, who forcefully rebutted Forsyth's testimony that he told Sheridan that Warren was a mile and a half to the rear; Benyaurd; and four members of the Ninety-First New York. The five latter witnesses all testified to seeing Warren lead the charge on the western edge of the Gilliam field, and several of the men from the Ninety-First placed a cavalry officer they believed to be Custer at the left and south of their position in the Gilliam field, thus making it impossible that he could have earlier turned the Confederate right. On the 11th another cavalryman testified to Warren's "moody and depressed" demeanor, to be followed by Humphreys, who gave a clear and cogent description of the fighting on the White Oak Road on March 31.[42]

Humphreys also cleared up a point which had been vexing the inquiry. Grant had allegedly warned Meade the evening of March 30 that an attack was being prepared against Warren, and Warren's being taken by surprise the next morning was another factor in Grant's disenchantment with the Fifth Corps commander. Warren had denied that any such warning was received by him, and Humphreys now made it apparent that the warning had been directed to Ord and his corps, not Warren.[43]

On November 17, General Joseph J. Bartlett, who commanded a brigade in the First Division of Warren's corps, and was called by one Fifth Corps officer "a witness bitterly hostile to General Warren," testified to what his brigade and Griffin's division had done on the two days in question. He testified about his position in the rear of the Confederate cavalry in the early evening of March 31 (ordered there by Warren) and his unhappiness at being ordered to retrace his steps back to Griffin's division rather than attack, although he understood that that was at Meade's insistence. He testified, in addition, that Sheridan's statement to Locke when the latter brought the message from Warren close to the end of the battle was different from what Locke (and Melcher) said it was. Bartlett quoted Sheridan as saying, "Tell General Warren that I do not consider him in command of the Fifth Army Corps. I do not see him where the fighting is." While this was an interesting twist on the quotation which Locke wrote down, at most it represented an opinion from Sheridan which did not actually change the command structure.[44]

Two days later, after the court heard from a second lieutenant in Ransom's Confederate brigade who testified to the severity of the fighting at Five Forks, Warren took the stand again as the final witness, with the number of spectators exceeded only by that on the day that Grant appeared. "He wore an anxious look," a reporter wrote, but "with an air of earnestness that intensified the resolution that usually marks his countenance he seated himself as a witness." Warren went over again what had happened at the White Oak Road on March 31; "Ever so many times it has been spoken by persons during this examination, and in the press, that the whole Fifth Corps was driven back. That was not so." Griffin's division, the largest in the corps, "was not driven an inch . . . and the other divisions rallied behind it. The corps took care of itself." On the morning of April 1, he stated, "My conversation with him [Sheridan] was very full and earnest." The two men talked "ten or fifteen minutes at least."[45]

Warren then went through the case point by point, categorically denying various allegations made by Sheridan's witnesses. The only time he was east of Five Forks was when he "was going back after having been relieved." He was not on the White Oak Road east of the Forks until after the engagement was over. While he was in the middle of the Gilliam field, he said, he saw Custer passing "westwardly and northwardly." Warren said, "He came up from my left, upon my left flank and passed me, at that time our most advanced point." "We were then ahead of any cavalry," he said.[46]

Gardner's cross-examination, a newsman said, "was ably and skillfully conducted, but elicited no new points of especial interest." Counsel and the witness rehashed both March 31 and April 1, but the only score Gardner made was with Warren's admission that a few details in his postwar pamphlet on Five Forks turned out to be mistaken, even though based on Crawford's official report. Warren's examination finished late in the afternoon of November 19.[47]

For a couple more days Warren went over his testimony and clarified it for the printed record. On Monday the 22nd Warren and Gardner indulged in a further colloquy, but that was the end of it. Counsel wrangled some over the procedures to be followed in making their closing arguments, but Augur said the court would not rule on anything further until the record was printed and the court reconvened at his call, probably in January.[48]

Warren, comforted by Emily's presence with him in New York as the court was winding down, wrote to Will the next day, "I do feel greatly relieved for now my efforts whether successful or not or the best that could have been made, have been the best that I could do . . . I have so often felt this past year, as the investigation seemed so interminable, is not this a waste of life after all? . . . I have got rid of the matter as far as I am responsible, feeling I have done all that has been in my power to do." [49]

But of course he had not gotten rid of the matter at all.

CHAPTER TWENTY-EIGHT

THE LAWYERS HAVE THEIR SAY

S HORTLY BEFORE THE COURT OF INQUIRY under Generals Augur and Newton concluded its taking of testimony, Gouverneur K. Warren wrote to his wife about the experience. "This Court of Inquiry," Warren said, "is taking my record as a rolling mill does a molten mass of metal and is pounding and hammering and rolling it into shape. It is what no other man's military record in our war in a successful battle has ever been subjected to." He went on, "It gives me importance if I can bear it manfully, but I have been sick, and weak, and it is hard to stand this test 15 years after the occurrences." [1]

Warren was much interested in a story which came out of Washington, that Sheridan and Grant were angry at Sherman for permitting the court of inquiry to be called. Sherman, it was reported, favored the court "on the ground that it would be well to smooth over old difficulties and differences in the army," while Sheridan felt it put him and Grant on trial. Warren thought the story "striking in its nature if it is true." He doubted that Sheridan and Grant would *show* animosity toward Sherman, "however much they may feel." He felt perhaps the article was meant as a signal to Augur and Newton "of what is expected of them if S & G's friendship is to be retained." [2]

With the evidentiary phase of the inquiry concluded, Warren presumed that what still lay ahead of him was several days of argument by the lawyers, a few days for Augur, Newton, and Langdon to analyze the record, argue about what had been presented, and put their judgments down in black and white, and then a few weeks of military procedure to be undergone before the whole thing was publicly promulgated. Warren, who spoke confidently of escaping "the thralldom of the Court of Inquiry," could hardly anticipate what was going to happen. [3]

He told Andrew Humphreys, after his testimony was finished, that "I shall not worry about the results of the investigation. My part is done in it, and all that I could ask my friends to help me so they have done." But his work was not done. There was still Stickney's argument, and Warren could hardly stand aside and not take his full part in shaping that.[4]

Financial difficulties continued to bedevil Warren. His sister Emily tried to ease these for him. Early in January, she sent him another thousand dollars, in exchange for a mortgage he insisted on giving her on the Cold Spring house, so that he would not be forced to sell it at a bad time. "I suppose you will feel more contented if you arrange everything in a business like way," she told her brother, "but as far as I am concerned I would not have you worry yourself about giving me a mortgage." He would use the funds to pay Albert Stickney, but Emily Roebling comforted him in this by adding, "I do not feel that you could possibly have invested your money better for your children than in using it on this investigation, and I am sure as they grow old enough to understand the value of your reputation they will prize it more than money."[5]

When his wife told of their children's being ill, Warren confessed himself "depressed . . .with your account of conditions at home." "I do not know what I should do," he went on, "if I lost any of you. I have had a load on my heart so long I think it would kill me to have this added."[6]

He tried to reassure his wife about their finances: "Don't feel worried about money. We are even with the world take us at our worst in this line: paying all that is claimed of us, and losing all we lose. That is honorable, and honor is worth more than money." He despaired of getting much from the Chase estate: "I never could see how he [Emily's father] could accumulate property with his nature, unless he was in luck. He never seemed to have any luck." With Emily and the children in Newport, Warren was tied to New York by his work with Stickney. "It is very cold," he said. "I sit hovering over my coal grate fire much of the time . . .working away. . . . tho' the end seems even yet far off."

"Be happy with the children," he admonished her. "Take good care of them. Enjoy yourself sociably when you can among your friends. In all our affairs there is no crushing misfortune, although there are trials no doubt." Warren's effort to buck up his wife soon ran afoul of his bleak cast of mind:

> I had it, in my young life visions, to be possessor of money in my declining years. I threw myself away, in ardent service to my country. I drew you in to the same fate. You, whose loveliness no woman could excel. Who would have adorned in simple nature the highest station. I was at the summit of my ambition at Five Forks—my corps victorious—myself a leader in the final work, with my banner in my hand, and a careful director of all the force. I was cut right down, and the storied Iron Mask was put upon me. It has stifled all my life. It is killing me today as this work lingers along. The end will come however, and the life that is left in me shall still be recognized. As Danton said on the scaffold—I doubt not of my name being remembered in History.[7]

Asa Bird Gardner was serving as judge advocate in a court-martial looking into the mistreatment of Johnson C. Whittaker, a black cadet at West Point. His involvement in that proceeding necessitated further delay in the resolution of Warren's case. Argument of counsel before Augur and Newton had to await the conclusion of Gardner's work in the Whittaker case.

Fitz John Porter, who had been exonerated by an army court-martial and now awaited action by Congress to restore him to good standing, wrote to Warren, who had given material assistance to Porter's case, saying, "My persistence in demand helps you in public opinion, and in the belief that wrongs, deep ones, were committed during the war & the demands for redress are just." A curious thing about the Porter case was that Grant had made a turnabout and now championed justice for Porter. This was easier for him to do there than in Warren's situation, of course, since he had not been involved with Porter's disgrace in the beginning.[8]

Gouverneur Warren, ill and frustrated, sat in his room in the Stevens House and wondered when his court might ever come to an end. He vowed not to leave New York until it was behind him, writing to Emily on the first of July, "never will I carry the shadow of the great grievance which I am oppressing across my own door sill again. It has spread all over your young life, and Syd and Emily were born under its bitterness. When I leave here again I mean to leave this behind me, or not leave at all."[9]

The next day Warren was thunderstruck with the rest of the country to learn of the attempted assassination of President Garfield in Union Station, Washington. At first believing Garfield dead, he was relieved to hear that the chief executive was only seriously wounded.[10]

Stickney was ready for his argument on July 11, but Gardner asked for a postponement to the 20th. Warren wrote Emily, "My room in Newport will not be used by me this summer . . . [M]ake it a spare room." A few days later, he wrote, "I shall be so glad to have it over that it makes me somewhat indifferent to the further results."[11]

On July 19, Warren reported that the court's meeting was put off again, this time to July 25. "We anticipated this somewhat," he said, "and will be glad if it is not again put off." Stickney, he said, "is getting worn out." Four days later he prayed to be let "out of this long drawn out inquisition" which "leaves me in a state of suspended animation." His engineering work, he said, "would be like a boy's play to me."[12]

Finally, the court resumed on July 25, and Albert Stickney began his closing argument. "General Warren," he said, "should, undoubtedly, be held to a very high standard, to the highest standards of his profession . . . That is his own wish. He does not come here to make excuses." At the same time, he said, "a corps commander is something more than a mere conduit pipe to his subordinates for the orders of his superiors. He is to do something more than blindly follow the letter of the orders he receives."

A corps commander, Stickney went on, is entitled to the presumption "that in all the ordinary situations of war he did his whole duty." He is not required to prove "for every single minute his personal whereabouts, or to account for his every personal movement, as if he were a suspected criminal." He need not be "at the front" at all times. "He is to be the brain and moving will of his command . . . at most times, in a central position at the rear, where he can be found, where he can get reports often and easily from all parts of his command." The handling of his subordinate units should be left to the commanders of those organizations. "If the corps commander is doing the work of subordinates," he asked, "how is he to do his own, and who is to do it for him?" There come times, Stickney said, when a corps commander must literally lead his men. "But those times come seldom. At all ordinary times, the corps commander is 'at the front' when he is in the rear of his men." [13]

Stickney discussed the veracity of several of Gardner's witnesses, demonstrating that both Forsyths and Frank Sherman were clearly wrong in several vital instances, because their testimony was refuted by so many other credible witnesses. He then launched into his minute analysis of the many points of evidence before the court. Warren called it "a lovely touching summing up." [14]

Stickney continued his argument on July 26 and concluded it the next day. In his summation, he called the court's attention to the "thorough accuracy" of Warren's testimony on every point of the case, confirmed by the testimony of other witnesses of high rank and unquestioned veracity. He used Sheridan's words to support Warren's position on several disputed issues. In regard to the confusion at the start of the attack at Five Forks, he paraphrased Sheridan's testimony: "I was on the point of attacking the earth-works of the enemy with a corps of 12,000 infantry: and I delivered the attack with that corps three-quarters of a mile to the right of where I should have delivered it." Moreover, Sheridan said, in effect, "I had during the whole of that forenoon 8,000 cavalry . . . with whom I could have ascertained with precise accuracy the exact position of those works; I allowed those six hours to go by; and I never then knew, and do not to this day know, where the position of the enemy was against which I was going to launch my corps of infantry." Warren and his subordinates, Stickney went on, were forced to rectify Sheridan's error, and Warren had to spend most of his efforts on that field correcting the effects of that error. [15]

Stickney then addressed the "imputation" that Warren did not wish Sheridan's planned action to be a success. That, he said solemnly, "is something like a charge of high treason." Even more than a charge of cowardice, he said, "this is the most serious charge that can be made—that a man is 'secretly aiding the enemy'—that is what it means." He quoted Gardner's putting on the record that "no one questions the fact" that Warren "was as brave an officer as the army had . . . that General Sheridan does not mean to dispute it." That, Stickney said, is the point questioned by that imputation, and that is the point at which the court must sustain Warren." [16]

As to Warren's "manner" on April 1, Stickney simply cited Chamberlain's testimony as conclusive. He paraphrased Sheridan again on his actual knowledge of what happened that day:

> The most singular feature of this whole case . . . is the fact that a witness comes here and says: "Although I was in command of the United States forces in the field on that day, I saw only the attack of General Ayres on that earthwork at the end; I know nothing of Griffin's movements: I know nothing of Crawford's movements; I do not know that Crawford became engaged with Munford, or that he had any fighting at any point in the woods; I do not know anything of what the commander of the Fifth Corps did during the operations of that day; and I cannot give"—for those are his words—"I cannot give any account of my own personal movements after Ayres's assault. Yet I have had the glory of that day for sixteen years. And I still claim it![17]

Stickney scored Sheridan's statement that he had no prior knowledge of Warren by quoting Chamberlain again, that when he met Sheridan early on April 1 the cavalryman, on learning that Warren was with the rearguard, said, "Just where I expected him to be." Sheridan had claimed that he resolved to replace Warren after the battle was over in light of his worry that Lee would strike him in the rear; Stickney refuted this claim with the testimony of Griffin's aide that Sheridan told Griffin he was in command of the corps midway through the fight. Taking into consideration the oral authorization received from Grant and what that message conveyed, Stickney said, "I think we shall have no difficulty in coming to the conclusion that General Sheridan's resolution to relieve Warren was formed early in the progress of that battle, if not before the battle began." [18]

Warren's relief meant, "until the act is disavowed," that despite his record and his conduct throughout the war, "that such a man, with such a record, had been guilty of cowardice, or something equivalent to it, upon the field of battle." Warren now looked to a board of soldiers for redress. If soldiers' reputations are "injured by any one, no matter how powerful a man he may be, if their reputation is attacked unjustly, they have the right to a court of soldiers to do them justice." Now, Stickney concluded, sixteen years "after these imputations were made against General Warren's military reputation," he looked to a military court as "a full and sufficient safeguard" of his military reputation. [19]

Gardner began his main argument the same day, July 27, and concluded it the next day. Warren reported it to his wife as "about 120 pages long and . . . full of lies and . . . a torrent of vile misrepresentation and abuse of me . . . I staid away after hearing the opening part[.] It was too much for me to listen to in silence. Stickney advises me never to read it." [20]

There was no reason to expect Gouverneur Warren to be pleased with the argument of Sheridan's attorney. Gardner's reading of the evidence before the court, as might be expected, was diametrically opposed to that of Stickney. Every conceivable inference was made to Warren's detriment, and every cavalryman's testimony was brought forth to prove that Warren was negligent or disobedient on March 31 and April 1. However, since Gardner was there to protect Sheridan's interests, and Sheridan was determined to resist to the bitter end any suggestion that he might have made a mistake in his judgment of Warren, Gardner was only doing what a zealous advocate was supposed to do. The tenor of Gardner's address makes clear that Sheridan never directed him to go easy on Warren.

He began with a specious argument against the calling of the court itself, stating that it was unfair to force Sheridan to explain something done sixteen years earlier, since Warren, after two early efforts in 1865 and 1866, made no attempt to obtain a court during Johnson's or Grant's administrations and "only obtains one in the last year of the term of President Hayes." [21] Everyone in the room knew that further attempts during the Johnson and Grant administrations would have been futile.

Gardner speculated whether Warren "ever before that time undertook, of his own volition, any *independent* military movement sufficiently extensive to require the co-operation of an entire corps in action," concluding that "I am inclined to believe that the previous movements of the Fifth Corps, while under his command in action, in which any success was obtained" must have been "under the immediate observation of some superior military commander." [22]

Gardner repeatedly attacked Warren's mental state on the two crucial days, saying that Warren "seems either to have been bewildered and incapable of sound judgment, or else he had an overweening opinion of his own military abilities and a proportionate undervaluation of those superior to himself with whom he was called upon to serve, which made him fail to give efficient support in an emergency." Ticking off what he said were Warren's failures on the night of March 31, Gardner said these were "all circumstances which bear hard against this applicant and which would not, probably, have come under the notice of the historian but for his unfortunate application for this court of inquiry." [23]

He criticized Warren for his failure to report to Sheridan in a timely manner on the morning of April 1, an issue on which Warren was eminently vulnerable and for which his excuse seemed like so much pettifogging. Gardner went on to Warren's alleged lack of enthusiasm in carrying out Sheridan's plans:

> From these evidences it is quite manifest that General Warren entered
> upon that day's action either under great apprehensions for the safety of the

Fifth Corps, from the position in which he was placed, and want of confidence in the commanding general successfully to carry out his plan of
operations, or else from a reluctance to assist a general from another army
in winning a great and conclusive victory, or from a want of comprehen-
sion of the true military situation, or because of bewilderment and physical
depression.

Referring to the actual battle of Five Forks, Gardner claimed that Warren's
conduct during the fight "was that of a man who was uncertain as to exactly
what he should do," citing his "moving toward Ayres, then rushing off after
Crawford, then coming back to the open south of the White Oak road, then
rushing after Crawford again, and returning again to the road, and then following him up through the woods and finally meeting him by the Ford road . . . ,
sending his staff hither and thither, and actually taking no part in the serious
action of the day, while the battle was raging and before it had been won." [24]

Gardner claimed, contrary to most of the evidence, that Locke had delivered to Warren Sheridan's verbal order relieving him *before* the attack in the
Gilliam field, which he called "a trifling occurrence at the close of the day."
This order, Gardner said, awoke Warren "to the disagreeable fact that a great
victory had been won and that he had no especial part in it." He saw "that his
military reputation . . . might be irretrievably ruined, unless he did something
that would attract attention." Then followed the charge against "a little body
of the enemy cooped in at the western side of the Gilliam field." [25]

"General Warren," Gardner concluded, "had, for the two days just passed,
failed to meet the emergency, and having deliberately formed that conclusion, General Sheridan's duty was plain. He accepted the responsibility without a moment's hesitation, and to make assurance doubly sure, he put the
gallant Griffin in command." [26]

The speech was a *tour de force* on Gardner's part, taking a one-sided and partisan view of the evidence before the court and hammering hard on those
points where Warren was vulnerable. What the court would make of it would
remain a puzzle for some time.

On July 29, after Gardner's main argument was ended, Stickney asked leave
to respond to it, which request Gardner opposed vigorously. The court permitted him to do so, and Stickney summarized the main points of his case. He
concluded with a plea that the court take the case up for consideration at the
earliest possible moment, for, if a decision should be long delayed, "who can
tell whether the lives of the members of this court will be spared, or that the
life of the person who is most interested in its decision will be spared." [27]

Gardner claimed the same privilege of rebuttal. As a result the court sat
once again on July 30. In his summation, Gardner claimed that "had General
R.E. Lee attacked down the White Oak road while those two divisions

[Griffin's and Crawford's] were in such confusion in the woods they would have been destroyed," a dubious assertion of the "if pigs had wings the sky would be full of flying bacon" variety. Lee would have had to fight his way through the Second Corps and Mackenzie's cavalry before he could have turned his weary marchers into the woods to find Griffin and Crawford.[28]

At 4:30 on that day, the court adjourned, subject to being reconvened by Augur when the entire record was completed for its consideration. "The wearing work is over," Warren wrote, and, indeed, aside from some proofreading and minor corrections Stickney had to do on the text of his argument, there was nothing more to do but wait. "Our side," Warren said, "feels that everything possible has been done by us."

CHAPTER TWENTY-NINE

THE FRUSTRATION OF WAITING

W ARREN RETURNED TO NEWPORT AND SPENT the balance of the summer trying to recover his health. Will expressed concern to him that the inquiry had "been such a terrible mental and physical wear upon you," and Warren referred to himself as "a feeble man" and said that his "special ailment" had not abated. He took up his engineering assignments again, and he tried to get out of doors as much as he could, often on excursions with Sidney. But his health, which had never been robust since his breakdown during the Mississippi River bridge days, continued to be a problem.[1]

Money and finances were constant concerns, and Warren was involved in a nasty dispute over the cost of printing maps with a lithographer named Von Arx. His sister Emily tried to reassure him about her continuing assistance. When Gouv sent her a check for $114 for interest on the money she had loaned him, she said, "I never meant you to pay the interest on this money . . . and should much rather send it back to you if you will let me." The other money he owed, she said, "I can assume that too for you . . . I feel sorry to have you worried about money if I can help you as there are so many other things that annoy you that no one can help you with."[2] But he would accept no charity from her, devoted as they were to one another.

Another shadow over him was the deteriorating condition of President Garfield, about which Warren commented frequently in his letters. After a summer of rising and falling hopes, of optimistic and pessimistic medical bulletins, Garfield passed away on September 19, 1881, at Elberon, New Jersey. The virtually unknown Chester Alan Arthur of New York City assumed the presidency. Warren knew Arthur only slightly, having made his acquaintance early in the war when Arthur was New York's quartermaster general under Edwin D. Morgan. He knew that Arthur, despite his early political sponsorship by Morgan, had become the chief lieutenant of Roscoe Conkling's New York Republican machine and that Conkling was Grant's primary political ally.

Arthur had been fired as Collector of the Port of New York by Hayes as part of a reform of the New York Customs House and had been placed on the 1880 ticket by Garfield as a sop to Conkling and the disappointed Grant supporters. While Arthur was far more able than his detractors supposed, his presence in the White House promised to complicate the course of the Warren Court of Inquiry.

Augur and Newton got together with Colonel Langdon, the recorder, on October 21, 1881, to begin their deliberations. They went over the record thoroughly, considered the "imputations" against Warren in Sheridan's report, argued, analyzed, and finally put together an opinion and report. The *World* predicted on October 28 that they would "probably reach a verdict in about a week."[3] The two old soldiers spent fifteen days on this final part of their labors and finished up on November 8, 1881.

Several weeks later, in a letter sending Stickney a hundred dollars on account for the final thousand-dollar legal bill, Warren said, "[O]f course, it would please me to have the 'opinion' vindicate me explicitly, but I have never been very sanguine that they would do it after Hancock withdrew." He was just as much prepared, he said, "for an unsatisfactory opinion, because there is the record anyhow and it is sufficient, much more valuable than an opinion." He would be happy to have a favorable opinion on his attorney's account, "and to defeat Gardner, whose slanders and perversions in summing up the case I think 'conduct unbecoming an officer and a gentleman.'"[4]

Through the early months of 1882, Gouverneur Warren waited patiently, for he knew that there was a set procedure that the court's opinion must follow: consideration by the judge advocate general, approval by the commanding general, recommendation by the secretary of war, and finally direction by the president of the United States.

In the beginning of February, Warren sent Albert Stickney another hundred dollars, saying regretfully that "I find so many things about home that require attention that I shall not be able to send you any more for some time to come." He hoped that his lawyer's affairs were not disconcerted by his inability to pay more at the moment, and he trusted that Stickney was "getting along well yourself and have plenty of fat fees."[5]

Warren's health was causing concern to his friends and relatives. He looked drawn and sickly, and he had very little strength. Will wrote him late in March of uneasiness about "the feeble state of your health," saying that "the constant drain, mental and physical, upon you from the very time you entered West Point, is what is now telling upon you, and rest is absolutely necessary."[6]

As the months drifted by, however, and Warren seemed to become weaker, he and his lawyer worried about the continuing delay in publishing the report of the court, as well as what if anything they could do about it. "I suppose we will hear something about the report of the Inquiry soon," Warren told Stickney. "I do not think it advisable to make any move in the matter, but abide the President's convenience." Referring to rumors that Secretary of War Robert Lincoln might be removed by the new president, Warren said, "If we are going to have a new Secy of War it may be left over till he is determined on."[7]

Stickney replied, "I suppose it is wise to simply wait for the President's action. It is a shame that his action is so delayed. I do not mean that [he] is personally greatly to be blamed, if at all. For nothing can get his attention that is not strongly pressed upon him."[8]

Warren wrote to Fitz John Porter, saying, "No matter what may be the outcome of my Court of Inquiry I have the satisfaction of feeling I have done my best. You surely have done so, and have a right to the same consolation." He told Porter that his health was much improved, but any improvement was on the surface only. Warren wrote to Crawford that he was unable to attend Decoration Day ceremonies at Gettysburg and admonished his former division commander, "Don't let the name of Genl Meade be forgotten, nor any note of detraction go unsilenced on that field."[9]

On April 29, Warren told Humphreys that he was preparing "to have a quiet time for a while," but he solicited his friend's thoughts on what should be done "to call the attention of the President to my court." He was in no hurry personally, Warren said, but was "willing to await the President's time for acting." He then showed his true feeling by asking, "Do I injure my cause by too much waiting?"[10]

A few days later Will wrote from Washington that he had met with a Colonel Winthrop from the judge advocate's office

> and he mentioned to me that he has recently reviewed the papers in your case, which you know was referred to the Judge Advocate General. He said he went over the case with a very great deal of interest and was glad for one reason that he hadn't a personal friendship to have any effect in warping his judgment—or words to that effect—and added that he didn't know how far his views would have weight with the Head of the Department. I said I hoped some conclusion in the case would soon be reached for you had been held in suspense long enough. He quite agreed with me and rather intimated there was no reason why the action should have been delayed so long.[11]

A week later Will reported Humphreys' strong feeling that some prominent friend in Washington should be recruited to "bring your case favorably to the notice of the higher authorities." Will told Humphreys that he had read that ex-governor Morgan was coming to visit Arthur at the White House, and Humphreys rejoined that Morgan was just the man he had in mind. Will worried that Morgan might be "a little too close to President Arthur—staying at his house," but Humphreys sensibly saw that as no objection.[12]

Another week brought a frustrating letter from Langdon, the court recorder, asking if *Warren* could let *him* know "about when the Executive will act upon and promulgate your case." Warren wrote back, saying, "I know nothing about it. I hardly know whether I am expected to do anything more or not. I suppose it is best to await the action of the superior authorities in silence."[13]

Warren's interest in Fitz John Porter's case continued to take some of his time and strength. Porter's 1863 court-martial conviction had been reversed by a board of officers headed by John M. Schofield, but congressional action was required to restore him to his rank. Porter asked Warren to intervene for him with Jimmy Wadsworth, Warren's former aide, who was now in Congress but not in favor of Porter's bill. Warren duly sent off a letter to Wadsworth, saying, "I have always defended General Porter . . . I know *from personal observation* and participation in the events, that he did all he could to *sustain General Pope.*" He pointed out that Grant now took Porter's side; "this is hard upon my feelings, but I even forget my own grievances at Grant's treatment of me, if he will help Porter."[14]

A couple of days later Warren got a letter from Rufus Dawes, former commander of the Sixth Wisconsin in the Fifth Corps, also now a member of Congress, saying Wadsworth had shown him Warren's letter on Porter. "You, General," Dawes said, "I fully believe were 'wronged'—But your case I have always regarded as an intense opposite of Porter's." Wadsworth, too, wrote back, saying that even with Warren's letter, "I hardly feel willing to change my position" in regard to Porter.[15]

While Warren's unsuccessful lobbying for Porter was going on, he wrote to Stickney that "I think the time has about come to do something." What was wanted, he thought, was a copy of the court's report, "and it can give no offense to anyone to ask for that. I do not expect it to be a very strong document in my favor—probably as non-committal as possible." With the opinion in hand, "then we could see whether it would embarrass him [Arthur] politically to approve of the report. Non-action on his part leaves this matter open, but if we force him by any embarrassing pressure he might disapprove the finding and that would end the matter. This last course would hurt me very much in future history and with the public at present." The continuing delay, he knew, meant "the Grant influence again rules against me."[16]

Stickney suggested that Warren write directly to the president, but Warren demurred. "No doubt you are more practical, and better know what influences to use," he said, in a letter which he then did not send, "and deem a publication of my Court's 'opinion' (mark you it is only an *opinion* not a *judgement*) a matter of importance which I do not. It is only two men's opinions, or two different opinions, and has no more weight than any other one two or three generals or others who may study the record which is already public."

Warren, fearing Grant's influence with Arthur, felt "the case is now wholly a matter for executive consideration. The inquiry is terminated. He the president has the right I think to entirely suppress the opinion of the court, or to approve it or disapprove of it according to his ideas of what is best for the 'public service.'" He warned that "a direct address to the president must not even appear to run against his prerogatives, especially from an army officer, who must obey his orders even if he perish under them in the public service." Perhaps the thing to do now, he suggested, was to address General Sherman, as an army matter. Warren concluded, wearily, "I will be satisfied with everything and want a rest." [17]

He was pleased to receive a letter from Rufus Dawes, explaining that their differences on the Porter case in no way affected his feelings toward Warren. Describing his command of the Sixth Wisconsin from Spotsylvania to the Petersburg Mine, he said, "Your own intrepid bearing at the battle front, for you were always there, commanded my admiration and friendship." [18]

Finally, Warren, Stickney, and Humphreys decided that a letter from Warren to the army adjutant general, strictly within military channels, might be the best way to move along the publication of the court opinion. Warren sent Stickney a draft of a proposed letter on June 9, saying to his lawyer, "I do not dare ask any friend who is in [a] political situation to do anything for me . . . My case is now purely military, and such I prefer it shall hereafter remain. In this line all the efforts will be matters of record . . . Hence my official appeal to the Adjutant General [Richard C. Drum]. I know he is my friend. He will do his duty however regardless of that. I think Genl Sherman is my friend too, but he prefers I think to act on the matter entirely impersonally— so he should." [19]

Will wrote a somewhat alarmist letter from Washington on June 11, decrying the possible passage of an army retirement bill then before Congress, one which did not pass as then written. Among its other provisions the bill would have caused Sherman's immediate retirement, with Sheridan taking his place as commanding general, with what possibilities of mischief one could only imagine. Will also reported rumors of Asa Bird Gardner's impending promotion within the judge advocate's bureau and the problems that might cause. He suggested that these factors mitigated in favor of the least delay possible in having the court of inquiry's report promulgated. [20]

Drafts of the proposed letter went back and forth among Warren in Newport, Humphreys in Washington, and Stickney in New York, as various forms of language came under consideration. On June 15 one of the drafts was inadvertently picked up by an overzealous clerk in Newport and mailed off to its putative addressee, complete with strikeovers and erasures. Adjutant General Drum coolly sent it back to Warren with his notation, "Is this not the draft of the letter & sent by mistake?" Warren sent Drum a personal note saying it was indeed a mistake and "there was not the remotest intention of taking such a way to sound you unofficially." All he wanted, he said, was "to be entirely under the control of the regulations of the Army, as an officer of the Army, and for the good of the Army." [21]

In the meantime, Stickney admonished his client, "You would be an excellent adviser in some other man's case. But no man is a wise adviser in his own case. Especially is it so when a man has carried a wrong for so many years as you have this. I suggest that you turn this matter [of whom to solicit] over entirely to me." [22]

Warren was still preparing drafts of a possible letter to the adjutant general, and writing a friend that "I have been hard at work as I could stand, fixing up my public affairs to make life easier or die." He was so physically weak, he said, that he could not accept an invitation to go to the mountains. His wife Emily, he went on, "is wearied with the cares and disappointments of our life." He added that the Roeblings were there in Newport with them.[23]

Late in June leaks about the court's report started appearing in the New York papers, apparently emanating from the judge advocate general's office, which had by then passed the matter along to the secretary of war. The *New York Post* reported the interpretation of the case by Judge Advocate General Swaim, a Grant partisan, saying that reasonable grounds existed for Sheridan's doing what he did and that his motivations were the highest. Swaim also doubted the propriety of the inquiry so long after the events in question. On June 28, however, Charles Dana's editorial in the *Sun* said that "it is confidently believed by General Warren's numerous friends, who have carefully read the evidence, that the verdict will go far toward satisfying his expectations, in completely vindicating his reputation, after a patient and almost hopeless contest maintained through seventeen years." The next day several papers reported that the opinion "vindicated in several particulars the course pursued by Gen. Warren." [24]

Fitz John Porter wrote Warren that "at last the 'Sun' is shining for you, though I presume your heart has been kept alive by the consciousness that the cloud must disperse. I hope this is true—and Dana knows if any one." Warren was not so sanguine. He wrote to Stickney, "I don't know who wrote the article in the Sun. It does me no good, though kindly intended." He also said, a bit testily, "I think you don't understand me in this matter. I want to forget it. *My duty* is done. I am getting involved in a large correspondence about it, which affects my health. I only meant to respectfully call the attention of the Adjutant General to it so that it might duly reach the proper authority for action, and not allow it to be *forgotten* there. I never meant to urge the president." [25]

Since the news reports all agreed that the court's opinion had moved on to the secretary of war, Warren was hopeful that it would soon be published, though it had languished for an unreasonably long time in Swaim's hands. On July 10, while the question of a letter to the president was being kicked around again, Warren met with Morgan in Newport. Morgan told him "he had never conversed with President Arthur on the subject," but "the President was an intelligent well-informed man, and knew my record well, which Gov M spoke very highly of. (That takes a large part out of the proposed letter) Gov M said he would not advise writing to the President now. He would undoubtedly see justice done me when he could—thought that Grant had asked for *no haste!* in the matter. Otherwise it would have been passed upon already." "Grant's influence not permanent," he added hopefully.

"Gov M said to me," he recounted, "let the whole matter rest on my part and he would know how to address a letter on his own knowledge and position to the Secretary of War Mr. Lincoln and his information on the result of this would enable him to give the advice for me next to take." So, once again, as he had sixteen years earlier, Warren rested his hopes on the chance that Morgan would actually undertake something on his behalf. He recognized, though, that his rights in this matter would never be looked after "independent of partisan and personal politics." [26]

The next day he wrote to a friend that "my health is feeble so I must rest all I can." Several days later Warren told Humphreys of his meeting with Morgan and why the letter to Arthur had been scratched for the time being. "My strength does not return as I hoped for," he said to his old comrade, "but in fact I still have too much worry to rest as I need to." [27]

Humphreys answered that he was satisfied with not writing to the president. "What Gov. Morgan will do will be sufficient," he wrote. Ruefully he added, "I should regret to be obliged to believe that Genl G. had endeavored to delay and perhaps suppress the Rept. and Proceedings of the Court." Warren told Stickney Humphreys' opinion, that "it will be just as well for me not to write at all." He concluded, "Thus endeth this consultation for the present." [28]

Will reported another interview with Winthrop of the judge advocate's office, who hinted that what the papers had reported about the court's conclusions "were in the main correct." Winthrop was "impressed with the fact of your vindication" and wished that the paper *he* had prepared had gone forward with the record instead of the one Swaim attached to it. [29]

When the press reported Swaim's opinion that the whole proceeding had been unnecessary because the statute of limitations or laches or public policy protected Sheridan from a court-martial after such a passage of time, Warren protested that that statement was designed "to make a false issue and deceive the public." The court of inquiry "was not called to investigate Sheridan or give any opinion about him, and it ruled out anything not leading up to me." He said that Swaim's function was simply to make sure the proceedings complied with law, "and it is highly improper for him to give an opinion upon the action of ex-president Hayes." [30]

CHAPTER THIRTY

WHERE MALEVOLENCE
CANNOT REACH

W ITH ALL OF THE PLANS AND PROJECTS considered by Warren, Humphreys, and Stickney, the opinion of the court of inquiry remained unpublished as the summer of 1882 moved along. Soon the failure of the executive branch to release the report became academic.

On Monday, July 31, Gouverneur Warren went to Fort Adams, south of Newport's town center, to check on some work being done there, and he was seen riding on Bellevue Avenue with Sidney and little Emily. On Tuesday, after a day spent around his house and headquarters, Warren ate a good supper, sat on the terrace outside his house for a cigar, and fell asleep. When he awakened an hour or so later he was chilled by the evening air, and he spent a restless and uncomfortable night, as his worn-down constitution came to a point of collapse. The family physician called the next morning and found Warren to be quite ill. By August 3, he was in and out of consciousness. A reporter noted that "he rallied repeatedly, but his constitution would not admit of any permanency to the few favorable symptoms which were noticed." He told those around him that his work was done and he was ready to die.

For three days Warren was unconscious, but he rallied on the 7th when Will arrived from Washington. As his brother leaned over his wasted body, Gouv put his arm around Will's neck and held on so tightly that it was found necessary to disengage him, as the effort was costing him needed strength. He made known his desire that his funeral not be a military one and that he be buried in civilian dress. "Convey me quietly to my grave without pageant or show," he was reported to have said to Emily; "I die a disgraced soldier." His last hours were peaceful, and on August 8, at 6 P.M., Gouverneur Kemble Warren passed away, in his fifty-third year.[1]

The cause of death was diabetes, aggravated by a liver problem, but his friends and partisans were quick to claim that Warren died of a broken heart, with the responsibility to be meted out among Grant, Sheridan, Gardner, Swaim, Arthur, and anyone else who had frustrated his drive for vindication. No doubt the mental stress and physical effort of two and a half years with the court of inquiry and its aftermath weakened a constitution which had never been robust since the breakdown on the Mississippi. Death had marked Warren's visage for some time before his actual demise, and Emily received several letters of consolation from friends who were surprised that Gouverneur had not died earlier.[2]

The press dutifully reported Warren's death, with canned accounts of his career as an engineer and soldier and euphemistic descriptions of "the untoward events" or "unfortunate misunderstanding" at Five Forks. The *Washington Post* noted that Warren had gone "where neither the malevolence nor the justice of this world can reach him. He had enough of the former; and denial of the latter not only embittered the closing months of his life, but undoubtedly hastened his end."[3]

A few journalists took the opportunity to review more fully the circumstances of Warren's case and its lack of finality. The *American* decried those who, like Sheridan, Sherman, and Grant, looked upon something like Warren's discomfiture as simply "one of the unpleasant incidents of the war" and Warren himself "as a man with a grievance." It noted the existence of "a small residuum of old army officers . . .who are not content with any such statement as conclusive of Warren's case. They look on it as an injustice inflicted on a soldier of tried merit, by one whose career has been a series of brilliant good luck, and who might with great credit to himself have exercised the small generosity of acknowledging an injury done a brave soldier, and thus put himself even more in the right."[4]

Another editor contended that "Sheridan must feel that it is no longer Warren's reputation as a soldier but his own reputation as a man that is on trial." He said, "It is too late for the tardy acknowledgment of General Sheridan to do any good to General Warren; it is not too late for it to do some good to General Sheridan."[5]

Sheridan apparently never acknowledged or paid the least attention to the death of Gouverneur Warren. It was not a part of his style or coarse-grained nature to do so. His malevolence toward Warren continued unabated. But Emily Warren did receive kind words from those who meant more to her, among the many notes of consolation which poured in. Margaretta Meade wrote, "Genl Meade & Genl Warren were so closely united during the war that I feel as if I myself had lost a friend." Hancock expressed "the heart-felt regrets of very many good people," and immediately left for Newport to attend the funeral. Albert Stickney wrote that "it is seldom that any man who has done his country so noble service suffers so great injustice."[6]

One of the most moving tributes came from Loomis L. Langdon, the official recorder of the court of inquiry. Langdon wrote,

> It was with a most painful shock I learned this noon of dear General Warren's death. By the newspapers, I knew he was very ill, and though he has often shown the elasticity of his constitution by recovering from severe attacks of illness I dreaded the worst, because I knew as well as those nearer and very dear to him how much he had been worried by the events which formed the basis of the inquiry by his Court . . .

> I had never met General Warren till he came before his Court of Inquiry of which I was the recorder. Since then I have been as much thrown with him as two officers could be who were examining papers connected with the same public affairs. I learned to value his good opinion—and while I admired his great patience, his wonderful energy, his habit of concentration, his vast learning and untiring application, I loved him for his tenderness, gentleness and charity, even for those whom he believed had combined to do him a cruel wrong; and I admired him for his nobleness of character and his courage and unselfish patriotism.[7]

Gouverneur K. Warren was buried, dressed in a plain black suit, at the Island Cemetery in Newport after a simple funeral service in All Saints' Chapel on August 11, 1882. Two Episcopalian clerics conducted the service, which was attended by Hancock, Crawford, and John Parke, as well as by ex-governor Morgan. Humphreys was called away before the service because of the sudden serious illness of his son. The mayor and postmaster of Newport were among the pallbearers. The only military aspect of the proceedings was the playing of a dirge by the Fort Adams band while Warren's polished oak casket was lowered into the ground.[8]

The marble slab over the grave bears the simple inscription, "Gouverneur K. Warren, Major General, U.S.V.; He Has Written His Own Epitaph with Sword and Pen." Incised upon the base of it are the symbols of the Corps of Engineers, the Second Corps, and the Fifth Corps, and the years 1830–1882. Next to it are stones marking the resting places of his wife, son, and daughter.[9]

On August 16, Albert Stickney wrote directly to the president, on behalf of Warren's family and the people of the United States, asking "that final action on the Report be taken, and that the Report of the Court may be published, at as early a date as your other official duties will allow." On September 7, he wrote to Secretary of War Robert Todd Lincoln. On the 20th, Lincoln replied that, while it was true "that the record in this case was for a long time in the hands of the Judge Advocate General," it had come to him only after receiving Sherman's endorsement on July 15. Lincoln had then directed that the report be put in print "for my examination" and before that could take place Warren died. The Secretary said he understood that it was "not customary to make the usual publication" when the person most affected has died. However, he went on, if the family really desired it, the report could be printed, a statement the absurdity of which must have struck Lincoln even as he wrote it. He enclosed a proof sheet of the report, to be shown in confidence to Mrs. Warren, and if she requested he would direct its publication "in the usual way." [10]

Attached to the report of Augur and Newton were two additional commentaries, one by Swaim, the judge advocate general, the other by Sherman, both unfavorable to Warren. It now became the object of Stickney and Humphreys to have the report of the court published without these appendages. "It was the Court's views Genl W. asked," Humphreys wrote, "not Genl Sherman's or anybody else's." [11]

Finally, on November 21, 1882, Lincoln issued the following statement: "The foregoing proceedings and report having been laid before the President, he directs that the findings and opinion of the court of inquiry be published." While its publication without Swaim's and Sherman's additions appeared to be a small victory for Stickney, who said Sherman's comments "would have hurt General Sherman and no one else in the end," it was quickly vitiated by the issuance of two hundred copies *with* Swaim and Sherman annexed and by Sheridan's having a thousand copies of Sherman's statement printed. [12]

Nevertheless, despite the attachments, the report and opinion of the court were now in the public domain, and those who had followed the course of the case were interested to see what the court's conclusions might be.

The court's opinion dealt in good logical army fashion with the four imputations identified by Warren as having cast the stigma upon his reputation. The first imputation was found in Grant's report of the fighting on March 31. "On the morning of the 31st," Grant had written, "General Warren reported favorably to getting possession of the White Oak road, and was directed to do so. To accomplish this, he moved with one division instead of his whole corps," and Ayres and Crawford were then driven back. After analyzing the evidence, the court found that "there seems to be no evidence that General Warren on the morning of March 31st, or at any other time, reported favorably to getting possession of the White Oak road," and it denied that Meade directed him to do so. The court, however, felt that Warren "should have been with his advanced divisions" and "should have started earlier to the front." [13]

The "second imputation" was in Sheridan's report, in the statement that "had General Warren moved according to the expectations of the Lieutenant General, there would appear to have been but little chance for the escape of the enemy's infantry in front of Dinwiddie Court House." The court found that "it was not practicable for the 5th Corps to have reached General Sheridan at 12 o'clock on the night of March 31st." The court felt also, however, that Warren "should have moved the two divisions by the Crump road" during the night, even though neither Meade nor Sheridan contemplated having this column attack before morning and even though Meade and Warren both correctly anticipated the enemy in front of Sheridan withdrawing during the night because of the position of the Fifth Corps in his rear.[14]

The third imputation, and the most serious, was Sheridan's statement that "Warren did not exert himself to get up his corps as rapidly as he might have done, and his manner gave me the impression that he wished the sun to go down before dispositions for the attack could be completed." The court found "that there was no unnecessary delay in this march of the 5th Corps, and that General Warren took the usual methods of a corps commander to prevent delay." It waffled on the question of Warren's "manner," calling the charge "too intangible" and the evidence "too contradictory," Gardner's squadron of cavalry witnesses on this point apparently offsetting the testimony of such as Chamberlain. However, the court went on, "his actions, as shown by the evidence, do not appear to have corresponded with such wish, if ever he entertained it." [15]

Finally, the fourth "imputation" was connected with the attack itself, when a portion of his line allegedly "gave way when not exposed to a heavy fire" and, according to Sheridan, "General Warren did not exert himself to inspire" the necessary confidence. This had always been the most absurd statement in Sheridan's report, and the court had little difficulty with it. After detailing the divergence of Griffin and Crawford and Warren's efforts, the court expressed its opinion.

> General Warren's attention appears to have been drawn, almost immediately after Ayres received the flank fire from the "return" and his consequent change of front, to the probability of Crawford with Griffin diverging too much from and being separated from Ayres, and by continuous exertions of himself and staff substantially remedied matters; and the court thinks that this was for him the essential point to be attended to, which also exacted his whole efforts to accomplish.[16]

And that was it. The report of the court ended abruptly at this point, leaving its readers to analyze its findings and opinions and to figure where Warren came out as a result. Albert Stickney wrote, "Looking . . . at the findings I boil. The intimation of a doubt as to Warren's honest zeal is contemptible." [17] Perhaps Stickney was too close to the case, because it is difficult to find such a doubt, except perhaps in the failure to reach a conclusion on his "manner." The court's findings were largely in Warren's favor, although not unreservedly so, an appropriate result for an analysis of a battle in which his actions, while certainly not deserving the treatment meted out by Sheridan, were not above criticism in some respects. The opinion was surely a worthy effort by two senior officers who had to continue service in an army soon to be commanded by Phil Sheridan.

On the first charge, Generals Augur and Newton found that Grant was wrong in his description of the preliminaries and fight of March 31, although they suggested that Warren should have gone to the front sooner rather than staying in telegraphic communication with Meade, certainly a debatable and not damaging criticism. As to the second "imputation," they found that Sheridan's expectation of a midnight arrival was unrealistic, although Warren should have moved Griffin and Crawford sooner than he did, as ordered by Meade. Even here, the court conceded the perplexities which occupied Warren's mind on that confused night and early morning. Finally, on the third and fourth "imputations," the court found squarely in Warren's favor, despite reaching no conclusion as to his "manner." [18]

Swaim, the judge advocate general, after a long, argumentative, and repetitious review of the evidence and the court's opinion, concluded that the recorder should have prosecuted the case and proved the truth of the imputations against Warren, with Warren then required to disprove the case made against him. Few readers paid much attention to Swaim's tendentious opinion, but Sherman's addition was another matter. Sherman was highly regarded, and his views were much more succinctly expressed. [19]

Sherman misstated the opinion of the court, stating that its opinion was "that the tactical handling of the 5th Corps by General Warren was unskillful" and that the victory was achieved "in spite of the misdirection of two of the three divisions of the 5th Corps, for which the corps commander was held responsible." Sheridan then relieved him, and "there," Sherman said, "the matter ought to have ended." Reversing the position he took in endorsing the granting of the inquiry by Hayes, he said, "[I]t would be an unsafe and dangerous rule to hold the commander of an army in battle to a technical adherence to any rule of conduct for managing his command." Showing that perhaps the resentment toward him attributed to Grant and Sheridan had affected him, Sherman concluded that Sheridan "was perfectly justified in his action in this case, and he must be fully and entirely sustained if the United States expects great victories by her armies in the future," another debatable verdict. [20]

And there it rested. Sheridan printed and distributed Sherman's opinion, ignoring the court's report, and he circulated all over the country printed copies of Gardner's argument, which can be found in libraries across the nation to this day. Some of Warren's friends trumpeted the court's report as the vindication he sought, which in truth it was, although somewhat more ambiguous than he would have liked. Others, including Fitz John Porter, deplored the court's opinion; John A. Kellogg, commander of the "pivot" brigade in Crawford's division, said "the wishy washy verdict of the Court has lessened my respect for all military tribunals." [21]

Emily Warren found herself upon her husband's death with virtually no assets, a residence which was really the army's, two children, one sixteen and one eight years old, and severely limited prospects. While a movement was set on foot to have Congress pass a special bill granting Warren's widow a pension, his friends undertook to raise a fund to provide a home for her. General George W. Cullum, the former superintendent of West Point, chaired this effort, which raised over $16,700 from such diverse donors as Theodore Lyman, Hiram Duryea, Fred Locke, John Codman Ropes, William B. Franklin, Loomis Langdon, Horace Porter of Grant's staff, and numerous old Fifth Corps soldiers, enlisted men as well as officers. The fund was used to buy a lot and build a house on Gibbs Avenue in Newport, and on May 15, 1884, Cullum sent Emily a check for $1,270.44, the amount left over.[22]

In the meantime, the House Committee on Invalid Pensions reported out Congressman Jimmy Wadsworth's bill to grant a pension of fifty dollars a month to Mrs. Warren, and the bill was passed and signed by President Arthur. An effort was made to double this several years later, when a Senate report mentioned that her uncertain and limited income had required her to go to work. The higher pension was passed in 1889.[23]

Hiram Duryea created and chaired a committee to have a statue of Warren erected on Little Round Top. Fred Locke headed a subcommittee which contracted with Karl Gerhardt of Hartford to create the statue, which was cast by the Henry Bonnard Bronze Company of New York. The funds came primarily from the Fifth New York Association, and the statue, eight feet high and weighing fifteen hundred pounds, was dedicated on August 8, 1888, six years after the general's death. Gouverneur K. Warren is immortalized in bronze, sword in one hand, binoculars in the other, standing on the spot from which he first discovered Hood's advancing Confederates.[24]

Sidney Warren went off to Harvard and later moved to Buffalo for business. He died in 1907. Emily, Warren's widow, lived on in Newport until her death in 1928 at the age of eighty-five. The Warrens' beloved daughter Emily never married but devoted her life to the preservation and enhancement of the memory of her father. While Mrs. Warren considered some sort of memoir of her husband but never followed through on it, their daughter engaged a writer named Emerson Gifford Taylor to write a biography of the general. Warren himself had arranged his vast collection of papers in chronological order, his wife had carefully preserved them, and their daughter had added to them. Now Emily Warren made the papers available to Taylor.

His book came out in 1932, and its overall thrust, certainly pleasing to the general's daughter, was that Warren had been one of the great generals in American history. The reviews were not so pleasing. Taylor wrote that the court of inquiry had sustained Warren in every respect, and historian Henry Steele Commager jumped on this assertion. "The court did no such thing," Commager wrote. "It found against Warren on the first two charges," itself a dubious statement, "and vindicated him on the third and fourth." Taylor's

Statue of Warren on Little Round Top

statement, he wrote, "inevitably inspires distrust of the correctness and impartiality of the entire narrative." The book's value, Commager said, lay in its "generous selection from the letters and diaries of the young commander of the famous Fifth Corps." A reviewer in the *Boston Transcript* called the book "a splendid piece of biography," but T. R. Hay, in the *American Historical Review*, said that "as a critical history or biography it has little value." [25]

So what verdict should history render on Gouverneur Kemble Warren? He was a highly intelligent, well read, and rational man. Even in religion, he stated, "As for myself I am a liberal Christian . . . I believe what I can and nothing more and am willing that anybody else shall believe as much more or less as they can. Honest belief cannot be forced, and to say we believe what we don't is falsehood." [26]

Yet Warren suffered from chronic depression, whether clinical or not, and this affected those around him. His bleak outlook on life, already a part of his nature before Five Forks, was magnified by his grudge against Sheridan and Grant and by his persistent ill health after the war.

As a person, the postwar engineer suffering from his supposed disgrace is a far more sympathetic figure than the arrogant and hypercritical young general of 1863, 1864, and 1865. The quick and sulphurous temper which he displayed during the Virginia campaign of 1864 worked against Warren by making him unnecessary enemies and dismaying his friends. There is little chance that Sheridan would have found Warren a congenial figure in any event, but the latter's angry outbursts against Sheridan's cavalry laid up obvious trouble for him. When the crisis came Warren had so alienated Meade that he received no help from his commander.

Warren's curious mixture of military characteristics made him one of the enigmas of the Army of the Potomac. His physical courage was unquestioned, except by Sheridan, and he was frequently seen in the front lines, as testified to by Rufus Dawes, who once had to pull him to the ground to keep him from being shot. His tactical initiatives were usually well carried out. He had a bad habit of second-guessing the plans of his superiors, and Meade was certainly not enthralled to receive Warren's long letters replete with strategic advice. Warren's hesitance to obey orders which he could see promised no success in his immediate front was a more serious matter; it nearly cost him his command at the Wilderness and Spotsylvania and did so finally at Five Forks.

Grant, in his memoirs, after a description of the battle of Five Forks so muddled as to be almost unrecognizable, commented on Warren:

> He was a man of fine intelligence, great earnestness, quick perception, and could make his dispositions as quickly as any officer, under difficulties where he was forced to act. But I had before discovered a defect which was beyond his control, that was very prejudicial to his usefulness in emergencies . . . He could see every danger at a glance before he had encountered it. He would

not only make preparations to meet the danger which might occur, but he would inform his commanding officer what others should do while he was executing his move.[27]

James Wilson, a division commander in Sheridan's cavalry who had his share of run-ins with Warren in 1864, called him an "officer of great experience and fine ability, who was generally regarded as one of the most capable corps commanders our army ever had, but . . . captious and impatient of control." "Certain it is," Wilson went on, "that toward the latter part of his career he hardly ever received an order which he did not criticize nor a suggestion which he did not resent." Nevertheless, Wilson acknowledged, no man in the army knew better than Warren "the difference between discussion looking to delay or to change of plan and prompt obedience to a positive order from his superior." [28]

The black and despondent moods which characterized Warren during much of the Virginia campaign of 1864 and after certainly contributed to the hesitancy referred to. He was sickened by the great loss of life entailed in Grant's campaign style, and he loathed ordering his men into doomed assaults which promised nothing but death and destruction. Warren felt that his finest hour had been, not at Little Round Top, but at Mine Run, when he had preserved thousands of Union soldiers from pointless death. But he stubbornly refused to recognize that his preferred means of waging war—in the style of his ideal, George McClellan—would have stretched the war far beyond the end which Grant was able to achieve.

Civil War generals can be judged as to both their leadership and their generalship. Warren's leadership was generally of a high character. He drilled and disciplined his men to a high point of excellence, and he led them in battle with bravery and skill. For the most part he took care that they were not thrown into suicidal situations, and he looked after their welfare. His leadership qualities were unfortunately compromised by the rages into which he fell as he attained higher command, although these were apparently visited more upon his staff than upon those in the ranks.

Warren's generalship is more problematical to assess. Even those most critical of him agree that he was skilled in the tactical handling of his troops in combat. It is on the higher level of generalship that Warren seems to fall short. His hectoring of Meade, whether on general principles, proposed strategic initiatives, or the failings of his colleagues, was counterproductive, as was his frequent delay in carrying out orders to advance or attack while he checked on peripheral matters which had already presumably been considered by his superior. Yet his cautious attitude permitted Warren to avoid the deadly blunders which some of his fellow commanders committed.

Gouverneur Warren possessed one of the finest intellects in the Union army; he was an excellent engineer, an accomplished topographer, and a highly regarded scientist. But in the crucible of war it was his military qualities which were of the highest moment. And those qualities were mixed in such a way that he was not the soldier that his intellectual inferiors like Grant and Sheridan were. The two of them, whom Warren despised to the point of hatred after Five Forks, were gifted with a kind of tunnel vision that made them aggressive and successful commanders. Warren was handicapped by the breadth of his vision, normally a quality greatly to be desired, but a mixed blessing in the context of Civil War command. It did not prevent him from carrying out his orders, but it imparted to his actions a doubtful character which exasperated his superiors. Warren was a complex man, much more so than such simpler figures as Sheridan, Grant, even Hancock. The battlefields of Virginia were, unfortunately, not the proper theater for Warren's complexity.

NOTES

Abbreviations

Battles and Leaders	Robert Underwood Johnson and Clarence Clough Buell, eds., *Battles and Leaders of the Civil War* (New York: Century, 1884–1887), 4 vols.
Davenport Letters	Alfred Davenport Letters, New-York Historical Society
GKW	Gouverneur Kemble Warren
Humphreys Papers	Andrew Atkinson Humphreys Papers, Historical Society of Pennsylvania
Official Records	*War of the Rebellion: A Compilation of the Official Records of the Union and Confederate Armies* (Washington, D.C.: Government Printing Office, 1880–1901).
Proceedings	*Proceedings, Findings, and Opinions of the Court of Inquiry Convened by Order of the President of the United States . . . in the Case of Gouverneur K. Warren, Late Major-General U.S. Volunteers; Commanding the Fifth Army Corps in the Campaign of Five Forks, Va., 1865* (Washington, D.C.: Government Printing Office, 1883)
Roebling Papers	Roebling Family Collection, Special Collections and University Archives, Rutgers University Libraries
Warren Papers	Gouverneur Kemble Warren Papers, New York State Library

Preface

1. *Newport Mercury,* July 29, 1882; letter of Alfred Davenport, Feb. 25, 1863, Davenport Letters; David S. Sparks, ed., *Inside Lincoln's Army: The Diary of Marsena Rudolph Patrick, Provost Marshal General, Army of the Potomac* (New York and London: Thomas Yoseloff, 1964), 381 (diary entry of June 6, 1864); Worthington Chauncey Ford, ed., *A Cycle of Adams Letters, 1861–1865* (Boston and New York: Houghton Mifflin, 1920), vol. 2, 72; Harold Adams Small, ed., *The Road to Richmond: The Civil War Memoirs of Major Abner R. Small of the Sixteenth Maine Volunteers* (Berkeley: University of California Press, 1939), 195; Allan Nevins, ed., *A Diary of Battle: The Personal Journals of Colonel Charles S. Wainwright, 1861–1865* (New York: Harcourt Brace and World, 1962), 405; C. H. Morgan to GKW, March 8, 1868, Warren Papers.

1. Cold Spring and West Point

1. William J. Blake, *The History of Putnam County, N.Y.* (New York: Baker and Scribner, 1849), 240, 245.

2. For Scott's attendance at Kemble's dinners, see John S. D. Eisenhower, *Agent of Destiny: The Life and Times of General Winfield Scott* (New York: The Free Press, 1997), 144–45.

3. GKW to Emily Warren, Oct. 23, 1863, quoting an earlier letter of Oct. 5, 1863, to him from his sister Emily, in which she describes a visit from Uncle Harry (Sylvanus's brother), who talked about old Samuel and the understanding that "some trouble made him leave his home and that he took care none of his relatives should know what had become of him." Warren Papers.

4. The family background is taken from a note in Warren's hand, located in the Warren Papers, and from Blake, *The History of Putnam County, N.Y.*, 234–35.

5. G. Kemble to Sylvanus Warren, Nov. 12, 1839, and Nov. 22, 1839; official appointment of Sylvanus Warren as assistant marshal for Putnam County by U.S. Marshal William C. H. Waddell, Nov. 25, 1839; A. J. Bleecker to Sylvanus Warren, Jan. 30, 1840; G. Kemble to Sylvanus Warren, May 25, 1840; all in Warren Papers.

6. Blake, *The History of Putnam County, N.Y.*, 77, 144.

7. Ibid., 149; David McCullough, *The Great Bridge* (New York: Simon and Schuster, 1982 [orig. pub. 1972]), 457.

8. GKW to Sylvanus Warren, Sept. 1, 1858, Warren Papers.

9. U.S. Military Academy, Cadet Application Papers, 1805–1866, Record Group 94, Records of the Adjutant General's Office, National Archives. Woodworth was an undistinguished one-term congressman from Hyde Park who was denied renomination by the Democrats. Woodworth's nomination of Gouverneur Warren to the military academy was undoubtedly the high point of his congressional career.

10. Ibid. Appointments to the academy were "conditional" until the appointee passed the actual entrance examination at the Point.

11. GKW to Phoebe Warren, February, 1848, Warren Papers. "Give my love to all my little brothers and sisters," Gouv wrote his mother.

12. GKW to Phoebe Warren, March 19, 1848, Warren Papers. Bankhead held on to graduate thirty-fifth in his class, and he won a promotion to brevet brigadier general for service at Five Forks, under Warren.

13. GKW to Sylvanus Warren, Jan. 11, 1848, Warren Papers.

14. GKW to Phoebe Warren, May 20, 1849, Warren Papers.

15. Blake, *The History of Putnam County, N.Y.*, 240, 245.

16. Ibid.

2. Topographical Engineer

1. GKW to Sylvanus Warren, Oct. 21, 1850, Warren Papers.

2. John M. Barry, in his *Rising Tide: The Great Mississippi Flood of 1927 and How It Changed America* (New York: Simon and Schuster, 1997), 32–45, gives a comprehensive summary of the problem of the Mississippi and the government's efforts to combat it. His work is marred only by a strong bias against Humphreys.

3. GKW to Sylvanus Warren, Oct. 21, 1850, Warren Papers.

4. GKW to Sylvanus Warren, Nov. 1, 15, Dec. 20, 1850, Warren Papers.

5. Warren Journal 1851, Jan. 1, Warren Papers.

6. Warren Journal 1851, Jan. 8, 9, Warren Papers.

7. GKW to Sylvanus Warren (with addition to Eliza Warren), Jan. 18, 1850, Warren Papers.

8. Warren Journal 1851, Feb. 1, 11, Warren Papers.

9. Warren Journal 1851, Feb. 21, 22, 28, Warren Papers.

10. GKW to Sylvanus Warren, March 2, 1851; Warren Journal 1851, March 8; both in Warren Papers.

11. Warren Journal 1851, May 5–11, 14, 15; GKW to Sylvanus Warren, May 17, 1851; both in Warren Papers.

12. GKW to W. J. Warren, June 24, 1851, Warren Papers.

13. Warren Journal 1851, June 24–30 and various entries in July; GKW to Sylvanus Warren, July 15, 1851; both in Warren Papers.

14. GKW to Sylvanus Warren, July 25, 1851, Warren Papers.

15. Andrew A. Humphreys and Henry Abbot, *Report upon the Physics and Hydraulics of the Mississippi River* (Philadelphia: J. B. Lippincott, 1861). In 1872, Humphreys described his work as "a series of investigations which developed the law governing the formation of the bars and shoals at the mouth of that river, from which most important consequences have followed for the improvement of navigation and the increase of commerce." *Philadelphia North American and United States Gazette*, Nov. 19, 1872. In 1862, Humphreys had written to his wife that with the Mississippi River report "my name will be better known a century hence than it is now, ten times over. As a professional man I feel satisfied; I am contented with the reputation that I have with my fellows, and satisfied that it will grow yearly as the Delta Report becomes more read. It will always be a standard work and the facts it records will make it live for ever." A. A. Humphreys to Becky Humphreys, July 29, 1862, Humphreys Papers.

16. Warren Journal 1851, Oct. 24, Nov. 6; GKW to Sylvanus Warren, Oct. 6, 1851; both in Warren Papers.

17. GKW to Sylvanus Warren, Oct. 17, Nov. 20, 1851; Warren Journal 1851, Dec. 8; both in Warren Papers.

18. Warren Journal 1851, Dec. 31, Warren Papers.

19. While watching to see if Congress would pass the army appropriation, "the whole army is very like a water mill in a drought, almost completely idle. The officers and men are employed and kept on duty, but in our corps for instance it is in doing things that would be left undone if there was a more active employment." GKW to Sylvanus Warren, May 22, 1852, Warren Papers.

20. Undated newspaper clipping, Warren Papers.

21. GKW to Sylvanus Warren, Jan. 7, 1852; Warren Journal 1852; both in Warren Papers.

22. Warren Journal 1853, Dec. 12; "Journal, Survey of Rapids, Miss. R."; both in Warren Papers.

3. Into the West with Harney

1. Jefferson Davis, "Report of the Secretary of War on the Several Pacific Rail Road Explorations" (1855).

2. A. A. Humphreys, Feb. 5, 1855, in A. A. Humphreys and G. K. Warren, *An Examination by Direction of the Hon. Jefferson Davis, Secretary of War, of the Reports of Explorations for Railroad Routes from the Mississippi to the Pacific, Made under the Orders of the War Department in 1853–'54* (Washington, D.C.: A. O. P. Nicholas, 1855), 5–6.

3. GKW to Spencer Baird, Sept. 15, 1854, U.S. National Museum, Asst. Secretary, 1850–1877, Incoming Correspondence, Smithsonian Institution Archives, appears to be

the earliest item in the voluminous correspondence between the two men. Baird had been a professor at Dickinson College for several years before coming to Washington. Joseph Henry, of course, the former Princeton professor, was one of the leading American men of science at the time, particularly for his experiments and findings in the field of electromagnetism.

4. GKW to W. J. Warren, Aug. 5, 1854, Warren Papers.

5. Davis, "Report of the Secretary of War on the Several Pacific Rail Road Explorations"; Warren Journal 1855, April 21, Warren Papers; James A. Hanson, *Little Chief's Gatherings: The Smithsonian Institution's G. K. Warren 1855–1856 Plains Indian Collection and the New York State Library's 1855–1857 Warren Expedition Journals* (Crawford, Nebr.: The Fur Press, 1996), 93.

6. Robert M. Utley, *Frontiersmen in Blue: The United States Army and the Indian, 1848–1865* (New York: Macmillan, 1967), 113–14.

7. GKW to Spencer Baird, from Missouri River, June 8, 1855, U.S. National Museum, Asst. Secretary, 1850–1877, Incoming Correspondence, Smithsonian Institution Archives.

8. GKW to Baird, ibid.; Warren Journal 1855, July 16; both in Warren Papers. On July 15, for example, when Warren thought they were finally going to arrive, he recorded in his journal, "Met with a great deal of detention today, and only reached the mouth of the Little Missouri."

9. James D. McLaird and Lesta V. Turchen, "The Dacota Explorations of Lieutenant Gouverneur Kemble Warren, 1855–1856–1857," *South Dakota History*, vol. 3, no. 4 (Fall 1973), 366; Warren Journal 1855, Aug. 8, Warren Papers. Montgomery apparently overlooked the fact that this second lieutenant had recently had an hour's tête-à-tête with the secretary of war.

10. Lt. G. K. Warren, *Explorations in the Dacota Country, in the Year 1855* (Washington, D.C.: A. O. P. Nicholson, 1856), 21.

11. Warren Journal 1855, Aug. 22, Warren Papers.

12. Warren Journal 1855, Aug. 30, Sept. 2, 3, Warren Papers.

13. Warren Journal 1855, Sept. 3, Warren Papers, contains Warren's lengthy description of the Blue Water fight and its aftermath. He reported that there were thirty-one lodges of Brulés and eleven of Oglalas in Little Thunder's camp, and that sixty to seventy prisoners—women and children—were taken. From the evidence of the artifacts collected by Warren, some Miniconjou Sioux and Cheyennes were present as well.

14. Hanson, *Little Chief's Gatherings*, 17. There is no doubt that the collection came from Warren, who was on the lookout for things to send back to Baird, even though these were not in Baird's zoological line. Secretary Davis's calendar for December 8, 1856, mentions a note from Joseph Henry that "Lt. Gouverneur K. Warren has brought back many artifacts." Lydia Lasswell Crist and Mary S. Dix, eds., *The Papers of Jefferson Davis* (Baton Rouge and London: Louisiana State University Press, 1989), vol. 6, 519. Hanson speculates about Warren's motive in remaining silent about his collection. He believes Warren was distressed by the unequal Blue Water fight and chagrined to have had a part in attacking the Sioux. Further, he feels Warren suffered "remorse and embarrassment for having looted the possessions of a vanquished foe," even though what he did not gather up was consigned to the flames by Harney's order. *Little Chief's Gatherings*, 17.

15. Warren Journal 1855, Sept. 22, Warren Papers. Among the prominent Sioux chieftains whose presence Warren noted were Man Afraid of His Horses, Red Leaf, Big Partisan, and Spotted Tail. It was apparently at or around this gathering that Warren picked

up the nickname given him by the Sioux, "Little Chief," both from his position as an aide to Harney and from his small size. Hanson, *Little Chief's Gatherings*, 4.

16. Warren Journal 1855, Sept. 29–Oct. 19, Warren Papers. The "Mauvaises terres" were reached on October 10.

17. Ibid., Oct. 22–Dec. 21.

4. The Black Hills

1. Lt. G. K. Warren, *Explorations in the Dacota Country, in the Year 1855* (Washington, D.C.: A. O. P. Nicholson, 1856), 19.

2. "Portion of Journal Kept by Lt. Warren in 1856," Warren Papers; Frank N. Schubert, "Troublesome Partnership: Gouverneur K. Warren and Ferdinand V. Hayden on the Northern Plains in 1856 and 1857," *Earth Sciences History*, vol. 3, no. 2 (1984), 143–44. "You may expect a pretty thorough business," Hayden wrote to George Engelmann, a leading botanist and founder of the Academy of Science of St. Louis. F. V. Hayden to George Engelmann, Feb. 18, 1856, George Engelmann Papers, Missouri Botanical Garden.

3. Mike Foster, *Strange Genius: The Life of Ferdinand Vandeveer Hayden* (Niwot, Colo.: Roberts Rinehart, 1994), 73.

4. "Portion of Journal Kept by Lt. Warren in 1856," April 22, Warren Papers; F. V. Hayden to George Engelmann, June 18, 1856, from Fort Pierre, Engelmann Papers.

5. Augustus Meyers, in "Dakota in the Fifties," *South Dakota Historical Collections*, vol. 10 (Pierre, S.Dak.: State Publishing, 1920), 168–69, says the *Genoa* arrived while the council was on, bringing Warren and his party. This is clearly incorrect, as Warren makes it clear in his journal that they arrived by foot, and the *Genoa* did not pull in until the 24th.

6. "Portion of Journal Kept by Lt. Warren in 1856," Warren Papers; GKW to Spencer Baird, May 24, 1856, U.S. National Museum, Asst. Secretary, 1850–1877, Incoming Correspondence, Smithsonian Institution Archives. Along with this letter, Warren sent Baird a box of 291 bird skins, five hare skins, and three squirrel skins.

7. Foster, *Strange Genius*, 74.

8. GKW to Spencer Baird, May 24, 1856, U.S. National Museum, Asst. Secretary, 1850–1877, Incoming Correspondence. Hayden came near getting himself killed at Fort Clark, when he leveled his rifle at some Arikaras who threw pebbles at him while he was fossil hunting. The steamboat captain shouted at Hayden not to fire, recognizing that the Indians would kill him if he did so. Foster, *Strange Genius*, 74.

9. "Portion of Journal Kept by Lt. Warren in 1856," July 26, Warren Papers.

10. GKW to Spencer Baird, Oct. 4, 1856, U.S. National Museum, Asst. Secretary, 1850–1877, Incoming Correspondence, Smithsonian Institution Archives.

11. Foster, *Strange Genius*, 75.

12. G. K. Warren, *Preliminary Report of Explorations in Nebraska and Dakota in the Years 1855–'56–'57* (Washington, D.C.: reprint, 1875), 16.

13. Warren Journal, Nebraska Expedition 1857, Warren Papers; Foster, *Strange Genius*, 77. Hayden had tried to get a job inoculating Indians of the Upper Missouri for the Office of Indian Affairs, or a post with the Northern Boundary Survey.

14. Warren Journal, Nebraska Expedition 1857, Warren Papers. Later, on July 19, Warren recorded that McMillan's escort consisted of sixteen men and two noncommissioned officers, the remainder of the original thirty.

15. Warren Journal, Nebraska Expedition 1857, Aug. 7, Warren Papers. "Our greatest wish," Warren said about the Loup, "is to get away from it as soon as possible and never return."

16. GKW to Sylvanus Warren, Sept. 3, 1857, Warren Papers. The encounter with the Brulés took place on August 11 and 12.

17. Warren, *Preliminary Report*, 18.

18. Warren Journal, Nebraska Expedition 1857, Sept. 5, Warren Papers.

19. George W. Kingsbury, *History of Dakota Territory* (Chicago: S. J. Clarke, 1915), vol. 1, 862.

20. Warren Journal, Nebraska Expedition 1857, Sept. 9, Warren Papers.

21. Ibid., Sept. 16.

22. Warren, *Preliminary Report*, 19.

23. Warren Journal, Nebraska Expedition 1857, Sept. 16, Warren Papers. What Warren called the North Fork of the Cheyenne is now the Belle Fourche River, and the L'eau Qui Court is the Niobrara.

24. Ibid.; Warren, *Preliminary Report*, 20.

25. Warren Journal, Nebraska Expedition 1857, Sept. 17, Warren Papers.

26. Ibid., Sept. 18.

27. Ibid., Sept. 20.

28. Ibid., Sept. 22, 23.

29. Ibid., Sept. 24 (erroneously 23 in the original).

30. Ibid., Sept. 30.

31. Ibid., Oct. 31.

32. GKW to Sylvanus Warren, Sioux City, Nov. 16, 1857, Warren Papers.

33. Doane Robinson, "Black Hills Bygones," *South Dakota Historical Collections*, vol. 12 (Pierre, S.Dak.: State Publishing, 1924), 204. See also Robert J. Casey, *The Black Hills and Their Incredible Characters* (Indianapolis and New York: Bobbs-Merrill, 1949), 118.

34. Warren, *Preliminary Report*, 30.

35. Ibid., 51.

36. Ibid., 51–54.

37. Ibid., 54.

5. The Explorer Becomes a Soldier

1. GKW to Spencer Baird, Feb. 16, 1858, U.S. National Museum, Asst. Secretary, 1850–1877, Incoming Correspondence, Smithsonian Institution Archives.

2. Hayden said that Warren had called on him to produce "a catalogue of the specimens in Geology and Natural History to be published with the President's Message & documents." He said he succeeded "after a good deal of trouble in getting together a Catalogue of about 500 species of plants." Dr. Engelmann, he said, identified most of them, "though I was familiar with many species." F. V. Hayden to Asa Gray, Dec. 30, 1858, and F. V. Hayden to George Engelmann, Nov. 19, Dec. 1, 1858, George Engelmann Papers, Missouri Botanical Garden.

3. GKW to Sylvanus Warren, Sept. 1, 1858, Warren Papers. Edgar's education, of course, included a tour of Nebraska and the Black Hills, complete with confrontations with threatening Dakotas, that Gouv's had lacked in his formative years.

4. GKW to Sylvanus Warren, Dec. 9, 1858, Warren Papers.

5. GKW to A. S. Chase, Nov. 23, 1863, Warren Papers; letter of Feb. 23, 1859, quoted in E. G. Taylor, *Gouverneur Kemble Warren: The Life and Letters of an American Soldier, 1830–1882* (Boston and New York: Houghton Mifflin, 1932), 44.

6. The details of the Sylvanus Warren estate, whose administration and distribution was not completed until March 4, 1863, can be found in the Warren Papers. The Surrogate spelled the widow's name "Phebe."

7. GKW to Spencer Baird, Aug. 20, 1859, U.S. National Museum, Asst. Secretary, 1850–1877, Incoming Correspondence, Smithsonian Institution Archives. In the letter to Baird, Warren not only discusses his assignment to the Point but also remarks, "No definite news from Raynold's party."

8. O. O. Howard, *Autobiography of Oliver Otis Howard, Major General, United States Army* (New York: Baker and Taylor, 1907), vol. 1, 102.

9. "Journal from April 24, 1861 to February 2, 1863," April 24–30, 1861, Warren Papers; Howard, *Autobiography of Oliver Otis Howard*, vol. 1, 105.

10. "Journal from April 24, 1861 to February 2, 1863," May 2, 8, 1861, Warren Papers. The order of Secretary of War Simon Cameron to the superintendent of the academy specified that Warren's leave was to be granted "if in your judgement he can be spared from the Mathematical Department," but it was endorsed on May 6 by E. D. Townsend, Assistant Adjutant General, who wrote that Warren's services at the academy were "just now not required . . . because of the reduced numbers of the classes." Special Orders No. 61, Headquarters, Military Academy, officially granted Warren his leave. Both documents in Warren Papers.

11. Howard, *Autobiography of Oliver Otis Howard*, vol. 1, 106; "Journal from April 24, 1861 to February 2, 1863," May 8–9, 14–15, 23, 1861, Warren Papers; Alfred Davenport, *Camp and Field Life of the Fifth New York Volunteer Infantry (Duryée Zouaves)* (New York: Dick and Fitzgerald, 1879), 26. For the trip from Fort Schuyler, across Manhattan, and then on to the steamer *Alabama* for the voyage to Virginia, see ibid., 30–31.

12. On May 31, 1861, Warren noted in his journal, "Col. Duryee turned command of Regt over to me." "Journal from April 24, 1861 to February 2, 1863," Warren Papers. "[T]he duty of drilling the battalion has devolved upon Lieut. Col. Warren," wrote Davenport, "who handles the regiment in a scientific manner. In field maneuvers the men are taught movement and tactics they never dreamed of before, and were never performed by the militia at home." Davenport, *Camp and Field Life of the Fifth New York Volunteer Infantry*, 87.

13. *New York Times*, Nov. 22, 1862. This letter was signed "C., Late Captain Duryee's Zouaves," but Cambrilling wrote to Warren, explaining that he had written the letter after reading an article in the paper giving credit to then-general Duryée for the achievements of the Fifth New York. "I considered that great injustice was done you," he told Warren. Cambrilling to Warren, Nov. 22, 1862, Warren Papers. Cambrilling's letter to the paper did give Duryée credit for organizing and supplying the regiment. Cambrilling was apparently a variant spelling of the family name Cambreleng, a well-known name in New York political circles.

14. "Journal from April 24, 1861 to February 2, 1863"; Philip L. Wilson to John E. White, March 2, 1889; both in Warren Papers.

15. Benjamin F. Butler, *Butler's Book: Autobiography and Personal Reminiscences* (Boston: A. M. Thayer, 1892), 270–71.

16. GKW to R. B. Ayres, Feb. 27, 1876; Warren's handwritten report, dated June 15, 1861; both in Warren Papers. Greble's father wrote to Warren, thanking him for "your noble and courageous conduct in bringing his body from the fatal field, along with the limber of the gun he so bravely used against the enemies of his country." Edwin Greble to GKW, June 20, 1861, Warren Papers.

17. W. J. Warren to Edgar Warren at Cold Spring, June 12, 1861, Warren Papers.

18. *Report of the Joint Committee on the Conduct of the War*, Rep. Com. No. 108, 37th Cong., 3d sess. (1863), pt. 3, 384.

19. "Journal from April 24, 1861 to Feb. 2, 1863," July 23, 1861, Warren Papers.

20. Ibid., Aug. 19, 30, Sept. 2, 11, 1861.

21. Warren was called before the Committee on the Conduct of the War on January 28, 1862, to answer questions about Lockwood's having assured Virginia slaveowners that the army would find and restore to them any escaped slaves. Warren was unable to help the committee in that area, but he hardly bothered to hide his feeling that the whole movement had been a great waste of time and energy. *Report of the Joint Committee* (1863), 380–82.

22. Algernon Chase was not quite the sober and uninteresting merchant he might have appeared to be. In his youth he had had a serious romance with Charlotte Cushman, a budding opera singer who would become one of America's most famous mid-century actresses. The young man's family, however, looked askance at actresses, and Charlotte was not particularly interested in matrimony, so the two became lifelong friends instead. See Warren's letter of Feb. 20, 1863, to Emily Chase, Warren Papers, for reference to the Valentine's Day party. See also Davenport, *Camp and Field Life of the Fifth New York Volunteer Infantry*, 143, who says that the ball "did not terminate till daybreak."

23. It should be noted, however, that Warren *did* make reference to Hill as "your old beau" after defeating him at the North Anna, "same as it was at Bristow. I think he must begin to feel unkindly towards me." GKW to Emily Warren, May 24, 1864, Warren Papers.

24. Handwritten notes of Emily B. Warren, Warren Papers. For an enlisted man's sour comments on the ball, see the letter of Alfred Davenport, Feb. 16, 1862, Davenport Letters.

25. GKW to Emily Chase, Feb. 22, 1862, Warren Papers.

26. GKW to Emily Chase, March 15, 1862, Warren Papers.

27. GKW to Emily Chase, March 16, 1862, Warren Papers.

28. Davenport, *Camp and Field Life of the Fifth New York Volunteer Infantry*, 150–51; *Baltimore American*, March 31, 1862.

6. On the Virginia Peninsula

1. Pvt. Warren Lee Goss, "Yorktown and Williamsburg," *Battles and Leaders*, vol. 2, 189.

2. GKW to Emily Chase, April 1862, from "camp 5 miles from Ft Monroe," Warren Papers.

3. "Journal from April 24, 1861 to February 2, 1863," April 2, 5, 1862, Warren Papers.

4. Pvt. Warren Lee Goss, "Campaigning to No Purpose," *Battles and Leaders*, vol. 2, 157–58.

5. "Journal from April 24, 1861 to February 2, 1863," April 10, 11, 1862, Warren Papers; Alexander S. Webb, *The Peninsula: McClellan's Campaign of 1862* (New York: Charles Scribner's Sons, 1881), 47; Jos. E. Johnston to R. E. Lee, April 22, 1862, *Official Records*, vol. 11, pt. 3, 456. For Johnston's dismay after examining the Yorktown defenses, see Steven H. Newton, *Joseph E. Johnston and the Defense of Richmond* (Lawrence: University Press of Kansas, 1998), 88–89.

6. Régis de Trobriand, *Four Years with the Army of the Potomac*, trans. George K. Dauchy (Boston: Ticknor and Co., 1889), 175.

7. GKW to Emily Chase, April 21, 1862, Warren Papers; Alfred Davenport, *Camp and Field Life of the Fifth New York Volunteer Infantry (Duryée Zouaves)* (New York: Dick and Fitzgerald, 1879), 163. Davenport wrote, "We all like him as a man and a soldier; he is strict but he knows all the wants of a soldier from experience, and seldom taxes our endurance too much." Ibid.

8. A. S. Webb to GKW, April 26, 1862, and GKW to W. J. Warren, May 1, 1862, Warren Papers; Newton, *Joseph E. Johnston*, 130.

9. Undated clipping from *Baltimore American*, Warren Papers.

10. Webb, *The Peninsula*, 69; GKW to Emily Warren, May 7, 1862, Warren Papers.

11. G. B. McClellan, "The Peninsular Campaign," *Battles and Leaders*, vol. 2, 172–73. The regimental historian describes how Warren borrowed a drill field usually used by the regulars and then put the Fifth New York through a set of complicated drills which impressed both the regulars and Sykes himself. Davenport, *Camp and Field Life of the Fifth New York Volunteer Infantry*, 156.

12. Davenport, *Camp and Field Life of the Fifth New York Volunteer Infantry*, 175. McClellan had been told by a Virginia civilian that there was a force of seventeen thousand rebels at Hanover Court House, and he always believed such reports. In actuality, the Confederates there, under the command of General Lawrence Branch, numbered about four thousand. Stephen W. Sears, *To the Gates of Richmond: The Peninsula Campaign* (New York: Ticknor and Fields, 1992), 113–14.

13. Sears, *To the Gates of Richmond*, 176; George Brinton McClellan, *McClellan's Own Story: The War for the Union* (New York: C. L. Webster, 1887), 370, 373; F. T. Locke, Asst. Adj. Gen., Fifth Corps, to GKW, May 24, 1862, Warren Papers; GKW to F. T. Locke, May 30, 1862, *Official Records*, vol. 11, pt. 3, 202; "Journal from April 24, 1861 to February 2, 1863," May 28, 29, 1862, Warren Papers. See also Fitz John Porter, "Hanover Court House and Gaines's Mill," *Battles and Leaders*, vol. 2, 322. McClellan said that Porter's operations were "entirely successful, and resulted in completely clearing our flank, cutting the railroads . . . destroying bridges, inflicting a severe loss upon the enemy, and fully opening the way for the advance of McDowell's corps." McClellan, "The Peninsular Campaign," *Battles and Leaders*, vol. 2, 175–76.

14. GKW to W. J. Warren, June 2, 11, 1862, Warren Papers.

15. Report of GKW, June 16, 1862, *Official Records*, vol. 11, pt. 1, 1029–30; GKW to W. J. Warren, June 16, 1862, Warren Papers.

16. Sears, *To the Gates of Richmond*, 189.

17. "Journal from April 24, 1861 to February 2, 1863," June 26, 1862, Warren Papers.

18. A recent work has considered McClellan, the workings of his mind, and his standing in Civil War historiography and concluded that the general has not been treated fairly; Thomas J. Rowland, *George B. McClellan and Civil War History: In the Shadow of Grant and Sherman* (Kent, Ohio, and London: Kent State University Press, 1998), particularly chapter 2, 16–44.

19. Surgeon Joseph S. Smith, a captive within the Confederate lines, told Warren that "from their generals down through all grades they all coincided that they never had seen the superiors of the 'red legs' for unflinching courage & coolness." J. S. Smith to GKW, July 28, 1862, Warren Papers.

20. GKW to Emily Chase, July 8, 1862, Warren Papers.

21. Report of GKW, July 4, 1862, Warren Papers. Warren wrote a letter to the editor of *Harper's* after the war, stating, "Of one thing I am certain and that the part of the line where I was did not give way simultaneous with the rest . . . Sykes division with the reinforcements they had never gave way materially at all." March 9, 1866, Warren Papers.

22. Davenport, *Camp and Field Life of the Fifth New York Volunteer Infantry*, 225. McClellan told Warren that his brigade saved the right wing of the army at Gaines's Mill. Letter of Alfred Davenport, July 8, 1862, Davenport Letters.

23. Fitz John Porter, "The Battle of Malvern Hill," *Battles and Leaders*, vol. 2, 409; McClellan, *McClellan's Own Story*, 433.

24. F. C. Barlow to his mother, July 4, 1862, Francis Channing Barlow Papers,

Massachusetts Historical Society; Trobriand, *Four Years with the Army of the Potomac*, 272; Webb, *The Peninsula*, 35. The standard defense of McClellan for his failure in the Peninsular Campaign is set forth in one of his biographies: "It was not McClellan that Lee had beaten, but the Union government, which, in its fear for the capital, had wrecked the campaign at its most critical period by keeping from the army 50,000 men [a slight stretch for McDowell's 40,000] McClellan should have had. In reaching out for that promised reinforcement, he had been compelled to divide his army by the Chickahominy, thereby laying himself open to attack. Since McDowell did not come—was, in fact, never designed to come—McClellan could not have maintained himself in front of Richmond with a supply base on the Pamunkey River. He did the only thing possible under the circumstances in moving to the James River." Hamilton James Eckenrode and Bryan Conrad, *George B. McClellan: The Man Who Saved the Union* (Chapel Hill: University of North Carolina Press, 1941), 120. This argument was not very convincing in 1941 and is not very convincing now.

25. Allan Nevins and Milton Halsey Thomas, eds., *The Diary of George Templeton Strong: The Civil War 1860–1865* (New York: Macmillan, 1952), 235; A. A. Humphreys to Becky Humphreys, July 5, 1862, Humphreys Papers.

26. GKW to W. J. Warren, July 6, 1862, Warren Papers.

27. GKW to Emily Chase, July 8, 1862, Warren Papers.

28. GKW to W. J. Warren, July 20, 1862, Warren Papers.

29. Letter of Alfred Davenport, July 21, 1862, Davenport Letters. Several weeks later, when an order from the Surgical Board directed that all sick and convalescent men be sent away, Warren was said to be "crazy mad" in opposition to the order. Letter of Alfred Davenport, Aug. 10, 1862. In the same letter, Davenport, who generally admired Warren, wrote, "If Col. W gets down on a man, he might as well have a snake against him."

30. GKW to Emily Chase, July 27, 1862, Warren Papers.

31. GKW to Emily Chase, Aug. 8, 11, 1862, Warren Papers.

32. GKW to Emily Chase, Aug. 14, 1862, Warren Papers.

33. *Official Records*, vol. 12, pt. 3, 473–74, for Pope's "address."

7. From Second Manassas to Fredericksburg

1. John J. Hennessy, *Return to Bull Run: The Campaign and Battle of Second Manassas* (New York: Simon and Schuster, 1993), 468.

2. GKW to Emily Chase, Aug. 24, 27, 1862; "Journal from April 24, 1861 to February 2, 1863," Aug. 26, 27, 1862; all in Warren Papers.

3. For Pope's order to McDowell to "bag" Jackson, see *Official Records*, vol. 12, pt. 2, 71.

4. Rufus R. Dawes, *Service with the Sixth Wisconsin Volunteers* (Madison: State Historical Society of Wisconsin, 1962), 69.

5. Hennessy, *Return to Bull Run*, 230.

6. For the "joint order," see *Official Records*, vol. 12, pt. 2, 76.

7. "Journal from April 24, 1861 to February 2, 1863," Aug. 29, 1862, Warren Papers; *New York Evening Telegram*, March 12, 1880. In a letter to Will written on September 5, Warren said, "Porter's Corps should have then attacked on the enemy's right flank but McDowell would not let us." GKW to W. J. Warren, Sept. 5, 1862, Warren Papers.

8. *Official Records*, vol. 12, pt. 2, 503. The historian Ropes wrote of Warren's movement, "Warren, with great promptitude, takes his little brigade, with Sykes' approval, to the left, and endeavors to maintain himself against a heavy attack which the enemy do not fail to make immediately upon his small command. But he . . . was overwhelmed

by superior numbers." John Codman Ropes, *The Army under Pope* (New York: Charles Scribner's Sons, 1881), 136.

9. *Official Records*, vol. 12, pt. 2, 469, 504.

10. Andrew Coats of the Fifth New York ("vortex"), quoted in Brian C. Pohanka, "'Boys, Won't I Make a Fine Looking Corpse?' Duryée's Zouaves at Second Bull Run," *Civil War Regiments*, vol. 1, no. 2 (1991); *Official Records*, vol. 12, pt. 2, 504; Chas. F. McKenna, in *Pittsburgh Dispatch*, July 29, 1888. McKenna continued, more dubiously, "Their last stand, covering the retreat of the Potomac army to the intrenchments in Washington, is a matter of history established to the nation's satisfaction in the many investigations which that battle subsequently gave rise to." This was a claim which Warren did not make. Richard Robins, in "The Battles of Groveton and Second Bull Run," wrote, "General Warren, commanding a brigade, seeing a break in our line, without orders, held the enemy with his old regiment of zouaves, the Fifth New York, until a new line could be established." *Military Essays and Recollections: Papers Read before the Commandery of the State of Illinois*, Military Order of the Loyal Legion of the United States, Commandery of the State of Illinois (Chicago: Dial Press, 1899), vol. 3, 95–96. This, although still somewhat exaggerated, is a more defensible statement of what Warren's brigade accomplished. A private in the brigade, calling Warren's getting off safely "a miracle," described his colonel "with his red cap in his hand, his horse running at the top of his speed." Letter of Alfred Davenport, Sept. 25, 1862, Davenport Letters.

11. GKW to W. J. Warren, Sept. 5, 1862, Warren Papers.

12. GKW to Emily Chase, Sept. 5, 1862, Warren Papers.

13. GKW to Emily Chase, Sept. 9, 12, 1862, Warren Papers.

14. A copy of Lee's operational plan was found wrapped around three cigars near Frederick, when a Federal unit camped on a site where the Confederates had been a couple of days earlier.

15. George Brinton McClellan, *McClellan's Own Story: The War for the Union* (New York: Charles L. Webster, 1887), 601. Casualties on September 17 came to more than twenty-six thousand in killed, wounded, and missing on both sides.

16. Charles Carleton Coffin, "Antietam Scenes," *Battles and Leaders*, vol. 2, 685.

17. "Journal from April 24, 1861 to February 2, 1863," Sept. 22, 25, 26, 1862; GKW to Emily Chase, Sept. 22, 27, 1862; all in Warren Papers. Warren's new commission, of course, was as a brigadier general of volunteers, and it had no effect upon his permanent rank in the army. It was at about this time, after Antietam, that Davenport said that his company commander "and Col. Warren, both under the influence of liquor," drilled the unit in a place where it was subject to rebel sharpshooters. Letter of Alfred Davenport, Sept. 25, 1862, Davenport Letters.

18. *Rochester Democrat and Chronicle*, Oct. 15, 1877.

19. GKW to W. J. Warren, Nov. 5, 1862, Warren Papers; *New York Times*, Nov. 9, 1862.

20. GKW to Emily Chase, Nov. 26, 1862, Warren Papers.

21. GKW to Emily Chase, Dec. 9, 1862, Warren Papers.

22. Mary Genevie Green Brainard, *Campaigns of the One Hundred and Forty-Sixth Regiment New York State Volunteers* (New York and London: G. P. Putnam's Sons, 1915), 31.

23. Walter H. Hebert, *Fighting Joe Hooker* (Indianapolis and New York: Bobbs-Merrill, 1944), 159.

24. *Official Records*, vol. 21, 429–30, 402.

25. *Rochester Democrat and Chronicle*, Oct. 29, 1877.

26. GKW to W. J. Warren, Dec. 18, 1862, Warren Papers.

27. GKW to Emily Chase, Dec. 25, 1862, Warren Papers.

8. With Hooker

1. "Journal from April 24, 1861 to February 2, 1863," Jan. 20, 22, 1863, Warren Papers.

2. A. A. Humphreys to Becky Humphreys, Jan. 24, 1863, Humphreys Papers.

3. *New York Times*, Feb. 12, 1863; John Gibbon, *Personal Recollections of the Civil War* (New York and London: Putnam's, 1928), 107; Francis Winthrop Palfrey, *The Antietam and Fredericksburg* (New York: Charles Scribner's Sons, 1882), 55.

4. Francis A. Walker, *History of the Second Army Corps in the Army of the Potomac* (New York: Charles Scribner's Sons, 1886), 202. Hooker's biographer wrote that Butterfield "did not . . . have the detailed knowledge of military science so important to the work of Chief of Staff." Walter H. Hebert, *Fighting Joe Hooker* (Indianapolis and New York: Bobbs-Merrill, 1944), 172. See Edwin B. Coddington, *The Gettysburg Campaign: A Study in Command* (New York: Charles Scribner's Sons, 1968), 26–30, for a description of Hooker's changes.

5. Letter of Alfred Davenport, Jan. 26, 1863, Davenport Letters.

6. GKW to W. J. Warren, Jan. 30, 1863, Warren Papers.

7. GKW to W. J. Warren, Feb. 3, 1863, Warren Papers. Special Orders No. 33, from the headquarters of the Army of the Potomac, dated February 2, 1863, officially assigned Warren to the staff position.

8. GKW to Col. James C. Biddle, May 26, 1877, Warren Papers; A. A. Humphreys to Becky Humphreys, Sept. 1, 1864, Humphreys Papers.

9. GKW to Emily Chase, Feb. 20, 1863; J. C. Woodruff to GKW, Feb. 23, 1863; both in Warren Papers. On February 19, General Orders No. 12, from the Army of the Potomac headquarters, directed that all topographical work, whether at corps, division, or brigade level, was to be coordinated through Warren. *Official Records*, vol. 25, pt. 2, 89.

10. GKW to Emily Chase, Jan. 26, March 9 (telegram), 1863, Warren Papers.

11. GKW, Daily Memoranda, March 10, 1863, Warren Papers.

12. GKW to Emily Chase, March 20, 1863, Warren Papers.

13. GKW to Emily Chase, April 17, 1863 (first), Warren Papers.

14. GKW to Emily Chase, April 17, 1863 (second), Warren Papers.

15. GKW to Emily Chase, April 22, 1863, Warren Papers.

16. GKW to Emily Chase, April 23, 1863 (first), Warren Papers.

17. GKW to Emily Chase, April 23, 1863 (second), Warren Papers.

18. GKW to Emily Chase, April 27, 28, 1863, Warren Papers.

19. GKW to Emily Chase, April 29, 1863, Warren Papers; *Official Records*, vol. 25, pt. 1, 197.

29. *Report of the Joint Committee on the Conduct of the War*, 38th Cong., 2d sess. (1865), vol. 1, 43.

21. Ibid.; GKW to Emily Chase, April 30, 1863, Warren Papers.

22. General Orders No. 47, *Official Records*, vol. 25, pt. 1, 171. Hooker that night told a newspaper reporter, "The rebel army . . . is now the legitimate property of the Army of the Potomac. They may as well pack up their haversacks and make for Richmond. I shall be after them." William Swinton, *Campaigns of the Army of the Potomac* (1866; reprint, New York: Charles Scribner's Sons, 1882), 275.

23. *Official Records*, vol. 25, pt. 1, 196–97.

24. Report of GKW, *Official Records*, vol. 25, pt. 1, 198; D. N. Couch, "The Chancellorsville Campaign," *Battles and Leaders*, vol. 3, 159. Washington Roebling, assigned to Hooker's staff, later said that Hooker drank to excess to celebrate the unhindered crossing of the Rapidan and consequently slept in a deep stupor until almost 10 A.M.

the next morning, when orders for the day's march were finally issued. W. A. Roebling to Gamaliel Bradford, Dec. 15, 1914, Roebling Papers.

25. Report of Couch, *Official Records*, vol. 25, pt. 1, 306; report of GKW, *Official Records*, vol. 25, pt. 1, 199.

26. Abner Doubleday, *Chancellorsville and Gettysburg* (New York: Charles Scribner's Sons, 1882), 14; D. N. Couch, "The Chancellorsville Campaign," *Battles and Leaders*, vol. 3, 159; *Official Records*, vol. 25, pt. 1, 199. Hooker's biographer said, "This was the supreme decision of his military career. It climaxed the almost twenty years he had devoted to the profession of soldiering. The honors won in Mexico and in the last year of solid fighting would be forgotten by many in view of this fatal decision. When he called in his advance, the battle became Lee's, not his." Hebert, *Fighting Joe Hooker*, 199.

27. Swinton, *Campaigns of the Army of the Potomac*, 280.

28. Darius N. Couch to GKW, Nov. 20, 1876, Warren Papers.

29. Walker, *History of the Second Army Corps*, 224.

30. *Official Records*, vol. 25, pt. 1, 199.

31. GKW to Daniel E. Sickles, Feb. 15, 1875, Warren Papers. See also GKW to Darius N. Couch, Nov. 17, 1876, Warren Papers.

32. *Official Records*, vol. 25, pt. 1, 200; O. B. Curtis, *History of the Twenty-Fourth Michigan of the Iron Brigade* (Detroit: Winn and Hammond, 1891), 133; *Report of the Joint Committee* (1865), vol. 1, 127 (Hooker's testimony).

33. With both Jackson and A. P. Hill wounded, Lee placed Jeb Stuart in command of the portion of his army formerly under Jackson.

34. *Official Records*, vol. 25, pt. 1, 201.

35. Stephen W. Sears, *Chancellorsville* (Boston and New York: Houghton Mifflin, 1996), 309. Warren was subsequently angered when Hooker breached his confidence by relating to "that outrageous Committee on the Conduct of the War" what Warren had said about Sedgwick not attacking had he [Warren] not been present. Sedgwick's friends were unhappy with Warren when they heard this, but what Warren said he meant "was that Hooker's order was so unreasonable [and] so misstated the facts . . . that it was enough to destroy all confidence, and this confidence my presence and a knowledge of me revived." Warren considered Hooker's attempt to cast the blame for Chancellorsville upon Sedgwick "one of the meanest of the mean things which this mean lot of men ever attempted." GKW to Col. James C. Biddle, May 26, 1877, Warren Papers.

36. *Official Records*, vol. 25, pt. 1, 202, pt. 2, 393.

37. *Official Records*, vol. 25, pt. 1, 203. Warren told Ben Wade's joint committee, "I know I urged a different arrangement of the troops before we got to that place." *Report of the Joint Committee* (1865), vol. 1, 48.

38. Sears, *Chancellorsville*, 389. The grim toll was 21,357 casualties.

39. *Official Records*, vol. 25, pt. 2, 396.

40. Warren memorandum, *Official Records*, vol. 25, pt. 1, 512; GKW to Col. James C. Biddle, May 26, 1877, Warren Papers.

41. *Official Records*, vol. 25, pt. 1, 511.

42. Report of GKW, May 12, 1863, *Official Records*, vol. 25, pt. 1, 204. I have corrected the text's "or the Rapidan."

43. *Under the Maltese Cross: Antietam to Appomattox* (Pittsburgh: 155th Regimental Association, 1910), 139–40.

44. Edward Hagerman, *The American Civil War and the Origins of Modern Warfare*

(Bloomington and Indianapolis: Indiana University Press, 1988), 91; Doubleday, *Chancellorsville and Gettysburg,* 73.

45. *Official Records,* vol. 25, pt. 1, 204. John Gibbon, who had commanded a Second Corps division that Hooker kept back at Fredericksburg for the entire battle, talked to Reynolds after it was over, to learn what had happened. "He was the picture of woe and disgust," wrote Gibbon, "and said plainly that we had been badly outgeneraled and whipped by half our number." Gibbon, *Personal Recollections of the Civil War,* 119.

9. *To Little Round Top*

1. GKW to W. J. Warren, May 8, 1863, Warren Papers. "Thirty thousand" refers to those whose terms of enlistment had expired as well as the killed, wounded, and captured.

2. GKW to Emily Chase, May 11, 1863, Warren Papers.

3. *Official Records,* vol. 25, pt. 2, 471.

4. GKW to Emily Chase, May 14, 1863, Warren Papers.

5. GKW to Emily Chase, May 16, 1863, Warren Papers.

6. GKW to Emily Chase, May 9, 17, 1863, Warren Papers.

7. GKW to Emily Chase, May 20, 1863, Warren Papers. Charles Francis Adams, Jr., writing on May 24 to his father in London, called Sickles, Butterfield, and Hooker "the disgrace and bane of this army . . . three humbugs, intriguers and demagogues." Worthington Chauncey Ford, ed., *A Cycle of Adams Letters, 1861–1865* (Boston and New York: Houghton Mifflin, 1920), vol. 2, 14–15.

8. GKW to Emily Chase, May 21, 22, 27, 30 (telegram), 1863; Emily Chase to GKW, May 26, 1863; all in Warren Papers.

9. GKW to Emily Chase, June 5, 1863, Warren Papers.

10. GKW to Emily Chase, June 11, 1863, Warren Papers.

11. Allan Nevins, ed., *A Diary of Battle: The Personal Journals of Colonel Charles S. Wainwright, 1861–1865* (New York: Harcourt Brace and World, 1962), 202; Edwin B. Coddington, *The Gettysburg Campaign: A Study in Command* (New York: Charles Scribner's Sons, 1968), 36–37.

12. Circular to the corps commanders, also D. Butterfield to John F. Reynolds, both June 13, 1863, *Official Records,* vol. 27, pt. 3, 88–89.

13. Special Orders No. 161, Headquarters, Army of the Potomac, June 13, 1863, *Official Records,* vol. 51, pt. 1, 1053; D. Butterfield to GKW, June 14, 1863, *Official Records,* vol. 27, pt. 3, 101.

14. GKW to Emily Chase, June 14, 1863, and GKW to W. S. Hancock, June 15, 1863, Warren Papers; GKW to Seth Williams, June 16, 1863, *Official Records,* vol. 27, pt. 3, 147.

15. Special Orders No. 163, Headquarters, Army of the Potomac, June 17, 1863, *Official Records,* vol. 51, pt. 1, 1059.

16. For the Potomac fords, see GKW to D. Butterfield, June 16, 1863, 5.15 P.M., *Official Records,* vol. 27, pt. 3, 148–49.

17. GKW's whereabouts before and after the wedding can be followed in the entries from June 16 through June 20 in his untitled journal, Feb. 3 to August 12, 1863, Warren Papers. D. Butterfield to GKW (telegram), June 19, 1863, 10:10 P.M., Warren Papers.

18. GKW to Emily Warren, June 21, 1863, Warren Papers.

19. GKW to Emily Warren, June 22, 1863, Warren Papers.

20. GKW to Emily Warren, June 23, 1863, Warren Papers.

21. GKW to Emily Warren, June 24, 25, 1863, Warren Papers.

22. Thos. L. Livermore, "The Gettysburg Campaign," *Civil and Mexican Wars, 1861, 1846,* Military Historical Society of Massachusetts (Boston: The Military Historical Society of Massachusetts, 1913), vol. 13, 506.

23. GKW to J. A. Hooker, June 24, 1863, Warren Papers (also in *Official Records,* vol. 27, pt. 3, 292); Coddington, *The Gettysburg Campaign,* 122, 125. Hooker's biographer felt that Warren's study "may have . . . inspired" Hooker to start moving. Walter H. Hebert, *Fighting Joe Hooker* (Indianapolis and New York: Bobbs-Merrill, 1944), 243.

24. *Official Records,* vol. 27, pt. 1, 60, 61; Coddington, *The Gettysburg Campaign,* 131.

25. G. G. Meade to Col. G. G. Benedict, March 16, 1870, in "The Meade-Sickles Controversy," *Battles and Leaders,* vol. 3, 413; Freeman Cleaves, *Meade of Gettysburg* (Norman: University of Oklahoma Press, 1960), 124–25; GKW to Porter Farley, Oct. 23, 1877, in Oliver Willcox Norton, *The Attack and Defense of Little Round Top, Gettysburg, July 2, 1863* (New York: Neale, 1913), 314–15. Oliver Norton was the flag-bearer for Strong Vincent's brigade at Little Round Top.

26. GKW to Emily Warren, June 28, 1863, Warren Papers.

27. Cleaves, *Meade of Gettysburg,* 133. The Pipe Creek Circular is in *Official Records,* vol. 27, pt. 3, 458–59.

28. GKW to Emily Warren, June 30, 1863, Warren Papers.

29. GKW to Emily Warren, July 2, 1863, Warren Papers.

30. Henry J. Hunt, "The Second Day at Gettysburg," *Battles and Leaders,* vol. 3, 297; Coddington, *The Gettysburg Campaign,* 337; Charles Elihu Slocum, *The Life and Services of Major-General Henry Warner Slocum* (Toledo: Slocum, 1913), 104; George Meade, *The Life and Letters of George Gordon Meade* (New York: Charles Scribner's Sons, 1913), vol. 2, 68; Cleaves, *Meade of Gettysburg,* 144.

31. GKW to Porter Farley, July 13, 1872, in Norton, *The Attack and Defense of Little Round Top,* 309. Warren and Porter Farley, a Rochester man who had been the adjutant for the 140th New York Volunteers, carried on an extensive correspondence, mostly about the events on and about Little Round Top, between 1872 and 1878. Farley was engaged in writing a regimental history, but Warren's half of the correspondence is published in Norton's book. Farley's description of the Little Round Top fight was published as the ninth serial of his regimental history in the *Rochester Democrat and Chronicle,* December 3, 1877.

32. *Rochester Democrat and Chronicle,* December 3, 1877; see also the report of Capt. Lemuel B. Norton, Chief Signal Officer, in *Official Records,* vol. 27, pt. 1, 202. Warren's statement about having Smith fire a shot to make the rebels reveal themselves is reported, but with some skepticism, in both Coddington, *The Gettysburg Campaign,* 740, and Harry W. Pfanz, *Gettysburg: The Second Day* (Chapel Hill and London: University of North Carolina Press, 1987), 506. Roebling, in a letter written almost exactly fifty years after the fact, says he was the first one up Little Round Top, and "one glance sufficed to note the head of Hood's Texans coming up the rocky ravine" between the Round Tops. W. A. Roebling to Col. Smith, July 5, 1913, Roebling Papers.

33. Norton, *The Attack and Defense of Little Round Top,* 309–310. See R. S. Mackenzie to G. G. Meade, March 22, 1864, *Official Records,* vol. 27, pt. 1, 138.

34. There is some dispute about the route taken by Vincent's brigade, with the alternative possibility being the direct route from the Wheatfield Road, then in front of the western side of Little Round Top, across Plum Run, and straight up the southwestern slope of the hill. But it is hard to see how Warren could have missed seeing a thousand-man brigade marching directly across his line of sight. Norton, who rode beside Vincent, is clear that the route was behind (on the east side of) Little Round Top.

35. Warren wrote, "I did not see Vincent's brigade come up, but I suppose it was

about this time they did, and coming up behind me through the woods and taking post to the left (their proper place) I did not see them." Norton, *The Attack and Defense of Little Round Top*, 310.

36. Weed, a native New Yorker, was a member of the West Point class of 1854. A month earlier, on June 6, 1863, he had been promoted from captain to brigadier general and given the brigade command. O'Rorke, born in Ireland but a resident of Rochester, graduated from West Point in 1861. Warren's words are from a statement by Captain Joseph Leeper of the 140th New York in the John B. Bachelder Papers, New Hampshire Historical Society, cited in Pfanz, *Gettysburg: The Second Day*, 225. Roebling called O'Rorke Warren's "favorite pupil at West Point." W. A. Roebling to Col. Smith, July 5, 1913, Roebling Papers.

37. In his letter to Porter Farley of July 24, 1872, Warren describes how he and some Third Corps stragglers lifted the carriage of one gun over some rocks. Norton, *The Attack and Defense of Little Round Top*, 310. Roebling also described his part in hauling the guns up the hill. W. A. Roebling to Col. Smith, July 5, 1913, Roebling Papers.

38. Porter Farley to le Comte de Paris, Oct. 21, 1877, copy in Warren Papers. Farley was sure that "Hazlett's battery and the 140th N.Y. Vols. were the troops and the only troops who held Little Round Top till the struggle for its possession was virtually over." One of Weed's aides, who received some attention for his part in the movements of the brigade, was Warren's younger brother, Edgar, whom we last heard of when he accompanied Gouv on the jaunt into the Black Hills.

39. Warren told Emily, "I got slightly wounded by a bullet grazing my throat. It was a narrow escape." GKW to Emily Warren, July 3, 1863, Warren Papers. See also Mary Genevie Green Brainard, *Campaigns of the One Hundred and Forty-Sixth Regiment New York State Volunteers* (New York and London: G. P. Putnam's Sons, 1915), 121. Hood himself was severely wounded in the arm and carried from the field after about twenty minutes of fighting. John Bell Hood, *Advance and Retreat: Personal Experiences in the United States and Confederate States Armies* (1880; reprint, Bloomington: Indiana University Press, 1959), 59.

40. Chamberlain won the Medal of Honor for his work on July 2, 1863.

41. Untitled GKW journal, Feb. 3 to Aug. 12, 1863; GKW to A. A. Humphreys, Feb. 4, 1878; both in Warren Papers.

42. Abner Doubleday, *Chancellorsville and Gettysburg* (New York: Charles Scribner's Sons, 1882), 178; A. L. Long, *Memoirs of Robert E. Lee: His Military and Personal History* (New York, Philadelphia, and Washington, D.C.: J. M. Stoddart, 1887), 284; S. W. Crawford to GKW, July 29, 1872, Warren Papers.

10. *The Aftermath of Gettysburg*

1. Pfanz summarizes the day's activities: Sickles "had abandoned vital terrain, isolated his corps, and put the entire army at special risk. It was a grievous error mitigated only by the hard and costly fighting of his corps and by the assistance given it by the corps of Hancock and Sykes. Sykes secured the Little Round Top area with the Fifth Corps, and Hancock, as usual, conducted himself magnificently. It was through Hancock's efforts in great part that the Federals were able to reestablish their position on Cemetery Ridge." Harry W. Pfanz, *Gettysburg: The Second Day* (Chapel Hill and London: University of North Carolina Press, 1987), 425.

2. John Gibbon, "The Council of War on the Second Day," *Battles and Leaders*, vol. 3, 313; Edwin B. Coddington, *The Gettysburg Campaign: A Study in Command* (New York: Charles Scribner's Sons, 1968), 449. The corps commanders present were New-

ton (First), Gibbon (Second, although Hancock was really the commander), Birney (Third), Sykes (Fifth), Sedgwick (Sixth), Howard (Eleventh), and Alpheus Williams (Twelfth, while Slocum had his higher responsibilities). In 1864, Butterfield and Birney accused Meade before the Committee on the Conduct of the War of wanting to retreat, saying that only the vote of his generals kept him at Gettysburg for another day. Virtually all of the other men present called such a charge totally wrong. Warren could be of no help to Meade on this point.

3. Thomas L. Livermore, *Days and Events, 1860–1866* (Boston and New York: Houghton Mifflin, 1920), 260.

4. Freeman Cleaves, *Meade of Gettysburg* (Norman: University of Oklahoma Press, 1960), 161; Coddington, *The Gettysburg Campaign*, 498. Actually, although the Union guns were firing beyond their targets (the Confederate artillery), their shells were doing considerable damage among the infantry waiting concealed in the trees on Seminary Ridge.

5. Cleaves, *Meade of Gettysburg*, 168.

6. GKW to Emily Warren, July 4, 1863, Warren Papers.

7. Untitled GKW journal, Feb. 3 to Aug. 12, 1863, Warren Papers.

8. GKW to Emily Warren, July 4, 1863, Warren Papers. For an assessment of Meade's reasoning on a counterattack, see Coddington, *The Gettysburg Campaign*, 532–34.

9. George Meade, *The Life and Letters of George Gordon Meade* (New York: Charles Scribner's Sons, 1913), vol. 2, 116; *Official Records*, vol. 27, pt. 3, 517.

10. *Official Records*, vol. 27, pt. 3, 554.

11. Meade, *Life and Letters*, vol. 2, 125–26; Emily Warren to GKW, July 6, 1863, Warren Papers. Cleaves wrote that Butterfield was relieved because he issued improper orders which sent the Third and Fifth corps off to Middletown; Cleaves, *Meade of Gettysburg*, 175.

12. Untitled GKW journal, Feb. 3 to Aug. 12, 1863, July 14, Warren Papers. Warren wrote to Emily, "Terrible has been the ruin of the rebel hopes as I told you it would be if they invaded the north. But we have not yet destroyed Lee's Army and the campaign must go on." GKW to Emily Warren, July 14, 1863, Warren Papers.

13. GKW to A. A. Humphreys, Oct. 24, 1881, Warren Papers; GKW to Major Woodruff, July 14, 1863, 3 P.M., *Official Records*, vol. 27, pt. 3, 691. Warren wrote to his wife that the first person he saw that he knew at Harper's Ferry was her brother Lewis, "corporal of the guard over some Commissary stores." GKW to Emily Warren, July 16, 1863, Warren Papers. Lewis Chase, Emily's ne'er-do-well brother, would be a source of vexation to his brother-in-law many times over the years to come.

14. Morris Schaff, *The Battle of the Wilderness* (Boston and New York: Houghton Mifflin, 1910), 30–31.

15. G. G. Meade to H. W. Halleck, July 19, 1863, *Official Records*, vol. 27, pt. 1, 96–97; also a copy in the Warren Papers. "I consider the efficiency and spirit of this army will be greatly promoted by making this appointment," Meade wrote. On Hays, one staffer wrote of the general's great fondness for whiskey, with sugar and water, but that he "made it a rule not to drink before 10 A.M.," although he sometimes breached that rule. Livermore, *Days and Events*, 285.

16. GKW to Emily Warren, July 12, 21, 1863, Warren Papers.

17. GKW to Emily Warren, July 22, 1863, Warren Papers.

18. H. W. Halleck to G. G. Meade, July 26, 1863, *Official Records*, vol. 27, pt. 1, 101; GKW to Emily Warren, July 26, 1863, Warren Papers.

19. GKW to W. J. Warren and GKW to Emily Warren, both July 30, 1863, Warren Papers.

20. Untitled GKW journal, Feb. 3 to Aug. 12, 1863, Aug. 3–12, Warren Papers; the order naming GKW to the Second Corps post is in *Official Records*, vol. 51, pt. 1, 1084, as well as in the Warren Papers. It was later stated that the dating back to May 3, a mark of Meade's favoritism, caused resentment, because it made Warren outrank David Birney and Alfred Pleasonton, whose promotions dated from May 29 and June 1, respectively. *(Washington) Sunday Herald*, Aug. 13, 1882.

21. *Official Records*, vol. 29, pt. 2, 120; Francis A. Walker, *History of the Second Army Corps in the Army of the Potomac* (New York: Charles Scribner's Sons, 1886), 1, 3. Hancock wrote to Warren, "I was glad when you got command of the Corps. It was my wish, so expressed to Genl Meade." W. S. Hancock to GKW, Sept. 24, 1863, Warren Papers.

22. GKW to Emily Warren, Aug. 16, July 9, 1863, both in Warren Papers.

23. GKW to Emily Warren, Aug. 24, 1863, Warren Papers. Col. Rufus Dawes of the Sixth Wisconsin, a regiment in the First Corps, wrote to his fiancée Mary Beman Gates on November 1, 1863, "General G. K. Warren of the second corps is the rising young general of this army." Rufus R. Dawes, *Service with the Sixth Wisconsin Volunteers* (Madison: State Historical Society of Wisconsin, 1962), 219. This opinion, of course, was after Bristoe Station, but it reflected a feeling widespread because of Warren's youth and rapid and merited rise.

24. GKW to Emily Warren, Aug. 27, 31, 1863, Warren Papers. In the latter missive Warren said he would provide if asked for Emily's brother Lewis, but Lewis really should go back to school. "In my experience," he wrote, "I have invariably found that educated men were always in demand and preferment was always awaiting them if they were industrious."

11. Second Corps Interlude

1. Freeman Cleaves, *Meade of Gettysburg* (Norman: University of Oklahoma Press, 1960), 193; Seth Williams to Cmdg Officer, Second Corps, Sept. 11, 1863, 10:10 P.M., *Official Records*, vol. 29, pt. 2, 169. John Newton, commanding the First Corps, got his nose out of joint at his corps' not getting the assignment. He wrote to Seth Williams that "the Officers and men of the First Corps are disappointed and mortified at . . . the inference that . . . the First Corps was not qualified." Sept. 13, 1863, *Official Records*, vol. 29, pt. 2, 176. Meade had Williams respond the next day with his reasons but then added that "he does not admit the right of any subordinate commander to call in question his acts, and he regrets that you should have thought it proper to do so." Seth Williams to John Newton, Sept. 14, 1863, *Official Records*, vol. 29, pt. 2, 181.

2. G. G. Meade to GKW, Sept. 13, 1863; GKW to Emily Warren, Sept. 14, 1863; both in Warren Papers.

3. Thomas L. Livermore, *Days and Events, 1860–1866* (Boston and New York: Houghton Mifflin, 1920), 288.

4. Andrew A. Humphreys, *From Gettysburg to the Rapidan: The Army of the Potomac July, 1863, to April, 1864* (New York: Charles Scribner's Sons, 1883), 11.

5. Livermore, *Days and Events*, 296.

6. Ibid., 297. Some time later, Roebling wrote that Warren "is such a perfect gentleman when he is sober—but 2 glasses of ale Oh Lord!" W. A. Roebling to (Miss) Emily Warren, April 3, 1864, Roebling Papers. Such tales as these, together with one or two comments made by Alfred Davenport in his letters home, indicate that Warren on occasion drank more than he should have, not altogether surprising in wartime conditions. There is virtually no evidence that he did so when action was near or that alcohol was any real problem for him. Haskell, a Dartmouth graduate and a lawyer in Madison,

Wisconsin, was actually two years older than Warren. A hero at Gettysburg as Gibbon's chief aide, Haskell left the Second Corps on November 10, 1863, and soon received promotion to lieutenant colonel and command of a regiment, at whose head he was killed at Cold Harbor. Bingham, a prominent Republican congressman after the war, won the Medal of Honor for heroism in the Wilderness, and received a brevet as a brigadier general on the last day of the war.

7. GKW to Emily Warren, Sept. 19, 22, 1863, Warren Papers.

8. GKW to Emily Warren, Oct. 5, 6, 1863, Warren Papers. Warren received a brief message, at the Chase home, reading, "Gen. Meade desires that you return at once." Seth Williams to GKW, Oct. 9, 1863, Warren Papers.

9. St. Clair A. Mulholland, *The Story of the 116th Regiment, Pennsylvania Infantry* (Philadelphia: F. McManus, Jr., 1899), 155–56, 157–58. For the orders to the Second Corps, first to cross the Rappahannock to the north, next to return to Brandy Station, and finally to return to Bealeton "immediately," see *Official Records*, vol. 29, pt. 1, 287, 295, and 298. The third order was sent at 9:15 P.M., but of course it took time to reach Warren.

10. For Meade's intention to seize Centreville Heights ahead of Lee, see the circular to the Army of the Potomac, October 13, 1863, *Official Records*, vol. 29, pt. 2, 304.

11. See William Swinton, *Campaigns of the Army of the Potomac* (1866; reprint, New York: Charles Scribner's Sons, 1882), 381–83, for the encounter at Auburn. Caldwell's report, in *Official Records*, vol. 29, pt. 1, 253–54, describes his men's reaction to the unexpected shelling, and Warren's remark is in his report. *Official Records*, vol. 29, pt. 1, 239.

12. A. A. Humphreys to GKW, Oct. 14, 1863, 10 A.M. and noon, Warren Papers.

13. G. Sykes to GKW, Oct. 14, 1863 (twice), Warren Papers.

14. Report of Hill, Oct. 26, 1863, *Official Records*, vol. 29, pt. 1, 426–27.

15. Francis A. Walker, *History of the Second Army Corps in the Army of the Potomac* (New York: Charles Scribner's Sons, 1886), 349; James I. Robertson, Jr., *General A. P. Hill: The Story of a Confederate Warrior* (New York: Random House, 1987), 236.

16. James L. Morrison, Jr., ed., *The Memoirs of Henry Heth* (Westport, Conn., and London: Greenwood Press, 1974), 180. Taylor, in his biography of Warren, writes that after the battle Warren sent Hill a message: "Hill, I have not only whipped you, but married your old sweetheart." Emerson Gifford Taylor, *Gouverneur Kemble Warren: The Life and Letters of an American Soldier, 1830–1882* (Boston and New York: Houghton Mifflin, 1932), 114. He cites no evidence for this tale.

17. G. Sykes to GKW, Oct. 14, 1863, Warren Papers. Warren's description of his reaction to this ill-timed message is in his letter to Sykes, Oct. 29, 1863, Warren Papers.

18. Report of GKW, *Official Records*, vol. 29, pt. 1, 243–44; Frank L. Byrne and Andrew T. Weaver, eds., *Haskell of Gettysburg: His Life and Civil War Papers* (Madison: State Historical Society of Wisconsin, 1970), 222; Charles D. Page, *History of the Fourteenth Regiment, Connecticut Vol. Infantry* (Meriden, Conn.: Horton Printing, 1906). Warren's letter to Emily described "one of the most trying days of my life. We had to move at 2 in the morning, were attacked all around at daybreak. We forced away the cavalry in the direction we were going . . . Marched then about 6 miles and was attacked by Hill A.P.'s corps which we repulsed capturing 500 men two battle flags, and five pieces of artillery. We held our ground fighting till after dark and then withdrew in the night, marching to this place [Centreville] and the corps getting in position all safe except losses in battle of killed." GKW to Emily Warren, Oct. 15, 1863, Warren Papers. See also Edward G. Longacre, *To Gettysburg and Beyond: The Twelfth New Jersey Volunteer Infantry, II Corps, Army of the Potomac, 1862–1865* (Hightstown, N.J.: Longstreet

House, 1988), 158, which describes "the killing march" in which "Warren pushed the column mercilessly, as though willing to sacrifice men for speed."

19. General Orders No. 96, Headquarters, Army of the Potomac, Oct. 15, 1863, *Official Records*, vol. 29, pt. 1, 250. Warren told Meade the next day that the order had been "received with enthusiasm by officers and men." He added that the corps "is satisfied if it receives no other praise than his, and is ready to perform its part of the plans of the commanding general in the future, as it has done in the past." Ibid.

20. GKW to G. Sykes, Oct. 29, 1863, Warren Papers. Swinton's article, in the Oct. 23, 1863, *New York Times*, said that Warren received from Sykes "the comforting intelligence that he 'was moving off slowly and in good order.'"

21. G. Sykes to GKW, Oct. 30, 1863, Warren Papers.

22. GKW to G. Sykes, Oct. 31, 1863, Warren Papers.

23. GKW to Emily Warren, Oct. 20, 1863, Warren Papers.

24. *Official Records*, vol. 29, pt. 1, 247. Morgan served in the Second Corps until Hancock left it and then served under Hancock to war's end. He finally received promotion to brigadier general of volunteers on May 21, 1865, shortly before reverting to his permanent rank of captain. On March 24, 1864, Morgan, having just read Warren's report on Bristoe, wrote to Warren to say he was "extremely gratified at the very handsome manner in which you alluded to my services." C. H. Morgan to GKW, Warren Papers.

25. Cornelius Hook to GKW, Oct. 21, 1863, and GKW to Emily Warren, Nov. 5, 1863, Warren Papers. Emily and her young brother Willie did get to Cold Spring for the wedding.

26. Letter of Oct. 31, 1863, Byrne and Weaver, eds., *Haskell of Gettysburg*, 225.

27. GKW to Emily Warren, Nov. 11, 13, 1863, Warren Papers. "Genl Meade won't let anyone go nor has he ever been willing to do it since he came in command. He seems to be afraid to let one man off, and in this I think he makes a great mistake. Thousands of us are quite miserable from this weary life and a little change or hope of it would probably strengthen and enliven us." GKW to Emily Warren, Nov. 15, 1863, Warren Papers.

28. GKW to Emily Warren, Nov. 15, 16, 1863, Warren Papers.

29. GKW to Emily Warren, Nov. 18, 1863, Warren Papers. Warren eventually became good friends with the flamboyant cavalryman.

30. GKW to Emily Warren, Nov. 26, 1863, Warren Papers. For French, see Meade's testimony to the Committee on the Conduct of the War, printed in George Meade, *The Life and Letters of George Gordon Meade* (New York: Charles Scribner's Sons, 1913), vol. 2, 373–74. Warren cited French's failures in this campaign as "proof of utter incompetency." GKW to A. A. Humphreys, Dec. 3, 1863, Warren Papers.

31. Curiously, in later testimony before the Committee on the Conduct of the War, Warren said, "I wish to have it distinctly understood that it was no scheme of mine at all to attack this place . . . [That] the plan of that fight did not depend on anything that I said that night is apparent from the fact that the troops on the right were already in position for the attack before I got to General Meade. I put the best face that I could on it then." *Report of the Joint Committee*, 38th Cong., 2d sess. (1865), vol. 1, 386–87. This appears to be disingenuous and may be explained by another statement he made, "I am personally a great deal on trial about Mine Run." Ibid. Marsena Patrick, no admirer of Warren, told the committee that Warren assured Meade he could carry the position "without having examined sufficiently." Ibid., 474.

32. *Official Records*, vol. 29, pt. 2, 516.

33. Mulholland, *Story of the 116th Regiment*, 166; Livermore, *Days and Events*, 301.

34. Report of GKW, *Official Records*, vol. 29, pt. 1, 697–98; W. A. Roebling to J. F. Rusling, Feb. 8, 1916, Roebling Papers. Regimental histories confirm the pinning of

names to the uniform: Page, *History of the Fourteenth Regiment*, 202, and Longacre, *To Gettysburg and Beyond*, 167. "No assault could have succeeded," Roebling said. "Ten thousand men would have been slaughtered." This is of course an opinion from fifty-three years later, but the point of it is still clear: there would have been fearful losses.

35. A. A. Humphreys to GKW, Nov. 30, 1863, 6:30 A.M., Warren Papers; Livermore, *Days and Events*, 303–304; George R. Agassiz, ed., *Meade's Headquarters, 1863–65: Letters of Colonel Theodore Lyman from the Wilderness to Appomattox* (Boston: Atlantic Monthly, 1922), 56. Warren's note to Meade, marked 7:45 A.M., said that the position and strength of the enemy "seem so formidable in my present front that I advise against making the attack here. The full light of the sun shows me that I cannot succeed." *Official Records*, vol. 29, pt. 2, 517.

36. David S. Sparks, ed., *Inside Lincoln's Army: The Diary of Marsena Rudolph Patrick, Provost Marshal General, Army of the Potomac* (New York and London: Thomas Yoseloff, 1964), 317; *New York Tribune*, Dec. 5, 1863. Harry Heth, whose men were behind the defenses confronting Warren, hoped he would attack "in order that I might square accounts with him for his treatment of me at Bristoe Station." Morrison, ed., *The Memoirs of Henry Heth*, 180.

37. The circular assigning troop movements to liquidate the campaign is dated December 1, 1863. *Official Records*, vol. 29, pt. 2, 530–32.

12. *Fallout, 1863–1864*

1. GKW to Emily Warren, Dec. 3, 4, 1863; GKW to W. J. Warren, Dec. 4, 1863; all in Warren Papers.

2. GKW to Emily Warren, Dec. 7, 1863, Warren Papers.

3. GKW to A. A. Humphreys, Dec. 3, 1863, Warren Papers. Henry Prince and Henry D. Terry were the two division commanders named.

4. Thomas L. Livermore, *Days and Events, 1860–1866* (Boston and New York: Houghton Mifflin, 1920), 308–309.

5. George Meade, *The Life and Letters of George Gordon Meade* (New York: Charles Scribner's Sons, 1913), vol. 2, 157; Lt. Col. J. H. Lockwood, Seventh (West) Virginia, to GKW, Dec. 5, 1863, Warren Papers; Rufus Dawes to Mary B. Gates, Dec. 2, 1863, Dawes, *Service with the Sixth Wisconsin Volunteers* (Madison: State Historical Society of Wisconsin, 1962), 225.

6. Mary Genevie Green Brainard, *Campaigns of the One Hundred and Forty-Sixth Regiment New York State Volunteers* (New York and London: G. P. Putnam's Sons, 1915), 145; Livermore, *Days and Events*, 304.

7. W. S. Hancock to GKW, Sept. 24, 1863, Warren Papers; Special Orders No. 7, Jan. 8, 1864, and report of a commission on Hancock's absence, approved by Meade, Jan. 8, 1864, Letters Received, Commission Branch, Adj. Gen. Office, 1863–1870, National Archives; *Official Records*, vol. 51, pt. 1, 1139; *Official Records*, vol. 33, 1.

8. GKW to Emily Warren, Dec. 8, 1863, Warren Papers.

9. GKW to Emily Warren, Dec. 10, 1863, Warren Papers.

10. Special Orders No. 281, Second Corps, Dec. 13, 1863, Roebling Papers; GKW to Emily Warren, Dec. 12, 16 (telegram), 1863, Jan. 7, 1864; entries, Jan. 1–8, 1864, Journal, Warren Papers.

11. GKW to Emily Warren, Jan. 11, 13, 16, 1864, Warren Papers; W. A. Roebling to J. A. Roebling, Jan. 9, 1864, Roebling Papers. On the 16th, Hancock wrote Warren from Harrisburg, Pa., assuring him, "If you do not get a corps . . . I rely upon you for one of the Divisions in this operation." W. S. Hancock to GKW, Jan. 16, 1864, Warren Papers.

12. Lizzie W. Burnass to GKW, Jan. 27, 1864 (telegram), Warren Papers; A. A. Humphreys to Becky Humphreys, Jan. 28, 1864, Humphreys Papers.

13. Report of GKW, *Official Records*, vol. 33, 114, 515–16 (orders for the demonstration). A captain in the Fourteenth Connecticut named William H. Hawley later wrote that Warren, rather than being unwell, was in fact drunk. Since he said that Hays, commanding the division, and Charles Powers, the brigade commander, were also drunk, since Warren was not present and thus not under Hawley's observation, and since no one else seems to have noticed or mentioned any of this, the story may be doubted. Charles D. Page, *History of the Fourteenth Regiment, Connecticut Vol. Infantry* (Meriden, Conn.: Horton Printing, 1906), 225. We can note, too, that Warren was always conscientious about the performance of his duties, no matter what his other failings may have been, and it seems inconceivable for him to get drunk when he knew there was a military operation immediately ahead.

14. GKW to Emily Warren, Feb. 6, 1864, Warren Papers. Warren, of course, had had first-hand experience of Butler's bumbling, at Big Bethel in 1861.

15. Washington *Daily Chronicle*, Feb. 27, 1864; G. G. Meade to Mrs. Meade, Feb. 24, 1864, Meade, *Life and Letters*, vol. 2, 167; A. S. Chase to GKW (telegram), Feb. 28, 1864, and GKW to Emily Warren, March 1, 1864, Warren Papers.

16. GKW to Emily Warren, March 3, 1864 (misdated '63), Warren Papers.

17. War Dept., Special Orders No. 103, March 3, 1864, ordered Warren to report to the chairman of the Committee "at such time as the exigencies of the service will justify"; Meade wired Warren March 7, 1864, at 8:45 P.M., to "get before the Committee as soon as possible"; both in Warren Papers.

18. *Report of the Joint Committee on the Conduct of the War*, 38th Cong., 2d sess. (1865), vol. 1, 384, 388. Warren's testimony on Chancellorsville on March 9, 1864, is printed in the report on pp. 43–50, and on Gettysburg on pp. 376–82 (March 9) and pp. 382–88 (March 10).

19. Seth Williams to GKW, March 21, 1864, Warren Papers.

20. Seth Williams to GKW, March 23, 1864, 2.10 P.M., Warren Papers, and also in *Official Records*, vol. 33, 718.

21. War Dept., General Orders No. 115, March 23, 1864, *Official Records*, vol. 33, 717–18; W. A. Roebling to J. F. Rusling, Feb. 8, 1916, Roebling Papers.

22. Freeman Cleaves, *Meade of Gettysburg* (Norman: University of Oklahoma Press, 1960), 221; A. A. Humphreys to Becky Humphreys, March 25, 1864, Humphreys Papers; Allan Nevins, ed., *A Diary of Battle: The Personal Journals of Colonel Charles S. Wainwright, 1861–1865* (New York: Harcourt Brace and World, 1962), 335; W. A. Roebling to (Miss) Emily Warren, April 10, 1864, Roebling Papers.

23. GKW to Emily Warren, March 24, 1864, Warren Papers; Edward G. Longacre, *To Gettysburg and Beyond: The Twelfth New Jersey Volunteer Infantry, II Corps, Army of the Potomac, 1862–1865* (Hightstown, N.J.: Longstreet House, 1988), 178; *Under the Maltese Cross: Antietam to Appomattox* (Pittsburgh: 155th Regimental Association, 1910), 233; Nevins, ed., *A Diary of Battle*, 338.

24. GKW to Emily Warren, March 24, 25, 1864, Warren Papers.

25. George R. Agassiz, ed., *Meade's Headquarters, 1863–1865: Letters of Colonel Theodore Lyman from the Wilderness to Appomattox* (Boston: Atlantic Monthly, 1922), 82. Grant's aide Adam Badeau wrote that "Sheridan had almost grown up as a general under Grant's own eye, until finally the chief declared the subordinate the peer of any soldier of any time . . . The history of their relation is like a story from Homer . . . the friendship of chieftains, the love of strong men who had stood side by side in war, and

watched each other's deeds." Adam Badeau, *Grant in Peace: From Appomattox to Mount McGregor* (Hartford, Conn.: S. S. Scranton, 1887), 95.

26. GKW to Emily Warren, March 26, 1864, Warren Papers.

27. General Orders No. 10, Army of the Potomac, March 24, 1864, *Official Records*, vol. 33, 722; S. W. Crawford to GKW, March 23, 1864, Warren Papers.

28. Draft of report in GKW's hand to Seth Williams, early Sept. 1864, Warren Papers.

29. Harold Adams Small, ed., *The Road to Richmond: The Civil War Memoirs of Major Abner R. Small of the Sixteenth Maine Volunteers* (Berkeley: University of California Press, 1939), 149.

30. Andrew A. Humphreys, *The Virginia Campaign of '64 and '65* (New York: C. Scribner's Sons, 1883), 13.

31. GKW to Emily Warren, March 27, 1864, Warren Papers.

32. GKW to Emily Warren, March 31, 1864, Warren Papers; W. A. Roebling to (Miss) Emily Warren, April 1, 1864, Roebling Papers.

33. Nevins, ed., *A Diary of Battle*, 338–39.

34. (Miss) Emily Warren to GKW, April 7, 1864. Emily continued to her brother, "I have always clung to you with a peculiar devotion. Your marriage has not in the least altered our feeling for each other and I trust that mine would not." On the sword, see W. A. Roebling to (Miss) Emily Warren, April 21, 1864, Roebling Papers. Roebling, who had received his father's hearty consent to the proposed match, was fearful of the reaction of "that fraternal relative of yours known familiarly as GeKay." He said, "[I]f I didn't stand in official relationship with your brother I wouldn't feel half the delicacy that I do." W. A. Roebling to (Miss) Emily Warren, April 4, 1864, Roebling Papers. He was quite happy that Emily took it upon herself "to tell Gouv," relieving him of the chore. W. A. Roebling to (Miss) Emily Warren, April 5, 1864, Roebling Papers.

35. GKW to Emily Warren, April 26, 30, 1864, Warren Papers.

36. St. Clair A. Mulholland, *The Story of the 116th Regiment, Pennsylvania Infantry* (Philadelphia: F. McManus, Jr., 1899), 170.

13. Into the Deep, Dark Woods

1. Sartell Prentice, "The Opening Hours in the Wilderness in 1864," *Military Essays and Recollections: Papers Read Before the Commandery of the State of Illinois*, Military Order of the Loyal Legion of the United States, Commandery of the State of Illinois (Chicago: Dial Press, 1894), vol. 2, 101.

2. Andrew A. Humphreys, *The Virginia Campaign of '64 and '65* (New York: Charles Scribner's Sons, 1883), 14. The three infantry corps contained 3506 officers and 69,884 men, and the artillery comprised 274 pieces. With more than 19,000 men in the Ninth Corps, the combined total surpassed 90,000 men, to Lee's estimated 62,000. J. H. Wilson to GKW, from Germanna Ford, 4:40 A.M., 5:50 A.M., May 4, 1864, Warren Papers (also in *Official Records*, vol. 36, pt. 2, 377); Morris Schaff, *The Battle of the Wilderness* (Boston and New York: Houghton Mifflin, 1910), 86.

3. William Swinton, *Campaigns of the Army of the Potomac* (1866; reprint, New York: Charles Scribner's Sons, 1882), 412; Ulysses S. Grant, *Personal Memoirs of U. S. Grant* (Cleveland: World Publishing, 1952), 414.

4. GKW to Emily Warren, May 1, 1864 (completed May 3, for he concludes, "As soon as I send this letter . . . I mount my horse"), Warren Papers.

5. Allan Nevins, ed., *A Diary of Battle: The Personal Journals of Colonel Charles S. Wainwright, 1861–1865* (New York: Harcourt Brace and World, 1962), 347–48.

6. Harold Adams Small, ed., *The Road to Richmond: The Civil War Memoirs of Major Abner R. Small of the Sixteenth Maine Volunteers* (Berkeley: University of California Press, 1939), 130–31.

7. Schaff, *The Battle of the Wilderness*, 57–58; *Under the Maltese Cross: Antietam to Appomattox* (Pittsburgh: 155th Regimental Association, 1910), 241.

8. Humphreys, *Virginia Campaign*, 11. General Alexander Webb estimated these trains as taking up sixty-five miles; he said they "were until 2 P.M. of May 5th in passing over Culpeper Mine Ford and Germanna Ford." A. S. Webb, "Through the Wilderness," *Battles and Leaders*, vol. 4, 153.

9. W. A. Roebling to O. W. Norton, July 13, 1915; W. A. Roebling to H. G. Pearson, Dec. 1910; both in Roebling Papers.

10. GKW to A. A. Humphreys, 3:50 P.M., May 4, 1864, Warren Papers (also *Official Records*, vol. 36, pt. 2, 378); Schaff, *The Battle of the Wilderness*, 98.

11. Headquarters, Army of the Potomac, 6 P.M., May 4, 1864; Fifth Corps orders, 8:30 P.M., May 4, 1864; both in Warren Papers, and in *Official Records*, vol. 36, pt. 2, 371, 378–79.

12. GKW to C. H. Porter, Nov. 21, 1875, Warren Papers.

13. GKW to A. A. Humphreys, May 5, 1864, 5 A.M., Warren Papers (also *Official Records*, vol. 36, pt. 2, 413); Schaff, *The Battle of the Wilderness*, 126.

14. *Official Records*, vol. 36, pt. 2, 415 (also in Warren Papers). "I do not believe that Warren ever had a greater surprise in his life," wrote Morris Schaff, "but his thin, solemn, darkly sallow face was nowhere lightened by even a transitory flare." Schaff, *The Battle of the Wilderness*, 126. Jenkins, the commander of the pickets on the turnpike, was killed in the fighting of that morning.

15. GKW to his division commanders, May 5, 1864, 6 A.M., Warren Papers; Fred. C. Locke (the corps chief of staff) to C. Griffin, May 5, 1864, 6:20 A.M., *Official Records*, vol. 36, pt. 2, 416; GKW to A. A. Humphreys, May 5, 1864, 6 A.M., *Official Records*, vol. 36, pt. 2, 413. The "such demonstrations" sentence was also included in the messages to the Fifth Corps division commanders and may have remained in the message to Meade by inadvertence.

16. G. G. Meade to U. S. Grant, May 5, 1864 (recd. 7:30 A.M.), *Official Records*, vol. 36, pt. 2, 403.

17. U. S. Grant to G. G. Meade, 8:24 A.M., May 5, 1864, ibid.

18. G. G. Meade to GKW, May 5, 1864, *Official Records*, ibid., 404.

19. Mary Genevie Green Brainard, *Campaigns of the One Hundred and Forty-Sixth Regiment New York State Volunteers* (New York and London: G. P. Putnam's Sons, 1915), 187–88. The Confederates Crawford spotted on the plank road were in fact from Heth's division, the vanguard of Hill's corps.

20. GKW to C. H. Porter, Nov. 21, 1875, Warren Papers; Schaff, *The Battle of the Wilderness*, 128. Schaff wrote that he was within ten feet of Meade when he heard the general make this statement.

21. F. T. Locke to S. W. Crawford, May 5, 1864, 7:30 A.M., *Official Records*, vol. 36, pt. 2, 417; GKW to S. W. Crawford, May 5, 1864, ibid., 418; GKW to S. W. Crawford, May 5, 1864, 11:50 A.M., ibid., 419; Humphreys, *Virginia Campaign*, 24–25.

22. Schaff, *The Battle of the Wilderness*, 129; see also the report of Capt. F. H. Cowdrey, aide to Wadsworth, on Wadsworth's operations of May 5–6, 1864, Warren Papers. It was here that a staffer pointed out a bare knoll to Warren and suggested that it would be a good place for a battery; Warren "coolly observed that when he wanted advice from his staff he would ask for it." Schaff, *The Battle of the Wilderness*, 129. Schaff was appalled at the mean-spiritedness of this reply but allowed that Warren was under considerable pressure at the time.

23. Schaff, *The Battle of the Wilderness*, 138. Warren noted in his letterbook on May 5, "These records of this day's operations do not show what passed between the corps commander and Genl Meade. He and Genl Grant were personally so close at hand that nearly all important communications were made verbally." He also wrote, "The death of Genl Wadsworth on the 6th and the serious wound of Genl Robinson prevented my getting copies from them of any field dispatches and instructions which I had not time to copy myself." Warren Papers.

24. William Swan, "The Battle of the Wilderness," *Papers of the Military Historical Society of Massachusetts*, vol. 6 (Boston: The Military Historical Society of Massachusetts, 1907), 129–30.

25. GKW to C. H. Porter, Nov. 21, 1875, Warren Papers; Brainard, *Campaigns of the One Hundred and Forty-Sixth Regiment*, 187–88; W. A. Roebling to Morris Schaff, May 18, 1909; W. A. Roebling to J. F. Rusling, Jan. 14, 1910; both in Roebling Papers.

26. Swan, "The Battle of the Wilderness," 150.

27. Prentice, "The Opening Hours in the Wilderness in 1864," 116–17.

28. Prentice, "The Opening Hours in the Wilderness in 1864," 117; Gordon C. Rhea, *The Battle of the Wilderness, May 5–6, 1864* (Baton Rouge and London: Louisiana State University Press, 1994), 152–55. Rhea's book is the best study written of this confused and confounding battle.

29. Report of W. A. Roebling, 8, Warren Papers. Warren noted, on his copy of Roebling's report, "The responsibility of sending this section of Artillery with the advance, rests upon me. G. K. Warren." Porter Farley, adjutant of the 140th New York, wrote later that Warren told him he had ordered up the guns "so that when the enemy should be broken the guns might open fire, and their sound being heard along the line, thus give confidence to our men." *Under the Maltese Cross*, 246.

30. Humphreys, *Virginia Campaign*, 27. Roebling's report said that "the brigade of McCandless had been handled even worse than the rest, being almost surrounded and losing about two whole regiments by capture." Report of W. A. Roebling, 7, Warren Papers.

31. George R. Agassiz, ed., *Meade's Headquarters, 1863–1865: Letters of Colonel Theodore Lyman from the Wilderness to Appomattox* (Boston: Atlantic Monthly, 1922), 91. See also Schaff, *The Battle of the Wilderness*, 166.

32. Brainard, *Campaigns of the One Hundred and Forty-Sixth Regiment*, 185; Nevins, ed., *A Diary of Battle*, 351.

33. GKW to C. H. Porter, Nov. 21, 1875, Warren Papers. "This is not an afterthought of mine," Warren continued. "I saw it at once at the time." Rhea commented, "There was no excuse for his [Meade's] forcing Warren forward until he was ready and until Wright's full weight could be brought to bear . . . Delaying an hour or two would have made no appreciable difference in Ewell's strength but could have materially increased Warren's chance of success." Rhea, *Wilderness*, 173.

34. F. T. Locke to A. A. Humphreys, 5:45 P.M., May 5, 1864, *Official Records*, vol. 36, pt. 2, 414.

35. Schaff, *The Battle of the Wilderness*, 188–89; Rhea, *Wilderness*, 231.

36. A. A. Humphreys to GKW, 6 P.M., May 5, 1864, *Official Records*, vol. 36, pt. 2, 415; Rhea, *Wilderness*, 246.

37. Report of W. A. Roebling, May 5, 1864, 9–10, Warren Papers.

38. Schaff, *The Battle of the Wilderness*, 209–210. "After that," Schaff wrote, "I always doubted reports of casualties until officially certified." Ibid. Rhea comments that Warren's "reputation headed Meade's casualty list . . . Never again would the compulsive New Yorker command Grant's and Meade's unquestioning respect." Rhea, *Wilderness*, 252.

39. Prentice, "The Opening Hours in the Wilderness in 1864," 118–19.

40. G. G. Meade to GKW, 10 P.M., May 5, 1864, *Official Records*, vol. 36, pt. 2, 415 (4:30 attack); G. G. Meade to U. S. Grant, 10:30 P.M., May 5, 1864, ibid., 404–405; Lt. Col. W. R. Rowley to G. G. Meade, May 5, 1864, ibid., 405; A. A. Humphreys to GKW, 11:30 P.M., May 5, 1864, ibid., 415 (change to 5:00 A.M.).

41. GKW to A. A. Humphreys, 5:30 A.M., May 6, 1864, Warren Papers, also *Official Records*, vol. 36, pt. 2, 449.

42. G. G. Meade to U. S. Grant, 6 A.M., May 6, 1864, *Official Records*, vol. 36, pt. 2, 438; GKW to A. A. Humphreys, 6:25 A.M., May 6, 1864, *Official Records*, vol. 36, pt. 2, 450; report of GKW, *Official Records*, vol. 36, pt. 1, 540; A. A. Humphreys to GKW, 6 A.M., May 6, 1864, *Official Records*, vol. 36, pt. 2, 449.

43. A. A. Humphreys to GKW, 7:15 A.M., May 6, 1864, *Official Records*, vol. 36, pt. 2, 450.

44. At 9:30 A.M., Humphreys sent a dispatch to Warren to "suspend your operations on the right & send some force to prevent the enemy from pushing past your left near your Head Q. They have driven in Cutler in disorder & are following him." A. A. Humphreys to GKW, 9:30 A.M., May 6, 1864, Warren Papers, also *Official Records*, vol. 36, pt. 2, 451.

45. A. A. Humphreys to GKW, 10:35 A.M., May 6, 1864, *Official Records*, vol. 36, pt. 2, 451–52.

46. GKW to W. J. Warren, May 7, 1864, Warren Papers. "The afternoon was accordingly spent in making the necessary preparation," Roebling wrote, "getting off the wagons and wounded; the ambulance trains did not move until the last moment; 500 wounded were left owing to want of transportation; they were recovered a week afterwards . . . under a flag of truce." Report of W. A. Roebling, 18, Warren Papers.

14. Bloody Spotsylvania

1. "Make all preparations during the day for a night march, to take position at Spotsylvania Court-House with one army corps . . . I think it would be advisable . . . to leave Hancock where he is until Warren passes him." U. S. Grant to G. G. Meade, 6:30 A.M., May 7, 1864, *Official Records*, vol. 36, pt. 2, 481. The order directing the Fifth Corps to "move to Spotsylvania Courthouse, by way of Brock road and Todd's Tavern" was a general order issued to the army by Meade at 3 P.M., May 7, *Official Records*, vol. 36, pt. 2, 483–84.

2. Report of W. A. Roebling, 18–19, Warren Papers. Roebling stated the order of march to be Cutler, Robinson, Crawford, and Griffin, but there is doubt about that, as Robinson's division seems to have been the first one on the road. The order of march given here was considered "probable" in William D. Matter, *If It Takes All Summer: The Battle of Spotsylvania* (Chapel Hill and London: University of North Carolina Press, 1988), 46.

3. *Under the Maltese Cross: Antietam to Appomattox* (Pittsburgh: 155th Regimental Association, 1910), 266; Allan Nevins, ed., *A Diary of Battle: The Personal Journals of Colonel Charles S. Wainwright, 1861–1865* (New York: Harcourt Brace and World, 1962), 355; Charles Camper and J. W. Kirkley, *Historical Record of the First Regiment Maryland Infantry* (Washington, D.C.: Gibson Bros., 1871), 131.

4. *Rochester Democrat and Chronicle*, Jan. 30, 1878.

5. Matter is quite hard on Warren for not being "at the head of his command during this critical movement," while Cleaves said, "With Warren some miles back, in his proper position, watching the withdrawal, Meade took steps to remove the obstruc-

tion." Matter, *If It Takes All Summer,* 48; Freeman Cleaves, *Meade of Gettysburg* (Norman: University of Oklahoma Press, 1960), 241.

6. G. G. Meade to Torbert or Merritt, First Cavalry Division, 1 A.M., May 8, 1864, *Official Records,* vol. 36, pt. 2, 552. At the same time, Meade fired off a message to Sheridan: "I find Generals Gregg and Torbert [he meant Merritt] without orders. They are in the way of the infantry and there is no time to refer to you. I have given them the inclosed orders, which you can modify today after the infantry corps are in position." *Official Records,* vol. 36, pt. 2, 551.

7. Report of W. A. Roebling, 20, Warren Papers; Nevins, ed., *A Diary of Battle,* 356.

8. Nevins, ed., *A Diary of Battle,* 356.

9. GKW to A. A. Humphreys, May 8, 1864, 5 A.M., 6:45 A.M., *Official Records,* vol. 36, pt. 2, 538–39.

10. Nevins, ed., *A Diary of Battle,* 356; GKW to A. A. Humphreys, 8 A.M., May 8, 1864, *Official Records,* vol. 36, pt. 2, 539.

11. Col. Charles L. Pierson, the regimental commander, quoted in Alfred S. Roe, *The Thirty-Ninth Regiment, Massachusetts Volunteers, 1862–65* (Worcester, Mass.: Regimental Veteran Assn., 1914), 180; report of W. A. Roebling, 21, Warren Papers.

12. Morris Schaff, *The Battle of the Wilderness* (Boston and New York: Houghton Mifflin, 1910), 229–30. Schaff speculates that this may have been the same sharpshooter who shot and killed Sedgwick at virtually the same place the next day. Several observers commented on Warren's dress on this occasion; see, for example, Donald L. Smith, *The Twenty-Fourth Michigan of the Iron Brigade* (Harrisburg, Pa.: Stackpole, 1962), 192. Warren, after Spotsylvania, dressed in "the plain fatigue dress of his rank." *Under the Maltese Cross,* 264.

13. Harold Adams Small, ed., *The Road to Richmond: The Civil War Memoirs of Major Abner R. Small of the Sixteenth Maine Volunteers* (Berkeley: University of California Press, 1939), 126; Roe, *The Thirty-Ninth Regiment,* 180. In his report, Roebling confirms that "up to this time we thought we were fighting cavalry." Report of W. A. Roebling, 22, Warren Papers.

14. Schaff, *The Battle of the Wilderness,* 91.

15. Charles H. Morgan, the chief of staff of the Second Corps, later wrote Warren that he had been told by a member of Ayres's staff that Ayres's troops were thrown piecemeal, "by Regiment—or otherwise," into the fight, that one of his regiments was pitched into the action without Ayres's knowledge, "giving the idea generally that the fight was precipitated while the column was en route." Ayres had, by remarks to his staff, complained "that he was forced into action without preparation." C. H. Morgan to GKW, March 8, 1868, Warren Papers.

16. Camper and Kirkley, *Historical Record of the First Regiment Maryland Infantry,* 132; report of W. A. Roebling, 22–23, Warren Papers; GKW to A. A. Humphreys, 10:15 A.M., May 8, 1864, *Official Records,* vol. 36, pt. 2, 539–40.

17. John Sedgwick to A. A. Humphreys, 12:10 P.M., May 8, 1864, *Official Records,* vol. 36, pt. 2, 544; Matter, *If It Takes All Summer,* 66.

18. Meade endorsement on GKW dispatch of 10:15 A.M., May 8, 1864, and G. G. Meade to GKW, noon, May 8, 1864, both in *Official Records,* vol. 36, pt. 2, 540; GKW to A. A. Humphreys, 12:30 P.M., May 8, 1864, ibid., 540–41. Around noon., Warren sent a courier to Hancock at Todd's Tavern, asking him to "send me down a good division," and ammunition, too, if he could spare any. Warren feared "I cannot do much more if I am attacked." Hancock, apparently assuming Warren had cleared this request with Meade, promptly sent Gibbon down the road, but he said he had no spare ammunition. GKW to W. S. Hancock, May 8, 1864, and W. S. Hancock to GKW, 12:25 P.M.,

May 8, 1864, ibid., 532. Meade subsequently turned Gibbon's division around. As to the two divisions of Longstreet's corps, Warren was correct; by this time Charles W. Field's division had joined Kershaw.

19. One authority suggests that Warren did not have his men entrench before going into battle, as he customarily would have done, because he knew they were so tired that he did not want to give them any more labor before the fighting started. Edward Hagerman, *The American Civil War and the Origins of Modern Warfare* (Bloomington and Indianapolis: Indiana University Press, 1988), 257. Warren himself, in the personal journal he kept for this battle, described the morning's activities as follows: The cavalry "gave it up about 6 A.M. *May 8th* and got out of our way. Genl Robinson's division immediately went forward lead by himself. We at once cleared out the enemy's cavalry and the wood with which they had obstructed the road and advancing rapidly struck the advance of Longstreet's corps near the Block house. This we forced back till we gained a good position and were compelled then to await reinforcements." GKW Journal, May 4–19, mailed by GKW to Emily Warren, May 20, 1864, Warren Papers.

20. G. G. Meade to GKW, 1:30 P.M., A. A. Humphreys to GKW, 2 P.M., GKW to G. G. Meade, 2 P.M., all May 8, 1864, all in *Official Records*, vol. 36, pt. 2, 541.

21. James Harrison Wilson, *Under the Old Flag* (New York and London: D. Appleton, 1912), vol. 1, 395–96. Wilson wrote that Warren told him this story several years after the war; it is *not* the report of any witness. The dispute with Sheridan was over the role the cavalry played (or did not play) in the march of the night before. In the course of the shouting, Sheridan had occasion to chastise the Fifth Corps, saying there was no force worth speaking of in front of it that day. Roe, *The Thirty-Ninth Regiment*, 182. This seems to be the first manifestation of any ill feeling between Sheridan and Warren. Wash Roebling later wrote, "Sheridan's hatred of Warren dates back to the night march from the Wilderness to Spottsylvania when Sheridan's cavalry got in the way and prevented the 5th Corps from reaching Spottsylvania in time. Warren complained of him at HdQrtrs and Sheridan never forgot it." W. A. Roebling memorandum, apparently 1914, Roebling Papers.

22. GKW to G. G. Meade, 9 P.M., May 8, 1864, Warren Papers (slightly different in *Official Records*, vol. 36, pt. 2, 542). Charles Dana, the undersecretary of war, who exhibited an unremitting hostility to Warren, described the day's activities in a letter to Stanton: "General Grant at once [after the Confederates fell back to Laurel Hill] gave orders for attacking these troops with the whole of Warren's corps, to whose support Sedgwick was hurrying up, in order to destroy them before the rest of the rebel army could arrive. Warren, however, proceeded with extreme caution, and when he finally did attack, sent a single division at a time, and was constantly repulsed. The general attack which Generals Grant and Meade directed was never made, for reasons which I have not yet been able to learn, but successive assaults were made upon this and that point in the rebel positions, with no decisive results." *Official Records*, vol. 36, pt. 1, 64. One wonders from whom Dana was getting his information.

23. A. A. Humphreys to John Sedgwick, 6:30 A.M., May 9, 1864, *Official Records*, vol. 36, pt. 2, 576–77; A. A. Humphreys to GKW, 10:30 A.M., May 9, 1864, and memorandum of W. A. Roebling, 7:40 A.M., May 9, 1864, both ibid., 574.

24. Mark De Wolfe Howe, ed., *Touched with Fire: Civil War Letters and Diary of Oliver Wendell Holmes, Jr., 1861–1864* (Cambridge: Harvard University Press, 1946), 109–110; Special Orders No. 21, Headquarters, Armies of the United States, May 9, 1864, *Official Records*, vol. 36, pt. 2, 577.

25. GKW to A. A. Humphreys, 9:30 A.M., May 9, 1864, Warren Papers. This letter was marked "*never sent*" but a notation on it dated Nov. 21 reads, "In looking over my dis-

patches I find this one which was written and never sent. As I have however no reason to change the views expressed in it I retain it. G. K. Warren."

26. Nevins, ed., *A Diary of Battle*, 360.

27. G. G. Meade to GKW, May 9, 1864 (recd. 5:40 P.M.), *Official Records*, vol. 36, pt. 2, 575.

28. G. G. Meade to GKW, 10 A.M., May 10, 1864, ibid., 604.

29. John Gibbon, *Personal Recollections of the Civil War* (New York and London: Putnam's, 1928), 218–19.

30. G. G. Meade to U. S. Grant, 3:30 P.M., May 10, *Official Records*, vol. 36, pt. 2, 596; A. A. Humphreys to W. S. Hancock, 3:30 P.M., May 10, 1864, ibid., 600; report of W. A. Roebling, 32–33, Warren Papers; Gibbon, *Personal Recollections of the Civil War*, 219. Rhea implies that this accelerated attack was urged by Warren solely because Hancock was temporarily absent so he, Warren, could lead it. Gordon C. Rhea, *The Battles for Spotsylvania Court House and the Road to Yellow Tavern, May 7–12, 1864* (Baton Rouge and London: Louisiana University Press, 1997), 143.

31. Rufus Dawes to Emily Warren, Jan. 24, 1887, Warren Papers. The same incident is described in Rufus R. Dawes, *Service with the Sixth Wisconsin Volunteers* (Madison: State Historical Society of Wisconsin, 1962), 265–66.

32. Nevins, ed., *A Diary of Battle*, 364.

33. C. A. Dana to E. M. Stanton, 7 A.M., May 11, 1864, *Official Records*, vol. 36, pt. 1, 66–67; Adam Badeau, *Military History of Ulysses S. Grant, from April, 1861, to April, 1865* (New York: D. Appleton, 1885), vol. 2, 163.

34. Nevins, ed., *A Diary of Battle*, 362–63.

35. Ibid., 364; U. S. Grant to H. W. Halleck, 8:30 A.M., May 11, 1864, *Official Records*, vol. 36, pt. 2, 627; U. S. Grant to G. G. Meade, 3 P.M., May 11, 1864, ibid., 629.

36. GKW to S. W. Crawford (copies to other division commanders), 5 A.M., May 12, 1864, *Official Records*, vol. 36, pt. 2, 666–67; G. G. Meade to GKW, 6 A.M., May 12, 1864, and GKW to G. G. Meade, 6:15 A.M., May 12, 1864, both ibid., 661.

37. G. G. Meade to GKW, 7:30 A.M., May 12, 1864; G. G. Meade to GKW, 8 A.M., May 12, 1864; GKW to G. G. Meade, May 12, 1864; all ibid., 662.

38. Report of W. A. Roebling, 36, Warren Papers; GKW to A. A. Humphreys, 9:10 A.M. (twice), May 12, 1864, *Official Records*, vol. 36, pt. 2, 662, 663.

39. A. A. Humphreys to GKW, 9:15 A.M., May 12, 1864, and A. A. Humphreys to GKW ("Dear Warren"), 9:30 A.M., May 12, 1864, *Official Records*, vol. 36, pt. 2, 663; GKW to C. Griffin, 9:30 A.M., May 12, 1864, ibid., 668; GKW to Lysander Cutler, 9:30 A.M., May 12, 1864, ibid., 671; GKW to S. W. Crawford, 9:30 A.M., May 12, 1864, ibid., 669.

40. Andrew A. Humphreys, *The Virginia Campaign of 1864 and 1865* (New York: Charles Scribner's Sons, 1883), 101 nn; G. G. Meade to U. S. Grant, May 12, 1864, and U. S. Grant to G. G. Meade, 10:40 A.M., May 12, 1864, both in *Official Records*, vol. 36, pt. 2, 654.

41. Humphreys wrote to his wife on May 13, "I had an evidence yesterday of being held in some esteem from Genl Grant which I will not mention even to you just now." A. A. Humphreys to Becky Humphreys, May 13, 1864, Humphreys Papers. Presumably this "evidence" was Grant's willingness to confer corps command upon him, so Humphreys at least knew that the change was under serious consideration.

42. Horace Porter, *Campaigning with Grant* (New York: Century, 1897), 108. That these are Grant's exact words, of course, is highly dubious. Adam Badeau, whose postwar book was understood to reflect Grant's views, was extremely critical of Warren's May 12 actions, holding him responsible for the entire failure to convert Hancock's early success into overwhelming victory. "Both Grant and Meade," he wrote, "were

greatly chagrined at this delay [failure to attack at once at 8 A.M.], for it was losing all the advantages that Hancock's brilliant achievement had obtained." Later he observed that, because of the concentration of force at the Angle, "the rebel flanks were doubt-less weakened, so that the Fifth and Ninth corps had a comparatively easy task." When two of Warren's divisions were sent elsewhere, and no attack was made upon the diluted Fifth Corps line, Badeau said, "the general-in-chief was confirmed in his belief that there had been no important force in front of Warren, and that a vigorous assault on the rebel left would have been successful earlier in the day." "Warren's feebleness," he said, " . . . especially prevented Grant from following up the advantage that Hancock had obtained." Badeau, *Military History*, 177, 178, 180–81, 183. But even Dana, in his report of the day, after saying that "Warren alone has gained nothing," conceded that "the rebel works in his front were very strong." C. A. Dana to E. M. Stanton, 7 P.M., May 12, 1864, *Official Records*, vol. 36, pt. 1, 68.

15. *Around Lee's Right*

1. GKW to Emily Warren, 9 A.M., May 13, 1864, Warren Papers; GKW to G. G. Meade, May 13, 1864, *Official Records*, vol. 36, pt. 2, 718; Allan Nevins, ed., *A Diary of Battle: The Personal Journals of Colonel Charles S. Wainwright, 1861–1865* (New York: Harcourt Brace and World, 1962), 368; Special Order, 5:45 P.M., May 13, 1864, *Official Records*, vol. 36, pt. 2, 700.

2. Report of W. A. Roebling, 39–40, Warren Papers; Mary Genevie Green Brainard, *Campaigns of the One Hundred and Forty-Sixth Regiment New York State Volunteers* (New York and London: G. P. Putnam's Sons, 1915), 205–206; GKW to Emily Warren, 11 P.M., May 14, 1864, Warren Papers; GKW to A. A. Humphreys, 4 A.M., May 14, 1864, *Official Records*, vol. 36, pt. 2, 755; GKW to A. A. Humphreys, 6:30 A.M., ibid., 756.

3. Nevins, ed., *A Diary of Battle*, 377. Warren reported that he fired about eighteen hundred rounds that day. GKW to A. A. Humphreys, 8 P.M., May 18, 1864, *Official Records*, vol. 36, pt. 2, 876. Swinton called the Army of the Potomac's barrage an "im-mense waste of ammunition—result *nil*." William Swinton, *Campaigns of the Army of the Potomac* (1866; reprint, New York: Charles Scribner's Sons, 1882), 456n.

4. GKW to Emily Warren, May 20, 1864, Warren Papers.

5. GKW to Emily Warren, May 19, 1864, Warren Papers.

6. GKW to Emily Warren, 7:30 A.M., May 21, 1864, Warren Papers.

7. GKW to Emily Warren, 11:30 P.M., May 21, 1864, Warren Papers.

8. GKW to W. S. Hancock, 11:30 A.M., May 23, 1864, *Official Records*, vol. 36, pt. 3, 117; *Under the Maltese Cross: Antietam to Appomattox* (Pittsburgh: 155th Regimental Association, 1910), 276, 578; Swinton, *Campaigns of the Army of the Potomac*, 473.

9. Andrew A. Humphreys, *The Virginia Campaign of '64 and '65* (New York: Charles Scribner's Sons, 1883), 128–29; GKW to W. S. Hancock, 1:30 P.M., May 23, 1864, *Official Records*, vol. 36, pt. 3, 118; Donald L. Smith, *The Twenty-Fourth Michigan of the Iron Brigade* (Harrisburg, Pa.: Stackpole, 1962), 201–202.

10. William Henry Locke, *The Story of the Regiment* (Philadelphia: J. B. Lippincott, 1868), 343.

11. Lt. Col. Chas. S. Venable, in an address at the Lee Memorial Meeting in Rich-mond, November 3, 1870, quoted in Humphreys, *Virginia Campaign*, 132 n; Francis J. Parker, *The Story of the Thirty-Second Regiment, Massachusetts Infantry* (Boston: C. W. Calkins, 1880), 217; Nevins, ed., *A Diary of Battle*, 383, 387; David S. Sparks, ed., *Inside Lincoln's Army: The Diary of Marsena Rudolph Patrick, Provost Marshal General, Army of the Potomac* (New York and London: Thomas Yoseloff, 1964), 376. When Meade

congratulated Warren's "gallant corps" for its victory at the North Anna, Wainwright said, "I presume he includes the batteries in the corps, but I think that they ought to have had especial mention." Nevins, ed., *A Diary of Battle*, 383–84.

12. GKW to Emily Warren, 9 A.M., May 24, 1864, Warren Papers. Meade's message to Warren that evening said, "I congratulate you and your gallant corps for the handsome manner in which you repulsed the enemy's attack." G. G. Meade to GKW, 10:30 P.M., May 23, 1864, *Official Records*, vol. 36, pt. 3, 129. Roebling said the repulse of Hill "is a great feather in our cap." W. A. Roebling to (Miss) Emily Warren, May 24, 1864, Roebling Papers.

13. GKW to Emily Warren, May 24, 1864, Warren Papers.

14. GKW to Emily Warren, 10 P.M., May 26, 1864, Warren Papers. Warren's order to his corps for the recrossing of the North Anna is found in *Official Records*, vol. 36, pt. 3, 223.

15. Brainard, *Campaigns of the One Hundred and Forty-Sixth Regiment*, 213; Nevins, ed., *A Diary of Battle*, 390.

16. Nevins, ed., *A Diary of Battle*, 393; report of W. A. Roebling, 71–72, Warren Papers; Freeman Cleaves, *Meade of Gettysburg* (Norman: University of Oklahoma Press, 1960), 249; GKW to A. A. Humphreys, 7 A.M., May 30, 1864, *Official Records*, vol. 36, pt. 3, 336; GKW to S. W. Crawford, 3 P.M., May 30, 1864, ibid., 351; GKW to C. Griffin, 3 P.M., May 30, 1864, Warren Papers.

17. Special Orders No. 128, Fifth Corps, May 29, 1864, *Official Records*, vol. 36, pt. 3, 304–305. Before the war, Lockwood had resigned his army commission and spent many years teaching mathematics and astronomy in the navy, and he was a professor at the Naval Academy when the war started. After the Civil War, Lockwood returned to teaching at Annapolis, where he is buried.

18. GKW to Emily Warren, 5 A.M., May 31, 1864, Warren Papers.

19. Nevins, ed., *A Diary of Battle*, 396; C. A. Dana to E. M. Stanton, 5 P.M., June 1, 1864, *Official Records*, vol. 36, pt. 1, 85. For various messages concerning the morning's activities among Warren, Meade, and Washington Roebling, see *Official Records*, vol. 36, pt. 3, 446–48. Badeau repeated Dana's charge in his war history of Grant, attributing it to "those peculiarities [of Warren's] already described, which made this officer hesitate so often and so long, before an action." Badeau, *Military History*, 276–78. He described Grant as "bitterly disappointed" at this failure. In postwar correspondence with Warren, Charles H. Porter, who was on picket in front of the Fifth Corps and found Early's corps "in good position and awaiting attack," concluded that the column which Badeau and Dana thought Warren was supposed to strike, under Anderson, passed to the rear of Early's line "and in order to have reached him you would have to smash Early & then get Anderson, always supposing that you had got over Early." C. H. Porter to GKW, Nov. 28, 1881, Warren Papers. Warren responded the next day: "I was very seldom favored with an idea of what was expected during Grant's command, so I do not think I had any instruction whatever in regard to Anderson's movement." GKW to C. H. Porter, Nov. 29, 1881, Warren Papers. Indeed, no orders regarding this movement appear in the *Official Records*.

20. Ulysses S. Grant, *Personal Memoirs of U. S. Grant* (Cleveland: World Publishing, 1952), 440; G. G. Meade to U. S. Grant, 10:15 P.M., June 1, 1864, *Official Records*, vol. 36, pt. 3, 433. John Rawlins, Grant's chief of staff, reported that the heaviest attack was made on Warren's front, and repulsed three times. James Harrison Wilson, *The Life of John A. Rawlins* (New York: Neale, 1916), 225.

21. Harold Adams Small, ed., *The Road to Richmond: The Civil War Memoirs of Major Abner R. Small of the Sixteenth Maine Volunteers* (Berkeley: University of California Press, 1939), 148; C. A. Dana to E. M. Stanton, 6 A.M., June 2, 1864, *Official Records*,

vol. 36, pt. 1, 86; GKW to G. G. Meade, June 1, 1864, *Official Records*, vol. 36, pt. 3, 451–52. At 11 P.M., Meade wrote to Warren that "an order will be sent in the morning relieving Brigadier-General Lockwood from command. You can now make a good division for Crawford." Ibid., 452.

22. Special Orders No. 26, Armies of the United States, June 2, 1864, and Special Orders No. 131, Fifth Army Corps, June 2, 1864, *Official Records*, vol. 36, pt. 3, 494–95.

23. A. A. Humphreys to GKW, 1:30 P.M., June 2, 1864, *Official Records*, vol. 36, pt. 3, 491; Nevins, ed., *A Diary of Battle*, 399–400.

24. A. L. Long, *Memoirs of Robert E. Lee: His Military and Personal History* (New York, Philadelphia, and Washington, D.C.: J. M. Stoddart, 1887), 348; Grant, *Personal Memoirs*, 444–45; U. S. Grant to G. G. Meade, 12:30 P.M., June 3, 1864, *Official Records*, vol. 36, pt. 3, 526.

25. Nevins, ed., *A Diary of Battle*, 404–405.

26. Roebling wrote to Emily Warren that "your brother G. K. now spends half his waking hours in cursing the damned fate that keeps him away from his wife; he feels a misery now to which he was a stranger previous to last year." W. A. Roebling to (Miss) Emily Warren, June 28, 1864, Roebling Papers.

27. For the order for "regular approaches," see Seth Williams to corps commanders, 1:30 P.M., June 3, 1864, *Official Records*, vol. 36, pt. 3, 528–29.

16. Standoff at Petersburg

1. Mary Genevie Green Brainard, *Campaigns of the One Hundred and Forty-Sixth Regiment New York State Volunteers* (New York and London: G. P. Putnam's Sons, 1915), 219.

2. General Orders No. - [no number given], Fifth Army Corps, June 5, 1864, *Official Records*, vol. 36, pt. 3, 613–14; Seth Williams, Orders, 4 P.M., June 5, 1864, ibid., 603.

3. GKW to A. A. Humphreys, 1 A.M., June 5, 1864, and A. A. Humphreys to GKW, 1:50 A.M., June 5, 1864, both ibid., 609; A. A. Humphreys to P. H. Sheridan, 1:40 A.M., June 5, 1864, ibid., 627; P. H. Sheridan to A. A. Humphreys, June 5, 1864, and A. A. Humphreys to P. H. Sheridan, 8:30 A.M., June 5, 1864, both ibid., 628.

4. GKW to A. A. Humphreys, 4:30 A.M., June 6, 1864, ibid., 649.

5. William Henry Locke, *The Story of the Regiment* (Philadelphia: J. B. Lippincott, 1868), 350; A. A. Humphreys to GKW, 9:45 P.M., June 6, 1864, *Official Records*, vol. 36, pt. 3, 650; Allan Nevins, ed., *A Diary of Battle: The Personal Journals of Colonel Charles S. Wainwright, 1861–1865* (New York: Harcourt Brace and World, 1962), 409; GKW to Emily Warren, 11 P.M., June 10, 1864, Warren Papers. Wainwright, while valuable as an observer, is perhaps less so as an analyst.

6. A. A. Humphreys to GKW, 7:30 P.M., June 10, 1864, *Official Records*, vol. 36, pt. 3, 730–31; GKW to A. A. Humphreys, 6:30 P.M., June 11, 1864, ibid., 750.

7. Nevins, ed., *A Diary of Battle*, 414–15.

8. James Harrison Wilson, *Under the Old Flag* (New York and London: D. Appleton, 1912), vol. 1, 398–99. Wilson went on to describe meeting Warren the next day, telling him how offended he was to receive the message he had, and being surprised to hear that Warren barely remembered the incident and offered a sincere apology for his rudeness. Several days later Wilson told the story of the incident at the Chickahominy to Grant, who responded, "Well, I'll take care of Warren anyhow." Ibid., 401.

9. Report of W. A. Roebling, 92–93, Warren Papers. Any uncorroborated tale about Warren by a cavalry officer, after Five Forks and after the Court of Inquiry, is subject to some skepticism.

10. GKW to A. A. Humphreys, 10 P.M., June 12, 1864, *Official Records*, vol. 36, pt. 3, 762; GKW to A. A. Humphreys, 5 A.M., June 13, 1864, *Official Records*, vol. 40, pt. 2, 6.

11. Locke, *The Story of the Regiment*, 351.

12. Fifth Corps, Special Orders No. 141½, June 13, 1864, *Official Records*, vol. 40, pt. 2, 8; Brainard, *Campaigns of the One Hundred and Forty-Sixth Regiment*, 223–24; Rufus R. Dawes, *Service with the Sixth Wisconsin Volunteers* (Madison: State Historical Society of Wisconsin, 1962), 290; John G. Nicolay and John Hay, *Abraham Lincoln: A History* (New York: Century, 1890), vol. 9, 406–407.

13. G. G. Meade to GKW, 8:30 P.M., June 15, 1864, *Official Records*, vol. 40, pt. 2, 63; report of W. A. Roebling, 97, Warren Papers.

14. A. A. Humphreys to GKW, noon, June 16, 1864, and GKW to G. G. Meade, 2 P.M., June 16, 1864, both in *Official Records*, vol. 40, pt. 2, 94; C. B. Comstock to GKW, 2:30 P.M., June 16, 1864, and G. G. Meade to GKW, 9:30 P.M., June 16, 1864, both ibid., 95.

15. GKW to Emily Warren, June 17, 1864, Warren Papers.

16. G. G. Meade to GKW, 5:15 A.M., June 18, 1864, *Official Records*, vol. 40, pt. 2, 172; GKW to G. G. Meade, 5:50 A.M., and G. G. Meade to GKW, 6:30 A.M., both June 18, 1864, ibid., 173; G. G. Meade to GKW, 7:10 A.M., June 18, 1864, ibid., 174; G. G. Meade to GKW, 10 A.M., and GKW to G. G. Meade, 10:30 A.M., both June 18, 1864, ibid., 175; G. G. Meade to GKW (same to Generals Burnside, Birney, and Martindale), 11 A.M. (sent 11:34 A.M.), June 18, 1864, ibid., 176.

17. GKW to G. G. Meade, 11:36 A.M., *Official Records*, vol. 40, pt. 2, 176; G. G. Meade to GKW, 11:45 A.M., GKW to G. G. Meade, 11:50 A.M., and G. G. Meade to GKW, 11:55 A.M., all June 18, 1864, ibid., 177.

18. GKW to G. G. Meade (with endorsement by A. E. Burnside), 2 P.M., and G. G. Meade to GKW and A. E. Burnside, 2:20 P.M., both June 18, 1864, *Official Records*, vol. 40, pt. 2, 179.

19. T. Lyman to G. G. Meade, 2:40 P.M., GKW to G. G. Meade, 4 P.M., both June 18, 1864, *Official Records*, vol. 40, pt. 2, 180; Joshua Lawrence Chamberlain, *The Passing of the Armies: An Account of the Final Campaign of the Army of the Potomac* (1915; reprint, Dayton, Ohio: Morningside Bookshop, 1991), 26–27; Dawes, *Service with the Sixth Wisconsin Volunteers*, 290–91. Chamberlain himself was wounded in the attack, mortally, it was at first thought, the ball passing through his pelvis and bladder. Warren recommended that he be promoted to brigadier general before he died, which was done, and he then survived to serve for the rest of the war. GKW to G. G. Meade, 9:16 P.M., June 19, 1864, *Official Records*, vol. 40, pt. 2, 216–17. Chamberlain's promotion is in Special Orders No. 39, Headquarters, Armies of the United States, June 20, 1864, *Official Records*, vol. 40, pt. 2, 236.

20. G. G. Meade to GKW, 6:30 P.M., June 18, 1864, *Official Records*, vol. 40, pt. 2, 180; Nevins, ed., *A Diary of Battle*, 426.

21. GKW to G. G. Meade, 9:30 A.M., June 20, 1864, *Official Records*, vol. 40, pt. 2, 242–43; C. A. Dana to E. M. Stanton, 5 P.M., June 20, 1864, *Official Records*, vol. 40, pt. 1, 26; GKW to Emily Warren, June 20, 1864, Warren Papers. Warren went on to tell his wife, "I am so dirty and so tired out and so hopeless of the result we have all prayed and fought for that death will be no pang to me." Later the same day, Warren wrote about his "dismal" note, saying that he thought his "understanding with Genl Meade" was "a good thing" and that the army would approve it and regard him "as 'the rat that belled the cat.'" GKW to Emily Warren, June 20, 1864, Warren Papers.

22. C. A. Dana to E. M. Stanton, 11 A.M., July 1, 1864, *Official Records*, vol. 40, pt. 1, 28.

23. Several weeks having passed, it appears that Meade may have gotten June 19 and June 20 confused.

24. The letter which Meade wrote, addressed to John A. Rawlins, June 21, 1864, but never sent, is in the George Gordon Meade Papers, Historical Society of Pennsylvania.

25. *Pittsburg Commercial*, July 14, 1864; GKW to G. G. Meade, July 22, 1864, *Official Records*, vol. 40, pt. 3, 393; G. G. Meade to GKW, July 22, 1864, ibid., 393–94.

26. S. W. Crawford to C. Griffin, June 21, 1864, with first endorsement by Griffin, dated June 22, 1864, and second endorsement by GKW, dated June 23, 1864, *Official Records*, vol. 40, pt. 2, 280.

27. GKW to G. G. Meade, June 23, 1864 (recd. 1:15 P.M.), G. G. Meade to U. S. Grant, 2 P.M., June 23, 1864, and G. G. Meade to GKW, 2:10 P.M., June 23, 1864, all in *Official Records*, vol. 40, pt. 2, 332–33; GKW to G. G. Meade, June 23, 1864, ibid., 346. Warren's plan is discussed by Edward Hagerman, *The American Civil War and the Origins of Modern Warfare* (Bloomington and Indianapolis: Indiana University Press, 1988), 269, who concludes that "any risk in strategic maneuver had been displaced by the relative security of attrition."

28. GKW to A. A. Humphreys, 11:40 A.M., June 24, 1864, *Official Records*, vol. 40, pt. 2, 385.

29. GKW to Emily Warren, June 25, 1864, Warren Papers.

30. GKW to Emily Warren, June 25, 1864 (second letter), Warren Papers.

31. GKW to A. A. Humphreys, 2 P.M., July 13, 1864, *Official Records*, vol. 40, pt. 3, 214; Nevins, ed., *A Diary of Battle*, 436. On July 17, Wainwright commented on the great size of one redoubt; "I can hardly suppose that there was any call for quite so large a work, and am inclined to think that it was a hobby of Warren's." Ibid., 437.

32. *Under the Maltese Cross: Antietam to Appomattox* (Pittsburgh: 155th Regimental Association, 1910), 306.

33. GKW to Emily Warren, July 1, 1864, Warren Papers.

34. U. S. Grant to G. G. Meade, 10:30 A.M., and G. G. Meade to U. S. Grant, noon, both July 3, 1864, *Official Records*, vol. 40, pt. 2, 599; G. G. Meade to GKW, noon, July 3, 1864, ibid., 603–604; GKW to G. G. Meade, 12:30 P.M., July 3, 1864, ibid., 604.

35. GKW to G. G. Meade, July 4, 1864, ibid., 624.

36. GKW to G. G. Meade, 11 A.M., July 4, 1864, ibid., 624–25. Meade answered that "when I called on you for your opinion I designed the question . . . as a military one, and had no reference myself to the willingness or boldness independent of military considerations." G. G. Meade to GKW, July 4, 1864, ibid., 625.

37. C. A. Dana to E. M. Stanton, 8 A.M., July 7, 1864, *Official Records*, vol. 40, pt. 1, 35–36.

38. Circular signed by GKW, July 12, 1864, *Official Records*, vol. 40, pt. 3, 192.

39. C. S. Wainwright to H. J. Hunt, July 15, 1864, and H. J. Hunt to A. A. Humphreys, July 18, 1864, both in Henry Jackson Hunt Papers, Library of Congress; also *Official Records*, vol. 40, pt. 3, 318; Edward G. Longacre, *The Man behind the Guns: A Biography of General Henry Jackson Hunt, Chief of Artillery, Army of the Potomac* (South Brunswick and New York: A. S. Barnes, 1977), 203.

40. GKW to A. A. Humphreys, July 20, 1864, *Official Records*, vol. 40, pt. 3, 350.

41. H. J. Hunt to C. S. Wainwright, June 3, 1864, Henry Jackson Hunt Papers, Library of Congress; Seth Williams to GKW, July 21, 1864, *Official Records*, vol. 40, pt. 3, 367.

42. Nevins, ed., *A Diary of Battle*, 440.

43. GKW to Emily Warren, July 20, 1864, Warren Papers.

44. GKW to Emily Warren, July 24, 1864, Warren Papers.

17. The Mine and the Railroad

1. A. A. Humphreys to GKW, 8 P.M., July 26, 1864, *Official Records*, vol. 40, pt. 3, 468, explains to Warren the Second Corps movement, what was hoped from it, and the consequences for the attack after the springing of Burnside's mine.

2. Seth Williams, Orders, Headquarters, Army of the Potomac, July 29, 1864, *Official Records*, vol. 40, pt. 3, 596–97.

3. G. G. Meade to GKW, 1:30 P.M., July 28, 1864, *Official Records*, vol. 40, pt. 1, 446; GKW to A. A. Humphreys, 4 P.M., July 29, 1864, ibid., 446–47.

4. F. T. Locke, Circular, Headquarters, Fifth Army Corps, July 29, 1864, ibid., 448.

5. GKW to Emily Warren, July 29, 1864, Warren Papers.

6. William Marvel, *Burnside* (Chapel Hill and London: University of North Carolina Press, 1991), 400.

7. A. A. Humphreys to GKW, 5:50 A.M., GKW to A. A. Humphreys, 6 A.M., and GKW to A. A. Humphreys, 6:15 A.M., all July 30, 1864, *Official Records*, vol. 40, pt. 1, 449. Warren later testified that he had no more chance of success by attacking the enemy in front of him that day than on any other day; "I had, with more men," he said, "failed in my attack before." *Report of the Joint Committee on the Conduct of the War,* "Battle of Petersburg," 38th Cong., 2d sess. (1865), vol. 1, 82.

8. A. A. Humphreys to A. E. Burnside, 6:05 A.M., A. E. Burnside to G. G. Meade, 6:20 A.M., both July 30, 1864, *Official Records*, vol. 40, pt. 1, 141; G. G. Meade to A. E. Burnside, 6:50 A.M., July 30, 1864, ibid., 141–42.

9. A. A. Humphreys to GKW, 6:30 A.M., GKW to S. W. Crawford, 6:40 A.M., and GKW to A. A. Humphreys, 6:40 A.M., all July 30, 1864, ibid., 450; report of W. A. Roebling, 125, Warren Papers.

10. Testimony of GKW, Mine Court of Inquiry, Aug. 30, 1864, *Official Records*, vol. 40, pt. 1, 80; GKW to A. A. Humphreys, 7:50 A.M., A. A. Humphreys to GKW (no time), and G. G. Meade to GKW (no time), all July 30, 1864, ibid., 451.

11. GKW to Emily Warren, July 31, 1864, Warren Papers. Warren went on in the same letter to say, "I no longer give myself any concern about my relations with Genl Meade or even with Genl Grant. I trust they will never injure me, I mind my own affairs too well, to get in their way or make them wish another in my place."

12. Testimony of GKW, Mine Court of Inquiry, Aug. 29, 30, 1864, *Official Records*, vol. 40, pt. 1, 80–81.

13. Marvel, *Burnside*, 403.

14. Testimony of G. G. Meade, Mine Court of Inquiry, Aug. 8, 1864, *Official Records*, vol. 40, pt. 1, 51.

15. *New York Herald*, July 24, 1878; Findings of the Mine Court of Inquiry, *Official Records*, vol. 40, pt. 1, 127. Badeau, Grant's aide and apologist, later wrote that both Warren and Hancock "replied in the negative" when asked by Meade if they could support Burnside by attacks in their fronts, even though "many, spectators and participants, believed, at the time and afterwards," that the lines in their fronts could have been "easily carried." "The corps commanders, however," he said, "were learned in their art; and not being at the front himself, Meade could hardly do other than accept their judgments." Adam Badeau, *Military History of Ulysses S. Grant, from April, 1861, to April, 1865* (New York: D. Appleton, 1885), vol. 2, 485–86. Grant, obviously, was not the only one rewriting the history of the Petersburg mine.

16. Thomas L. Livermore, *Days and Events, 1860–1866* (Boston and New York: Houghton Mifflin, 1920), 386; testimony of Major J. C. Duane, Mine Court of Inquiry,

Sept. 3, 1864, *Official Records*, vol. 40, pt. 1, 112; *Report of the Joint Committee* (1865), vol. 1, 81.

17. U. S. Grant to H. W. Halleck, Aug. 1, 1864, *Official Records*, vol. 40, pt. 1, 17; Walter C. Newberry, "The Petersburg Mine," *Military Essays and Recollections: Papers Read before the Commandery of the State of Illinois*, Military Order of the Loyal Legion of the United States, Commandery of the State of Illinois (Chicago: Dial Press, 1899), vol. 3, 123; Allan Nevins, ed., *A Diary of Battle: The Personal Journals of Colonel Charles S. Wainwright, 1861–1865* (New York: Harcourt Brace and World, 1962), 443.

18. GKW to Emily Warren, Aug. 14, 1864, Warren Papers.

19. A. A. Humphreys to GKW, 2:30 P.M., Aug. 17, 1864, *Official Records*, vol. 42, pt. 2, 251.

20. GKW to Emily Warren, Aug. 17, 1864, Warren Papers; GKW to A. A. Humphreys, 4 A.M., Aug. 18, 1864, *Official Records*, vol. 42, pt. 2, 271.

21. Mary Genevie Green Brainard, *Campaigns of the One Hundred and Forty-Sixth Regiment New York State Volunteers* (New York and London: G. P. Putnam's Sons, 1915), 237–38.

22. GKW to A. A. Humphreys, 9 A.M. and 10 A.M., both Aug. 18, 1864, *Official Records*, vol. 42, pt. 2, 272; GKW to A. A. Humphreys, 11 A.M. and 2:30 P.M., Aug. 18, 1864, ibid., 273; GKW to A. A. Humphreys, 4 P.M., Aug. 18, 1864, ibid., 274.

23. GKW to A. A. Humphreys, 7 P.M., Aug. 18, 1864, ibid., 275; GKW to Emily Warren, 9 P.M., Aug. 18, 1864, Warren Papers.

24. U. S. Grant to H. W. Halleck, 11 A.M., Aug. 21, 1864, *Official Records*, vol. 42, pt. 2, 353.

25. A. A. Humphreys to GKW, 10 P.M., Aug. 18, 1864, ibid., 276; GKW to S. W. Crawford, 8 P.M., Aug. 18, 1864, ibid., 278; A. A. Humphreys to J. G. Parke, 1:45 P.M., Aug. 18, 1864, ibid., 280; G. W. Gowan to J. G. Parke, 4:30 P.M., Aug. 18, 1864, ibid., 281; GKW to J. G. Parke, 10 P.M., Aug. 18, 1864, ibid., 283–84; J. G. Parke to GKW, 11 P.M., Aug. 18, 1864, ibid., 284.

26. U. S. Grant to G. G. Meade, 11:15 P.M., Aug. 18, 1864, and G. G. Meade to GKW, 12:05 A.M., Aug. 19, 1864, both ibid., 266.

27. GKW to A. A. Humphreys, 11 A.M., Aug. 19, 1864, ibid., 306; William Henry Locke, *The Story of the Regiment* (Philadelphia: J. B. Lippincott, 1868), 358–59; report of GKW, Aug. 25, 1864, *Official Records*, vol. 42, pt. 1, 429–30; Alan D. Gaff, *On Many a Bloody Field: Four Years in the Iron Brigade* (Bloomington and Indianapolis: Indiana University Press, 1996), 377; Brainard, *Campaigns of the One Hundred and Forty-Sixth Regiment*, 239.

28. Locke, *The Story of the Regiment*, 359–60; Charles Camper and J. W. Kirkley, *Historical Record of the First Regiment Maryland Infantry* (Washington, D.C.: Gibson Bros., 1871), 170; Brainard, *Campaigns of the One Hundred and Forty-Sixth Regiment*, 239–40; Robert Garth Scott, ed., *Forgotten Valor: The Memoirs, Journals, and Civil War Letters of Orlando B. Willcox* (Kent, Ohio, and London: Kent State University Press, 1999), 568; GKW to G. G. Meade, Aug. 19, 1864 (recd. 12:15 A.M., Aug. 20), *Official Records*, vol. 42, pt. 2, 310; report of W. A. Roebling, 147, Warren Papers.

29. GKW to Emily Warren, 9 P.M., Aug. 20, 1864, Warren Papers.

30. Isaac Hall, *History of The Ninety-Seventh Regiment, New York Volunteers ("Conkling Rifles") in the War for the Union* (Utica, N.Y.: L. C. Childs and Son, 1890), 221, 226.

31. Ibid., 226.

32. Report of W. A. Roebling, 152, 153, Warren Papers; Gaff, *On Many a Bloody Field*, 378; Nevins, ed., *A Diary of Battle*, 453.

33. David S. Sparks, ed., *Inside Lincoln's Army: The Diary of Marsena Rudolph Patrick, Provost Marshal General, Army of the Potomac* (New York and London: Thomas Yoseloff, 1964), 417.

34. GKW to Emily Warren, Aug. 22, 1864, Warren Papers.

35. GKW to A. A. Humphreys, 3 P.M., Aug. 21, 1864, *Official Records*, vol. 42, pt. 2, 369.

18. West to Peebles' Farm

1. George Meade, *The Life and Letters of George Gordon Meade* (New York: Charles Scribner's Sons, 1913), vol. 2, 224.

2. See G. G. Meade to U. S. Grant, 6 P.M., Aug. 23, 1864, *Official Records*, vol. 42, pt. 2, 420.

3. For speculation about the Confederate movements, see GKW to A. A. Humphreys, 9 P.M., Aug. 24, 1864, and A. A. Humphreys to GKW, 9:10 P.M., Aug. 24, both in *Official Records*, vol. 42, pt. 2, 452, and C. H. Morgan to D. M. Gregg, 11 P.M., Aug. 24, 1864, ibid., 455.

4. Allan Nevins, ed., *A Diary of Battle: The Personal Journals of Colonel Charles S. Wainwright, 1861–1865* (New York: Harcourt Brace and World, 1962), 457; David M. Jordan, *Winfield Scott Hancock: A Soldier's Life* (Bloomington: Indiana University Press, 1988), 161–62.

5. GKW to Emily Warren, Aug. 26, 1864, Warren Papers; Nevins, ed., *A Diary of Battle*, 459–60.

6. GKW to Emily Warren, Aug. 27, 1864, Warren Papers.

7. GKW to R. B. Ayres (same to S. W. Crawford), 9 A.M., Aug. 27, 1864, *Official Records*, vol. 42, pt. 2, 546.

8. Nevins, ed., *A Diary of Battle*, 459. The reorganization of the Fifth Corps was formalized in General Orders No. 35, Headquarters, Fifth Corps, issued Sept. 12, 1864; *Official Records*, vol. 42, pt. 2, 800–801.

9. GKW to A. A. Humphreys, Sept. 10, 1864, *Official Records*, vol. 42, pt. 2, 778.

10. U. S. Grant to G. G. Meade, Sept. 27, 1864, ibid., 1046–47.

11. Orders, Headquarters, Army of the Potomac, Sept. 28, 1864, ibid., 1069; GKW to A. A. Humphreys, 11 A.M., Sept. 28, 1864, Warren Papers (also in *Official Records*, vol. 42, pt. 2, 1074).

12. A. A. Humphreys to GKW, 12:15 A.M., Sept. 30, 1864, *Official Records*, vol. 42, pt. 2, 1130; A. A. Humphreys to GKW, 8:50 A.M., Sept. 30, 1864, ibid., 1131.

13. Richard J. Sommers, *Richmond Redeemed: The Siege at Petersburg* (Garden City, N.Y.: Doubleday, 1981), 190.

14. Ibid., 241–42; Nevins, ed., *A Diary of Battle*, 467.

15. GKW to A. A. Humphreys, 11 A.M., Sept. 30, 1864, *Official Records*, vol. 42, pt. 2, 1131.

16. Sommers, *Richmond Redeemed*, 242–43.

17. J. A. Rawlins to Mrs. Rawlins, Dec. 12, 1864, in James Harrison Wilson, *The Life of John A. Rawlins* (New York: Neale, 1916), 292.

18. GKW to Emily Warren, Oct. 1, 1864, Warren Papers.

19. Sommers, *Richmond Redeemed*, 247–49, describes all these problems, which he says added to Warren's "personal hesitancy to precipitate battle."

20. Ibid., 251.

21. Charles Camper and J. W. Kirkley, *Historical Record of the First Regiment Maryland Infantry* (Washington, D.C.: Gibson Bros., 1871), 176; GKW to A. A. Humphreys,

2:20 P.M., Sept. 30, 1864, *Official Records*, vol. 42, pt. 2, 1132; GKW to A. A. Humphreys, 1:30 P.M., Sept. 30, 1864, ibid., 1131; F. T. Locke to Seth Williams, 6 P.M., Sept. 30, 1864, ibid., 1132; Sommers, *Richmond Redeemed*, 253–54.

22. Sommers, *Richmond Redeemed*, 260.

23. Nevins, ed., *A Diary of Battle*, 468; Sommers, *Richmond Redeemed*, 272; U. S. Grant to G. G. Meade at Warren's headquarters, recd. 3:25 P.M., Sept. 30, 1864, *Official Records*, vol. 42, pt. 2, 1119. Parke, in his official report of the battle, wrote, "Learning that Griffin's division, of the Fifth Corps, was to advance in support of the right of the Second Division [Potter's], I ordered the brigade of the First Division [Willcox's] that was in support to move to the left . . . [After Potter advanced] the enemy attacked vigorously . . . and forced it to retire, Griffin's division not having effected the connection with Potter's right." Report of J. G. Parke, Nov. 5, 1864, *Official Records*, vol. 42, pt. 1, 546.

24. GKW to A. A. Humphreys, 10 P.M., Sept. 30, 1864, *Official Records*, vol. 42, pt. 2, 1133; GKW to S. W. Crawford, 9 P.M., Sept. 30, 1864, ibid., 1135. For losses, see *Official Records*, vol. 42, pt. 1, 139–42, which gave the Ninth Corps loss as 2,010, and ibid., 546 (Parke's report), which gave it as 1,994.

25. A. A. Humphreys to GKW, 7:45 P.M., Sept. 30, 1864, *Official Records*, vol. 42, pt. 2, 1132–33; A. A. Humphreys to GKW, 11:45 P.M. (sent at midnight), Sept. 30, 1864, ibid., 1133; GKW to A. A. Humphreys, 8 A.M., Oct. 1, 1864, *Official Records*, vol. 42, pt. 3, 18; Sommers, *Richmond Redeemed*, 312.

26. Sommers, *Richmond Redeemed*, 327.

27. Ibid., 336; GKW to A. A. Humphreys, Oct. 1, 1864, *Official Records*, vol. 42, pt. 3, 18.

28. GKW to Emily Warren, 6 P.M., Oct. 1, 1864, Warren Papers; GKW to G. G. Meade, evening, Oct. 1, 1864, *Official Records*, vol. 42, pt. 3, 19–20.

29. A. A. Humphreys to GKW, 7 P.M., Oct. 1, 1864, *Official Records*, vol. 42, pt. 3, 19.

30. A. A. Humphreys to GKW (same to J. G. Parke), 11:15 A.M., Oct. 2, 1864, ibid., 41.

31. Sommers, *Richmond Redeemed*, 432–33, 436. It will be recalled that Sommers had defined "grand tactics" as "that realm of military art dealing with movements just outside the actual field of combat." Ibid., 243.

19. To the End of 1864

1. GKW to Emily Warren, Oct. 2, 1864, Warren Papers.

2. G. G. Meade to GKW, 7 P.M., Oct. 6, 1864, *Official Records*, vol. 42, pt. 3, 96; ibid., 106; GKW to Emily Warren, Oct. 20, 1864, Warren Papers; GKW to Seth Williams, Oct. 21, 1864, *Official Records*, vol. 42, pt. 3, 296; W. A. Roebling to (Miss) Emily Warren, Oct. 23, 1864, Roebling Papers.

3. GKW to Emily Warren, Oct. 31, 1864, Warren Papers. Gouv concluded the letter by assuring his wife that "I was not shot in the face the other day as one of the correspondents said."

4. Allan Nevins, ed., *A Diary of Battle: The Personal Journals of Colonel Charles S. Wainwright, 1861–1865* (New York: Harcourt Brace and World, 1962), 476; GKW to Emily Warren, Oct. 23, 1864, Warren Papers.

5. Donald L. Smith, *The Twenty-Fourth Michigan of the Iron Brigade* (Harrisburg, Pa.: Stackpole, 1962), 228.

6. Worthington Chauncey Ford, ed., *A Cycle of Adams Letters, 1861–1865* (Boston and New York: Houghton Mifflin, 1920), vol. 2, 207.

7. Orders, Oct. 25, 1864, *Official Records*, vol. 42, pt. 3, 341.

8. Hancock reported at 9 P.M. that he had "not been able to find General Crawford since about 4 P.M." W. S. Hancock to A. A. Humphreys, 9 P.M., Oct. 27, 1864, ibid., 382.

9. G. G. Meade to U. S. Grant, 8 P.M., Oct. 27, 1864, ibid., 373. In the same message, Meade said, "Crawford moved up the run after driving in their skirmishers and confronted the enemy on their bank, but owing to the very dense thicket through which he had to move and the slashed timber in the run, did not succeed in finding a practicable place to attack." Ibid., 374.

10. U. S. Grant to G. G. Meade, Oct. 28, 1864, ibid., 402–403.

11. G. G. Meade to U. S. Grant, 11 A.M., Oct. 28, 1864, ibid., 403. Crawford took two hundred prisoners from Mahone; G. G. Meade to Lt. Col. Bowers, Oct. 28, 1864, ibid., 406. As an example of how bad the country was in which Crawford was trying to move, Wash Roebling brought in a party of eight Confederates and two Federals; "these men of ours had been taken prisoners by the rebels in the first place, but not one of the whole party knew where they were, so they had made up their minds to follow the first man who knew where anywhere was." Statement of Major W. A. Roebling, *Official Records*, vol. 42, pt. 1, 442.

12. GKW to Emily Warren, Oct. 27, 28, 1864; GKW to W. J. Warren, Oct. 29, 1864; all in Warren Papers.

13. GKW to Emily Warren, Nov. 1, 1864, Warren Papers.

14. GKW to Emily Warren, Nov. 7, 1864, Warren Papers.

15. Ibid.; GKW to Emily Warren, Nov. 8, 9, 1864, Warren Papers. Warren reported the election results in the Fifth Corps, overwhelmingly for Lincoln, in *Official Records*, vol. 42, pt. 3, 576–77.

16. GKW to Emily Warren, Nov. 11, 1864, Warren Papers; A. A. Humphreys to Becky Humphreys, Nov. 12, 1864, Humphreys Papers; GKW to Emily Warren, Nov. 22, 1864, Warren Papers.

17. GKW to Emily Warren, Nov. 29, 30, 1864, Warren Papers.

18. GKW to Emily Warren, Dec. 3, 1864, Warren Papers. Ironically, August Belmont is buried in the same cemetery in Newport, Rhode Island, in which Warren and his family are interred.

19. GKW to Emily Warren, Dec. 4, 1864, Warren Papers.

20. GKW to Emily Warren, 10 P.M., Dec. 6, 1864, Warren Papers.

21. G. G. Meade to J. A. Rawlins, 3:40 P.M., Dec. 4, 1864, *Official Records*, vol. 42, pt. 3, 795.

22. Report of S. W. Crawford, Dec. 19, 1864, *Official Records*, vol. 42, pt. 1, 497; William Henry Locke, *The Story of the Regiment* (Philadelphia: J. B. Lippincott, 1868), 365–66.

23. Mary Genevie Green Brainard, *Campaigns of the One Hundred and Forty-Sixth Regiment New York State Volunteers* (New York and London: G. P. Putnam's Sons, 1915), 250–51; report of GKW, Dec. 14, 1864, *Official Records*, vol. 42, pt. 1, 444. See the report of Chaplain Lorenzo Barber, of the Second U.S. Sharpshooters, Second Corps, for a graphic description of tearing up and burning the tracks; ibid., 355–56. "The sight presented by the burning road, bridges, piles of wood, and fences," Chaplain Barber said, "was sad and grand in the extreme—a terrible comment on the waste and ravages of war."

24. Report of GKW, *Official Records*, vol. 42, pt. 1, 444–45; Brainard, *Campaigns of the One Hundred and Forty-Sixth Regiment*, 252.

25. Report of GKW, *Official Records*, vol. 42, pt. 1, 445–46; Brainard, *Campaigns of the One Hundred and Forty-Sixth Regiment*, 253; Charles Camper and J. W. Kirkley, *Historical Record of the First Regiment Maryland Infantry* (Washington D.C.: Gibson Bros., 1871), 183–84.

26. Report of G. G. Meade, Dec. 14, 1864, *Official Records*, vol. 42, pt. 1, 38; report of GKW, ibid., 445–46; Brainard, *Campaigns of the One Hundred and Forty-Sixth Regiment*, 253; James I. Robertson, Jr., *General A. P. Hill: The Story of a Confederate Warrior* (New York: Random House, 1987), 308–309; J. A. Rawlins to Mrs. Rawlins, Dec. 12, 1864, in James Harrison Wilson, *The Life of John A. Rawlins* (New York: Neale, 1916), 292; report of Fifth Corps, *Official Records*, vol. 42, pt. 1, 56–57. During the raid to Hicksford, there were several instances of Union soldiers confiscating quantities of apple-jack; "they made merry with the seductive liquids made from immortal cider." One soldier, having consumed three fingers of the booze, happily slapped Warren himself on the back, calling him "The Little Corporal." This appellation thereafter clung to him, but it is not recorded how Warren reacted. Alfred S. Roe, *The Thirty-Ninth Regiment, Massachusetts Volunteers, 1862–65* (Worcester, Mass.: Regimental Veteran Association, 1914), 266–67.

27. GKW to Emily Warren, Dec. 12, 13, 1864, Warren Papers.

28. GKW to Emily Warren, Dec. 14, 24, 1864, Warren Papers.

29. GKW to Seth Williams, Dec. 20, 1864, *Official Records*, vol. 42, pt. 3, 1047; Special Orders No. 356, Headquarters, Army of the Potomac, Dec. 31, 1864, ibid., 1109.

20. Beginning of the End

1. GKW to Emily Warren, Jan. 29, 1865, Warren Papers.

2. GKW to Emily Warren, Jan. 30, 31, 1865, Warren Papers.

3. GKW to Emily Warren, Feb. 2, 4, 1865, Warren Papers.

4. GKW to Emily Warren, Feb. 4, 1865, Warren Papers. Warren's specific orders for the movement on the morning of the 5th came in a dispatch from Alexander Webb, Humphreys's successor as Meade's chief of staff; Feb. 4, 1865, *Official Records*, vol. 46, pt. 2, 377–78.

5. Mary Genevie Green Brainard, *Campaigns of the One Hundred and Forty-Sixth Regiment New York State Volunteers* (New York and London: G. P. Putnam's Sons, 1915), 280–81; GKW to A. S. Webb, 11:30 A.M., Feb. 5, 1865, *Official Records*, vol. 46, pt. 2, 400; GKW to A. S. Webb, 4:30 P.M., Feb. 5, 1865, ibid., 401; GKW to Emily Warren, 8 P.M. (before Meade's subsequent order to withdraw), Feb. 5, 1865, Warren Papers.

6. H. E. Tremaine (Gregg's aide-de-camp) to GKW, 4:30 P.M., Feb. 5, 1865, and A. S. Webb to GKW, 5 P.M., Feb. 5, 1865, both in *Official Records*, vol. 46, pt. 2, 401. See also D. M. Gregg to GKW, 4:20 P.M. (recd. 5:30 P.M.), Feb. 5, 1865, ibid., 410, describing "but few wagons passing on the Boydton plank road."

7. A. S. Webb to GKW, 9 P.M., Feb. 5, 1865, ibid., 402–403; GKW to C. Griffin, 9:30 P.M., Feb. 5, 1865, ibid., 404; Brainard, *Campaigns of the One Hundred and Forty-Sixth Regiment*, 281. Webb mistakenly thought Humphreys outranked Warren and directed the latter to take orders from Humphreys. Warren replied that "I presume you do not mean this literally." GKW to A. S. Webb, 9:15 P.M., Feb. 5, 1865, *Official Records*, vol. 46, pt. 2, 403. He was not making any kind of fuss about the error, and obviously he and Humphreys could work together if anyone could, but he did not wish to let the mistake slip by unremarked. Humphreys, the next morning, told Webb gently, "Warren's commission is a little older than mine." A. A. Humphreys to A. S. Webb, 6:40 A.M., Feb. 6, 1865, ibid., 422.

8. Report of GKW, Feb. 15, 1865, *Official Records*, vol. 46, pt. 1, 254.

9. Allan Nevins, ed., *A Diary of Battle: The Personal Journals of Colonel Charles S. Wainwright, 1861–1865* (New York: Harcourt Brace and World, 1962), 497.

10. GKW to Emily Warren, Feb. 13, 1865, Warren Papers; report of GKW, *Official Records*, vol. 46, pt. 1, 255–56. It was of this battle that a veteran from the 118th Pennsylvania wrote to Mrs. Warren after the general's death: "[O]ur line was slowly advancing when to the extreme front I observed Gen. Warren sitting upon his milk white steed, apparently unmindful of the danger he was in. It was at a moment when the bullets by the thousand rent the air. Expecting each moment to see our beloved commander shot down, I felt that I must go to [him] and beg him to withdraw, but was deterred doing so as shortly after, being outflanked by the enemy, we had to retire from the position." J. L. Smith to Emily Warren, March 24, 1884, Warren Papers.

11. Report of GKW, *Official Records*, vol. 46, pt. 1, 256; G. G. Meade to U. S. Grant, 5:15 P.M., Feb. 7, 1865, *Official Records*, vol. 46, pt. 2, 448.

12. G. G. Meade to Mrs. Meade, Feb. 7, 1865, George Meade, *The Life and Letters of George Gordon Meade* (New York: Charles Scribner's Sons, 1913), vol. 2, 261; GKW to Emily Warren, Feb. 13, 1865, Warren Papers.

13. GKW to Emily Warren, Feb. 8, 10, 11, 14, 1865, Warren Papers.

14. GKW to Emily Warren, Feb. 16, 1865, Emily Warren to GKW (telegram), Feb. 17, 1865, and GKW to Emily Warren, Feb. 27, 1865, all in Warren Papers; W. T. Gentry (acting asst. adj. gen., Fifth Corps) to A. S. Webb, Feb. 23, 1865 (recd. 10 A.M.), *Official Records*, vol. 46, pt. 2, 658.

15. GKW to Emily Warren, March 5, 1865, Warren Papers; Freeman Cleaves, *Meade of Gettysburg* (Norman: University of Oklahoma Press, 1960), 304.

16. GKW to Emily Warren, March 5, 1865; W. J. Warren to GKW, March 12, 1865; both in Warren Papers. Will had problems of his own; early in March he was drafted for the army and had quickly to make arrangements to procure a substitute. W. J. Warren to GKW, March 6, 1865, Warren Papers.

17. GKW to Emily Warren, March 10, 1865, Warren Papers. See GKW to A. S. Webb, 4 P.M., March 10, 1865, *Official Records*, vol. 46, pt. 2, 916: "It seems to be the general belief in the rebel army that their cause is hopeless. Rations are very scarce."

18. U. S. Grant to E. M. Stanton, Feb. 21, 1865, *Official Records*, vol. 46, pt. 2, 608; U. S. Grant to P. H. Sheridan, 2 P.M., Feb. 21, 1865, and P. H. Sheridan to U. S. Grant, same day, both ibid., 619. Hancock was named to command the Middle Military Division. David M. Jordan, *Winfield Scott Hancock: A Soldier's Life* (Bloomington: Indiana University Press, 1988), 174–75.

19. GKW to G. D. Ruggles, 6:55 A.M., March 25, 1865, *Official Records*, vol. 46, pt. 3, 129; G. D. Ruggles to GKW, 7:06 A.M., GKW to G. D. Ruggles, 7:50 A.M., and G. D. Ruggles to GKW, 8:20 A.M., all March 25, 1865, ibid., 130; J. G. Parke to U. S. Grant, 6:10 A.M., March 25, 1865, ibid., 145; J. G. Parke to U. S. Grant, 8:30 A.M., March 25, 1865, ibid., 146. Parke discovered early in the attack that Meade was absent and that he as senior officer was in command of the Army of the Potomac, not just the Ninth Corps.

20. GKW to Emily Warren, March 26, 1865, Warren Papers.

21. To the White Oak Road

1. GKW to Emily Warren, March 28, 1865, Warren Papers.

2. *Official Records*, vol. 46, pt. 1, 569–70. On Crawford and Coulter, see Joshua Lawrence Chamberlain, *The Passing of the Armies: An Account of the Final Campaign of the Army of the Potomac* (1915; reprint, Dayton, Ohio: Morningside Bookshop, 1991), 94. All of the brigade commanders were brigadier generals except for Colonel Kellogg.

3. U. S. Grant to P. H. Sheridan, March 19, 1865, *Official Records*, vol. 46, pt. 3, 46.

4. Orders issued by G. D. Ruggles, asst. adj. gen., March 28, 1865, ibid., 224; U. S. Grant to P. H. Sheridan, March 28, 1865, ibid., 234.

5. Allan Nevins, ed., *A Diary of Battle: The Personal Journals of Colonel Charles S. Wainwright, 1861–1865* (New York: Harcourt Brace and World, 1962), 507; Mary Genevie Green Brainard, *Campaigns of the One Hundred and Forty-Sixth Regiment New York State Volunteers* (New York and London: G. P. Putnam's Sons, 1915), 288–89; A. S. Webb to GKW, 8:45 A.M. (recd. 10:20 A.M.), and GKW to A. S. Webb, 10:30 A.M., both March 29, 1865, *Official Records*, vol. 46, pt. 3, 254.

6. A. S. Webb to GKW, 11:20 A.M., and GKW to A. S. Webb, noon, both March 29, 1865, *Official Records*, vol. 46, pt. 3, 255; Nevins, ed., *A Diary of Battle*, 507.

7. Report of GKW, Feb. 21, 1866, *Official Records*, vol. 46, pt. 1, 801–802; report of Chas. Griffin, April 29, 1865, ibid., 846; A. S. Webb to GKW, 7 P.M., March 29, 1865, *Official Records*, vol. 46, pt. 3, 256. See Chamberlain's report, April 21, 1865, *Official Records*, vol. 46, pt. 1, 847–48, and Chamberlain, *The Passing of the Armies*, 44. Chamberlain subsequently received a brevet major general's commission for his performance on March 29.

8. Chris M. Calkins, *The Appomattox Campaign, March 29–April 9, 1865* (Conshohocken, Pa.: Combined Books, 1997), 16–17.

9. GKW to Emily Warren, 9 P.M., March 29, 1865, Warren Papers.

10. Nevins, ed., *A Diary of Battle*, 509.

11. Report of GKW, Feb. 21, 1866, *Official Records*, vol. 46, pt. 1, 806–807, 809–810.

12. Calkins, *The Appomattox Campaign*, 20.

13. GKW to Emily Warren, March 30, 1865, Warren Papers.

14. Philip Henry Sheridan, *The Personal Memoirs of P. H. Sheridan* (1888; reprint, New York: Da Capo Press, 1992), 350.

15. U. S. Grant to P. H. Sheridan, March 29, 1865, *Official Records*, vol. 46, pt. 3, 266; Chamberlain, *The Passing of the Armies*, 49–50.

16. William Swinton, *Campaigns of the Army of the Potomac* (1866; reprint, New York: Charles Scribner's Sons, 1882), 588–89.

17. GKW to R. B. Ayres, 8:15 A.M., March 30 [31], 1865, *Official Records*, vol. 46, pt. 3, 369; A. S. Webb to GKW, 8:25 A.M. (recd. 8:40 A.M.), March 31, 1865, in report of GKW, *Official Records*, vol. 46, pt. 1, 812; William Henry Locke, *The Story of the Regiment* (Philadelphia: J. B. Lippincott, 1868), 383; GKW to A. S. Webb, 9:40 A.M. (recd. 10:30 A.M.), March 31, 1865, and A. S. Webb to GKW, 10:30 A.M. (recd. 11:40 A.M.), March 31, 1865, both in *Official Records*, vol. 46, pt. 3, 362.

18. Alfred S. Roe, *The Thirty-Ninth Regiment, Massachusetts Volunteers, 1862–65* (Worcester, Mass.: Regimental Veteran Association, 1914), 282; Swinton, *Campaigns of the Army of the Potomac*, 590; GKW to A. S. Webb, 1 P.M., March 31, 1865, *Official Records*, vol. 46, pt. 3, 362. A dispute arose between the Fifth and Second corps as to whether or not Miles "occupied" the White Oak Road before falling back and whether, if he did so, he did it before or after Griffin did. Because this dispute was between Warren and Humphreys, it was carried on very politely and with none of the venom which embittered countless postwar arguments about wartime occurrences. See GKW to A. A. Humphreys, July 6, 1865, A. A. Humphreys to GKW, July 11, 1865, GKW to A. A. Humphreys, July 17, 1865, GKW to C. Griffin, July 17, 1865, A. A. Humphreys to GKW, July 19, 1865, and J. L. Chamberlain to GKW, Nov. 7, 1865, all in Warren Papers. As Warren wrote in his letter to Humphreys of July 6, "The error into which you have been led [by Miles's allegedly erroneous report] would be a small thing to me at most times but now everything connected with that day's operations are very important to me."

19. Sylvanus Cadwallader, *Three Years with Grant*, ed. Benjamin P. Thomas (New York: Alfred A. Knopf, 1955), 299, 301. Cadwallader's partiality for Grant and resultant dislike of Warren, together with the numerous errors which infest this work, written in 1896, when both Warren and Crawford were dead, should be kept in mind in assessing this story, although Cadwallader's description of Warren's ill temper matches those penned by Wainwright. Crawford's friendship with and support for Warren after the war suggests that this story was either a fiction or a great exaggeration by Cadwallader.

20. Report of GKW, Feb. 21, 1866, *Official Records*, vol. 46, pt. 1, 815; U. S. Grant to G. G. Meade, 1 P.M., March 31, 1865, *Official Records*, vol. 46, pt. 3, 337.

21. Report of GKW, Feb. 21, 1866, *Official Records*, vol. 46, pt. 1, 815–17. Chamberlain reports that just after sunset he and Warren crept on their hands and knees to within two hundred yards of the enemy position to assess its strength. Chamberlain, *The Passing of the Armies*, 67.

22. Horace Porter, "Five Forks and the Pursuit of Lee," *Battles and Leaders*, vol. 4, 711.

23. P. H. Sheridan to U. S. Grant and U. S. Grant to P. H. Sheridan, both March 31, 1865, *Official Records*, vol. 46, pt. 3, 380.

24. A. S. Webb to GKW, 4:30 P.M., and A. S. Webb to GKW, 5:15 P.M. (recd. 5:45 P.M.), March 31, 1865, ibid., 363; GKW to A. S. Webb, 5:50 P.M., March 31, 1865, ibid., 364. An alleged eyewitness claims he saw Warren's mounting distress at hearing the retreating sounds of gunfire, apparently indicating Sheridan's repulse. At last Warren was said to have exclaimed, "I can endure this no longer, and without orders I will endeavor to send aid to Sheridan. Bartlett's old brigade must endeavor to make its way to Sheridan's relief." "Sketches of Army Life" by "AN OLD PRIVATE," *Newport (R.I.) Mercury*, June 24, 1882.

25. A. S. Webb to GKW, March 31, 1865, GKW to A. S. Webb, 6:30 P.M., March 31, 1865, and G. G. Meade to GKW, 7:30 P.M. (recd. 8 P.M.), March 31, 1865, all in *Official Records*, vol. 46, pt. 3, 364.

26. GKW to A. S. Webb, 8:20 P.M., A. S. Webb to GKW, 8:30 P.M. (recd. 8:35 P.M.), and GKW to A. S. Webb, 8:40 P.M., all March 31, 1865, ibid., 365.

27. U. S. Grant to G. G. Meade, 8:45 P.M., March 31, 1865, ibid., 340; G. G. Meade to U. S. Grant, 9:45 P.M., March 31, 1865, ibid., 341; U. S. Grant to G. G. Meade, 10:15 P.M., March 31, 1865, ibid., 342.

28. A. S. Webb to GKW, 9 P.M. (recd. 9:17 P.M.), March 31, 1865, Warren Papers; Fifth Corps General Orders No. [23], 9:35 P.M., March 31, 1865, *Official Records*, vol. 46, pt. 3, 368; A. S. Webb to GKW, 9:20 P.M. (recd. 9:45 P.M.), March 31, 1865, ibid., 366.

29. GKW to A. S. Webb, 10 P.M., March 31, 1865, ibid., 366.

30. W. H. H. Benyaurd to GKW, July 10, 1880, Warren Papers.

31. A. S. Webb to GKW, 9:40 P.M. (recd. 10:15 P.M.), March 31, 1865, *Official Records*, vol. 46, pt. 3, 366; G. G. Meade to GKW, 10:15 P.M. (recd. 10:48 P.M.), March 31, 1865, and GKW to G. G. Meade, 10:55 P.M., March 31, 1865, both ibid., 367; report of GKW, Feb. 21, 1866, *Official Records*, vol. 46, pt. 1, 822. In the *Official Records*, the last sentence of Warren's 10:55 P.M. dispatch omits the word "otherwise," thereby changing the meaning substantially. When Warren dictated this dispatch, he said "otherwise," but the staff officer transcribing it apparently left the word out of the message that went to Meade.

32. Report of GKW, Feb. 21, 1866, *Official Records*, vol. 46, pt. 1, 822.

33. U. S. Grant to P. H. Sheridan, 10:45 P.M., March 31, 1865, *Official Records*, vol. 46, pt. 3, 381. Stephen Sears contends, however, that "it was obvious to anyone on the scene who read the dispatch that Grant had been misinformed about the situation" and that

Sheridan seems not to have actually expected the Fifth Corps by midnight. Stephen W. Sears, *Controversies and Commanders: Dispatches from the Army of the Potomac* (Boston and New York: Houghton Mifflin, 1999), 272. Nevertheless, in his memoirs, Sheridan describes midnight as "the hour fixed" for the arrival of the Fifth Corps, though he magnanimously "assumed that there were good reasons for its non-appearance." Sheridan, *Personal Memoirs*, 372.

34. G. G. Meade to GKW, 11:45 P.M., March 31, 1865 (recd. 1 A.M., April 1, 1865), *Official Records*, vol. 46, pt. 3, 367.

35. Report of GKW, Feb. 21, 1866, *Official Records*, vol. 46, pt. 1, 823; Calkins, *The Appomattox Campaign*, 27.

36. P. H. Sheridan to GKW, 3 A.M. (recd. 4:50 A.M.), April 1, 1865, *Official Records*, vol. 46, pt. 3, 419–20. Sheridan called his 3 A.M. message "instructions," which seems a strange characterization of these ruminations. Report of P. H. Sheridan, April 2, 1865, *Official Records*, vol. 46, pt. 1, 1104.

37. In his memoirs, Sheridan said he "never once doubted that measures would be taken to comply with my dispatch of 3 A.M.," even though he still seemed not to understand where the Fifth Corps divisions actually were. Sheridan, *Personal Memoirs*, 372.

22. *All Fools' Day*

1. Report of R. B. Ayres, April 12, 1865, *Official Records*, vol. 46, pt. 1, 869.

2. Joshua Lawrence Chamberlain, *The Passing of the Armies: An Account of the Final Campaign of the Army of the Potomac* (1915; reprint, Dayton, Ohio: Morningside Bookshop, 1991), 80.

3. Report of GKW, Feb. 21, 1866, *Official Records*, vol. 46, pt. 1, 826; Chamberlain, *The Passing of the Armies*, 89.

4. Andrew A. Humphreys, *From Gettysburg to the Rapidan: The Army of the Potomac, July, 1863, to April, 1864* (New York: Charles Scribner's Sons, 1883), 356. See letter of E. R. Warner to H. J. Hunt, Aug. 30, 1875, extracted to GKW, Sept. 1, 1875, Warren Papers.

5. Horace Porter, "Five Forks and the Pursuit of Lee," *Battles and Leaders*, vol. 4, 711; Sylvanus Cadwallader, *Three Years with Grant*, ed. Benjamin P. Thomas (New York: Alfred A. Knopf, 1955), 302.

6. GKW to Col. James C. Biddle, May 26, 1877, Warren Papers. "My feelings," Warren went on in this letter, "are quite strong against certain members of Grant's and Sheridan's staffs." C. H. Morgan to GKW, March 14, 1868, Warren Papers.

7. *Proceedings*, vol. 1, 741–42. See also Porter, "Five Forks and the Pursuit of Lee," 711.

8. Report of P. H. Sheridan, May 16, 1865, *Official Records*, vol. 46, pt. 1, 1104.

9. Ibid., 1105. One commentator said that Warren, while "using every exertion that he deemed necessary . . . did not ride around swearing and cursing at a fearful rate." Charles H. Porter, "The Fifth Corps at the Battle of Five Forks," *Papers of the Military History Society of Massachusetts*, vol. 6 (1907), 250.

10. Cadwallader, *Three Years with Grant*, 302. Cadwallader then goes on to say that Warren's attitude "so incensed Sheridan that he removed him from command on the spot," placed Griffin in command, and then rushed the corps into battle. One would think that by 1896 Cadwallader could have gotten the basic facts of the battle straight. See S. W. Crawford to GKW, July 17, 1865, R. B. Ayres to GKW, June 24, 1865, and C. Griffin to GKW, June 26, 1865, all in Warren Papers, for confirmation from Warren's division commanders that he had ordered prompt movements into position and that these were in fact carried out.

11. Thos. L. Rosser to Jas. Longstreet, Oct. 22, 1892, quoted in Chris Calkins, "The Battle of Five Forks: Final Push for the South Side," *Blue & Gray Magazine*, vol. 9, no. 4 (April 1992), 48.

12. Mary Genevie Green Brainard, *Campaigns of the One Hundred and Forty-Sixth Regiment New York State Volunteers* (New York and London: G. P. Putnam's Sons, 1915), 293–94.

13. Report of R. B. Ayres, April 12, 1865, *Official Records*, vol. 46, pt. 1, 869; William Henry Locke, *The Story of the Regiment* (Philadelphia: J. B. Lippincott, 1868), 388.

14. Chamberlain, *The Passing of the Armies*, 99.

15. George Alfred Townsend, *Campaigns of a Non-Combatant, and His Romaunt Abroad during the War* (New York: Blelock, 1866), 323.

16. See J. A. Kellogg to GKW, Dec. 23, 1878, describing Sheridan's staffer (he thinks it was Forsyth) ordering his brigade forward when it was supposed to be "the pivot of the change of front." Kellogg is a little hazy on some of the facts but is clear on the order to advance.

17. Testimony of Frederick T. Locke and Holman S. Melcher at the Warren Court of Inquiry, May 24 and 29, 1880, *New York Times*, May 25, 30, 1880. Melcher was the corps postmaster.

18. W. Porter Snell to S. W. Crawford, April 13, 1865 (from his 'Notes on the Campaign'), Warren Papers; report of GKW, Feb. 21, 1866, *Official Records*, vol. 46, pt. 1, 835; H. S. Melcher to GKW, Feb. 18, 1880, Warren Papers. Richardson wrote to Warren a few months later, saying, "I saw you lead the *final grand charge* through the open field beyond and at right angles with the works captured of the enemy, with your Corps flag in hand, followed by a single scout, riding at least five rods in advance of the front line of battle." H. Richardson to GKW, Jul. 20, 1865, Warren Papers. Swinton, in his history, said of Warren's charge, "The history of the war presents no equally splendid illustration of personal magnetism." William Swinton, *Campaigns of the Army of the Potomac* (1866; reprint, New York: Charles Scribner's Sons, 1882), 600.

19. Gen. Nelson Miles, commanding a division in the nearby Second Corps, wrote that "the advance of the Fifth Corps, ably commanded and gallantly led by Warren, in conjunction with the advance of the cavalry, resulted in a crushing defeat of the Confederate forces." Nelson Appleton Miles, *Serving the Republic: Memoirs of the Civil and Military Life of Nelson A. Miles* (New York and London: Harpers, 1911), 83.

20. Field Orders No. - [no number given], April 1, 1865, *Official Records*, vol. 46, pt. 3, 420.

21. Chamberlain, *The Passing of the Armies*, 114.

22. From a letter Warren wrote to Secretary of War Stanton, dated April 1865, never sent but preserved in the Warren Papers. Warren concluded by noting that he said nothing to Grant "about what I with every officer and man of the army regarded as frequent the unneccessary slaughter to which we had been ordered, and which beyond the appalling inhumanity of the loss of so many lives, really perilled the success of our cause."

23. Ibid., Warren Papers. Meade learned of Warren's dismissal in a singular way. At 9:25 P.M., he sent to Grant, after learning of the Five Forks victory, "I am truly delighted with the news from Sheridan. What part did Warren take? I take it for granted he was engaged." Grant's reply, received at 11:10 P.M., said, "The Fifth Corps was in and did splendidly, but Sheridan had to relieve Warren on the field after the fight began," which was of course quite untrue. G. G. Meade to U. S. Grant, 9:25 P.M., and U. S. Grant to G. G. Meade, recd. 11:10 P.M., both April 1, 1865, *Official Records*, vol. 46, pt. 3, 398, 399.

23. A Soldier's Good Name

1. Alfred S. Roe, *The Thirty-Ninth Regiment, Massachusetts Volunteers, 1862–65* (Worcester, Mass.: Regimental Veteran Association, 1914), 286; William Henry Locke, *The Story of the Regiment* (Philadelphia: J. B. Lippincott, 1868), 393. Richard Coulter, commander of Crawford's third brigade, wrote Warren that Sheridan's action "was as deeply mortifying to your command as . . . to yourself." R. Coulter to GKW, March 21, 1866, Warren Papers.

2. A. B. Farnham to GKW, May 24, 1872, and H. Baxter to GKW, April 18, 1866, both in Warren Papers; Mary Genevie Green Brainard, *Campaigns of the One Hundred and Forty-Sixth Regiment New York State Volunteers* (New York and London: G. P. Putnam's Sons, 1915), 296. On April 12, Warren rode out from Petersburg to survey the area of the fighting around Five Forks, and he found there Colonel Farnham, badly wounded with a ball in his lung and attended by just one man. "He was very glad to see me," Warren wrote, particularly since the general arranged to have Farnham brought in to the hospital on a stretcher. GKW to Emily Warren, April 12, 1865, Warren Papers.

3. Allan Nevins, ed., *A Diary of Battle: The Personal Journals of Colonel Charles S. Wainwright, 1861–1865* (New York: Harcourt Brace and World, 1962), 513–14; C. S. Wainwright to GKW, March 15, 1866, Warren Papers.

4. *New York World*, April 4, 1865.

5. *New York Herald*, April 4, 1865. In his book published long after, Cadwallader wrote that "this moderate statement provoked a fierce quarrel with a few of Warren's real and pretended friends." Sylvanus Cadwallader, *Three Years with Grant*, ed. Benjamin P. Thomas (New York: Alfred A. Knopf, 1955), 304. Both Hendricks's and Cadwallader's dispatches mistakenly named Gibbon as the new commander of the corps.

6. James Harrison Wilson, *The Life of John A. Rawlins* (New York: Neale, 1916), 316; C. A. Dana to E. M. Stanton, 11:30 A.M., April 5, 1865, *Official Records*, vol. 46, pt. 3, 574; GKW to W. J. Warren, Nov. 22, 1877, Warren Papers.

7. GKW to Emily Warren, April 2, 1865, Warren Papers.

8. GKW to Emily Warren, April 4, 1865, Warren Papers. The orders assigning Warren to his new command were Special Orders No. 68, Headquarters, Armies of the United States, April 2, 1865, *Official Records*, vol. 46, pt. 3, 462; Special Orders No. 85, Headquarters, Army of the Potomac, April 3, 1865, ibid., 514; and T. S. Bowers, asst. adj. gen., to GKW, April 3, 1865, ibid., 536.

9. GKW to A. S. Webb, April 7, 1865, endorsed by Meade "to the lieutenant-general commanding," April 8, 1865, *Official Records*, vol. 46, pt. 3, 636.

10. Emily Warren to GKW, April 5, 1865; GKW to Emily Warren, April 6, 8, 9, 1865; all in Warren Papers.

11. GKW to Emily Warren, April 11, 1865; W. J. Warren to GKW, April 10, 1865; GKW to W. J. Warren, April 22, 1865; all in Warren Papers.

12. G. G. Meade to U. S. Grant, 10 A.M., April 18, 1865, *Official Records*, vol. 46, pt. 3, 822; T. S. Bowers to G. G. Meade, April 18, 1865 (recd. 7:20 P.M.), ibid., 823.

13. G. G. Meade to U. S. Grant, 1 P.M., May 1, 1865, ibid., 1055; U. S. Grant to G. G. Meade, 9:10 P.M., May 1, 1865, and General Orders No. 78, War Dept., Adjt. Gen.'s Office, May 1, 1865, both ibid., 1056.

14. Joshua Lawrence Chamberlain, *The Passing of the Armies: An Account of the Final Campaign of the Army of the Potomac* (1915; reprint, Dayton, Ohio: Morningside Bookshop, 1991), 228–29. Another writer felt that the "vociferous cheers" of the Fifth Corps gave Warren "one vindication which he might have valued more than any

other." John J. Pullen, *The Twentieth Maine: A Volunteer Regiment in the Civil War* (Philadelphia and New York: J. B. Lippincott, 1957), 280.

15. Emily Warren to A. S. Chase, May 1, 1865; GKW to "My dear friend," April 22, 1865; both in Warren Papers.

16. W. J. Warren to GKW, May 1, 1865, Warren Papers.

17. GKW to J. A. Rawlins, April 9, 1865, *Official Records*, vol. 46, pt. 3, 679.

18. Warren's letters of April 9, to Rawlins, and of April 22, to Bowers, and Grant's reply of May 6, 1865, were all published along with a letter to the editor from Warren in the *New York Times* of May 25, 1865.

19. GKW to Emily Warren, May 10, 11, 14, 1865, Warren Papers.

20. GKW to Emily Warren, May 15–18, 1865 (one letter), Warren Papers.

21. GKW to Emily Warren, May 20, 1865, Warren Papers; E. R. S. Canby to GKW, May 20, 1865, and GKW to adjutant general, U.S. Army, May 20, 1865, both in *Official Records*, vol. 48, pt. 2, 520.

22. *New York Times* and *New York Herald*, both May 25, 1865, and *Vicksburg Daily Herald*, May 30, 1865.

23. GKW to Emily Warren, May 28, 31, 1865, Warren Papers. The conduct of Confederate troops under Forrest after the surrender of Union defenders at Fort Pillow on April 12, 1864, toward black Union soldiers (and white soldiers who fought with them) was labeled the "Fort Pillow massacre," although Confederate authorities denied that it merited such an appellation. Sheridan's man Forsyth, who remained in the army after the war, later gained notoriety as the commander of the army troops who shot down unarmed Sioux at the misnamed "battle" of Wounded Knee in 1890.

24. An Engineer, Again

1. Report of P. H. Sheridan, May 16, 1865, *Official Records*, vol. 46, pt. 1, 1103; also published in the *Army and Navy Gazette*, June 13, 1865.

2. *Official Records*, vol. 46, pt. 1, 1104–105.

3. Ibid., 1105–106.

4. GKW to T. S. Bowers, Feb. 21, 1866 (Warren report of Five Forks, Dec. 1, 1865), ibid., 829; *Army and Navy Journal*, March 3, 1866; G. K. Warren, *An Account of the Operations of the Fifth Army Corps, Commanded by Maj.-Gen. G. K. Warren, at the Battle of Five Forks, April 1, 1865, and the Battles and Movements Preliminary to It* (New York: D. Van Nostrand, 1866), 3.

5. The printing bill from William M. Franklin for $233.02, dated Feb. 27, 1866, is in the Warren Papers.

6. W. S. Hancock to GKW, March 18, 1866; H. L. Abbot to GKW, March 25, 1866; both in Warren Papers. Fred Locke, the longtime adjutant general of the Fifth Corps, told Warren the pamphlet "completely refutes the unwarranted aspersions cast upon you by Genl. Sheridan. Had I not been satisfied of this on the *field*, your able defence would have removed all doubts." F. T. Locke to GKW, March 19, 1866, Warren Papers.

7. T. Lyman to GKW, March 13, 1866, Warren Papers.

8. *New York World*, March 8, 1866; *The Nation*, March 29, April 5, 1866. William Swinton, in a letter to Warren, called "A Staff Officer" who wrote the letter in *The Nation* "an infamous scoundrel." Wm. Swinton to GKW, April 6, 1866, Warren Papers.

9. Wm. Swinton to GKW, April 6, 1866; William Swinton, *Campaigns of the Army of the Potomac* (1866; reprint, New York: Charles Scribner's Sons, 1882), 601.

10. GKW to Emily Warren, March 24, 1866, Warren Papers.

11. GKW to Emily Warren, April 10, 14, 1866, Warren Papers.

12. GKW to D. H. Mahan, April 10, 1866 (not sent), Warren Papers.

13. GKW to Emily Warren, "Tuesday evening," April 20, 1866, Warren Papers.

14. GKW to Emily Warren, April 22, 1866, Warren Papers.

15. GKW to Emily Warren, April 27, 1866, Warren Papers. The threat of "counter charges" after vindication gives credence to a note Roebling wrote years later, saying, "I have heard men like Humphreys & others say that Grant was inclined to give Warren an investigation, but that Warren demanded that Sheridan should be publicly reprimanded for having done a cowardly & unsoldierlike act—and in choosing between the two he finally shielded Sheridan." W. A. Roebling memorandum, 1914, Roebling Papers.

16. GKW to Emily Warren, April 30, 1866, Warren Papers.

17. GKW to Emily Warren, April 30, May 1, 2, 1866, Warren Papers. For Stanton's deference to Grant, see Benjamin P. Thomas and Harold M. Hyman, *Stanton: The Life and Times of Lincoln's Secretary of War* (New York: Alfred A. Knopf, 1962), 471.

18. GKW to Emily Warren, Aug. 3, 1866, Warren Papers. Warren's official title was Superintending Engineer of Surveys and Improvements of the Upper Mississippi and its Tributaries.

19. GKW to Emily Warren, Aug. 17, 1866, Warren Papers.

20. GKW to Emily Warren, Aug. 21, 26, 31, Sept. 2, 15, 1866, Warren Papers.

21. GKW to Emily Warren, Sept. 7, 1866, Warren Papers.

22. GKW to Emily Warren, Sept. 17, 1866, Warren Papers.

23. GKW to Emily Warren, Sept. 26, Oct. 15, 30, Nov. 2, 6, 1866; A. A. Humphreys to GKW, Nov. 12, 1866; all in Warren Papers.

24. See letter of GKW to Emily Warren, June 20, 1868, from Washington, referring to baby Sidney for the first time, Warren Papers.

25. A. A. Humphreys to GKW, Nov. 8, Dec. 19, 1866, Warren Papers. In the December 19 letter, Humphreys took note of the blessed event in the Warren family by post-scripting, "I am glad to hear such fine accounts of the young *Guvner* & his mama."

26. GKW to Emily Warren, Jan. 17, 1867; W. J. Warren to GKW, Feb. 1, 1867; GKW to Emily Warren, April 16, 18, May 1, 1867; all in Warren Papers.

27. GKW to Emily Warren, May 7, 24, 1867, Warren Papers. In the latter note, Warren reported that Hancock was expected in St. Louis momentarily, having "lately concluded a repetition of the military performance of the King of France" (from the old ditty, "The good old King of France, he had ten thousand men, he marched them up a hill and he marched them down again"), referring to Hancock's having marched four thousand men across Kansas after the Cheyennes, losing the tribes, and returning empty-handed. See David M. Jordan, *Winfield Scott Hancock: A Soldier's Life* (Bloomington: Indiana University Press, 1988), 188–95.

28. GKW to Emily Warren, May 31, June 9, 1867, Warren Papers.

29. GKW to Emily Warren, June 24, Aug. 8, Nov. 24, Dec. 12, 1867, Warren Papers.

30. GKW to Emily Warren, Dec. 14, 19, 22, 1867, Warren Papers.

31. GKW to E. D. Morgan, March 16, 23, 1868, Edwin D. Morgan Papers, New York State Library. Morgan wrote to Warren on March 20 with the requested statement. GKW to Emily Warren, Oct. 24, 1868, for the visit that day with Young; GKW to Emily Warren, Sept. 20, 1868, for Hancock (telling of the distress Hancock was suffering from his Gettysburg wound); GKW to Emily Warren, Aug. 21, 1868, for the visit of the Agassiz party; all in Warren Papers.

32. GKW to Emily Warren, Nov. 12, 1868, Warren Papers.

33. Ibid.

34. GKW to Emily Warren, Nov. 16, 17, 1868, Warren Papers.

35. GKW to Emily Warren, Nov. 20, 22, Dec. 4, 1868, Warren Papers.

36. GKW to Emily Warren, Jan. 22, 29, 1869, Warren Papers.

37. GKW to Emily Warren, Feb. 4, 7, 11, 25, March 7, 12, 1869, Warren Papers.

38. GKW to Emily Warren, March 18, 1869, Warren Papers. How this letter was to get through if the mails were stopped by the snow is not indicated.

39. GKW to Emily Warren, Feb. 28, 1871, Warren Papers.

40. Edgar Warren to GKW, Jan. 31, 1870; W. J. Warren to GKW, Feb. 8, 1870; Emily Roebling to GKW, March 6, 1870; A. A. Humphreys to GKW, Feb. 16, 18, 1870; all in Warren Papers.

41. GKW to Emily Warren, Jan. 29, Feb. 2, 8, 10, 17, 18, 1870, Warren Papers.

42. GKW to Emily Warren, Feb. 20, 1870, Warren Papers.

43. GKW to Emily Warren, Feb. 22, 1870, Warren Papers.

44. GKW to Emily Warren, April 28, 30, 1870; GKW to adjutant general, April 30, 1870; Special Orders No. 102, Headquarters of the Army, Adjutant General's Office, Washington, May 3, 1870; all in Warren Papers.

25. Newport

1. A. S. Chase to GKW, May 25, 1870; A. A. Humphreys to GKW, June 10, 1870; A. A. Humphreys to Wilson G. Hunt, July 13, 1870 (though this letter never got beyond Warren); GKW to A. S. Chase, May 28, 1870; all in Warren Papers. Early in 1870, Will Warren was pressing Rufus Ingalls for a job, and Ingalls mentioned to him that he was interested in an engineering project "and if it was a success they wanted you, and would give you a big salary." W. J. Warren to GKW, Jan. 24, 1870, Warren Papers. Like all the other projects, nothing came of this. Will did manage to get a job in 1870 with the Census Bureau, headed by Francis A. Walker, former adjutant general of the Second Corps.

2. *Newport (R.I.) Daily News*, July 20, 1908. The house was owned by Daniel T. Swinburne, who was the corps' landlord. In 1908, the newspaper said, it "is now occupied as an Italian tenement house."

3. W. J. Warren to GKW, Oct. 24, 1870; GKW to Emily Warren, Nov. 27, 1870; GKW to A. S. Chase, Jan. 15, 1870; all in Warren Papers. Second Lieutenant Lewis Chase was court-martialed in Vicksburg on Jan. 5, 1869, for a drunken escapade on December 10/11, 1868, after his earlier acquittal on other charges in return for a pledge of total abstinence from alcohol. Lewis was convicted and dismissed from the service, the sentence being confirmed on April 20, 1869.

4. GKW to Emily Warren, Nov. 11, 1870, Warren Papers. After Siddy's query about the tricycle, Warren said, "I won't forget the look he gave me when he asked that question, to my dying day."

5. J. H. Wilson to GKW, Oct. 2, 1870; GKW to Emily Warren, Nov. 19, 20, 1870; all in Warren Papers.

6. GKW to Emily Warren, Aug. 16, Sept. 13, Oct. 18, Nov. 11, 1871, Warren Papers.

7. GKW to Emily Warren, Feb. 2, 19, March 23, April 4, Dec. 23, 25, 1872, Warren Papers.

8. H. N. Babcock to GKW, Jul. 18, 1872; A. S. Chase to GKW, Aug. 5, 1872; both in Warren Papers. C. R. Mather, one of those involved, had the cheek, after being dismissed from his job, to ask Warren for a letter of reference. C. R. Mather to GKW, Jul. 20, 1872, Warren Papers.

9. J. H. Dwight to GKW, June 19, 1872; GKW to Dwight, June 21, 1872; both in Warren Papers.

10. GKW to Emily Warren, Sept. 1 (Chicago), Nov. 13 (Detroit), Nov. 25 (Louisville), Nov. 27, 28 (New Orleans), 1873; Special Orders No. 83, Headquarters, Corps of

Engineers, June 30, 1873, ordering GKW to Antietam; GKW to G. H. Mandell, July 10, 1873; GKW to A. A. Humphreys, Nov. 8, 1873, recommending full allowance of the claim; all in Warren Papers.

11. GKW to Emily Warren (actually addressed to "My darling Emmie & little daughter), April 14, 1874, Warren Papers.

12. *Chicago Times*, May 17, 1874; GKW to Emily Warren, May 29, 1874, Warren Papers. The Chicago reporter said of Sheridan, "Since the glory of his life began and ended in a carnival of hate, it is not surprising that he should look with apprehension upon the rapidly accumulating evidences that his day is passed, and the time has come when the country has no use for the man who made the Shenandoah valley a dreary waste." He said the ovation for Warren "must have given Sheridan a premonition of the manner in which history will deal with him."

13. GKW to Emily Warren, Dec. 17, 1874, Warren Papers.

14. GKW to Emily Warren, April 14, May 1, 1874, Warren Papers.

15. W. J. Warren to GKW, May 23, 1875; GKW to Gouverneur Paulding, Sept. 19, 1875; both in Warren Papers.

16. A. S. Chase to GKW, Sept. 14, 1875; Lewis S. Chase to GKW, Aug. 18, 1876, advising that Morriss & Chase, Gentlemen's Fine Clothing, was "doing the largest clothing business that is done any where in this part of the South"; both in Warren Papers.

17. Extract from *Utah Evening Mail*, Jan. 24, 1876; Emily Roebling to GKW, March 8, 1876; both in Warren Papers.

18. GKW to Emily Warren, [late] April 1876; GKW to Emily Warren, Sept. 22, 1876; both in Warren Papers. Earlier, on Sept. 2, 1874, Warren had been made a member of the American Society of Civil Engineers.

19. *Washington Sunday Herald*, June 25, 1876.

20. GKW to Dr. Mercer, July 27, 1876, Warren Papers.

21. A. A. Humphreys to GKW, July 10, 1877; T. A. Adams to GKW, Aug. 12, 1877; A. P. Martin to GKW, Sept. 24, 1877; all in Warren Papers. McClellan was then a candidate (a successful one, as it turned out) for governor of New Jersey.

22. GKW to N. A. Miles, Oct. 10, 1877, Warren Papers.

23. Shortly after Warren's death, Emily wrote to Albert Stickney "that I have received no money or income from the estate of my father . . . as many of my friends erroneously suppose." Emily Warren to A. Stickney, Aug. 21, 1882, Warren Papers. Warren described the difficulties he as executor was having with Chase's former business partner and the fact that "there is no income from the estate" in a letter to Emily of March 13, 1879, Warren Papers. Many years later, Warren's daughter Emily wrote that "the one real home I have known was in the old house on Thames Street, Newport, R.I." Note, ca. 1931, Warren Papers.

24. GKW to A. A. Humphreys, Nov. 10, 1878, Warren Papers.

25. A. A. Humphreys to GKW, Nov. 13, 1878, Warren Papers.

26. Eliza Hook to GKW, Jan. 8, 1879; A. A. Humphreys to GKW, Feb. 18, 1879; both in Warren Papers.

27. GKW to Emily Warren, April 2, 8, 20, 1879, Warren Papers.

28. A. A. Humphreys to GKW, May 19, 1879. Horatio G. Wright had commanded the Sixth Corps after Sedgwick's death; Edward O. C. Ord led what was formerly Butler's army in the final campaign; Henry L. Hunt was the artillery commander of the Army of the Potomac; John Gibbon had been a division commander in the Second Corps before getting the Eighteenth and later Twenty-Fourth Corps; and Thomas H. Ruger had been a division commander in Sherman's army.

29. GKW to A. A. Humphreys, May 31, 1879. Parke, the erstwhile Ninth Corps commander, was a colleague in the Engineers; John M. Schofield, who had a distinguished career in the western army, had served briefly as secretary of war under Johnson and led the board that reviewed Fitz John Porter's case; Alfred H. Terry, who was Custer's superior in the Sioux campaign of 1876, had also served on the Porter board; and Henry Abbot, of course, was Warren's close friend and engineering colleague, while Emory Upton was one of the up-and-coming stars of the army.

30. A. A. Humphreys to GKW, June 7, 1879; GKW to A. A. Humphreys, June 11, 1879; both in Warren Papers. When anti-Hayes, pro-Grant Republicans in the Senate blocked McCrary's nomination from immediate consideration, Warren said this "more satisfies my mind that he is a level-headed man." Ibid.

31. Memorandum in GKW's hand dated Oct. 2, 1879, Warren Papers.

32. GKW to Emily Warren, Nov. 18, 1879, Warren Papers.

33. GKW to Emily Warren, Nov. 21, 1879; E. D. Morgan to R. B. Hayes, Nov. 13, 1879; both in Warren Papers. On December 1, his sister Emily wrote to Warren that she was glad "to hear you speak so cheerfully of the success of your enterprise in Washington." Emily Roebling to GKW, Dec. 1, 1879, Warren Papers.

34. Special Orders No. 277, Headquarters of the Army, Adjutant General's Office, Dec. 9, 1879.

26. The Court Begins

1. GKW to Emily Warren, Dec. 11, 1879, Warren Papers.

2. Proceedings, vol. 1, 6–7.

3. GKW to Emily Warren, Dec. 26, 30, 1879, Warren Papers. In the latter, Warren told Emily he could not come to Newport that week, "as this is the crisis of my affairs," and added, "Don't let it interfere with your tea party however." Also, GKW to Emily Warren, Jan. 1, 1880, Warren Papers. The receipt for the rental of the horses, dated Dec. 27, 1879, for a total of twelve dollars, is in the Warren Papers.

4. Proceedings, vol. 1, 6, 9.

5. Ibid., 30; New York Times, Jan. 8, 1880. Hancock later advised Warren that he would have at least to the first of April to prepare. GKW to A. Stickney, Jan. 27, 1880, Warren Papers.

6. GKW to Emily Warren, Jan. 5, 1880; GKW to A. B. Gardner, Jan. 15, 1880; GKW to A. Stickney, Jan. 19, 1880; GKW to A. Stickney, March 11, 1880; all in Warren Papers.

7. A letter of Warren to his wife details the financial arrangements with his lawyer, obviating the "need to call upon your income or my salary to meet this affair." GKW to Emily Warren, March 15, 1880, Warren Papers.

8. GKW to Emily Warren, Jan. 8, 1880, Warren Papers.

9. GKW to A. Stickney, Jan. 27, 1880, Warren Papers. "Have patience with me," Warren told his lawyer; "I shall get through if I keep well." GKW to A. Stickney, Feb. 5, 1880, Warren Papers.

10. GKW to A. Stickney, Jan. 27, 1880, Warren Papers. Griffin died in New Orleans of yellow fever.

11. See W. J. Warren to GKW, March 1, April 2, 4, 1880, Warren Papers. Gouv wrote to Will, "You have done so much, and so well, that I realize what it is to have a brother." GKW to W. J. Warren, April 10, 1880, Warren Papers.

12. Proceedings, vol. 1, 31 (Langdon), 36 (Warner's testimony).

13. GKW to Emily Warren, April 30, May 2, 1880, Warren Papers.

14. *Proceedings*, vol. 1, 45 (Sheridan's letter), 49 (Newhall); *New York Times*, May 4, 1880.

15. *Proceedings*, vol. 1, 56.

16. Ibid., 67; *New York Times* and *New York World*, both May 5, 1880. Sheridan later revised his testimony to read five miles per hour "for a short space of time" and forty-five miles between daylight and dusk in Oregon. *Proceedings*, vol. 1, 67. The damage to Sheridan's credibility, however, was done.

17. GKW to Emily Warren, May 4, 1880, Warren Papers.

18. *New York Times*, May 6, 7, 1880. On May 10, Stickney asked Sheridan, "You had no knowledge at the time of what General Warren did do in this battle after you parted with him at the beginning of the attack?" "No," said Sheridan, "I had no knowledge." "Nor did you make any inquiry to find out what he had done?" persisted Stickney. "I didn't have time," Sheridan responded. *Proceedings*, vol. 1, 128.

19. *Proceedings*, vol. 1, 100, 114–15. Later Sheridan testified that he did not really mean the commendatory terms by which he described the Fifth Corps in his report but omitted the criticisms he should have included, saying, "it was not my purpose to antagonize the Fifth Corps, nor to make the officers of the Fifth Corps nor the men of the Fifth Corps feel bad." Ibid., 118. On "Bobby Lee," Sheridan may have been thinking of Warren's description of Lee's giving his corps "a field day" on March 31.

20. *New York Times*, May 7, 1880.

21. *Proceedings*, vol. 1, 94.

22. GKW to Emily Warren, May 12, 1880, Warren Papers; *Proceedings*, vol. 1, 139.

23. GKW to Emily Warren, May 13, 1880, Warren Papers.

24. *Proceedings*, vol. 1, 146 (Newhall), 208 (J. Forsyth), 219 (Kellogg). Benyaurd took the stand on May 14, Wadsworth and James Forsyth the next day, and George Forsyth, Michael V. Sheridan, and Kellogg on the 15th. Warren was "perfectly delighted" by Wadsworth, who "remembers everything as clear as day," while "the mean [James] Forsyth . . . had forgot almost everything, and his voice was pitiable feeble, and his manner nervous and evasive." GKW to Emily Warren, May 15, 1880, Warren Papers.

25. *Proceedings*, vol. 1, 236. Chamberlain told Warren that when he attended the court Michael Sheridan, the general's brother, told him that Sheridan "would have been glad to compromise the matter with Warren if he could," but since "that was impossible he was going to make the fight with whatever 'club' he could get hold of." GKW memorandum, Nov. 1880, Warren Papers. There is no other evidence of any attempt by Sheridan "to compromise the matter" or any terms for doing so.

26. *New York Sun*, May 17, 1880; *New York Times*, May 13, 1880; *Brooklyn Eagle*, May 17, 1880.

27. *Proceedings*, vol. 1, 250, 252, 254; *New York World* and *New York Times*, both May 18, 1880.

28. *Proceedings*, vol. 1, 269.

29. Ibid., 272, 282, 285, 292, 303–304. Swan said he was not sure who the Sheridan staffer was who met Ayres. Sheridan had said on May 10 that if Ayres's attack failed, Griffin's and Crawford's divisions would have been captured and marched off to Libby Prison. Ibid., 133. Brinton, from Griffin's staff, said that on seeing Warren lead the final charge in the Gilliam field he remarked to another officer, "Why, we have two commanders; both General Warren and General Griffin are commanding the corps; a singular thing." Ibid., 304.

30. GKW to Emily Warren, May 15, 18, 1880, Warren Papers. The reference is to the denouement of Gilbert and Sullivan's popular *H.M.S. Pinafore*.

31. *Proceedings*, vol. 1, 315–16, 333; *New York Times* and *New York World*, both May 22,

1880. Among the interested spectators on Governor's Island that day was the governor of New Jersey, George B. McClellan. Another witness that day, W. J. Denslow, of the Ninety-First New York, had seen Warren seize the corps colors and ride toward the Confederate line. "I asked my men then," he said, "if they were going to allow their corps commander to go alone through there, and they said 'No,' and they followed right after." *Proceedings*, vol. 1, 335.

32. *Proceedings*, vol. 1, 338, 341, 366–67, 373, 379; *New York Times* and *New York World*, both May 25, 1880; *New York Times*, May 26, 1880.

33. *Proceedings*, vol. 1, 443, 454.

34. Ibid., 471, 491; *New York Times*, June 2, 1880.

35. *Proceedings*, vol. 1, 497, 510.

36. Ibid., 532; *New York Times*, *New York World*, and *Brooklyn Eagle*, all June 9, 1880; GKW to Emily Warren, June 9, 1880, Warren Papers. In this letter, Warren referred to "my first great personal enemy . . . Rawlins Grant's Chief of Staff." Again meaning Rawlins, who died of tuberculosis within six months of Grant's naming him secretary of war in 1869, Warren said, "He died by the hand of God—*One*. Grant goes under by the voice of the Republican party—*Two*. I am fighting Sheridan now. Shall that be *Three!*"

37. *New York Times* and *New York World*, both June 16, 1880; GKW to Emily Warren, June 15, 1880, Warren Papers.

38. GKW to Emily Warren; GKW to W. J. Warren; both June 17, 1880, Warren Papers.

39. GKW to Emily Warren, June 23, 1880, Warren Papers.

40. David M. Jordan, *Winfield Scott Hancock: A Soldier's Life* (Bloomington: Indiana University Press, 1988), 280; A. A. Humphreys to GKW, June 24, 1880, Warren Papers.

27. *The Court Resumes*

1. *Proceedings*, vol. 1, 654.

2. *New York World*, June 30, 1880; *Proceedings*, vol. 1, 663.

3. R. C. Drum, adjutant general, to W. S. Hancock, June 29, 1880, *Proceedings*, vol. 1, 683; *Philadelphia Inquirer*, June 30, 1880; GKW to Emily Warren, June 30, 1880, and W. J. Warren to GKW, June 29, 1880, Warren Papers. In his letter to Emily, Warren added, "Hancock being now off my Court makes my position towards him less delicate than it was before."

4. *Proceedings*, vol. 1, 736–37.

5. Ibid., 741–42.

6. Ibid., 744, 746.

7. Ibid., 748; the ruling against Custer's letter is at page 640.

8. Ibid., 750–51.

9. Ibid., 752.

10. Ibid., 790.

11. Ibid., 791–92.

12. Ibid., 793–94.

13. *New York World*, July 4, 1880.

14. GKW to Emily Warren, July 4, 1880, Warren Papers. Later on, he said, "I dont think I shall personally care much what these witnesses may say against me. Some of them I know are my friends." GKW to A. Stickney, Sept. 22, 1880, Warren Papers.

15. GKW to Emily Warren, July 6, 8, 1880, Warren Papers.

16. *Proceedings*, vol. 1, 805; GKW to Emily Warren, July 15, 1880, Warren Papers.

17. GKW to A. Stickney, July 22, Sept. 22, 1880, Warren Papers.

18. W. J. Warren to GKW, Aug. 24 (telegram and letter), 30, 1880; GKW to W. J. Warren, Sept. 3, 1880; all in Warren Papers.

19. A. A. Humphreys to GKW, Sept. 13, 1880, Warren Papers. On the Miles testimony, see GKW to A. A. Humphreys, Sept. 19, 1880; A. A. Humphreys to GKW, Sept. 21, 1880; both in Warren Papers.

20. *New York Evening Telegram*, Sept. 29, Oct. 2, 1880.

21. GKW to Emily Warren, Oct. 2, 1880, Warren Papers; *Proceedings*, vol. 2, 820, 823; *New York Times*, Oct. 2, 1880. In recommending a promotion for Mackenzie during the war, Warren had written Meade that "Mackenzie is a gem of a man. I know him well, because I taught him mathematics for two years. Saving that he is young and inexperienced, there is not a better man in all my acquaintance than he." GKW to G. G. Meade, June 9, 1864, *Official Records*, vol. 36, pt. 3, 713–14.

22. *Proceedings*, vol. 2, 935 (Gillespie), 988 (McGonnigle).

23. GKW to Emily Warren, Oct. 6, 1880, Warren Papers; David M. Jordan, *Winfield Scott Hancock: A Soldier's Life* (Bloomington: Indiana University Press, 1988), 289; A. A. Humphreys to GKW, Oct. 13, 1880, Warren Papers. The attack on Hancock, Warren said, "puts us both in the same attitude toward Grant and his piratical crew." GKW to Emily Warren, Oct. 7, 1880, Warren Papers.

24. *Proceedings*, vol. 2, 901; *New York Times*, Oct. 12, 1880. Babcock was deeply implicated in the Whiskey Ring frauds centered around St. Louis, and only Grant's intervention (and possible perjury) kept him from going to jail. For a description of this complex matter, see William S. McFeely, *Grant: A Biography* (New York and London: W. W. Norton, 1981), 405–416.

25. *Proceedings*, vol. 2, 908–909, 911, 919; GKW to Emily Warren, Oct. 12, 1880, Warren Papers.

26. GKW to Emily Warren, Oct. 12, 1880, Warren Papers.

27. *Proceedings*, vol. 2, 974.

28. *New York Evening Telegram*, Oct. 19, 21, 1880; *Proceedings*, vol. 2, 999–1012, for Stickney's cross-examination; GKW to Emily Warren, Oct. 22, 1880, Warren Papers. Tarbell said that during the march up to Gravelly Run Church his troops were all over the road when Warren rode by and said, "Why don't you order left oblique or right oblique?" in what Tarbell considered a censorious tone, and he had been nursing his grudge ever since. *Proceedings*, vol. 2, 997, 1010.

29. *Proceedings*, vol. 2, 1026–27. The *Newport (R.I.) Daily News*, reprinting on October 26, 1880, an item from the *New York Evening Mail*, said "the greeting between Gen. Grant and Gen. Warren, when the former appeared before the Court of Inquiry, shows the existence of a personal feeling of friendliness between the two." This is highly unlikely, in view of Warren's repeated statements of hostility toward Grant. The *New York Times*, in reporting Grant's appearance, said the ex-president "had no communication with Warren either before or after the examination." *New York Times*, Oct. 24, 1880. This certainly seems far closer to the truth.

30. *Proceedings*, vol. 2, 1028, 1030.

31. Ibid., 1030; *New York Times*, *New York Tribune*, and *New York Sun*, all Oct. 24, 1880.

32. *Proceedings*, vol. 2, 1041; *New York Tribune*, Oct. 24, 1880.

33. *Proceedings*, vol. 2, 1044.

34. Ibid., 1046; *New York Sun*, Oct. 24, 1880.

35. GKW to Emily Warren, Oct. 25, 1880, Warren Papers.

36. *Proceedings*, vol. 2, 1049.

37. Ibid., vol. 2, 1058 (testimony of Archer N. Martin), 1060–64 (Sheridan's statement); *Brooklyn Eagle*, Oct. 29, 1880.

38. Jordan, *Winfield Scott Hancock*, 306; GKW to Emily Warren, Nov. 3, 1880, Warren Papers.

39. *Proceedings*, vol. 2, 1084.

40. Ibid., 1087.

41. Ibid., 1091–92, 1094.

42. Ibid., 1102 (Locke), 1134 (Charles F. Gillies).

43. Ibid., 1145; *New York Times*, Nov. 12, 1880.

44. *Proceedings*, vol. 2, 1167, 1172; *New York Times*, Nov. 18, 1880; William W. Swan, "The Five Forks Campaign," *Papers of the Military History Society of Massachusetts*, vol. 6, 329.

45. *New York Herald*, Nov. 20, 1880; *Proceedings*, vol. 2, 1203–204.

46. *Proceedings*, vol. 2, 1208–209.

47. *New York Times*, Nov. 20, 1880.

48. *New York Herald*, Nov. 21, 1880; *New York Times*, Nov. 21, 23, 1880; *Army and Navy Journal*, Nov. 27, 1880.

49. GKW to W. J. Warren, Nov. 23, 1880, Warren Papers.

28. The Lawyers Have Their Say

1. GKW to Emily Warren, Nov. 12, 1880, Warren Papers.

2. *Boston Daily Advertiser*, Dec. 22, 1880; GKW to A. Stickney, Dec. 23, 1880, Warren Papers.

3. GKW to Emily Warren, Nov. 16, 1880, Warren Papers. The reporter for the *Times*, on November 13, 1880, analyzed what was left to do, including additional testimony and the arguments of counsel, and predicted that "the case may be left to the court" at the close of the session on November 19. *New York Times*, Nov. 13, 1880. He missed by about eleven months.

4. GKW to A. A. Humphreys, Nov. 24, 1880, Warren Papers.

5. Emily Roebling to GKW, Jan. 6, 1881, Warren Papers.

6. GKW to Emily Warren, Jan. 11, 1881, Warren Papers.

7. GKW to Emily Warren, Jan. 29, 1881, Warren Papers. Earlier he had told Emily that as a result of the inquiry he had "probably more permanently established my name than if no ill treatment had been endured." GKW to Emily Warren, Jan. 7, 1881, Warren Papers.

8. F. J. Porter to GKW, April 25, 1881, Warren Papers.

9. GKW to Emily Warren, July 1, 1881, Warren Papers.

10. GKW to Emily Warren, July 2, 1881, Warren Papers. Garfield was shot by a disappointed office-seeker named Charles Guiteau.

11. GKW to Emily Warren, July 5, 10, 1881, Warren Papers.

12. GKW to Emily Warren, July 19, 23, 1881, Warren Papers.

13. *Proceedings*, vol. 2, 1340.

14. Ibid., 1341–45; GKW to Emily Warren, July 25, 1881, Warren Papers.

15. *Proceedings*, vol. 2, 1400, 1402. The *Philadelphia Times*, in an editorial of July 29, 1881, stated that what was made evident by Stickney's address "was the saving of the Union front by Warren's rectification of Sheridan's incompetent and muddle-headed mismanagement of the movement."

16. *Proceedings*, vol. 2, 1403.

17. Ibid., 1404.

18. Ibid., 1408.

19. Ibid., 1408–409.

20. GKW to Emily Warren, July 28, 1881, Warren Papers. "General Warren has absented himself from the court-room while the argument of Major Gardner has been in progress . . . pacing restlessly about . . . The reason assigned for this action is the severity of Major Gardner's criticisms on his conduct." *New York Times,* July 29, 1881.

21. *Proceedings,* vol. 2, 1410–11.

22. Ibid., 1421.

23. Ibid., 1441–42.

24. Ibid., 1464.

25. Ibid., 1509, 1521–22.

26. Ibid., 1526.

27. Ibid., 1532–33.

28. Ibid., 1538. Humphreys had marked up for Warren a copy of his "Report of Operations of the Second Army Corps, from March 29 to April 9, 1865," and penciled in a note which read, "Warren, The paragraphs I have marked . . . show that at dusk of April 1 . . . the White Oak road . . . was not open for the enemy to move against Sheridan at Five Forks, as stated by him to the Court, May 4th [1880]." Report as marked in Warren Papers.

29. *The Frustration of Waiting*

1. W. J. Warren to GKW, Aug. 11, 1881; GKW to A. Stickney, Nov. 1, 15, 1881; both in Warren Papers. The "special ailment" referred to was presumably the diabetes which was to kill him.

2. Emily Roebling to GKW, Sept. 8, 1881, Warren Papers.

3. *New York World,* Oct. 28, 1881.

4. GKW to A. Stickney, Dec. 2, 1881, Warren Papers.

5. GKW to A. Stickney, Feb. 1, 1882, Warren Papers.

6. W. J. Warren to GKW, March 26, 1882, Warren Papers.

7. GKW to A. Stickney, April 14, 1882, Warren Papers.

8. A. Stickney to GKW, April 15, 1882, Warren Papers.

9. GKW to F. J. Porter, April 19, 1882; GKW to S. W. Crawford, April 24, 1882; both in Warren Papers. Meade had died in 1872.

10. GKW to A. A. Humphreys, April 29, 1882, Warren Papers.

11. W. J. Warren to GKW, May 3, 1882, Warren Papers.

12. W. J. Warren to GKW, May 10, 1882, Warren Papers. Humphreys suggested to Warren that he should get a friendly senator to see the secretary of war about the case. A. A. Humphreys to GKW, May 7, 1882, Warren Papers.

13. L. L. Langdon to GKW, May 16, 1882; GKW to L. L. Langdon, May 18, 1882; both in Warren Papers.

14. F. J. Porter to GKW, May 19, 1882; GKW to J. W. Wadsworth, May 21, 1882; both in Warren Papers.

15. Rufus Dawes to GKW, May 24, 1882; J. W. Wadsworth to GKW, May 27, 1882; both in Warren Papers. Warren wrote a letter back to Dawes, which he did not send, defining his position toward Grant as "unqualified hatred of his tyrannical acts of cruelty and injustice, and defiance of right." GKW to Rufus Dawes, May 27, 1882, Warren Papers. The bill restoring Porter's rank was finally passed in 1886 and signed by President Grover Cleveland.

16. GKW to A. Stickney, May 24, 1882, Warren Papers.

17. GKW to A. Stickney (not sent), May 28, 1882, Warren Papers.

18. Rufus Dawes to GKW, June 8, 1882, Warren Papers.

19. GKW to A. Stickney, June 9, 1882, Warren Papers.

20. W. J. Warren to GKW, June 11, 1882, Warren Papers.

21. GKW to R. C. Drum, June 15, 1882 (draft), with undated notation by Drum; GKW to R. C. Drum, June 19, 1882; both in Warren Papers.

22. A. Stickney to GKW, June 17, 1882, Warren Papers.

23. GKW to R. C. Drum, June 20, 1882 (draft); GKW to A. Child, June 21, 1882; both in Warren Papers.

24. *New York Post*, June 26, 1882; *New York Sun*, June 28, 1882; *New York Herald, New York Tribune, New York Times*, all June 29, 1882.

25. F. J. Porter to GKW, June 28, 1882; GKW to A. Stickney, June 30, 1882; both in Warren Papers.

26. GKW to A. Stickney, July 10, 1882, Warren Papers.

27. GKW to W. H. Morris, July 11, 1882; GKW to A. A. Humphreys, July 16–17, 1882; both in Warren Papers.

28. A. A. Humphreys to GKW, July 19, 1882; GKW to A. Stickney, July 21, 1882; both in Warren Papers.

29. W. J. Warren to GKW, July 23, 1882, Warren Papers.

30. Associated Press dispatch, July 26, 1882, reporting Swaim's opinion; GKW to W. J. Warren, July 31, 1882, Warren Papers.

30. *Where Malevolence Cannot Reach*

1. *New York Herald*, Aug. 10, 1882; *Under the Maltese Cross: Antietam to Appomattox* (Pittsburgh: 155th Regimental Association, 1910), 667, from a speech by Col. A. L. Pearson at the 155th Pennsylvania reunion in Pittsburgh, Sept. 12, 1894.

2. Rhode Island Death Records, book 21, p. 762, Rhode Island State Archives; Ann M. King to Emily Warren, Aug. 27, 1882, E. S. Eldredge to Emily Warren, Aug. 23, 1882, Lily S. Clymer to Emily Warren, Aug. 28, 1882, all in Warren Papers.

3. *Philadelphia North American*, Aug. 11, 1882; *New York Times*, Aug. 9, 1882; *Washington Post*, Aug. 10, 1882.

4. *The American*, Aug. 19, 1882.

5. *New York World*, Aug. 11, 1882.

6. M. Meade to Emily Warren, Aug. 10, 1882; W. S. Hancock to Emily Warren, Aug. 10, 1882; A. Stickney to Emily Warren, Aug. 15, 1882; all in Warren Papers.

7. L. L. Langdon to Emily Warren, Aug. 9, 1882, Warren Papers.

8. *Newport (R.I.) Daily News*, Aug. 12, 1882; *New York Times*, Aug. 13, 1882.

9. The birth year on daughter Emily's stone, 1875, is incorrect, as she was born the year before.

10. A. Stickney to C. A. Arthur, Aug. 16, 1882; R. T. Lincoln to A. Stickney, Sept. 20, 1882; both in Warren Papers.

11. A. A. Humphreys to A. Stickney, Oct. 10, 1882, Warren Papers. Swaim's opinion took up thirty-five printed pages, while Sherman's was but two.

12. *Proceedings*, vol. 2, 1561; A. Stickney to J. P. Cotton, Dec. 9, 1882, A. A. Humphreys to A. Stickney, Feb. 22, 1883, Warren Papers.

13. *Proceedings*, vol. 2, 1545, 1549–50. The report and opinion of the court of inquiry is found in General Orders No. 132, Headquarters of the Army, Adjutant General's Office, Nov. 23, 1882.

14. *Proceedings*, vol. 2, 1550, 1558–59.

15. Ibid., 1559.

16. Ibid., 1560–61.

17. A. Stickney to J. P. Cotton, Dec. 9, 1882, Warren Papers.

18. Warren's aide Cotton wrote up an analysis for Stickney. On Warren's staying back to be in communication with Meade on the 31st, "That," Cotton said, "was for Warren to decide on the ground." On the confused actions of that night, the court's opinions "are made up after knowing all of the conditions and not as Warren had to do that night, knowing as he did but little of the situation of Sheridan and the enemy." On Warren's manner, "they were not willing to come out squarely and give that charge the 'black eye' that it deserved, but they do not give Sheridan any comfort." J. P. Cotton to A. Stickney, Oct. 25, 1882, Warren Papers.

19. *Proceedings*, vol. 2, 1598.

20. Ibid., 1602.

21. F. J. Porter to Emily Warren, July 5, 1886; J. A. Kellogg to Emily Warren, Oct. 21, 1882; both in Warren Papers. The Sheridan Papers in the Library of Congress show that Sheridan sent copies of Gardner's speech to the governor of Michigan, the postmaster general, the Union League Club of New York, the Calumet Club of Chicago, John Codman Ropes, Theodore Lyman, the Connecticut Historical Society, Prince Otto von Bismarck, and the Minnesota Historical Society, and to the libraries at West Point, Amherst, Princeton, Yale, and Harvard, as well as to many similar recipients. Lyman, who supported Warren, wrote diplomatically to Sheridan in acknowledging receipt, "There is *one* fight we shall know about, and that is Five Forks!" T. Lyman to P. H. Sheridan, Nov. 14, 1881, Sheridan Papers.

22. G. W. Cullum to Emily Warren, May 15, 1884, Warren Papers.

23. H.R. Report No. 1830, 47th Cong., 2d sess., Dec. 16, 1882; Sen. Report No. 1649, 50th Cong., 1st sess.

24. H. Duryea to Emily Warren, Dec. 28, 1887, Warren Papers.

25. *New York Herald Tribune*, May 28, 1933; *Boston Transcript*, Jan. 28, 1933; *American Historical Review*, July 1933.

26. GKW to Emily Warren, July 15, 1881, Warren Papers.

27. Ulysses S. Grant, *Personal Memoirs of U. S. Grant* (Cleveland: World Publishing, 1952), 534.

28. James Harrison Wilson, *Under the Old Flag* (New York and London: D. Appleton, 1912), vol. 1, 397.

BIBLIOGRAPHY

Manuscripts and Papers

American Philosophical Society Archives

Francis Channing Barlow Papers, Massachusetts Historical Society

George W. Cullum File, Special Collections Division, United States Military Academy Library

Alfred Davenport Letters, New-York Historical Society

Ferdinand J. Dreer Collection, Historical Society of Pennsylvania

George Engelmann Papers, Missouri Botanical Garden

John Gibbon Papers, Maryland Historical Society

Gilliam Family Papers, Alderman Library, University of Virginia

Simon Gratz Collection, Historical Society of Pennsylvania

Andrew Atkinson Humphreys Papers, Historical Society of Pennsylvania

Henry Jackson Hunt Papers, Library of Congress

Anne Bachman Hyde Papers, Southern Historical Collection, University of North Carolina Library

LeConte Papers, American Philosophical Society

George Gordon Meade Papers, Historical Society of Pennsylvania

Fielding B. Meek Papers, Smithsonian Institution Archives

Edwin D. Morgan Papers, New York State Library

National Archives of the United States

> Record Group 57, Records of the U.S. Geological Survey, Predecessor Surveys, Ferdinand V. Hayden, Personal Letters Received, 1853–1862, 1864–1874, v. M–W
> Record Group 94, Records of the Adjutant General's Office
> U.S. Military Academy, Cadet Application Papers, 1805–1866
> Appointment, Commission and Personal Branch Document File General Papers and Books Union Staff Officers File

Roebling Family Collection, Special Collections and University Archives, Rutgers University Libraries

Philip Henry Sheridan Papers, Library of Congress

Smithsonian Institution, Office of the Secretary, 1863–1879, Incoming Correspondence, Smithsonian Institution Archives

Smithsonian Institution, Office of the Secretary, 1865–1891, Outgoing Correspondence, Smithsonian Institution Archives

Smithsonian Institution, Office of the Secretary, 1879–1882, Incoming Correspondence, Smithsonian Institution Archives

U.S. National Museum, Assistant Secretary, 1850–1877, Incoming Correspondence, Smithsonian Institution Archives
U.S. National Museum, Assistant Secretary, 1850–1877, Outgoing Correspondence, Smithsonian Institution Archives
Gouverneur Kemble Warren Papers, New York State Library

U.S. Government Publications

Cadets Arranged in Order of Merit in Their Respective Classes, as Determined at the General Examination in June, 1847 [annually through June, 1850].
Davis, Jefferson. "Report of the Secretary of War on the Several Pacific Rail Road Explorations" (1855).
House Exec. Doc. No. 194, 43d Congress, 1st sess. (1874), "Saint Louis and Illinois Bridge across the Mississippi River."
House Exec. Doc. No. 76, 43d Congress, 2d sess. (1875), "Minnesota River."
House Exec. Doc. No. 41, 44th Congress, 2d sess. (1877), "Navigation of the Mississippi River."
Humphreys, Andew A. "Annual Report of Captain A. A. Humphreys, Topographical Engineers, in Charge of Office of Explorations and Surveys, War Department, December, 1858." Washington, 1859.
Humphreys, Andrew A., and G. K. Warren. An Examination by Direction of the Hon. Jefferson Davis, Secretary of War, of the Reports of Explorations for Railroad Routes from the Mississippi to the Pacific, Made under the Orders of the War Department in 1853–54. Washington, D.C.: A. O. P. Nicholas, 1855.
Proceedings, Findings, and Opinions of the Court of Inquiry Convened by Order of the President of the United States in Special Orders No. 277, Headquarters of the Army, Adjutant General's Office, Washington, D.C., Dec. 9, 1879, in the Case of Gouverneur K. Warren, Late Major-General U.S. Volunteers; Commanding the Fifth Army Corps in the Campaign of Five Forks, Va., 1865. 3 vols. Washington, D.C.: Government Printing Office, 1883.
Report of the Joint Committee on the Conduct of the War. Rep. Com. No. 108, 37th Cong., 3d sess. (1863).
Report of the Joint Committee on the Conduct of the War. 38th Cong., 2d sess. (1865).
Senate Exec. Doc. No. 32, 35th Congress, 2d sess. (1859). "Colonel Wright's Late Campaign against the Indians in Oregon and Washington Territories."
War of the Rebellion: A Compilation of the Official Records of the Union and Confederate Armies. 128 vols. Washington, D.C.: Government Printing Office, 1880–1901.
Warren, Lt. G. K. Explorations in the Dacota Country, in the Year 1855. Washington, D.C.: A. O. P. Nicholson, 1856.
———. Preliminary Report of Explorations in Nebraska and Dakota in the Years 1855–'56–'57. Washington, D.C.: reprint, 1875.

Newspapers and Journals

American
Army and Navy Journal
Atchison (Kans.) Champion
Boston Commercial Bulletin
Boston Daily Advertiser

Boston Post
Brooklyn Daily Eagle
Cleveland Leader
Grand Army Review
LaCrosse (Wis.) Republican

New York Evening Telegram
New York Herald
New York Sun
New York Times
New York Tribune
New York World
Newport (R.I.) Daily News
Philadelphia American
Philadelphia Evening Telegraph
Philadelphia Inquirer
Philadelphia North American

Philadelphia Press
Philadelphia Times
Pittsburgh Dispatch
Pittsburgh Leader
Richmond Whig
Rochester Democrat and Chronicle
Toledo Daily Blade
Utica Morning Herald
Vicksburg Daily Herald
Washington Post
(Washington) Sunday Herald

Books and Articles

Abbot, Henry L. "Gouverneur Kemble Warren." *Science*, March 7, 1884.

Agassiz, George R., ed. *Meade's Headquarters, 1863–1865: Letters of Colonel Theodore Lyman from the Wilderness to Appomattox*. Boston: Atlantic Monthly, 1922.

Arnold, James R. *The Armies of U. S. Grant*. London: Arms and Armour Press, 1995.

Athearn, Robert G. *Forts of the Upper Missouri*. 1967. Reprint, Lincoln: University of Nebraska Press, 1972.

Badeau, Adam, *Grant in Peace: From Appomattox to Mount McGregor*. Hartford, Conn.: S. S. Scranton, 1887.

———. *Military History of Ulysses S. Grant, from April, 1861, to April, 1865*. 3 vols. New York: D. Appleton, 1868–1881.

Barry, John M. *Rising Tide: The Great Mississippi Flood of 1927 and How It Changed America*. New York: Simon and Schuster, 1997.

Batchelder, George Alexander. *A Sketch of the History and Resources of Dakota Territory*. Yankton, S.D.: Press Steam Power Printing Co., 1870.

Bates, Samuel P. *History of Pennsylvania Volunteers, 1861–5*. 5 vols. Harrisburg, Pa.: B. Singerly, State Printer, 1869–1871.

Blake, William J. *The History of Putnam County, N.Y.* New York: Baker and Scribner, 1849.

Brainard, Mary Genevie Green. *Campaigns of the One Hundred and Forty-Sixth Regiment New York State Volunteers*. New York and London: G. P. Putnam's Sons, 1915.

Butler, Benjamin F. *Butler's Book: Autobiography and Personal Reminiscences*. Boston: A. M. Thayer, 1892.

Butterfield, Julia Lorrilard Safford, ed. *A Biographical Memorial of General Daniel Butterfield*. New York: Grafton Press, 1904.

Byrne, Frank L., and Andrew T. Weaver, eds. *Haskell of Gettysburg: His Life and Civil War Papers*. Madison: State Historical Society of Wisconsin, 1970.

Cadwallader, Sylvanus. *Three Years with Grant*. Edited by Benjamin P. Thomas. New York: Alfred A. Knopf, 1955.

Calkins, Chris M. *The Appomattox Campaign, March 29–April 9, 1865*. Conshohocken, Pa.: Combined Books, 1997.

———. "The Battle of Five Forks: Final Push for the South Side." *Blue & Gray Magazine*, vol. 9, no. 4 (April 1992).

Camper, Charles, and J. W. Kirkley. *Historical Record of the First Regiment Maryland Infantry*. Washington, D.C.: Gibson Bros., 1871.

Carmichael, Peter S. "The Battle of Five Forks, March 31–April 1, 1865." *Civil War,* April 1998.

Casey, Robert J. *The Black Hills and Their Incredible Characters.* Indianapolis and New York: Bobbs-Merrill, 1949.

Catton, Bruce. *Grant Takes Command.* Boston and Toronto: Little, Brown and Co., 1968.

Chamberlain, Joshua Lawrence. *The Passing of the Armies: An Account of the Final Campaign of the Army of the Potomac.* 1915. Reprint, Dayton, Ohio: Morningside Bookshop, 1991.

Cleaves, Freeman. *Meade of Gettysburg.* Norman: University of Oklahoma Press, 1960.

Coburn, Jeff. L. "A Visit to the Battlefield of Dinwiddie Court House." *The Maine Bugle,* January 1895.

Coddington, Edwin B. *The Gettysburg Campaign: A Study in Command.* New York: Charles Scribner's Sons, 1968.

Conyngham, D. P. *The Irish Brigade and Its Campaigns.* New York: Fordham University Press, 1994.

Crawford, Mark J. "Dinwiddie Court House: Beginning of the End." *America's Civil War,* vol. 12 no. 1 (March 1999).

Crist, Lynda Lasswell, and Mary S. Dix, eds. *The Papers of Jefferson Davis.* Vol. 6. Baton Rouge and London: Louisiana State University Press, 1989.

Cullen, Joseph P. *The Peninsula Campaign 1862: McClellan and Lee Struggle for Richmond.* Harrisburg, Pa.: Stackpole Books, 1973.

Cullum, George W. *Biographical Register of the Officers and Graduates of the U.S. Military Academy at West Point, N.Y., From its Establishment, in 1802, to 1890.* Boston and New York: Houghton, Mifflin and Co., 1891.

Curtis, O. B. *History of the Twenty-Fourth Michigan of the Iron Brigade.* Detroit: Winn and Hammond, 1891.

Dana, Charles A. *Recollections of the Civil War.* New York: D. Appleton and Co., 1899.

Davenport, Alfred. *Camp and Field Life of the Fifth New York Volunteer Infantry (Duryée Zouaves).* New York: Dick and Fitzgerald, 1879.

Dawes, Rufus R. *Service with the Sixth Wisconsin Volunteers.* Madison: State Historical Society of Wisconsin, 1962.

Doubleday, Abner. *Chancellorsville and Gettysburg.* New York: Charles Scribner's Sons, 1882.

Eaton, Clement. *Jefferson Davis.* New York: The Free Press, 1977.

Eisenhower, John S. D. *Agent of Destiny: The Life and Times of General Winfield Scott.* New York: The Free Press, 1997.

Eisenschiml, Otto. *The Celebrated Case of Fitz John Porter: An American Dreyfus Affair.* Indianapolis and New York: Bobbs-Merrill, 1950.

Feis, William B. "Neutralizing the Valley: The Role of Military Intelligence in the Defeat of Jubal Early's Army of the Valley, 1864–1865." *Civil War History,* September 1993.

Ferris, Loraine. "Gouverneur Kemble Warren—The Man." *Nebraska History,* October–December 1938.

Fisher, Donald M. "Born in Ireland, Killed at Gettysburg: The Life, Death, and Legacy of Patrick Henry O'Rorke." *Civil War History,* vol. 39 no. 3 (September 1993).

Flanagan, Vincent J. "Gouverneur Kemble Warren, Explorer of the Nebraska Territory." *Nebraska History,* Summer 1970

Ford, Worthington Chauncey, ed. *A Cycle of Adams Letters, 1861–1865.* 2 vols. Boston and New York: Houghton Mifflin, 1920.

Foster, Mike. *Strange Genius: The Life of Ferdinand Vandeveer Hayden*. Niwot, Colo.: Roberts Rinehart, 1994.

14th Annual Reunion of the Association of the Graduates of the United States Military Academy, at West Point, June 12, 1883. Philadelphia: Times Printing House, 1883.

Freeman, Douglas Southall. *Lee's Lieutenants: A Study in Command*. 3 vols. New York: Charles Scribner's Sons, 1942–1944.

Furgurson, Ernest B. *Chancellorsville, 1863: The Souls of the Brave*. New York: Alfred A. Knopf, 1992.

Gaff, Alan D. *On Many a Bloody Field: Four Years in the Iron Brigade*. Bloomington and Indianapolis: Indiana University Press, 1996.

Gallagher, Gary W., ed. *The Spotsylvania Campaign*. Chapel Hill and London: University of North Carolina Press, 1998.

———. *The Wilderness Campaign*. Chapel Hill and London: University of North Carolina Press, 1997.

Gardner, Asa Bird. *The Battles of "Gravelly Run," "Dinwiddie Court-House," and "Five Forks," Va., 1865*. Chicago, 1881.

Gibbon, John. *Personal Recollections of the Civil War*. New York and London: G. P. Putnam's Sons, 1928.

Grant, Ulysses S. *Personal Memoirs of U. S. Grant*. Cleveland: World Publishing, 1952.

Hagerman, Edward. *The American Civil War and the Origins of Modern Warfare*. Bloomington and Indianapolis: Indiana University Press, 1988.

Hall, Isaac. *History of the Ninety-Seventh Regiment, New York Volunteers ("Conkling Rifles") in the War for the Union*. Utica, N.Y.: L. C. Childs and Son, 1890.

Hanson, James A. "A Forgotten Fur Trade Trail." *Nebraska History*, Spring 1987.

———. *Little Chief's Gatherings: The Smithsonian Institution's G. K. Warren 1855–1856 Plains Indian Collection and the New York State Library's 1855–1857 Warren Expedition Journals*. Crawford, Nebr.: The Fur Press, 1996.

Haskell, Frank Aretas. *The Battle of Gettysburg*. Wisconsin Historical Commission, 1910.

Hebert, Walter H. *Fighting Joe Hooker*. Indianapolis and New York: Bobbs-Merrill, 1944.

Heenehan, Jim. "The Little Round Top Regiments." *America's Civil War*, vol. 12 no. 4 (September 1999).

Henderson, Gertrude. "Ferries on the Big Sioux near Sioux City." *South Dakota Historical Collections*. Vol. 23. Pierre, S.Dak.: State Publishing, 1947.

Hennessy, John J. *Return to Bull Run: The Campaign and Battle of Second Manassas*. New York: Simon and Schuster, 1993.

Hergesheimer, Joseph. *Sheridan: A Military Narrative*. Boston and New York: Houghton Mifflin, 1931.

Hood, John Bell. *Advance and Retreat: Personal Experiences in the United States and Confederate States Armies*. 1880. Reprint, Bloomington: Indiana University Press, 1959.

Howard, O. O. *Autobiography of Oliver Otis Howard, Major General, United States Army*. 2 vols. New York: Baker and Taylor, 1907.

Howe, Mark De Wolfe, ed. *Touched with Fire: Civil War Letters and Diary of Oliver Wendell Holmes, Jr., 1861–1864*. Cambridge: Harvard University Press, 1946.

Humphreys, Andrew A. *From Gettysburg to the Rapidan: The Army of the Potomac, July, 1863, to April, 1864*. New York: Charles Scribner's Sons, 1883.

———. *The Virginia Campaign of '64 and '65*. New York: C. Scribner's Sons, 1883.

Humphreys, Henry H. *Andrew Atkinson Humphreys*. Philadelphia: John C. Winston, 1924.

Jackson, Huntington W. "The Battle of Chancellorsville." In *Military Essays and Recollections: Papers Read before the Commandery of the State of Illinois*, Military Order of the Loyal Legion of the United States, Commandery of the State of Illinois. Vol. 3. Chicago: Dial Press, 1894.

Johnson, Robert Underwood, and Clarence Clough Buell, eds. *Battles and Leaders of the Civil War.* 4 vols. New York: Century, 1884–1887.

Jordan, David M. *Winfield Scott Hancock: A Soldier's Life.* Bloomington: Indiana University Press, 1988.

Kelly, Michael T. *"I Will Have Justice Done": Gen. Gouverneur K. Warren, U.S.A.* Gettysburg, Pa.: Farnsworth Military Impressions, 1997.

Kingsbury, George W. *History of Dakota Territory.* Vol. 1. Chicago: S. J. Clarke, 1915.

Krick, Robert E. L. "Weldon Railroad August 18–21, 1864." *Civil War,* April 1998.

Kurtz, Henry I. "Five Forks: The South's Waterloo." *Civil War Times Illustrated,* October 1964.

Livermore, Thomas L. *Days and Events, 1860–1866.* Boston and New York: Houghton Mifflin, 1920.

Locke, William Henry. *The Story of the Regiment.* Philadelphia: J. B. Lippincott, 1868.

Long, Armistead L. *Memoirs of Robert E. Lee: His Military and Personal History.* New York, Philadelphia, and Washington, D.C.: J. M. Stoddart, 1887.

Longacre, Edward G. "Gouverneur K. Warren: A Personality Profile." *Civil War Times Illustrated,* January 1972.

——. *The Man behind the Guns: A Biography of General Henry Jackson Hunt, Chief of Artillery, Army of the Potomac.* South Brunswick and New York: A. S. Barnes, 1977.

——. *To Gettysburg and Beyond: The Twelfth New Jersey Volunteer Infantry, II Corps, Army of the Potomac, 1862–1865.* Hightstown, N.J.: Longstreet House, 1988.

Longstreet, James. *From Manassas to Appomattox: Memoirs of the Civil War in America.* Philadelphia: Lippincott, 1895; 2nd rev. ed., 1912.

Mahan, Dennis Hart. *A Complete Treatise on Field Fortification.* New York: Wiley and Long, 1836.

Marbaker, Thos. D. *History of the Eleventh New Jersey Volunteers from Its Organization to Appomattox.* Toronto: MacCrellish and Quigley, 1898.

Marvel, William. *Burnside.* Chapel Hill and London: University of North Carolina Press, 1991.

Matter, William D. *If It Takes All Summer: The Battle of Spotsylvania.* Chapel Hill and London: University of North Carolina Press, 1988.

Mattes, Merrill J. "Report on Historic Sites in the Fort Randall Reservoir Area, Missouri River, South Dakota." *South Dakota Historical Collections,* vol. 24. Pierre, S.Dak.: State Publishing, 1949.

McClellan, George Brinton. *McClellan's Own Story: The War for the Union.* New York: C. L. Webster, 1887.

——. *Report on the Organization and Campaigns of the Army of the Potomac.* New York: Sheldon and Co., 1864.

McCullough, David. *The Great Bridge.* New York: Simon and Schuster, 1982 (originally published 1972).

McElfresh, Earl B. *Maps and Mapmakers of the Civil War.* New York: Harry N. Abrams, 1999.

McFeely, William S. *Grant: A Biography.* New York and London: W. W. Norton, 1981.

McKenzie, John D. "Confrontation at Five Forks: Sheridan vs. Warren." *Civil War,* March–April 1993.

McLaird, James D., and Lesta V. Turchen. "The Dacota Explorations of Lieutenant
    Gouverneur Kemble Warren, 1855–1856–1857." *South Dakota History*, vol. 3, no.
    4 (Fall 1973).

Meade, George. *The Life and Letters of George Gordon Meade*. 2 vols. New York:
    Charles Scribner's Sons, 1913.

Meyers, Augustus. "Dakota in the Fifties." *South Dakota Historical Collections*, vol. 10.
    Pierre, S.Dak.: State Publishing, 1920.

Miles, Nelson Appleton. *Serving the Republic: Memoirs of the Civil and Military Life
    of Nelson A. Miles*. New York and London: Harpers, 1911.

Morris, Roy, Jr. *Sheridan: The Life and Wars of General Phil Sheridan*. New York:
    Crown, 1992.

Morrison, James L., Jr., ed. *The Memoirs of Henry Heth*. Westport, Conn., and London:
    Greenwood Press, 1974.

Mulholland, St. Clair A. *The Story of the 116th Regiment, Pennsylvania Infantry*. Phil-
    adelphia: F. McManus, Jr., 1899.

Murfin, James V. *The Gleam of Bayonets: The Battle of Antietam and the Maryland
    Campaign of 1862*. New York and London: Thomas Yoseloff, 1965.

Nash, Eugene A. *A History of the Forty-Fourth Regiment New York Volunteer Infantry
    in the Civil War, 1861–1865*. Chicago: R. R. Donnelley and Sons, 1911.

Neul, Robert C. "Too Late the Hero: Warren at Five Forks." *Civil War*, July–August
    1990.

Nevins, Allan, ed. *A Diary of Battle: The Personal Journals of Colonel Charles S. Wain-
    wright, 1861–1865*. New York: Harcourt Brace and World, 1962.

Nevins, Allan, and Milton Halsey Thomas, eds. *The Diary of George Templeton Strong:
    The Civil War, 1860–1865*. New York: Macmillan, 1952.

Newberry, Walter C. "The Petersburg Mine." In *Military Essays and Recollections: Pa-
    pers Read before the Commandery of the State of Illinois*, Military Order of the
    Loyal Legion of the United States, Commandery of the State of Illinois. Vol. 3.
    Chicago: Dial Press, 1899.

Newhall, Fred C. "With Sheridan in Lee's Last Campaign." *The Maine Bugle*,
    January–April 1895.

Newton, Steven H. *Joseph E. Johnston and the Defense of Richmond*. Lawrence: Uni-
    versity Press of Kansas, 1998.

New York Monuments Commission. *Dedication of the New York Auxiliary State
    Monument on the Battlefield of Gettysburg*. Albany: J. B. Lyon, 1926.

Nichols, Edward J. *Toward Gettysburg: A Biography of General John F. Reynolds*. New
    York: Pennsylvania State University Press, 1958.

Nicolay, John G., and John Hay. *Abraham Lincoln: A History*. 10 vols. New York: Cen-
    tury, 1890.

Niven, John. *Connecticut for the Union: The Role of the State in the Civil War*. New
    Haven and London: Yale University Press, 1965.

Norton, Oliver Willcox. *The Attack and Defense of Little Round Top, Gettysburg, July
    2, 1863*. New York: Neale, 1913.

Page, Charles D. *History of the Fourteenth Regiment, Connecticut Vol. Infantry*. Meri-
    den, Conn.: Horton Printing, 1906.

Palfrey, Francis Winthrop. *The Antietam and Fredericksburg*. New York: Charles Scrib-
    ner's Sons, 1882.

Parker, Francis J. *The Story of the Thirty-Second Regiment, Massachusetts Infantry*. Bos-
    ton: C. W. Calkins, 1880.

Peattie, Roderick, ed. *The Black Hills*. New York: Vanguard Press, 1952.

Pfanz, Harry W. *Gettysburg: The Second Day*. Chapel Hill and London: University of North Carolina Press, 1987.

Pleasants, Henry, Jr., and George H. Straley. *Inferno at Petersburg*. Philadelphia and New York: Chilton, 1961.

Pohanka, Brian C. " 'Boys, Won't I Make a Fine Looking Corpse?' Duryée's Zouaves at Second Bull Run." *Civil War Regiments*, vol. 1, no. 2 (1991).

——. "Charge Bayonets: The 5th New York at the Battle of Gaines' Mill." *Civil War Times Illustrated*, vol. 33 no. 2 (May–June 1994).

——. "Duryée's Zouaves: The 5th New York Volunteer Infantry." *Civil War Regiments*, vol. 1, no. 2 (1991).

Porter, Charles H. "The Fifth Corps at the Battle of Five Forks." In *Papers of the Military Historical Society of Massachusetts*, Military Historical Society of Massachusetts. Vol. 6. Boston: The Military Historical Society of Massachusetts, 1907.

——. "Operations of the Fifth Corps on the Left, March 29, to Nightfall March 31, 1865; Gravelly Run." *Papers of the Military Historical Society of Massachusetts*, Military Historical Society of Massachusetts. Vol. 6. Boston: The Military Historical Society of Massachusetts, 1907.

Powell, William H. *The Fifth Army Corps (Army of the Potomac): A Record of Operations during the Civil War in the United States of America, 1861–1865*. New York and London: G. P. Putnam's Sons, 1896.

Prentice, Sartell. "The Opening Hours in the Wilderness in 1864." In *Military Essays and Recollections: Papers Read before the Commandery of the State of Illinois*, Military Order of the Loyal Legion of the United States, Commandery of the State of Illinois. Vol. 3. Chicago: Dial Press, 1894.

Pullen, John J. *The Twentieth Maine: A Volunteer Regiment in the Civil War*. Philadelphia and New York: J. B. Lippincott, 1957.

Rawley, James A. *Edwin D. Morgan, 1811–1883: Merchant in Politics*. New York: Columbia University Press, 1955.

Ray, Frederic E. *"Our Special Artist": Alfred R. Waud's Civil War*. Mechanicsburg, Pa.: Stackpole Books, 1994.

Reid, Brian Holden. "Another Look at Grant's Crossing of the James, 1864." *Civil War History*, vol. 39 no. 4 (December 1993).

Rhea, Gordon C. *The Battle of the Wilderness, May 5–6, 1864*. Baton Rouge and London: Louisiana State University Press, 1994.

——. *The Battles for Spotsylvania Court House and the Road to Yellow Tavern, May 7–12, 1864*. Baton Rouge and London: Louisiana University Press, 1997.

Richardson, James D. *A Compilation of the Messages and Papers of the Presidents, 1789–1908*. Vol. VII. Washington, D.C.: Bureau of National Literature and Art, 1908.

Ritchie, Norman L., ed. *Four Years in the First New York Light Artillery: The Papers of David F. Ritchie*. Hamilton, N.Y.: Edmonston Publishing, 1997.

Robertson, James I., Jr. *General A. P. Hill: The Story of a Confederate Warrior*. New York: Random House, 1987.

Robertson, James I., Jr., ed. *The Civil War Letters of General Robert McAllister*. New Brunswick: Rutgers University Press, 1965.

Robins, Richard. "The Battles of Groveton and Second Bull Run." In *Military Essays and Recollections: Papers Read before the Commandery of the State of Illinois*, Military Order of the Loyal Legion of the United States, Commandery of the State of Illinois. Vol. 3. Chicago: Dial Press, 1899.

Robinson, Doane. "Black Hills Bygones." *South Dakota Historical Collections*, vol. 12. Pierre, S.Dak.: State Publishing, 1924.

Robinson, Will G. "Digest of Reports of the Commissioner of Indian Affairs—1853–1869." *South Dakota Historical Collections*, vol. 27. Pierre, S.Dak.: State Publishing, 1954.

Roe, Alfred S. *The Thirty-Ninth Regiment, Massachusetts Volunteers, 1862–65.* Worcester, Mass.: Regimental Veteran Association, 1914.

Rogan, George. "Salem Church: Final Federal Assault at Chancellorsville." *America's Civil War*, January 1999.

Ropes, John Codman. *The Army under Pope.* New York: Charles Scribner's Sons, 1881.

Rowland, Thomas J. *George B. McClellan and Civil War History: In the Shadow of Grant and Sherman.* Kent, Ohio, and London: Kent State University Press, 1998.

———. "In the Shadows of Grant and Sherman: George B. McClellan Revisited." *Civil War History*, vol. 40 no. 3 (September 1994).

Savage, Henry, Jr. *Discovering America, 1700–1875.* New York: Harper and Row, 1979.

Schaff, Morris. *The Battle of the Wilderness.* Boston and New York: Houghton Mifflin, 1910.

Schubert, Frank N. "Troublesome Partnership: Gouverneur K. Warren and Ferdinand V. Hayden on the Northern Plains in 1856 and 1857." *Earth Sciences History*, vol. 3, no. 2 (1984).

Scott, Robert Garth, ed. *Forgotten Valor: The Memoirs, Journals and Civil War Letters of Orlando B. Willcox.* Kent, Ohio, and London: Kent State University Press, 1999.

———. *Into the Wilderness with the Army of the Potomac.* Bloomington: Indiana University Press, 1985.

Sears, Stephen W. *Chancellorsville.* Boston and New York: Houghton Mifflin, 1996.

———. *Controversies and Commanders: Dispatches from the Army of the Potomac.* Boston and New York: Houghton Mifflin, 1999.

———. *George B. McClellan: The Young Napoleon.* New York: Ticknor and Fields, 1988.

———. "Gouverneur Kemble Warren and Little Phil." *North & South*, vol. I, no. 5 (1998).

———. *Landscape Turned Red: The Battle of Antietam.* New Haven and New York: Ticknor and Fields, 1983.

———. *To the Gates of Richmond: The Peninsula Campaign.* New York: Ticknor and Fields, 1992.

Sheridan, Philip Henry. *The Personal Memoirs of P. H. Sheridan.* 1888. Reprint, New York: Da Capo Press, 1992.

Simon, John Y., ed. *The Papers of Ulysses S. Grant.* 20 vols. Carbondale and Edwardsville, Ill.: Southern Illinois University Press, 1967–1995.

Simpson, Brooks D. *Ulysses S. Grant: Triumph over Adversity 1822–1865.* Boston and New York: Houghton Mifflin, 2000.

Slocum, Charles Elihu. *The Life and Services of Major-General Henry Warner Slocum.* Toledo: Slocum, 1913.

Small, Harold Adams, ed. *The Road to Richmond: The Civil War Memoirs of Major Abner R. Small of the Sixteenth Maine Volunteers.* Berkeley: University of California Press, 1939.

Smith, Donald L. *The Twenty-Fourth Michigan of the Iron Brigade.* Harrisburg, Pa.: Stackpole, 1962.

Sommers, Richard J. "The Battle of Pegram's Farm and First Squirrel Level Road, September 29–October 2, 1864." *Civil War*, April 1998.

———. *Richmond Redeemed: The Siege at Petersburg.* Garden City, N.Y.: Doubleday, 1981.

Sparks, David S., ed. *Inside Lincoln's Army: The Diary of Marsena Rudolph Patrick, Provost Marshal General, Army of the Potomac*. New York and London: Thomas Yoseloff, 1964.

Steere, Edward. *The Wilderness Campaign*. Harrisburg, Pa.: Stackpole, 1960.

Sutherland, Daniel E. *Fredericksburg and Chancellorsville: The Dare Mark Campaign*. Lincoln and London: University of Nebraska Press, 1998.

Swan, William W. "The Battle of the Wilderness." In *Papers of the Military Historical Society of Massachusetts*, Military Historical Society of Massachusetts. Vol. 6. Boston: The Military Historical Society of Massachusetts, 1907.

———. "The Five Forks Campaign." In *Proceedings of the Military Historical Society of Massachusetts*, Military Historical Society of Massachusetts. Vol. 6. Boston: The Military Historical Society of Massachusetts, 1907.

Swanberg, W. A. *Sickles the Incredible*. New York: Charles Scribner's Sons, 1956.

Swinton, William. *Campaigns of the Army of the Potomac*. 1866. Reprint, New York: Charles Scribner's Sons, 1882.

Taylor, Emerson Gifford. *Gouverneur Kemble Warren: The Life and Letters of an American Soldier, 1830–1882*. Boston and New York: Houghton Mifflin, 1932.

Taylor, Walter H. *Four Years with General Lee*. New York: D. Appleton and Co., 1877.

Thomas, Benjamin P., and Harold M. Hyman. *Stanton: The Life and Times of Lincoln's Secretary of War*. New York: Alfred A. Knopf, 1962.

Townsend, George Alfred. *Campaigns of a Non-Combatant, and His Romaunt Abroad during the War*. New York: Blelock, 1866.

Tremain, Henry Edwin. *Last Hours of Sheridan's Cavalry: A Reprint of War Memoranda*. New York: Bonnell, Silver and Bowers, 1904.

Trinque, Bruce A. "Hancock's 'Well-Conducted Fizzle.'" *America's Civil War*, vol. 9 no. 6 (January 1997).

Trobriand, Régis de. *Four Years with the Army of the Potomac*. Translated by George K. Dauchy. Boston: Ticknor and Co., 1889.

Trudeau, Noah Andre. *The Last Citadel: Petersburg, Virginia, June 1864–April 1865*. Baton Rouge: Louisiana State University Press, 1991.

———. *Out of the Storm: The End of the Civil War, April–June 1865*. Baton Rouge: Louisiana State University Press, 1994.

Tyler, Mason Whiting. *Recollections of the Civil War*. New York and London: G. P. Putnam's, 1912.

Under the Maltese Cross: Antietam to Appomattox. Pittsburgh: 155th Regimental Association, 1910.

Urban, John W. *Battle Field and Prison Pen*. Philadelphia: Hubbard Brothers, 1882.

Utley, Robert M. *Frontiersmen in Blue: The United States Army and the Indian, 1848–1865*. New York: Macmillan, 1967.

Walker, Francis A. *History of the Second Army Corps in the Army of the Potomac*. New York: Charles Scribner's Sons, 1886.

Warren, G. K. *An Account of the Operations of the Fifth Army Corps, Commanded by Maj.-Gen. G. K. Warren, at the Battle of Five Forks, April 1, 1865, and the Battles and Movements Preliminary to It*. New York: D. Van Nostrand, 1866.

———. *Geographical Surveys in the United States, Remarks upon Professor J. D. Whitney's Article in the North American Review, July, 1875, Concluding with an Account of the Origination of the Pacific Railroad*. Washington, D.C.: Judd and Detweiler, 1877.

Washburn, George H. *A Complete Military History and Record of the 108th Regiment N.Y. Vols., from 1862 to 1894*. Rochester, N.Y.: E. R. Andrews Press, 1894.

Waugh, John C. *The Class of 1846: From West Point to Appomattox—Stonewall Jackson, George McClellan and Their Brothers.* New York: Warner Books, 1994.

Webb, Alexander S. *The Peninsula: McClellan's Campaign of 1862.* New York: Charles Scribner's Sons, 1881.

Wilson, James Grant, and Titus Munson Coan, eds. *Personal Recollections of the War of the Rebellion: Addresses Delivered before the New York Commandery of the Loyal Legion of the United States,* Military Order of the Loyal Legion of the United States, New York Commandery. New York, 1891.

Wilson, James Harrison. *The Life of John A. Rawlins.* New York: Neale, 1916.

———. *Under the Old Flag.* 2 vols. New York and London: D. Appleton, 1912.

Wukovits, John F. "Hold at All Hazards." *America's Civil War,* May 1990.

INDEX

ABOUT THE AUTHOR

DAVID M. JORDAN, a native of Philadelphia, a graduate of Princeton University, and a practicing attorney, has previously published biographies of New York political boss Roscoe Conkling, Union general Winfield Scott Hancock, and left-handed pitcher Hal Newhouser, as well as a history of the Philadelphia Athletics.